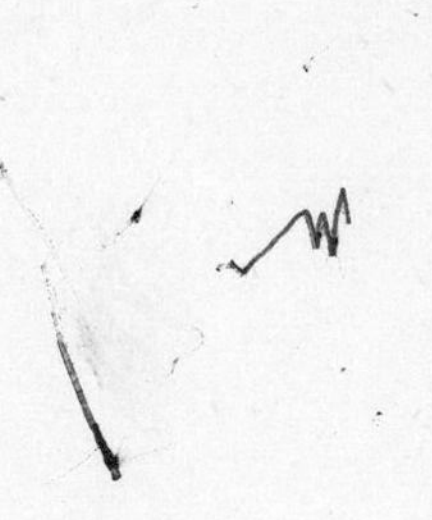

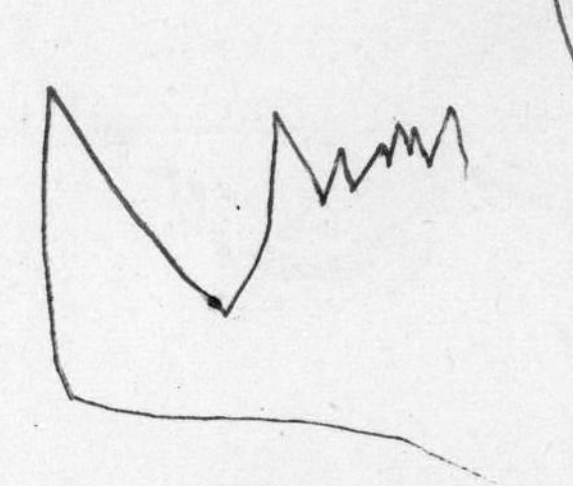

BASIC ACCOUNTING

Victor L. D'Amico, B.A., M.Ed.

Maurice D. Obonsawin, B.Comm.

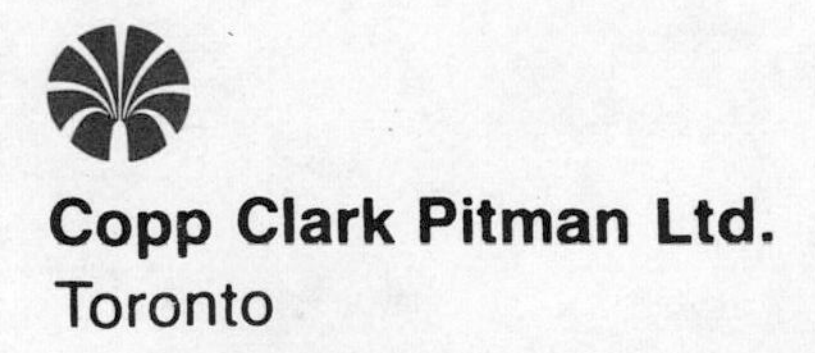

ISBN 0-7730-4254-7

Australia – Pitman Publishing Pty. Ltd., Melbourne
New Zealand – Pitman Publishing New Zealand Ltd., Wellington
U.K. – Pitman Publishing Ltd., London
U.S.A. – Fearon-Pitman Publishers Inc., Belmont, California

Copp Clark Pitman Ltd.
495 Wellington Street West
Toronto, Ontario M5V 1E9

Printed and bound in Canada

Contents

Part One The Basic Accounting Cycle

Part Two Accounting Systems and Procedures

Preface

Basic Accounting has been developed with several premises in mind. The authors feel that an accounting text should include:

- a complete package of curriculum materials for students and teachers
- a practical system of individualized learning
- extensive practice material with several levels of difficulty
- realistic case studies, source documents, accounting systems, and career descriptions

Using Basic Accounting The theory, exercises, and case studies in *Basic Accounting* are designed to be completed over two school years. Most classes will be able to cover the first thirteen chapters in one year and the balance of the book in a second year. The extensive exercise materials will challenge the best students and provide teachers with great flexibility when planning lessons. However, it may not be possible for some students to complete all the cases, the four projects, and the exercises within the two year period.

Exercises in each chapter are divided into three levels of difficulty: A, B, and C. The A and B sections include all the theory covered in each chapter. These exercises are short to intermediate in length. The exercises in part C are longer and more complex. A teacher may decide to assign the part C exercises to some students only, or to eliminate parts of each exercise in part C. Teachers may also decide to be selective in their assignment of the four major projects.

Individualized Learning Many people, including the authors, believe that learning is a highly individualized process. We all learn in different ways and at different speeds. For these reasons, the *Basic Accounting* package has been designed as an individualized program to facilitate student progress through the learning process.

The *Basic Accounting* text contains 53 individualized units of learning in its 21 chapters. The two study guides for *Basic Accounting* are correlated with these individualized units to greatly extend the scope of traditional workbooks currently being used in the classroom. In addition to providing the necessary working papers for the completion of the exercises, the study guides contain instructions for a step-by-step coverage of the entire course. Thus, it is possible for students to proceed at their own pace, with minimal help from the teacher. Students who so desire, may even follow the instructions to teach themselves all the aspects of basic accounting.

Case Studies Throughout *Basic Accounting,* case studies are used to introduce and to reinforce accounting theory. Real cases are used as often as possible in order to present relevant systems, procedures, and case dilemmas. It is hoped that these cases will broaden the general business background of students as well as present an opportunity for critical and analytical thinking. As students learn accounting theory, the cases may be used to develop interpretative and decision making skills.

Values Cases A number of case studies present values dilemmas. These cases are included in the text so that students, in small groups or in class discussion, may examine their personal beliefs and come to the realization that everyone has a highly personal values system. Hopefully, students will learn to see that in any values dilemma there are several possible alternatives and that different consequences follow from each alternative. Also, each individual should be aware of the responsibilities attached to the various alternatives available in any decision based on personal values.

Career Profiles A wide variety of careers related either directly or indirectly to accounting are included at the end of every chapter. We have attempted to present some of the job opportunities that are open to accounting students by describing job profiles of people who are enjoying accounting oriented careers. The authors would like to sincerely thank all those persons who kindly provided personal descriptions of their jobs and career development.

Source Documents and Accounting Systems Throughout the text real source documents have been used as a basis for business transactions and theory development. We greatly appreciate the assistance of the companies who provided these documents and hope that such material will provide a more realistic course of study.

An attempt has been made to introduce other techniques of processing accounting data in addition to the traditional manual systems. Automated and one-write systems are described using actual business practices from such companies as INCO Ltd., Metropolitan Life Insurance, Teleaccount, Warrendon Sports, Renfrew Printing, and Macval Developments.

Acknowledgements We sincerely appreciate the materials, encouragement, and ideas provided to us in the preparation of *Basic Accounting*. Case studies, source documents, illustrations, and descriptions of accounting systems were supplied by:
Mary and Joseph Galotta, The Cascade Inn, Niagara Falls; L.G. Moulds, C.A., Vice-President, Macval Developments, Ottawa; Warren Creighton, Partner, Warrendon Sports, Ottawa; W. MacAdam, President, Renfrew Printing, Renfrew; W. Rorison, H. Prince, and R. Beaver, INCO Ltd., Sudbury; M.L. Gettler, Comptroller, Anchor Cap & Closure Corp., Toronto; D. Bolt, The Big "A" Co., Toronto; Peter Kenwood, Treasurer, Kenwood Moving and Storage, Montréal; John Kisel, Accounting Manager, Pollock, Lyttle & Co., Welland; W.J. Costello, Vice-President, Robert Hunt Co. Ltd., London; G.F. Reimer, Vice-President, Reimer Express Lines Ltd., Winnipeg; B.G. Young, Comptroller, Canadian Ingersoll Rand Ltd., Sherbrooke; W. Foley, Comptroller, Domcor Distribution Ltd., Calgary; C. Smith, Accountant, Scotiabank, Ottawa and Arnprior; T. Wiseman, C.A., Comptroller, Van Leeuwen Boomkamp Ltd., Ottawa; W.G. Corcoran, R.L. Crain Ltd., Ottawa; Panda/Miller Services Limited for Figure 1.1.

Teachers who have used and commented on the individualized learning materials include Lloyd Moon, Harry Ralph, Carol Gusen, Gene Daly, and Bob

Morin. We thank them and their students at Ottawa High School of Commerce. We have been greatly encouraged by, and received ideas from, a respected colleague, Guy Drolet of the Ottawa Board of Education. Several ideas have been borrowed from Bob Harkness of the Hamilton Board of Education and his dedicated group of accounting teachers. Many teaching concepts have been refined through the presentation of workshops on individualized learning organized by Clarence Webb of the Ontario Business Education Association and by dedicated teachers such as Tom Davis of Peterborough, John Allen of Sudbury, and Terry Murphy of Kingston. We would like to thank W. Squire, principal of Ottawa High School of Commerce who has been supportive of all our experimentation, and Pat Trant, a friend and supporter who first encouraged us to develop this material. A mountain of manuscript has been efficiently organized and typed by Myrna Zeitoun, Linda Obonsawin, and Cecilia D'Amico.

Finally, we are specially grateful for the understanding and encouragement shown by our families who suffered through the birth of the book. We are lucky to have such beautiful families and thank Linda, Russell and Tanyss, and Cecilia, Mike, Cathy, Ann Marie and Tom for their support.

PART ONE

The Basic Accounting Cycle

Part One of this text introduces the theory of accounting and the tasks performed in the accounting period following the steps in the basic accounting cycle.

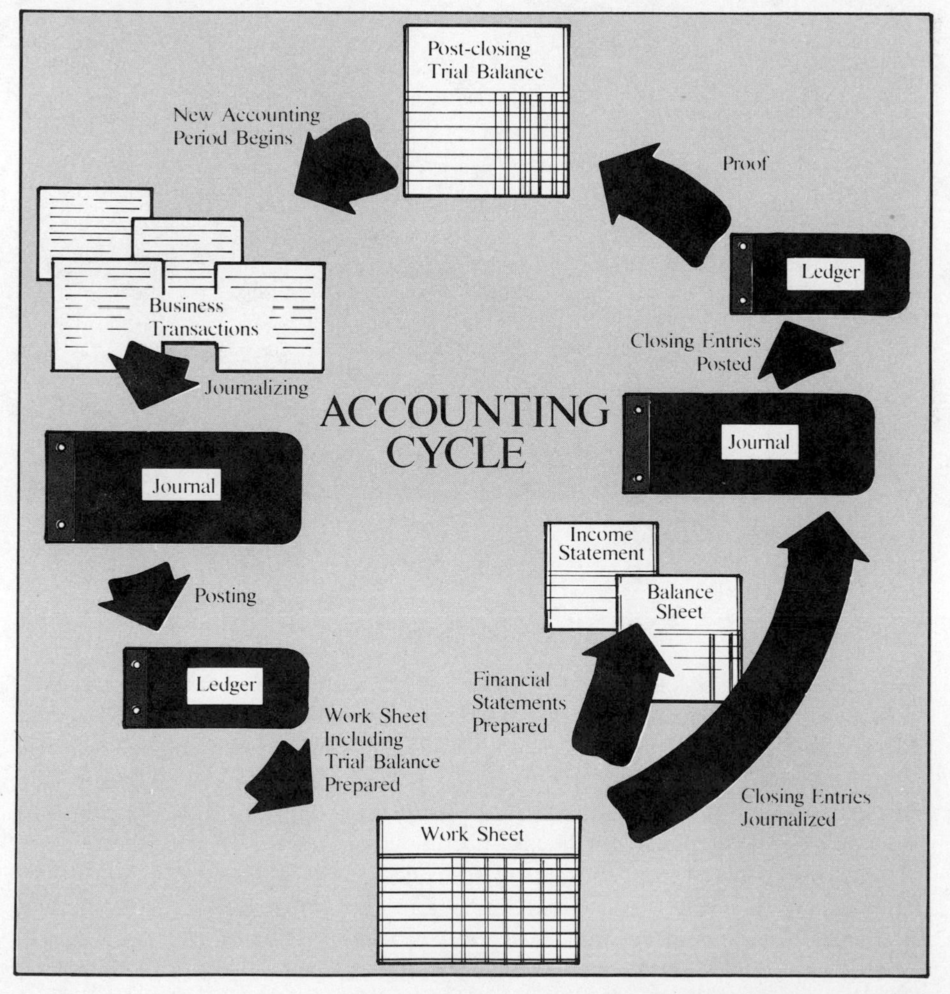

CHAPTER 1

The Balance Sheet

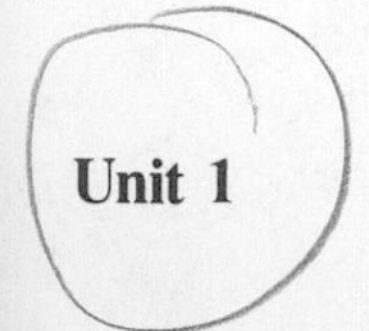

Figure 1.1 *Niagara Falls*

The Cascade Inn

*1

Joseph and Mary Galotta live in Niagara Falls, Ontario. For a number of years, Joseph worked for a local industry and Mary looked after their home as well as their three young sons. Joseph at first liked his office position very much and worked extremely hard. Gradually though, he began to become unhappy with his job. He felt the routine office duties that he was performing did not use his business knowledge and potential to its fullest. After much discussion between themselves, the Galottas decided to open their own business.

Niagara Falls is widely known as a tourist attraction and resort city, so something associated with tourism seemed like a good business possibility. Also the Galottas owned a large lot near the famous Falls. Because of these factors the Galottas decided to go into the motel business and began to make plans to build a small motel.

The decision to start a business had been a difficult one. Joseph and Mary owned their own home, earned a good income, and had three boys to raise. Life was very good, but they wanted something more – the challenge of owning their own business. Once the decision to actually go ahead had been made, the problems and questions really began to come to light. *Where would the money come from to start the business? Would the business provide enough income for them to live on? Would the business be successful?* These were only some of the questions that they asked themselves.

The source of money to start the business was the first hurdle to be passed. Luckily, they already owned the land, but now it was necessary to put up a building. To raise some money, the Galottas sold their house and moved into a rented home. They hired carpenters, electricians, and plumbers and started construction. Soon a modest 12-room motel called *The Cascade Inn* was open for business.

For a number of reasons, the business has been successful in spite of stiff competition from about 140 other motels in the city. There is a great demand for motel accommodation in Niagara Falls, and the Cascade is very close to the Falls. Most important, the Cascade is well managed. Expenses are kept to a minimum through the hard work of the family. Guests like the personal treatment they receive and many of them return year after year. Today, the Cascade is a 67-room inn, having expanded four times in 12 years to include a restaurant, gift shop, sweet shop, and sightseeing tour services.

The Cascade Inn is a successful business. *Why is this so? Why are some businesses not successful and forced to close down?* The success of a business

Figure 1.2 *The Cascade Inn*

depends on the profit it makes for its owners. *What is profit? How does a business keep records of its day-to-day activities? How did the Galottas know that they could afford to expand their motel from 12 to 67 rooms?* All these types of questions are very much related to the purpose of accounting and will be examined during the course of this book.

The Purpose of Accounting

***2**

The purpose of accounting is to provide financial information for decision-making.

The Galotta family had to make many decisions in developing their motel into a successful business. The accounting system developed for the Cascade provided information which helped in making these decisions. Every accounting system must:

- record the day-to-day activities of the business
- summarize and report information in a useful form

In this chapter, the study of accounting will begin with a report called a *balance sheet* which provides information in a useful form, and a device called a *transaction sheet* which is used to record and analyse daily business activities. In later chapters, more sophisticated methods of recording business transactions will be studied.

The Balance Sheet

***3**

A balance sheet is a financial statement which lists the assets, liabilities and owner's equity at a specific date.

What does the Cascade own? What does it owe to others? What is it worth to the owners? Answers to these questions are found in a financial statement called a balance sheet. A recent balance sheet of the Cascade, dated September 30, is shown in Figure 1.3.

The Cascade Inn
Balance Sheet
September 30, 19__

Assets		Liabilities	
Cash	5 000 00	Accounts Payable	24 000 00
Motel Supplies	7 000 00	Bank Loan	15 000 00
Office Equipment	3 000 00	Mortgage Payable	100 000 00
Room Furniture	110 000 00	Total Liabilities	139 000 00
Building	500 000 00		
Land	50 000 00	Owner's Equity	
		Galotta, Capital	536 000 00
		Total Liabilities	
Total Assets	675 000 00	and Owner's Equity	675 000 00

Figure 1.3 *Example of a balance sheet for The Cascade Inn*

As the Cascade Inn earned profits, the profits were used to pay off debts and to pay for additions to the building. The balance sheet shows the financial position of the Cascade as we might imagine it to be, because although this is an actual case study, the figures presented are fictitious.

It *owns* the following:

Cash (in bank and on hand)	$ 5 000
Motel Supplies	7 000
Office Equipment	3 000
Room Furniture	110 000
Building	500 000
Land	50 000
Total	$675 000

It has the following *debts:*

Accounts Payable	$ 24 000
Bank Loan	15 000
Mortgage Payable	100 000
Total	$139 000

How much is the business worth to its owners? This can be determined by subtracting the debts from the total owned.

$$\$675\ 000 - \$139\ 000 = \$536\ 000$$

Thus it can be said that the business is worth $536 000 to the owners.

Assets On the left side of the balance sheet in Figure 1.3 are listed the things of value owned by the business. These are called *assets* and are listed under the heading Assets. The total of the assets owned by the Cascade is $675 000. Included in this total are Cash, Motel Supplies, Office Equipment, Room Furniture, Building, and Land.

An asset is something of value owned by a business or person.

Cash includes money in the bank and cash on hand. Motel Supplies are things such as towels, soap and mops. The asset Office Equipment includes cash registers, a typewriter, and a calculator. The asset Room Furniture comprises such items as beds, chairs, dressers, television sets, tables and lamps.

A liability is a debt owed to others by a business or person.

Liabilities Money and debts owed to others are found on the right side of the balance sheet in Figure 1.3 These are called *liabilities* and are listed under the heading Liabilities on the right side of the balance sheet. The liabilities of the Cascade total $139 000. They include money owed to other companies (Accounts Payable), a bank loan, and money owing on the building (Mortgage Payable).

Owner's equity is the owner's claim against the assets of a business.

Owner's Equity The worth of the business to the owner or owners (which is the owner's financial interest in the business) is shown on the right side of the balance sheet under the heading *Owner's Equity*. In Figure 1.3, the Galottas' financial interest in The Cascade Inn is $536 000. There are two sources for owner's equity. It comes from the owner's investment in the business and from the past profitable operations of the business.

The owner's equity may be calculated by subtracting the liabilities from the assets. For example:

Assets ($675 000) – **Liabilities** ($139 000) = **Owner's Equity** ($536 000)

*4

Claims against the Assets All businesses require assets in order to operate. *Where did the Galottas obtain the assets to start their business?* The Galottas contributed the land and some cash from their savings and the sale of their home. The rest of the assets were obtained by borrowing. Money was borrowed from a bank and also from a trust company (the Mortgage Payable).

Some of the supplies, equipment, and furniture were bought on credit from other businesses. The debts owed to these businesses are called *accounts payable*. The term *creditors* is also used to describe a company which has given *credit*. The creditors of the Cascade would include a bank, a trust company, and the companies which have supplied various items on credit.

As has been shown, there are two sides to the balance sheet in Figure 1.3: a left side and a right side. On the left side are listed the items owned, or the assets of the business. On the right side are listed those who have provided the assets and therefore have a claim against them. The assets of the Cascade came from two sources:

- the owners
- the creditors

Creditors have a claim against assets.

Since $139 000 is still owing to the creditors, that amount is their claim against the assets.

An equity is a claim against assets.

The remainder of the assets were provided by the owners and the profitable operation of the business. Thus the claim or equity of the owners is $536 000. Remember, the term Owner's Equity is used to indicate the owner's claim against the assets of the business. Figure 1.4 illustrates the claims against the assets of the Cascade.

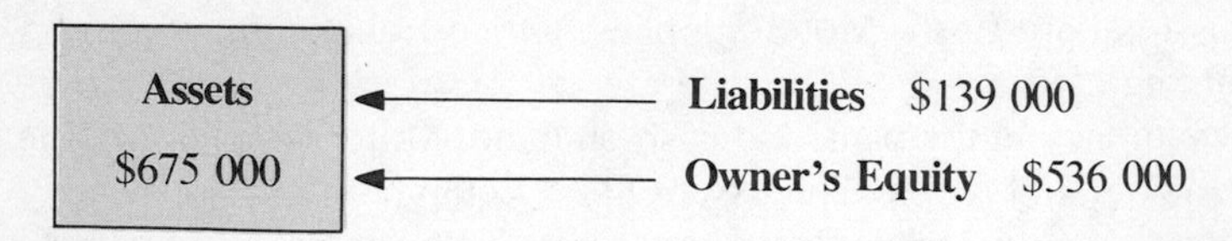

Figure 1.4 *Claims against the assets of The Cascade Inn*

A convenient way of expressing this relationship is with the equation:

Assets	=	**Liabilities**	+	**Owner's Equity**
$675 000	=	$139 000	+	$536 000

There are two claims on the assets of a business: the claim of the creditors and the claim of the owners. If a company goes out of business the creditors have *first* claim on the assets. Any assets that remain *after* the creditors' claims have been satisfied, belong to the owners.

The Accounting Equation

The items on the balance sheet may be expressed in the form of an equation:

$$A = L + OE$$

This is called the *accounting equation*. It is a mathematical expression of how the balance sheet works. In a mathematical equation, the left side equals the right side. In the accounting equation, the left side (assets) must always equal the right side (liabilities and owner's equity). The original basis of the accounting equation is the fact that:

Assets = Claims against the Assets

This simple relationship of assets and claims against the assets is very important. Many accounting concepts are developed from this basic relationship. Also, many of the mathematical checks on the accuracy of accounting are based on the concept that:

Left Side = Right Side
Assets = Claims against the Assets
Assets = Liabilities + Owner's Equity

Common Recording Practices

Unit 2
***5**

Remember to follow these common recording practices when using this book and in practical situations.

1. When ruled accounting paper is used, dollar signs, decimals, and cent signs are not required.
2. A single, ruled line indicates addition or subtraction.
3. A double, ruled line indicates that the work is complete and accurate.

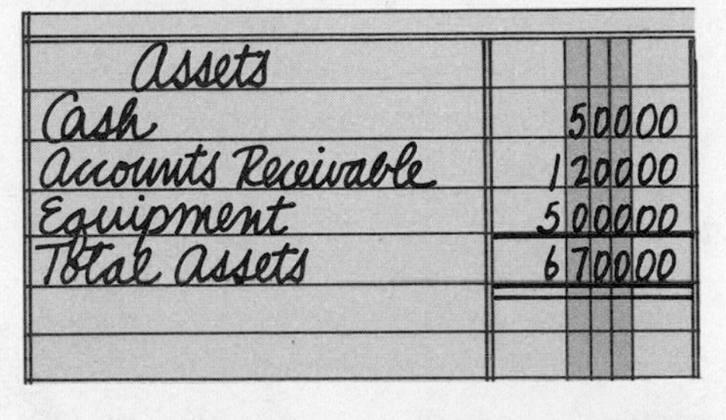

4. Errors are corrected by ruling a single line through the error and writing the correction above or below the error.

560.00
~~600.00~~

5. When ruled accounting paper is not used, place a dollar sign beside the first figure in a column and all subtotals and totals in the column.

Liabilities	
Accounts Payable	$2800.00
Bank Loan	1000.00
Total Liabilities	$3800.00
Owner's Equity	
W. Holloway, Capital	2900.00
Total Liabilities and Owner's Equity	$6700.00

Order of the Assets on the Balance Sheet It is a general rule in accounting to list the assets on the balance sheet in the order in which they may be converted into cash. Therefore Cash is always listed first. Next is Accounts Receivable because it represents money which will be received in the near future. Next come assets such as Office Supplies, Furniture, Office Equipment, Delivery Truck, and Building. These assets are not normally converted into cash but are used in the day-to-day operations of the business.

Steps in Preparing a Balance Sheet

*6

The following five steps should be observed when preparing a balance sheet.

1. Write the three-line heading at top centre of the page. The heading answers three questions:

Who?	The Cascade Inn	← Name of the business
What?	Balance Sheet	← Name of the statement that follows
When?	September 30, 19--	← Date of the statement

2. List and total the assets on the left side of the page under the heading Assets. Write Total Assets opposite the total amount.

Assets			
Cash	5 000 00		
Motel Supplies	7 000 00		
Office Equipment	3 000 00		
Room Furniture	110 000 00		
Building	500 000 00		
Land	50 000 00		
Total Assets	675 000 00		

3. List and total the liabilities on the right side of the page under the heading Liabilities.

		Liabilities	
		Accounts Payable	24 000 00
		Bank Loan	15 000 00
		Mortgage Payable	100 000 00
		Total Liabilities	139 000 00

4. Show the owner's investment (Capital) under the heading Owner's Equity and below the Liabilities on the right side of the page. Leave a blank space between the liability and equity sections.

		Owner's Equity	
		Galotta, Capital	536 000 00
		Total Liabilities	
		and Owner's Equity	675 000 00

5. Total Assets and Total Liabilities and Owner's Equity are written on the same line and double rules are drawn below the two totals.

		Total Liabilities	
Total Assets	675 000 00	and Owner's Equity	675 000 00

Accounting Terminology

*7

Cash is currency (bills and coins), bank deposits, cheques, and money orders.

The understanding of accounting terminology is very important. For example, the term *cash* represents not only currency (bills and coins), but also bank deposits, cheques, and money orders.

A business may give credit to its customers. When it does, the customers owe money to the business. This money is an asset because the business has the right to collect the money. When it is collected it becomes part of the company's asset Cash. Until the money is received a record is kept showing the amounts owed to the business by its customers. This record is called *accounts receivable*. Another term for an account receivable is *debtor*. Accounts receivable are assets since they are something of value owned by the business (the amount of the accounts receivable will eventually be received).

Accounts receivable are amounts owed to a business by customers.

An amount owed by a business to another business for things bought on credit is called an *account payable*. Another term for account payable is *creditor*. Accounts payable are liabilities since they are owed by the business (the amount of accounts payable will eventually be paid).

Accounts payable are amounts owed to others for purchases on credit.

A small business could list the names of all the accounts receivable and the names of all the accounts payable individually on the balance sheet. However, a business with numerous debtors and creditors usually shows only the total amount opposite the words Accounts Receivable and Accounts Payable on the balance sheet.

As you should remember, the owner's claim on the assets of a business is called *owner's equity*. Other less commonly used terms for owner's equity are *capital, net worth,* and *proprietorship*. Throughout this text the heading Owner's Equity is used on the balance sheet. The owner's claim is shown below this heading and is described as *capital* as in *Galotta, Capital* (Figure 1.3).

Unit 3 Thurs

*8

Transactions

The balance sheet reproduced in Figure 1.3 represents a picture of the financial position of The Cascade Inn at a specific date, September 30, 19__. However, this position changes frequently as business events occur. For example, a customer pays for use of a room, supplies are purchased, or a debt is paid. Each of these events, called *transactions,* causes changes on the balance sheet.

A transaction is an exchange of things of value.

A transaction always includes an exchange of things of value:

Transaction

Something of value is given.

Something of value is received.

A business transaction causes changes in the values of items on the balance sheet. If the next balance sheet is to be correct, the changes caused by the transactions must be recorded. Remember that one of the purposes of accounting is to record the day-to-day activities or transactions of a business. The recording aspect of accounting will be examined by looking at some transactions of a small appliance repair shop called Speedy Appliance Repairs.

Figure 1.5 is the October 1 balance sheet for Speedy Appliance Repairs. The following three transactions will cause changes on the balance sheet:

1. Received $90 cash from a customer
2. Paid $500 cash to a creditor
3. Bought new equipment worth $200 on credit

Speedy Appliance Repairs Balance Sheet October 1, 19__			
Assets		Liabilities	
Cash	1 900 00	Accounts Payable	1 500 00
Accounts Receivable	1 200 00		
Equipment	13 900 00	Owner's Equity	
		C. Moore, Capital	15 500 00
		Total Liabilities	
Total Assets	17 000 00	and Owner's Equity	17 000 00

Figure 1.5 *Balance sheet for Speedy Appliance Repairs*

The Transaction Sheet

A device used to assist in analysing transactions is called a *transaction sheet*. A transaction sheet (Figure 1.6) is basically a balance sheet re-arranged so that changes may be recorded. Notice that the transaction sheet contains a column for each of the items on the balance sheet.

*9

Transaction 1: Received $90 cash from a customer In transaction 1, $90 cash was received from a customer. *Which items on the balance sheet change?* If you said Cash and Accounts Receivable you were correct. Since cash was received, the Cash total increases from $1 900 to $1 990. Notice how the increase and the new balance for Cash is shown on the transaction sheet (Figure 1.6).

TRANSACTION SHEET					
	ASSETS			= LIABILITIES +	OWNER'S EQUITY
	CASH +	ACCOUNTS RECEIVABLE +	EQUIPMENT =	ACCOUNTS PAYABLE +	C. MOORE, CAPITAL
Beginning Balances	1 900 00	1 200 00	13 900 00	1 500 00	15 500 00
Transaction 1	+ 90 00	− 90 00			
New Balances	1 990 00	1 110 00	13 900 00	1 500 00	15 500 00
	$17 000			$17 000	

Figure 1.6 *Transaction 1*

When a customer (Accounts Receivable) pays part of a debt, what happens to the balance of the debt? Does it increase or decrease? Of course, it decreases! The Accounts Receivable balance of $1 200 decreases to $1 110. This is shown on the transaction sheet (Figure 1.6). The balances for Equipment ($13 900), Accounts Payable ($1 500), and C. Moore, Capital ($15 500) do not change.

After transaction 1 is recorded on the transaction sheet, the asset total of $17 000 still equals the liability and owner's equity total of $17 000. The left side of the equation equals the right side.

Transaction 2: Paid $500 cash to a creditor *As a result of this transaction, which items on the balance sheet change?* Cash and Accounts Payable change. Cash decreases and Accounts Payable also decreases because part of the debt owed to a creditor has been paid.

Figure 1.7 shows this transaction and the new balances on the transaction sheet. If the assets are now totalled they still equal the liabilities plus owner's equity. Both totals are now $16 500.

Transaction 3: Bought new equipment worth $200 on credit *Which balance sheet items change?* Equipment changes and must increase because more equipment is now owned. Accounts Payable changes because the equipment was bought on credit and thus the amount owing to creditors increases.

Figure 1.8 illustrates the changes caused by transaction 3. Notice that after this transaction is recorded, the two sides still balance. The left side equals $16 700 and the right side equals $16 700.

*10

The accounting procedures which have been illustrated for Speedy Appliance Repairs cover two main aspects of accounting. These are:
- recording of daily transactions
- preparation of reports

Balance Sheet

↓

Transactions

↓

Analyse and Record

↓

Balance Sheet

First, the three transactions were analysed and recorded. The next step is to prepare a new balance sheet. Figure 1.9 is the balance sheet for Speedy Appliance Repairs which is prepared after the transactions have been recorded. Notice the new date of October 5. It has been assumed that only three transactions took place since the last balance sheet was prepared on October 1.

TRANSACTION SHEET					
	ASSETS			= LIABILITIES +	OWNER'S EQUITY
	CASH	+ ACCOUNTS RECEIVABLE	+ EQUIPMENT	= ACCOUNTS PAYABLE	+ C. MOORE, CAPITAL
Beginning Balances	1 900 00	1 200 00	13 900 00	1 500 00	15 500 00
Transaction 1	+ 90 00	− 90 00			
New Balances	1 990 00	1 110 00	13 900 00	1 500 00	15 500 00
Transaction 2	− 500 00			− 500 00	
New Balances	1 490 00	1 110 00	13 900 00	1 000 00	15 500 00
	$16 500			$16 500	

Figure 1.7 *Transaction 2*

TRANSACTION SHEET					
	ASSETS			= LIABILITIES +	OWNER'S EQUITY
	CASH	+ ACCOUNTS RECEIVABLE	+ EQUIPMENT	= ACCOUNTS PAYABLE	+ C. MOORE, CAPITAL
Beginning Balances	1 900 00	1 200 00	13 900 00	1 500 00	15 500 00
Transaction 1	+ 90 00	− 90 00			
New Balances	1 990 00	1 110 00	13 900 00	1 500 00	15 500 00
Transaction 2	− 500 00			− 500 00	
New Balances	1 490 00	1 110 00	13 900 00	1 000 00	15 500 00
Transaction 3			+ 200 00	+ 200 00	
New Balances	1 490 00	1 110 00	14 100 00	1 200 00	15 500 00
	$16 700			$16 700	

Figure 1.8 *Transaction 3*

Speedy Appliance Repairs Balance Sheet October 5, 19__			
Assets		Liabilities	
Cash	1 490 00	Accounts Payable	1 200 00
Accounts Receivable	1 110 00		
Equipment	14 100 00	Owner's Equity	
		C. Moore, Capital	15 500 00
Total Assets	16 700 00	Total Liabilities and Owner's Equity	16 700 00

Figure 1.9 *New balance sheet for Speedy Appliance Repairs after the three transactions have been recorded*

The Accounting Period

Financial reports such as the balance sheet are prepared at the end of the *accounting period.* The length of the accounting period varies from company to company. A very small firm may only require financial reports once a year. For such a firm, the accounting period is a year. Other firms may wish to have reports every month. For them, the accounting period is one month.

Additional Transactions

*11

Figures 1.10, 1.11, and 1.12 are further examples of how transactions cause changes to the balance sheet, how the transaction sheet is used to analyse these changes, and how a new balance sheet is prepared using the balances from the transaction sheet. First, the beginning balance sheet for Holloway Appliance Service is shown in Figure 1.10.

Holloway Appliance Service
Balance Sheet
October 20, 19__

Assets		Liabilities	
Cash	1 900 00	Accounts Payable	1 000 00
Accounts Receivable	700 00	Bank Loan	3 000 00
Supplies	500 00	Total Liabilities	4 000 00
Delivery Truck	9 000 00		
		Owner's Equity	
		W. Holloway, Capital	8 100 00
		Total Liabilities	
Total Assets	12 100 00	and Owner's Equity	12 100 00

Figure 1.10 *Balance sheet for Holloway Appliance Service*

The following transactions occurred after the October 20 balance sheet was prepared:

1. P. Pasqua, debtor (Accounts Receivable), pays a debt of $49.
2. W. Holloway, the owner of the business, invests an additional $2 000 in the business.
3. A payment of $250 is made to a creditor (Accounts Payable).
4. A new delivery van is purchased from Capital Ford Ltd. A cash down payment of $2 000 is given to Capital Ford. The price of the van is $6 000. The balance of $4 000 is to be paid in six months and is now considered an account payable.
5. An invoice (bill) for $50 of supplies purchased from Sylvan Electric is received.
6. The bank loan is reduced by paying the bank $1 000.

Now follow the record of these transactions on the transaction sheet illustrated in Figure 1.11.

TRANSACTION SHEET							
	ASSETS				= LIABILITIES	+ OWNER'S EQUITY	
	CASH	+ ACCOUNTS RECEIVABLE	+ SUPPLIES	+ DELIVERY TRUCK	= ACCOUNTS PAYABLE	+ BANK LOAN	+ W. HOLLOWAY, CAPITAL
Beginning Balances	1 900 00	700 00	500 00	9 000 00	1 000 00	3 000 00	8 100 00
Transaction 1	+ 49 00	− 49 00					
New Balances	1 949 00	651 00	500 00	9 000 00	1 000 00	3 000 00	8 100 00
Transaction 2	+2 000 00						+2 000 00
New Balances	3 949 00	651 00	500 00	9 000 00	1 000 00	3 000 00	10 100 00
Transaction 3	−250 00				−250 00		
New Balances	3 699 00	651 00	500 00	9 000 00	750 00	3 000 00	10 100 00
Transaction 4	−2 000 00			+6 000 00	+4 000 00		
New Balances	1 699 00	651 00	500 00	15 000 00	4 750 00	3 000 00	10 100 00
Transaction 5			+ 50 00		+ 50 00		
New Balances	1 699 00	651 00	550 00	15 000 00	4 800 00	3 000 00	10 100 00
Transaction 6	−1 000 00					−1 000 00	
New Balances	699 00	651 00	550 00	15 000 00	4 800 00	2 000 00	10 100 00
	$16 900				$16 900		

Figure 1.11 *Transaction Sheet for Holloway Appliance Service*

After the changes caused by the transactions have been recorded, a new balance sheet is prepared as illustrated in Figure 1.12.

Holloway Appliance Service Balance Sheet October 31, 19__			
Assets		Liabilities	
Cash	699 00	Accounts Payable	4 800 00
Accounts Receivable	651 00	Bank Loan	2 000 00
Supplies	550 00	Total Liabilities	6 800 00
Delivery Truck	15 000 00		
		Owner's Equity	
		W. Holloway, Capital	10 100 00
Total Assets	16 900 00	Total Liabilities and Owner's Equity	16 900 00

Figure 1.12 *New balance sheet for Holloway Appliance Service after the six transactions have been recorded*

Facts to Remember

The *purpose of accounting* is to provide financial information for decision-making.

Financial statements such as the balance sheet provide financial information.

A *balance sheet* is a financial statement which lists the assets, liabilities, and owner's equity at a specific date.

An *asset* is something of value owned by a business or person.

A *liability* is a debt owed to others by a business or person.

Equity is a claim against assets.

Owner's equity is the owner's claim against assets.

Cash is currency (bills and coins), bank deposits, cheques, and money orders.

The *accounting equation* is Assets = Liabilities + Owner's Equity (A = L + OE).

Accounts receivable are amounts owed to a business by customers.

Accounts receivable are assets.

Debtor is another name for an account receivable.

Accounts payable are amounts owed to others for purchases on credit.

An *account payable* is a liability.

Creditor is another name for an account payable.

Creditors have a claim against assets.

A *transaction* is an exchange of things of value.

Checking Your Reading

Questions

1. Why did Joseph and Mary Galotta decide to go into business for themselves?
2. How did the Galottas finance their motel business?
3. What risks did they take? Why?
4. What is the purpose of accounting?
5. What is a balance sheet?
6. Define asset. Give five examples of different assets.
7. Define liabilities. Give three examples of different liabilities.
8. How is the owner's equity calculated?
9. What items are recorded on the left side of the balance sheet? What items are recorded on the right side?
10. On which sides of the accounting equation are the assets, the liabilities, and the owner's equity?

11. What is the accounting equation?
12. What does a single ruled line on a financial statement indicate? What does a double ruled line mean?
13. When may dollar signs, decimals, and cent signs be omitted in financial statements?
14. How are recording errors corrected?
15. What information is provided by the three lines in the heading of a balance sheet?
16. What are the other terms for accounts receivable and accounts payable?
17. Define the term transaction.

Applying Your Knowledge

Exercises Part A

1. Leslie goes to college seven months of the year and works weekends and during the summer. Leslie *owes* $250 in tuition fees to Algonquin College and $200 to Hi-Lo Stereo Ltd. Following is a list of things *owned* by Leslie:

Cash	$ 50
Savings Bank Account	650
Stereo Components	700
Clothes	750
Sports Equipment	250
Record and Tape Collection	300
Books and Personal Items	300

a) What is Leslie worth?
b) Prepare a personal balance sheet for Leslie dated September 28, 19__.

2. The Algonquin Apartment Hotel rents light housekeeping rooms on a daily, weekly, or monthly basis. Classify each of the following items concerning the Algonquin Apartment Hotel as either an asset, a liability, or the owner's equity:

land and building, cash, owner's claim on the business, mortgage payable on buildings, accounts receivable from tenants (or money owed by tenants), furniture and fixtures, money due to suppliers, room supplies, bank loan.

3. Complete the following equations in your Study Guide or your notebook.

Assets	=	Liabilities	+	Owner's Equity
$100 000	=	$30 000	+	?
29 500	=	5 000	+	?
?	=	17 800	+	$23 200
130 000	=	?	+	90 000

4. On January 31, 19__ the assets and liabilities for Dr. Kingsbury, a general practitioner, were as follows:

bank $9 000; money due from patients $6 000; money due from the Provincial Health Insurance Plan $14 000; supplies $2 000; equipment $30 000; money owing to suppliers $4 000; bank loan $7 000.

In your notebook:
a) classify each item as an asset, liability, or owner's equity;
b) calculate the doctor's equity;
c) prepare the balance sheet using the format in Figure 1.3 (page 4 of the text).

5. On May 31, 19__, the assets and liabilities for C. Klink, a lawyer, were as follows:

cash $8 000; money due clients $17 000; office supplies $500; office equipment $3 400; bank loan $6 000.

a) classify each as an asset, liability, or owner's equity;
b) calculate Klink's equity;
c) prepare the balance sheet in your Study Guide.

6. Metro Dry Cleaners, owned by Jack Hill, specializes in drapery cleaning and has a drive-in service. On October 31, 19__, assets and liabilities of the business were as follows:

cash $5 400; due from customers $34 000; supplies $7 000; equipment $50 000; land and building $150 000; trucks $21 600; due to suppliers $12 300; mortgage on building $75 000; bank loan $4 700.

Calculate the owner's equity and prepare a balance sheet for Metro Dry Cleaners.

7. Arabian Nights is a restaurant owned by Mr. Michael Nihmey. On August 1, 19__ the restaurant's assets and liabilities were as follows:

cash $17 000; stock on hand $4 000; supplies $6 000; furniture and fixtures $19 600; equipment $40 000; land and buildings $175 000; due to suppliers $10 300; mortgage payable $110 000.

Calculate the owner's equity and prepare the restaurant's balance sheet.

Exercises Part B

8. Davis Driving School is owned by Karen Davis. On July 1, 19__, the school's assets, liabilities and owner's equity were as follows:

office supplies $3 500; automobiles $35 000; accounts payable/Bill's Service Station $4 000; accounts payable/Kwik Body Repairs $2 400; cash $22 000; bank loan $5 000; accounts receivable/clients $5 000; equipment $7 000; K. Davis, capital $61 100.

Prepare the balance sheet.

9. Ambassador Travel Services, owned by W. Corcoran, provides travel and accommodation reservations throughout the world. On July 1, 19__, assets, liabilities and owner's equity of the business were as follows:

cash $50 000; accounts receivable/hotels $75 000; office supplies $5 000; office equipment $25 000; deposits owed to travellers $30 000; bank loan $15 000; W. Corcoran, capital $110 000.

Prepare the balance sheet.

10. Following is the balance sheet for Bookkeeping Services as of October 1.

Bookkeeping Services Balance Sheet October 1, 19__			
Assets		**Liabilities**	
Cash	1 900 00	Accounts Payable	2 000 00
Accounts Receivable	1 100 00		
Office Equipment	3 000 00	**Owner's Equity**	
Furniture	9 000 00	R. King, Capital	13 000 00
		Total Liabilities	
Total Assets	15 000 00	and Owner's Equity	15 000 00

The following transactions took place before October 11.

October 2 Bought new furniture for $300 cash.
5 Bought a new typewriter for $200 cash.
6 Paid $500 cash to Mr. Jones, a creditor (Accounts Payable).
9 Bought new office equipment worth $300 from Kerwin Suppliers on account (the $300 will be paid next month).
10 R. King, the owner, invested $6 000 cash in the business.
11 R. King, the owner took $1 000 from the bank account of the business and placed it in his own personal account.

a) Prepare a transaction sheet and record the transactions that are given. Follow the format of the transaction work sheet in Figure 1.6 (page 11).
b) Prove the accuracy of your work after the last transaction by seeing if the Assets = Liabilities + Owner's Equity.
c) Prepare a new balance sheet after the last transaction dated October 11.

Exercises
Part C

11. Following is the balance sheet for Fisher's Body Repairs as of July 1.

Fisher's Body Repairs
Balance Sheet
July 1, 19__

Assets		Liabilities	
Cash	7 500 00	Accounts Payable	3 400 00
Accounts Receivable	15 300 00	Bank Loan	1 500 00
Equipment	55 000 00	Total Liabilities	4 900 00
		Owner's Equity	
		L. Fisher, Capital	72 900 00
		Total Liabilities	
Total Assets	77 800 00	and Owner's Equity	77 800 00

The following transactions took place during July.

July 3 Received $450 cash from K. Bell, a customer.
4 Purchased a new $1 500 air compressor from K. D. Manufacturers on account.
5 Borrowed $2 000 cash from the bank.
8 Paid $600 on account to General Auto Parts, a supplier.
15 Made a $500 cash payment on the bank loan.
20 The owner, L. Fisher, invested a further $3 000 in the business.

a) Prepare a transaction sheet for Fisher's Body Repairs and record the transactions.
b) After the last transaction, prove the arithmetical accuracy of your calculations by seeing if the left side total equals the right side total.

12. Mail-O-Matic Printing prints material such as advertising brochures and flyers for retail stores and distributes them door-to-door. Following are several transactions that occurred during March and the balance sheet for Mail-O-Matic Printing.

March 4 Purchased $950 worth of paper from Cooper Products on account.
5 Some of the paper received from Cooper Paper Products was damaged during delivery. Paper worth $200 was returned.
9 Paid $700 on account to Clear Chemicals Ltd., a supplier.
10 Purchased a new $15 000 printing press from Conway Manufacturers. A down payment of $3 000 cash was made, and the balance of $12 000 is to be paid later.

March 14 Bargain Stores, a customer, paid $2 500 cash on account.
17 S. Zimic, the owner, invested another $6 000 cash in the business.

Mail-O-Matic Printing Balance Sheet March 1, 19__			
Assets		Liabilities	
Cash	14 000 00	Accounts Payable	6 500 00
Accounts Receivable	23 000 00		
Printing Supplies	8 900 00	Owner's Equity	
Equipment	97 000 00	S. Zimic, Capital	136 400 00
		Total Liabilities	
Total Assets	142 900 00	and Owner's Equity	142 900 00

a) Complete a transaction sheet for Mail-O-Matic.
b) After the last transaction, prove the arithmetical accuracy of your calculations.

Accounting in Action

Case 1

How Much was the Profit? At the beginning of the year a company's assets, liabilities, and capital were $110 000, $60 000 and $50 000 respectively. During the year a profit was made. The owner did not invest additional capital or withdraw any capital. At the end of the year the assets were $150 000, the liabilities were $70 000, and the capital (owner's equity) was $80 000.

How much was the profit?

Case 2

Withdrawals and the Owner's Equity At the beginning of the year the financial position of Miller & Sons was:

A $250 000 = **L** $140 000 + **OE** $110 000

At the end of the year the financial position is:

A $230 000 = **L** $130 000 + **OE** $100 000

If the owner did not withdraw or invest any funds during the year, how much profit did the business earn during the year?

Case 3

What is a Business Worth? George Harris, a friend of yours, owns his own business. He offers to sell you half of the business for $40 000. George suggests that this is an excellent price since the assets of the business total $135 000.

The balance sheet of the company follows. What do you think of the deal offered to you?

George Harris & Company Balance Sheet September 30, 19__			
Assets		Liabilities	
Cash	1 500 00	Accounts Payable	10 000 00
Accounts Receivable	2 000 00	Bank Loan	30 000 00
Supplies	500 00	Mortgage Payable	90 000 00
Equipment	9 000 00	Total Liabilities	130 000 00
Land & Building	122 000 00		
		Owner's Equity	
		G. Harris, Capital	5 000 00
		Total Liabilities	
Total Assets	135 000 00	and Owner's Equity	135 000 00

Case 4

Errors on a Balance Sheet There are several mistakes in the set-up and content of this balance sheet. Can you locate them?

M. Mancini & Company Balance Sheet August 31, 19__			
Assets		Liabilities	
Cash	1 000 00	Accounts Receivable	3 000 00
Accounts Payable	2 000 00	Equipment	5 000 00
Supplies	1 000 00	Bank Loan	30 000 00
Building	90 000 00	Total Liabilities	38 000 00
		Owner's Equity	
		M. Mancini, Capital	68 000 00
		Total Liabilities	
Total Assets	94 000 00	and Owner's Equity	106 000 00

Profit and Owner's Equity R. McLean is the owner of a small business. The present financial position of the company is:

Case 5

A \$150 000 = **L** \$40 000 + **OE** \$110 000

During the current year, McLean withdrew \$12 000 cash and \$2 000 worth of merchandise for personal use. No record was made of these transactions. Express, in equation form, the correct financial position of the business to reflect these withdrawals.

Preparing a Balance Sheet Janet Russell began a business on September 1. The first transactions of the company follow.

Case 6

- Janet Russell invested \$25 000 in the business
- purchased equipment for \$7 000 cash
- purchased supplies on account, \$1 000
- purchased a building worth \$80 000 (made a down payment of \$10 000 and signed a \$70 000 mortgage)

What are the total assets, liabilities, and owner's equity of the business? Prepare the balance sheet.

The Owner's Claim on Assets Josie Clarke, the owner of a retail store, has come to you for advice. She shows you her latest balance sheet. The assets total \$200 000, the liabilities \$130 000, and the owner's equity is \$70 000. Included in the assets are old equipment and merchandise at a value of \$120 000. Realistically, these assets are now worth \$40 000.

Case 7

Josie is considering selling all the assets. She feels she could get about \$120 000 cash if all the assets were sold. She would then take her investment (equity of \$70 000) and close down the business. The remaining \$50 000 from the sale of the assets would be available to the creditors as their claim against the assets.

What advice would you give Josie concerning her proposal?

Credit One of the assets which appears on the balance sheet is accounts receivable. This asset represents money owed to a business by its customers. The business has entered into an agreement with a customer in which the customer promises to pay at a future time for goods or services received at the present time. That is, the customer has bought *on credit.*

Case 8

In the next seven chapters case studies will examine these aspects of credit:

- using credit wisely
- how a company decides if credit is to be granted
- the operations of a credit bureau
- how overdue debts are collected
- bank credit cards
- the operations of a collection agency
- women and credit

Using Credit Wisely Can you imagine living in a country without credit? How would houses be financed without mortgages (which are a form of credit)? How would people buy automobiles, appliances, and all the other things they need and want *now* but do not have money for? Credit is a part of everyday life in Canada. It can bring benefits or trouble depending on its use.

Advantages of Credit

- Credit makes it possible to buy goods and services as they are needed and to pay for them with future income.
- Credit helps handle unexpected emergencies, for example automobile breakdowns that occur away from home.
- Credit is an easy way to buy things without having to carry large sums of money.
- Credit enables shoppers to take advantage of sales.

Disadvantages of Credit

- Credit may encourage a person to live beyond his or her income.
- Credit costs money and increases the cost of goods and services.
- Credit encourages impulse buying.

The Sources of Credit Credit may be obtained from a variety of sources including:

- banks
- credit unions
- trust companies
- consumer loan companies
- sales finance companies
- life insurance companies
- credit card companies
- retail stores

Obtaining Credit A person's credit rating determines whether or not credit is granted. Those who grant credit often base their decisions on the *four C's* of credit:

- character
- capacity
- capital
- common sense

Character refers to a sincere attitude towards the paying of bills and to a person's reputation.

Capacity refers to a person's ability to pay debts. It generally refers to a good employment record.

Capital refers to a person's wealth or what he or she owns and indicates a person's ability to save part of his/her income and generally manage money wisely.

Common sense is the ability to manage one's affairs successfully. The ability to use credit wisely and to avoid financial problems is included in common sense.

Conduct a survey of the families of each of your classmates to determine:

- the credit cards and charge accounts used
- the types of goods purchased on credit
- the credit limit (that is the maximum amount of credit allowed by the credit grantor)
- the reasons why goods are bought on credit
- the number of families that never buy on credit

Career Profiles

Look in the newspaper employment section and you will see numerous jobs in the accounting field.

All organizations do some accounting, whether they are a business, a government, a non-profit organization, or an educational institution. They all keep records, pay their employees, prepare reports, and plan their spending. It is not surprising that a variety of employment opportunities exist in accounting.

Levels of Jobs There are three work levels in accounting:

- beginning
- supervisory
- management

Beginning Level At this level, there are many recording and clerical positions such as accounts receivable clerks, payroll clerks, inventory control clerks, and general accounting clerks. They are concerned with recording, classifying, and summarizing the daily transactions of a business.

Supervisory Whenever there is a group of workers, there is usually someone appointed to be responsible for planning the work, hiring and training, and for controlling the quality of the work performed. A person who has been successful at the basic level, who is mature and reliable, and who gets along well with others has the opportunity to obtain a position such as accounting supervisor, office manager, assistant accountant, or payroll supervisor.

Management Treasurer, comptroller, senior accountant, auditor, cost accountant, tax accountant, and manager of accounting departments such as budgeting, taxation, accounts receivable, payroll, accounts payable, forecasting, credit, and collections are types of management opportunities in accounting.

Broad experience and education in general business and accounting as well as personal qualities such as leadership, ability to make decisions, ability to work under pressure, and human relations skills are requirements at this level.

The Accounting Profession There are three professional accounting designations in Canada: Chartered Accountant (C.A.), Certified General Accountant (C.G.A.), and Registered Industrial Accountant (R.I.A.). These certifications are granted to a person who has completed the educational and on-the-job training requirements of the Canadian Institute of Chartered Accountants, the Certified General Accountants Association, or the Society of Management Accountants. The provincial addresses for each of these groups are found in Appendix B, page 566. Write them to obtain complete descriptions of their programs.

The professional accountant is generally concerned with designing accounting systems, preparing financial reports, interpreting and analysing reports, planning and making financial recommendations, and checking the accounting systems and procedures used by companies.

An accountant may work for a business or in the government, or he or she may operate his or her own business and offer accounting services to others. The public accountant *provides* accounting services, in particular the preparation of financial reports and the provision of tax advice, to the general public for a fee. Another important service provided by the accountant is auditing – the examination and appraisal of the financial records and procedures of a business.

At the end of each chapter in this book you will find a *Career Profile*. These profiles are descriptions of people and their careers in the accounting field. These profiles will help explain the many different jobs available and the relevance of this accounting course to your future both in private life and for career opportunities.

CHAPTER 2

Balance Sheet Accounts

The Account

Unit 4

*1

In the last chapter, a device called a transaction sheet was used for teaching purposes to illustrate the fact that every business transaction results in at least two changes in items on the balance sheet. However, a transaction sheet is a cumbersome method of recording transactions and it is not suitable for recording a large number of transactions.

In this chapter, a more convenient recording form called a *T-account* is used to develop basic accounting procedures. In later chapters, a columnar form for recording transactions similar to those used by businesses will be introduced.

What is an Account? "Put it on my account" or "Charge it to my account" are instructions that customers often give when they make a purchase. Such customers enjoy the privilege of buying on credit. When a customer buys on credit, the seller must record the fact that money is owed to the business by the customer. For each customer, an *account* is kept. In each customer's account, the amount owing to the business is recorded. When a customer pays a portion of the amount owing, the account is lowered by this amount. When the customer charges additional purchases, the account is raised.

An account is a form on which changes caused by transactions are recorded.

Every transaction involving a customer and the business causes changes in the customer's account balance. These changes are recorded in the account kept for each customer.

The T-Account

*2

Following is a simple form of account called the T-account – for a reason that you can probably guess simply by looking at it. Notice that it has a title and two sides (a left side and a right side) just like the balance sheet.

Account Title

Left Side	Right Side

Debit refers to the left side of an account.

Credit refers to the right side of an account.

Using accounting terminology, *debit* refers to the left side of an account and *credit* refers to the right side of an account. *Do not place any additional meanings on these words.* In accounting, these two words refer *only* to the left (debit) and the right (credit) sides of an account.

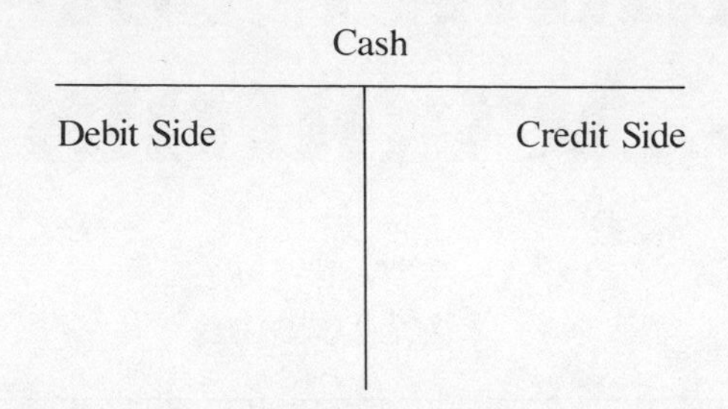

Recording the Balance Sheet in T-Accounts

*3

A separate account is required for each asset, for each liability, and for the owner's equity shown on the balance sheet. These separate accounts are required to record the day-to-day transactions of the business and the resulting changes these transactions cause in the items on the balance sheet. *How many accounts are required for the balance sheet in Figure 2.1?*

Martin Painting Contractors Balance Sheet November 1, 19__			
Assets		**Liabilities**	
Cash	1 675 00	Accounts Payable	250 00
Paint Supplies	900 00	Bank Loan	3 000 00
Equipment	2 500 00	Total Liabilities	3 250 00
Truck	6 000 00		
		Owner's Equity	
		K. Martin, Capital	7 825 00
Total Assets	11 075 00	Total Liabilities and Owner's Equity	11 075 00

Figure 2.1 *Balance sheet for Martin Painting Contractors*

Seven accounts are required to record this balance sheet: one for each of the four assets, one for each of the two liabilities, and one for owner's equity, K. Martin, Capital. These seven accounts are shown in Figure 2.2. Notice that each account has a title, a left side (debit), and a right side (credit).

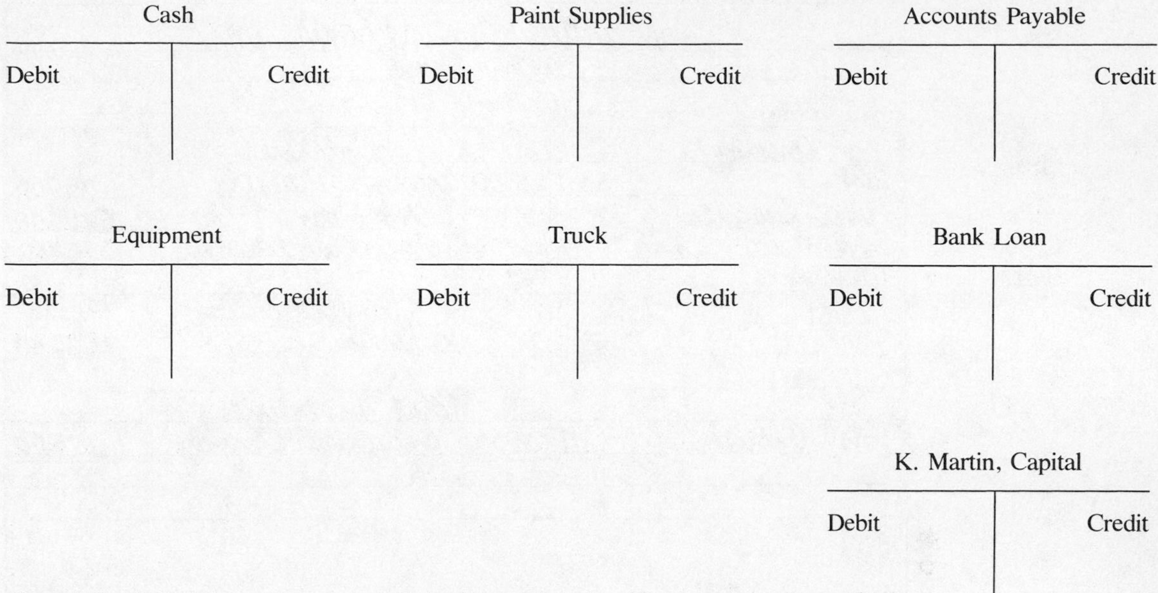

Figure 2.2 *Seven T-accounts to record the Martin Painting Contractors' balance sheet*

Recording Beginning Balances The beginning amount entered in an account from the balance sheet is called the *beginning balance*. Using Martin Painting Contractors as an example, the beginning balance for Cash is $1 675 and the beginning balance for Paint Supplies is $900.

*4

Cash	
1 675	

Paint Supplies	
900	

Since assets are located or originate on the left side of the balance sheet, the beginning balance of an asset is recorded on the left or debit side of its account. Similarly, liabilities are located or originate on the right side of the balance sheet so the beginning balance of each liability is recorded on the right or credit side of its account. The owner's equity balance is recorded on the credit or the right side of its account for the same reason. The rules for recording beginning balances are illustrated in Figure 2.3.

The beginning balance is the amount taken from the balance sheet and entered in an account.

After recording the balance sheet items in the T-accounts, some of the accounts have debit balances and others have credit balances. If all the debit balances are added, the total is $11 075. If all the credit balances are added, the total is also $11 075. Thus, just as the left side of the balance sheet equals the right side, the total of the debit balances in the accounts *always* equals the total of the credit balances.

Assets ($11 075) = **Liabilities** ($3 250) + **Owner's Equity** ($7 825)

Martin Painting Contractors
Balance Sheet
November 1, 19__

Assets		Liabilities	
Cash	1 675 00	Accounts Payable	250 00
Paint Supplies	900 00	Bank Loan	3 000 00
Equipment	2 500 00	Total Liabilities	3 250 00
Truck	6 000 00		
		Owner's Equity	
		K. Martin, Capital	7 825 00
		Total Liabilities	
Total Assets	11 075 00	and Owner's Equity	11 075 00

Asset account balances are recorded on the left side of their accounts.

Liability and owner's equity account balances are recorded on the right side of their accounts

Cash	
1 675	

Paint Supplies	
900	

Accounts Payable	
	250

Equipment	
2 500	

Truck	
6 000	

Bank Loan	
	3 000

K. Martin, Capital	
	7 825

Figure 2.3 *On which side of the T-accounts are the assets, liabilities, and owner's equity recorded?*

The Ledger

*5

A ledger is a group of accounts.

Seven accounts were required to record the opening balances for Martin Painting Contractors as shown in Figure 2.3. These accounts as a group are called a *ledger*. The process of recording opening balances from the balance sheet in accounts is called *opening the ledger*. In the past, a ledger was a book with each page being one account. Now the ledger may also consist of cards in a file, punched cards, computer tape, or magnetic discs.

Recording Transactions in T-Accounts

Unit 5

*6

Every business transaction causes changes in the assets, liabilities, or owner's equity of a business. These changes are recorded in the accounts or the ledger of the business. The balances of the accounts may increase or decrease depending on the type of transaction that occurs. In the four examples following, you will see that every transaction causes at least two changes in the accounts and you will learn the rules for recording changes in T-accounts.

Transaction 1 On November 3, Martin Painting Contractors buys paint supplies for $100 cash. This transaction immediately causes changes in Martin's accounts. First of all, the Paint Supplies account changes. It increases because the company now has more paint supplies. Since paint supplies increase, the $100 is recorded on the debit side of the Paint Supplies account below the opening balance of $900. Secondly, the Cash account changes. It decreases because Martin's now has less cash. In the Cash account, the $100 is recorded on the credit side, the side opposite the opening balance. *Can you determine why?*

An account increases on the same side as its opening balance.

An account decreases on the side opposite its opening balance.

Paint Supplies	
900	
100	

Cash	
1 675	100

There are logical reasons for recording a transaction on the left (debit) or right (credit) side of a T-account. Following is the reasoning involved.

1. The opening balance of asset accounts is recorded on the *left* side of the account because assets appear on the *left* side of the balance sheet. In other words, the side of origin of assets is the left side of the balance sheet.
2. An account increases on the same side as its opening balance.
3. Asset accounts increase on the *debit* side.
4. An account decreases on the side *opposite* to its opening balance. Asset accounts decrease on the *right* side or the *credit* side.

Assets increase on the debit side.

Assets decrease on the credit side.

*7

Transaction 2 On November 5, a new paint sprayer worth $200 is purchased on account. No cash is paid. *What are the changes in the accounts?*

The asset, Equipment, increases and the liability, Accounts Payable, also increases. The company now owns more equipment, but it now has more debts. It owes an additional $200.

Refer to the reasons given in Transaction 1 for recording transactions on the debit or credit side of accounts and apply them to this transaction. Because the Equipment account increases, the $200 is written below the opening balance on the debit side.

Equipment	
2 500	
200	

Accounts Payable	
	250
	200

Because Accounts Payable also increases, the $200 is written below the opening balance on the credit side. Following is the reasoning involved.

1. The opening balance of liability accounts is recorded on the *right* side of the account because liabilities appear on the *right* side of the balance sheet. The side of origin of liabilities is the right side of the balance sheet.
2. An account increases on the same side as its opening balance.
3. Liability accounts increase on the *credit* side.
4. An account decreases on the side *opposite* to its opening balance. Liability accounts decrease on the *left* side or *debit* side.

Liabilities increase on the credit side.

Liabilities decrease on the debit side.

*8

Transaction 3 On November 7, $1 000 cash is paid to the bank to reduce the bank loan. This transaction causes the account, Cash, to decrease and the account, Bank Loan, to also decrease. The company has less cash. The amount owing on the bank loan has decreased. *Is Cash debited or credited? Is Bank Loan debited or credited?*

The T-accounts that follow show how this transaction is recorded. Notice that although both Cash and Bank Loan decrease, the Cash account is *credited* and the Bank Loan account is *debited.*

Cash	
1 675	100
	1 000

Bank Loan	
1 000	3 000

*9

Transaction 4 On November 10, the owner, K. Martin, decides to improve the cash balance of Martin Painting Contractors and invests $700 of personal savings in the business. The effect of this transaction is to increase the company's Cash account. Martin's investment is also increased. The owner's investment is recorded in the account, K. Martin, Capital. Therefore the account, K. Martin, Capital, increases. In recording this transaction, Cash is debited because it increases. *Is K. Martin, Capital debited or credited?* The following reasoning will help you to decide.

1. The opening balance of the capital account is recorded on the *right* side of the

account because Owner's Equity or Capital appears on the right side of the balance sheet. The side of origin of Owner's Equity or Capital is the right side of the balance sheet.

Owner's Capital increases on the credit side.

2. An account increases on the same side as its opening balance.
3. The Capital account increases on its *credit* side.
4. An account decreases on the side *opposite* to its opening balance. The Capital account decreases on the *left* side or *debit* side.

Owner's Capital decreases on the debit side.

Cash	
1 675	100
700	1 000

K. Martin, Capital	
	7 825
	700

Rules for Recording Debits and Credits

*10

After recording the four transactions, the ledger of Martin Painting Contractors looks like Figure 2.4. Notice the dates that the opening balances were recorded and also the dates when each transaction occurred are now written beside each entry. As the number and complexity of accounts and transactions increase, the dates will prove to be a valuable reference and help to maintain the accuracy of the accounts.

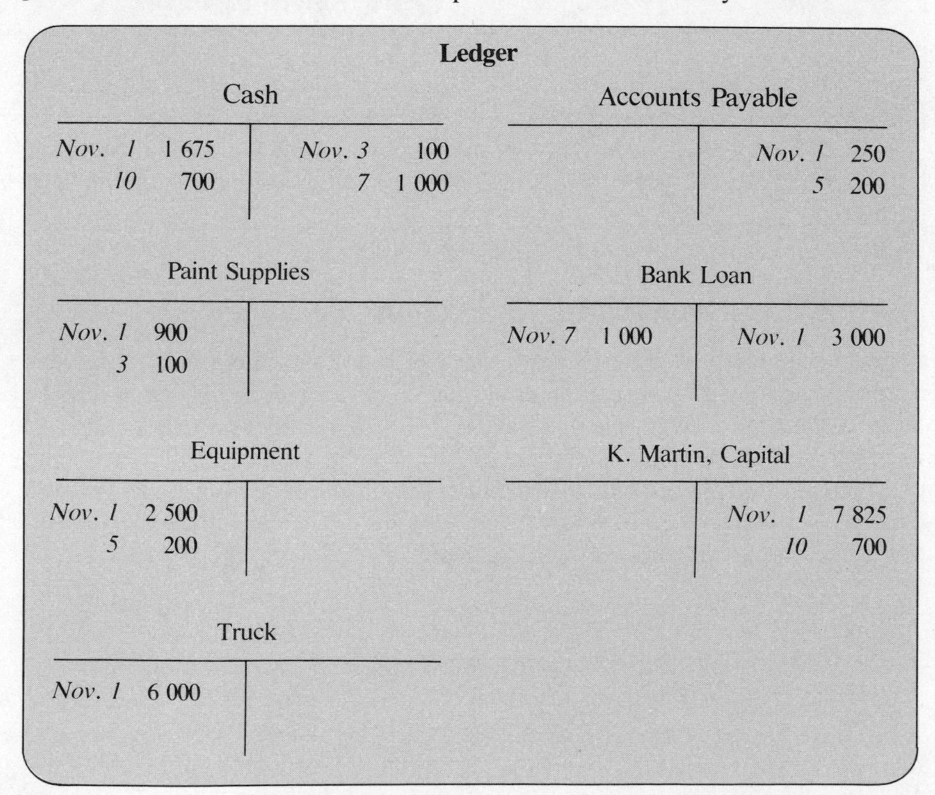

Figure 2.4 *T-account ledger after the four transactions have been recorded*

The four transactions given in the examples were recorded using the following basic rules for recording debits and credits:

- An account increases on the side of origin (the side on which it appears on the balance sheet).
- An account decreases on the side opposite the side of origin.

These basic rules are illustrated in Figure 2.5.

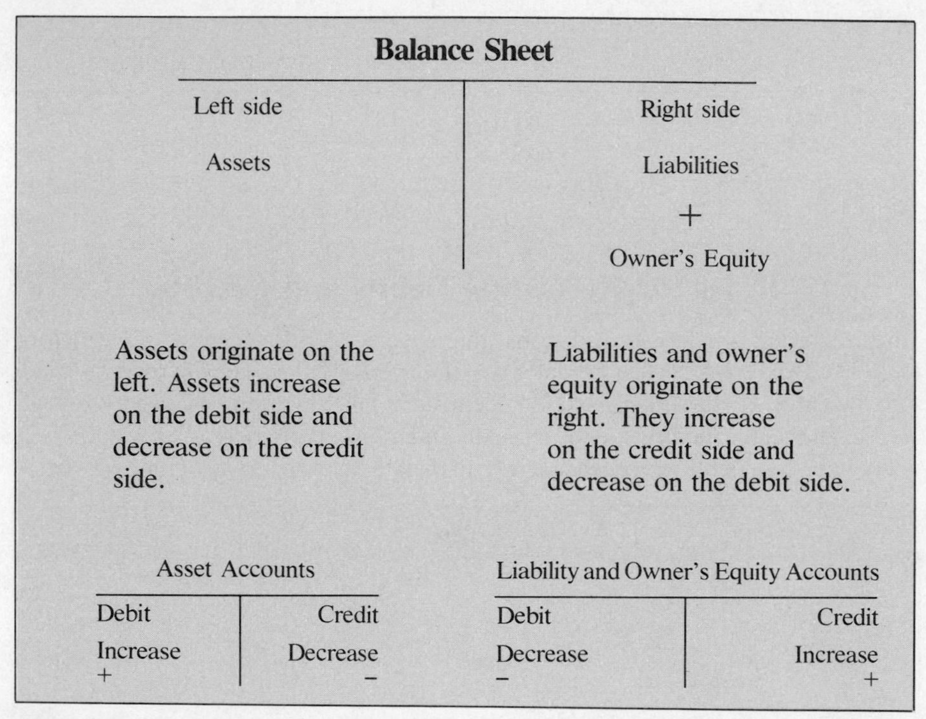

Figure 2.5 *Basic rules for recording transactions in accounts*

Unit 6

Determining T-Account Balances

*11

The difference between the two sides of an account is called the account balance.

Figure 2.4 shows the ledger of Martin Painting Contractors after transactions have been recorded as debits and credits. *How much cash does the business now have? What is the value of the equipment owned?* To answer these questions, it is necessary to find the *balances* of the accounts. To find the balance of an account, calculate the total of each side, then subtract the smaller total from the larger one. The Cash account in Figure 2.6 is an example of this procedure. All the accounts in the ledger would be balanced in this manner.

Cash

Nov. 1	1 675	*Nov. 3*	100
10	700	*7*	1 000
	2 375		1 100
Balance	1 275		

Figure 2.6 *Balancing the Cash account*

In Figure 2.6, the debits total $2 375 and the credits total $1 100 in the Cash account. Note that the balance of $1 275 (2 375 – 1 100 = 1 275) is written on the side of the account with the larger total, which is the debit side in this example. If the total on the debit side of an account is larger than the total on the credit side, the account is said to have a debit balance. If the total on the credit side is larger then the total on the debit side (as is the case in the Bank Loan account), the account is said to have a credit balance.

Assets normally show debit balances. Liabilities and owner's equity accounts normally show credit balances.

The Trial Balance

The mathematical accuracy of the ledger is tested by preparing a list of the account balances in what is called a *trial balance*. The total of the debit account balances should equal the total of the credit account balances.

The ledger for Martin Painting Contractors is shown in Figure 2.7. For each of the accounts, the balance has been determined.

*12

A trial balance is a procedure for testing the equality of debit and credit account balances in the ledger.

Ledger

Cash

Nov. 1	1 675	*Nov. 3*	100
10	700	*7*	1 000
	2 375		1 100
Balance	1 275		

Accounts Payable

		Nov. 1	250
		5	200
		Balance	450

Paint Supplies

Nov. 1	900		
3	100		
Balance	1 000		

Bank Loan

Nov. 7	1 000	*Nov. 1*	3 000
		Balance	2 000

Equipment

Nov. 1	2 500		
5	200		
Balance	2 700		

K. Martin, Capital

		Nov. 1	7 825
		10	700
		Balance	8 525

Truck

Nov. 1	6 000		
Balance	6 000		

Figure 2.7 *T-account ledger with the account balances*

A trial balance for the ledger is shown in Figure 2.8. The trial balance is simply a list of all the accounts in the ledger, with their balances. The list shows the accounts with debit balances and the accounts with credit balances. The total of the debit balances should equal the total of the credit balances.

1	Who? Martin Painting Contractors			
	What? Trial Balance			
	When? November 10, 19__			
	ACCOUNT TITLE	ACC. NO.	DEBIT	CREDIT
2	Cash		1 275 —	
	Paint Supplies		1 000 —	
	Equipment		2 700 —	
	Truck		6 000 —	
	Accounts Payable			450 —
	Bank Loan			2 000 —
	K. Martin, Capital	3		8 525 —
		4	10 975 —	10 975 —

Figure 2.8 *Trial balance for Martin Painting Contractors*

Steps in Preparing a Trial Balance

1. Write the heading, showing the name of the business *(Who?)*, the name of the statement *(What?)*, and the date *(When?)*.
2. List each account in the order in which it appears in the ledger and write the balance in the correct debit or credit column.
3. Rule a single line under both columns and add the columns.
4. If the two columns are equal, write the totals below the single line and rule double lines below the totals.

*13

Accuracy of the Trial Balance The trial balance provides a checking procedure to test the accuracy of the entries in the accounts. First, it checks that the beginning balances were recorded correctly. Secondly, it checks that a debit and an equal credit were recorded for each transaction. Finally, the trial balance proves that the debit totals in the accounts equal the credit totals.

The trial balance can be considered to be a preliminary check on the accuracy of the accounting procedures. After the trial balance has been completed and is in balance, the balance sheet is prepared from the information on the trial balance.

If a trial balance does not balance, an error has been made and must be corrected before the balance sheet is prepared. Although the mathematical accuracy of the ledger can be tested and proven by the preparation of a trial balance, a ledger which is in balance is not necessarily correct. For instance, it is possible to record an equal debit or credit correctly, but in the wrong accounts, or to record incorrect amounts such as $100 instead of $1 000. It is important to realize that a ledger which is in balance may still contain errors. Errors can only be avoided through careful work on your part and will be less likely to occur as you gain more experience in accounting procedures. Detailed procedures for locating errors are outlined in Chapter 5 on page 99.

Double-Entry Accounting

All the transactions illustrated in this chapter affected two accounts. The transactions caused changes in the accounts with the changes being recorded as debits or credits. For every transaction a debit and an equal credit was recorded. In accounting, the process of entering a debit and a credit of equal amounts is called *double-entry* accounting. The important principle of double-entry accounting is that the left side always equals the right side. This principle provides a mathematical check on the accuracy of accounting procedures.

*14

Double-entry accounting is a system by which every transaction is recorded with equal debit and credit amounts.

Equality of Debits and Credits To demonstrate the principle of double-entry accounting, look at the summary of accounting procedures that have been covered in this chapter as illustrated in Figure 2.9.

Facts to Remember

An *account* is a form on which changes caused by transactions are recorded. There is one account for each asset and liability, and for the owner's capital.

Debit refers to the left side of an account.

Credit refers to the right side of an account.

Assets, which are on the left side of the balance sheet, have their balances recorded on the left side, the debit side, of their accounts.

Assets increase on their debit side and decrease on credit side.

Liabilities and owner's equity, which are on the right side of the balance sheet, have their balances recorded on the right side, the credit side, of their accounts.

Liabilities and owner's equity accounts increase on the credit side and decrease on the debit side.

A *ledger* is a group of accounts.

A trial balance is a procedure for testing the equality of debit and credit account balances in the ledger.

Double-entry accounting is a system by which every transaction is recorded with equal debit and credit amounts.

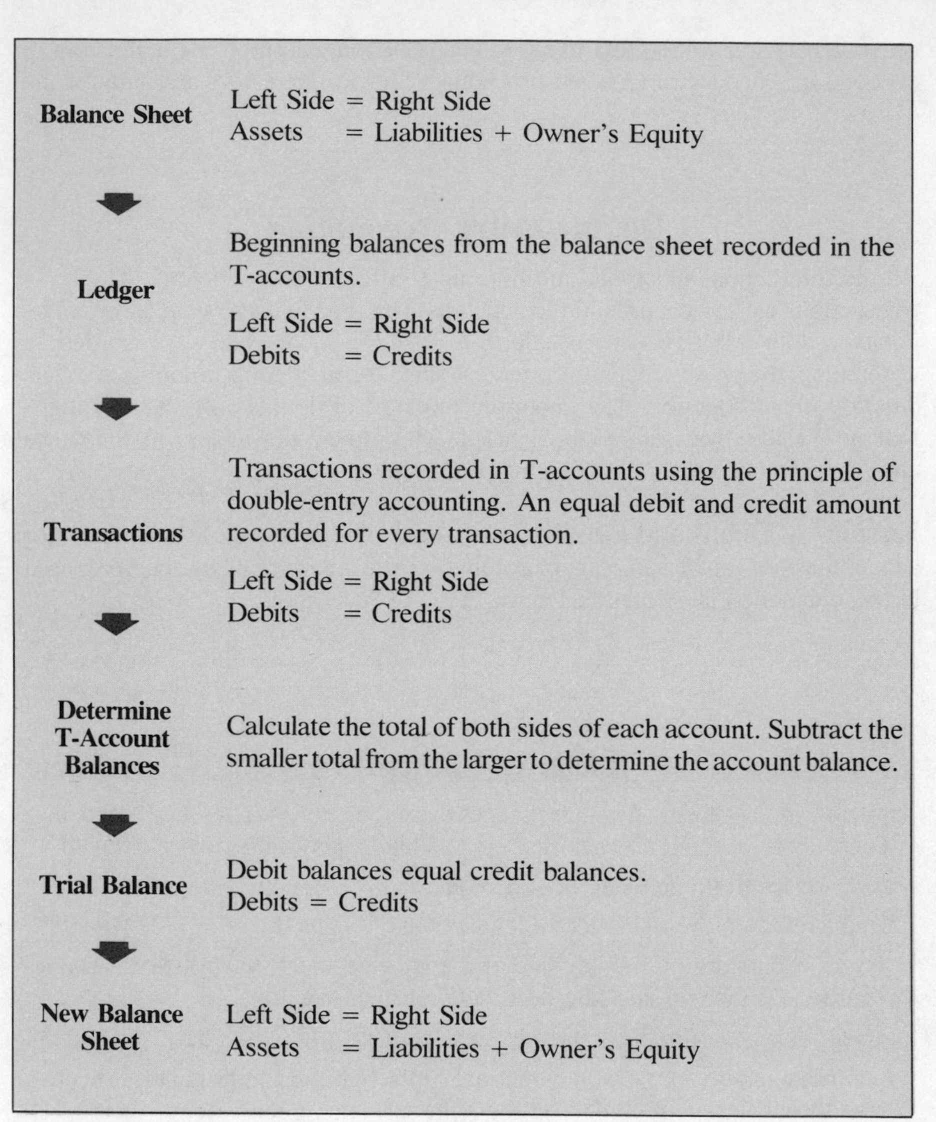

Figure 2.9 *Summary of accounting procedures discussed in this chapter*

Summary of Debit and Credit Theory

A = **L** + **OE**

Asset Accounts		Liability Accounts		Owner's Equity Account	
Debit	Credit	Debit	Credit	Debit	Credit
Increase	Decrease	Decrease	Increase	Decrease	Increase
+	−	−	+	−	+

Checking Your Reading

Questions

1. What is an account?
2. What is the left side of an account called?
3. What is the right side of an account called?
4. What determines the number of accounts required to record the beginning balances of a business?
5. On which side of an account is the beginning balance of an asset recorded? Why?
6. On which side of the account is the beginning balance of a liability recorded? Why?
7. On which side of the account is the beginning balance of the owner's equity recorded? Why?
8. What is a ledger?
9. What is the increase side for an asset account? Why? What is the decrease side?
10. What is the increase side for a liability and owner's equity account? Why? What is the decrease side?
11. How is an account balance calculated?
12. What is a trial balance?
13. List the steps followed in preparing a trial balance.
14. What can you safely assume about the ledger if the trial balance indicates that the totals of the debits and credits are equal?
15. What is double-entry accounting?
16. Prepare a summary of the rules for recording transactions as debits and credits. Your summary, if written on a slip of paper or on a card, can be used as a bookmark and ready reference source.

Applying Your Knowledge

Exercises Part A

1. High-Rise Cleaners have contracts to wash the windows of large office buildings. Using the information from their balance sheet, set up accounts and record the opening balances. Since there are four assets, two liabilities, and the capital, you will need seven T-accounts.

High-Rise Cleaners Balance Sheet May 1, 19__			
Assets		Liabilities	
Cash	3 500 00	Accounts Payable	700 00
Cleaning Supplies	1 400 00	Bank Loan	4 300 00
Equipment	5 000 00	Total Liabilities	5 000 00
Truck	7 500 00		
		Owner's Equity	
		B. Hill, Capital	12 400 00
		Total Liabilities	
Total Assets	17 400 00	and Owner's Equity	17 400 00

2. Action Auction Sales provides auctioneering services as well as complete sales facilities. Open their ledger on June 1, 19__ with the following accounts and balances:

   Assets: Cash $9 600; Accounts Receivable $17 300; Supplies $3 000; Land & Building $92 000; Furniture & Fixtures $8 500; Truck $7 000.
   Liabilities: Accounts Payable $5 600; Mortgage $35 000.
   Owner's Equity: M. John Henry, Capital $96 800.

3. Open the ledger for Dr. Kingsbury on February 1, 19__ with the following accounts and balances:

   Cash $9 000; Due from Patients $6 000; Due from Provincial Health Plan $14 000; Supplies $2 000; Equipment $30 000; Due to Suppliers $4 000; Bank Loan $7 000; Dr. Kingsbury, Capital $50 000.

4. Bradley Air Service provides aviation training and leases or rents aircraft. Open their books on March 1, 19__ with the following accounts and balances:

   Cash $8 500; Accounts Receivable $12 600; Equipment $45 000; Aircraft Fleet $150 000; Accounts Payable $14 700; Bank Loan $5 200; Mortgage Payable $75 100; D. Bradley, Capital $121 100.

5. Open the ledger for the Arabian Nights Restaurant on August 1, 19__ with the following accounts and balances:

   Cash $17 000; Supplies $10 000; Furniture and Fixtures $19 600; Equipment

$40 000; Land and Building $175 000; Due to Suppliers $10 300; Mortgage Payable $110 000; M. Nihmey, Capital $141 300.

6. Calculate the balance for each of the following accounts using the procedure that accompanies Figure 2.6.

Cash	
1 500	250
400	750
2 000	

Accounts Receivable	
2 000	500
3 700	250
1 800	50

7. For the following T-account ledger:
   a) calculate the balance for each account;
   b) prepare a trial balance on December 10, 19__ using the format in Figure 2.8.

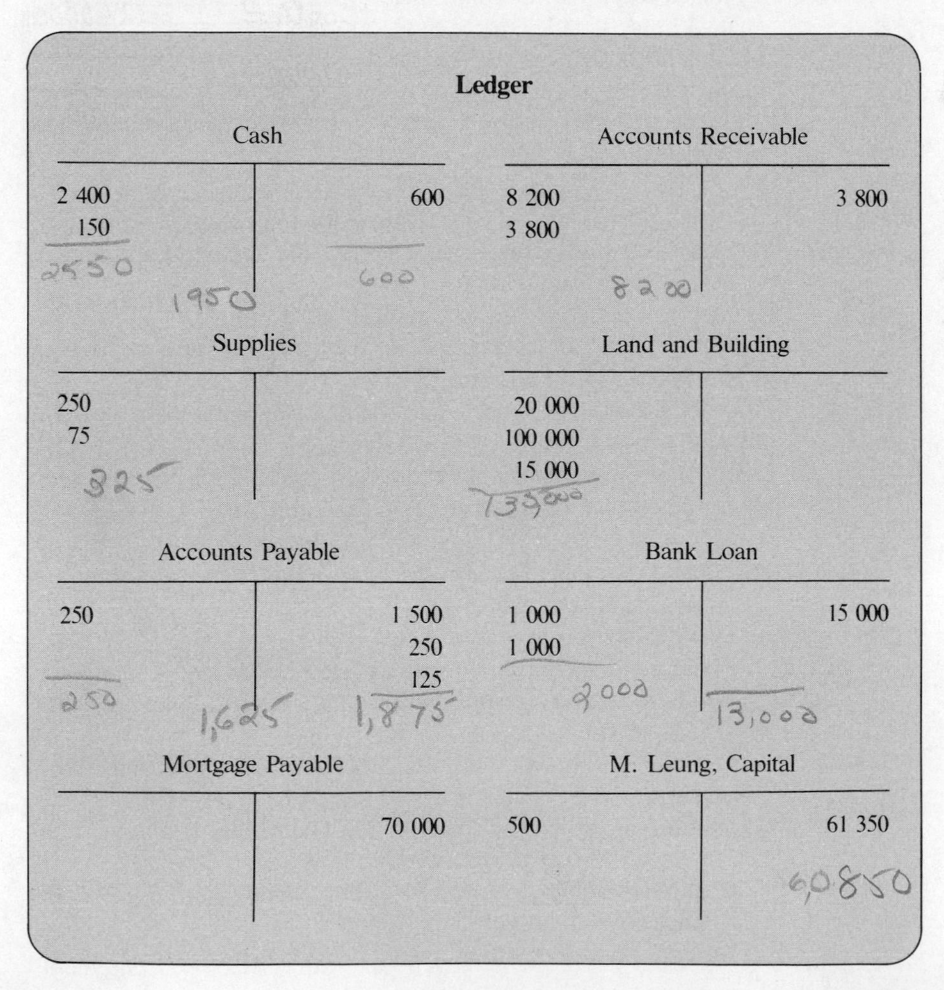

8. In the ledger you opened for High-Rise Cleaners in exercise 1:
   a) record the following transactions;
   b) prepare a balance sheet on May 9, 19__.

May 4 Bought soap, towels, and other cleaning supplies for $150 cash.
6 Bought a new hoist for the scaffolds. The hoist is valued at $1 500, but will be paid for at a later date.
8 Cash of $800 was paid to the bank to reduce the bank loan.
9 Mr. Hill invested $2 000 of his personal savings into High-Rise Cleaners.

9. In the ledger you opened for Action Auction Sales in exercise 2:
   a) record the following transactions;
   b) prepare a balance sheet on June 15, 19__.

June 2 M. Kelly, a client, paid $550 cash on his account.
6 Bought some supplies for $50 cash.
7 Installed new shelves (fixtures) for which Action Auction Sales promised to pay V. Gorman, the carpenter, $260 at a later date.
9 Paid $370 to B. Soles, a creditor, on account.
11 Made a $500 payment on the mortgage.
15 M. John Henry increased his investment in Action Auction Sales by $2 000 by taking the money from his personal savings and giving it to his business.

Exercises Part B

10. In the set of books you opened for Dr. Kingsbury in exercise 3:
    a) record the following transactions and calculate the account balances;
    b) prepare a trial balance on February 7, 19__.

Feb 1 C. Patten, a patient, paid $55 cash on his account.
3 Bought surgical bandages and other medical supplies from Medical Suppliers for $78 on account.
5 Returned $43 worth of supplies to Medical Suppliers since they had not sent what Dr. Kingsbury had ordered.
6 Paid $90 to Pharmaceutical Products, a creditor, on account.
7 Made the regular $200 payment on the bank loan.

11. In the set of books you opened for Bradley Air Services in exercise 4:
    a) record the following transactions;
    b) prepare a trial balance on March 15, 19__.

March 2 Made a regular monthly payment of $700 on the mortgage.
3 Purchased a new compressed air pump from Cadence Industries for $1 700 on account.
6 D. Bradley, the owner, invested $4 000 more cash from personal savings.
7 Secured a further bank loan of $15 000 to buy a new aircraft.
11 Purchased a new aircraft worth $24 000 from Airways Manufacturing by paying a $14 000 downpayment; the $10 000 balance to be paid later.
15 Received $2 500 cash on account, from L. Rosewood

12. In the set of books you opened for the Arabian Nights in exercise 5:
a) record the following transactions;
b) prepare a trial balance on August 8, 19__.

Aug 1 Made the regular monthly payment of $880 on the mortgage.
2 Purchased a new oven from Restaurant Suppliers for $780 on account.
4 Paid $1 300 on account to Wholesale Foods Limited.
5 Purchased a new table and four chairs from Owens Furniture for $280 cash.
8 Mr. Nihmey invested $3 000 cash into the business.

Exercises Part C

13. Disc Jockeys Unlimited provide music and a disc jockey service for dances and other functions. From the information supplied:
a) open their books on April 1, 19__;
b) record the transactions;
c) calculate the new balances in each account;
d) prepare a trial balance on April 15, 19__

Accounts and Balances on April 1, 19__
Cash $2 500; Accounts Receivable/Skilite Hotel $300; Accounts Receivable/Trimble High School $120; Record Library $6 600; Equipment $7 800; Accounts Payable/Columbia $600; Accounts Payable/RCA $300; Bank Loan $1 200; K. Potter, Capital $15 220.

Transactions

April 1 Received $120 cash from Trimble High School in full payment of their account.
3 Received a $250 shipment of records from RCA. The bill will be paid at a later date.
4 Some of the records were damaged when received and were sent back to RCA for a $50 credit.
5 Paid Columbia $100 on account.
8 Bought a new set of speakers from Trevor Electronics for $1 750 cash.
10 Made a $400 payment on the bank loan.

14. a) Open the books for Clare's Beauty Salon with the accounts and balances given on October 1, 19__.
b) Record the October transactions.
c) Calculate the new balances in each account.
d) Prepare a trial balance on October 7, 19__.

Accounts and Balances on October 1, 19__
Cash $4 800; Accounts Receivable/Visa $3 600; Supplies $2 400; Equipment $40 000; Land & Building $120 000; Accounts Payable/Beauty Products $800; Bank Loan $700; Mortgage $90 000; C. Williams, Capital $79 300.

Transactions

Oct. 1 Purchased shampoo, hair spray, and other beauty supplies from Beauty Products for $250 on account.

Oct. 2 Returned some of the supplies to Beauty Products for a credit of $75 since they were not what had been ordered.
2 Received $2 200 cash from Visa.
3 Made the regular $700 payment on the mortgage.
4 Bought 4 new hair dryers worth $12 000 from Beauty Products. The business put a $3 000 cash deposit on the dryers, and the balance of $9 000 is to be paid later.
5 Secured a bank loan of $10 000, part of which will be used to pay for the hair dryers.
7 Paid $9 000 cash to Beauty Products to pay for the balance owing on the hair dryers.

Accounting in Action

Case 1

T-Account Errors There are several errors in the Cash T-account. What are they? What is the correct balance?

Cash

5 000.	1 000
2 000.	3 000
4 000.	1 500
11 000	6 500
	balance 4 500

Case 2

Trial Balance Errors A trial balance has been prepared and balances with total debits of $150 000 and total credits of $150 000. However the following errors were made:

- a $1 000 transaction was recorded (both debit and credit) as $100
- a $250 transaction was omitted entirely (both debit and credit)

What is the correct trial balance total?

Case 3

Transaction Errors A $300 payment was made to a creditor. In recording the transaction both cash and accounts payable were credited. This was the only error made.

a) Is the cash account balance correct?
b) Is the accounts payable account correct?
c) What will the difference be between the debit and the credit totals of the trial balance?

Case 4

Double-Entry Accounting A student has learned the double-entry method of accounting. The student states that it is based on the idea that:

Items owned = Claims against items owned.

Further, because of this relationship, debits must always equal credits if the accounting equation, A = L +OE, is to remain in balance.

The student then states this false conclusion: "In recording a transaction, an asset must change and either a liability or the owner's equity must also change."

Using your knowledge of double-entry accounting, explain the fallacy in the student's thinking.

Case 5

The Trial Balance An accounting student claims that there is no purpose served by the trial balance. She states that a balance sheet can be made directly from the data in the ledger.

a) Is she correct? Give reasons for your answer.
b) How would you explain the purpose served by the trial balance to her?

Case 6

Interpreting Accounting Data A relative of yours has just passed away. In the will you are named to inherit a small fuel business called Crowland Fuels Co. The records of the company provide the following information:

Things Owned by the Company	Cost Price
Two fuel trucks (each)	$20 000
Cash in the bank	2 000
Storage Tanks	10 000
Fuel Inventory	17 000
Equipment	5 000
Office Supplies	200
Office Equipment	4 000
Miscellaneous Assets	2 000
Debts of the Company	
Accounts Payable	$12 000
Salaries Owing	500
Taxes Owing	2 000
Bank Loan	20 000

Other Information The two trucks are over five years old. None of the assets is less than two years old except the fuel inventory. The company employs two full-time truck drivers, a service repairman and an office clerk. During the busy season two part-time employees are hired. The company has contracts to supply fuel to 200 customers. The average purchase per customer is $400 per year.

a) What is the business worth to you?
b) Would you keep the business or sell it?
c) What other information would you like to have in order to answer b)?
d) A very large multinational corporation, Exodus Ltd., has offered you $12 000 in return for the assets, liabilities, and customer contracts. Would you accept? Why?

You probably have found it quite difficult to confidently answer the questions.

This case study is designed to illustrate that owners and managers need accurate and up-to-date information to help them make decisions about their companies. One of the main purposes of accounting is to provide such information. People who work in accounting provide financial information and also interpret the information for their employers.

Case 7

Charge Accounts We are all familiar with bank credit cards such as Master Charge and Visa. Many large department stores such as Eaton's, The Bay, and Simpsons-Sears grant their own credit cards to their customers. Here is how one store, *Z Department Store** decides whether or not a person will receive the privilege of using its credit card.

1. Complete a standard application form. Call the credit references supplied on the form. Call the employer to verify employment. If these steps indicate that the person has a job and has a good payment record for the last six months, *approve* the application at once. If this information is not available, proceed to step two.
2. Call the Credit Bureau. If the person receives a favourable credit check, *approve* the application at once. If there is no file on the person, proceed to step three.
3. Confirm the person's employment. If working full time, *approve* the application at once. If unemployed, *reject*.

If a charge account is granted to a customer, then a credit limit is set. This is the maximum amount which may be outstanding in the customer's account. The limit is set by completion of this guide:

A	**Marital Status**	Married	Single	Widowed	Other
	Points	+2	+1	+4	0

B	**Years Married**	0-2	2-5	5-10	10 or more
	Points	0	+2	+3	+5

C	**Residence**	Own	Own a Mobile Home	Rent	Live with Parents
	Points	+5	+3	0	+2

D	**Years at Address**	2 yrs	2-5	5 or more
	Points	0	+2	+3

E	**Spouse's Age**	up to 30	30-36	36-45	45 or more
	Points	0	+2	+3	+5

F	**Telephone**	Yes	No
	Points	+4	0

Points are allocated to the answers to A to F. If a person obtains less than 12 points, a charge account is not issued. If a person obtains 13 to 18 points, a credit limit of $600 is established with a monthly minimum payment of $50. If a person obtains a total over 19 points, a limit of $800 is established with monthly payments of $60.

*The name has been changed.

a) What is your opinion of the advantages and disadvantages of this system of granting charge accounts?
b) Can you suggest a better method?

What Employers Look for in Job Applicants Many people apply for jobs but some are continually turned down and never seem lucky enough to get hired. Why? To answer this question, a survey was made of employers and 1 695 answered questions concerning how and why they hired and fired employees. Following is a summary of this survey. **Case 8**

Sources for Obtaining Job Applicants Employers were asked to indicate how they get job applicants. The five leading sources, in order, are:

1. word-of-mouth
2. people applying without knowing if an opening is available
3. newspaper want ads
4. government agency
5. private employment agencies

Reasons for Rejecting Job Applicants The 10 leading reasons employers give for rejecting job applicants after the job interview are, in order:

1. little interest or poor reasons for wanting a job
2. applicant has a past history of job-hopping
3. inability of applicant to communicate during job interview
4. health record
5. immaturity (other than chronological age)
6. personal appearance
7. manners and mannerisms
8. personality
9. lack of job-related skills
10. poorly filled-out job application form

Causes for Terminating Employees Employers cited as the five primary causes for employee termination, in order:

1. absenteeism
2. lack of interest in the job
3. continuously makes costly mistakes
4. does not follow instructions
5. shows an unwillingness to learn

Areas in Which Improvement is Needed Employers were also asked about improvements they believe are needed in those areas that prepare people for entry into full-time work. Areas in which improvement is most needed are, in order:

1. a concern for productivity
2. a pride of craftsmanship and quality of work
3. responsibility and the ability to follow through on an assigned task
4. dependability
5. work habits
6. attitudes toward company and employer
7. the ability to write and speak effectively

8. the ability to follow instructions
9. the ability to read and apply printed matter to the job
10. ambition/motivation/desire to get ahead

Case 9

Punishing the Innocent Along with the Guilty The following article appeared in an Ottawa newspaper.

Jaws:

$600 missing – theatre fires 13

The management of a local theatre fired 13 employees – mostly teenagers working part-time at the concession stand or as ushers. Letters advising the employees of their dismissal were mailed following the disappearance of about $600.

A spokesman for the theatre defended the firing by saying, "Money has been disappearing for a number of weeks. We were unable to determine who the thief was so we decided to fire everyone who had access to the cash register."

"We didn't notify the police. By keeping it quiet we thought we might protect the reputations of 12 innocent people. It's unfortunate that everyone has to suffer for the actions of one thief, but we acted within the letter of the law."

The theft was discovered by an analysis of the concession inventory. Each week a count is made of all candy, soft drinks, etc., on hand. To the total obtained, the purchases of goods during the week is added. From this total, the inventory of goods on hand at the end of the week is subtracted. The result is the cost of the goods sold during the week. The management is able to determine the cash that should be on hand from the cost of the sales.

a) Do you think the theatre management was justified in firing all 13 employees since they could not determine which one was guilty?
b) What would you do if you were one of the innocent persons fired?
c) What do you think of the statement that the firings protected the reputations of 12 innocent people?
d) If you were one of the 13 employees and were aware that one of your fellow workers was stealing money, what would you do?

Career Profile

A Financial Analyst Ray Thomas attended the High School of Commerce in Ottawa. While in high school he took a number of business courses including three accounting courses. After graduating, Ray took a three-month holiday. In September, he entered the School of Business at Algonquin College and graduated after three years from the Business Administration program.

Ray's first job after college was with the federal government as a trainee in the Auditing Branch. The work in accounting proved to be enjoyable and rewarding.

His superiors encouraged him to continue his studies and to work towards a professional degree in accounting.

After working for three years, Ray decided to begin the studies required to become a *Registered Industrial Accountant* (R.I.A.). Ray continued to work with the civil service during the day and took night lectures at Carleton University. His employers recognized his industriousness and paid the tuition fees for these courses.

It was a very tiring and time-consuming period. After working all day, Ray had to spend about 15 hours each week on his R.I.A. studies. However, he was able to benefit from an educational program offered by his employers. For six months he went to classes full time at Algonquin College and was able to accumulate a number of credits towards the R.I.A. certification. The best part was that he was still being paid his full salary! Thus, only three years after starting the program, Ray graduated with his R.I.A. degree.

Ray is now a financial systems analyst with the Canadian Department of Supply and Services. His duties include the preparation of financial management reports, cost studies, and the development of financial systems to control government costs and revenues.

CHAPTER 3

The Income Statement

Unit 7

Reviewing the Purpose of Accounting

*1

RECORDING
↓
REPORTS
↓
DECISIONS

In Chapter 1, the purpose of accounting was expressed as a system to provide information which is used to make decisions. This involves two types of accounting activity:

- recording daily transactions
- preparing reports which summarize daily transactions

In Chapters 1 and 2 you learned how daily business transactions were recorded and how a statement called a balance sheet was prepared. The balance sheet presented the assets, liabilities, and owner's equity at a specific date. In this chapter and in Chapter 4, you will learn how a statement called an *income statement* is prepared.

Profit and Loss

TRANSACTIONS
↓
LEDGER

People go into business for themselves for a variety of reasons. Mary and Joe Galotta, the owners of The Cascade Inn, started their motel business:

- to use their personal talents and abilities to the fullest
- because of the pride they felt in ownership of their own business
- for the personal satisfaction of building a successful business
- to earn a profitable living for themselves

Once the Cascade was established, it grew and became successful. It is successful because it is *profitable*. A business cannot survive for very long unless it earns a *profit*.

*2

Goods are products sold to customers.

Services are things done for customers.

What is a Profit? What is a Loss? A business sells *goods* such as cameras, automobiles, clothes, and furniture or it sells *services* like television repairs, transportation, and hair styling. The money or the promise of money received from the sale of goods or services is called *revenue*.

In order to sell goods and services, money is spent to operate the business. Money is spent on salaries, advertising, delivery, and many other things required to run a business. These items are called *expenses*. More formal definitions of revenue and expenses are given on page 52.

Figure 3.1 shows a camera which has a selling price of $80. The seller had to spend $45 in selling the camera. *When the camera was sold, did the seller make a profit or was there a loss?* Of course there was a profit of $35.

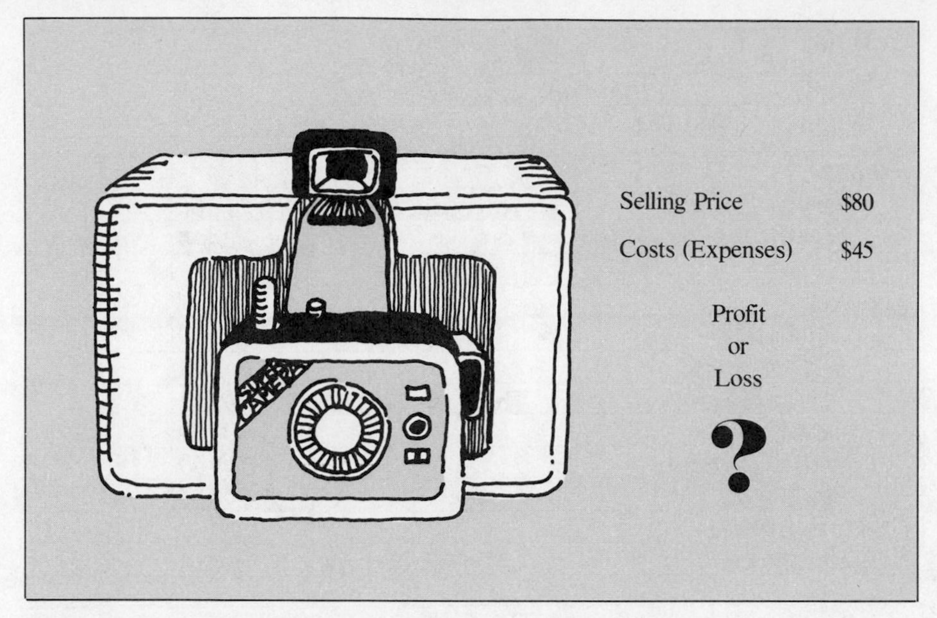

Figure 3.1 *Is there a profit or a loss on the sale of the camera?*

As the camera example illustrates, when the revenue is greater than the expenses there is a profit or *net income*.

Revenue – Expenses = Profit or Net Income

Net income is the difference between revenue and expenses when revenue is greater than expenses.

However, the total of the expenses may be greater than the revenue and then the difference between the revenue and the expenses is called a loss or *net loss*.

Revenue – Expenses = Loss or Net Loss

The terms net income and net loss are the preferred accounting terms for profit and loss respectively and will be used in the balance of this book. The following equation mathematically illustrates how the net income or net loss on the sale of the camera is determined.

Net loss is the difference between revenue and expenses when expenses are greater than revenue.

Revenue (Selling Price)	–	**Expenses** (Costs and Expenses)	=	**Net Income or Net Loss**
$80	–	$45	=	$35 (Net Income)
$80	–	$95	=	– $15 (Net Loss)

The Income Statement

Figure 3.2 illustrates a financial statement, called an *income statement,* that was prepared to determine the net income or net loss of The Cascade Inn. *3

To begin with, look at the various parts of the income statement. Just like the balance sheet, it has a three-part heading which answers the questions *Who?, What?,* and *When?* The major difference in the two statements is that a balance sheet presents the assets, liabilities, and owner's equity at a particular *point in time*.

An income statement is a financial statement which presents the revenue, expenses, and net income or net loss for a specific period of time.

Who? Cascade Inn			
What? Income Statement			
When? For the Month of June, 19__			
Revenue:			
Room Rentals	1 Revenue Section	25 000 00	
Restaurant Sales		6 000 00	31 000 00
Expenses:			
Salaries		10 000 00	
Advertising		1 000 00	
Telephone	2 Expense Section	200 00	
Laundry		3 600 00	
Maintenance		6 000 00	
Interest		2 000 00	
Total Expenses			22 800 00
Net Income	3 Net Income		8 200 00

Figure 3.2 *Income statement for The Cascade Inn*

An income statement presents the revenue, expenses, and net income or net loss covering a *period of time*. In Figure 3.2, the period of time is the month of June.

After the heading there are three parts to the income statement: *revenue, expenses,* and *net income* (or *net loss*).

Revenue is an inflow of assets from the sale of goods and services.

Revenue The revenue of a business comes from customers who buy goods or services supplied by the business. The revenue for the Cascade came from two sources – room rentals and restaurant sales. Revenue is usually in the form of cash or accounts receivable.

The income statement of The Cascade Inn shows that the business has sold the use of its rooms ($25 000) and food and beverages in its restaurant ($6 000) for a total revenue of $31 000.

Expenses are the costs of goods or services used in the operation of a business.

Expenses In order to bring in the $31 000 revenue, the management of the Cascade had to spend money. Management had to pay for items such as salaries, advertising, telephone, laundry, maintenance, and interest. These items are *expenses.*

Net income is the difference between revenue and expenses when revenue is greater than expenses.

Net Income or Net Loss *Did The Cascade Inn make any money in June or did the business lose money? How much?* If the inn made money, the amount is identified by the accounting term *net income*. The last line of the income statement illustrated in Figure 3.2 reveals that The Cascade Inn had a net income of $8 200 in June. For this particular month, the revenue of $31 000 was greater than the expenses of $22 800. The difference of $8 200 was the net income for the month.

Revenue	–	**Expenses**	=	**Net Income (or Net Loss)**
$31 000	–	$22 800	=	$8 200

The Cascade Inn Balance Sheet June 30, 19__				
Assets		Liabilities		
Cash	4 000 00	Accounts Payable	30 000 00	
Motel Supplies	9 000 00	Bank Loan	16 000 00	
Office Equipment	3 000 00	Mortgage Payable	115 000 00	
Room Furniture	110 000 00	Total Liabilities		161 000 00
Building	500 000 00			
Land	50 000 00	Owner's Equity		
		Galotta, Capital, June 1	506 800 00	
		Net Income for June	8 200 00	
		Galotta, Capital, June 30		515 000 00
Total Assets	676 000 00	Total Liabilities and Owner's Equity		676 000 00

Figure 3.3 *Balance sheet for The Cascade Inn showing net income added to owner's capital*

When a business earns a net income, the owner's equity increases because the net income belongs to the owner. A *net loss* decreases the owner's equity. Revenue generates or creates the surplus which becomes the net income; thus revenue increases owner's equity. Expenses do the opposite. They decrease or cancel any surplus; thus expenses decrease equity.

Net loss is the difference between revenue and expenses when expenses are greater than revenue.

The Balance Sheet Figure 3.3. is the balance sheet for the Cascade that was prepared on June 30. Notice that the $8 200 net income for the month was added to the owner's capital. The owner's investment has increased because the business earned a net income in June. Remember that the net income figure is required to complete the balance sheet so the income statement must always be prepared before the balance sheet.

***4**

The functions of the revenue and expense accounts and the income statement as a whole will be examined more thoroughly in Chapter 4. First, several more new concepts must be introduced.

The Accounting Period

The *accounting period* is the period of time covered by the income statement and the length of the period may vary depending on the accounting practices of particular businesses. Every business prepares a yearly income statement for tax purposes, but many businesses prefer to prepare statements more frequently. For example, the income statement in Figure 3.2 shows a one-month accounting period. A business may be able to take action to improve its operations if, for

***5**
The accounting period is the period of time covered by the income statement.

instance, the income statement shows a net loss during a short period of time. If a business only finds out after a year that it is operating at a loss, it may be too late to do anything about it.

The term *fiscal period* is often used in place of the term accounting period. A *fiscal year* (or an accounting year) is, therefore, any 12-month accounting period. This is not to be confused with the *calendar year* which is the 12 months beginning January 1 and ending December 31.

Unit 8

The Owner's Equity Accounts

*6

The owner's equity accounts are vital to the understanding of correct debit and credit procedures for the revenue and expense accounts. Since the transactions affecting the revenue and expense accounts will be covered in Chapter 4, be sure you understand the discussion of the owner's equity accounts that follows before proceeding to the next chapter.

There can be two owner's equity accounts in the ledger. They are the *owner's Capital account* and the *owner's Drawing account*. Both also appear on the balance sheet.

R. Reynolds, Capital

Debit	Credit
Decrease	Increase

The Capital Account

The Capital account is a record of the owner's investment in the business. The Capital account increases when additional investments are made. It also increases if there is net income from operations. The owner's Capital account decreases when a net loss is incurred or when the owner decides to permanently withdraw part of the investment.

*7

Withdrawal of Assets by the Owner When the owner of a business needs cash for personal use, the cash may be withdrawn from the business. By doing so, the owner is decreasing the investment in the business. Therefore, the owner's equity decreases and this decrease is recorded by debiting the Capital account.

The Drawing Account

The owner's Drawing account records the withdrawal of assets from the business by the owner.

When the owner makes a regular practice of withdrawing money for personal use, a separate account called the *Drawing account* is used. Since the withdrawal of assets affects the owner's investment, the owner's Drawing account is an equity account. This account appears in the equity section of the balance sheet and it decreases the owner's equity. The Drawing account normally has a debit balance since withdrawals by the owner decrease owner's equity.

The owner's Drawing account is debited whenever assets are withdrawn by the owner for personal use. Examples of this are:

- withdrawal of cash
- removal of merchandise for personal use
- taking of equipment from the business for personal use
- using company funds for personal expenses of the owner or the owner's family

R. Reynolds, Drawing

Debit	Credit
Withdrawals are recorded as debits because they *decrease* capital.	

For example, on October 15, R. Reynolds, the owner of a business withdrew $1 000 cash from the business for personal use. The effect of this withdrawal is illustrated by these T-accounts:

Cash

	1 000

R. Reynolds, Drawing

1 000	

The Owner's Salary A salary may be paid by a business to the person who owns that business. However, for income tax purposes, the business may not record the payment in an expense account such as the Salaries account. Therefore, payment of wages or salaries to the owners must be recorded in the owner's Drawing account.

Equity Accounts on the Balance Sheet

*8

The owner's Capital account appears in the owner's equity section of the balance sheet. The Capital account is a record of the owner's investment in the business. It is the owner's claim against the assets. The Capital account increases if there is a net income earned or if the owner increases the assets of the business from personal sources. The Capital account decreases if there is a net loss or if the owner withdraws assets from the business for personal use. The results of increases or decreases in the Capital account are shown in the equity section of the balance sheet.

Figures 3.4, 3.5, and 3.6 show the owner's equity section of three balance sheets. In the October balance sheet (Figure 3.4), the Capital increases because R. Reynolds, Drawing is less than the net income.

Owner's Equity			
R. Reynolds, Capital October 1		15 000 00	
Add Net Income for October	3 000 00		
Less R. Reynolds, Drawing	1 000 00		
Increase in Capital		2 000 00	
R. Reynolds, Capital October 31			17 000 00

Figure 3.4 *Capital increases — drawing is less than net income for October*

Owner's Equity			
R. Reynolds, Capital November 1		17 000 00	
Add Net Income for November	800 00		
Less R. Reynolds, Drawing	1 200 00		
Decrease in Capital		400 00	
R. Reynolds, Capital November 30			16 600 00

Figure 3.5 *Capital decreases — drawing is greater than net income for November*

Owner's Equity			
R. Reynolds, Capital December 1		16 600 00	
Less Net Loss for December	400 00		
Less R. Reynolds, Drawing	1 000 00		
Decrease in Capital		1 400 00	
R. Reynolds, Capital December 31			15 200 00

Figure 3.6 *Capital decreases — drawing is added to a net loss for December*

In the November balance sheet (Figure 3.5), the Capital decreases because R. Reynolds Drawing is greater than net income.

In the December balance sheet (Figure 3.6), the Capital decreases because the business suffered a net loss of $400 which was added to R. Reynolds, Drawing of $1 000 to reduce capital by a total of $1 400.

The Report Form of Balance Sheet

*9

The final concept to be introduced in this chapter is a new form for writing a balance sheet. Up to this point, the *account form* of balance sheet has been used as in Figure 3.3. The account form of balance sheet was essential to establishing the concept:

Left Side = Right Side

From this concept, the accounting equation was established:

Assets = Liabilities + Owner's Equity

The accounting equation is an inflexible rule and the basis of the double-entry accounting system.

The account form of the balance sheet lists the assets on the left side and the liabilities and owner's equity on the right side.

The balance sheet does not always appear in the account format. Another form of balance sheet is the *report form* as shown in Figure 3.7. In the report form, the assets, liabilities, and owner's equity are listed vertically. You will find that the vertical arrangement of the report form is more convenient for handwritten balance sheets than the account form which is prepared horizontally.

The report form of the balance sheet lists the assets, liabilities, and owner's equity vertically.

The Cascade Inn Balance Sheet June 30, 19__		
Assets		
Cash	4 000 00	
Motel Supplies	9 000 00	
Office Equipment	3 000 00	
Room Furniture	110 000 00	
Building	500 000 00	
Land	50 000 00	
Total Assets		676 000 00
Liabilities		
Accounts Payable	30 000 00	
Bank Loan	16 000 00	
Mortgage Payable	115 000 00	
Total Liabilities		161 000 00
Owner's Equity		
Galotta, Capital, June 1	506 800 00	
Net Income for June	8 200 00	
Galotta, Capital, June 30		515 000 00
Total Liabilities and Owner's Equity		676 000 00

Figure 3.7 *Report form of balance sheet*

Of course, the initial step in deriving the accounting equation, Left Side = Right Side, no longer applies as the balance sheet is written vertically and there is no left side and right side. Remember, though, that *the accounting equation still applies.*

The Ledger

*10

The study of the ledger in the last two chapters can now be summarized. You have learned that a ledger is a group of accounts. In the ledger there is one account for each asset, for each liability, and for the owner's equity. As transactions occur, the changes caused by the transactions are recorded in these accounts. There is also an account required in the ledger for each revenue account and for each expense account and for the Drawing account.

At the end of the accounting or fiscal period, a trial balance is prepared. The assets, liabilities, and owner's equity accounts (including the Drawing account) are used to prepare the balance sheet. The revenue and expense accounts are used to prepare the income statement. A complete summary of some typical ledger accounts, the account classifications, and the financial statement prepared from these accounts is shown in Figure 3.8.

Facts to Remember

Goods are products sold to customers.

Services are things done for customers.

An *income statement* is a financial statement which presents the revenue, expenses, and net income or net loss for a specific period of time.

Revenue is an inflow of assets from the sale of goods and services.

Expenses are costs of goods and services used in the operation of a business.

Net income is the difference between revenue and expenses when revenue is greater than expenses.

Net loss is the difference between revenue and expenses when expenses are greater than revenue.

Net income increases equity.

Net loss decreases equity.

The *accounting period* or *fiscal period* is the period of time covered by the income statement.

A *fiscal year* is any 12-month accounting period.

The *owner's Drawing account* records the withdrawal of assets from the business by the owner.

The *account form* of the balance sheet lists the assets on the left side and the liabilities and owner's equity on the right side.

The *report form* of the balance sheet lists the assets, liabilities, and owner's equity vertically.

The *accounting equation* is Assets = Liabilities + Owner's Equity no matter which form the balance sheet takes.

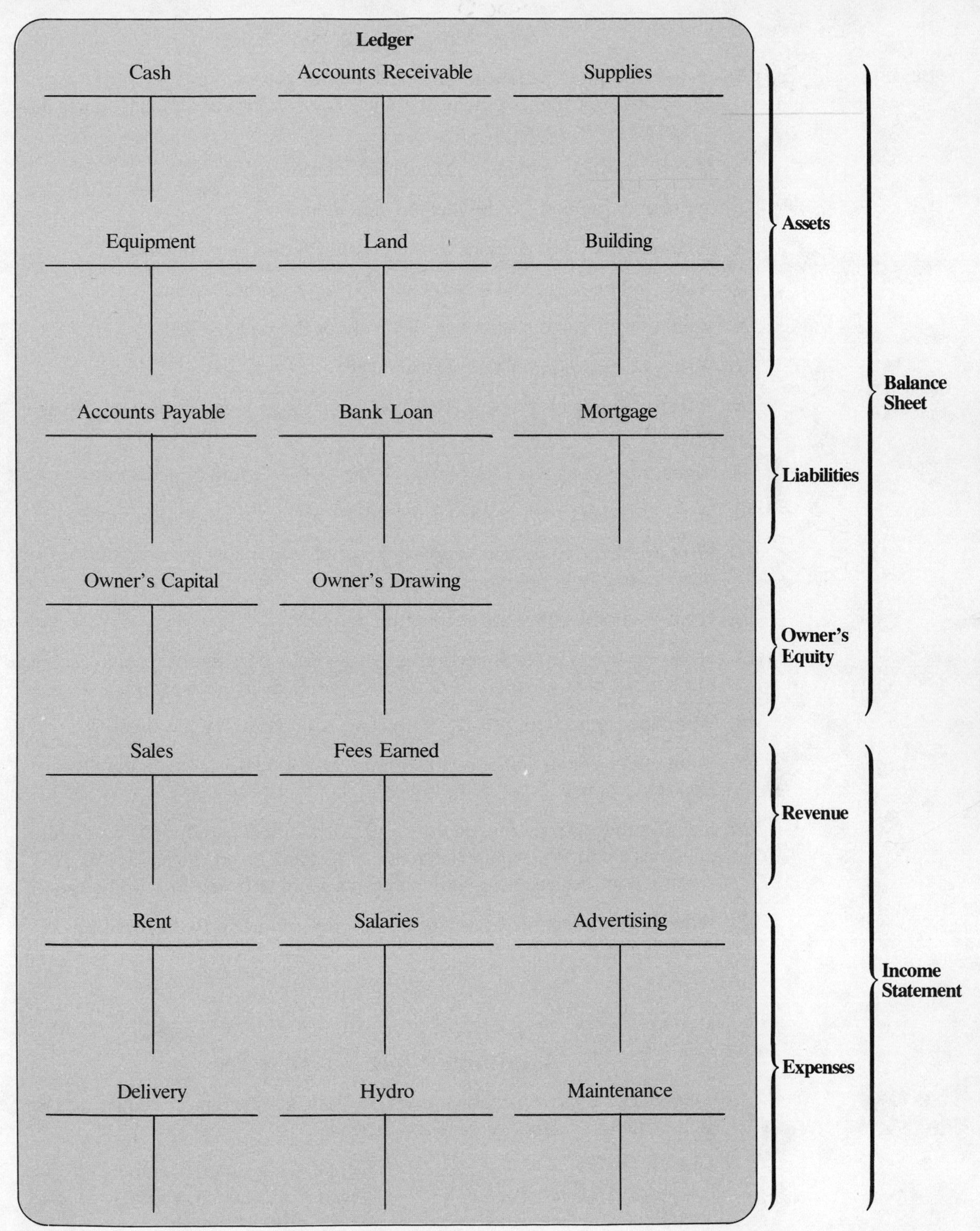

Figure 3.8 *Summary of some typical ledger accounts*

Checking Your Reading

Questions

1. a) Why do most people go into business for themselves?
   b) What do you think would be the single most important reason for going into business for yourself?
2. Define: revenue, expense, net income, net loss.
3. Write the equation for the income statement.
4. What are the three sections in the body of the income statement?
5. Name the two financial statements you have studied so far.
6. What are the three sections in the body of the balance sheet?
7. Write the equation for the balance sheet.
8. Which statement is prepared first, the income statement or the balance sheet? Why?
9. What effect does a net loss have on the Owner's Equity account?
10. What effect does net income have on the Owner's Equity account?
11. Why do many businesses prepare financial statements every month rather than waiting until the end of the year?
12. What is another term for accounting period?
13. a) Give two examples of occurances that would increase the Capital account.
    b) Give two examples of occurances that would decrease the Capital account.
14. What special account records withdrawals of assets by the owner?
15. What effect does a withdrawal of assets by the owner have on the Owner's Equity account?
16. If J. Conrad's equity on August 1, 19__ is $45 000 and during the month drawings are $1 500, what will the owner's equity be on August 31, 19__? Assume that the business showed no net income or net loss in the month.
17. What is the difference between the account form and the report form of balance sheet?

Applying Your Knowledge

Exercises Part A

1. Following is a list of accounts used by Dr. Chamberlain, a dentist. Classify each of them as either revenue or expense:

Rent on Office	Dental Association Membership Fees
Telephone Expense	Salary – Dental Hygienist
Fees Received from Customers	Salary – Receptionist
Supplies Used	Interest Earned on Bank Account

2. Following is a list of accounts in the ledger of Welland South Movers. Classify each as either revenue or expense:

Truck Repairs
Gasoline and Oil
Driver's Wages
Office Salaries
Moving Revenue
Office Rent
Advertising
Storage Fees Earned
Taxes

3. Following are the ledger balances for Morgan Cleaners on September 30. Prepare the income statement for the month of September:

Cleaning Service Revenue, $27 000; Advertising Expense, $770; Salaries Expense, $2 000; Wages Expense, $11 000; Telephone Expense, $450.

4. Prepare the income statement for Dr. Winters for the year ended December 31 by using the following accounts from her ledger:

Income from Fees; $85 000; Investment Income, $9 500; Automobile Expense, $1 800; Supplies Expense, $4 600; Rent Expense, $4 000; Salaries Expense, $13 600; Donations Expense, $2 500.

5. Following is a list of accounts for Welland South Movers. Classify each account as either an asset, a liability, an owner's equity, a revenue or an expense and indicate on which financial statement it appears. The first one is done for you.

Cash
Bank Loan
Advertising
Storage Fees Earned
Salaries
Delivery Equipment
Accounts Receivable
Truck Expense
Warehouse (owned)
G. Rossi, Capital
Accounts Payable
Moving Revenue

Account	Balance Sheet (A,L,OE)	Income Statement (R,E)
Cash	Asset	

6. a) From the trial balance for Morrison Moving, classify each account as an asset, a liability, an owner's equity, a revenue, or an expense and indicate whether it appears on the balance sheet or on the income statement.

   Example: Cash – An asset which appears on the balance sheet.

   b) Using the appropriate accounts, prepare the income statement for Morrison Moving for the year ended June 30, 19__.

   c) Prepare a balance sheet for Morrison Moving on June 30, 19__

Morrison Moving
Trial Balance
June 30, 19__

ACCOUNT TITLE	ACC. NO.	DEBIT	CREDIT
Cash		25 000 —	
Accounts Receivable		65 000 —	
Equipment		65 200 —	
Land and Buildings		175 000 —	
Accounts Payable			24 000 —
Bank Loan			31 000 —
A. Morrison, Capital			200 000 —
Storage Fees Revenue			26 500 —
Moving Service Revenue			185 000 —
Salaries Expense		95 300 —	
Truck Expense		32 000 —	
Utilities Expense		9 000 —	
		466 500 —	466 500 —

7. a) Prepare the income statement for Office Services from the trial balance given for the month ended March 31, 19__.
   b) Prepare a balance sheet for Office Services on March 31, 19__.

Office Services
Trial Balance
March 31, 19__

ACCOUNT TITLE	ACC. NO.	DEBIT	CREDIT
Cash		3 500 —	
Accounts Receivable		15 000 —	
Office Supplies		900 —	
Office Equipment		4 100 —	
Furniture and Fixtures		15 000 —	
Accounts Payable			2 900 —
Bank Loan			2 600 —
S. Layman, Capital			30 000 —
Commissions Earned			9 100 —
Salaries Expense		5 000 —	
Office Expense		700 —	
General Expense		400 —	
		44 600 —	44 600 —

Exercises Part B

8. a) Using the appropriate accounts, prepare the income statement for Kaplan's T.V. Repairs for the month ended January 31, 19__.
   b) Prepare a balance sheet for Kaplan's T.V. Repairs on January 31, 19__.

Kaplan's T.V. Repairs
Trial Balance
January 31, 19__

ACCOUNT TITLE	ACC. NO.	DEBIT	CREDIT
Cash		1 200 —	
Accounts Receivable		3 500 —	
Parts Inventory		2 700 —	
Equipment		46 000 —	
Truck		6 200 —	
Accounts Payable			1 600 —
Bank Loan			2 000 —
C. Kaplan, Capital			55 000 —
Fees from Repairs			10 200 —
Salaries Expense		4 000 —	
Parts Expense		3 800 —	
Truck Repairs & Maintenance Expense		1 200 —	
General Expense		200 —	
		68 800 —	68 800 —

9. Complete the following chart by indicating the amount of increase or decrease in the Capital and showing the amount of the Capital.

	Beginning Capital	Net Income	Net Loss	Drawing	Inc. or Dec. in Capital	Ending Capital
a)	$10 000	$1 000	—	$ 500	?	?
b)	25 000	1 000	—	1 500	?	?
c)	18 000	—	2 000	600	?	?
d)	12 000	3 000	—	1 000	?	?

10. From the following information about Corrigan Landscaping, prepare a balance sheet on July 31, 19__.

Assets: Cash, $4 600; Accounts Receivable, $5 300; Supplies, $1 200; Truck, $6 100

Liabilities: Accounts Payable, $2 400; Bank Loan, $3 000

Owner's Equity: C. Corrigan, Capital, $10 300; Net Income for the month of July, $3 200; C. Corrigan, Drawing, $1 700

11. From the following information about Conway Painters, prepare a balance sheet on October 31, 19__.

Assets: Cash, $2 300; Accounts Receivable, $4 700; Painting Supplies, $900; Equipment, $14 000

Liabilities:	Accounts Payable, $3 000
Owner's Equity:	L. Conway, Capital, $20 000; L. Conway, Drawing, $700; Net Loss for October, $400

Exercises Part C

12. N. Corbett's capital on April 1 is $25 000. Use the data below to prepare the Owner's Equity section of his balance sheet for April, May, and June.

a) April:	Net Income	$2 500
	Drawing	1 500
b) May:	Net Income	$1 000
	Drawing	1 500
c) June:	Net Loss	($1 000)
	Drawing	1 500

13. a) Prepare the income statement for Bell's Plumbing for the month of February.

b) Prepare the balance sheet for Bell's Plumbing on February 28, 19__.

Bell's Plumbing
Trial Balance
February 28, 19__

ACCOUNT TITLE	ACC. NO.	DEBIT	CREDIT
Cash		6 500 —	
Accounts Receivable/C. Carter		1 600 —	
Plumbing Supplies		7 000 —	
Equipment		26 000 —	
Truck		7 000 —	
Accounts Payable			2 600 —
Bank Loan			4 500 —
C. Bell, Capital			37 600 —
C. Bell, Drawing		1 700 —	
Sales			14 600 —
Advertising Expense		900 —	
Rent Expense		1 100 —	
Salaries Expense		7 000 —	
General Expense		500 —	
		59 300 —	59 300 —

Accounting in Action

The Income Statement There are several errors in the following income statement. Can you find them?

Case 1

Income Statement		
L. Kretchner and associates		
April 30, 19__		
Revenue		
Sales		50 000 00
Investment Income		2 000 00
Cash		7 000 00
		59 000 00
Expenses		
Advertising	2 000 00	
Salaries	40 000 00	
Accounts Payable	5 000 00	
Rent	8 000 00	
General	1 000 00	56 000 00
Net Income		3 000 00

Changes in Owner's Equity Cathy Dillabough is the owner of a profitable business. The March income statement showed net income of $2 500. The balance sheet dated March 31 showed that the Capital balance had decreased by $600. How is it possible to have a decrease in capital when a net income of $2 500 was earned in March?

Case 2

Income Tax and the Business Owner B. Joanisse owns the Hillside Distributing Company. The company is organized as a *sole proprietorship;* that is, it is owned by one person, B. Joanisse. Hillside Distributing is very successful and Joanisse receives a monthly salary of $4 000 for managing the business. For the last fiscal year, the company's operating results were:

Case 3

Revenue	–	**Expenses**	=	**Net Income**
$370 000	–	$340 000	=	$30 000

Included in the expense total is $48 000 paid to Joanisse as a salary for managing the business. Joanisse has no other personal income. In preparing his personal income tax return, Joanisse feels justified in paying personal income tax only on his income or salary of $48 000.

Read the following income tax and accounting principles and then answer the questions.

I. A sole proprietorship does not pay income tax on its net income. However, the net income is considered to be the income of the owner.

II. For tax purposes, a proprietorship must record salary payments to its owner in the owner's Drawing account.

a) Applying the preceding principles, correctly complete this equation:

Revenue	–	**Expenses**	=	**Net Income**
$370 000	–	?	=	?

b) For personal income tax purposes, what is Joanisse's income for the year?
c) In the company ledger, what is the year-end balance in the Drawing account? Assume there were no other withdrawals than those mentioned.

Case 4

Operating a Business Discuss the questions that follow after looking at the income statement of Bill's T.V. Repairs.

Bill's T.V. Repairs
Statement of Income and Expenditure
For the Year Ended June 30

Income from Services		28 000 00
Less Operating Expenses		
Advertising	500 00	
Light, Heat and Water	300 00	
Rent	2 000 00	
Tools and Equipment	1 700 00	
Supplies	800 00	
Salaries	12 000 00	
Truck	2 000 00	
Taxes and Licenses	1 000 00	
Total Operating Expenses		20 300 00
Net Income		7 700 00

a) How much was the net income of the business?
b) How can the business increase its net income?
c) Why does Bill not buy a building and save the rent expense?
d) Why do you think Bill went into business?
e) Bill has two employees. What responsibility does Bill have that his employees do not have?
f) What advantages does Bill have that the employees do not enjoy?
g) How does the community benefit from Bill's business?

Case 5

Recording Transactions National Products is a very large manufacturer of household products. It has several factories producing items which are sold by 45 branch offices located throughout the country. As an incentive for the branch managers, a bonus is offered if yearly budgeted net income figures are exceeded.

You are the accountant for a branch office of National Products. The manager of the branch is Eliot Mathews. You are aware that Mr. Mathews has obtained a new position and plans to leave National Products early in January. Late in December he instructs you to omit from your records several large expenses including insurance, overtime pay for December, and fuel and hydro expenses. He tells you to pay these expenses as usual in December but to delay recording the items until some time in the new year.

a) What will be the effect of not recording the expenses in December?
b) What would you do? What are your alternatives? What are the consequences of each alternative?

Case 6

The Credit Bureau Tracy is known as a *skip* to retail stores. This is because Tracy buys on credit as far as possible, but very rarely pays for credit card purchases. Tracy moves (skips) whenever a large credit balance has built up. Businesses have trouble locating Tracy and often are stuck with bad debts. Tracy continually obtains new charge accounts and avoids paying credit charges by skipping town.

The Credit Bureau exists because of people like Tracy. Credit bureaus can be found in every large metropolitan area in Canada. They provide a service to *credit grantors*. Any firm which offers credit to its customers is called a credit grantor. The credit bureau provides information to businesses which helps them to decide if credit should be given to a particular person. In order to obtain information, a credit grantor must join the credit bureau and pay a membership fee.

How the Credit Bureau Works The credit bureau maintains files on consumers. It obtains the information from credit grantors who are members of the credit bureau, from employers, and from public records. A typical file contains information about a person's job history and credit record with various companies. Figure 3.9 illustrates the basic operations of a credit bureau.

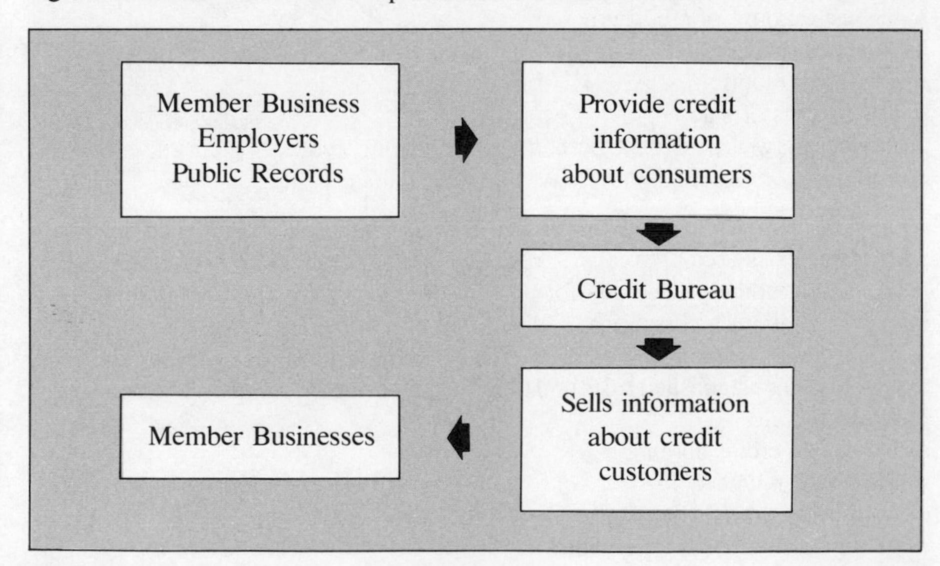

Figure 3.9 *Operations of a credit bureau*

Sources of Information When credit grantors join the credit bureau they agree to report the paying habits of their customers. They may be asked questions about the credit history of a customer by the bureau. They are asked to report overdue customer charge accounts to the credit bureau.

Information Provided about Consumers Each member of the credit bureau is identified by a code. For example, the Ann Marie's Boutique code might be C-117. When the boutique requires information about a customer, it telephones the credit bureau and identifies itself by name and code. The person requesting the information must give his or her name.

The person requesting information must also provide accurate details about the consumer being investigated. This includes the consumer's name, address, occupation, place of employment, age, social insurance number, and any other identifying data. This is to ensure that the correct consumer will be reported on.

The credit bureau then locates the consumer's file and gives the credit grantor such information as:

- the consumer's name, address, date of birth, and number of dependents
- estimated salary
- whether a home is owned or rented
- former addresses and occupations
- spouse's employer, position, estimated salary, and when employed
- credit history
- collection items
- public record items

The credit history of the consumer is the most useful information provided. It includes:

- kind of businesses the consumer has bought from
- dates charge accounts were opened
- highest amount of credit granted
- balances owing
- past-due amounts
- usual terms of sale

A service charge is paid to the bureau by the company requesting information on a consumer.

Legal Regulations Provincial governments have passed laws controlling such agencies as credit bureaus. These laws outline how credit reports are to be used. They outline procedures for ensuring the accuracy and confidentiality of information about a consumer.

The credit bureaus are linked by the Associated Credit Bureaus of Canada. This association has established rules and policies governing the manner in which credit bureaus operate.

a) What is a credit bureau?
b) How is it financed?
c) Who joins a credit bureau?
d) What services does it provide?
e) Who benefits from the services of the credit bureau?

f) What may consumers do if they suspect that incorrect information is in their file?
g) What controls do you feel should be placed on credit bureaus?
h) Why did credit bureaus come into existence?

Income Statement Analysis The accountant for Crowland Fuels Co. has prepared an income statement which shows net income of $9 000 for the year. The following factors were not considered in the preparation of the statement:

Case 7

- Interest expense on a bank loan of $400 is owed to the bank.
- Two customers owing a total of $890 left town over six months ago and cannot be located.
- Salaries expense of $500 is owed to the workers.

a) What effect does the omission of the three items have on the net income?
b) What is the correct net income?

Career Profile

An Office Manager A knowledge of accounting is useful in many jobs. The career of Jackie Lentini shows how accounting skills have been useful to her in a variety of jobs.

Jackie developed excellent skills in shorthand and typing while in high school. Although she specialized in secretarial subjects she also took several accounting courses. Jackie's first job after graduation from high school was with a law firm. She was hired as a secretary and was able to make good use of her shorthand and typing skills. Her duties also involved some accounting and she assisted the company bookkeeper on a regular basis. After three years, Jackie took a position wth A. H. Fitzsimmons Ltd., a real estate firm.

At Fitzsimmons, Jackie was a secretary and also kept property management records for clients. Records were kept of rental collections and of expenses of maintaining properties. A monthly statement summarizing the income and expenses was prepared for each client.

After three years, Jackie left to become the office manager for Kemper Realty Ltd. In her present position with Kemper, Jackie is responsible for the administration of two offices and 25 employees. As well as acting as liason between the two offices and between the employees and senior management, Jackie performs much of the accounting work for her firm.

Among her duties are: accounts receivable, accounts payable, payroll, and banking, including the monthly bank reconciliation. She is involved in handling all the sales contracts and deals with the lawyers for the real estate sales of her company. Jackie has an assistant to help her with these tasks.

Jackie's present position is a responsible one. She is called upon to use judgement and tact in dealing with clients, company employees, and lawyers. Many problems occur which require human relations skills in order to solve them. In fact, Jackie feels that handling problems is the major task in her daily routine.

Chapter 4

Income Statement Accounts

Review of Balance Sheet Accounts

Unit 9

*1

The purpose of setting up accounts is to record changes in items on the balance sheet.

The purpose of setting up accounts is to record changes in items on the balance sheet. Debit and credit entries in accounts are used to record the increases and decreases caused by business transactions. At the end of the fiscal period, the balance of each asset, liability, and equity account is calculated and used in the preparation of the balance sheet (Figure 4.1).

Revenue and Expense Accounts

An account is required for each item on the income statement just as an account is required for each item on the balance sheet. Revenue is earned as goods and services are sold to customers. Expenses are incurred as items are used in the daily operations of the business. Thus, there are transactions (exchanges of value) involving revenue and expense accounts just as there are transactions affecting asset, liability, and equity accounts. These transactions are recorded in the revenue and expense accounts. At the end of the fiscal period the balance of each revenue and expense account is used in the preparation of the income statement (Figure 4.1).

Transactions

▼

Accounts
(Revenue, Expense, Asset, Liability, Owner's Equity)

▼

Trial Balance

▼

Income Statement
and
Balance Sheet

Figure 4.1 *Summary of accounting steps discussed in the first three chapters*

*2

Recording Transactions Figure 4.2 summarizes the theory for recording debits and credits in balance sheet accounts. This chapter examines how transactions are recorded when income statement accounts (revenue and expenses) are affected.

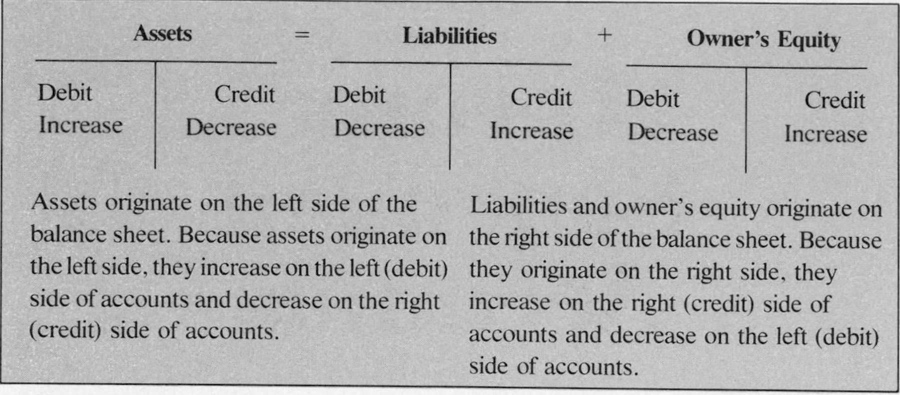

Figure 4.2 *Theory summary for recording debits and credits in balance sheet accounts*

As was shown in Chapter 3, net income causes an increase in the owner's equity (capital). Equity increases on the credit side and revenue causes the increase in equity. Therefore, when revenue accounts are increased, the increase is recorded on the credit side of the revenue account.

Owner's Equity

Debit Decrease	Credit Increase
	Revenue increases owner's equity

*3

A net loss decreases owner's equity. Equity decreases on the debit side. A net loss can be said to be caused by expenses. Therefore, expenses are recorded as debits.

Owner's Equity

Debit Decrease	Credit Increase
Expenses decrease owner's equity	

*4

Summary Debits and credits in revenue and expense accounts are determined by the effect on owner's equity. Revenue increases equity and is recorded as a credit. Expenses decrease equity and are recorded as debits.

*5

Reason for Revenue and Expense Accounts If revenue increases equity, expenses decrease equity, and net income is eventually added to the owner's equity on the balance sheet, *why are revenue and expense accounts necessary? Why not enter transactions directly into the equity account?*

One of the main purposes of accounting is to provide information to management about the operations of the business. Separate accounts for items of revenue and

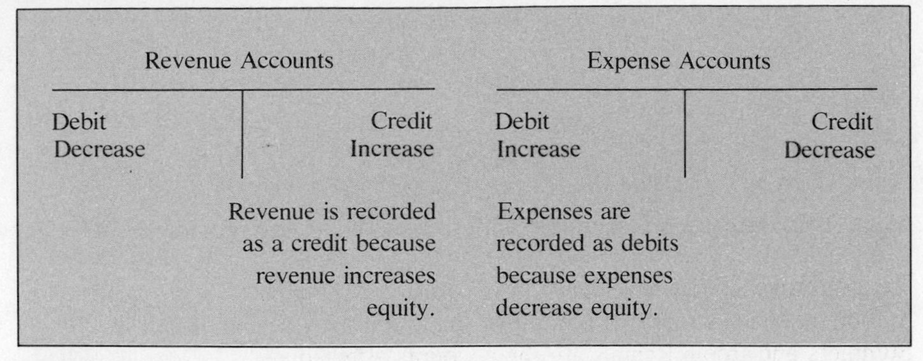

Figure 4.3 *Theory summary for recording debits and credits in income statement accounts*

expense show at a glance which accounts are bringing in the company's revenue and which expenses are increasing too rapidly. Individual accounts for revenue and expenses provide managers with detailed information which helps them to make decisions about the business they are running and to control expenses, increase revenue, and operate the business effectively.

Analysing Transactions

Unit 10

***6**

At least two accounts are involved in every business transaction. There is an equal debit amount recorded for every credit amount. In this chapter you will see that the same principles of double-entry accounting apply when recording transactions involving revenue and expense accounts. For every debit amount, an equal credit amount is recorded. The transactions in this chapter will involve five types of accounts: asset, liability, equity, revenue, and expense.

Following are four transactions for The Cascade Inn. Examine carefully how each transaction is analysed and the position of the debit and the credit in the T-accounts.

Transaction 1: An asset and a revenue transaction Cash of $45 is received from a motel customer. Cash and Room Rentals are the accounts affected.

- Cash is an asset account.
- Cash increases by $45.
- Assets increase on the debit side.
- Therefore Cash is debited $45.

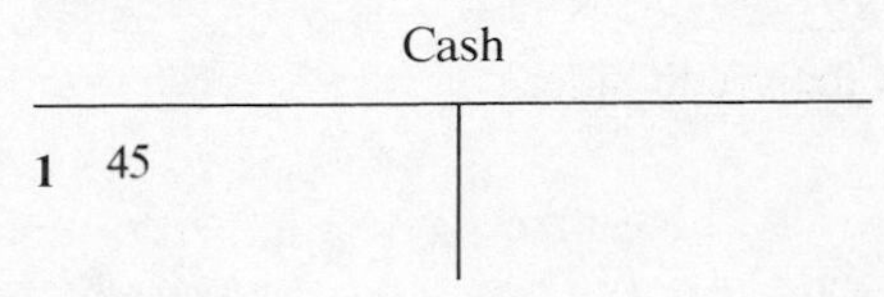

- Room Rentals is a revenue account.
- Revenue increases owner's equity.
- Owner's equity increases on the credit side.
- Therefore Room Rentals is credited $45.

Room Rentals

	1 45

Note: This transaction is recorded with a debit of $45 and a credit of $45.

Transaction 2: An asset and a revenue transaction A customer, Bob Summers, charges room rent of $28 to his account. Accounts Receivable/B. Summers and Room Rentals are the accounts affected.

- Accounts Receivable/B. Summers is an asset account.
- Accounts Receivable/B. Summers increases by $28.
- Assets increase on the debit side.
- Therefore Accounts Receivable/B. Summers is debited $28.

Accounts Receivable
B. Summers

2 28	

- Room Rentals is a revenue account.
- Revenue increases owner's equity.
- Owner's equity increases on the credit side.
- Room Rentals is credited $28.00

Note: This transaction is recorded wth a debit of $28 and a credit of $28.

Room Rentals

	1 45
	2 28

*7

Transaction 3: An expense and an asset transaction A $25 telephone bill is paid. Cash and Telephone Expense are affected.

- Cash is an asset.
- Cash decreases by $25.
- Assets decrease on the credit side.
- Cash is credited $25.

Cash

1 45	3 25

- Telephone Expense is an expense account.
- Expenses decrease owner's equity.
- Owner's equity decreases on the debit side.
- Telephone Expense is debited $25.

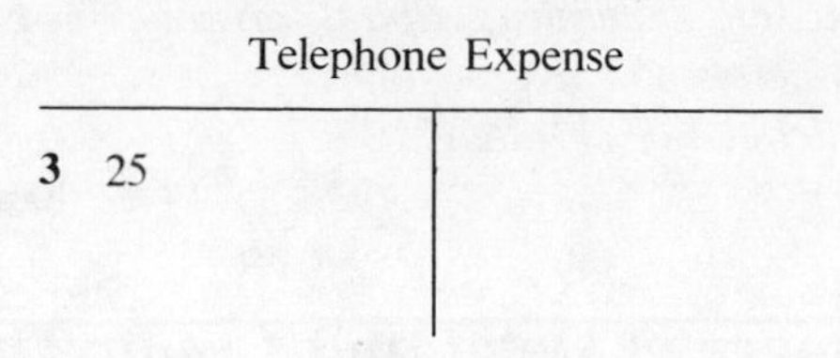

Note: This transaction is recorded with a debit of $25 and a credit of $25.

Transaction 4: An expense and a liability transaction A $200 bill for advertising was received from the *Niagara Falls Courier* but not paid. The accounts affected are Advertising Expense and Accounts Payable/*Niagara Falls Courier*.

- Advertising is an expense.
- Expenses decrease owner's equity.
- Owner's equity decreases on the debit side.
- Advertising Expense is debited $200.

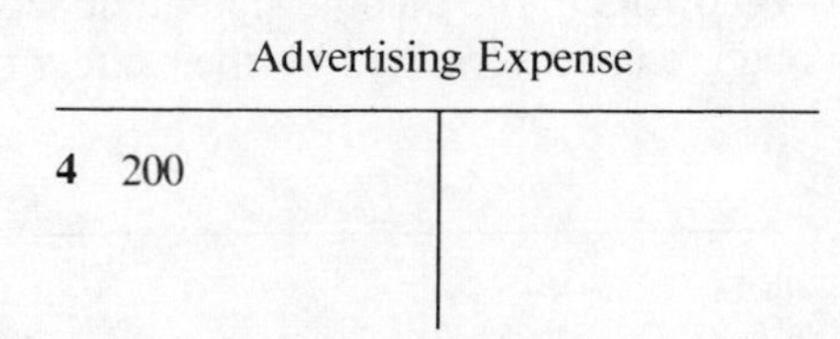

- Accounts Payable/*N.F. Courier* is a liability.
- Accounts Payable increases by $200.
- Liabilities increase on the credit side.
- Accounts Payable/*N.F. Courier* is credited $200.

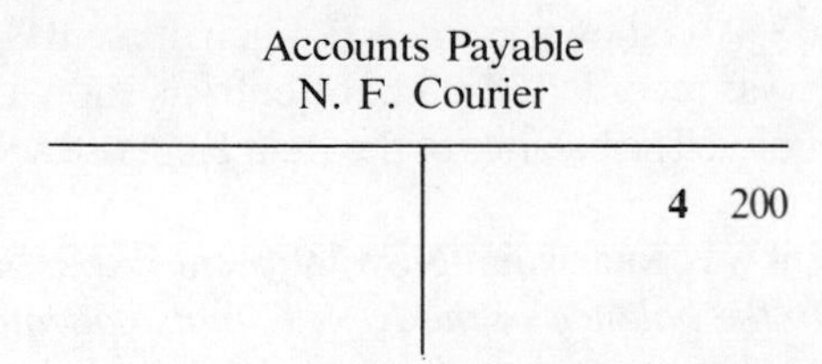

Note: This transaction is recorded with a debit of $200 and a credit of $200. All four transactions have had an equal debit and credit entry.

Steps in Analysing a Transaction

*8

When you analyse a transaction, ask yourself these questions:

- *What accounts are affected?*
- *Are the accounts assets, liabilities, capital, revenue, or expenses?*
- *Does the account increase or decrease?*
- *Are the accounts debited or credited?*

Summary of Debit and Credit Theory

*9

Balance Sheet Accounts The debits and credits for balance sheet accounts are determined by the accounting equation.

Assets		=	**Liabilities**		+	**Owner's Equity**	
Debit	Credit		Debit	Credit		Debit	Credit
Increase	Decrease		Decrease	Increase		Decrease	Increase

*10

Income Statement Accounts The income statement accounts (revenue and expense) have debits and credits determined by their effect on equity.

Revenue accounts increase on the credit side.

Expense accounts increase on the debit side.

Equity	
Debit	Credit
Decrease	Increase
Expenses	Revenue

Expense Accounts Rent of $500 was paid on January 1. Because an expense *decreases* equity, the $500 is shown as a *debit*. When the rent was paid on February 1, another $500 debit was recorded. Again, the entry is shown as a debit because expenses decrease equity. The balance of the Rent Expense account is now $1 000. It has increased.

On March 1 the rent was paid again. Now the Rent Expense balance is $1 500. *What is happening to the balance of the Rent Expense account each time rent is recorded? Why is Rent Expense (and all expenses) recorded as a debit?* If you can answer these two questions you understand why expenses increase on the debit side.

Rent Expense		
Debit		Credit
Jan. 1	500	
Feb. 1	500	
March 1	500	
Balance	1 500	

Account Titles The names given to accounts in the ledger vary from company to company. Many firms use titles such as Building, Office Supplies, Equipment, Advertising, Property Taxes, Truck, and so on. However, some account titles are determined by the nature of the business. Some examples of different revenue account titles are shown in Figure 4.4.

*11

Account Title	Type of Business
Fees Income Fees Earned	Professionals such as Doctors, Lawyers, and Dentists
Sales	Retail Stores, Wholesalers, Manufacturers
Moving Revenue Storage Revenue	Cartage, Moving Firms

Figure 4.4 *Examples of different revenue account titles*

Facts to Remember

One account is required for every item on the balance sheet and *one account* is required for each item on the income statement.

Revenue increases equity and is recorded as a credit in the revenue account.

Revenue accounts increase on their credit side.

Expenses decrease equity and are recorded as debits in the expense accounts.

Expense accounts increase on their debit side.

Checking Your Reading

Questions

1. Name the two financial statements studied so far.
2. Name the three types of accounts found on the balance sheet.
3. Name the two types of accounts found on the income statement.
4. a) How is the increase side for assets, liabilities, and owner's equity determined?
   b) What is the increase side for each of these three types of account?
5. a) How is the increase side for revenue and expense accounts determined?
   b) What is the increase side for each of these two types of account?
6. What four questions should you ask in analysing transactions?
7. Write a summary of the rules for recording transactions as debits and credits for balance sheet accounts.

8. Write a summary of the rules for recording transactions as debits and credits for income statement accounts.

9. Expenses decrease (debit) equity. Expenses increase on their debit side. Explain this apparent contradiction.

Applying Your Knowledge

Exercises Part A

1. A company made a sale to a customer and received $100 cash. Sales is one of the accounts affected.
   a) What is the other?
   b) For each of the two accounts affected, answer these questions:
      i) What type is the account (A, L, OE, R, or E)?
      ii) Does the account increase or decrease?
      iii) Is the account debited or credited?

2. A company paid $500 for its monthly office rent.
   a) Name the accounts affected.
   b) Answer the following questions for each account:
      i) What type of account is it?
      ii) Does the account increase or decrease?
      iii) Is the account debited or credited?

3. Record the following transactions in a ledger with five T-accounts. The names of the accounts are: Cash; Accounts Receivable/B. Scinto; Accounts Receivable/J. Hill; Accounts Receivable/R. Wilson; Sales.

Nov. 1	Sold goods for cash, $200.
3	Sold goods on account to R. Wilson, $600.
4	Sold goods on account to B. Scinto, $500
5	Sold goods to J. Hill, $300; terms half cash, balance on account.
8	B. Scinto returned $100 worth of the goods sold Nov. 4. The goods were not what was wanted.
9	Received $100 from R. Wilson.

Calculate the balance of each account (see Figure 2.6, page 34) and prepare a trial balance on November 9.

4. Record the following transactions in a ledger with these six accounts: Cash; Equipment; Accounts Payable/Acme Ltd.; C. Clarke, Capital; Salaries; Advertising Expense; Rent Expense.

Oct. 1	C. Clarke invested $9 000 cash in a business.
2	Paid $150 cash to the *Bowmanville Chronicle* for advertising.
3	Bought equipment worth $500 on account from Acme Ltd.
6	Paid rent, $600.
7	Paid Wilco Printers $200 cash for advertising circulars.
8	Paid salaries, $900 cash.
8	Paid $100 cash to Acme Ltd.

Balance the accounts and prepare a trial balance on October 8.

5. Record the following transactions in the ledger of the Capital Theatre. The accounts are Cash; A. Ryholm, Capital; Ticket Sales; Refreshment Sales; Salaries Expense; Film Rental Expense; Hydro Expense.

Nov.	1	A. Ryholm invested $12 000 cash.
	8	Ticket sales for the week, $14 000.
	8	Refreshment sales, $1 900.
	10	Paid for film rental, $4 000 cash.
	15	Paid salaries, $2 000 cash.
	15	Ticket sales, $9 900 cash.
	15	Refreshment sales, $1 300 cash.
	15	Paid hydro, $50 cash.

Balance the accounts and prepare a trial balance on November 15.

Exercises Part B

6. J. Pearce wishes to start a landscaping business. Record the following transactions in a ledger with these five accounts: Cash; Equipment; J. Pearce, Capital; Sales; Equipment Repairs Expense.

June	1	J. Pearce invested $3 000 cash in a gardening business.
	3	Paid $1 500 cash for gardening equipment.
	5	Received $150 cash from T. Hunt for work done on a lawn.
	7	Paid $70 cash to Tony's Repairs for repairing gardening equipment.

Balance the accounts and prepare a trial balance on June 7.

7. Record the following transactions in a ledger for Stokes Driving School with these accounts: Cash; Accounts Receivable/L. Starr; Equipment; Automobiles; Accounts Payable/Grant's Esso; R. Stokes, Capital; Revenue from Lessons; Salaries Expense; Advertising Expense; Automobile Expense; Utilities Expense.

Aug.	1	R. Stokes invested $25 000 cash.
	2	Purchased equipment for $2 000 cash.
	4	Purchased 2 cars from Dardick Motors for $12 000 cash.
	5	Received $700 cash from customers taking driving lessons.
	7	Paid $300 cash for instructor's salaries for the first week.
	9	Paid $15 cash to the telephone company.
	10	Received $800 cash from customers taking driving lessons.
	11	Issued an invoice (bill) of $50 to L. Starr, a customer who is taking lessons, but will pay at a later date.
	11	Received a $30 invoice from Grant's Esso for gas and oil used by the cars.
	12	Paid $20 cash for hydro and electricity.
	13	Sent a $70 cheque to the *Daily Star* for advertising space.
	14	Received $50 cash from L. Starr, to pay off the account.

a) Balance the accounts and prepare a trial balance.

b) Prepare an income statement for the two weeks ended August 14.

8. On April 1, Ted's Golfing School had the following accounts and balances:

Ted's Golfing School Partial Trial Balance April 1, 19--			
ACCOUNT TITLE	ACC. NO.	DEBIT	CREDIT
Cash		3 000 —	
Accounts Receivable/P. Moores		150 —	
Accounts Receivable/L. Troop		—	
Equipment		4 700 —	
Accounts Payable/Jack's Repair Shop			750 —
T. Craig, Capital			7 100 —
Fees Income			—
Advertising Expense		—	
Rent Expense		—	
Equipment Repairs Expense		—	
Utilities Expense		—	

a) Set up the General Ledger for Ted's Golfing School on April 1 and record the following transactions:

April	2	Received $300 cash from customers for golfing lessons.
	2	Issued a $45 invoice to L. Troop for lessons which will be paid for later.
	3	Paid $400 cash to United Realty for the monthly rent.
	4	Received $50 cash from P. Moores.
	5	Received a $175 invoice (bill) from Jack's Repair Shop for repairing equipment.
	8	Received $450 cash from customers for lessons.
	8	Issued another $45 invoice to L. Troop for lessons.
	9	Received $100 cash from P. Moores who paid the balance of his account.
	10	Received a $500 invoice for a piece of equipment bought from Jack's Repair Shop. The amount is to be paid at a later date.
	12	Paid $20 cash for electricity and water.
	12	Paid $300 cash to Jack's Repair Shop on account.
	12	Paid $55 cash to the *Gazette* for advertising.

b) On April 12, balance the accounts and prepare a trial balance, an income statement for the two weeks, and a balance sheet.

9. On October 1, the Luckville Beavers Hockey Team owned by R. Branch had the following accounts and balances:

ACCOUNT TITLE	ACC. NO.	DEBIT	CREDIT
Cash		12 000 —	
Accounts Receivable/Stokes Dept. Stores		—	
Equipment		4 000 —	
Bus		15 000 —	
Accounts Payable/Klaman Motors			5 300 —
R. Branch, Capital			25 700 —
Ticket Sales			—
Income from Concessions			—
Players' Salaries Expense		—	
Bus Maintenance Expense		—	
Arena Rental Expense		—	
Advertising Expense		—	

a) Set up the general ledger for the hockey team, on October 1, and record the following transactions for the month of October:

Oct. 2 Received $120 000 cash from sales of season's tickets.
4 Purchased equipment for $3 000 cash.
8 Received a $250 invoice from Klaman Motors for repairs to the team bus.
9 Issued an invoice of $2 100 to Stokes Department Stores who bought a block of 500 tickets for the team's opening home game. (The store will use the tickets for promotional purposes.)
10 Paid $350 rental fee for use of the arena for the last two weeks' practice.
14 Issued cheques for $10 400 to pay the players' salaries for the past two weeks.
16 Paid $350 cash to KCV T.V. for advertising the first home game on October 26.
17 Paid $470 to the *Daily Reporter* for advertising.
20 The week's sale of tickets for the opening game brought in $3 500.
24 Paid $50 cash for gas and oil for the bus on the first away-from-home game.
26 Received a further $8 700 cash for ticket sales on the opening game.
26 Received $1 100 cash in revenue on the snack bar concessions.
28 Paid $2 100 cash to the arena for rental for the last two weeks.
29 Issued cheques for $9 800 to pay the players' salaries for the rest of the month.

b) On October 31, balance the accounts and prepare a trial balance, an income statement for the month, and a balance sheet.

Accounting in Action

Case 1

Comparing Net Incomes for Two Years The revenue and expense accounts for Hollingsworth and Associates for the last two years are:

	This Year		Last Year	
Service Revenue		45 000 00		43 000 00
Advertising Expense	4 000 00		900 00	
Office Expense	2 000 00		1 800 00	
Truck Expense	1 000 00		900 00	
Salaries Expense	20 000 00		19 000 00	
Miscellaneous Expense	500 00		500 00	
Utilities Expense	300 00		280 00	
Total Expenses		27 800 00		23 380 00
Net Income		17 200 00		19 620 00

The owners of the business are concerned because the net income has decreased. What advice can you give them?

Case 2

Is the accounting system adequate? Ed and Cindy Baker operate a small craft shop. They look after their own books. Their accounting procedures include the following simple steps:

- Sales are recorded in a sales account.
- Expenses are recorded in an account called Expenses.
- The difference between the two accounts is their net income.

What are your comments on their accounting system?

Case 3

Fraud by Employees The following article appeared in an Ottawa newspaper. Names and addresses have been changed.

The Invisible Employees

Five employees of a building cleaning firm have been charged with theft and uttering forged documents after the firm they worked for was defrauded of up to $50 000.

The firm called in Ottawa police fraud squad members following a lengthy investigation by a private detective. The detective, who had been hired by the company, had obtained evidence showing that a series of payroll cheques had been issued to non-existent employees.

Charged with theft by conversion are Luke Preston, a supervisor in charge of hiring personnel, his wife Karen and their three sons Michael, Paul, and Anthony, all of Orleans. Charged with uttering forged documents is Catherine Marino of Cumberland.

Police say other charges may also be laid as the investigation continues.

a) What may have caused the firm to become suspicious and to hire a private detective?
b) What precautions can you suggest to prevent a company from being defrauded by its own people who have the responsibility for hiring workers?

Case 4

Personal Withdrawals Jean Brisbois is the owner of a management consulting firm. For the month of June, sales were $30 000 and expenses were $20 000. Jean paid herself a salary of $4 000.
a) What account should be debited for Jean's salary of $4 000?
b) What is the net income of the business for the month of June?

Case 5

Owner's Capital Jean Brisbois' capital at the beginning of July was $29 000. The net income for the month was $8 000. Jean withdrew $4 000 for personal use during the month. What is Brisbois' capital at the end of July?

Case 6

Management Information Dale Barnes operates a motel. Revenue is received from room rentals, a restaurant, a gift shop, and soft drink and cigarette machines. All revenue is credited to an account called Sales. Expenses are recorded in these accounts: Salaries, General Expense, and Cleaning Expense. Although the business as a whole is operating at a profit, Dale suspects that the gift shop is operating at a loss.

Suggest changes in the accounting system which will provide more useful information to the owner.

Case 7

Income Statement Analysis The owner of Giancarlo's, a chain of beauty salons, has come to you for advice. During the past year three new operators were added; one at the beginning of the year, one on May 1, and one on September 1. The end of the year income statement indicated that net income was earned. However, Giancarlo says he knows very little about accounting and would like to know if he should hire more people or if he has already hired too many.

	Jan. 1 to April 30	May 1 to Aug. 31	Sept. 1 to Dec. 31	Total for the Year
Sales	$100 000	$120 000	$130 000	$350 000
Salaries Expense	52 000	62 000	72 000	186 000
Rent Expense	10 000	10 000	10 000	30 000
Supplies Expense	12 000	14 000	16 000	42 000
Advertising Expense	2 000	2 200	2 400	6 600
Equipment Expense	4 000	4 800	5 200	14 000
Miscellaneous Expense	5 000	5 200	5 400	15 600
Total Expenses				$294 200
Net Income				$ 55 800

In order to advise him you go over the year's records and prepare three separate income statements covering each four-month period, and a fourth income statement for the entire year.

a) Calculate the net income for each of the statements.

b) What advice would you give Giancarlo?

Case 8

Collecting Outstanding Customer Accounts Not all customers pay their debts on time. Some *forget* to pay. Some *cannot* pay. Some *will not* pay. Bestway Hardware has the following system to collect money owing to it by customers.

First of all, Bestway attempts to eliminate risks by allowing credit only to those customers it feels will pay their debts. It does this by applying the four C's of credit (see Chapter 1) and by using the services of a credit bureau. Bestway also sets a credit limit for each customer so that the customer does not charge more goods than he or she can afford. The credit limit ranges from $100 to $800 depending on factors such as the customer's income, number of dependants, and number of other charge accounts. The credit limit is shown on the ledger account. When the balance reaches the limit the customer is not allowed to make more credit purchases.

Following is an example of what is done when a customer does not pay on time. Suppose B. Baillor made a purchase of $815.58 on December 15. A down payment of $100 was made leaving a balance of $715.58. This balance is due on January 15.

	Dec. 15	The sale is made.
Step 1	Jan. 15	A statement of account is mailed to Baillor. Payment is expected within 10 days.
Step 2	Feb. 15	If payment has not been received, 1.5% interest per month is added to the account. Another statement is sent to the customer. This has a *past finger* stamped on the statement.
Step 3	March 15	Another month's interest is added and the *friendly reminder* stamp is placed on the statement mailed to the customer.

Step 4	April 15	The customer is telephoned and an attempt is made to have a payment schedule worked out. Several calls may be involved.
Step 5	May 15	Another statement plus interest is mailed. The brightly coloured *Past Due, Please Remit Today* sticker is attached to the statement.
Step 6	June 15	Another statement with the coloured sticker is mailed.
Step 7	July 15	If payment is not received after the June 15 statement, the account is turned over to a collection agency. This company attempts to collect the outstanding debt. It keeps a percentage of the amount collected as a commission. The collection agency may take legal action against the customer if necessary.
Step 8		If collection cannot be made, Bestway *writes off* the account as a bad debt.

Career Profile

A Co-operative Education Student Lise Crete is currently a grade 12 student at the Ottawa High School of Commerce. She attends classes in the morning, but in the afternoon she goes to work in a business office. Lise is a participant in what is called a co-operative education program. This program is approved by the Ministry of Education in Ontario. Lise receives academic credits for the subjects she studies in the morning (English, Law, Accounting, and Ceramics) and also receives academic credits for her work performed in the afternoon in a business office.

Following is a description of what Lise does in the afternoon. By 13:00 she has made her way by bus from the High School of Commerce to the office of McGrath of Canada Ltd. This company is a collection agency responsible for collecting outstanding debts for its 3 000 customers.

Among the duties performed by Lise are: recording sales in the customer accounts using a Burroughs Sensimatic posting machine, recording cash received in the customer accounts, recording cash payments and purchases, preparing end-of-month reports.

Lise enjoys her work at McGrath because, although she is still a student, she is treated as an employee and is given the responsibilities of a permanent employee. One of her favourite subjects at school is accounting and the afternoon work gives her the opportunity to apply what she has been learning in the classroom.

As part of the co-operative program, Lise's supervisor has trained Lise to do a variety of clerical duties including those of a receptionist, cash control clerk, mail clerk, and invoice clerk. Lise will soon graduate from high school and has already accepted a permanent job in accounting at McGrath of Canada Ltd.

CHAPTER 5

The Journal and the Ledger

Unit 11

Avoiding Human Error in Accounting Systems

*1

Few systems, including accounting systems, are safe from human error. The fact must be accepted that people make mistakes, but accountants have worked through the years to develop systems that reduce the risk of errors. Accountants have also shared another concern: to avoid guesswork and time-consuming checking in tracking down mistakes that do occur.

Imagine a business, such as a major department store, that has to operate with a very large number of accounts. Imagine also that an accountant suspects that a transaction has been incorrectly recorded in the ledger. *How would the incorrect entry be traced?* The accountant would have to go through all the accounts until the incorrect entries were located. The accounts could be in widely separated parts of the ledger and it would take a long time to locate particular accounts, especially in a large business. This difficulty is eliminated by the use of a *journal.*

The Journal

A journal is a book where transactions are recorded in chronological order.

A journal is sometimes called a *book of original entry* because this is where transactions are first recorded. In a journal, the date, debit and credit, and explanation for each transaction are recorded together. Transactions can be conveniently located because they are recorded chronologically, that is, in the order in which they take place. The main journal of a business is often called the *General Journal.* Other types of journals will be discussed in later chapters.

Figure 5.1 *Transactions are first recorded in a journal*

Journal Entries Each transaction recorded in a journal is called an *entry*. The process of recording transactions in a journal is called *journalizing*. Each journal entry has four parts as shown in Figure 5.2:

Journalizing is the recording of transactions in a journal.

1. date of the transaction
2. account debited and amount
3. account credited (indented) and amount
4. an explantion giving details of the transaction

Sample Transactions Figure 5.2 illustrates how the following three transactions appear when they are recorded in the General Journal.

October 1 Sold services for $300 cash.
3 Paid $75 for advertising.
5 Paid secretary's salary, $200.

GENERAL JOURNAL — PAGE 11

	DATE		PARTICULARS	PR	DEBIT	CREDIT
1	Oct. 19--	1	Cash 2		2 300 —	
			Sales 3			3 300 —
		4	Sold services to A. Baker			
			for cash			
		3	Advertising Expense		75 —	
			Cash			75 —
			Paid for a newspaper ad			
		5	Salaries Expense		200 —	
			Cash			200 —
			Paid secretary's weekly salary			

Figure 5.2 *Transactions recorded in a General Journal*

Notice that in the General Journal illustrated in Figure 5.2, debits and credits are determined according to the same rules as those you learned in previous chapters. Note also that there is a consistent procedure for recording debits and credits in the General Journal: debits are recorded first and credits are recorded second and are indented.

In a journal, the first entry on each page must show the year, the month, and the day. Only the day of the month needs to be recorded for other entries on the page unless the month changes before a page is completed. In that event, the new month is shown in the date column.

The year is shown on each journal page.

The names of the accounts debited and credited in a journal should always be written in exactly the same way as the titles of the accounts appear in the ledger. For example, if cash is received, the appropriate account title would be Cash, not Cash Received.

*2

Advantages of the Journal Although transactions may be recorded directly into the ledger accounts, many businesses prefer to record transactions in a journal first for the following reasons.

- The complete transaction is recorded in one place.
- The use of a journal reduces errors. When entries are recorded directly into ledger accounts, it is easy to make a mistake by recording two debits and no credits or by recording only the debit or only the credit. Such errors are less likely to occur in a journal, but if they do happen, they are easy to spot. A quick check of each page in a journal will soon reveal any entry which does not show a debit and an equal credit.
- A journal represents a chronological history of all the business transactions recorded by date.
- It is possible to determine the daily, weekly or monthly volume of business and to identify busy periods more easily.

A journal presents a history of all the company's transactions.

*3

Journal Systems The basic journal, or the General Journal as it is called, is the type described in this chapter, but it is not the only kind. The type and number of journals are determined by the nature of the business and the number of transactions to be recorded. There can even be a *journalless system* where transactions are recorded directly into the ledger accounts.

Unit 12

Posting to the Ledger

*4

The General Journal is a systematic record of all transactions. It shows the accounts debited and credited for every transaction in the order in which the transactions occur. However, the General Journal does not provide the balance for each account. The General Journal does not tell the accountant how much cash is on hand and it also does not record the balance of each of the items that will appear on the financial statements. This type of information is found in the accounts in the ledger. The information in the General Journal (as well as in the other journals to be discussed later in the book) is transferred to the ledger by a process called *posting*.

Posting is the transfer of information from a journal to the ledger accounts.

Balance-column Form of Ledger Account

The T-account was introduced in Chapter 2 as a simple form for recording transactions in ledger accounts. It is an ideal form for learning the rules of debit and credit, but a T-account is not very practical for use in business. The most widely used form of account is the *balance-column account* which is sometimes called a three-column account (Figure 5.5).

In Figure 5.4 a number of transactions are recorded in a Cash T-account. Exactly the same transactions appear in Figure 5.5 in the form of a balance-column account. *Why is it called a balance-column form of account?*

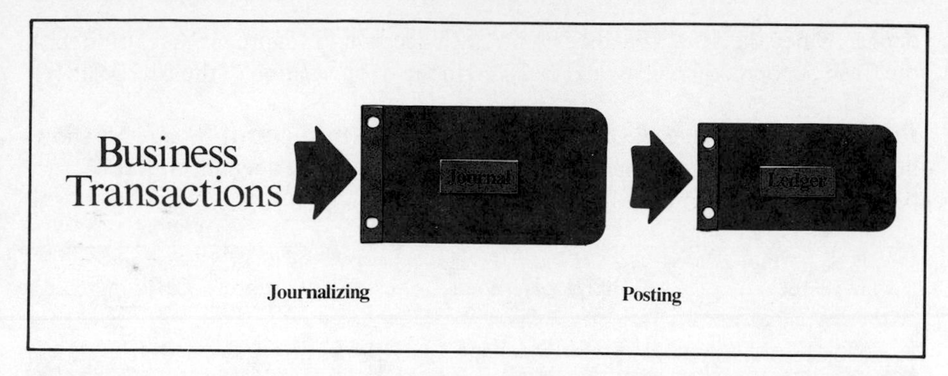

Figure 5.3 *Posting is the transfer of information from a journal to the accounts in the ledger*

Cash

Nov. 1	2 000	*Nov. 3*	150
3	75	*6*	200
5	100		350
	2 175		
Balance	1 825		

Figure 5.4 *Transactions recorded in a Cash T-account*

ACCOUNT Cash NO. 101

DATE		PARTICULARS	PR	DEBIT	CREDIT	DR CR	BALANCE
Nov. 19--	1		J1	2 000 —		DR	2 000 —
	3		J1	75 —		DR	2 075 —
	3		J1		150 —	DR	1 925 —
	5		J2	100 —		DR	2 025 —
	6		J3		200 —	DR	1 825 —

Figure 5.5 *Transactions shown in Figure 5.4 recorded in a balance-column ledger account*

Compare the information in the T-account in Figure 5.4 with the same information shown in the balance form of account in Figure 5.5. Notice that in the balance-column form of account a running balance is provided on each line. The accountant can see at a glance how much cash the company has at the close of each transaction. The *DR/CR* (debit/credit) column indicates that the balance in the example is a debit balance; that is, the debits are larger than the credits. Although entries in the account on November 3 and 6 are credits, the DR/CR column on these dates indicates that the balance is still a debit balance. The DR/CR column of the account also indicates the column of the trial balance in which the account will

The DR/CR column indicates whether the account balance is a debit or a credit.

appear. Since the $1 825 balance in the Cash account in Figure 5.5 is a DR (debit), the Cash account balance would be listed in the debit column of the trial balance.

*5

Posting to a Balance -Column Form of Ledger Account Figure 5.6 shows how a $300 General Journal entry is posted to the Cash account in the balance-column form of ledger account.

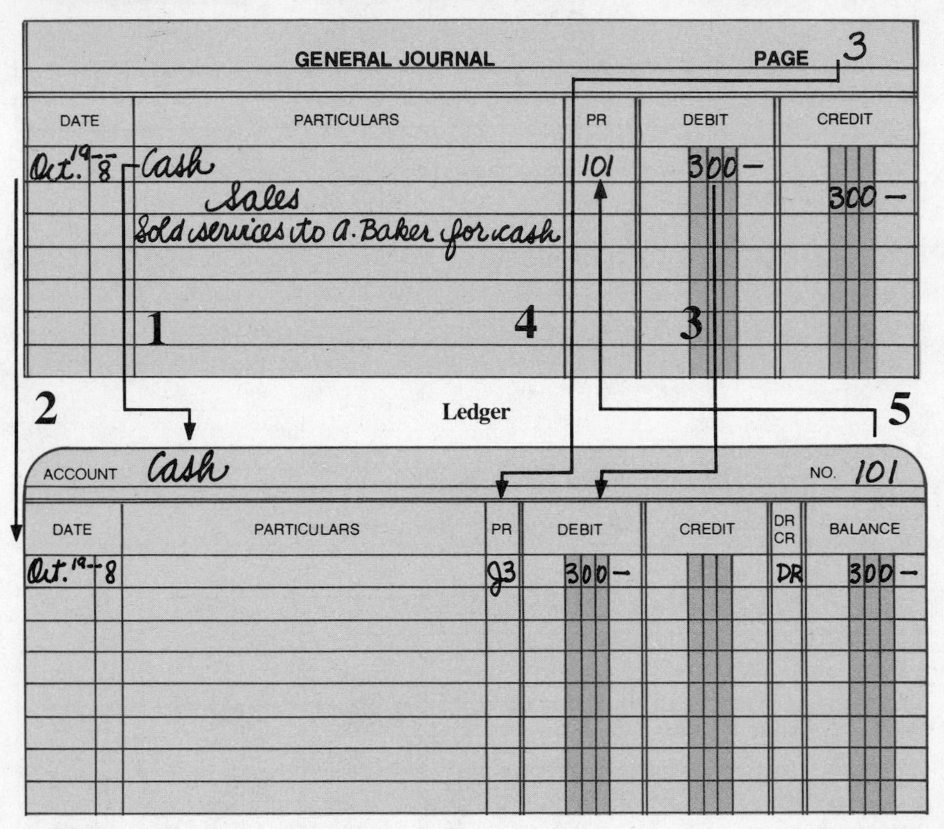

Figure 5.6 *Steps for posting the General Journal to the ledger*

Steps in Posting To avoid mechanical errors in the posting procedure, follow these steps.

1. Locate the ledger account shown on the first line of the General Journal entry.
2. Record the date in the date column of the ledger account.
3. Enter the amount of the debit in the debit column (or credit in the credit column) of the account and calculate and record the new balance. Indicate whether the balance is a debit or credit balance.
4. Enter the General Journal page number from which the amount was posted in the posting reference column of the ledger account. The page number is preceded by the letter *J* to indicate that the amount came from the General Journal.
5. Copy the account number from the ledger account into the *PR* (posting reference) column of the General Journal. This number recorded in the General

Journal indicates that the amount in the General Journal has been posted to the ledger.

The Posting Reference Column Numbers in the posting reference columns serve an important purpose. They are cross references that link particular journal entries to corresponding postings to the ledger accounts. *6

A journal page number in the ledger account posting reference column indicates where more information about the transaction can be found. For instance, the information explaining the transaction with A. Baker (Figure 5.6) can be located by referring to page three of the General Journal.

The ledger account number in a journal posting reference column indicates that the amount has been posted. It tells the accounting clerk where he or she left off in posting to the ledger.

Periodically, all companies have their records audited by an outside accountant. An audit is a systematic check of accounting records and procedures. The cross reference provided by posting reference numbers helps the auditor to check the accuracy of the journalizing and posting of transactions. The posting reference numbers allow the transactions to be traced from a journal to the ledger and also from the ledger to a journal.

The Ledger after Posting Figure 5.7 represents page 12 of a General Journal used by Martin Painting Contractors. Figure 5.8 is a portion of the company's ledger to which the transactions have been posted. Trace the transactions from the General Journal to the ledger. The posting reference column will help you. *7

GENERAL JOURNAL PAGE 12

DATE		PARTICULARS	PR	DEBIT	CREDIT
Nov. 19--	1	Cash	101	1300 —	
		Sales	400		1300 —
		Sold services to W. Mason			
	3	Advertising Expense	500	275 —	
		Cash	101		275 —
		Paid Ottawa Journal for a			
		newspaper advertisement			
	5	Salaries Expense	501	250 —	
		Cash	101		250 —
		Paid secretary's salary			
	6	Cash	101	700 —	
		Sales	400		700 —
		Painted house for M. Blais			

Figure 5.7 *Page 12 of the General Journal for Martin Painting Contractors*

ACCOUNT *Cash* NO. 101

DATE		PARTICULARS	PR	DEBIT	CREDIT	DR CR	BALANCE
Nov. 19—	1	Forwarded				DR	4000 —
	1		J12	1300 —		DR	5300 —
	3		J12		275 —	DR	5025 —
	5		J12		250 —	DR	4775 —
	6		J12	700 —		DR	5475 —

ACCOUNT *Sales* NO. 400

DATE		PARTICULARS	PR	DEBIT	CREDIT	DR CR	BALANCE
Nov. 19—	1		J12		1300 —	CR	1300 —
	6		J12		700 —	CR	2000 —

ACCOUNT *Advertising Expense* NO. 500

DATE		PARTICULARS	PR	DEBIT	CREDIT	DR CR	BALANCE
Nov. 19—	3		J12	275 —		DR	275 —

ACCOUNT *Salaries Expense* NO. 501

DATE		PARTICULARS	PR	DEBIT	CREDIT	DR CR	BALANCE
Nov. 19—	5		J12	250 —		DR	250 —

Figure 5.8 *Portion of the ledger for Martin Painting Contractors affected by the transactions in Figure 5.7*

Opening the Books

*8

Figures 5.7 and 5.8 illustrated how routine transactions are recorded in the General Journal and then are posted to a ledger. The special procedures followed when a business first begins operations will now be examined.

The Opening Entry A special entry, called an *opening entry,* is prepared when a business first begins operations. Following are the procedures K. Martin used when he started his painting business.

On September 1, K. Martin borrowed money from a bank and started a painting business. He invested $4 000 cash, a small truck worth $6 500, and equipment worth $1 900. The assets of the new business are:

Cash	$ 4 000
Equipment	1 900
Delivery Truck	6 500
Total	$12 400

The business has one liability:

Bank Loan $5 000

Martin's equity is calculated by applying the equation:

A	=	L	+	OE
$12 400	=	$5 000	+	$7 400

Martin's equity is $7 400.

To open the books of the business, the General Journal is set up and the business' assets, liability, and owner's equity are recorded. This first entry as illustrated in Figure 5.9 is called the opening entry.

GENERAL JOURNAL — PAGE 1

DATE		PARTICULARS	PR	DEBIT	CREDIT
Dec. 19--	1	Cash		4 000 —	
		Equipment		1 900 —	
		Delivery Truck		6 500 —	
		Bank Loan			5 000 —
		K. Martin, Capital			7 400 —
		Started a painting business			
		with the above assets,			
		liabilities, and owner's equity			

Figure 5.9 *Opening entry in the General Journal for Martin Painting Contractors*

The opening entry records the assets, liabilities, and owner's equity when a business first begins operations.

Notice that the opening entry shows three debits and two credits with the three debit amounts ($12 400) equal to the two credit amounts ($12 400). An entry, such as this opening entry, that shows more than one debit or credit, is called a *compound entry*. However, all entries must have equal debit and credit amounts. After the opening entry is journalized, the daily entries of the business can be recorded.

A compound entry is an entry that has more than one debit or more than one credit.

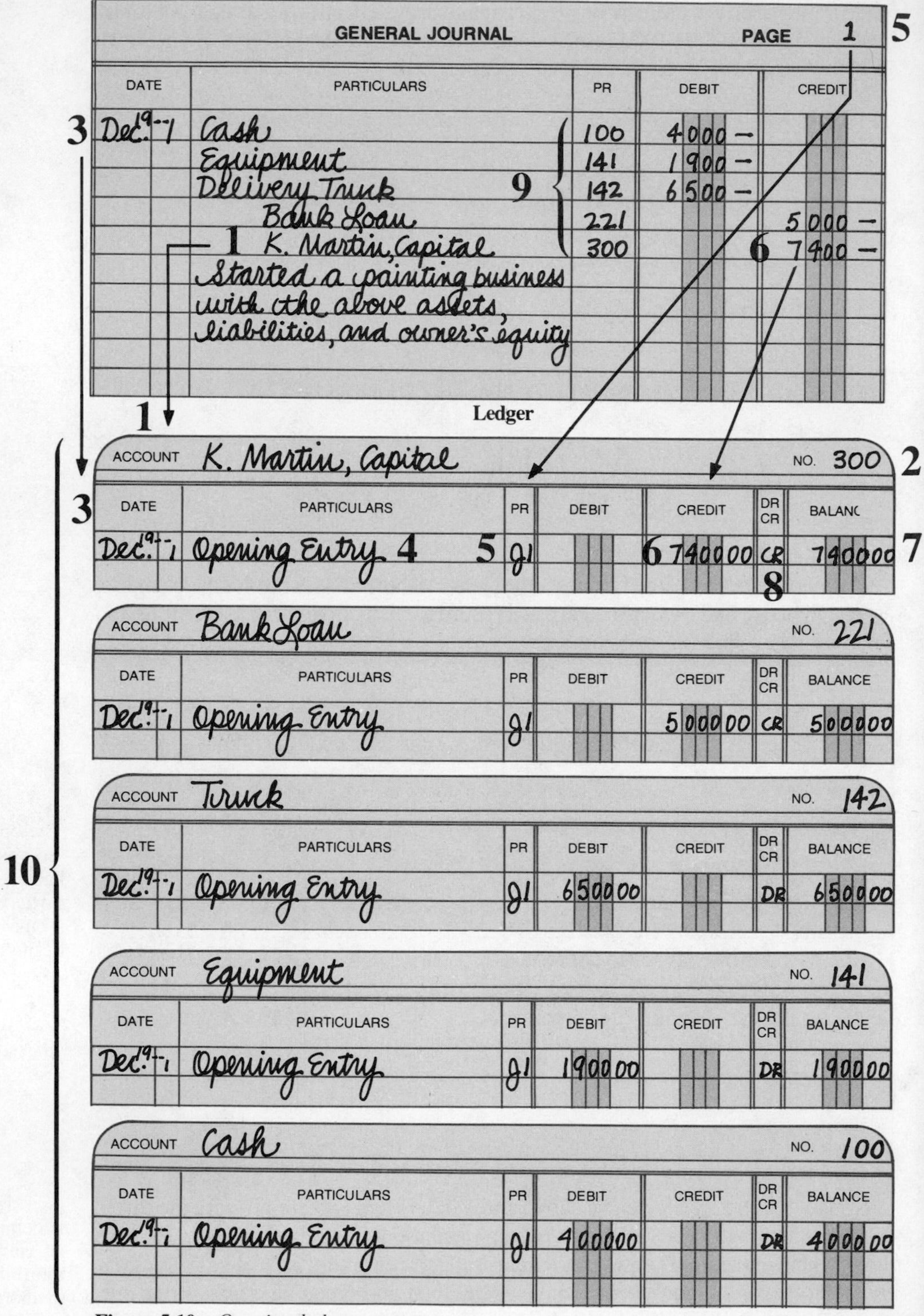

GENERAL JOURNAL — PAGE 1

DATE		PARTICULARS	PR	DEBIT	CREDIT
Dec.19--	1	Cash	100	4 000 —	
		Equipment	141	1 900 —	
		Delivery Truck	142	6 500 —	
		Bank Loan	221		5 000 —
		K. Martin, Capital	300		7 400 —
		Started a painting business with the above assets, liabilities, and owner's equity			

Ledger

ACCOUNT K. Martin, Capital — NO. 300

DATE		PARTICULARS	PR	DEBIT	CREDIT	DR CR	BALANCE
Dec.19--	1	Opening Entry	J1		7 400 00	CR	7 400 00

ACCOUNT Bank Loan — NO. 221

DATE		PARTICULARS	PR	DEBIT	CREDIT	DR CR	BALANCE
Dec.19--	1	Opening Entry	J1		5 000 00	CR	5 000 00

ACCOUNT Truck — NO. 142

DATE		PARTICULARS	PR	DEBIT	CREDIT	DR CR	BALANCE
Dec.19--	1	Opening Entry	J1	6 500 00		DR	6 500 00

ACCOUNT Equipment — NO. 141

DATE		PARTICULARS	PR	DEBIT	CREDIT	DR CR	BALANCE
Dec.19--	1	Opening Entry	J1	1 900 00		DR	1 900 00

ACCOUNT Cash — NO. 100

DATE		PARTICULARS	PR	DEBIT	CREDIT	DR CR	BALANCE
Dec.19--	1	Opening Entry	J1	4 000 00		DR	4 000 00

Figure 5.10 *Opening ledger accounts*

Opening Ledger Accounts Next, the ledger is prepared by opening the accounts required to post the opening entry (Figure 5.10). As business transactions occur, they are journalized. As new accounts are required they are opened in the ledger. Follow these procedures when opening a new balance-column account. *9

1. Write the name of the account to the right of the word Account.
2. Write the account number at the far right on the top line.
3. Write the date in the Date column.
4. Write *Opening Entry* on the first line in the column identified by the heading *Particulars*. This will help distinguish the opening entry from the changes that will occur to the account as business transactions take place.
5. Write *J1* for General Journal Page 1 in the posting reference column.
6. Record the amount in the correct debit or credit column.
7. Enter the balance in the Balance column.
8. Write *DR* or *CR* depending on the balance in the DR/CR column.
9. Enter the ledger account number in the posting reference column of the General Journal.
10. Insert the account in numerical sequence in the ledger.

Forwarding Procedure The active accounts of a business show many transactions recorded on the pages of the ledger. When an account page is filled, a new page is opened according to the following procedure. *10

1. Head up a new page using the same account name and number (Figures 5.11 and 5.12).
2. Write *Forwarded* on the last line of the old page in the Particulars column (Figure 5.11).

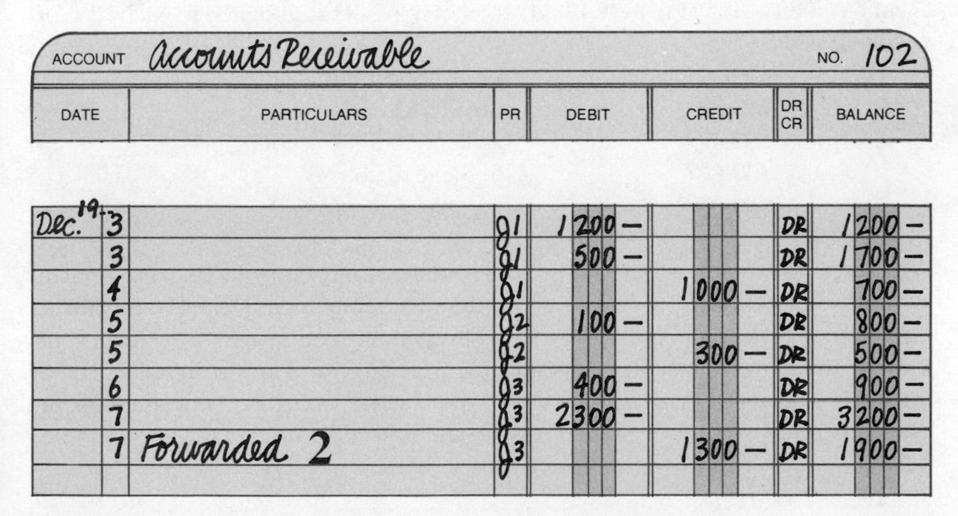

ACCOUNT Accounts Receivable NO. 102

DATE		PARTICULARS	PR	DEBIT	CREDIT	DR CR	BALANCE
Dec. 19--	3		J1	1200 —		DR	1200 —
	3		J1	500 —		DR	1700 —
	4		J1		1000 —	DR	700 —
	5		J2	100 —		DR	800 —
	5		J2		300 —	DR	500 —
	6		J3	400 —		DR	900 —
	7		J3	2300 —		DR	3200 —
	7	Forwarded 2	J3		1300 —	DR	1900 —

Figure 5.11 *A ledger page that has been filled and forwarded*

3. On the first line of the new page, write the date (year, month, day), *Forwarded* in the Particulars column, and the balance in the Balance column. Indicate the type of balance. Place a check-mark in the posting reference column as shown in Figure 5.12.

ACCOUNT Accounts Receivable						NO. 102
DATE	PARTICULARS	PR	DEBIT	CREDIT	DR CR	BALANCE
Dec. 7	Forwarded	✓			DR	1900 —

Figure 5.12 *A new ledger page*

Note that aside from the *Opening Entry* and *Forwarded* notations, the Particulars column is seldom used. If further information is required about a transaction, use the posting reference numbers to trace the entry back to the General Journal where more detailed information can be found.

Chart of Accounts

A chart of accounts is a list of the names and account numbers of all the accounts in the ledger.

Each account in the ledger has an account title and an account number. Accounts are placed in the ledger in numerical sequence so that they may be located quickly. A list of the account names and numbers called a *chart of accounts* is used by accounting employees. The chart of accounts is an aid in deciding which accounts may be used when transactions are journalized and in locating accounts when posting to the ledger.

The accounts in the ledger are numbered in the same order as they appear on the balance sheet and income statement. Notice that in the chart of accounts for Martin Painting Contractors (Figure 5.13), a series of numbers is assigned to each type of account:

100-199	Asset accounts
200-299	Liability accounts
300-399	Owner's equity accounts
400-499	Revenue accounts
500-599	Expense accounts

In large companies, a four-digit series of numbers may be required to cover all the accounts. For example asset accounts might be numbered 1000-1999 and liability accounts might be numbered 2000-2999. This system is suitable for a business with a large number of accounts. Appendix A, page 564, provides a sample chart of accounts used by a Canadian Tire Corporation store. In computer accounting, the account number becomes a numeric code and is used in place of the account title.

The Trial Balance

*11

At regular intervals, usually monthly, a trial balance is prepared. A trial balance is proof of the mathematical accuracy of the ledger. As you learned in Chapter 2, a trial balance is a list of the debit account balances and the credit account balances. The total of the debit balances should equal the total of the credit balances. The

Martin Painting Contractors
Chart of Accounts

Assets

100	Cash
101	Accounts Receivable/A. Baker
102	Accounts Receivable/L. Carter
131	Painting Supplies
141	Equipment
142	Truck

Liabilities

200	Accounts Payable/International Paints
201	Accounts Payable/Hardware Supply Corp.
221	Bank Loan
231	Mortgage Payable

Owner's Equity

300	K. Martin, Capital
301	K. Martin, Drawing

Revenue

400	Sales

Expenses

500	Advertising
501	Rent
502	Salaries

Figure 5.13 *Chart of accounts for Martin Painting Contractors*

formal trial balance for Martin Painting is illustrated in Figure 5.14.

A trial balance is proof of the mathematical accuracy of the ledger.

The trial balance may take several forms:

- a formal trial balance (Figure 5.14)
- a list of the debit and credit account balances in which the debit total equals the credit total (Figure 5.15)
- a machine tape listing the account balances in which the debits minus the credits equals zero (Figure 5.16)

Martin Painting Contractors Trial Balance November 30, 19--			
ACCOUNT TITLE	ACC. NO.	DEBIT	CREDIT
Cash	100	1 200 —	
Accounts Receivable / A. Baker	101	295 —	
Accounts Receivable / L. Carter	102	150 —	
Equipment	141	2 250 —	
Truck	142	6 500 —	
Accounts Payable / International Paints	200		695 —
Accounts Payable / Hardware Supply Corp.	201		315 —
Bank Loan	221		5 000 —
K. Martin, Capital	300		4 385 —
		10 395 —	10 395 —

Figure 5.14 *Formal trial balance*

Martin Painting Contractors
Trial Balance
November 30, 19--

Debits	Credits
$1 200	$ 695
295	5 000
150	315
6 000	4 385
2 750	
$10 395	$10 395

Figure 5.15 *List form of trial balance – total debits equal total credits*

MARTIN PAINTING CONTRACTORS
Trial Balance
NOVEMBER 30, 19--

```
   0.00 *

1200.00 +
 295.00 +
 150.00 +
6000.00 +
2750.00 +
 695.00 -
5000.00 -
 315.00 -
4385.00 -
   0.00 *
```

Figure 5.16 *Machine tape form of trial balance – debits minus credits equals zero*

Unit 13

*12

The Accounting Cycle

You have seen that business transactions are first recorded in a journal and are then posted to the ledger. If the ledger is in balance, the financial statements (the income statement and the balance sheet) are then prepared. These steps are completed in sequence in each accounting period and together are called the *accounting cycle*.

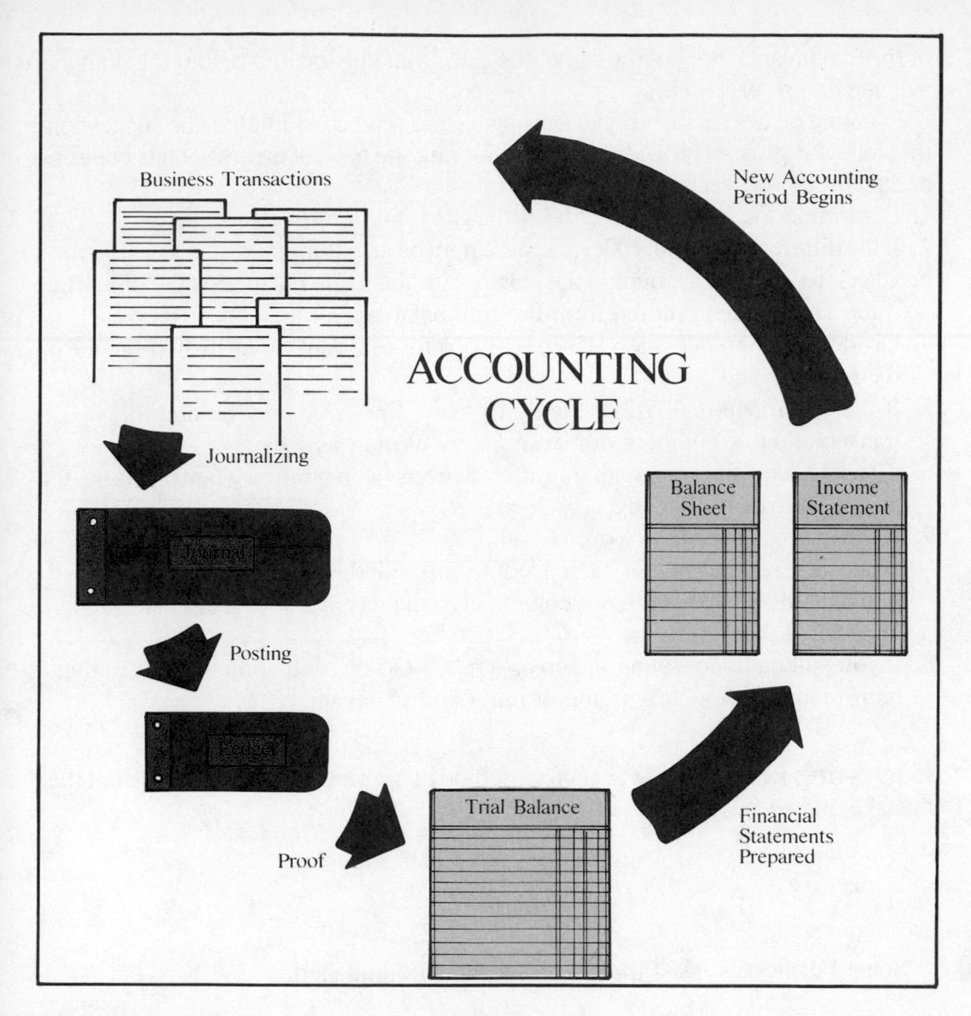

Figure 5.17 *The accounting cycle*

The accounting cycle is the set of accounting procedures performed in each accounting period.

Errors Made in Posting

*13

By following the steps in posting listed on page 90 , the following types of errors can be avoided:

- not posting an entire transaction
- not posting either the debit or credit part of a transaction
- posting to the correct side but to the wrong account
- posting to the wrong side of an account
- calculating the balance incorrectly
- transposing figures (posting 96 instead of 69)

Locating Trial Balance Errors The trial balance is a test or trial to prove that the ledger is mathematically in balance. If the totals of the debit and credit columns of the trial balance are not the same, the error must be located before the financial statements are prepared.

Locating errors can be very discouraging and time consuming. The suggestions that follow represent procedures for identifying the type of error that has occurred and methods for tracking it down.

1. Determine the difference between the debit and credit totals.
2. If the difference is 1, 10, 100, etc., there may be an addition or subtraction error.
3. Check to see if an account in the ledger with the same balance as the difference (Step 1) has been omitted from the trial balance.
4. Divide the difference (Step 1) by two. Look for that amount on the wrong side of the trial balance.
5. If the difference is divisible evenly by nine, the error may be due to a transposition of numbers (for example 97 written as 79).
6. Check to see if the amount of the difference has been omitted when it was posted from a journal to the ledger.
7. If the error still escapes you:
   a) check each balance in each account in the ledger;
   b) check the posting reference column of each journal to locate unposted items;
   c) recheck each posting.
8. If you still have not found the error – relax! Go on with something else, then return later with a clear frame of mind and try again.

*14

Correcting Errors The accepted method of correcting errors is to rule out the mistake and to rewrite the correction:

265
~~256~~

Some businesses insist that all corrections be initialled:

259 C.D.
~~195~~

Correcting Entries It may be inconvenient to correct an error by using a ruler and rewriting to correct the entry because of the number of changes required. For example, suppose the following entry has been journalized and posted, but the amount should read $500:

June	2	Equipment		50 —	
		Cash			50 —
		Purchased a calculator for			
		$500 cash invoice BL-2851			

Rather than making a series of corrections, make the following journal entry:

June	29	Equipment		450—	
		Cash			450—
		To correct June 2 entry.			
		amount should have been			
		$500. See invoice BL-2851.			

Checking for Accuracy Most accounting offices use machines such as a 10-key adding machine or an electronic printing calculator to check their mathematical calculations. When you use a machine, follow these procedures (see Figure 5.18). *15

1. Clear the machine.
2. Enter the data.
3. Label the tape.
4. If the totals being checked do not balance, audit the tape by checking the numbers on the tape against the source. This step will locate errors made in entering numbers on the machine keyboard.
5. Staple the labelled tape to the material being checked.

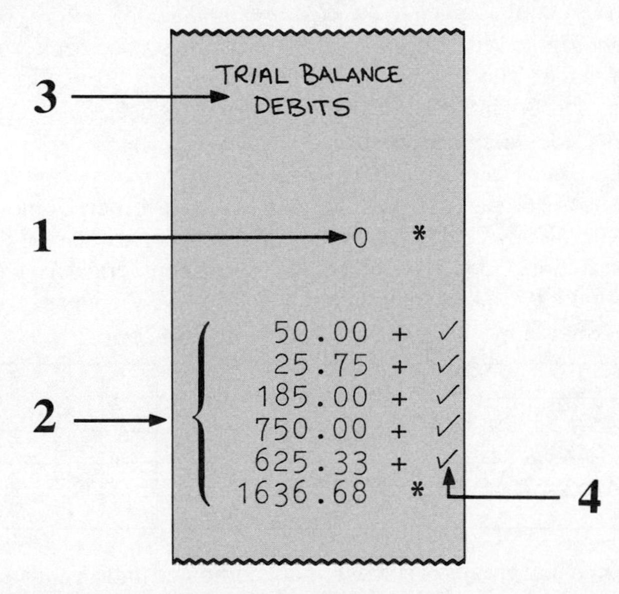

Figure 5.18 *Checking a trial balance by calculator*

Checking Accounts The balance of an account may be checked on a machine by entering each debit with the (+) bar and each credit with the minus (–) bar. Take the total after the last entry. Figure 5.19 illustrates this procedure.

Another method of checking accounts is to use the subtotal control bar to check the balance column after each entry (Figure 5.20). This technique specifically identifies the line on which an error may occur.

CASH ACCOUNT

```
      0     *
2190.00     +
  25.00     +
 395.00     -
 620.00     -
 895.60     +
   8.70     -
 699.20     +
2786.10     *
```

ACCOUNT *Cash* NO. *100*

DATE		PARTICULARS	PR	DEBIT	CREDIT	DR CR	BALANCE
19-- Nov.	1	Balance				DR	2190 —
	2		J16	25 —		DR	2215 —
	3		J16		395 —	DR	1830 —
	5		J16		620 —	DR	1200 —
	5		J17	895 60		DR	2095 60
	5		J17		8 70	DR	2086 90
	5		J18	699 20		DR	2786 10

Figure 5.19 *Checking accounts by calculator*

Source Documents

***16**
A source document is any business form that is the original source of information.

As business transactions occur, information about the transactions is recorded on some form of business document. For example, when a cash sale is made a sales slip is prepared. A copy is given to the customer and a copy is kept by the seller. The accountant for the seller uses the sales slip as the source of information that a sale has been made. The accountant for the buyer uses the copy of the same document as a source of information that a purchase has been made. This is where the term *source document* comes from.

Figure 5.21 is a cash sales slip similar to slips used by many retail stores. Three copies of this slip are prepared. Copy 1 is given to the customer. Copies 2 and 3 are kept by the seller. Copy 2 is used by the accounting department of the seller to record the transaction. Copy 3 is kept by the seller in a numerical file which serves as a record of all cash sales. Every sales slip must be accounted for in this file.

This entry is made by the seller's accountant from copy 2:

May	21	Cash		523	
		Sales			523
		Cash sales slip 43785			

CASH ACCOUNT

```
   0.00   T

2190.00
  25.00
2215.00   S

 395.00   -
1820.00   S

 620.00   -
1200.00   S

 895.60
2095.90   S

 699.20
2786.10   S
```

Figure 5.20 *Checking accounts by calculator – subtotal method*

It should be noted that groups of sales slips are combined and an entry similar to the preceding one is made to record the total of the group of slips.

The buyer uses the first copy as the source of information to record this entry:

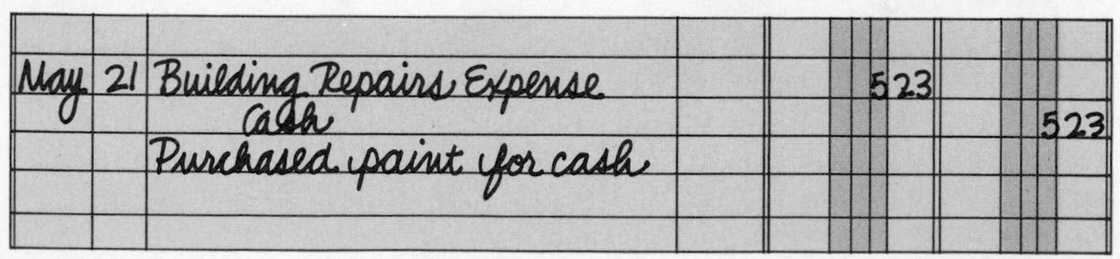

May	21	Building Repairs Expense		523	
		Cash			523
		Purchased paint for cash			

160 SPRUCE STREET OTTAWA, ONT. K1R 6P2 TEL (613) 236-0716

CASH SALE
VENTE AU COMPTANT
International Paints (Canada) Limited

Marine, Industrial, Railway, Aircraft & Household Finishes

Date May 21 19--

NAME / NOM Warrendon Sports

ADDRESS / ADRESSE Ottawa

CODE NUMBER NUMÉRO DU CODE	ORDERED COMM.	UNIT SIZE FORMAT	DESCRIPTION	UNIT PRIX L'UNITÉ	AMOUNT MONTANT	
CM230000	1	2L	Exterior Paint		4	89

CASH	CHX	REF		CHEQUE	PROV. TAX TAXE PROV.	0	34
✓							
SALESPERSON VENDEUR/EUSE R.H.					TOTAL	5	23

43785

CUSTOMER'S COPY
COPIE DU CLIENT

Figure 5.21 *Cash sales slip – a source document used by retail stores*

Sales Invoices and Purchase Invoices Figure 5.22 is an example of another source document. This type of invoice is generally used by manufacturers and wholesalers. It is a document which gives the details of a charge sale. Several copies are made depending on the needs of the business.

Copies 1 and 2 are sent to the customer. Copy 3 is used by the accounting department of the seller as the source of information to record the transaction. Copy 4 is kept by the sales department as a record of the sale. Copies 5 and 6 are given to the shipping department. Copy 5 is used to pack and label the shipment. Copy 6 is placed inside the shipment as a packing slip.

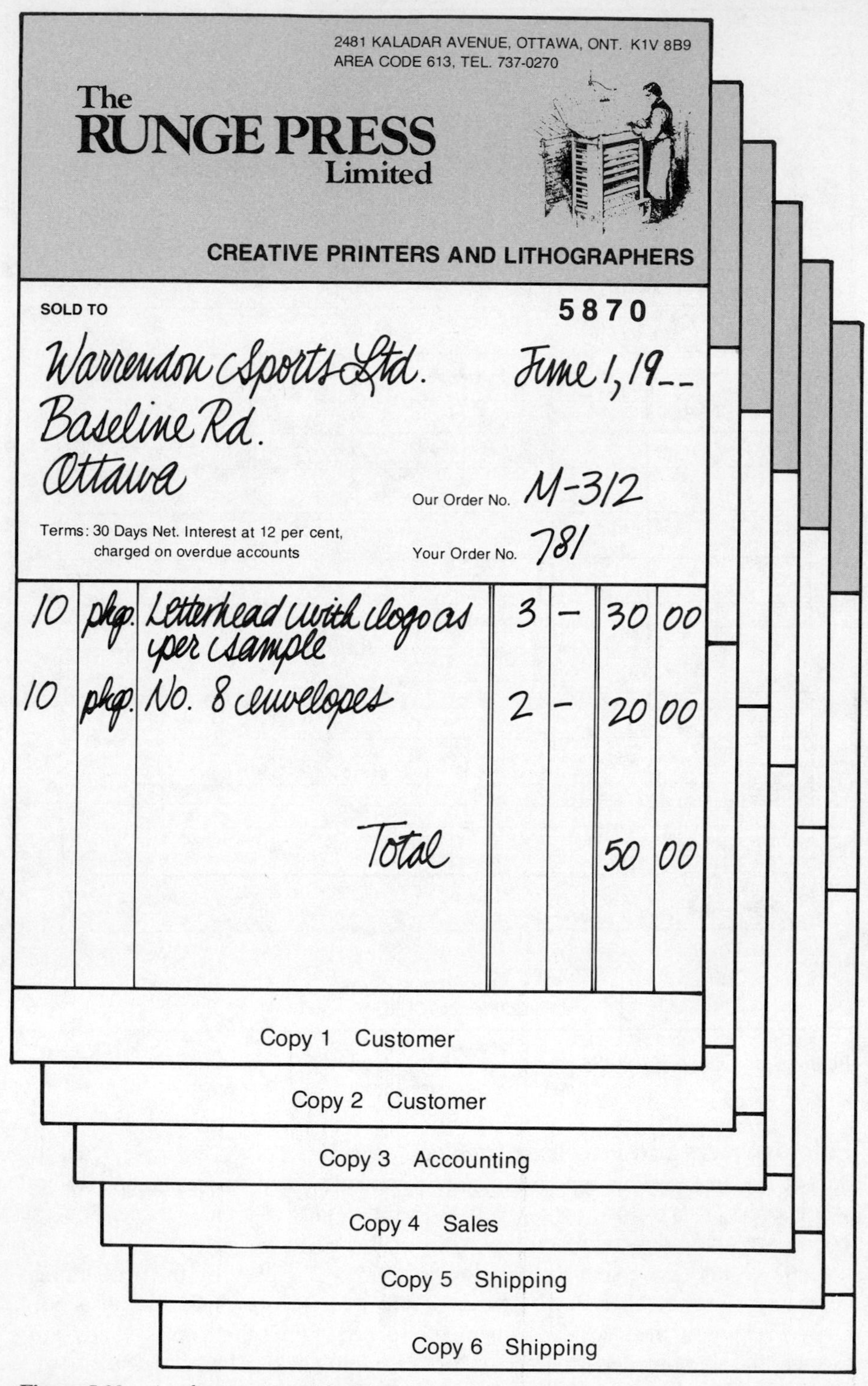

2481 KALADAR AVENUE, OTTAWA, ONT. K1V 8B9
AREA CODE 613, TEL. 737-0270

The RUNGE PRESS Limited

CREATIVE PRINTERS AND LITHOGRAPHERS

SOLD TO — 5870

Warrendon Sports Ltd. — June 1, 19__
Baseline Rd.
Ottawa

Our Order No. M-312

Terms: 30 Days Net. Interest at 12 per cent, charged on overdue accounts

Your Order No. 781

10	pkg.	Letterhead with logo as per sample	3	—	30	00
10	pkg.	No. 8 envelopes	2	—	20	00
		Total			50	00

Copy 1 Customer

Copy 2 Customer

Copy 3 Accounting

Copy 4 Sales

Copy 5 Shipping

Copy 6 Shipping

Figure 5.22 *A sales invoice with details of a charge sale*

This entry is made by the accounting department of the seller from copy 3.

				Debit	Credit
June	1	Acc. Rec./Warrendon Sports		50 —	
		Sales			50 —
		Invoice 5870, letterhead paper			
		and envelopes			

You can see that the same document is used to record the sale by the seller and the purchase by the customer. The sellers call their document a *sales invoice* and the buyers call their copy a *purchase invoice*.

Other Source Documents Sales slips, sales invoices, and purchase invoices are three commonly used source documents. Throughout this text you will be introduced to other documents including these:

- *Copies of cheques* When a payment is made by cheque, the payer may make a copy of the cheque and use it to record the payment.
- *Cheques received* Some companies use the cheques received from customers as sources of information for transactions. Others prefer to deposit the cheques in the bank and to use a daily list of cash received as the source of informaton.
- *List of cash received* Each day a list of all money received is prepared and used as the source of information for entries to record cash received.
- *Credit invoices, bank debit and credit memoranda, cash register tapes* These source documents are explained in later chapters.

Prenumbered Source Documents Source documents are prenumbered, and every document must be accounted for. The numbering of documents is a control procedure designed to prevent errors and losses due to theft or the use of false documents. Source documents are kept on file and must be made available to persons who have the authority to check a company's records. These include:

- owners and managers of the business
- outside accountants hired to check the records
- federal income tax personnel
- provincial sales tax and Department of Labour personnel
- officials of the courts

Source documents are an important part of a company's accounting system. Every business should take care to produce neat, legible documents which are numbered and filed in a well-organized manner.

Facts to Remember

A *journal* is a book where transactions are recorded in chronological order.

Journalizing is the recording of transactions in a journal.

A journal entry is any transaction recorded in a journal.

Every journal entry has four parts: the date; account and debit amount; account and credit amount; and an explanation of the transaction.

Posting is the transfer of information from a journal to the ledger accounts.

The *opening entry* records the assets, liabilities, and owner's equity when a business first begins operations.

A compound entry is an entry that has more than one debit or more than one credit.

A chart of accounts is a list of the names and account numbers of all the accounts in the ledger.

The *accounting cycle* is the set of accounting procedures performed in each accounting period.

A *source document* is any business form that is the original source of information.

Checking Your Reading

Questions

1. What is a journal?
2. Why is a journal sometimes called a book of original entry?
3. What is a journal entry?
4. What is journalizing?
5. Name the four parts of a journal entry.
6. Which part of a journal entry is indented?
7. a) Describe four advantages of using a journal.
   b) In what order do entries appear in a journal?
8. What is journalless accounting?
9. What is posting?
10. What are the five steps followed in posting?
11. What is written in the posting reference column of a journal and a ledger?
12. What is an opening entry?
13. What is a compound entry?
14. What is a chart of accounts?

15. a) The difference in the totals of a trial balance is $100. What type of error has probably been made?
b) If the difference is $270, what type of error may have been made?

16. a) What is a source document?
b) Give four examples of source documents.
c) Why are source documents prenumbered?
d) Name a source document for each of the following:
i) a cash sale
ii) a sale on account
iii) a purchase on account
iv) a payment by cheque

Applying Your Knowledge

Exercises Part A

1. Prepare a chart of accounts for The Cascade Inn. Number each of the accounts using the numbering system in Figure 5.13. The accounts in the ledger are as follows: Cash; Supplies; Equipment; Land; Building; Accounts Payable; Mortgage Payable; J. Galotta, Capital; J. Galotta, Drawing; Room Rental Revenue; Restaurant Revenue; Advertising Expense; General Expense; Salaries Expense; Telephone Expense; Utilities Expense.

2. Journalize the following transactions for the Capital Theatre using the accounts from the following chart of accounts:

101	Cash	501	Salaries Expense
300	A. Ryholm, Capital	502	Film Rental Expense
400	Ticket Sales	503	Hydro Expense
401	Refreshment Sales		

Nov. 1 A. Ryholm invested $12 000 cash.
8 Ticket sales for the week, $14 000.
8 Refreshment sales, $1 900.
10 Paid for film rental, $4 000 cash.
15 Paid salaries, $2 000 cash.
15 Ticket sales, $9 900 cash.
15 Refreshment sales, $1 300 cash.
15 Paid hydro bill, $49.75 cash.

3. Journalize the following transactions for the Stokes Driving School, using accounts from the following chart of accounts:

101	Cash	401	Revenue from Lessons
102	Accounts Receivable/L. Starr	501	Salaries Expense
103	Equipment	502	Advertising Expense
104	Automobiles	503	Automobile Expense
201	Accounts Payable/Grant's Esso	504	Utilities Expense
301	R. Stokes, Capital		

Aug. 1 R. Stokes invested $25 000 cash.
2 Purchased equipment for $2 000 cash.
4 Purchased 2 cars from Dardick Motors for $12 000 cash.
5 Received $700 cash from customers taking driving lessons.
7 Paid $300 cash for instructor's salaries for the first week.
9 Paid $15 cash to the telephone company.
10 Received $800 cash from customers taking driving lessons.
11 Issued an invoice (bill) of $50 to L. Starr, a customer who is taking lessons, but will pay at a later date.
11 Received a $30 invoice from Grant's Esso for gas and oil used by the cars.
12 Paid $20 cash for hydro and electricity.
13 Sent a $70 cheque to the *Daily Star* for advertising space.
14 Received $50 cash from L. Starr, to pay off the account.

4. Journalize the following transactions in a General Journal. Select appropriate accounts for each transaction.

Feb. 1 G. Sloan invested $9 000 cash in a business.
2 Sold services worth $600 to D. Ferris, for cash.
3 Sold services to W. Anderson, $250 on account.
4 Sold services to T. Tidey, $700 on account.
5 Received $100 cash from W. Anderson as part payment of his account balance.
8 Received $700 cash from T. Tidey in full payment of his account.

5. a) The following Cash account has incomplete DR/CR and balance columns. Prepare a copy of the account, completing the DR/CR column and the balance column on each line of the account.

ACCOUNT Cash NO. 100

DATE	PARTICULARS	PR	DEBIT	CREDIT	DR CR	BALANCE
Nov. 19-- 1	Balance Forwarded	✓			DR	500 —
2		J6	25 —			
3		J6	50 —			
5		J7		10 —		
5		J7		90 —		
6		J7	100 —			

b) Assume that the account page for Cash is filled. Apply the forwarding procedure and forward the balance to a new account page for Cash.

6. Following are three *mini* trial balances that do not balance. Calculate the difference in the debit and credit totals and indicate the probable type of error in each.

a) Debit	Credit
3 000	
1 000	
700	
420	
	2 950
	2 170
5 120	5 020

b) Debit	Credit
200	
300	
50	
	75
	25
	300
	200
550	600

c) Debit	Credit
3 000	
1 000	
700	
240	
	2 950
	2 170
4 940	5 120

7. On Feb. 1, M. Conway, an architect, opened a business.
   a) Journalize the February transactions using accounts from this chart of accounts:

100	Cash	400	Fees Earned
101	Accounts Receivable/Bak Contractors	505	General Expense
141	Office Equipment	507	Rent Expense
142	Automobile	508	Salaries Expense
200	Accounts Payable/Ajax Motors	510	Telephone Expense
300	M. Conway, Capital		

Feb. 1 M. Conway invested $10 000 cash in an architectural consulting business.
2 Bought office equipment, $3 000 cash.
3 Bought an automobile for business from Ajax Motors Ltd. on account. The cost price of the car was $7 000.
4 Received $500 cash for services provided to a customer.
5 Sent a bill for $1 000 to Bak Contractors for services provided.
5 Paid the February rent, $600 cash.
5 Paid office salaries, $450.
5 Paid $45 for the installation of a telephone.

   b) Open ledger accounts using account titles and numbers from the chart of accounts.
   c) Post the General Journal entries.
   d) Prepare a trial balance.

8. M. Teron began a consulting business on March 1. The opening day balance sheet follows. Prepare an opening entry in a General Journal to record the firm's assets, liabilities, and equity.

M. Teron, Consultants			
Balance Sheet			
March 1, 19__			
Assets		**Liabilities**	
Cash	3 000 00	Bank Loan	5 000 00
Equipment	10 000 00		
Automobile	6 000 00	**Owner's Equity**	
		M. Teron, Capital	14 000 00
	19 000 00		19 000 00

Exercises Part B

9. a) Journalize the following transactions in M. Conway's journal. (Refer to exercise 7 if necessary.)

Feb. 8. Received $500 cash from Bak Contractors to reduce their account.
8 Received $50 cash for professional services.
9 Purchased a typewriter for the office for $650 cash from Olivetti Ltd.
10 Received $250 cash for professional services.
11 Paid $200 cash for a company membership in the Architects' Association (General Expense).
12 Paid $15 cash for miscellaneous items needed in the office (General Expense).
13 Paid office salaries $450.
13 Received $500 cash from Bak Contractors. Account now paid in full.

10. Following is the December 1 balance sheet for the Valley Motel owned by J. Lebrun:

Valley Motel			
Balance Sheet			
December 1, 19__			
Assets		**Liabilities**	
Cash	3 000 00	Accounts Payable/Acme	
Supplies	2 000 00	Supply	3 000 00
Office Equipment	2 000 00	Bank Loan	25 000 00
Furniture	20 000 00	Mortgage Payable	60 000 00
Automobile	6 000 00	Total Liabilities	88 000 00
Building	150 000 00		
		Owner's Equity	
		J. Lebrun, Capital	95 000 00
		Total Liabilities	
Total Assets	183 000 00	and Owner's Equity	183 000 00

a) Journalize the opening entry. The chart of accounts contains the accounts shown on the balance sheet and the following:

301	J. Lebrun, Drawing	502	Salaries Expense
400	Room Rentals	503	Telephone Expense
500	Advertising Expense	505	Utilities Expense
501	General Expense	506	Automobile Expense

b) Journalize the December transactions using account titles found in the balance sheet and in the chart of accounts.

Dec. 1 Paid $50 cash for automobile expenses.
2 J. Lebrun withdrew $150 cash for personal use.
3 Paid $1 000 cash to Acme Supply to reduce the amount owing to Acme.
4 Paid $75 cash for the month's telephone charges.
5 Received cash $900 for room rentals for the week.
8 Purchased cleaning supplies from Acme Supply, $120, but did not pay for them.
10 Paid $25 cash for repairs to Lebrun's personal car.
11 Bought an electronic printing calculator for the office for $200 cash.
12 Received cash, $1 100 for room rentals for the week.
12 Paid $12 cash for postage stamps (General Expense).
12 Paid the hydro bill, $290 cash, and the water bill, $175 cash.
15 Paid $75 cash for the printing of an advertising brochure.
15 Paid $45 for a small advertisement in the local newspaper.

c) Open ledger accounts for the balance sheet accounts and for the accounts on the chart of accounts.
d) Post the opening entry and the December General Journal entries.
e) Prepare a trial balance.

11. Helen Young operates a real estate agency which earns money from three sources:

- commissions earned on sales of property
- management fees
- investment income

The management fees are a result of renting and maintaining homes and condominiums for owners who are not living in them, but who lease them to others. For a fee, H. Young manages such properties for the owners. The company has invested past net incomes (profits) in stocks and bonds. Interest and dividends received on these investments are recorded in the Investment Income account.

Record the January transactions on page 17 of a General Journal. Use the accounts from the chart of accounts.

Jan. 2 Received $2 900 cash as a commission for handling the sale of a house.

Jan.	2	Paid $700 cash for the month's rent for the office.
	3	Received a bill from Tom's Service Centre for $75 for gas, oil, and repairs to the company automobile. The bill is not to be paid until January 15.
	5	Received a bill for $150 for the printing of letterhead, envelopes, and sales contract forms from Willson's Stationery. This bill is to be paid on January 15.
	6	Paid $150 cash for a new filing cabinet for the office.
	8	Sold an old filing cabinet to a friend for $20. This cabinet was recorded in the Furniture and Equipment account at the original cost price of $70.
	8	Received $8 000 cash, commission for a sale of property.
	8	Paid office salaries, $350.
	11	Paid $290 cash for newspaper advertising.
	12	Received a $100 cash fee for renting a home owned by a client.
	13	H. Young, the owner, withdrew $1 000 for personal use.
	14	Received commissions totalling $5 500 from the sale of properties.
	14	Paid $75 cash for telephone expense.
	15	Paid Tom's Service Centre $75 for the invoice received on January 3.
	15	Paid Willson's Stationery $150 for the invoice received on January 5.
	15	Paid $150 for the hydro bill.
	15	Donated $20 to a charitable organization.
	15	Received $90 in dividends from investments owned.
	15	Purchased $2 000 worth of Government of Canada bonds.
	15	Paid office salaries $350.
	15	Paid $5 000 in commissions to salespeople who work for H. Young Agencies.

100	Cash	400	Commissions Income
131	Office Supplies	401	Management Fees Earned
141	Furniture and Equipment	402	Investment Income
142	Automobile	500	Advertising Expense
170	Investments	501	Automobile Expense
200	Accounts Payable/Tom's Service Centre	502	Commissions Expense
201	Accounts Payable/Willson's Stationery	503	Rent Expense
300	H. Young, Capital	504	Salaries Expense
301	H. Young, Drawing	505	Telephone Expense
		506	Utilities Expense
		507	Miscellaneous Expense
		508	Loss on Sale of Furniture and Equipment

12. Continue your accounting for the Valley Motel for which you did the General Journal entries for the first half of December in exercise 10.

a) Journalize the following transactions:

Dec.	16	Paid $250 cash to J. Lebrun, the owner, for his own use.
	16	Paid salaries for the first half of the month, $750 cash.
	18	The bank sent a memorandum (letter) informing J. Lebrun that $350 has been taken out of the business bank account to pay for interest on the bank loan. (Open a new account numbered 507 for Interest Expense.)
	19	Received $1 750 cash for room rentals for the week.
	22	Received a $225 bill from Acme Supply for new linen and towels.
	23	Received a $35 bill from Kelly Motors for gasoline and oil used in the business car. (A new account will have to be opened for Kelly Motors.)
	25	Paid $350 cash to Acme Supply on account.
	26	Received $1 525 cash for room rentals for the week.
	31	Paid salaries for the rest of the month, $765 cash.

b) Post the General Journal transactions to the same ledger accounts you used in exercise 10.

c) Prepare a trial balance as at December 31, 19__.

d) Prepare the income statement.

13. Continue your accounting for H. Young Agencies for which you did the January 1 - 15 General Journal entries in exercise 11.

a) Open a ledger using the chart of accounts provided in exercise 11.

b) Record the January 1 balances that follow in the ledger accounts. (Record the date, balance, and write a √ in the posting reference column.)

Cash	$ 3 500
Office Supplies	700
Furniture & Equipment	2 900
Automobile	7 100
Investments	20 000
H. Young, Capital	34 200

c) Post the January 1 - 15 General Journal entries.

d) Prepare a trial balance.

e) Prepare an income statement.

14. a) Using the trial balance on page 114, open the accounts in the ledger for Carlo's T.V. Repairs.

b) At the end of each day, Carlos Amato does his accounting from the source documents that he received or issued on that day. Record the source documents for November 15 in the General Journal. Assign page 26 to the General Journal. The source documents are shown on pages 114-117.

Carlo's T.V. Repairs Trial Balance November 15, 19__			
ACCOUNT TITLE	ACC. NO.	DEBIT	CREDIT
Cash	101	3 000 —	
Accounts Receivable/B. Dover	102	147 43	
Accounts Receivable/Drive-Inn Motor Hotel	103	98 76	
Accounts Receivable/L. Mansfield	104	25 50	
Equipment	110	25 000 —	
Truck	111	8 000 —	
Accounts Payable/Electronic Suppliers	201		47 50
Accounts Payable/Poulin's Service Station	202		276 89
C. Amato, Capital	301		35 947 30
Sales	401		—
Hydro Expense	501	—	
Truck Expense	502	—	
Equipment Repairs Expense	503	—	
		36 271 69	36 271 69

Sales Invoices:

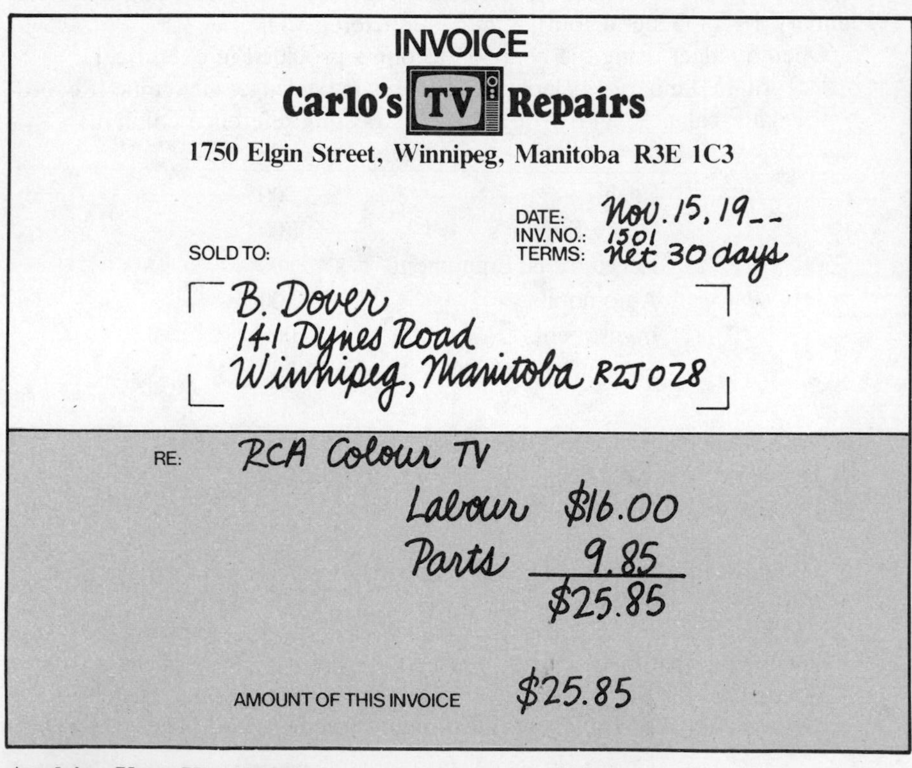

INVOICE

Carlo's TV Repairs

1750 Elgin Street, Winnipeg, Manitoba R3E 1C3

DATE: Nov. 15, 19__
INV. NO.: 1501
TERMS: net 30 days

SOLD TO:

B. Dover
141 Dynes Road
Winnipeg, Manitoba R2J 0Z8

RE: RCA Colour TV

Labour	$16.00
Parts	9.85
	$25.85

AMOUNT OF THIS INVOICE $25.85

INVOICE

Carlo's TV Repairs

1750 Elgin Street, Winnipeg, Manitoba R3E 1C3

DATE: Nov. 15, 19--
INV. NO.: 1502
TERMS: net 30 days

SOLD TO:

Drive-Inn Motor Hotel
1460 River Road
Winnipeg, Manitoba R2M 3Z8

RE: T.V.'s in rooms 117, 119 and 212

Labour $56.00
Parts 37.50
$93.50

AMOUNT OF THIS INVOICE $93.50

Purchase Invoices:

INVOICE

POULIN'S SERVICE STATION

1553 Park Drive, Winnipeg, Manitoba R3P 0H2

Date: Nov. 13/-- Terms: Net 15 days Inv. No. B-151

Part No.	Part Name	Total
X340	Oil Filter	$ 4.50
	4 L oil	5.25
316-092	Spark plugs	12.70
TOTAL PARTS FORWARD		$22.45

Make: GMC Truck
Licence: A-4597
Name: Carlo's T.V.
Address: 1750 Elgin Street Winnipeg

WORK COMPLETED	AMOUNT
Oil Change Tune-up	$24.00
TOTAL LABOUR	24.00
PARTS	22.45
TAX	1.57
PAY THIS AMOUNT	$48.02

ELECTRONIC SUPPLIERS

147 Industrial Blvd., Winnipeg, Manitoba R2W 0J7

Montreal
Toronto
Winnipeg
Vancouver

Tel: 475-6643

Terms: Net 15 days

SOLD TO	SHIP TO
Carlo's T.V. Repairs 1750 Elgin Street Winnipeg, Manitoba R3E 1C4	SAME

Fed. Sales Tax No.	Prov. Sales Tax No.	Date Invoiced	Invoice No.
S47354	435 70913	11 | 12 | --	7463

Quantity	Description	Unit Price		Amount	
1	EQUIPMENT	$453	90	$453	90

Cheques issued:

THE ROYAL BANK OF CANADA
3017 Leiland Road, Winnipeg, Manitoba R2K 0J7

No. **347**

Nov. 15 19--

PAY TO THE ORDER OF Electronic Suppliers-------------- $ 47.50

--Forty-seven---------------------------50 /100 DOLLARS

Carlo's TV Repair
1750 Elgin Street,
Winnipeg, Manitoba R3E 1C4

Carlo Amato

Account No. 49373

(Detach and retain this statement)

THE ATTACHED CHEQUE IS IN PAYMENT OF ITEMS LISTED BELOW

DATE	ITEM	AMOUNT	DISCOUNT	NET AMOUNT
Oct. 28	Inv. 7393	$47.50		$47.50

THE ROYAL BANK OF CANADA
3017 Leiland Road, Winnipeg, Manitoba R2K 0J7

No. **348**

Nov. 15 19--

PAY TO THE ORDER OF Winnipeg Hydro -------------------- $ 79.50

---Seventy-nine-------------------------50 /100 DOLLARS

Carlo's TV Repair
1750 Elgin Street,
Winnipeg, Manitoba R3E 1C4

Carlo Amato

Account No. 49373

(Detach and retain this statement)

THE ATTACHED CHEQUE IS IN PAYMENT OF ITEMS LISTED BELOW

DATE	ITEM	AMOUNT	DISCOUNT	NET AMOUNT
Nov. 15	Inv. B-741	$79.50		$79.50

Cash Receipts:

DAILY CASH RECEIPTS

November 15, 19--

Customer	Invoice	Amount
L. Mansfield	1370	$ 25.50
Drive-Inn Motor Hotel	1269	98.76
Cash Sales		156.63
		$280.89

c) Record the November 16 source documents in the General Journal.

Nov. 16 Sales invoices issued:
No. 1503 to L. Mansfield, $477.00
No. 1504 to Drive-Inn Motor Hotel, $573.60

Purchase invoices received:
From Electronic Suppliers, No. 7533, $134.50 for servicing the equipment

Cash receipts:
B. Dover, $147.43
Drive-Inn Motor Hotel, $93.50
Cash sales, $453.70

Copies of cheques issued:
No. 349 to Poulin's Service Station, $276.89 on account
No. 350 to Electronic Suppliers, $453.90 on account

d) Post the General Journal to the ledger and prepare a trial balance.

Accounting in Action

Case 1

The General Journal There are several errors in the following General Journal. Prepare a list of the errors.

GENERAL JOURNAL PAGE 17

DATE		PARTICULARS	PR	DEBIT	CREDIT
Nov. 19--	2	Cash		500 —	
		Sales			500 —
		Sold goods for cash			
	3	Supplies		100 —	
		Cash			100 —
	3	Cash			200 —
		Delivery Expense		200 —	
		Cheque 81 to Central Cartage			
Nov.		Accounts Receivable		500 —	
		Sales			500 —
		Inv. 871			
	5	Supplies		120 —	
		Accounts Payable		120 —	
		Inv. B-210, Grand & Toy			

The Journalless System Chris Lee is the accountant for Mac's Delivery Service. For many years the business was quite small and had only a few employees. Chris does not use a journal but simply records all transactions in the ledger. In the past year, business has increased greatly. The owner of the business has been advised to investigate using a journal. Chris is against the idea. Explain the advantages and disadvantages of the old system and of a new system using a journal. **Case 2**

Locating Errors The accountant for Mary Catherine's Boutique has made several errors in posting from the journal to the ledger. **Case 3**

a) Which of the following errors will cause the trial balance to be out of balance?
b) Which of the following errors will *not* be indicated by the trial balance?
   i) Both a $1 000 debit and a $1 000 credit were posted as $100.
   ii) A debit of $75 to General Expense was incorrectly posted to Delivery Expense.
   iii) A debit of $35 to General Expense was posted as a credit to General Expense.
   iv) A debit of $98.50 to W. Davis was posted in error to M. Davis' account.
   v) A debit and a credit of $875 were both posted as $785.

Transposition Errors You have learned that a transposition of figures is the reversing of the numbers of an amount. For example, $75 written as $57 is a transposition error. A transposition error may be indicated if the difference in a trial balance is exactly divisible by nine. If the difference in the two totals of a trial balance is $81 the difference may have been caused by transposition, since 81 is divisible evenly by nine. **Case 4**

Once a transposition error is suspected, it may be located by the following rule: *The number of times the amount of the difference is divisible by nine is the difference between the two digits transposed.*

Suppose the difference is 81. The difference is divisible by nine. (81 divided by 9 is 9). Therefore the difference between the two numbers transposed is 9. The only two numbers with a difference of 9 are 0 and 9. Therefore the amounts transposed must have been 90 written as 9 or 9 written as 90. By looking for 9 or 90 on the trial balance the error will be located.

Suppose the error is 63. Since 63 divided by 9 is 7, the difference between the transposed numbers is 7. Therefore the numbers transposed must be 7 and 0 or 2 and 9 or 8 and 1.

For each of the following trial balance differences state:

- the amount the difference is divisible by nine
- the combination of numbers which might be transposed

a) a difference of 72
b) a difference of 27
c) a difference of 36
d) a difference of 54

Accounting Procedures Gerri is an accountant responsible for journal entries and posting to the ledger. In order to get work done quickly, Gerri does not write **Case 5**

explanations in the journal and does not show posting references in the journal or in the ledger. What reasons would you give to convince Gerri that explanations and posting references should be used?

Case 6

Bank Credit Cards Buying on credit is a way of life for many people. Businesses realize that people want to buy on credit. They know that offering credit will probably increase sales. However, credit costs money. Records must be kept and clerical staff hired to maintain customer accounts, receive payments, and send out statements. Customers do not always pay their debts and the result is an expense called *bad debts*.

Many small businesses do not have the time or the money to organize their own credit plans. Groups of banks saw this as an opportunity to provide a service to businesses. The result was credit cards such as Master Charge and Visa which are both credit services operated by banks. The banks in effect, handle the charge accounts for businesses. They send out the statements and collect money owed by customers.

This system is appealing to consumers because it provides a single credit card which is acceptable in many stores. It is appealing to businesses because a great deal of clerical work is performed for them by the banks. In return for this service, the banks charge the stores between 3% and 5% of all credit card sales, depending on volume. The customer receives a monthly bill from the bank. Any amount which is not paid to the bank within 30 days is subject to an interest charge of approximately 18% a year. Figure 5.23 illustrates the operation of bank credit cards.

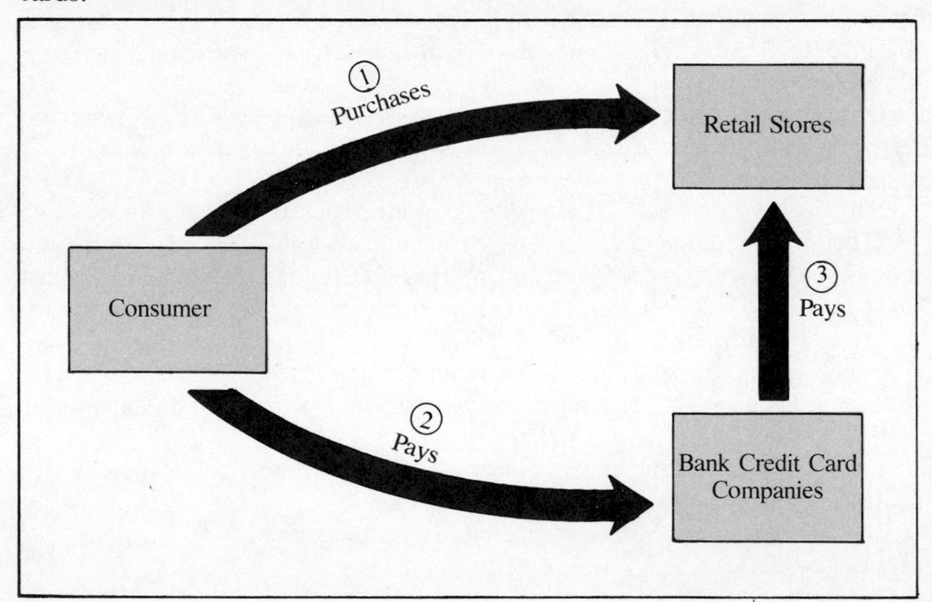

Figure 5.23 *The operation of bank credit cards*

1. *Consumer purchases merchandise from stores using the credit cards*

2. *Consumer receives a monthly statement from the credit card company. Interest is charged after one month. Payment is made to the bank credit card company*

3. *The credit card company pays the stores the total charged by customers, less a commission (3-5%)*

a) Discuss this statement: "Credit card companies such as Master Charge and Visa are simply providing an accounting service to businesses."
b) Leslie uses a credit card. The monthly statement shows an average balance of $215. Leslie pays this balance within the statement period of one month.
   Kelly has an average balance of $210 on a bank credit card. Kelly is not able to budget very well and is usually charged interest by the credit card company because payments are not received during the one-month statement period. How much interest does Kelly pay a year on the average monthly balance of $210?
c) Credit card companies charge 3% to 5% commission on their total billings to a business. This raises the cost of operating the business. The cost must be recovered by the business through the prices it charges its customers. Do you feel that a *cash discount* should be offered to customers who pay cash so that the cash customer is not subsidizing the customer who uses a credit card? Give reasons for your answer.
d) Conduct a survey by asking a group of people who use credit cards questions such as the following:
   - What cards do you use?
   - How often do you use a credit card?
   - What are the advantages and disadvantages of the use of credit cards?
   - What is the rate of interest charged by the credit card company?
   - What alternate sources of funds are available to finance consumer purchases?
   - Do you always pay within the statement period in order to avoid interest charges?

Career Profile

An Accountant Tony Pelosse is a young man who enjoys a lifestyle which combines travel, dedication to a service club, and a career in accounting.

After graduating from high school, Tony took a two-month vacation and travelled from Ottawa to Florida to British Columbia and back to Ottawa. It was then time to get a job in order to support himself. One of Tony's favourite subjects in high school had been accounting, so he looked for an accounting position. His first job was as an inventory clerk with General Supply Co. where he was responsible for maintaining an inventory system in a parts department. This involved checking extensions on sales invoices and raising and lowering stock card balances as items were sold and stock purchased. After about one year Tony was promoted to the position of manager of accounts payable. In this position he supervised three people. He was responsible for processing purchase invoices, for determining the availability of cash discounts, for paying bills, and for seeing that accounts payable records agreed with statements received from the company's creditors.

Tony had been in the accounts payable job for two years when he was faced with an important decision. He had to decide if he wanted to move to Toronto when his company transferred their entire operations to that city. Tony decided against

Toronto, left the company, and felt it was time for another vacation. This time his destination was Europe where he toured England, France, Belgium, Spain, and Italy. After an enjoyable two months in Europe, Tony returned home and went job hunting again.

Tony found his present job through contacts made at a Kiwanis Club meeting. He now works for The Runge Press Limited, a printing firm employing about 100 persons. Tony's job title is Accountant and it combines accounting and office supervisory duties. There are four main areas of accounting among his responsibilities. They are:

- accounts payable
- payroll
- collection of overdue accounts receivable
- job cost accounting

Tony is responsible for preparing the weekly payroll for all the employees. He also completes job cost sheets to determine if a net income or a net loss has been made on each printing job completed by the company. Tony's supervisory duties include responsibility for a receptionist and for three accounting clerks.

Each month a public accounting firm completes financial statements for The Runge Press. Tony works closely with this firm and supplies much of the data required for the monthly statements.

Tony is a dedicated member of the Kiwanis Club of south Ottawa. He is the administrator of 125 Key Clubs with over 3 000 student members in eastern Canada and in six Caribbean countries. Each year Tony's duties with Kiwanis require that he travel extensively throughout Canada, the U.S.A. and the Caribbean.

Tony's personal interests include skiing, reading and taking short trips on his motorcycle, a Kawasaki 400. His interest in accounting is indicated by the C.G.A. courses he takes through the extension department at Carleton University. In three years Tony will complete the requirements of the Certified General Accountants program.

CHAPTER 6

The Work Sheet and Classified Statements

The Work Sheet

Unit 14

*1

Figure 6.1 illustrates the steps in the accounting cycle as they have been described up to this point. The end of the fiscal period is a particularly important time for accountants because they do a great deal of work at that time. They must prove the mathematical accuracy of the ledger by preparing a trial balance; then they prepare the income statement and the balance sheet. As an aid in avoiding errors and to help organize their work, accountants use a device called a *work sheet*.

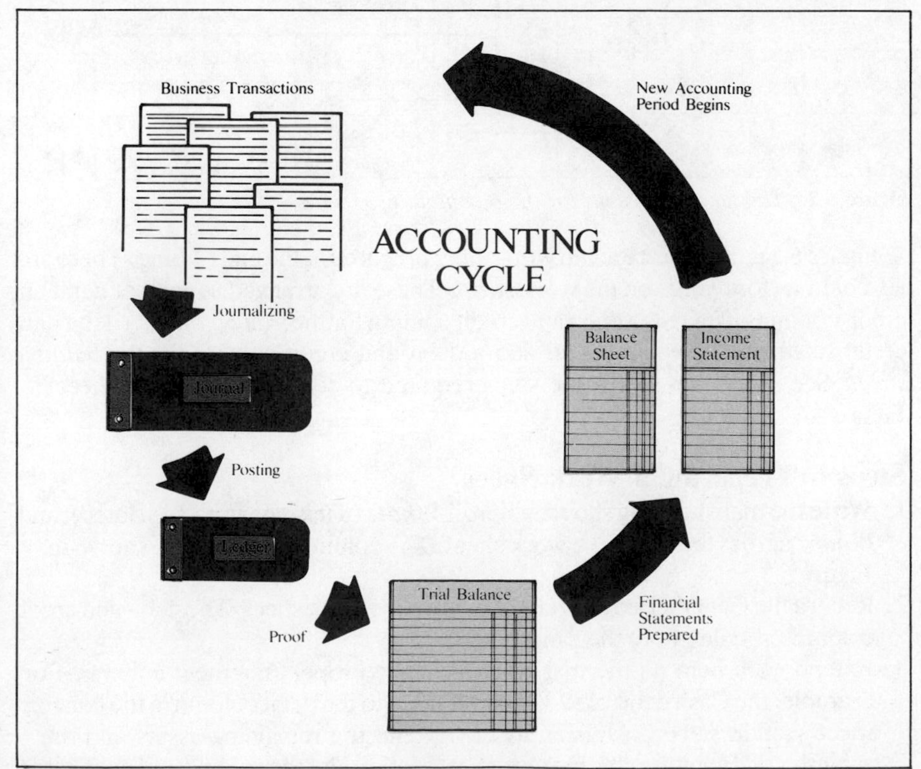

Figure 6.1 *The steps in the accounting cycle covered to this point*

A work sheet is a device that organizes accounting data required for the preparation of financial statements.

A work sheet is a large sheet of accounting paper used to organize data in the preparation of financial statements. It is one of the few forms that may be completed in pencil since it is not part of permanent accounting records. It is designed to discover and to eliminate errors before they become part of permanent records. The work sheet represents a rough draft of the work completed at the end of the accounting cycle and is sometimes called the accountant's *working papers*. It is *not* a formal statement provided for management or for the owners.

*2

6-Column Work Sheet Figure 6.2 illustrates the basic principles of the 6-column work sheet. The trial balance is written on the work sheet. The accounts on the trial balance are then transferred to either the income statement or the balance sheet sections of the work sheet.

ACCOUNT TITLE	ACC. NO.	TRIAL BALANCE		INCOME STATEMENT		BALANCE SHEET	
		DEBIT	CREDIT	DEBIT	CREDIT	DEBIT	CREDIT
Assets		XX				XX	
		XX				XX	
Liabilities			XX				XX
			XX				XX
Owner's Equity			XX				XX
Income			XX		XX		
Expenses		XX		XX			

Figure 6.2 *The basic principles for the 6-column worksheet*

Figure 6.3 is The Cascade Inn work sheet prepared at the end of June. There are six columns for figures on the work sheet. These are arranged in pairs of debit and credit columns. There is a debit and credit column for the *trial balance*, a debit and credit for the *income statement*, and a debit and credit column for the *balance sheet*. See if you can follow the steps required to complete the work sheet in Figure 6.3

*3

Steps in Preparing a Work Sheet

1. Write the main heading showing *Who?*, *What?* (if it is not already printed), and *When?* across the top of the work sheet. The column headings are shown in Figure 6.3.
2. Record the General Ledger trial balance on the work sheet. The debit and credit columns should show the same totals.

*4

3. Extend each item on the trial balance to the proper statement column. For example, the Cash debit of $9 300 is extended to the debit column in the balance sheet section since Cash is an asset. Extend the remaining assets and the liabilities and capital to the balance sheet section and the income and expenses to the income statement section.

1. Write the heading showing *Who, What,* and *When.*

The Cascade Inn
Work Sheet
Month of June, 19__

ACCOUNT TITLE	ACC. NO.	TRIAL BALANCE		INCOME STATEMENT		BALANCE SHEET	
		DEBIT	CREDIT	DEBIT	CREDIT	DEBIT	CREDIT
Cash	100	9 300 —				9 300 —	
Supplies	101	8 000 —				8 000 —	
Office Equipment	110	5 000 —				5 000 —	
Room Furniture	112	110 000 —				110 000 —	
Building	114	500 000 —				500 000 —	
Land	116	50 000 —				50 000 —	
Accounts Payable	200		24 000 —				24 000 —
Bank Loan	210		15 000 —				15 000 —
Mortgage Payable	220		100 000 —				100 000 —
Galotta, Capital	300		536 000 —				536 000 —
Galotta, Drawing	301	900 —				900 —	
Room Rentals	400		25 000 —		25 000 —		
Restaurant Income	401		6 000 —		6 000		
Salaries Expense	500	10 000 —		10 000 —			
Advertising Expense	501	1 000 —		1 000 —			
Telephone Expense	502	200 —		200 —			
Laundry Expense	503	3 600 —		3 600 —			
Maintenance Expense	504	6 000 —		6 000 —			
Interest Expense	505	2 000 —		2 000 —			
		706 000 —	706 000 —	22 800 —	31 000 —	683 200 —	675 000 —
Net Income				8 200 —			8 200 —
				31 000 —	31 000 —	683 200 —	683 200

2. Record the trial balance.

3. Extend each item from the trial balance to the proper statement.

4. Determine and record net income in the income statement debit column.

5. Record net income in the balance sheet credit column.

6. Rule double lines.

Figure 6.3 *Work sheet prepared for The Cascade Inn*

4. Rule a single line and add the income statement columns. Write the totals below the single line. The difference between the totals of these columns represents either the net income or the net loss made by the business. If the credit column exceeds the debit column, a net income has been made during the accounting period. The amount of this net income is entered below the total of the debit column, so that when these two amounts are added, the two columns are equal. *Net Income* is written in the account titles section opposite the amount of the net income. If the debit column exceeds the credit column, a net loss has occurred. The difference between the two columns is written in the credit column opposite the words *Net Loss.* *5
5. Rule a single line and add the balance sheet columns. Enter the net income amount below the total of the credit column of the balance sheet section. The net income represents the increase to the owner's capital for the period. If there has been a net loss, enter the amount of the loss below the debit column total. If the *6

amount of the net income or net loss added to the column total makes the column equal to the other balance sheet column total, the work sheet is mathematically correct.

*7

6. Rule double lines below the totals to indicate completion and proof that the work is mathematically correct.

*8

Using the Work Sheet When the work sheet is complete, it contains, in an organized, systematic and convenient form, all the information that the accountant needs to prepare formal financial statements.

The completed work sheet is used to prepare the financial statements at the end of the fiscal period.

The information from the income statement section is used to prepare the formal income statement. When the income column (credit) of the work sheet shows a greater total than the expense column (debit), the amount of the difference is the *net income*. When the expenses are greater, the difference is called *net loss*. When the formal income statement is complete, the conclusion (net income or net loss) should be the same as the matching conclusion on the work sheet.

The Income Statement The income statement shows the operating results for a business *over a period of time*. Figure 6.4 is the income statement of The Cascade Inn for the month of June. Notice that the heading clearly shows the period of time covered by the statement.

The information for the body of the income statement is taken from the income statement columns of the work sheet. The *revenue* information is found in the credit column of the income statement section of the work sheet. The *expense* data is found in the debit column. The net income of $8 200 appears both on the work sheet (Figure 6.3) and the income statement (Figure 6.4).

The Cascade Inn
Income Statement
For the month of June, 19__

Revenue		
Room Rentals	25 000 00	
Restaurant Income	6 000 00	31 000 00
Expenses		
Salaries	10 000 00	
Advertising	1 000 00	
Telephone	200 00	
Laundry	3 600 00	
Maintenance	6 000 00	
Interest	2 000 00	22 800 00
Net Income		8 200 00

Figure 6.4 *Income statement for The Cascade Inn prepared from the work sheet*

The Balance Sheet A balance sheet presents the financial position of a business *at a specific date*. Figure 6.5 is the balance sheet of The Cascade Inn prepared on June 30. It shows the assets, liabilities, and owner's equity at that specific date.

*9

Just as the information for the income statement originated in the work sheet, so does the information for the balance sheet. Notice that in Figure 6.5 all the data used on the balance sheet came from the balance sheet section of the work sheet. Notice also that the net income of $8 200 increases the capital in the owner's equity section of the balance sheet. The balance sheet in Figure 6.5 has been prepared in the report form.

The report form of balance sheet is prepared in vertical form.

The Cascade Inn Classified Balance Sheet June 30, 19__			
Assets			
Current Assets			
Cash		9 300 00	
Supplies		8 000 00	17 300 00
Fixed Assets			
Land		50 000 00	
Building		500 000 00	
Room Furniture		110 000 00	
Office Equipment		5 000 00	665 000 00
Total Assets			682 300 00
Liabilities and Owner's Equity			
Current Liabilities			
Accounts Payable			24 000 00
Long Term Liabilities			
Bank Loan		15 000 00	
Mortgage Payable		100 000 00	115 000 00
Owner's Equity			
Galotta Capital June 1		536 000 00	
Net Income for June	8 200 00		
Less Withdrawals	900 00		
Increase in Capital		7 300 00	
Galotta Capital June 30			543 300 00
Total Liabilities and Owner's Equity			682 300 00

Figure 6.5 *Balance sheet for The Cascade Inn prepared from the work sheet*

Classified Financial Statements

*10

The purpose of financial statements is to provide financial information about a company to the owners, management, creditors, and government. By classifying items on the statements into special categories, it is possible to provide more information and to provide it in a way which is more easily interpreted. For example, information to answer the following questions is provided in the classified balance sheet in Figure 6.5.

- *Which debts must be paid within a year?*
- *Is there sufficient cash (or assets) on hand to pay debts?*
- *Which debts must be paid in future years?*

Look at Figure 6.5 and answer the preceding questions.

Classified Balance Sheet

The June 30, 19__ balance sheet of The Cascade Inn, illustrated in Figure 6.5, includes the standard classifications usually found on balance sheets. The assets are divided into two main groups: *current* and *fixed*. The liabilities are divided into two groups: *current* and *long-term*.

Current assets are listed in order of liquidity.

Liquidity order is the order in which assets may be converted into cash.

Current Assets Assets which are converted into cash in the ordinary course of business, usually within one year, are called *current assets*. The list that follows provides some examples and the order in which current assets usually appear. They are listed in *order of liquidity*, that is the order in which assets may be converted into cash.

Current Assets
Cash
Government Bonds
Marketable Securities
Accounts Receivable
Merchandise Inventory
Prepaid Expenses

Fixed assets that have the longest life are listed first.

Fixed Assets *Fixed assets* are assets such as land, buildings, equipment, and trucks that are used in operating the business and which have a long life. The fixed assets that have the longest life are generally listed first.

*11

Current Liabilities The term *current liabilities* generally refers to liabilities that must be paid within a year or less. If possible, current liabilities are listed in the order that they are to be paid.

Current liabilities are liabilities due to be paid within one year.

Current Liabilities
Accounts Payable
Taxes Payable
Salaries Owing
Loans Payable

Long-term Liabilities *Long-term liabilities* are liabilities that are not due to be paid for at least one year. A loan payable in two years or a mortgage payable in 25 years are examples of long-term liabilities.

Long-term liabilities are liabilities that are not due to be paid for at least one year.

Owner's Equity Section of the Balance Sheet The owner's equity in a business increases when the business operates profitably. Owner's equity decreases when there has been a net loss and when the owner withdraws assets from the business.

*12

The owner's equity section of the balance sheet in Figure 6.5 is an example of equity increasing as a result of The Cascade Inn earning a net income which is greater than the owner's withdrawals from the business. Figure 6.6 shows how the equity section of a balance sheet is set up to record a net loss.

Owner's Equity			
T. Burns, Capital Nov. 1		90 000 00	
Less: Net Loss for the month	2 000 00		
Withdrawals	700 00		
Decrease in Capital		2 700 00	
T. Burns, Capital Nov. 30			87 300 00

Figure 6.6 *Net loss*

It is possible for a business to earn a net income yet still have a decrease in owner's equity. This happens when the withdrawals by the owner are greater than the net income. Figure 6.7 illustrates the set-up of the equity section when withdrawals are greater than net income.

Owner's Equity			
T. Burns, Capital Dec. 1		87 300 00	
Withdrawals	2 000 00		
Net Income for the month	1 400 00		
Decrease in Capital		600 00	
T. Burns, Capital Dec. 31			86 700 00

Figure 6.7 *Withdrawals greater than net income*

Classified Income Statement Discussion of classified income statements is reserved for Chapter 18. You will not be expected to classify income statements in the exercises in this chapter.

Facts to Remember

A *work sheet* is a device that organizes accounting data required for the preparation of financial statements.

Working papers is another term to describe a work sheet.

Current assets are assets that are converted into cash in the ordinary course of business, usually within one year.

Liquidity order is the order in which assets may be converted into cash.

Fixed assets are tangible assets used in operating a business.

Current liabilities are liabilities due to be paid within one year.

Long-term liabilities are liabilities that are not due to be paid for at least one year.

Checking Your Reading

Questions

1. What purpose is served by the work sheet?
2. What information is included in the main work sheet heading?
3. There are three sets of debit and credit columns in the work sheet. What is the heading for each set?
4. Which accounts from the trial balance are extended to the balance sheet section of the work sheet?
5. Which accounts from the trial balance are extended to the income section of the work sheet?
6. When the debit column total of the income section of the work sheet is greater than the credit column total, what is the difference called?
7. When the credit column total of the income section is greater than the debit column total, what is the difference called?
8. When is a work sheet considered to be mathematically correct?
9. What is the difference between the report form and the account form of the balance sheet?
10. What is a classified financial statement?
11. What are the "classifications" that appear on the balance sheet?
12. Explain the following terms:
    a) current asset;
    b) fixed asset;
    c) liquidity order;
    d) current liability;
    e) long-term liability.

13. What effect does a withdrawal of assets from the business by the owner have on owner's equity?
14. What effect does a net loss have on the owner's equity? On net income?
15. Prepare a diagram illustrating the steps in the accounting cycle.

Applying Your Knowledge

Exercises Part A

1. Following is a list of account titles. Prepare a form like the one in the example and indicate on which statement section and in which column of the work sheet each account would appear. The first one, Cash, is done for you.

Account Title	Income Statement		Balance Sheet	
	Debit	Credit	Debit	Credit
Cash			✓	
Supplies				
Rent Expense				
W. Hollingsworth, Capital				
Office Equipment				
Accounts Payable				
Advertising Expense				
Light, Heat, Water Expenses				
Bank Loan				
Sales				
Accounts Receivable				
Investment Income				
Land				

2. Prepare a work sheet for the month of April from the following trial balance.

J. Fioravanti Trial Balance For the month of April, 19__			
ACCOUNT TITLE	ACC. NO.	DEBIT	CREDIT
Cash		2 000 —	
Accounts Receivable		4 300 —	
Equipment		6 200 —	
Accounts Payable			2 500 —
J. Fioravanti, Capital			5 000 —
Sales			8 000 —
Salaries Expense		1 200 —	
General Expense		800 —	
Advertising Expense		1 000 —	
		15 500 —	15 500 —

3. a) Prepare a work sheet for the month of July from the trial balance that follows.

I. Grant Trial Balance For the month of July, 19__			
ACCOUNT TITLE	ACC. NO.	DEBIT	CREDIT
Cash		1 400 —	
Accounts Receivable		2 035 —	
Supplies		960 —	
Equipment		1 500 —	
Delivery Truck		7 800 —	
Accounts Payable			1 245 —
Loan Payable			1 400 —
I. Grant, Capital			10 500 —
I. Grant, Drawing		1 000 —	
Sales			8 970 —
Salaries Expense		6 000 —	
Rent Expense		500 —	
Miscellaneous Expense		540 —	
Office Expense		255 —	
Telephone Expense		125 —	
		22 115 —	22 115 —

b) Prepare an income statement from your completed work sheet.

c) From the same work sheet, prepare a balance sheet.

4. Classify each of the following as a current asset, fixed asset, current liability, or long-term liability:
   a) Accounts Receivable
   b) Land
   c) Bank Loan (6 months)
   d) Office Supplies
   e) Delivery Truck
   f) Prepaid Rent
   g) Automobile
   h) Mortgage Payable
   i) Taxes Owing
   j) Government Bonds
   k) Accounts Payable

5. a) List the current assets in question 4 in order of liquidity.
   b) List the fixed assets in question 4 in proper order.

6. The completed work sheet for the month of February for D. Adams, a lawyer, follows. Prepare the income statement and classified balance sheet.

D. Adams
Work Sheet
Feb. 28, 19__

ACCOUNT TITLE	ACC. NO.	TRIAL BALANCE DEBIT	TRIAL BALANCE CREDIT	INCOME STATEMENT DEBIT	INCOME STATEMENT CREDIT	BALANCE SHEET DEBIT	BALANCE SHEET CREDIT
Cash		3 000 —				3 000 —	
Accounts Receivable		500 —				500 —	
Office Equipment		6 000 —				6 000 —	
Automobile		8 000 —				8 000 —	
Willson Supply Ltd.			200 —				200 —
D. Adams, Capital			15 700 —				15 700 —
Fees Income			4 000 —		4 000 —		
Automobile Expense		100 —		100 —			
Rent Expense		800 —		800 —			
Salaries Expense		1 000 —		1 000 —			
General Expense		500 —		500 —			
		19 900 —	19 900 —	2 400 —	4 000 —	17 500 —	15 900 —
Net Income				1 600 —			1 600 —
				4 000 —	4 000 —	17 500 —	17 500 —

Cedar Hill Golf Club
Trial Balance
Three Months Ended September 30, 19--

ACCOUNT TITLE	ACC. NO.	DEBIT	CREDIT
Cash		3 000 —	
Supplies		9 000 —	
Equipment		30 000 —	
Land		200 000 —	
Accounts Payable			2 000 —
Bank Loan			95 000 —
G. Thompson, Capital			98 000 —
G. Thompson, Drawing		2 000 —	
Membership Fees			110 000 —
Salaries Expense		50 000 —	
Maintenance Expense		2 000 —	
Utilities Expense		7 000 —	
Office Expense		2 000 —	
		305 000 —	305 000 —

Cedar Hill Golf Club
Trial Balance
Three Months Ended December 31, 19--

ACCOUNT TITLE	ACC. NO.	DEBIT	CREDIT
Cash		3 500 —	
Supplies		2 000 —	
Equipment		30 000 —	
Land		200 000 —	
Accounts Payable			1 000 —
Bank Loan			91 000 —
G. Thompson, Capital			145 000 —
G. Thompson, Drawing		1 000 —	
Membership Fees			19 500 —
Salaries Expense		12 000 —	
Maintenance Expense		5 000 —	
Insurance Expense		1 500 —	
Utilities Expense		1 000 —	
Office Expense		500 —	
		256 500 —	256 500 —

7. a) Prepare a work sheet for the three months ended September 30, 19__ from the trial balance for Cedar Hill Golf Club at the top of page 134.
b) Prepare an income statement and balance sheet from the work sheet.

Exercises Part B

8. a) Prepare a work sheet for the three months ended December 31, 19__ for the Cedar Hill Golf Club. Use the trial balance at the bottom page 134.
b) Prepare an income statement and a classified balance sheet.

Exercise Part C

9. Trial balance figures for February and March for a business owned by T. Hood follow.
a) Prepare a work sheet, income statement, and balance sheet for February.
b) Prepare a work sheet and financial statements for March.

	February		March	
Cash	3 000		2 000	
Accounts Receivable	7 000		6 000	
Prepaid Insurance	800		600	
Land	30 000		30 000	
Building	90 000		90 000	
Furniture	5 000		5 000	
Accounts Payable		4 000		5 000
Taxes Owing		1 000		1 000
Bank Loan (2 year)		15 000		16 900
Mortgage Payable		40 000		38 000
T. Hood, Capital		72 100		75 800
T. Hood, Drawing	1 000		2 000	
Sales		20 000		14 000
Salaries Expense	12 000		13 000	
Delivery Expense	1 200		900	
Utilities Expense	700		700	
Advertising Expense	900		100	
Miscellaneous Expense	300		200	
Insurance Expense	200		200	
	152 100	152 100	150 700	150 700

Accounting in Action

Case 1

Monthly Financial Statements Reg Greer, the owner of a printing business, feels it is a waste of time to prepare a monthly work sheet and financial statements. He has them prepared only once a year at income tax time. What are some of the disadvantages of waiting until the end of a year to prepare the work sheet and financial statements?

Case 2

Work Sheet Errors The following work sheet contains several errors.

a) List the errors.
b) What is the correct net income?

A. Morena Co.
Work Sheet
May 31, 19__

ACCOUNT TITLE	ACC. NO.	TRIAL BALANCE DEBIT	TRIAL BALANCE CREDIT	INCOME STATEMENT DEBIT	INCOME STATEMENT CREDIT	BALANCE SHEET DEBIT	BALANCE SHEET CREDIT
Cash		3 000 —				3 000 —	
Accounts Receivable		8 000 —					8 000 —
Equipment		20 000 —				20 000 —	
Accounts Payable			500 —			500 —	
Bank Loan			2 000 —				2 000 —
A. Morena, Capital			21 000 —				21 000 —
A. Morena, Drawing		7 000 —		7 000 —			
Sales			80 000 —		80 000 —		
Rent Expense		3 000 —		3 000 —			
Salaries Expense		60 000 —		60 000 —			
Office Expense		1 900 —		1 900 —			
General Expense		600 —		600 —			
		103 500 —	103 500 —	72 500 —	80 000 —	23 500 —	31 000 —
Net Income				7 500 —		7 500 —	
				80 000 —	80 000 —	31 000 —	31 000 —

Case 3

The Cascade Inn The Cascade Inn incurs a relatively large amount of debt at the beginning of each tourist season. Supplies to operate the Inn are bought in large quantities. Repairs are made to television sets and to the plumbing. Painting and landscaping are done to spruce up the property. These debts are then paid off as money is received throughout the tourist season. Arrangements are made with creditors so that payments may be spread out over the summer.

a) Examine Figure 6.5. How would you assess the financial position of the business?
b) If you operated a television repair business would you do $800 worth of repair work for the Cascade, on credit? What other information might you require in order to make this decision?

Case 4

Office Rules With conditions of employment very much a topic of conversation, a document headed *Office Practices* and dated 1852, makes interesting reading. The document was found in a building being demolished. Do you think any of these rules should be applied to present day offices?

OFFICE PRACTICES

Godliness, Cleanliness and Punctuality are necessities of a good business.

This firm has reduced the hours of work, and the Clerical Staff will now only have to be present between the hours of 7 a.m. and 6 p.m. on weekdays.

Daily prayers will be held each morning in the Main Office. The Clerical Staff will be present.

Clothing must be of a sober nature. The clerical staff will not disport themselves in raiment of bright colours nor will they wear hose unless in good repair.

Overshoes and top-coats may not be worn in the office, but neck scarves and headwear may be worn in inclement weather.

No member of the Clerical Staff may leave the room without permission from Mr. Rogers. The calls of nature are permitted, and Clerical Staff may use the garden below the second gate.

No talking is allowed during business hours.

The craving of tobacco, wines or spirits is a human weakness and, as such, is forbidden to all members of the Clerical Staff.

Now that the hours of business have been drastically reduced the partaking of food is allowed between 11:30 a.m. and noon, but work will not, on any account, cease.

Members of the Clerical Staff will provide their own pens. A new sharpener is available, on application to Mr. Rogers.

Mr. Rogers will nominate a Senior Clerk to be responsible for the cleanliness of the Main Office and the Private Office and all Boys and Juniors will report to him 40 minutes before Prayers and will remain after closing hours for similar work. Brushes, Brooms, Scrubbers and Soap are provided by the owners.

The new increased Weekly Wages are hereunder detailed:

Junior Boys (to 11 years)	.15
Boys (to 14 years)	.25
Junior Clerks	1.05
Senior Clerks	2.50

The owners recognize the generosity of the new Labour Laws but expect a great rise in output of work to compensate for these near Utopian conditions.

Case 5

Financial Condition The current asset and current liability sections of a business follow.

Current Assets		Current Liabilities	
Cash	500 00	Accounts Payable	3 000 00
Accounts Receivable	2 000 00	Taxes Payable	700 00
Supplies	500 00	Salaries Payable	2 000 00

a) How would you describe the financial condition of this business?
b) What advice might you give management of the business?

Case 6

The Work Sheet and Financial Statements Roberta is a student who has just completed a work sheet and financial statements. She notes the following about her work:

- The net income obtained on the income statement is exactly the same as the net income obtained on the work sheet.
- The totals of the revenue and expenses on the income statement are the same as the corresponding totals on the work sheet.
- The total of the balance sheet debit column on the work sheet is higher than the total of the assets on the balance sheet.

Roberta does not understand why the asset total on the balance sheet is not the same as the debit column of the balance sheet section of the work sheet. Can you give her an explanation?

Case 7

Collection Agencies In the case studies on credit in previous chapters, you have seen the advantages and disadvantages of credit, how a business processes charge account applications, the purpose served by credit bureaus, how bank credit cards operate, and how a business attempts to collect overdue accounts.

Most businesses establish credit procedures that minimize losses due to bad debts (debts that cannot be collected). However, no matter how careful a business is in granting credit to customers, there are always customers who will not or who cannot pay their debts.

When a business has a customer from whom they cannot collect a debt or a customer whom they cannot locate, the services of a collection agency may be used. Generally, a collection agency is not used until the company has done its best to locate the customer and to collect amounts owing. The collection agency attempts to locate the customer and to arrange for payment of the debt. In return, the agency charges a fee for its services.

Collection agencies have facilities, equipment, and trained personnel to do the following:

- locate debtors
- offer financial counselling to debtors to encourage them to pay their debts
- use court action, if necessary, to collect debts

Most collection agencies belong to a collectors' association. This association offers a number of services to its members. They include:

- rules, policies, and a code of ethics
- workshops on credit and collection for members and credit grantors
- booklets on credit and collection
- information on the changes in credit laws
- means by which collection agencies throughout the country can co-operate in locating *skips* (a person who moves without paying debts or leaving a forwarding address is known as a *skip*)

a) Assume you own a business. Under what circumstances would you use the services of a collection agency?
b) Look in the yellow pages of your telephone directory to determine which collection agencies operate in your area.
c) Invite the manager of a local collection agency to speak to your class.
d) Write to your provincial government to obtain information on the laws and regulations governing collection agencies.

Career Profile

A Medical-Dental Secretary Professional legal, medical and dental practices are businesses which provide services to their clients. They keep records, pay taxes, and require employees to do accounting, just like any other business. In this career profile the position of medical-dental secretary, a job which involves quite a bit of accounting, will be examined.

Jane St. Denis is a dental secretary who attended St. Joseph's High School in Ottawa. After completing high school Jane enrolled in the one-year medical-dental program at Algonquin College. When she graduated from Algonquin, Jane obtained employment with a dentist as a dental secretary and while working, became certified as a dental assistant.

Jane's job includes a number of different responsibilities. Among the things she does are:

- scheduling appointments for patients
- acting as receptionist
- preparing customer invoices and statements
- maintaining the accounts receivable
- receiving payments from customers
- handling the bank account and preparing a monthly bank reconciliation statement
- preparing the payroll for the three employees in the office
- recording and paying accounts payable
- taking care of mail, ordering supplies, writing letters, and filing

Jane enjoys her work, especially the wide variety of tasks entrusted to her. Outside of her job, Jane's hobbies include ceramics, sewing, and knitting. As well she and her husband are avid campers in the summer and enjoy cross-country skiing in the winter.

CHAPTER 7

Closing the Books

Unit 16

The End of the Accounting Period

*1

The income statement is a means of calculating the net income or net loss that results from the operation of a business for a specific accounting period. The financial data required to determine the net income (or net loss) for the accounting period are found in the revenue and expense accounts. Remember:

Revenue – Expenses = Net Income (or Net Loss)

Revenue and expense accounts are closed at the end of the accounting period.

When one accounting period ends and a new one begins, the revenue and expense accounts should show zero balances so that in the new accounting period accounts contain only data that refer to the new period. The revenue and expense accounts are reduced to zero by a process called *closing the books*.

Closing the Books

*2

The process of closing the books of a business generally occurs once a year and only affects the revenue and expense accounts. Asset and liability accounts are *not* closed. The owner's equity accounts are affected, as you will see later.

Income Summary Account Revenue and expense accounts are closed by *transferring* their balances to an account called Income Summary. This procedure is illustrated in Figure 7.1. The credit balance in the Income Summary account indicates a net income was earned.

When the revenue and expense account balances have been transferred to the Income Summary account, the balance of the summary account is the net income or net loss. The balance in the Income Summary account should be the same as the net income (or net loss) shown on the work sheet.

Closing Entries The closing of revenue and expense accounts is first recorded in the form of debits and credits in the General Journal. These journal entries are called *closing entries*. After journalizing, the closing entries are posted to the General Ledger accounts. The four steps required to close the books follow.

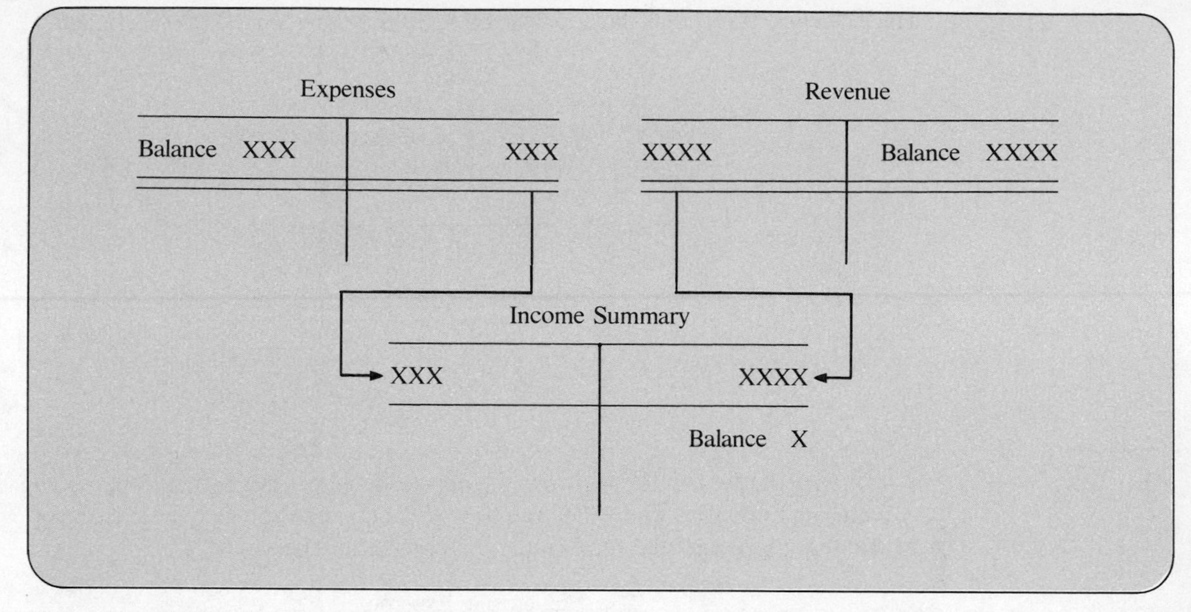

Figure 7.1 *Closing the revenue and expense accounts to the Income Summary account (Remember: debits must always equal credits.)*

1. Closing Revenue Accounts Revenue accounts have credit balances. The following Sales account shows a credit balance of $20 000 that represents the total sales for the year.

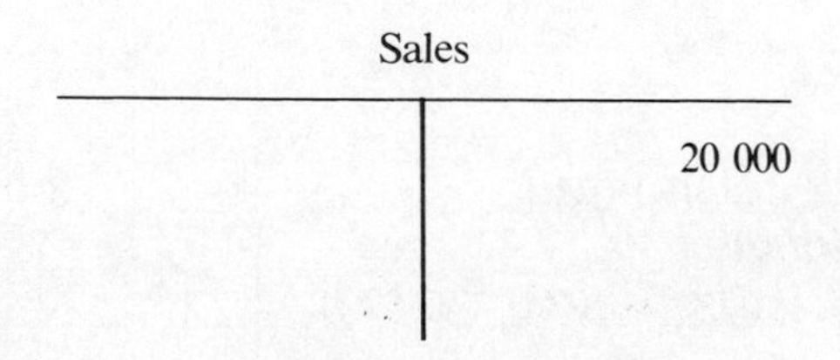

To close the Sales account means to reduce it to zero and to transfer the balance to the Income Summary account. This procedure is illustrated by the following journal entry:

GENERAL JOURNAL PAGE

DATE		PARTICULARS	PR	DEBIT	CREDIT
Dec.	31	Sales		20 000 —	
		Income Summary			20 000 —
		To close the Sales account			

The following T-accounts illustrate the effect of this entry on the two accounts:

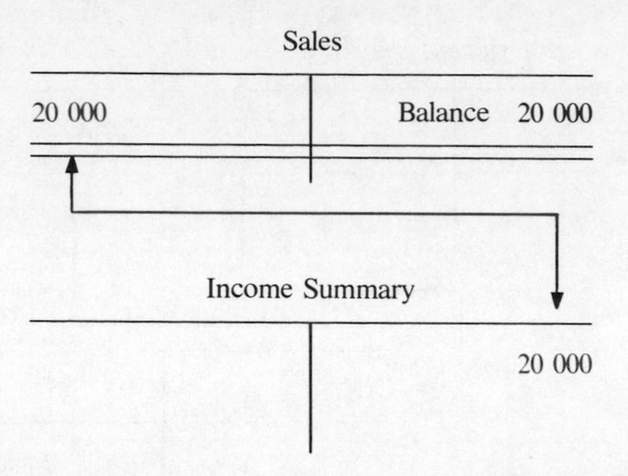

*3

2. Closing Expense Accounts Expense accounts have debit balances. The Advertising Expense account illustrated in the T-account shows a debit balance of $3 000 that represents the total of the advertising for the year.

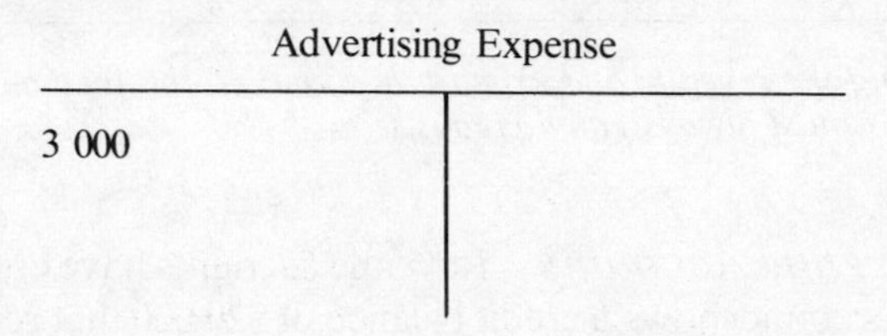

The following entry and the T-accounts illustrate the closing of an expense account.

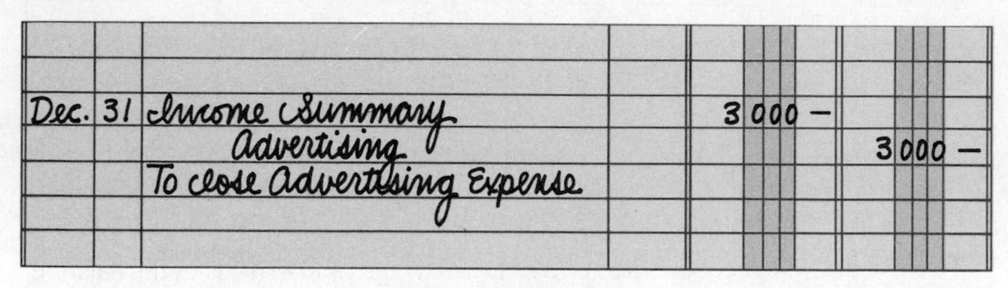

Dec.	31	Income Summary		3 000 —	
		Advertising			3 000 —
		To close Advertising Expense			

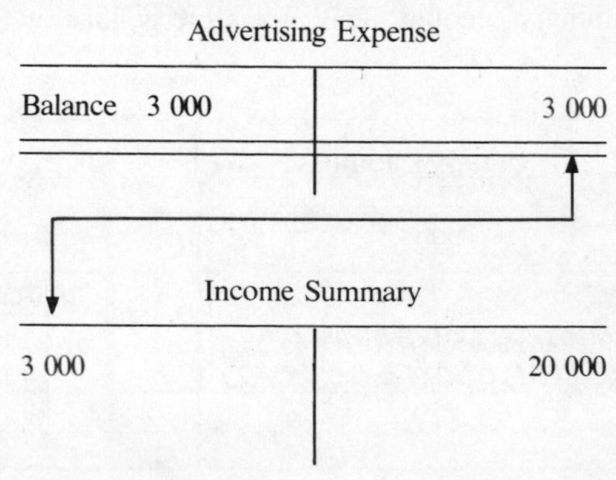

Each expense account in the ledger is closed in the same way. If a business has four expense accounts, they can be closed with four individual entries similar to the one for closing the Advertising Expense account. However, it is much simpler to make one compound entry such as the following:

Dec.	31	Income Summary		14 000 —	
		Advertising			3 000 —
		Salaries			10 000 —
		Telephone			500 —
		General			500 —
		To close the expense accounts			

3. Closing the Income Summary Account After the entries to close the revenue and expenses have been posted, the Income Summary account contains the revenue for the period on the credit side and the expenses for the period on the debit side. Since the credit side is larger, the $6 000 balance represents the net income for the period. *4

Income Summary

14 000	20 000
	Balance 6 000

The net income of $6 000 earned for the period increases the owner's equity or, in other words, the net income belongs to the owner. The balance of the Income Summary account is therefore transferred to the owner's Capital account by this closing entry:

Dec.	31	Income Summary		6 000 —	
		D. Adams, Capital			6 000 —
		To close the Income Summary account and transfer the net income to the Capital account			

The following T-accounts illustrate the effect of this entry on the two accounts:

Income Summary

Debit	Credit
14 000	20 000
6 000	Balance 6 000

D. Adams, Capital

Debit	Credit
	17 000
	6 000

*5

4. Closing the Owner's Drawing Account During the accounting period, withdrawals of cash and other assets by the owner are recorded in the owner's Drawing account. Since withdrawals by the owner affect the owner's investment, the Drawing account is closed with the following entry:

Dec.	31	D. Adams, Capital		2000 —	
		D. Adams, Drawing			2000 —
		To close the drawing account			

The following T-accounts illustrate the effects of this entry:

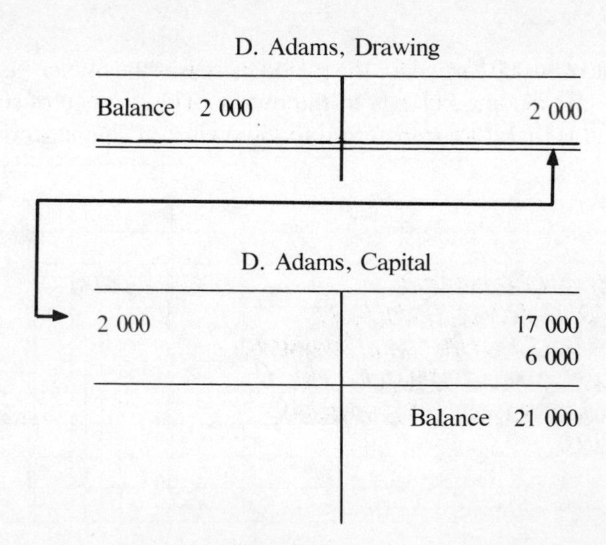

After these last two entries have been posted, the Income Summary account has been closed (reduced to zero), the Drawing account has been closed, and the Capital account has been updated so that it agrees with the balance for capital shown on the balance sheet.

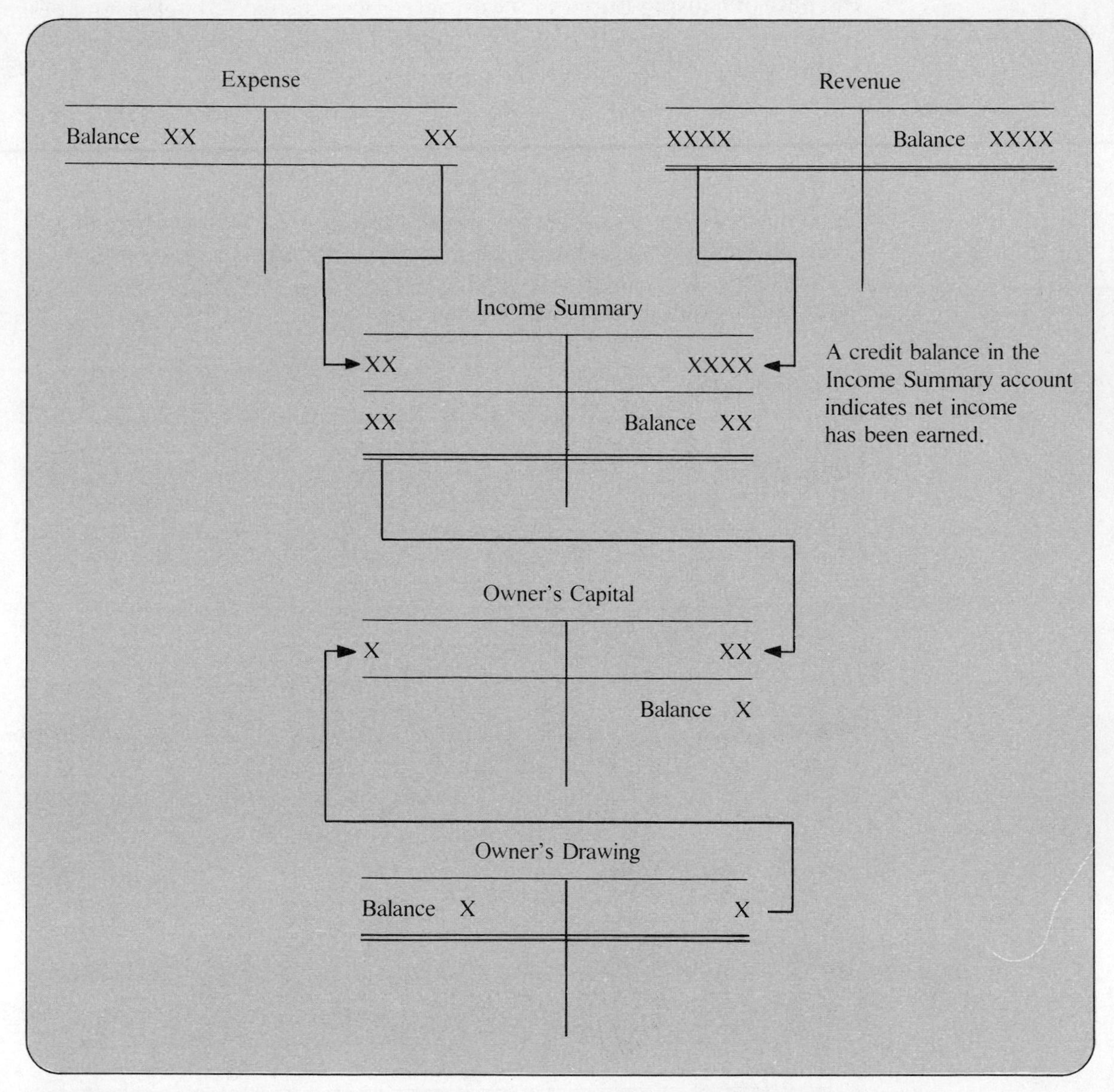

Figure 7.2 *Closing the books (Remember: debits must always equal credits.)*

Steps in Closing the Books In summary, there are four steps involved in closing the books . *6

1. Close the revenue accounts into the Income Summary account.
2. Close the expense accounts into the Income Summary account.

3. Close the Income Summary account into the Capital account.
4. Close the Drawing account into the Capital account.
See if you can follow the four steps in Figure 7.2.

Purpose of Closing Entries Two main purposes are served by closing entries:

- revenue and expense accounts are prepared for the next accounting period
- the Capital account is updated

Unit 17

*7

3-Column Ledger Accounts

Up to this point, the procedure for closing the books has been illustrated by T-accounts because it is easy to explain in this way. What follows is an explanation of how the books are closed using 3-column ledger accounts. Figure 7.3 is the ledger for D. Adams with the December 31 balances.

ACCOUNT *Cash* NO. *100*

DATE		PARTICULARS	PR	DEBIT	CREDIT	DR CR	BALANCE
19-- Dec.	31		✓			DR	2 000 —

ACCOUNT *Accounts Receivable* NO. *102*

DATE		PARTICULARS	PR	DEBIT	CREDIT	DR CR	BALANCE
19-- Dec.	31		✓			DR	4 500 —

ACCOUNT *Equipment* NO. *141*

DATE		PARTICULARS	PR	DEBIT	CREDIT	DR CR	BALANCE
19-- Dec.	31		✓			DR	9 000 —

ACCOUNT *Automobile* NO. *142*

DATE		PARTICULARS	PR	DEBIT	CREDIT	DR CR	BALANCE
19-- Dec.	31		✓			DR	8 000 —

ACCOUNT *Accounts Payable* NO. 200

DATE		PARTICULARS	PR	DEBIT	CREDIT	DR CR	BALANCE
Dec. 19--	31		✓			CR	2 500 —

ACCOUNT *D. Adams, Capital* NO. 300

DATE		PARTICULARS	PR	DEBIT	CREDIT	DR CR	BALANCE
Dec. 19--	31		✓			CR	17 000 —

ACCOUNT *D. Adams, Drawing* NO. 301

DATE		PARTICULARS	PR	DEBIT	CREDIT	DR CR	BALANCE
Dec. 19--	31		✓			DR	2 000 —

ACCOUNT *Sales* NO. 400

DATE		PARTICULARS	PR	DEBIT	CREDIT	DR CR	BALANCE
Dec. 19--	31		✓			CR	20 000 —

ACCOUNT *Advertising Expense* NO. 500

DATE		PARTICULARS	PR	DEBIT	CREDIT	DR CR	BALANCE
Dec. 19--	31		✓			DR	3 000 —

ACCOUNT *General Expense* NO. 501

DATE		PARTICULARS	PR	DEBIT	CREDIT	DR CR	BALANCE
Dec. 19--	31		✓			DR	500 —

ACCOUNT Salaries Expense						NO. 502
DATE	PARTICULARS	PR	DEBIT	CREDIT	DR CR	BALANCE
Dec. 31 19--		✓			DR	10 000 —

ACCOUNT Telephone Expense						NO. 503
DATE	PARTICULARS	PR	DEBIT	CREDIT	DR CR	BALANCE
Dec. 31 19--		✓			DR	500 —

Figure 7.3 *Ledger for D. Adams with December 31 balances*

Closing Entries The revenue and expense accounts in D. Adams' ledger are closed with the entries illustrated in the General Journal in Figure 7.4. Notice that there are four basic closing entries. The first entry closes the revenue accounts. The second entry closes the expense accounts. The third entry closes the Income Summary account and transfers the net income to the owner's Capital account. The fourth entry closes the Drawing account.

GENERAL JOURNAL					PAGE 34
DATE		PARTICULARS	PR	DEBIT	CREDIT
Dec. 19--	31	Sales		20 000 —	
		Income Summary			20 000 —
		To close the sales account			
	31	Income Summary		14 000 —	
		Advertising			3 000 —
		General			500 —
		Salaries			10 000 —
		Telephone			500 —
		To close the expense accounts			
	31	Income Summary		6 000 —	
		D. Adams, Capital			6 000 —
		To close the Income Summary account and transfer the net income to the Capital account			
	31	D. Adams, Capital		2 000 —	
		D. Adams, Drawing			2 000 —
		To close the Drawing account			

Figure 7.4 *Closing entries in the General Journal for D. Adams*

Posting Ledger Accounts after Closing the Books After the closing entries have been journalized, they are posted to the ledger accounts. Figure 7.5 illustrates the ledger for D. Adams after the closing entries have been posted. Notice that all the revenue and expense accounts have been closed and show a zero balance. They are now ready for the next accounting period. Double lines have been ruled and serve to separate the data for the two accounting periods.

Revenue and expense accounts show a zero balance after closing.

ACCOUNT Cash NO. 100

DATE		PARTICULARS	PR	DEBIT	CREDIT	DR CR	BALANCE
19-- Dec.	31		✓			DR	2000 —

ACCOUNT Accounts Receivable NO. 102

DATE		PARTICULARS	PR	DEBIT	CREDIT	DR CR	BALANCE
19-- Dec.	31		✓			DR	4500 —

ACCOUNT Equipment NO. 141

DATE		PARTICULARS	PR	DEBIT	CREDIT	DR CR	BALANCE
19-- Dec.	31		✓			DR	9000 —

ACCOUNT Automobile NO. 142

DATE		PARTICULARS	PR	DEBIT	CREDIT	DR CR	BALANCE
19-- Dec.	31		✓			DR	8000 —

ACCOUNT Accounts Payable NO. 200

DATE		PARTICULARS	PR	DEBIT	CREDIT	DR CR	BALANCE
19-- Dec.	31					CR	2500 —

ACCOUNT D. Adams, Capital — NO. 300

DATE		PARTICULARS	PR	DEBIT	CREDIT	DR CR	BALANCE
Dec. 19--	31		✓			CR	17 000 —
	31	Net Income	J34		6 000	CR	23 000 —
	31	Drawing	J34	2 000		CR	21 000 —

ACCOUNT D. Adams, Drawing — NO. 301

DATE		PARTICULARS	PR	DEBIT	CREDIT	DR CR	BALANCE
Dec. 19--	31		✓			DR	2 000 —
	31		J34		2 000 —	—	——

ACCOUNT Income Summary — NO. 302

DATE		PARTICULARS	PR	DEBIT	CREDIT	DR CR	BALANCE
Dec. 19--	31	Sales	J34		20 000 —	CR	20 000 —
	31	Expenses	J34	14 000 —		CR	6 000 —
	31	Net Income	J34	6 000 —		—	——

ACCOUNT Sales — NO. 400

DATE		PARTICULARS	PR	DEBIT	CREDIT	DR CR	BALANCE
Dec. 19--	31		✓			CR	20 000 —
	31		J34	20 000 —		—	——

ACCOUNT Advertising Expense — NO. 500

DATE		PARTICULARS	PR	DEBIT	CREDIT	DR CR	BALANCE
Dec. 19--	31		✓			DR	3 000 —
	31		J34		3 000 —	—	——

ACCOUNT General Expense — NO. 501

DATE		PARTICULARS	PR	DEBIT	CREDIT	DR CR	BALANCE
Dec. 19--	31		✓			DR	500 —
	31		J34		500 —	—	——

ACCOUNT Salaries Expense NO. 502

DATE		PARTICULARS	PR	DEBIT	CREDIT	DR CR	BALANCE
Dec. 19--	31					DR	10 000 —
	31		J34		10 000 —	—	——

ACCOUNT Telephone Expense NO. 503

DATE		PARTICULARS	PR	DEBIT	CREDIT	DR CR	BALANCE
Dec. 19--	31		✓			DR	500 —
	31		J34		500 —	—	——

Figure 7.5 *Closing entries posted to the ledger accounts. All the revenue and expense accounts have been closed and show a zero balance*

The capital account has been updated. The net income of $6 000 was added to the capital and the withdrawals of $2 000 were subtracted.

The balance of the Capital account is now $21 000. Before posting the closing entries, the Capital balance of $17 000 was not up to date because it did not include the net income or the withdrawals. The new Capital account balance of $21 000 now agrees with the new capital balance as shown on the balance sheeet.

Post-Closing Trial Balance

Once all the closing entries have been posted to the ledger, the ledger should be in balance; that is, the debits should equal the credits. A trial balance called the *post-closing trial balance* is prepared to ensure the mathematical accuracy of the ledger. Figure 7.6 shows the post-closing trial balance for D. Adams.

*8
The post-closing trial balance is prepared after the closing entries have been posted.

The post-closing trial balance contains only assets, liabilities, and capital accounts.

D. Adams
Post Closing Trial Balance
December 31, 19__

ACCOUNT TITLE	ACC. NO.	DEBIT	CREDIT
Cash	100	2 000 —	
Accounts Receivable	102	4 500 —	
Equipment	141	9 000 —	
Automobile	142	8 000 —	
Accounts Payable	200		2 500 —
D. Adams, Capital	300		21 000 —
		23 500 —	23 500 —

Figure 7.6 *Post-closing trial balance for D. Adams*

The post-closing trial balance contains only assets, liabilities, and capital accounts. The revenue and expense accounts and the Drawing and Income Summary accounts are not on this trial balance because they have been closed.

Since the debits equal the credits in this post-closing trial balance, no mathematical errors have been made in posting the closing entries. The ledger is ready for the transactions of the next accounting period.

The Accounting Cycle

Figure 7.7 illustrates the accounting cycle with the addition of the closing entries and the post-closing trial balance.

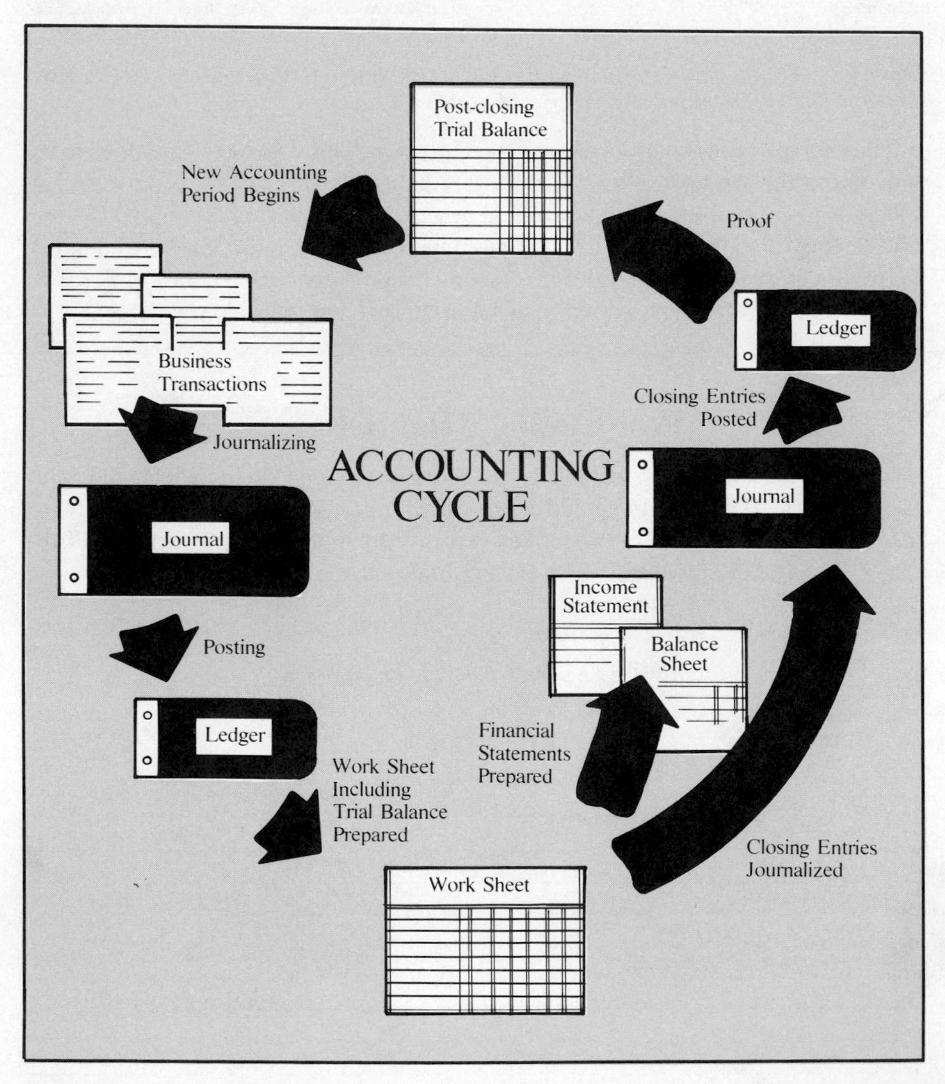

Figure 7.7 *The accounting cycle*

Facts to Remember

Revenue and expense accounts are closed at the end of the accounting period.

Closing entries are made to prepare the revenue and expense accounts for the next fiscal period and to update the Capital account.

Revenue and expense accounts show a zero balance after closing.

The *post-closing trial balance* is prepared after the closing entries have been posted.

The *post-closing trial balance* includes only assets, liabilities, and capital accounts.

Checking Your Reading

Questions

1. Name the types of accounts that are closed at the end of the accounting period.

2. The Sales account normally shows a credit balance. Is the Sales account debited or credited to close the account?

3. To which account is the balance of the Sales account transferred?

4. The Rent Expense account normally shows a debit balance. Is Rent Expense debited or credited to close the account?

5. What does the credit balance of $6 000 in the Income Summary account (page 143) represent?

6. Why is the balance of the Income Summary account transferred to the Capital account?

7. The following questions refer to D. Adams' ledger, Figure 7.3.
   a) What was the Cash balance before the closing entries were prepared?
   b) What was the balance of the Cash account after the closing entries were posted?
   c) What were the balances of the following accounts, before and after the closing entries were posted?
      i) Accounts Receivable
      ii) Sales
      iii) Advertising
      iv) Income Summary
      v) D. Adams, Drawing
      vi) D. Adams, Capital

8. What do the debit amounts in the Income Summary account represent?

9. What do the credit amounts in the Income Summary account represent?

10. What accounts remain open after the closing entries have been posted?

11. What purpose is served by the post-closing trial balance?

12. What accounts appear on the post-closing trial balance?

Applying Your Knowledge

Exercises Part A

1. From the following accounts, list those that would be closed at the end of the fiscal period:

   Cash; Accounts Receivable; Sales; Building; Rent Expense; Salaries Expense; Bank Loan; Investment Income; D. Adams, Drawing; D. Adams, Capital; Income Summary; General Expense.

2. Following is a T-account ledger.

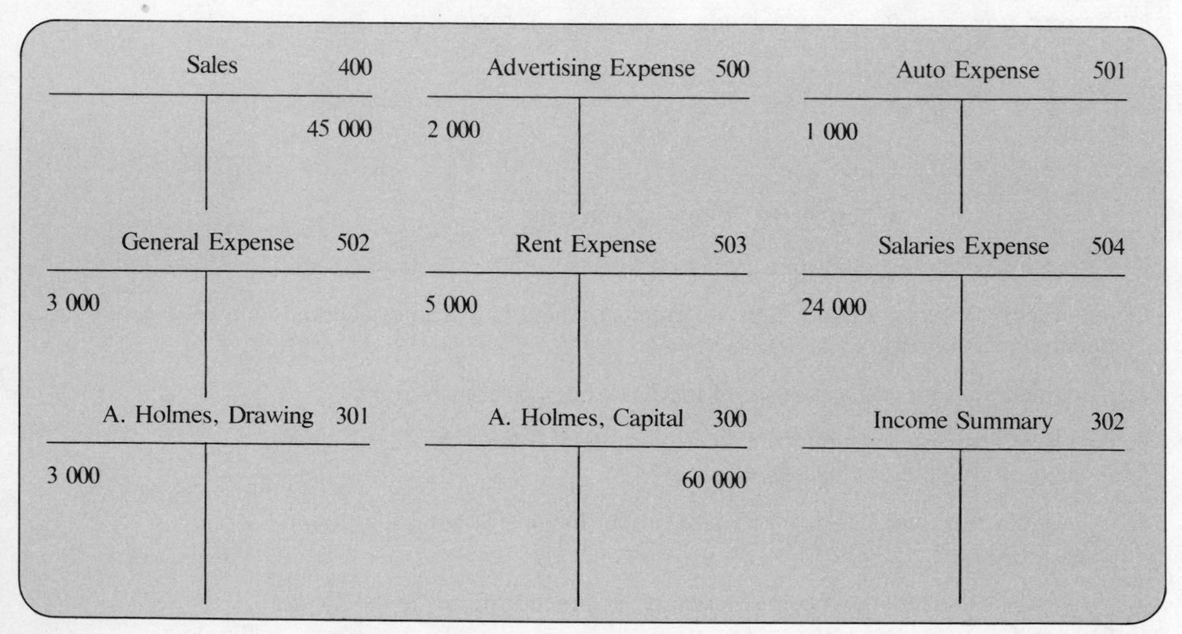

   a) Prepare the January 31 closing entries in a journal and post to the T-accounts.
   b) Calculate the final balance on January 31 in the A. Holmes, Capital account.

3. The account balances in the ledger of B. Whitton for the year ended December 31 are as follows:

   100 Cash *(DR)*, $4 700; 101 Accounts Receivable (*DR*), $10 000; 104 Supplies (*DR*), $2 600; 110 Equipment (*DR*), $17 000; 200 Accounts Payable (*CR*), $5 000; 300 B. Whitton Capital (*CR*), $25 100; 301 B. Whitton, Drawing (*DR*), $5 000; 400 Sales (*CR*), $60 000; 500 Rent Expense (*DR*), $4 800; 501 Delivery Expense (*DR*), $6 000; 502 Salaries Expense (*DR*), $40 000.

   a) Journalize the closing entries.
   b) Open a ledger and post the closing entries.

4. Prepare a trial balance for exercise 3 after the closing entries have been posted.

Exercises Part B

5. a) Open a ledger using the balances in the following trial balance. Include an Income Summary account, No. 302.

J. Fioravanti
Trial Balance
For the month of April, 19__

ACCOUNT TITLE	ACC. NO.	DEBIT	CREDIT
Cash	100	2 000 —	
Accounts Receivable	101	4 300 —	
Equipment	110	6 200 —	
Accounts Payable	200		2 500 —
J. Fioravanti, Capital	300		5 000 —
Sales	400		8 000 —
Salaries Expense	500	1 200 —	
General Expense	501	800 —	
Advertising Expense	502	1 000 —	
		15 500 —	15 500 —

b) Prepare the closing entries in a General Journal.
c) Post the closing entries.
d) Prepare a post-closing trial balance.

6. a) Open a ledger using the accounts and balances in the following trial balance.

I. Grant
Trial Balance
For the month of July, 19__

ACCOUNT TITLE	ACC. NO.	DEBIT	CREDIT
Cash	100	1 400 —	
Accounts Receivable	101	2 035 —	
Supplies	102	960 —	
Equipment	110	1 500 —	
Delivery Truck	112	7 800 —	
Accounts Payable	200		1 245 —
Loan Payable	210		1 400 —
I. Grant, Capital	300		10 500 —
I. Grant, Drawing	301	1 000 —	
Sales	400		8 970 —
Salaries Expense	500	6 000 —	
Rent Expense	501	500 —	
Miscellaneous Expense	502	540 —	
Office Expense	503	255 —	
Telephone Expense	504	125 —	
		22 115 —	22 115 —

b) Journalize the closing entries.
c) Post the closing entries. You will require account No. 302, Income Summary.
d) Is the balance of your Income Summary account correct? How do you know? (Check the work sheet you completed for exercise 3 in Chapter 6.)
e) Prepare a post-closing trial balance.

Exercises Part C

7. a) Open a ledger for The Cascade Inn. Your ledger should contain the accounts and balances found on the following work sheet and an Income Summary account, No. 302.

The Cascade Inn
Work Sheet
Month of June, 19__

ACCOUNT TITLE	ACC. NO.	TRIAL BALANCE DEBIT	TRIAL BALANCE CREDIT	INCOME STATEMENT DEBIT	INCOME STATEMENT CREDIT	BALANCE SHEET DEBIT	BALANCE SHEET CREDIT
Cash	100	9 300 —				9 300 —	
Supplies	101	8 000 —				8 000 —	
Office Equipment	110	5 000 —				5 000 —	
Room Furniture	112	110 000 —				110 000 —	
Building	114	500 000 —				500 000 —	
Land	116	50 000 —				50 000 —	
Accounts Payable	200		24 000 —				24 000 —
Bank Loan	210		15 000 —				15 000 —
Mortgage Payable	220		100 000 —				100 000 —
Galotta, Capital	300		536 000 —				536 000 —
Galotta, Drawing	301	900 —				900 —	
Room Rentals	400		25 000 —		25 000 —		
Restaurant Income	401		6 000 —		6 000 —		
Salaries Expense	500	10 000 —		10 000 —			
Advertising Expense	501	1 000 —		1 000 —			
Telephone Expense	502	200 —		200 —			
Laundry Expense	503	3 600 —		3 600 —			
Maintenance Expense	504	6 000 —		6 000 —			
Interest Expense	505	2 000 —		2 000 —			
		706 000 —	706 000 —	22 800 —	31 000 —	683 200 —	675 000 —
Net Income				8 200 —			8 200 —
				31 000 —	31 000 —	683 200 —	683 200 —

b) Journalize the closing entries.
c) Post the closing entries.
d) Is the balance of your Income Summary account correct? How do you know?
e) Prepare a post-closing trial balance.

8. a) Open a ledger using the accounts and balances in the following trial balance as well as Income Summary, No. 302.

T. Hood Trial Balance For the Month of February, 19__			
ACCOUNT TITLE	ACC. NO.	DEBIT	CREDIT
Cash	100	3 000 —	
Accounts Receivable	101	7 000 —	
Prepaid Insurance	102	800 —	
Land	110	30 000 —	
Building	120	90 000 —	
Furniture	122	5 000 —	
Accounts Payable	200		4 000 —
Taxes Owing	201		1 000 —
Bank Loan (2y)	202		15 000 —
Mortgage Payable	203		40 000 —
T. Hood, Capital	300		72 100 —
T. Hood, Drawing	301	1 000 —	
Sales	400		20 000 —
Salaries Expense	500	12 000 —	
Delivery Expense	501	1 200 —	
Utilities Expense	502	700 —	
Advertising Expense	503	900 —	
Miscellaneous Expense	504	300 —	
Insurance Expense	505	200 —	
		152 100 —	152 100 —

b) Journalize the closing entries.
c) Post the closing entries.
d) Compare the Capital account balance with the March Capital account balance given in exercise 9, Chapter 6.

Accounting in Action

Closing Entries Sandy H. is responsible for preparing closing entries in a journal. The ledger contains three revenue accounts, 15 expense accounts, an income summary account, and the owner's drawing account. Sandy has just spent considerable time journalizing 20 separate closing entries in a journal. Can you suggest a way in which the closing entries can be done much more efficiently with fewer than 20 journal entries? **Case 1**

Case 2

Closing Entry Errors

a) There are several errors in the following General Journal. Can you locate them?
b) What is the correct net income or net loss?

GENERAL JOURNAL PAGE 89

DATE		PARTICULARS	PR	DEBIT	CREDIT
19— Dec.	31	Sales		24 000 —	
		Advertising		1 000 —	
		Income Summary			25 000 —
	31	Income Summary		16 900 —	
		Rent Expense			500 —
		Salaries Expense			13 000 —
		Office Expense			400 —
		General Expense			1 000 —
		Selling Expense			2 000 —
	31	Income Summary		2 000 —	
		Owner's Drawing			2 000 —
	31	Owner's Capital		8 100 —	
		Income Summary			8 100 —

Case 3

Closing Entries

At the end of the fiscal period:

- the owner's equity section of the balance sheet shows capital of $29 000
- the Capital account in the ledger has a balance of $22 000
- the Drawing account has a balance of $2 000

a) Explain the difference in the balance sheet capital amount and the ledger Capital account balance.
b) What is the net income for the fiscal period?

Case 4

The Fiscal Period and Closing the Books

The revenue and expense accounts for McArthur Stores are summarized in these two T-accounts:

Revenue		Expenses	
Debit	Credit	Debit	Credit
	19_1 89 000	19_1 74 000	
	19_2 100 000	19_2 80 000	

At the end of year 19_1, a new accountant was hired. A net income of $15 000 was calculated by the accountant. At the end of 19_2, the accountant arrived at a net income of $35 000. The owner of the business feels an error has been made because the net income appears to be too high. What do you think?

Case 5

Women and Credit The use of credit is a privilege granted by business to its customers. However, everyone, regardless of sex or marital status, has the right to apply for credit and to be judged equally for credit-granting purposes. The governments of Ontario and other provinces have established equal credit opportunity guidelines to ensure that everyone is treated equally in the credit market.

The answers to the following series of questions may be obtained from the booklet "Credit and You, Women's Access to Credit in Ontario," which is available from the Ministry of Consumer and Commercial Affairs, Ontario, or from similar publications available from your provincial government.

a) May a woman obtain credit in her own name or must her married name be used?
b) May a company refuse credit to a woman solely because she is newly separated, divorced or widowed?
c) Can marriage affect credit status?
d) Is having a credit history important if one is married?
e) Can a person be asked for information about his or her spouse when applying for credit?
f) When is a wife responsible for a husband's debts?
g) When is a husband responsible for a wife's debts?
h) What can a person do if she or he is discriminated against when applying for credit?

Case 6

Starting a Business J. Fraser is considering opening a business in a new shopping plaza. He has spoken to government officials, bankers, and business friends. Here are some facts which Fraser has gathered.

- With good management the following results are forecast for the business:

Year 1	Net Loss	$ 8 000
Year 2	Net Loss	1 000
Year 3	Net Income	7 000
Year 4	Net Income	20 000
Year 5	Net Income	20 000

- After five years the average net income would be $30 000 per year.
- Personal loans of up to $50 000 are available to Fraser at 12% interest a year.
- Fraser has saved $20 000.
- $40 000 is required to start the business.
- Instead of starting a business, Fraser can invest the savings of $20 000 in mortgages at 10% interest a year.

a) What would you recommend to Fraser – should he start the business or invest in the mortgages? Why?
b) What other facts would you like to have before making a recommendation?

Career Profile

A Business Owner Tony Mariani has been out of high school for eight years. He is now part-owner and general manager of a holding company that operates the Mona Lisa Dining Lounge.

Tony enrolled in the three-year Business Administration program at Algonquin College after graduating from the High School of Commerce. In this program he specialized in management, marketing and accounting. Some of the courses he took were Accounting, Cost Accounting, Financial Management, Taxation, and Small Business Accounting.

After graduating from college, Tony obtained a job as a building management consultant for a large construction company. Tony specialized in planning and financing construction projects. He was responsible for obtaining short-term and long-term financing which meant constant contact with banks, trust companies, and other savings institutions.

One of Tony's projects was to prepare a management report for a restaurant. As a result of this report, Tony was given the opportunity of becoming part-owner of the restaurant. Tony accepted the challenge and is now vice-president of the company that owns the Mona Lisa Dining Lounge. He is completely responsible for the profitable operation of the restaurant. The Mona Lisa specializes in Italian food. Home-made pasta and a variety of veal dishes highlight the menu. Sales are just under $1 000 000 a year.

Tony enjoys being his own boss and realizes that he is responsible for the success or failure of the business. He hires, trains, and supervises 14 employees. He also handles the advertising, promotion, and accounting for the restaurant. Tony feels that a good accounting system is the key to any good business. His background in accounting helps him to ensure that the restaurant expenses are kept in line with its income.

The Basic Accounting Cycle

Project 1

This project includes all the steps in the accounting cycle covered to this point in *Basic Accounting*. You are required to journalize transactions, post to the ledger, prepare a work sheet and financial statements, prepare and post closing entries, and prepare a post-closing trial balance. It is a comprehensive review of Chapters 1 to 7. Good luck!

Playbill Cinema

Part A

The Playbill Cinema rents its premises from the Westbrook Shopping Centre. The operation has now been open for a month and the management wishes to find out how profitable the venture has been in that month. The following trial balance has been provided:

Playbill Cinema
Trial Balance
For the Month Ended January 31, 19__

ACCOUNT TITLE	ACC. NO.	DEBIT	CREDIT
Cash	100	5 653 —	
Equipment	110	89 563 —	
Accounts Payable	200		890 —
Bank Loan	201		10 387 —
V. Schulz, Capital	300		83 159 —
V. Schulz, Drawing	301	1 600 —	
Income Summary	302	—	—
Ticket Sales	400		20 453 —
Confection Income	401		2 407 —
Salaries Expense	500	6 801 —	
Advertising Expense	501	2 563 —	
Film Rental Expense	502	3 563 —	
Rent Expense	503	1 887 —	
Cleaning Expense	504	850 —	
Office Expense	505	1 235 —	
Equipment Repairs and Maintenance Expense	506	1 793 —	
Film Transportation Expense	507	248 —	
Heating Expense	508	658 —	
Electricity and Water Expense	509	532 —	
General Expense	510	350 —	
		117 296 —	117 296 —

1. Complete a work sheet.
2. Prepare an income statement for the month of January.
3. Prepare a balance sheet dated January 31, 19__.
4. Set up a General Ledger with the accounts and balances from the trial balance.
5. Journalize and post the closing entries.
6. Prepare a post-closing trial balance.

Part B

The following source documents came across the desk of the Playbill Cinema's accountant during the month of February.

1. Journalize the source documents and post to the General Ledger.
2. Prepare a trial balance.

Feb. 7 Cash register tapes from the box office for the week showing transactions No. 5345 to No. 6253 for total sales of $2 858. The money was deposited in the bank account.

Weekly sales report for the confection bar showing a net income of $225. The money was deposited in the bank account.

Purchase invoices were received from:
Electronics Canada Ltd., $256 for final adjustments to the projector
The Daily Sentinel, $750 for newspaper advertisements

Cheques issued:
No. 375 to City Hydro, $350 for electricity and water
No. 376 to Bell Canada, $45 (General Expense)

Feb. 14 Cash register tapes from the box office for the week showing transactions No. 6254 to No. 8871 for total sales of $7 534.

Weekly sales report for the confection bar showing a net income of $612.

Purchase invoices were received from:
International Film Distributors, $1 289 for rental of the film shown from February 1 to 7
Commercial Cleaners Ltd., $420 for cleaning the premises in the first half of the month
Cheques issued:
No. 377 to Craig stationers, $35 for office expenses
No. 378 to International Film Distributors, $890 on account
No. 379 to V. Schulz, the owner, $350 for personal drawings
No. 380 for a total of $2 890 for the salaries from February 1

Feb. 21 Cash register tapes from the box office for the week showing transactions No. 8872 to No. 11 608 for total sales of $8 132.
Weekly sales report for the confection bar showing a net income of $657.

Purchase invoices were received from:
Air Canada, $178 for transportation of film
CCHH Radio and TV, $371 for spot advertising
Stinson Fuels, $356 for oil

Cheques issued:
No. 381 to Electronics Canada Ltd., $256 on account
No. 382 to *The Daily Sentinel,* $750 on account

Feb. 28 Cash register tapes from the box office for the week showing transactions No. 11 609 to No. 14 142 for total sales of $7 483.

Weekly sales report for the confection bar showing a net income of $589.

Purchase invoices were received from:
International Film Distributors, $2 658 for rental of film from February 8 to 28
Commercial Cleaners Ltd., $435 for cleaning of premises

Cheques issued:
No. 383 to Commercial Cleaners Ltd., $420 on account
No. 384 to Westbrook Enterprises, $2 809 for the month's rent which is based on 10% of sales
No. 385 to V. Schulz, the owner, $350 for personal drawings
No. 386 for a total of $2 635 for the salaries from February 15.

Part C

At the end of the month of February, the following accounting procedures are to be completed for Playbill Cinema:

1. Prepare a work sheet.
2. Prepare an income statement for the month of February.
3. Prepare a balance sheet for February 28.
4. Journalize and post the closing entries.
5. Prepare a post-closing trial balance.

PART TWO

Accounting Systems and Procedures

Up to this point, you have learned the basic tasks performed during the accounting period. In theory, these tasks follow the sequence or cycle illustrated below. However, in practice, the steps of the accounting cycle are not always performed in this order – nor are all these steps necessarily performed. Some may be left out and others changed.

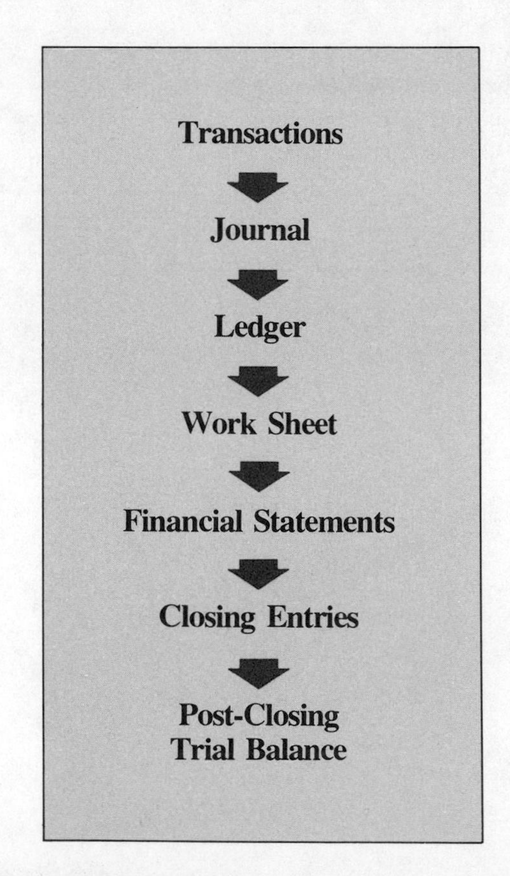

The sequence and the number of steps depend in part on the size of the business and the complexity of its operations. A large business, for instance, is seldom limited to one journal or one ledger; it may need several of each. If the business operates its accounting system through a computer, the computer may produce the journal and the ledger simultaneously.

Part Two of Basic Accounting examines refinements of the procedures described in Part One and various ways of doing accounting using manual, machine, and computer methods. Part Two also shows how the number of transactions, the information and controls desired by management, and the nature of a business, all affect accounting procedures.

The computer reduces the workload of the accountant by performing many of the repetitive accounting tasks.

CHAPTER 8

Subsidiary Ledgers

Unit 18

*1

Fraser Enterprises

In order to introduce the subject of subsidiary ledgers, the jobs of three people employed by a large business called Fraser Enterprises will first be examined. The practical day-to-day operation of this company's accounting system is a typical example of how subsidiary ledgers are used in business.

Accounts Payable Clerk

Fraser Enterprises purchases goods and services from a number of suppliers or creditors. Mary Houlton started as a typist at Fraser Enterprises, but after a few months she took over as accounts payable clerk in the Ottawa office. Now she is kept busy full-time, just handling transactions involving accounts payable.

A purchase invoice is a bill received from a creditor.

Figure 8.1 is an invoice received from a creditor, Western Manufacturing Ltd. Mary calls this a *purchase invoice* because Fraser Enterprises has purchased supplies and equipment from Western Manufacturing. To process this invoice, the following procedures have been established.

Processing Invoices Mary's first responsibility is to confirm that Fraser Enterprises ordered the goods specified in the invoice and that the total amount of the invoice is correct. In a file of purchase orders that she maintains, Mary locates purchase order No. 683, sent out about a month before by Fraser's to Western Manufacturing. She checks to see that the order price and the invoice price are the same and that there are no mathematical errors on the invoice.

Next, she must find out if the goods have actually been received. She checks her file of receiving reports and locates a report showing that the goods have been received. The three documents – the purchase order, the purchase invoice, and the receiving report – are presented to a supervisor for approval before they are recorded. The approved invoice is returned to Mary who records the amount owed to Western. First, Mary locates the account in her *Accounts Payable Ledger* and then raises the balance by entering a credit. (Remember, a liability increases on the credit side.) The Accounts Payable Ledger is a special ledger or *subsidiary ledger* that contains only creditors' accounts.

The Accounts Payable Ledger is a subsidiary ledger containing only creditors' accounts.

A subsidiary ledger is a group of accounts of one type.

The invoice, with the purchase order and receiving report attached, is now

SOLD TO: Fraser Enterprises
Ottawa, Ontario

DATE: Jan. 4, 19--

INVOICE NO: W-43

TERMS: Net 30 days

CUST. ORDER NO: 683

VIA: CN Express

QUANTITY	DESCRIPTION	PRICE	AMOUNT
2	Visual Card Files	$ 190	$ 380
10 000	Stock Cards	$5/1 000	50
	TOTAL		$ 430

P.O. NO. ______
REC. REP. NO. ______
PRICE O.K. ______
EXTENSIONS ______
A.P. LEDGER ______
JOURNAL ______

Figure 8.1 *Purchase invoice received from Western Manufacturing Ltd.*

placed in a date file until it is due to be paid – which will be within the 30-day period specified on the invoice.

Paying Creditors When the invoice is due to be paid on February 3, Mary removes the invoice from the date file. A cheque with a carbon copy is prepared and the original cheque is sent to the creditor. Using the carbon copy of the cheque as her source of information, Mary now decreases the creditor's account by entering a debit. This debit decreases the balance owed to Western. ***2**

Keeping Creditors' Accounts Up To Date It is Mary's job to maintain an accurate record of the amount owed to each creditor. She does this by recording purchases as credits and payments as debits. Figure 8.2 is a summary of Mary's duties. ***3**

Each month, Mary prepares a *schedule of accounts payable* as shown in Figure 8.3. This schedule is a listing of all the accounts payable with their balances. Figure 8.3 is a shortened version of a schedule of accounts payable. In reality it would contain many more creditor accounts and would be several pages in length.

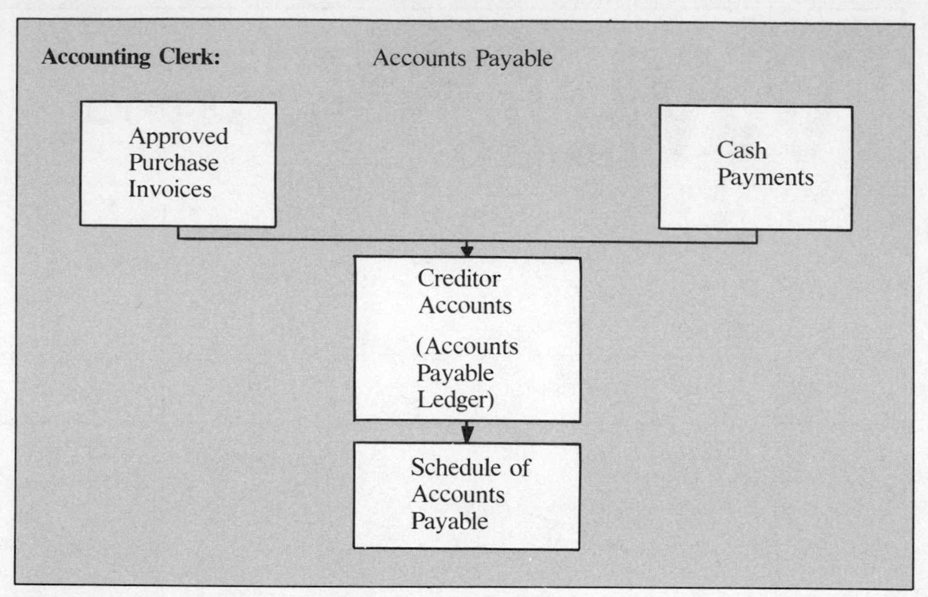

Figure 8.2 *Duties of an accounts payable clerk*

Fraser Enterprises Schedule of Accounts Payable January 31, 19__	
Acme Ltd.	200 00
Evans Co.	900 00
Falco Ltd.	400 00
Mentor Ltd.	500 00
	2 000 00

Figure 8.3 *Schedule of accounts payable*

Direct posting is the recording of information from source documents directly into ledger accounts.

Mary's job as accounts payable clerk does not include journalizing the purchase invoices. This is done by the accounting supervisor who journalizes the source documents after Mary is through with them. Mary *posts* information *directly* into the Accounts Payable Ledger from the invoices and cheque copies.

Unit 19

*4

Accounts Receivable Clerk

Fraser Enterprises has so many customers that Mary is unable to service their accounts and the accounts of creditors as well. A second accounting clerk, George Savard, handles transactions involving the customer accounts. His job title is accounts receivable clerk.

A sales invoice is a bill sent to a customer.

Figure 8.4 is a copy of a *sales invoice* sent to a customer, D. Meyer. When a sale was made to D. Meyer, an invoice was prepared in duplicate. The original copy was mailed to Meyer. The copy shown in Figure 8.4 was sent to George.

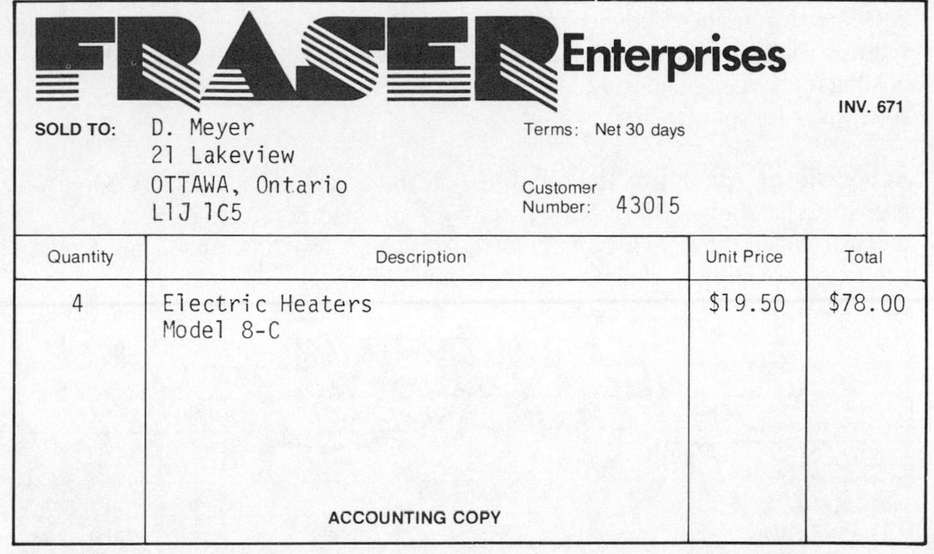

FRASER Enterprises

INV. 671

SOLD TO: D. Meyer
21 Lakeview
OTTAWA, Ontario
L1J 1C5

Terms: Net 30 days

Customer Number: 43015

Quantity	Description	Unit Price	Total
4	Electric Heaters Model 8-C	$19.50	$78.00

ACCOUNTING COPY

Figure 8.4 *Accounting department copy of the sales invoice sent to D. Meyer*

Processing Sales Invoices George's first task is to ensure that there are no errors on the invoice. He does this by checking the extensions (quantity × unit price) and the addition if necessary. George checks the extension of invoice No. 671 by multiplying the quantity (4) by the unit price ($19.50). This proves that the total ($78) shown on the invoice is correct. George then locates Meyer's account in the *Accounts Receivable Ledger* and increases the balance with a debit. (Remember, an account receivable is an asset and assets increase on the debit side.) The Accounts Receivable Ledger is a subsidiary ledger that contains only customer's accounts. George then initials the invoice and sends it along with others he has processed to his accounting supervisor.

*5

The Accounts Receivable Ledger is a subsidiary ledger containing only customers' accounts.

Processing Cash Received From Customers When cash (currency, cheques, or money orders) is received from customers, a list is prepared showing the customers' names, the invoices being paid, and the amounts received. The money is deposited in the bank each day. George does not actually see the money but is given a list like the one in Figure 8.5

Fraser Enterprises
Daily Cash Receipts
February 4, 19__

Customer	Amount
W. Turko	50 00
C. Bard	300 00
T. Roesler	200 00
Total Deposited	550 00

Figure 8.5 *List of daily cash receipts*

Cash received decreases customer account balances.

George locates the accounts of the customers shown on the cash receipts list and reduces the balances in these accounts with credits. When George is through posting the invoices and daily cash receipts, he passes them on to the accounting supervisor for journalizing.

*6

Schedule of Accounts Receivable At the end of each month, George prepares a list showing the balance owed by each customer. A shortened version of this list, called the *schedule of accounts receivable,* is shown in Figure 8.6. A summary of George's duties is presented in Figure 8.7.

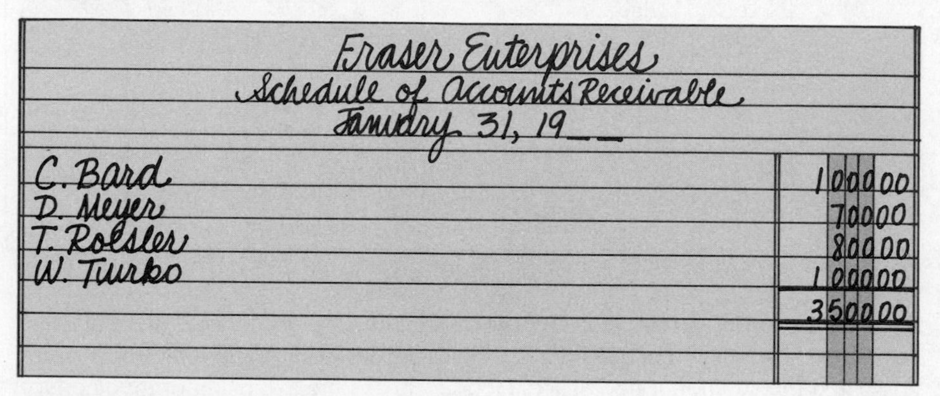
Fraser Enterprises
Schedule of Accounts Receivable
January 31, 19__

C. Bard	1 000 00
D. Meyer	700 00
T. Roesler	800 00
W. Turko	1 000 00
	3 500 00

Figure 8.6 *Schedule of accounts receivable*

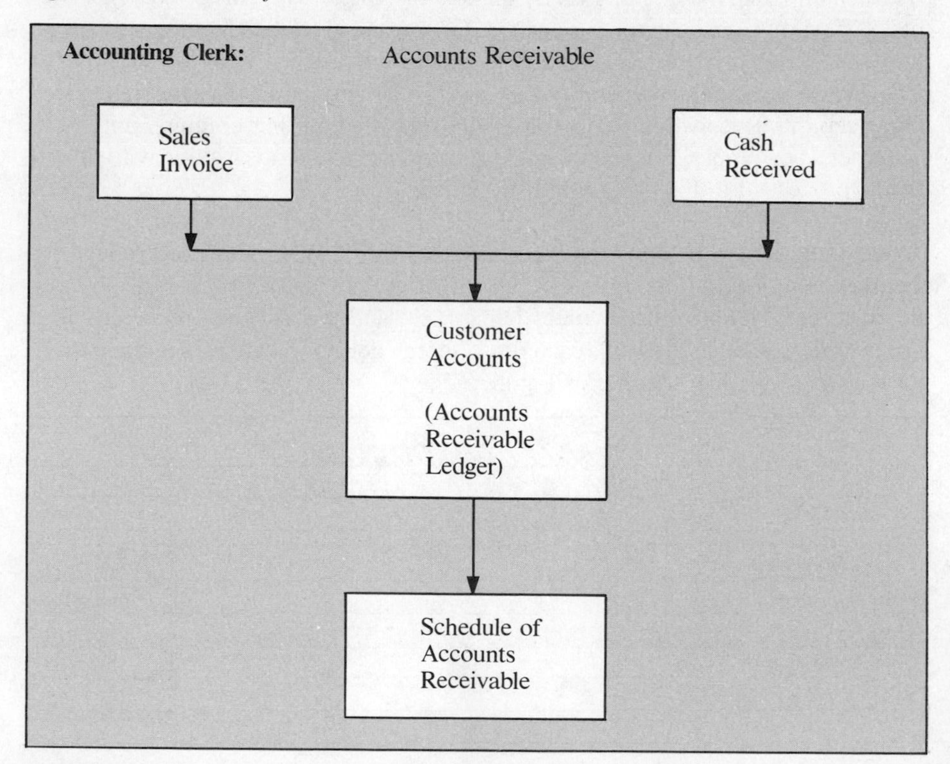

Figure 8.7 *Duties of an accounts receivable clerk*

Accounting Supervisor

*7

As has been shown in the first two job descriptions, Fraser Enterprises employs two accounting clerks: the accounts receivable clerk and the accounts payable clerk. Both clerks answer to an accounting supervisor who fills a third accounting position in the department. Marni Roberts is the accounting supervisor at Fraser Enterprises. While she was going to school, Marni worked at Fraser's as a part-time clerk. When she graduated from high school, she was hired as an accounts payable clerk. Several years later Marni was promoted to the position of accounting supervisor. Her job involves the supervision of the work of the accounting clerks and the preparation of journal entries. Marni is given source documents after they have been posted directly in the Accounts Receivable and Accounts Payable Ledgers by Mary and George. The source documents involved are:

- purchase invoices
- cheque copies
- sales invoice copies
- lists of cash receipts

Figure 8.8 illustrates how these documents are processed by the accounting supervisor.

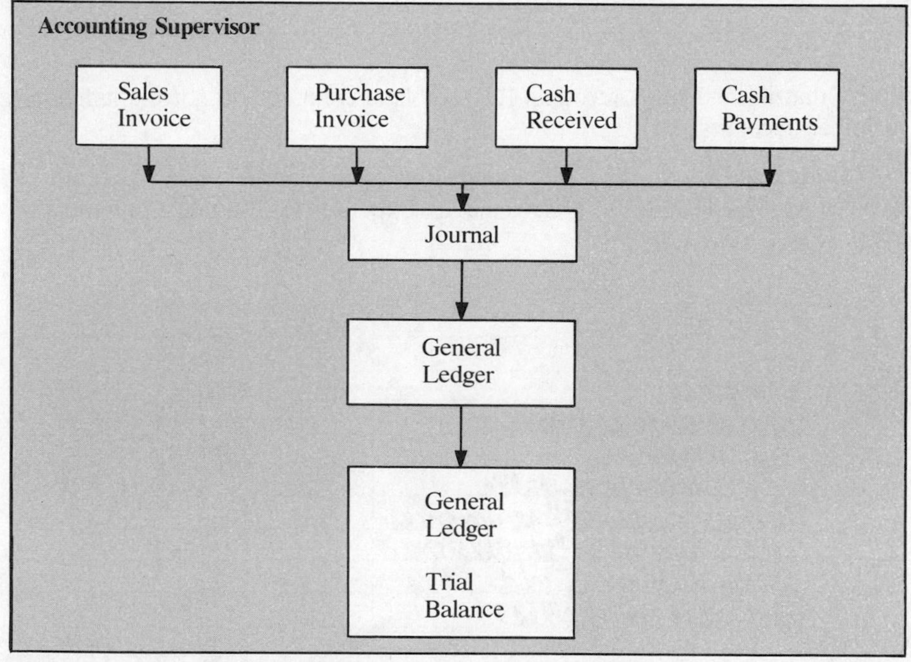

Figure 8.8 *Documents processed by an accounting supervisor*

Preparing Journal Entries

The journal entries on the next three pages are prepared to record the source documents sent to Marni from Mary and George.

Sales Invoices The journal entry to record sales invoices is as follows Notice that in this entry, individual customers are not debited. Instead, the Accounts Receivable account is debited. Also, several sales invoices (No.'s 671 to 675) are totalled and recorded in one entry.

Feb.	4	Accounts Receivable		730 —	
		Sales			730 —
		To record invoices 671-675			

List of Cash Receipts The entry to record the cash received from customers is as follows:

Feb.	4	Cash		550 —	
		Accounts Receivable			550 —
		To record cash receipts			
		for February 4			

Notice that in this entry Accounts Receivable is credited and not the individual customer accounts.

*8

Purchase Invoices The accounting supervisor's journal entry to record invoices for Supplies ($430), Miscellaneous Expenses ($170), and Equipment ($700) is as follows:

Feb.	4	Supplies		430 —	
		Miscellaneous Expense		170 —	
		Equipment		700 —	
		Accounts Payable			1 300 —
		To record purchase invoices			
		from Wilson's Ltd., Western			
		Manufacturing, and			
		Matheson Supplies			

Notice that in this entry, several invoices are recorded. Also, the Accounts Payable account is credited instead of the individual creditor accounts. *Can you explain why there are three accounts debited but only one account credited?*

*9

Cheque Copies The entry to record payments to creditors is shown at the top of page 173. This entry records several documents (cheques 71-73). The Accounts Payable account is debited instead of the individual creditor accounts.

Feb.	4	Accounts Payable		1200 —	
		Cash			1200 —
		To record cheques 71, 72, 73			

Posting the Journal Marni is also responsible for posting the journal entries to the *General Ledger*. When these entries have been posted to the General Ledger, the Accounts Receivable account in the General Ledger has the same balance as the total of the balances of the customer accounts in the Accounts Receivable Ledger. Remember that the sales invoices were recorded as debits in the customer accounts, and the cash received was recorded as credits in the customer accounts by George, the accounts receivable clerk.

*10

The General Ledger is the main ledger and contains all asset, liability, equity, revenue, and expense accounts.

The Accounts Payable account in the General Ledger also has the same balance as the total of the balances in the creditor accounts in the Accounts Payable Ledger. Remember that the purchase invoices and cash payments (cheque copies) were recorded by Mary, the accounts payable clerk.

All the source documents have been recorded twice: once by the accounting supervisor and once by the accounting clerks.

Other Journal Entries The accounting supervisor is responsible for journalizing all source documents, not just those involving accounts receivable and accounts payable. Some examples of other journal entries made by Marni follow:

*11

1. A $200 cash sale was made.

Feb.	8	Cash		200 —	
		Sales			200 —
		Cash sale			

2. The owner invested $5 000.

Feb.	8	Cash		5 000 —	
		D. Fraser, Capital			5 000 —
		Additional investment			

3. Cheque No. 74 for $500 was issued to pay the rent.

Date		Particulars	PR	Debit	Credit
Feb.	9	Rent Expense		500 —	
		Cash			500 —
		Cheque 74			

4. The owner withdrew $100 for personal use.

Date		Particulars	PR	Debit	Credit
Feb.	15	D. Fraser, Drawing		100 —	
		Cash			100 —
		Cheque 75, personal use			

Unit 21

*12

Subsidiary Ledgers

The three job descriptions have served as a basic introduction to subsidiary ledgers; a more detailed examination of the theory of subsidiary ledger accounting will now be made.

It is clear from the accounting procedures already covered in this chapter that a company like Fraser Enterprises needs more than one ledger to efficiently process and control the accuracy of its accounting data. Since Fraser Enterprises has numerous creditors and several hundred customers, it would, of course, be inconvenient to list them all on the balance sheet. Instead, the total owing by all the customers ($3 500) is indicated on the balance sheet by the Accounts Receivable account as shown in Figure 8.9. The total owing to all creditors ($2 000) is represented by the Accounts Payable account which is also shown in Figure 8.9. Both the Accounts Receivable and the Accounts Payable control accounts are found in the main or General Ledger.

The General Ledger is a file of all accounts used to prepare the financial statements.

In addition, the General Ledger contains all the asset, liability, equity, revenue, and expense accounts. As was explained in Chapter 5, the General Ledger is a file of all the accounts that are used to prepare the financial statements – both the income statement and the balance sheet.

A subsidiary ledger is a group of accounts of one type.

In order to effectively process the large number of customer and creditor account transactions, separate or *subsidiary ledgers* such as the Accounts Receivable Ledger and the Accounts Payable Ledger are used. A more detailed discussion of why subsidiary ledgers are required will follow on pages 175-178, once the functioning of these ledgers has been explained.

Before looking more closely at the two subsidiary ledgers used by Fraser Enterprises, remember that subsidiary ledgers are usually organized in alphabetical order. In the General Ledger, all accounts are numbered. For example, Cash may be number 100 and Capital may be number 300.

Fraser Enterprises Balance Sheet February 28, 19__		
Assets		
Cash	2 000 —	
Accounts Receivable	3 500 —	
Supplies	500 —	
Equipment	3 000 —	
Building	60 000 —	
Total Assets		69 000 —
Liabilities		
Accounts Payable	2 000 —	
Bank Loan	20 000 —	
		22 000 —
Owner's Equity		
D.S. Fraser, Capital		47 000 —
Total Liabilities and Owner's Equity		69 000 —

Figure 8.9 *Balance sheet for Fraser Enterprises*

Accounts Receivable Ledger In many firms like Fraser Enterprises, the Accounts Receivable accounts are removed from the General Ledger and placed in a special customers' *Accounts Receivable Ledger*. This subsidiary ledger is required to record the details of the large number of customer accounts of such businesses. Only the customer accounts are found in this Accounts Receivable Ledger.

*13

The Accounts Receivable Ledger is a subsidiary ledger containing only customers' accounts.

The customers' accounts are replaced in the General Ledger by a single account called the *Accounts Receivable Control account*. This account represents the total owing by all the customers and is necessary in order that the General Ledger remain in balance. The balance in the Accounts Receivable Control account should always equal the total of all the individual customer accounts in the Accounts Receivable Ledger – that is why it is called a control account. Customer accounts are usually filed alphabetically in the Accounts Receivable Ledger and new accounts are inserted as required.

Accounts Payable Ledger A business with many creditors often removes the creditors' accounts from the General Ledger and places them in a subsidiary ledger called the *Accounts Payable Ledger*. The creditors' accounts are replaced in the General Ledger by an *Accounts Payable Control account*.

The Accounts Payable Ledger is a subsidiary ledger containing only creditors' accounts.

The total of all the individual creditors' accounts in the Accounts Payable Ledger should equal the balance of the Accounts Payable Control account in the General Ledger. Accounts in the Accounts Payable ledger are also organized alphabetically. Figure 8.10 indicates the relationship of the three ledgers. Notice that the total of the Accounts Receivable Ledger is $3 500 ($1 000 + $800 + $700 +$1 000) and is equal to the balance in the Accounts Receivable Control account in the General Ledger.

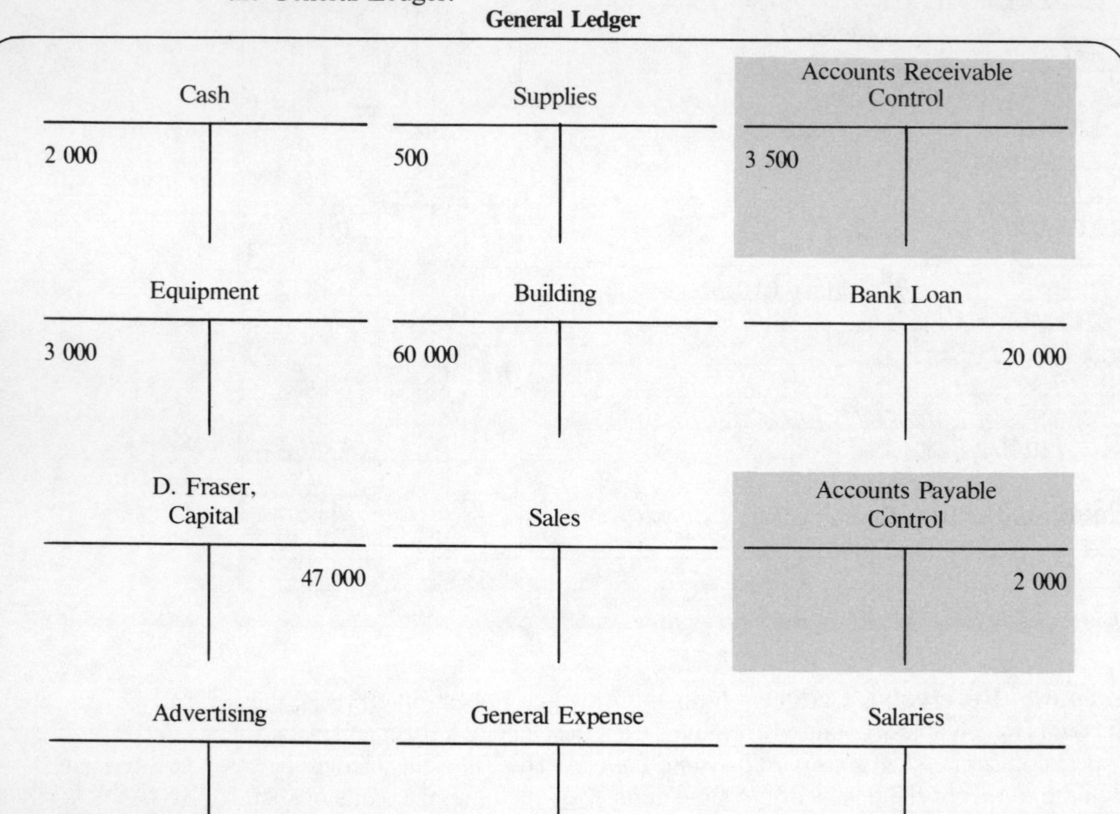

Accounts Receivable Ledger

Account	Debit	Credit
C. Bard	1 000	
T. Roesler	800	
D. Meyer	700	
W. Turko	1 000	

Accounts Payable Ledger

Account	Debit	Credit
Acme Ltd.		200
Evans Co.		900
Falco Ltd.		400
Mentor Ltd.		500

Figure 8.10 *A simplified example of the General Ledger and two subsidiary ledgers used by Fraser Enterprises*

Proof of Accuracy of Ledgers Each ledger should be proven to be mathematically accurate on a regular basis, for example monthly. The proof of the accuracy of the General Ledger is a trial balance in which the debit total equals the credit total as shown in Figure 8.11.

Fraser Enterprises
General Ledger Trial Balance
January 31, 19__

Account	Debit	Credit
Cash	2 000 —	
Accounts Receivable Control	3 500 —	
Supplies	500 —	
Equipment	3 000 —	
Building	60 000 —	
Accounts Payable Control		2 000 —
Bank Loan		20 000 —
Capital		47 000 —
	69 000 —	69 000 —

Fraser Enterprises
Schedule of Accounts Receivable
January 31, 19__

Customer	Amount
C. Bard	1 000 —
D. Meyer	700 —
T. Roesler	800 —
W. Turko	1 000 —
	3 500 —

Fraser Enterprises
Schedule of Accounts Payable
January 31, 19__

Acme Ltd.	200 —
Evans Co.	900 —
Falco Ltd.	400 —
Mentor Ltd.	500 —
	2 000 —

Figure 8.11 *Subsidiary ledger account totals must equal the balance of the related control account in the General Ledger*

The Accounts Receivable Ledger is proven to be correct if the total of the schedule of accounts receivable is equal to the balance of the Accounts Receivable Control account in the General Ledger. Similarly, the total of the schedule of accounts payable should be equal to the balance of the Accounts Payable Control account in the General Ledger. Remember this general rule:

For every subsidiary ledger, there is a control account in the General Ledger. The total of the accounts in the subsidiary ledger must equal the balance of the related control account in the General Ledger.

Advantages of Subsidiary Ledgers

*14

There are two main advantages of using subsidiary ledgers in an accounting system:

- division of labour
- accounting control

Division of Labour In a small business, one employee may be able to handle all of the accounting tasks from journalizing to the preparation of the financial statements. In a larger firm that must record many business transactions each day, one person cannot handle all of the accounting work. Large firms find it necessary and more efficient to divide the work among several people, each of whom specializes in an area of accounting. As has been shown in this chapter, Fraser Enterprises identifies these special accounting roles by the job titles: accounts receivable clerk, accounts payable clerk, and accounting supervisor. Other companies may use other titles for these same jobs, such as junior clerk, posting clerk, senior accountant, chief accountant, or accounting manager.

Accounting Control In a small business, the owner is involved in most of the transactions that take palce. The owner can spot irregularities or errors made by employees or by other businesses with which the owner deals. A large business has a number of people involved in the handling and recording of transactions. A good accounting system controls the recording, the accuracy, and the honesty of the people involved. The control accounts in the General Ledger must equal the totals of the schedules prepared for each of the subsidiary ledgers. When different people are responsible for each of the ledgers, they act as a check on the accuracy of each other's work.

Journalizing Batch Totals

*15

Journalizing batch totals is a technique used to efficiently record similar transactions that are frequently repeated. Suppose a business issues 35 invoices to customers over a short period of time. For each invoice, a journal entry such as this is made:

Feb.	5	Accounts Receivable		100 —	
		Sales			100 —
		To record invoice 101			

However, rather than record this entry 35 separate times for each invoice, a total may be taken of all the invoices, and this total recorded as follows:

Feb.	5	Accounts Receivable		4 200 —	
		Sales			4 200 —
		To record invoices 101 to 135			
		for sales on account			

This concept of grouping source documents and recording the total is called *journalizing batch totals*. It can be applied to a variety of documents. This is the entry made when cash receipts are batched:

Journalizing batch totals is the recording of the total of a number of source documents of one type in a single journal entry.

Feb.	5	Cash		2 200 —	
		Accounts Receivable			2 200 —
		To record cash received			
		from customers February 1-5			

Payments made to creditors may also be journalized in batches. For example, a series of cheque copies are journalized as follows:

Feb.	5	Accounts Payable		3 000 —	
		Cash			3 000 —
		Cheque copies 619 to 638			

Purchase invoices may be grouped together as well. However, the entry to record purchase invoices may have more than one debit if different items were purchased. The journal entry on page 180 illustrates this situation.

Feb.	5	Office Supplies		500 —	
		Equipment		2000 —	
		Heating Expense		300 —	
		Miscellaneous Expense		100 —	
		Accounts Payable			2900 —
		To record purchases			
		February 1-5			

Facts to Remember

A *purchase invoice* is a bill received from a creditor.

A *sales invoice* is a bill sent to a customer.

A business may have *more than one ledger* in its accounting records.

The main ledger is called the *General Ledger.*

The *General Ledger* is a file of all accounts used to prepare the financial statements.

A *subsidiary ledger* is a group of accounts of one type.

The *Accounts Receivable Ledger* and the *Accounts Payable Ledger* are two commonly used subsidiary ledgers.

Only customer accounts are found in the *Accounts Receivable Ledger.*

Only creditor accounts are found in the *Accounts Payable Ledger.*

There is a *control account* in the General Ledger for each subsidiary ledger.

The *total of the account balances* of a subsidiary ledger should equal the balance of its *control account.*

Directing posting is the recording of information from source documents directly into ledger accounts.

Journalizing batch totals is the recording of the total of a number of source documents of one type in a single journal entry.

Checking Your Reading

Questions

1. What source documents does an accounts payable clerk handle?

2. a) In the Accounts Payable Ledger, what documents are entered as debits?
b) What documents are entered as credits in the Accounts Payable Ledger?

3. Explain what is meant by direct posting.

4. Who receives the documents after the accounts payable clerk?

5. What is a schedule of accounts payable?

6. What is the accounts receivable clerk's first task with the copies of the sales invoices?

7. How does the accounts receivable clerk indicate that the sales invoices have been processed?

8. Specify whether the accounts receivable clerk records:
   a) sales invoices as debits or credits?
   b) cash receipts as debits or credits?

9. Who gets the sales invoices and the list of cash receipts after the accounts receivable clerk?

10. What is a schedule of accounts receivable?

11. List the source documents for which the accounting supervisor is responsible.

12. a) What two accounts are always affected by a sales invoice?
    b) Give an example of a journal entry resulting from a sales invoice.
    c) What is the advantage of combining many sales invoices into one journal entry?

13. a) What two General Ledger accounts are always affected by a list of cash receipts?
    b) Give an example of a journal entry resulting from a list of cash receipts.

14. a) What account is always credited when copies of cheques issued are journalized?
    b) Explain why the debit is not always the same when cheque copies are journalized.

15. a) What two General Ledger accounts are always affected by copies of cheques issued on account?
    b) Give an example of a journal entry resulting from a copy of a cheque on account.

16. What is a subsidiary ledger? Give an example.

17. What is a control account? Give an example.

18. What is the name given to the main ledger for a company that has more than one ledger?

19. Accounts in the General Ledger are numbered and organized in numerical sequence. How are the accounts in subsidiary ledgers usually organized?

20. What is the rule concerning the relationship between a subsidiary ledger and the General Ledger?

21. What is prepared to prove the accuracy of the General Ledger?

22. What is prepared to prove the accuracy of the Accounts Receivable Ledger?

23. What type of business uses more than one ledger in its set of books?

24. Explain the process of journalizing batch totals.

25. What are the two advantages of using subsidiary ledgers?

Applying Your Knowledge

Exercises Part A

1. You are the accounts payable clerk for Crawford Enterprises. Your duties include recording purchase invoices in creditor accounts.
   a) Head up the following accounts in your Accounts Payable Ledger:
   - Corbett's Service Station
   - Noonan Fuels Ltd.
   - Grant Equipment
   - Wilson Supply Ltd.

   b) The following purchase invoices represent purchases on account made by Crawford's. Record them in the Accounts Payable Ledger.

   Feb. 1 Noonan Fuels Ltd., No. 6931 for fuel oil, $120.
   Wilson Supply Ltd., No. K-213 for office supplies, $75.
   Grant Equipment, No. 316 for a typewriter, $495.
   2 Corbett's Service Station, No. 179 for gas and oil for company automobiles, $49.
   3 Grant Equipment, No. 391 for filing equipment, $260.
   Wilson Supply Ltd., No. K-272 for stationery, $50.
   8 Corbett's Service Station, No. 225 for car repairs, $160.
   Noonan Fuels Ltd., No. 6983 for furnace servicing, $40.
   9 Corbett's Service Station, No. 238 for gasoline, $35.
   Wilson Supply Ltd., No. K-317 for miscellaneous supplies, $24.
   15 Grant Equipment, No. 421 for cheque protecting machine, $175.

2. Your duties as accounts payable clerk for Crawford Enterprises also include recording payments made to creditors. Record the following copies of cheques issued in the Accounts Payable Ledger used for exercise 1.

   Feb. 10 No. 116 to Corbett's Service Station, $49 for invoice 179.
   No. 117 to Noonan Fuels Ltd., $120 for invoice 6931.
   15 No. 118 to Wilson Supply Ltd., $75 for invoice 213.
   No. 119 to Corbett's Service Station, $35 for invoice 238.
   20 No. 120 to Grant Equipment, $200 in part payment of invoice 316.
   No. 121 to Wilson Supply Ltd., $50 for invoice K-272.

3. Prepare a schedule of accounts payable dated February 28 for the Accounts Payable Ledger of Crawford Enterprises. Your schedule should total $954.

4. In this exercise, you will act as the accounts receivable clerk for Crawford Enterprises. Your duties include posting sales invoices directly into the customer accounts in the Accounts Receivable subsidiary ledger.

a) Head up the following accounts in your Accounts Receivable Ledger:
- T. Campbell
- W. Squire
- R. Mask
- G. Thompson

b) The following sales invoices represent sales on account made by your company to your customers. Post them directly into the Accounts Receivable Ledger.

Feb. 2 R. Mask, No. 76-15, 5 heaters at $40, total, $200.
G. Thompson, No. 76-16, $300.
3 W. Squire, No. 76-17, $500.
T. Campbell, No. 76-18, $195.
8 T. Campbell, No. 76-19, $205.
R. Mask, No. 76-20, $125.
10 W. Squire, No. 76-21, $95.
G. Thompson, No. 76-22, $175.
15 T. Campbell, No. 76-23, $430.
W. Squire, No. 76-24, $155.

5. The accounts receivable clerk's job at Crawford Enterprises includes recording money received from customers. Record the following cash receipts as credits in the customer accounts used in exercise 4.

Feb. 15 T. Campbell, $195 for invoice 76-18.
R. Mask, $200 for invoice 76-15.
G. Thompson, $100 towards payment of invoice 76-16.
18 T. Campbell, $205 for invoice 76-19.
W. Squire, $500 for invoice 76-17.
28 G. Thompson, $375 for invoices 76-16 and 76-22.
W. Squire, $95 for invoice 76-21.

6. Prepare a schedule of accounts receivable dated February 28 for the Accounts Receivable Ledger of Crawford Enterprises. Your schedule should total $710.

7. a) As the accounts receivable clerk for Crawford Enterprises, perform the following duties:

i) Set up the following accounts and balances in the Accounts Receivable Ledger:

• T. Campbell	$430
• R. Mask	125
• W. Squire	155
• G. Thompson	nil

ii) Post the following source documents directly to the Accounts Receivable Ledger:

March 2 Sales Invoices:
W. Squire, No. 76-25, $355
R. Mask, No. 76-26, $37

March 3 Sales Invoices:
R. Mask, No. 76-27, $670
G. Thompson, No. 76-28, $149

4 List of Cash Receipts:
R. Mask, $125 for inv. 76-20
W. Squire, $155 for inv. 76-24

5 Sales Invoices:
T. Campbell, No. 76-29, $476
R. Mask, No. 76-30, $275
G. Thompson, No. 76-31, $850

5 List of Cash Receipts:
T. Campbell, $430 for invoice 76-23
R. Mask, $707 for invoices 76-26 and 76-27
G. Thompson, $149 for invoice 76-28

iii) Prepare a schedule of accounts receivable dated March 5, 19__.

b) As the accounting supervisor for Crawford Enterprises, perform the following duties:

i) Set up the following accounts and balances in the General Ledger:

ACCOUNT TITLE	ACC. NO.	DEBIT	CREDIT
Cash	101	2109 —	
Accounts Receivable Control	102	710 —	
P. Crawford, Capital	300		2819 —
Sales	400		

ii) Journalize the source documents received from the accounts receivable clerk in exercise 7 a).

iii) Post the Journal to the General Ledger.

8. a) As the accounts payable clerk for Crawford Enterprises, perform the following duties:

i) Set up the following accounts and balances dated March 1 in the Accounts Payable Ledger:

Corbett's Service Station	$160
Grant Equipment	730
Noonan Fuels Ltd.	40
Wilson Supply Ltd.	24

ii) Post the following source documents directly to the Accounts Payable Ledger:

March 9 Purchase Invoices:
Wilson Supply Ltd., No. K-297 for office forms, $87

March 9 Grant Equipment, No. 420 for an office duplicator, $1 279

10 Purchase Invoices:
Corbett's Service Station, No. 247 for gas and oil, $12
Noonan Fuels Ltd., No. 7340 for fuel oil, $78

11 Copies of Cheques Issued:
No. 122 to Corbett's Service Station, $160 for invoice 225
No. 123 to Grant Equipment, $295 for the balance of invoice 316

13 Purchase Invoices:
Corbett's Service Station, No. 270 for towing the car and recharging the battery, $25
Wilson Supply Ltd., No. K-373 for stationery, $79

13 Copies of Cheques Issued:
No. 124 to Grant Equipment, $435 for invoices 391 and 421
No. 125 to Noonan Fuels Ltd., $40 for invoice 6983
No. 126 to Corbett's Service Station, $12 for invoice 247

iii) Prepare a schedule of accounts payable dated March 15, 19__.

b) As the accounting supervisor for Crawford Enterprises, perform the following duties:

i) Set up the following accounts and balances on March 9 in the General Ledger:

ACCOUNT TITLE	ACC. NO.	DEBIT	CREDIT
Cash	101	5750 —	
Office Supplies	103	—	
Office Equipment	110	—	
Accounts Payable Control	200		954 —
P. Crawford, Capital	300		4796 —
Car Expense	500	—	
Heating Expense	501	—	

ii) Journalize the source documents received from the accounts payable clerk.

iii) Post the above to the General Ledger.

iv) Prepare a trial balance dated March 15, 19__.

9. You are the accounting supervisor for C. Price, Consultants. Journalize the following source documents. Select appropriate account titles for your entries.

April 2 Sales Invoices:
No. 814 to E. Gartner, $450
No. 815 to Bartoch Industries, $976
No. 816 to C. Paterson, $350

April 3 Purchase Invoices:
Matlock Office Equipment, No. 6746, $560 for a new typewriter
Gladstone Service Centre, No. S-340, $129 for repairs to the company car

5 Cash Receipts:
$976, Bartoch Industries for invoice 815
$570 received for services provided to customers for cash

5 Cheque Copies:
No. 341 to Matlock Office Equipment, $560 for invoice 6736
No. 342 to C. Price, the owner, $725 for personal use
No. 343 to Olympia Realties, $950 for the April rent

Exercises Part B

10. a) Prepare an Accounts Receivable Ledger with the following customers' accounts:

- P. Blazyk
- B. McCleave
- W. Santini
- H. Krysiak
- L. Pasmore

b) Post the following source documents directly into the customer accounts:

March 1 Sales Invoices:
No. A-234, L. Pasmore, $75
No. A-235, H. Krysiak, $299
No. A-236, P. Blazyk, $99

4 Sales Invoices:
No. A-237, W. Santini, $250
No. A-238, P. Blazyk, $50
No. A-239, B. McCleave, $365

7 List of Cash Receipts:
P. Blazyk, $99 for invoice A-236
L. Pasmore, $75 for invoice A-234
H. Krysiak, $100, part payment of invoice A-235

10 Sales Invoices:
No. A-240, L. Pasmore, $179
No. A-241, B. McCleave, $325
No. A-242, W. Santini, $295

13 List of Cash Receipts:
P. Blazyk, $50 for invoice A-238
H. Krysiak, $199, balance of invoice A-235

c) Prepare an Accounts Payable Ledger with accounts with the following creditors:

- *The Daily Sentinel*
- Kars Stationers
- Dalton Motors
- Shavers Equipment

d) Post the following source documents directly into the creditor accounts:

March 16 Purchase Invoices:
Shavers Equipment, No. C-3478, $3 500 for typewriters
Kars Stationers, No. 6757, $250 for office supplies

March 19 Purchase Invoices:

The Daily Sentinel, No. 37E876, $450 for advertising space
Dalton Motors, No. S-73463, $147 for repairing the truck
Kars Stationers, No. 6816, $110 for envelopes and paper with letterhead

23 Cheque copies:

No. 430 to Shavers Equipment, $2 000 as part payment of invoice C-3478
No. 431 to *The Daily Sentinel,* $450 for invoice 37E876
No. 432 to Dalton Motors, $147 for invoice S-73463

24 Purchase Invoices:

Shavers Equipment, No. C-3650, $98 for servicing the typewriters
Dalton Motors, No. S-73774, $17 for gas and oil

28 Cheque copies:

No. 433 to Shavers Equipment, $1 500 for the balance of invoice 3478
No. 434 to Kars Stationers, $360 for invoices 6757 and 6816

e) Prepare a General Ledger with the following accounts and balances on March 1:

ACCOUNT TITLE	ACC. NO.	DEBIT	CREDIT
Cash	100	4600 —	
Accounts Receivable Control	101	—	
Office Supplies	102	—	
Equipment	103	—	
Truck	104	9500 —	
Accounts Payable Control	200		—
S. Blythe, Capital	300		14100 —
Sales	400		—
Advertising Expense	500	—	
Truck Expense	501	—	
Equipment Repairs Expense	502	—	

f) Journalize all source documents from parts b) and d).
g) Post the Journal to the General Ledger.
h) On March 31, prepare:
   i) a schedule of accounts receivable
   ii) a schedule of accounts payable
   iii) a trial balance of the General Ledger

11. The accounts and balances in the three ledgers for Holmes Consulting Services are as follows:

Holmes Consulting Services Schedule of Accounts Receivable February 28, 19__	
A. Battista Ltd.	250 —
S. Morgan & Co.	600 —
L. Quinn Inc.	85 —
M. Wong	1 250 —
	2 185 —

Holmes Consulting Services Schedule of Accounts Payable February 28, 19__	
Dustbane Enterprises	90 —
Matheson Office Supplies	195 —
Potter's Texaco	—
Underwood Equipment Ltd.	470 —
	755 —

Holmes Consulting Services
General Ledger Trial Balance
February 28, 19__

ACCOUNT TITLE	ACC. NO.	DEBIT	CREDIT
Cash	101	1 000 —	
Accounts Receivable Control	102	2 185 —	
Office Supplies	103	500 —	
Equipment	113	4 000 —	
Automobile	114	6 000 —	
Accounts Payable Control	200		755 —
A. Holmes, Capital	300		12 930 —
A. Holmes, Drawing	301	—	
Fees Income	400		—
Cleaning Expense	500	—	
Car Expense	501	—	
		13 685 —	13 685 —

In this exercise, you will perform the duties of three different employees of Holmes Consulting Services:

- the accounts receivable clerk
- the accounts payable clerk
- the senior accountant

a) Open three ledgers and record the balances from the preceding information.
b) Perform the accounts receivable clerk's job by posting the sales invoices and cash receipts from the March transactions listed below into customer accounts. Then prepare the March 31 schedule of accounts receivable.
c) Perform the accounts payable clerk's job by posting the purchase invoices and cheque copies into the creditor accounts. Then prepare the March 31 schedule of accounts payable.
d) Journalize all the following source documents and post to the General Ledger. Prepare the March 31 General Ledger trial balance.

March 1 Sales Invoices:
No. 309, L. Quinn Inc., $450
No. 310, M. Wong, $300
No. 311, A. Battista Ltd., $200
No. 312, S. Morgan & Co., $500

3 List of Cash Receipts:
$85, L. Quinn Inc.
$200, S. Morgan & Co.

5 Purchase Invoices:
Dustbane Enterprises, No. F-301, $90 for cleaning office
Potter's Texaco, $85, gasoline for the company's automobile
Underwood Equipment Ltd., No. 189, $300 for equipment

8 Sales Invoices:
No. 313, L. Quinn Inc., $200
No. 314, S. Morgan & Co., $450

10 Cheque Copies:
$90 to Dustbane Enterprises
$470 to Underwood Equipment Ltd.

15 Purchase Invoices:
Dustbane Enterprises, No. F-396, $90 for cleaning office
Matheson Office Supplies, No. M-201, $65 for office supplies
Potter's Texaco, $70 for repairs to the company car and $40 for gasoline for Holmes' family car, total $110

17 List of Cash Receipts:
$100 from A. Battista Ltd.
$400 from S. Morgan & Co.
$250 from M. Wong
$295 received from providing services to two customers for cash

March 20 Cheque Copies:
$85 to Potter's Texaco, on account
$195 to Matheson Office Supplies, on account
$500 to A. Holmes for personal use

24 List of Cash Receipts:
$150, A. Battista Ltd.
$450, L. Quinn Inc.
$300 received from cash services

31 Cheque Copies:
$180 to Dustbane Enterprises
$110 to Potter's Texaco

31 Sales Invoices:
No. 315, $500 to A. Battista Ltd.
No. 316, $285 to L. Quinn Inc.

31 Purchase Invoice:
$50 for gasoline for company car, Potter's Texaco

Exercises Part C

12. For this exercise you will perform the duties of three different employees of Carlo's T.V. Repairs:

- the accounts receivable clerk
- the accounts payable clerk
- the senior accountant

The accounts in the three ledgers with their balances are as follows:

Carlo's T.V. Repairs
Schedule of Accounts Receivable
May 3, 19__

B. Dover	35.60
Drive-Inn Motor Hotel	356.70
L. Malyk	26.70
	419.00

Carlo's T.V. Repairs
Schedule of Accounts Payable
May 3, 19__

Electronic Suppliers	675.83
Melvyn's Body Repairs	—
Poulin's Service Station	69.96
	745.79

Carlo's T.V. Repairs General Ledger Trial Balance May 3, 19__			
ACCOUNT TITLE	**ACC. NO.**	**DEBIT**	**CREDIT**
Cash	101	7 350 —	
Accounts Receivable Control	102	419 —	
Repair Parts	103	2 470 —	
Equipment	110	25 000 —	
Truck	111	8 000 —	
Accounts Payable Control	201		745 79
C. Amato, Capital	301		42 493 21
C. Amato, Drawing	302	—	
Sales	401		—
Truck Expense	502	—	
Rent Expense	504	—	
		43 239 —	43 239 —

a) Open the three ledgers and record the balances.
b) In the Accounts Receivable Ledger, record the appropriate source documents given on May 4 and May 5, then prepare a schedule of accounts receivable.
c) In the Accounts Payable Ledger, record the appropriate source documents and other transactions given on May 5, then prepare a schedule of accounts payable.
d) Record all source documents in the Journal, post to the General Ledger, and prepare a trial balance of the General Ledger.

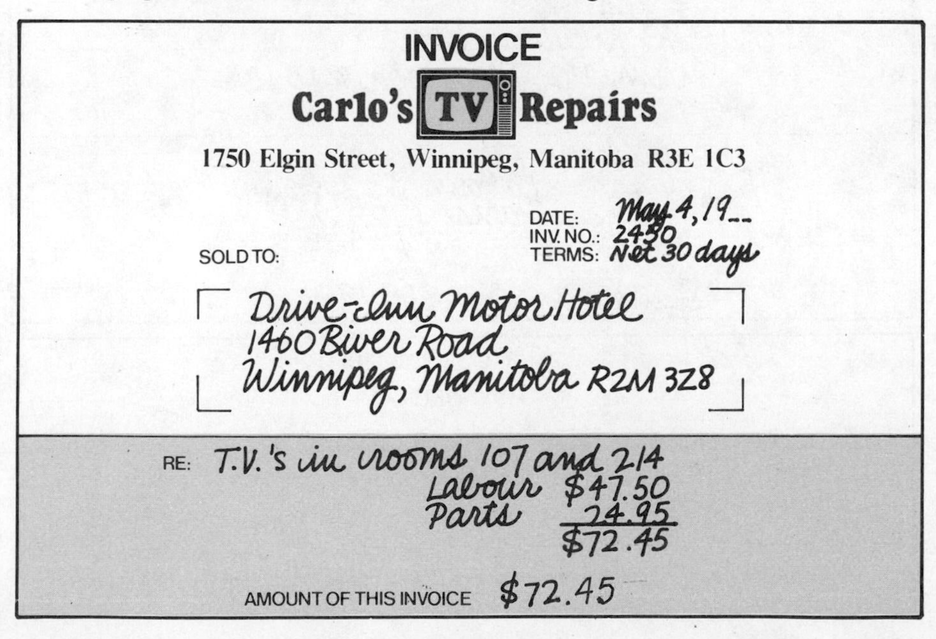
INVOICE

Carlo's TV Repairs

1750 Elgin Street, Winnipeg, Manitoba R3E 1C3

DATE: May 4, 19__
INV. NO.: 2450
TERMS: Net 30 days

SOLD TO:

Drive-Inn Motor Hotel
1460 River Road
Winnipeg, Manitoba R2M 3Z8

RE: T.V.'s in rooms 107 and 214
Labour $47.50
Parts 24.95
$72.45

AMOUNT OF THIS INVOICE $72.45

INVOICE

Carlo's TV Repairs

1750 Elgin Street, Winnipeg, Manitoba R3E 1C3

DATE: May 4, 19--
INV. NO.: 2451
TERMS: net 30 days

SOLD TO:

B. Dover
141 Dynes Road
Winnipeg, Manitoba R2K 0T9

RE: G.E. B/W T.V.

Labour $27.50
Parts 18.40
$45.90

AMOUNT OF THIS INVOICE $45.90

INVOICE

Carlo's TV Repairs

1750 Elgin Street, Winnipeg, Manitoba R3E 1C3

DATE: May 4, 19--
INV. NO.: 2452
TERMS: net 30 days

SOLD TO:

L. Malyk
543 Kilburn Street
Winnipeg, Manitoba R2B 1B1

RE: Sony Colour T.V.

Labour $32.45
Parts 22.74
$55.19

AMOUNT OF THIS INVOICE $55.19

DAILY CASH RECEIPTS

May 4, 19--

Customer	Invoice	Amount
L. Malyk	2340	$ 26.70
Drive-Inn Motor Hotel	2355	137.50
Cash Sales		247.65
Total Deposited		$411.85

ELECTRONIC SUPPLIERS

Montreal
Toronto
Winnipeg
Vancouver

147 Industrial Blvd., Winnipeg, Manitoba R2W 0J7

SOLD TO	Terms: Net 15 days	SHIP TO
Carlo's T.V. Repairs 1750 Elgin Street Winnipeg, Manitoba R3E 1C3		Same

Fed. Sales Tax No.	Prov. Sales Tax No.	Date Invoiced	Invoice No.
S 47354	435 70913	May 4, 19--	7463

Quantity	Description	Unit Price	Amount
15	X74S5 Tubes	$ 4.95	$ 74.25
27	TQ 347S Diodes	8.40	226.80
		Pay this amount ▶	$301.05

MELVYN'S BODY REPAIRS

4765 Borden Road, Winnipeg, Manitoba R2C 3C6
Telephone: 422-7368

Name: Carlo's T.V. Repairs **Inv. No.** 74709
Address: 1750 Elgin St. **Terms:** Net 30 days
Winnipeg, Manitoba
R3E 1C3
Make: GMC Truck **Licence:** A-4597
Date: May 4, 19--

Quantity	Description	Unit Price	Amount
1	Fender	$ 98.70	$ 98.70
4	Brackets	2.45	9.80
			$108.50
	Labour		287.45
		Pay this amount ▶	$395.95

Electronic Suppliers		May 4, 19--		Cheque No. 576
Date	Item	Amount	Discount	Net Amount
April 15	Inv. 6546	$203.76		
17	Inv. 6567	14.83		$218.59

Poulin's Service Station		May 4, 19--		Cheque No. 577
Date	Item	Amount	Discount	Net Amount
April 10	Inv. B-376	$24.50		
15	Inv. B-437	9.76		
20	Inv. B-533	35.70		$69.96

Cochran Realties		May 4, 19--		Cheque No. 578
Date	Item	Amount	Discount	Net Amount
Rent for May				$1 250.00

Other Transactions

May 5 Sales Invoices:
No. 2453 to Drive-Inn Motor Hotel, $157.65
No. 2454 to L. Malyk, $23.55

Daily Cash Receipts:
B. Dover, $35.60 on account
Cash Sales $367.30

Purchase Invoices:
Electronic Suppliers, No. 7510, $276.30 for parts
Poulin's Service Station, No. B-675, $81.50 for a tune-up on the truck

Cheque copies:
No. 579 to Melvyn's Body Repairs, $150 as part payment of invoice 74709
No. 580 to C. Amato, the owner, $270 for personal use

Accounting in Action

Case 1

What Would You Do? George S. is the accounts payable clerk for Clifford Enterprises. He is considered a reliable employee. Frank Clifford, the firm's owner, lets George "run his own show" and rarely checks the work done by George.

George is responsible for matching purchase orders, receiving reports, and purchase invoices. He audits the invoices and checks them for mathematical accuracy. Invoices are then initialed by George. A cheque is prepared, attached to the invoice, and presented to Mr. Clifford. The cheques are routinely signed by Mr.

Clifford. He assumes the invoice and cheque amounts are correct because "George never makes mistakes" and "George always catches overcharges made by suppliers."

One night, while having dinner with a friend, George meets Gord Chamberlain who is a major supplier of goods to Clifford Enterprises. Gord insists on paying George's check and buys him an expensive bottle of wine, saying, "It's the least we can do for such a good customer."

Soon afterwards, George is invited by Chamberlain to play golf at the Hunt Club. After a game of golf and dinner, George receives an offer: in return for accepting phoney invoices from Chamberlain's company and getting them paid by Mr. Clifford, George will be paid half the amount of each cheque. Chamberlain argues that George can earn $500 a month with no risk of being caught since he has the authority to approve invoices and his work is never questioned. George realizes he could get away with this plan without being caught.

a) If you were George, what would you do?
b) List several of the alternatives open to George.
c) What are the consequences of each alternative?

Case 2

Balancing the Accounts Receivable Ledger The following transactions were journalized and posted to the General Ledger of P & C Gusen Ltd. during May:

- Sales on account $10 800
- Cash received from customers 9 700
- Cash sales 4 200

The schedule of accounts receivable prepared on May 31 shows a total of $5 800 owed by customers.

a) Open a T-account for Accounts Receivable Control. The May 1 balance is $4 600.
b) Record the May transactions involving Accounts Receivable to the T-account. Determine the May 31 balance in the Accounts Receivable Control account.
c) Have any errors been made involving Accounts Receivable? Give reasons for your answer.

Case 3

Accounts Receivable Ledger Hamilton Clothiers has been a successful clothing store for a number of years. The business has a large number of faithful customers who have charge accounts, and an accounts receivable clerk is employed full-time to handle these customer accounts. The clerk's salary is $12 500.

In the last few years, many of the customers have begun to use credit cards such as Master Charge and Visa. The table below illustrates this trend:

Year	Total Charge Sales	Hamilton Clothier Charge Accounts	Master Charge and Visa Cards
19_1	$120 000	$100 000	$20 000
19_2	140 000	90 000	50 000
19_3	145 000	75 000	70 000
19_4	150 000	60 000	90 000

The general manager feels that a change should be made in the method of handling charge sales.

a) Prepare several alternatives for the manager's consideration. List the possible consequences of each alternative.
b) What other information would you like to have in order to solve this problem?

Case 4

Purchasing and Accounts Payable Systems Macval Developments is a builder of single and semi-detached homes. It completes and sells about 175 residences a year such as the one in Figure 8.12. It has 20 full-time and about 15 part-time employees.

Figure 8.12 *A home built by Macval Developments*

Although it appears to operate as an independent company, Macval is a wholly owned division of Campeau Corporation, a large land developer and builder. Macval is one of many divisions in the Campeau organization. Figure 8.13 illustrates how Macval is organized and administered.

Macval's Accounting System At Macval, the chief accountant is responsible for the payroll, payments, receipts, and banking. The accounts payable clerk receives, checks, and records purchase invoices. A one-write system (see Chapter 11) of accounting is used for payroll and accounts payable. Monthly summaries of all sources of original entry are sent to a public accounting firm which processes the data and prepares an updated General Ledger, a trial balance, and financial statements (income statement and balance sheet).

Purchasing System Macval purchases goods and services from about 200 creditors. A contracts manager negotiates contracts with subcontractors for a variety of building services such as bricklaying, electrical work, plumbing, foundation forming, framing, roofing, and drywall application. As well as purchasing these services, the contracts manager issues purchase orders for construction materials and other sundry items used by Macval.

Copies of each purchase order and of the service contracts are kept on file by the

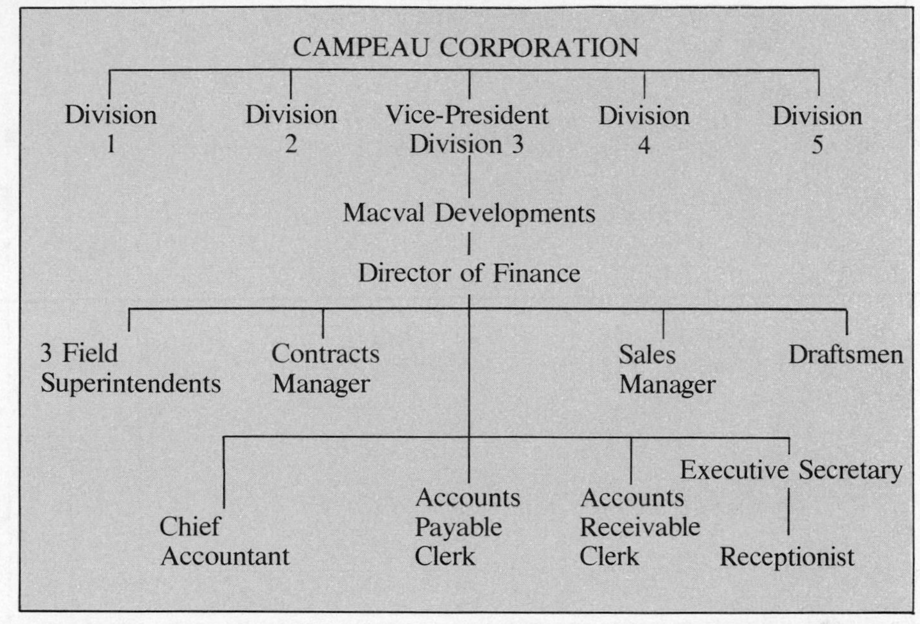

Figure 8.13 *Organization chart for Campeau Corporation and in particular Division 3*

accounts payable clerk. The chief accountant maintains a list of payment dates in order to plan the cash flow and to ensure that payments are made on time. Following is a description of the steps followed for a typical purchase of goods or services.

Work Completed Slip This form, shown in Figure 8.14, is required for all services and material used by Macval. It must be authorized by the field supervisor on the job site. A copy is kept by the contractor or supplier and a copy is sent to the accounts payable clerk, usually attached to the contractor's invoice (Figure 8.15).

Purchase Invoice When an invoice is received from a creditor by the accounts payable clerk, it is matched with the purchase order (Figure 8.16) and the work completed slip. The clerk checks the extensions for mathematical accuracy and then codes the invoice with the number of the General Ledger account to be debited.

Contracts Manager Since the contracts manager negotiates the price for the purchase, the invoice is initialed by the contracts manager if the price quoted is correct.

Director of Finance The complete set of documents supporting the purchase is examined and the General Ledger coding approved by the director of finance. The papers are then returned to the accounts payable clerk.

Accounts Payable Clerk When a batch of approved invoices has accumulated, the accounts payable clerk sets up the one-write board. The invoices are journalized and posted to the creditor's accounts. The documents are then filed in an unpaid file kept by the chief accountant.

WORK COMPLETED

SUB-TRADE: Drafting
FOREMAN: Glen McSweeney
PROJECT: Craig Henry
LOT-UNIT: M-17

ROUGHING	FINISHING
DATE: June	DATE: July

REMARKS:	OFFICE
Blueprints	

Macval Developments No. 3149

Macval Developments No. 3149

Macval Developments No. 3149

Figure 8.14 *Work completed slip*

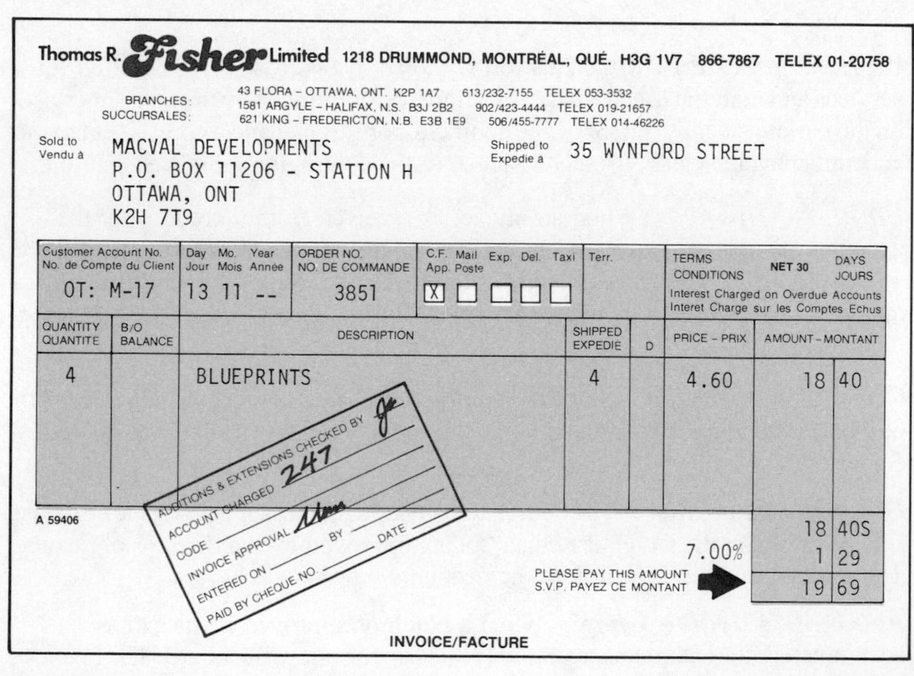

Thomas R. Fisher Limited 1218 DRUMMOND, MONTRÉAL, QUÉ. H3G 1V7 866-7867 TELEX 01-20758

BRANCHES: / SUCCURSALES:
43 FLORA – OTTAWA, ONT. K2P 1A7 613/232-7155 TELEX 053-3532
1581 ARGYLE – HALIFAX, N.S. B3J 2B2 902/423-4444 TELEX 019-21657
621 KING – FREDERICTON, N.B. E3B 1E9 506/455-7777 TELEX 014-46226

Sold to / Vendu à
MACVAL DEVELOPMENTS
P.O. BOX 11206 - STATION H
OTTAWA, ONT
K2H 7T9

Shipped to / Expedie a
35 WYNFORD STREET

Customer Account No. / No. de Compte du Client	Day Mo. Year / Jour Mois Année	ORDER NO. / NO. DE COMMANDE	C.F. App. / Mail Poste / Exp. / Del. / Taxi	Terr.	TERMS / CONDITIONS NET 30 DAYS / JOURS
OT: M-17	13 11 --	3851	X (C.F. App.)		Interest Charged on Overdue Accounts / Interet Charge sur les Comptes Echus

QUANTITY / QUANTITE	B/O / BALANCE	DESCRIPTION	SHIPPED / EXPEDIE	D	PRICE – PRIX	AMOUNT – MONTANT
4		BLUEPRINTS	4		4.60	18 40
						18 40S
					7.00%	1 29
					PLEASE PAY THIS AMOUNT / S.V.P. PAYEZ CE MONTANT	19 69

A 59406

ADDITIONS & EXTENSIONS CHECKED BY Jc
ACCOUNT CHARGED 247
CODE
INVOICE APPROVAL ____ BY ____ DATE ____
ENTERED ON
PAID BY CHEQUE NO.

INVOICE/FACTURE

Figure 8.15 *Invoice received November 13 from a supplier and attached to work completed slip for reference*

PURCHASE ORDER

macval developments

No. 3851
Show this Number on all Invoices

Date Nov. 1, 19--

This authorizes T. R. Fisher Ltd.
43 Flora Street
Ottawa, Ontario K2P 1A7

To supply the following Work or Material
Project
Location
Lot Number

Quantity	Description	Unit	Price
4	Blueprints	4.60	18.40
	SALES TAX 7%		1.29
	TOTAL		19.69

Checked By ____ Ordered by ____

Checked By ____ Ordered by ____

Checked By ____ Ordered by ____

Figure 8.16 *Purchase order prepared on November 1 to order blueprints*

Cheque Requisition The accountant completes a cheque requisition as shown in Figure 8.17 (usually covering several invoices) and sends the request along with the supporting documents to the director of finance. If everything is in order, the cheque request is authorized by the director of finance.

Voucher Cheque A pre-numbered cheque, Figure 8.18, is typed by the company receptionist who imprints the amount using a cheque protector. The cheque requires two signatures, those of the director of finance and the vice-president. The receptionist then mails the signed cheque to the creditor.

Cheque Register The chief accountant uses the cheque requisition as the source document for an entry in the cheque register and in the creditor's account. These entries are recorded by means of a one-write board.

Accounts Payable Clerk The tasks performed by the accounts payable clerk at Macval are summarized as follows:

- Match: purchase invoice
  purchase order
  work completed slip
- check and code invoice

macval developments

No. ________

CHEQUE REQUISITION

Date Nov. 20 19 --

NAME: T. R. Fisher

ADDRESS: 43 Flora Street, Ottawa, Ontario K3P 1A7

AMOUNT: $19.69

EXPLANATION: Invoice A59406
Our Order No. 3851
4 Blueprints @ $4.60 each
Sales tax $1.29

LEDGER ACCOUNT: 247

Approved by L. Moulds

Figure 8.17 *Cheque requisition prepared on November 20 to pay the invoice*

PAYMENT OF THE FOLLOWING INVOICES

REF	$	
A59406	19	69
	19	69

macval developments

G3820

A DIVISION OF CAMPEAU CORPORATION
Ottawa, Canada

Nov. 21 19--

PAYEZ A L'ORDRE DE
PAY TO THE ORDER OF T. R. Fisher $ 19.69

LA SOMME DE
THE SUM OF Nineteen -------------------- 69 /100 DOLLARS

THE BANK OF NOVA SCOTIA
OTTAWA, ONTARIO

GENERAL ACCOUNT

Per ________
Per ________

Figure 8.18 *Voucher cheque drawn up on November 21*

- journalize approved invoices
- post approved invoices to creditor accounts
- prepare monthly accounts payable summary

Accounting Control A good accounting system should reduce the possibility of error to a minimum and remove opportunities for employees and suppliers to be dishonest.

Some of the ways in which Macval achieves accounting control are:

- Division of tasks: The accounts payable clerk records approved invoices, the accountant records payments, and the receptionist prepares and mails the cheques.
- Numbered cheques: Numbered cheques, signed by two senior officers and printed by a cheque protector, are used.
- Supporting documents: Invoices and cheque requests must be supported by documents which indicate that the invoiced material was received, that prices were correct, and that correct accounts have been used to record the data.

Answer the following questions about Macval Developments; they will help you find out whether or not you understand the accounting operations of this business.

a) How many different people are involved in recording, authorizing, and paying a purchase invoice? Give their job titles. Why are so many people involved?
b) Why does Macval have the accounts payable clerk record the invoices and another person, the chief accountant, record the payment of the invoices?
c) How many signatures are required on each cheque?
d) Why are the cheques numbered?
e) Identify by title the individuals who would have to get together in order to cheat the Macval company by using phoney invoices to embezzle money.

Career Profile

An Accounts Receivable Clerk In this career profile we will examine Deanna Wong's job with D. S. Fraser & Co. Ltd. The company's head office is in Ottawa. It has branch offices in Moncton and Fredericton, New Brunswick, Halifax, Nova Scotia, and Pembroke, Sault Ste. Marie, Timmins, and Sudbury, Ontario. D. S. Fraser is a wholesaler of heating and refrigeration equipment. It buys from the manufacturer and sells to companies that in turn sell or install the equipment. Among Fraser's customers are fuel oil dealers, engineering firms, and mechanical equipment firms.

Deanna began work with Fraser's two years ago, immediately after graduating from high school. While in school, she took three accounting courses including applied accounting. The posting machine was taught in the applied accounting course; learning to use this machine was very helpful to Deanna on the job.

Deanna is also responsible for posting the cash received from customers. A list of all cheques received in head office is prepared in the mail room. The cheques are endorsed and immediately deposited in the bank. The list then is given to Deanna. From this list, Deanna posts credits (decreases) to the correct customer accounts.

Deanna enjoys working at Fraser's and the friendly people in her office. She has an aptitude for accounting and feels fortunate to have a career in this field.

CHAPTER 9

The Merchandising Company

Unit 22

Types of Business Operation

*1

A service company sells services.

Service Companies Up to this point, accounting procedures have been illustrated mainly by reference to businesses such as a motel, cinema, contractor, doctor, etc. All of these businesses offer services to their customers. They do not sell products like mouthwash or tires; they sell services and are called *service companies*.

A merchandising company sells a product.

Merchandising Companies Many businesses sell products, not services, and are known as *merchandising companies*. Both wholesalers and retailers are included in this group. Retailers usually buy merchandise from wholesalers or manufacturers and sell it to their customers at a price that covers their costs and provides a net income.

A manufacturing company makes a product.

Manufacturing Companies A firm that converts raw materials into saleable products is called a *manufacturing* company. Usually, a manufacturer sells its products to merchandising companies such as retailers and wholesalers.

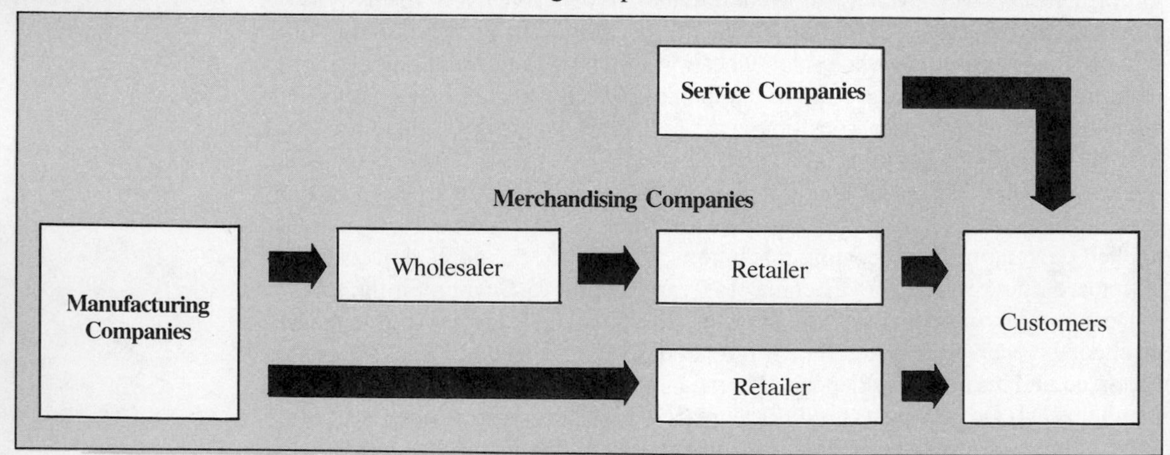

Figure 9.1 *There are three basic types of business operation*

Figure 9.2 *Warrendon Sports – a merchandising company*

Warrendon Sports

The accounting procedures of a merchandising company are a little different from those of a service company. The differences can be illustrated by examining Warrendon Sports, a retail store located in Ottawa.

*2

Goods bought for resale are called merchandise.

Warrendon Sports buys bicycles, hockey equipment, baseball equipment, and hundreds of other sporting goods from manufacturers such as Spalding, CCM, Winwell, and Slazenger. The goods bought from these manufacturers and sold to Warrendon's customers are called *merchandise*. The total dollar value of goods on hand is found in an account called *Merchandise Inventory*.

The Merchandise Inventory account represents the total dollar value of goods on hand.

Determining the Net Income for a Merchandising Company

*3

To calculate the net income for a service business, expenses are subtracted from the revenue. This calculation is illustrated by an equation as follows:

Revenue – Expenses = Net Income

A merchandising business must buy and pay for the merchandise it sells as well as pay the expenses of operating the business. These two equations illustrate how net income is calculated for a merchandising company.

Revenue – Cost of Goods Sold = Gross Profit
Gross Profit – Expenses = Net Income

Warrendon Sports Income Statement For the Month of March, 19__		
Revenue		
Sales		28 000 00
Cost of Goods Sold		
Cost of goods sold		17 000 00
Gross profit		11 000 00
Operating Expenses		
Advertising	1 200 00	
Delivery	400 00	
Office	300 00	
Miscellaneous	200 00	
Rent	1 300 00	
Salaries	2 700 00	
Utilities	200 00	
Total expenses		6 300 00
Net income		4 700 00

Figure 9.3 *Income statement for Warrendon Sports*

*4

In the income statement form used by Warrendon Sports, a single total, $17 000, appears in the cost of goods sold section. This total includes all the costs involved in purchasing the merchandise to be sold. It is arrived at by the completion of the schedule of cost of goods sold illustrated in Figure 9.4. The use of this schedule simplifies the presentation of the income statement.

Warrendon Sports Schedule of Cost of Goods Sold For March, 19__		
Merchandise inventory, March 1	8 000 00	
Add purchases of merchandise	18 000 00	
Total cost of merchandise	26 000 00	
Less merchandise inventory, March 31	9 000 00	
Cost of goods sold		17 000 00

Figure 9.4 *Schedule of cost of goods sold for Warrendon Sports*

The calculations performed in determining the cost of goods sold can be illustrated as follows.

Beginning Inventory	+	Purchases of Merchandise	−	Ending Inventory	=	Cost of Goods Sold
$8 000	+	$18 000	−	$9 000	=	$17 000

Chart of Accounts for a Merchandising Business

Unit 23

*5

As has been shown, the income statement for a merchandising business contains a new section – the cost of goods sold section. For each item in this section, there is an account in the General Ledger. Figure 9.5 lists the accounts usually found in the General Ledger of a merchandising company. Notice that there are six sections in the General Ledger of a merchandising company. The General Ledger of a service business has five sections. New accounts shown in Figure 9.5 are Sales Returns and Allowances, Purchases, Purchase Returns and Allowances, Transportation on Purchases, and Merchandise Inventory.

A Merchandising Company
Chart of Accounts

Section		No.	Title
1.	Assets	101	Cash
		102	Accounts Receivable
		103	Merchandise Inventory
		104	Store Supplies
		105	Office Supplies
		150	Land and Building
		151	Equipment
2.	Liabilities	200	Accounts Payable
		201	Bank Loan
		251	Mortgage Payable
3.	Equity	300	Owner's Capital
		301	Owner's Drawing
		302	Income Summary
4.	Revenue	400	Sales
		401	Sales Returns and Allowances
5.	Cost of Merchandise	500	Purchases
		501	Transportation on Purchases
		502	Purchases Returns and Allowances
6.	Expenses	600	Advertising
		601	Delivery
		602	Miscellaneous
		603	Office
		604	Salaries
		605	Utilities

Figure 9.5 *Chart of accounts for a merchandising company*

The cost of merchandise purchased for resale is recorded in the Purchases account.

Purchases The *Purchases account* is used to record the cost of merchandise bought for resale. The cost of goods purchased is one of the major costs of operating a merchandising business. Because costs (like expenses) decrease the net income and ultimately owner's equity, the Purchases account is debited when merchandise for resale is purchased. The following transactions illustrate the debit and credit theory for the new merchandising accounts.

Transaction 1 Warrendon Sports purchases $500 worth of sports equipment from CCM. A cheque is issued in payment. The two accounts involved are Cash and Purchases. Cash, an asset, decreases and is credited. Purchases, a cost account, is debited because it reduces owner's equity.

Cash	
	500

Purchases	
500	

*6

Transaction 2 Hockey equipment worth $200 is purchased on account from Spalding Ltd. Payment is to be made in 30 days. The two accounts involved are Purchases and Accounts Payable/Spalding Ltd. Spalding Ltd. is a liability account that increases and is credited. Purchases is a cost account and is debited because it reduces owner's equity.

Purchases	
500	
200	

Accounts Payable/ Spalding Ltd.	
	200

*7

The Transportation on Purchases account records the transportation charges on merchandise purchases.

Transaction 3 An invoice for $15 is received from CN Express for transporting merchandise from a manufacturer to Warrendon's store. The invoice is to be paid within 30 days. The cost of transporting merchandise from the supplier to the buyer's place of business is recorded in an account called *Transportation on Purchases.* Since this transaction adds to the costs of operating the business, owner's equity is reduced and therefore the Transportation on Purchases account is debited. The liability account, Accounts Payable/CN Express, increases and is credited.

Transportation on Purchases	
15	

Accounts Payable/ CN Express	
	15

The Delivery Expense account records cost of delivering merchandise to customers.

Transaction 4 Warrendon pays $25 to a local cartage firm for delivering sports equipment sold to customers. The expense of delivering goods to customers is recorded in the *Delivery Expense* account. Delivery expense reduces owner's equity and is debited. Cash, an asset, decreases, and is credited.

Delivery Expense	
25	

Cash	
	500
	25

Returns and Allowances There is always the chance that the buyer of merchandise may not be satisfied with the goods received. The goods may be the wrong size or colour, they may be defective, or they may be unsatisfactory for other reasons. Such goods are either returned to the seller for a full refund or the seller gives the customer an allowance on the selling price. The accounts, Purchases Returns and Allowances and Sales Returns and Allowances are used to record such a transaction.

*8

Transaction 5 A pair of skates is sold to a customer for $45 cash. Cash, an asset, increases and is debited and Sales, a revenue account, is credited because it increases owner's equity.

Cash	
45	500
	25

Sales	
	45

Transaction 6 On trying the skates (Transaction 5), the customer discovers that they are too small and returns them. Because there is no larger size in stock, Warrendon accepts the return of the skates and refunds the purchase price of $45 to the customer.

*9

The Sales account must now be reduced by $45 since the sale was originally recorded in that account (Transaction 5). The decrease side of Sales is the debit side. If returns by customers are infrequent, no special account is necessary and returns are simply recorded by decreasing the Sales account.

Cash	
45	500
	25
	45

Sales	
45	45

However, management may wish to know the amount of goods being returned by customers. In order to provide this information, an account called *Sales Returns and Allowances* is used. The return of the $45 skates is recorded as follows.

The Sales Returns and Allowances account records both the cost of goods returned by customers and the cost of allowances on the price granted to customers for defective merchandise.

Cash	
45	500
	25
	45

Sales Returns and Allowances	
45	

Cash, an asset, is decreased and is credited. The Sales Returns and Allowances account is debited because owner's equity is decreased.

Transaction 7 Tennis equipment worth $60 is sold to a customer, J. Jacques, who agrees to pay within two weeks. The transaction is recorded by debiting Accounts Receivable and crediting Sales.

Accounts Receivable/ J. Jacques	
60	

Sales	
	45
	60

Transaction 8 J. Jacques decides to return the tennis equipment. Warrendon values Jacques as a customer and agrees to accept the goods and to reduce the balance of Jacques' account.

The account Sales Returns and Allowances is debited because owner's equity is decreased. The asset, Accounts Receivable, is decreased with a credit.

Accounts Receivable/ J. Jacques	
60	60

Sales Returns and Allowances	
45	
60	

*10

The Purchases Returns and Allowances account records both the cost of goods returned to a supplier and the decrease in price allowed by a supplier on defective goods.

Transaction 9 In Transaction 1, Warrendon purchased $500 worth of sports equipment from CCM by cheque. Cash was credited and Purchases debited.

Suppose that $100 worth of this purchase is returned to CCM and a cash refund received. Since money is received, Cash is increased with a debit and *Purchases Returns and Allowances* is credited because owner's equity is increased by this transaction.

Cash	
45	500
100	25
	45

Purchases Returns and Allowances	
	100

Transaction 10 In Transaction 2, $200 worth of hockey equipment was purchased from Spalding Ltd. on account. Purchases was debited and Accounts Payable/Spalding Ltd. was credited. This equipment was defective, however, and was returned to Spalding Ltd. The Accounts Payable account, Spalding Ltd., decreases and is debited. The Purchases Returns and allowances account is credited because owner's equity increases.

Accounts Payable/ Spalding Ltd.	
200	200

Purchases Returns and Allowances	
	100
	200

Credit Invoice The source document that is completed when goods are returned is the *credit invoice* as shown in Figure 9.6. The credit invoice is prepared by the seller and sent to the customer. A copy is kept by the seller and used as the basis for the entry reducing the customer's account and for recording the return of merchandise in the Sales Returns account (see Transaction 8).

*11

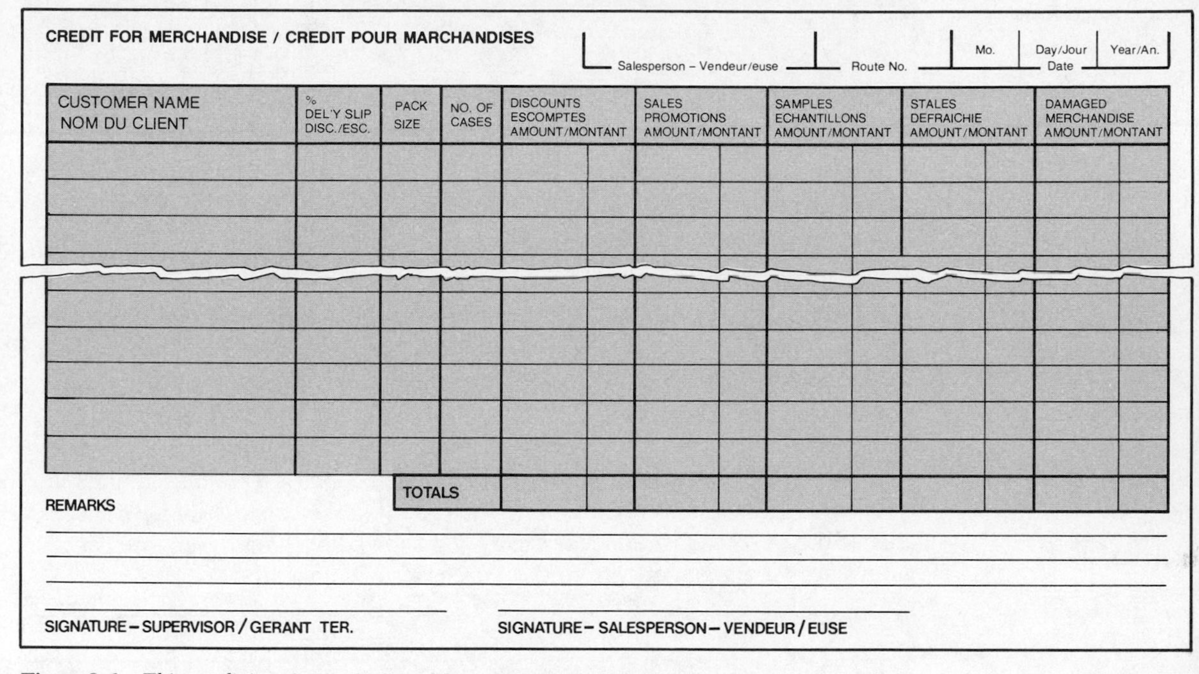

CREDIT FOR MERCHANDISE / CREDIT POUR MARCHANDISES

Salesperson – Vendeur/euse | Route No. | Date: Mo. | Day/Jour | Year/An.

CUSTOMER NAME NOM DU CLIENT	% DEL'Y SLIP DISC./ESC.	PACK SIZE	NO. OF CASES	DISCOUNTS ESCOMPTES AMOUNT/MONTANT	SALES PROMOTIONS AMOUNT/MONTANT	SAMPLES ECHANTILLONS AMOUNT/MONTANT	STALES DEFRAICHIE AMOUNT/MONTANT	DAMAGED MERCHANDISE AMOUNT/MONTANT
		TOTALS						

REMARKS

SIGNATURE – SUPERVISOR / GERANT TER.

SIGNATURE – SALESPERSON – VENDEUR / EUSE

Figure 9.6 *This credit invoice is designed for a manufacturer of food products.*

The credit invoice and its copy are used by both the seller and the buyer to record an entry. The seller records a *sales return* and the buyer, a *purchases return*. Figure 9.6 is an example of a credit invoice form used by Hostess Food Products.

The sample transactions introduced in this chapter deal with a number of new accounts. Since these accounts eventually appear on the income statement or the balance sheet, it is necessary to see how these transactions affect the financial statements.

A credit invoice is a source document issued by the seller to indicate the amount of credit allowed to a customer for returned or defective goods.

Income Statement

Unit 24

*12

Most of the new accounts introduced in this chapter affect one of three sections of the income statement.

Revenue The Sales Returns and Allowances account affects the revenue of a business. When goods are returned by customers, the total revenue is decreased. Figure 9.7 shows how Sales Returns and Allowances are subtracted from Sales to give a figure called *Net Sales*.

Net sales is the figure obtained when sales returns and allowances are subtracted from sales.

Warrendon Sports		
Partial Income Statement		
For the Month of March, 19__		
Revenue		
Sales	29 000 00	
Less Sales Returns and Allowances	1 000 00	
Net Sales		28 000 00

Sales – Sales Returns and Allowances = Net Sales

Figure 9.7 *The income statement, first shown in Figure 9.3, has been expanded to include Sales Returns and Allowances.*

Because the Sales Returns and Allowances account decreases revenue, it is sometimes called a *negative revenue account* or a *contra revenue account*.

*13

Cost of Goods Sold The Purchases, Purchases Returns and Allowances, and Transportation on Purchases accounts all appear in the schedule of cost of goods sold. Figure 9.8 shows that purchases increase the cost of goods sold and are added to the beginning inventory.

Purchases Returns and Allowances When goods are purchased, their cost is recorded in the Purchases account. When goods are returned to the supplier, the cost of the purchase is reduced. Figure 9.8 shows how Purchases Returns and Allowances are subtracted from the Purchases account total.

Warrendon Sports			
Schedule of Cost of Goods Sold			
For March, 19__			
Merchandise Inventory, March 1		8 000 00	
Purchases	21 000 00		
Less Purchases Returns and Allowances	4 000 00		
Net Purchases	17 000 00		
Add Transportation on Purchases	1 000 00	18 000 00	
Total Cost of Merchandise		26 000 00	
Less Merchandise Inventory, March 31		9 000 00	
Cost of Goods Sold			17 000 00

Net purchases is the figure obtained when purchases returns and allowances are subtracted from purchases.

Purchases – Purchases Returns and Allowances = Net Purchases

Figure 9.8 *The schedule of cost of goods sold, first shown in Figure 9.4, has been expanded to include Purchases Returns and Allowances and Transportation on Purchases.*

Transportation on Purchases Transportation charges increase the cost of goods purchased. Figure 9.8 shows that Transportation on Purchases is added to the net purchases.

Delivery Expense The cost of delivering merchandise to customers is recorded in the Delivery Expense account. This account appears in the expenses section of the income statement as shown in Figure 9.3.

*14

Physical Inventory

Before a balance sheet is prepared, someone has to take stock or *physical inventory* of all the merchandise on hand and assess its value. All the merchandise is counted and a total value is calculated. The total value of the merchandise is recorded in the Merchandise Inventory account and is entered on both the schedule of cost of goods sold (Figure 9.4) and the balance sheet. The Merchandise Inventory account appears in the current assets section of the balance sheet as shown in Figure 9.9.

*15

A physical inventory is an actual count of all merchandise on hand.

Warrendon Sports Partial Balance Sheet March 31, 19__		
Assets		
Current Assets		
Bank	4 000 00	
Accounts Receivable	27 000 00	
Merchandise Inventory	9 000 00	
Office Supplies	1 000 00	
Total Current Assets		41 000 00

The asset account, Merchandise Inventory, represents the value of all the merchandise owned.

Figure 9.9 *Current assets section of the balance sheet showing the Merchandise Inventory*

Accounts for a Merchandising Company

Several new accounts have been introduced in this chapter. Figure 9.10 summarizes the recording of debits and credits in these new accounts.

*16

Transactions involving four of the new accounts normally cause a decrease in owner's equity. They are Delivery Expense, Purchases, Transportation on Purchases, and Sales Returns and Allowances. These four accounts usually have a debit balance.

In previous chapters you learned that Sales increase the owner's equity and are recorded as credits. Purchases Returns and Allowances also increase the owner's equity and are recorded as credits. The Purchases Returns and Allowances account usually has a credit balance.

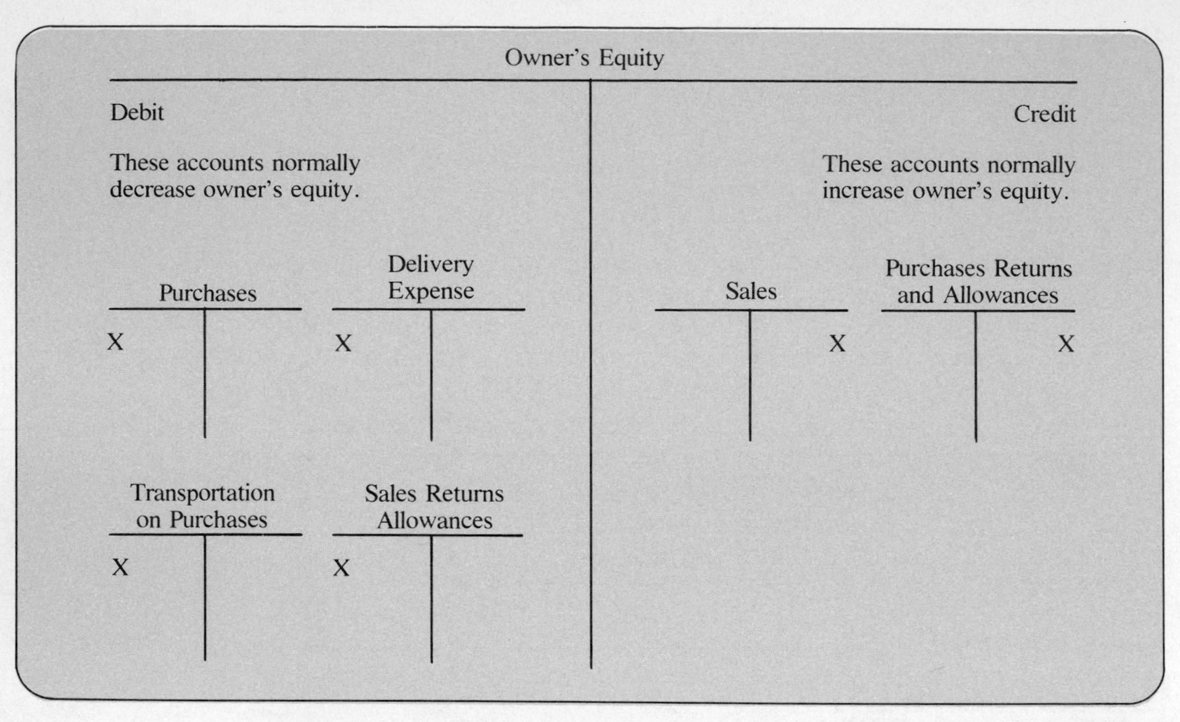

Figure 9.10 *Summary of debits and credits for the new accounts introduced in this chapter*

Facts to Remember

A *service company* sells services.

A *merchandising company* sells a product.

A *manufacturing company* makes a product.

Goods bought for resale are called *merchandise*.

The *Merchandise Inventory account* represents the total dollar value of goods on hand.

The cost of merchandise purchased for resale is recorded in the *Purchases account*.

The *Sales account* records the value of merchandise sold.

The *Transportation on Purchases account* records the transportation charges on merchandise purchased.

The *Delivery Expense account* records the cost of delivering merchandise to customers.

The *Sales Returns and Allowances account* records both the cost of goods returned by customers and the cost of allowances on the price granted to customers for defective merchandise.

The *Purchases Returns and Allowances account* records both the cost of goods returned to a supplier and any decrease in price allowed by a supplier on defective goods.

A *credit invoice* is a source document issued by the seller to indicate the amount of credit allowed to a customer for returned or defective goods.

Net Sales is the figure obtained when sales returns and allowances are subtracted from sales.

Net purchases is the figure obtained when purchases returns and allowances are subtracted from purchases.

The asset account, *Merchandise Inventory,* represents the value of all the merchandise owned.

A *physical inventory* is an actual count of all merchandise on hand.

Checking Your Reading

Questions

1. A business may be classified according to what it does. A company that sells services to customers is called a service business. Name two other types of business and describe what they do.
2. Prepare a list of firms in your area including the names of five companies in each of the three classifications identified in question 1.
3. Explain the terms:
   a) merchandise
   b) merchandise inventory
4. In what account would you record merchandise purchased for resale?
5. What is the difference between the Purchases account and the Office Supplies account?
6. What is the difference between the Purchases account and the Merchandise Inventory account?
7. What account is debited for each of the following items purchased by Johnson's Hardware?
   a) a desk and chair
   b) 10 ladders
   c) typing paper and carbons
   d) 2 000 bags for the check-out counter
   e) 150 lengths of rope for clothes lines
8. What is the difference between the Delivery Expense account and the Transportation on Purchases account?
9. What source document is prepared when goods are returned for credit?
10. Name the statement and section of the statement in which each of the following items appears. The first item is done for you.

Item	Statement	Section
a) Cash	*Balance Sheet*	*Current Asset*
b) Accounts Receivable		
c) Sales		
d) Office Supplies		
e) Purchases		
f) Sales Returns		
g) Salaries Expense		
h) Purchases Returns and Allowances		
i) Delivery Expense		
j) Transportation on Purchases		
k) Building		
l) Beginning Inventory		
m) Ending Inventory		

11. Name the increase side (debit or credit) for each of the following and give a reason for your answer.
a) Purchases
b) Delivery Expense
c) Transportation on Purchases
d) Purchases Returns and Allowances
e) Sales Returns and Allowances

Applying Your Knowledge

Exercises Part A

1. In January, Pelican Gifts had net sales of $2 400 and cost of goods sold of $1 100.
a) What is the gross profit?
b) If expenses totalled $900, what is the net income or net loss?

2. In February, Pelican Gifts' net sales were $3 600 and the cost of goods sold was $2 200. Expenses totalled $960.
a) What is the gross profit for the month?
b) What is the net income or net loss for the month?

3. Pelican Gifts' March figures showed the following: Net Sales $2 300; Cost of Goods Sold $1 200; Total Expenses $1 500.
a) What is the gross profit?
b) What is the net income or net loss?

4. The cost accounts of Lasalle Variety follow. Prepare a schedule of cost of goods sold for each of the following months.
a) Jan. 1: Inventory $5 000; Purchases $1 000; Jan. 31 Inventory $4 000
b) Feb. 1: Inventory $4 000; Purchases $3 000; Feb. 28 Inventory $3 500
c) March 1: Inventory $3 500; Purchases $2 900; Purchases Returns $300;

Transportation on Purchases $190; March 31 Inventory $3 100

d) April 1: Inventory $3 100; Purchases $5 600; Purchases Returns $600; Transportation on Purchases $320; April 30 Inventory $4 700

5. The following two documents have been received by Warrendon Sports:

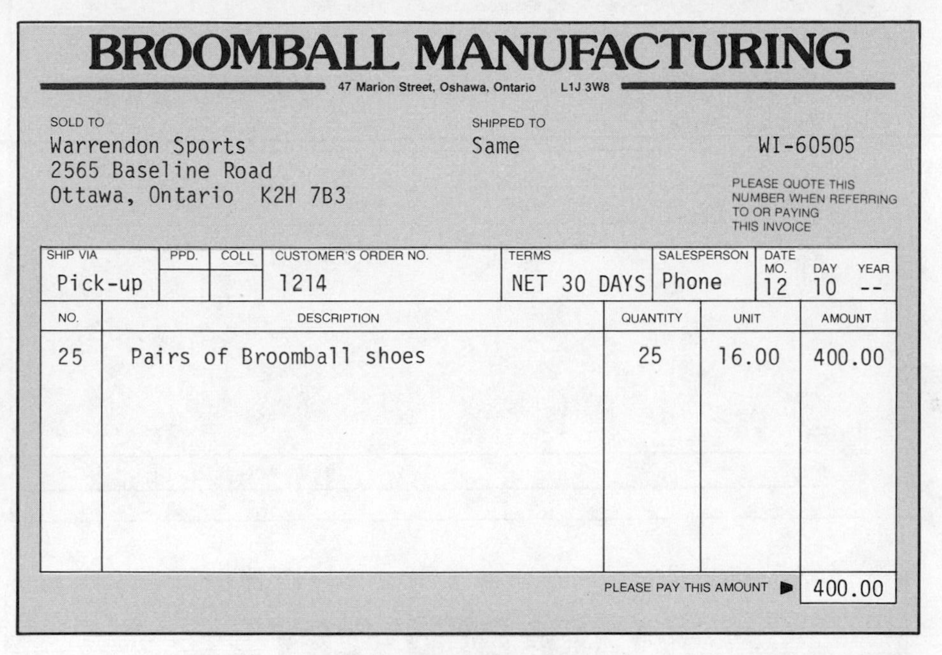

BROOMBALL MANUFACTURING

47 Marion Street, Oshawa, Ontario L1J 3W8

SOLD TO
Warrendon Sports
2565 Baseline Road
Ottawa, Ontario K2H 7B3

SHIPPED TO
Same

WI-60505

PLEASE QUOTE THIS NUMBER WHEN REFERRING TO OR PAYING THIS INVOICE

SHIP VIA	PPD.	COLL	CUSTOMER'S ORDER NO.	TERMS	SALESPERSON	DATE MO.	DAY	YEAR
Pick-up			1214	NET 30 DAYS	Phone	12	10	--

NO.	DESCRIPTION	QUANTITY	UNIT	AMOUNT
25	Pairs of Broomball shoes	25	16.00	400.00

PLEASE PAY THIS AMOUNT ▶ 400.00

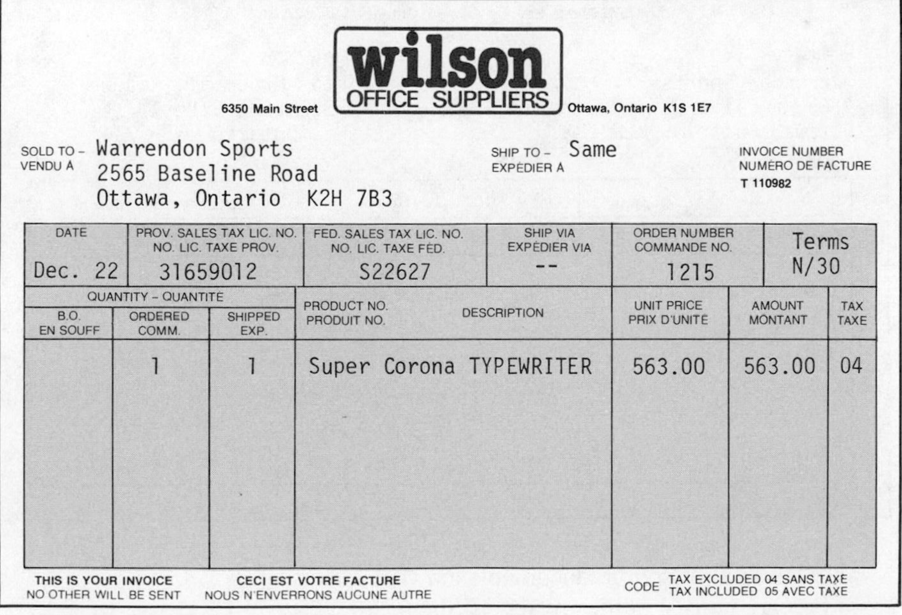

wilson OFFICE SUPPLIERS

6350 Main Street Ottawa, Ontario K1S 1E7

SOLD TO – VENDU A
Warrendon Sports
2565 Baseline Road
Ottawa, Ontario K2H 7B3

SHIP TO – EXPÉDIER A
Same

INVOICE NUMBER
NUMÉRO DE FACTURE
T 110982

DATE	PROV. SALES TAX LIC. NO. NO. LIC. TAXE PROV.	FED. SALES TAX LIC. NO. NO. LIC. TAXE FÉD.	SHIP VIA EXPÉDIER VIA	ORDER NUMBER COMMANDE NO.	
Dec. 22	31659012	S22627	--	1215	Terms N/30

QUANTITY – QUANTITÉ B.O. EN SOUFF	ORDERED COMM.	SHIPPED EXP.	PRODUCT NO. PRODUIT NO. / DESCRIPTION	UNIT PRICE PRIX D'UNITÉ	AMOUNT MONTANT	TAX TAXE
	1	1	Super Corona TYPEWRITER	563.00	563.00	04

THIS IS YOUR INVOICE
NO OTHER WILL BE SENT

CECI EST VOTRE FACTURE
NOUS N'ENVERRONS AUCUNE AUTRE

CODE TAX EXCLUDED 04 SANS TAXE
TAX INCLUDED 05 AVEC TAXE

a) What kind of source documents are they?

b) Prepare journal entries to record them.

6. The following two documents have been received by Warrendon Sports:

OVERLAND TRANSPORT

MONTREAL • OTTAWA • TORONTO

HEAD OFFICE: 1473 Blake Road, Montréal, Québec H3J 1E4

Shipper:

Broomball Manufacturing
49 Marion Street
Oshawa, Ontario L1J 3W8

Consignee:

Warrendon Sports
2565 Baseline Road
Ottawa, Ontario K2H 7B3

TERMS Net 30 days DATE Dec. 12, 19-- INV. NO. CK 4376

Quantity	Containers	Mass	Rate	Amount
3	Boxes	20 kg	0.25/kg	5.00

Pay this amount 5.00

CITY DELIVERY

576 Blythe Rd. Ottawa, Ontario K2A 3N6

Charge

Warrendon Sports
2565 Baseline Road
Ottawa, Ontario K2H 7B3

Deliver to

Carleton Broomball League
1476 Braeside Street
Ottawa, Ontario K1H 7J4

INV. NO. T-7437 TERMS Net 30 days DATE Dec. 20, 19--

Description	Amount
5 Boxes	5.65

a) What kind of source documents are they?
b) Prepare journal entries to record them.

7. The following two documents were issued by Warrendon Sports:

WARRENDON SPORTS

2565 Baseline Road, Ottawa, Ontario K2H 7B3

INVOICE

Order No.

Sold to
Laurentian High School
1357 Baseline Road
Ottawa, Ontario K2C 0A8

Ship to
Same

Date Jan. 3, 19--	Invoice No. 100	Terms net 30 days	Cash	Charge

Quantity	Description	Unit Price	Amount
1	Pr. Bauer Skates, size 10, Black Beauty	65 00	65 00

WARRENDON SPORTS

2565 Baseline Road, Ottawa, Ontario K2H 7B3

INVOICE

Order No.

Sold to
High School of Commerce
300 Rochester Street
Ottawa, Ontario K1R 7N4

Ship to
Same

Date Jan. 3, 19--	Invoice No. 101	Terms net 30 days	Cash	Charge

Quantity	Description	Unit Price	Amount
3	Volleyballs, vinyl specials	9 65	28 95

a) What kind of source documents are they?
b) Prepare journal entries to record them.

8. The following documents were issued by Warrendon Sports:

WARRENDON SPORTS

2565 Baseline Road, Ottawa, Ontario K2H 7B3

INVOICE

Order No.

Sold to
Woodroffe High School
2410 Georgina Drive
Ottawa, Ontario K2B 7M8

Ship to
Same

Date Jan. 4, 19--	Invoice No. 106	Terms net 30 days	Cash	Charge

Quantity	Description	Unit Price		Amount	
30	Hockey Sticks, Koho Supreme	6	50	195	00

WARRENDON SPORTS

2565 Baseline Road, Ottawa, Ontario K2H 7B3

CREDIT INVOICE

Sold to
Woodroffe High School
2410 Georgina Drive
Ottawa, Ontario K2B 7M8

No. 88
Date Jan. 10, 19--

Quantity	Description	Unit Price		Amount	
5	Re: Our invoice No. 106 - hockey sticks received in damaged condition	6	50	32	50

CREDIT

a) What kind of source documents are they?
b) Prepare journal entries to record them.

9. Record the following transactions in a Journal for Warrendon Sports. Use the accounts Cash, Accounts Receivable, Sales, and Sales Returns and Allowances.

March 1 Cash Register Summary:
Cash received from cash sales, $200.

2 Sales Invoices:
No. 301, Nepean Hockey Association, $195.
No. 302, Laurier High School, $85.
No. 303, S. Edgerton, $35.

3 Cash Refund Slip:
No. 29, for $25, refund for the return of a pair of children's skates.

8 Cash Register Summary:
Cash received from cash sales, $350.

9 Credit Invoices:
No. 89, for $75, hockey jackets returned by Nepean Hockey Association – wrong size.

10 Sales Invoices:
No. 304, Kanata Tennis Club, $150.
No. 305, H. Burger, $29.50.

15 Cash Receipts:
Cheques totalling $155 were received from Nepean Hockey Association ($120) and S. Edgerton ($35).

10. The following source documents were received by Warrendon Sports:

SPORTING EQUIPMENT

347 Tachereau Blvd., Montréal, Québec H2C 3B3

INVOICE NUMBER TR89–

SOLD TO Warrendon Sports
2565 Baseline Road
Ottawa, Ontario K2H 7B3

SHIPPED TO Same

Cust. Order No.	Our Order No.	Date Received	Date Shipped	Shipped Via	Invoice Date
1190	T6150	Dec. 13, 19--	Jan. 4, 19--	Our Truck	Jan. 10, 19--
I.C. Number	**Fed. Sales Tax**	**Prov. Sales Tax**	**Terms**	**F.O.B.**	**Salesperson**
	S22627	31659012	NET 30 DAYS		

Qty.	Description	Price	Total
50	Dolphin Clear Goggles	1.80	90.00

PRICES SUBJECT TO CHANGE WITHOUT NOTICE

ORIGINAL INVOICE

CREDIT MEMORANDUM

SPORTING EQUIPMENT

2565 Baseline Road, Ottawa, Ontario K2H 7B3

TO Warrendon Sports
2565 Baseline Road
Ottawa, Ontario K2H 7B3

January 12, 19--

CREDIT NUMBER 1195

WE CREDIT YOUR ACCOUNT AS SPECIFIED BELOW

Re: Invoice TR89-6153, dated January 10, 19--

6 damaged Dolphin Goggles @ $1.80	10.80
TOTAL CREDIT DUE	10.80

a) What kind of source documents are they?
b) Prepare journal entries to record them.

11. Journalize the following transactions for Warrendon Sports. Use the accounts Cash, Accounts Payable, Purchases, Purchases Returns and Allowances, Transportation on Purchases, and Delivery Expense.

March 1 Purchase Invoices:
Cooper Bros., $76.50 for hockey sticks.
CN Express, $8.50 for transportation charges on purchases.

2 Cheque copies:
No. 94, to Dinardo Delivery, $75 for delivery charges on sales to schools.
No. 95, to Merivale High School, $25 for return of unordered sporting goods.

10 Cheque copies:
No. 96, to Spalding Bros., $375 on account.
No. 97, to Tanyss Imports for tennis shoes, $219.50.

15 Purchase Invoices:
Hofstra Ltd., $339 for skis.
Smith Transport, $23.50, transportation charges on purchases.
Dinardo Delivery, $47 for delivery of goods to customers.

16 Credit note:
Cooper Bros., $36 for goods returned to them because they were received in a damaged condition.

Exercises Part B

12. Following are the March sales figures for Warrendon Sports: Sales $8 300; Sales Returns and Allowances $450.
    a) What is the net sales total for March?
    b) Determine the cost of goods sold for March for Warrendon Sports from the following: Beginning Inventory $35 000; March Purchases $6 000; Purchases Returns and Allowances $200; Transportation on Purchases $350; Ending Inventory $37 000.
    c) Determine the March gross profit for Warrendon Sports using the answers from parts a) and b) of this exercise.

13. Determine the cost of goods sold for Warrendon Sports from the following April figures: Beginning Inventory $37 000; April Purchases $7 500; Purchases Returns and Allowances $300; Transportation on Purchases $500; Ending Inventory $36 600.

14. Determine the net income for Warrendon Sports using the information in exercise 13 plus the following: Sales for April $10 800; Sales Returns and Allowances $500; Expenses $750.

15. a) Prepare a schedule of cost of goods sold for Warrendon Sports for May from the following figures: Beginning Inventory $36 600; Purchases $9 300; Purchases Returns and Allowances $400; Transportation on Purchases $600; Ending Inventory $33 800.
    b) Prepare an income statement for Warrendon Sports for May, using the cost of goods sold from part a) and the following figures: Sales for May $18 600; Sales Returns and Allowances $500; Salaries $3 200; Rent $2 700; Delivery Expense $1 100; Other Expenses $2 800.

16. a) Prepare a schedule of cost of goods sold for Warrendon Sports for June from the following figures: Beginning Inventory $33 800; June Purchases $7 200; Purchases Returns and Allowances $100; Transportation on Purchases $400; Ending Inventory $32 100.
    b) Prepare an income statement for Warrendon Sports using the cost of goods sold from part a) and the following figures: Sales for June $14 500; Sales Returns and Allowances $200; Salaries Expense $2 500; Rent Expense $2 700; Delivery Expense $600; Other Expenses $800.
    c) Prepare the current asset section of the balance sheet on June 30 using the following figures: Cash on hand $7 200; Accounts Receivable $2 700; Supplies $700. Remember that you must also use the figure for the ending inventory. Refer to part a) of this exercise.

17. Some of the account balances of Warrendon Sports for the month of July are shown on page 222.
    a) Prepare a schedule of cost of goods sold.
    b) Prepare an income statement.
    c) Prepare the current asset section of the balance sheet.

Beginning Inventory	$32 100
Purchases	9 100
Purchases Returns and Allowances	300
Transportation on Purchases	450
Ending Inventory	30 200
Sales	18 500
Sales Returns and Allowances	350
Salaries Expense	2 900
Rent Expense	2 700
Delivery Expense	700
Other Expenses	1 400
Cash on Hand	3 500
Accounts Receivable	2 900
Supplies on Hand	500

Exercises Part C

18. Using the information in the trial balance for Warrendon Sports of August 31, prepare the following for the month:
a) a schedule of cost of goods sold
b) an income statement
c) the current asset section of the balance sheet. (If you feel more adventurous, you may prepare a complete balance sheet instead.)

Warrendon Sports
Trial Balance
August 31, 19__

ACCOUNT TITLE	ACC. NO.	DEBIT	CREDIT
Cash	101	5300 —	
Accounts Receivable	102	2900 —	
Beginning Inventory	103	30200 —	
Supplies	104	600 —	
Furniture	150	45000 —	
Equipment	151	15000 —	
Truck	152	8000 —	
Accounts Payable	200		2900 —
Bank Loan (3 years)	201		6500 —
W. Creighton, Capital	300		93600 —
Sales	400		18600 —
Sales Returns and Allowances	401	400 —	
Purchases	500	8300 —	
Transportation on Purchases	501	600 —	
Purchases Returns and Allowances	502		400 —
Salaries Expense	600	2100 —	
Rent Expense	601	2700 —	
Delivery Expense	602	300 —	
Miscellaneous Expense	603	600 —	
		122000 —	122000 —

Note: The ending inventory is $27 100.

19. Using the information in the trial balance for Warrendon Sports of September 30, prepare the following for the month:

a) a schedule of cost of goods sold
b) an income statement
c) a balance sheet.

Warrendon Sports
Trial Balance
September 30, 19--

ACCOUNT TITLE	ACC. NO.	DEBIT	CREDIT
Cash	101	6 200 —	
Accounts Receivable	102	2 300 —	
Beginning Inventory	103	27 100 —	
Supplies	104	500 —	
Furniture	150	45 000 —	
Equipment	151	15 000 —	
Truck	152	8 000 —	
Accounts Payable	200		3 000 —
Bank Loan (3 years)	201		6 300 —
W. Creighton, Capital	300		94 500 —
W. Creighton, Drawing	301	500 —	
Sales	400		20 500 —
Sales Returns and Allowances	401	300 —	
Purchases	500	10 600 —	
Transportation on Purchases	501	900 —	
Purchases Returns and Allowances	502		500 —
Salaries Expense	600	3 500 —	
Rent Expense	601	2 700 —	
Delivery Expense	602	1 000 —	
Miscellaneous Expense	603	1 200 —	
		124 800 —	124 800 —

Note: The ending inventory is $25 900.

Accounting in Action

Case 1

Accounts Used by a Merchandising Company A new accountant began working for Nice Boy Stores on July 1. During the month of July the new accountant recorded the following group of purchase invoices.

Merchandise	$2 900
Office Supplies	300
Office Equipment	900
Delivery Expense	250

However, all four items were recorded as debits in the Purchases account.

a) For each of the invoices, name the account that should have been debited.
b) What effect will the incorrect recording of these invoices have on:
   i) the balance sheet
   ii) the schedule of cost of goods sold
   iii) the income statement

Case 2

Delivery Costs Vachon Stores offers free delivery service to its customers. For years a local cartage company has provided the delivery service. Business has increased substantially and on the average, 300 deliveries a month are made. The cartage firm has just increased its charges to $5 for every delivery.

K. Vachon, the owner of Vachon Stores, has asked the store accountant to compare the present delivery charges with the cost of buying and operating the company's own equipment. The accountant has determined several facts:

- A delivery van would cost $10 000
- The van would last four years and then would be worth $500 as a trade-in
- The driver's salary would be about $7 an hour, including all fringe benefits; the driver would work an average of 30 hours a week
- Insurance, repairs and maintenance, licences, and fuel would average $2 100 a year

a) What is more economical, buying the delivery equipment or using the services of the cartage firm?
b) List factors other than costs that could affect the decision.

Case 3

Sales Returns S. & S. Stores Ltd. is a large department store chain with stores in all the major cities in Canada. Their motto is "*Satisfaction guaranteed or your money cheerfully refunded.*"

The company has a policy of trying to maintain good customer relations no matter what the cost. As a result, some customers take advantage of the company policy. Merchandise is returned that has obviously been used for some time. Clothes which have been worn more than once are returned for refunds. Appliances and tools are returned for repairs after the warranty has expired.

In all these cases, the company accepts the returned goods.

a) Do you know of companies that have similar policies?
b) Why are such companies so generous to their customers?
c) Can you name companies which have a no-returns policy?

Returns and Allowances Accounts Company A does not use Sales or Purchase returns and Allowances accounts. Returns by customers are debited to the Sales account. Returns to creditors are credited to the Purchases account.

Case 4

Company B uses both a Sales Returns and Allowances account and a Purchases Returns and Allowances account. The income statement for Company B shows the amount of sales, the returns, and the net sales. The schedule of cost of goods sold shows the purchases, purchases returns, and net purchases. List the advantages and disadvantages of the two methods of handling returns.

Cost Prices and Selling Prices A customer found out that a company's cost price for the merchandise it sells is about half of the selling price. The customer complains to the owner that the net income on each item sold is about 100%. The customer feels that this is too much.

Case 5

The owner replies that there are many costs and expenses besides the cost of the goods sold to be considered.

a) To what costs and expenses is the owner referring?
b) If the customer is not happy with the answer provided by the owner, what can the customer do?

A Computer Accounting Service Accounting data is generally processed in four ways:

Case 6

- manually
- using a one-write board
- using accounting machines
- using electronic equipment

An organization may process its own data or have someone who offers an accounting service do it. This case study deals with a firm which offers an accounting service using the telephone and a computer.

Telaccount Limited is an accounting service company owned by the Bell Canada Group and The Bank of Nova Scotia. It offers a service to companies who do not have a computerized accounting system. Here is how it works:

- A company's own bookkeeper or accountant uses a standard touchtone telephone to transmit data to a computer owned by Telacount
- The computer processes the data and prints out the desired journals, ledgers, statements, etc.
- The print-outs are delivered the next day to a local Bank of Nova Scotia branch where they are picked up by the customer

Figure 9.11 illustrates the procedures followed.

Accounting Services Provided Telaccount designs a service to suit the customer's requirements. Typical print-outs are the journal, ledger, aged accounts receivable, customer statements, trial balance, and financial statements.

Aged accounts receivable is a listing of amounts owed by each customer showing the length of time each amount has been owed.

Advantages of This System Some of the advantages offered to customers:

- source documents never leave the customer's office
- flexibility – a variety of reports are available
- speed – next-day service
- reduction in routine clerical work

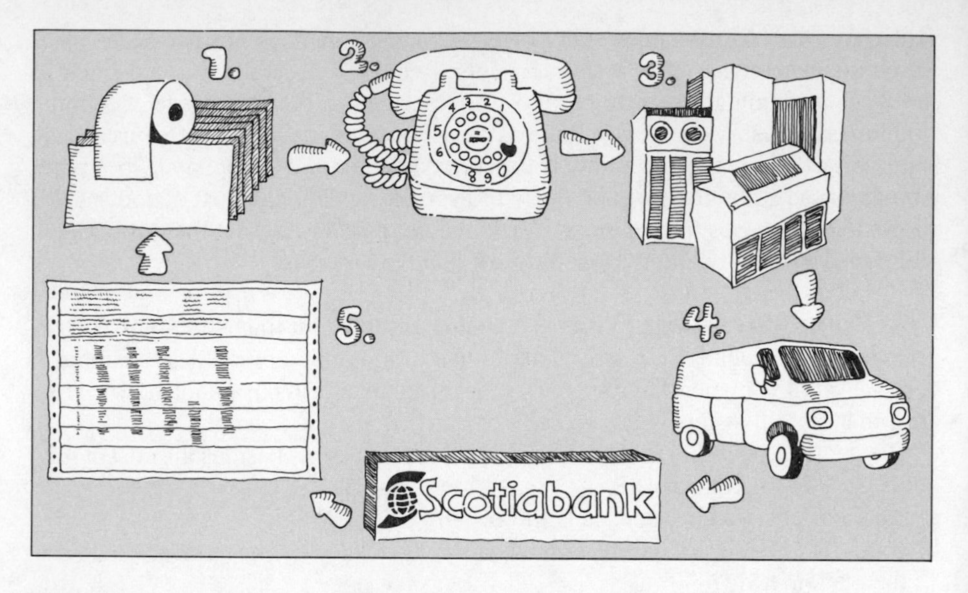

Figure 9.11 *Telacount computer accounting services*

Cost A monthly fee is charged. The fee is determined by the number of transactions handled and the number of accounting functions provided.

Does It Replace the Customer's Accountants? The Telaccounting service generally will reduce the amount of repetitive clerical work. However, trained accounting personnel are still required. The customer must still prepare source documents, check all data processed, and deal with its customers and creditors.

Suppose you are the accountant for a business and you receive a visit from a Telaccount Limited representative.

a) What questions would you ask the representative?
b) What factors would you consider in deciding to use this service?
c) What other information would you like to have before making a decision?

Career Profile

Setting Goals and Planning Your Future In each chapter of this text there is a description of a particular career. These careers range from students and their part-time jobs, to accounting clerks beginning their careers, to accountants working on their CGA, RIA, or CA degrees, to graduate professional accountants with senior positions in business.

Have you thought about your career? This is what the Career Profiles have been trying to get you to do. Have you thought about the stages you might progress through in your career? Have you begun to investigate the many careers open to you – not only those directly involving accounting? Try a little future-gazing by doing the following exercises.

On a sheet of paper write down the current year, and below the date, the answers to these questions.

a) With whom do you live?
b) Who provides your clothes, food, and shelter?
c) Who are your three closest friends or relatives?
d) To whom do you go to discuss your problems?
e) Where does your spending money come from?
f) What job(s), full-time or part-time, might you have in the next year or so?
g) What do you do with your spare time? (How much time do you spend studying? How much on personal entertainment, such as TV, music, visits with friends, etc.?)

Now write down the date five years from now and answer these questions.

h) Five years from now, will you still be going to a school? If the answer is yes, what type of school?
i) With whom will you be living?
j) Who will provide your clothes, food, and shelter?
k) Who will be your closest friends?
l) To whom will you go to discuss problems?
m) Will you be working (full-time or part-time)?
n) What type of job will you have?
o) What will you be doing with your time outside of school or your job?
p) Where will your money come from?

Now write down the date ten years from now and answer these questions.

q) Where will you be living ten years from now?
r) With whom will you be living ten years from now?
s) Will you be single or married? Will you have children?
t) Will you have completed your education?
u) Will you be studying part-time?
v) Who will provide your clothes, food, shelter, and spending money?
w) What will your hobbies and interests be?
x) Who will be your closest friends?
y) With whom will you discuss your problems?

To look into the future and to predict what you will be doing is a difficult task. It is necessary to set goals in order to plan for the future. However, it is necessary to do this in a way that doesn't produce anxiety and worry. It should be done with the realization that goals will change; that interests will change; that opportunities will occur unexpectedly; that there will be personal successes and failures; and that failure to reach a goal is not the end of the world.

By asking you to look into the future, these questions will have helped you realize that planning is necessary for personal fulfilment. Realistic goal-setting and planning can help to assure that each person reaches the fullest individual development. Good luck!

CHAPTER 10

Accounting for Purchases

Unit 25

Purchasing Systems

*1

Many documents and company departments are involved in a purchasing system. This is necessary in order to efficiently divide up the work load among a number of people and to control human error and possible dishonesty. Purchasing systems differ from business to business. Warrendon Sports is used in the examples that follow to illustrate standard principles used by many businesses.

Buying the Goods or Services Figure 10.1 illustrates the typical steps that are usually followed when buying goods or services in many businesses.

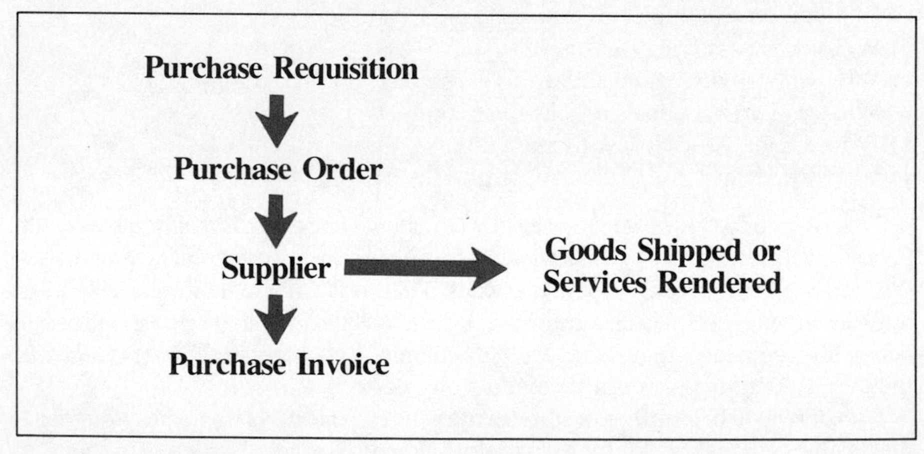

Figure 10.1 *Typical steps followed when buying goods or services*

A purchase requisition is a form sent to the purchasing department requesting that goods or services be ordered.

Purchase Requisition An employee wishing to purchase goods (or services) completes a request form called a *purchase requisition*. This form is sent to the purchasing department after it is approved by a supervisor. Figure 10.2 is an example of a purchase requisition used by Warrendon Sports.

WARRENDON SPORTS

2565 Baseline Road, Ottawa, Ontario K2H 7B3

PURCHASE REQUISITION

TO PURCHASING DEPARTMENT Please Purchase the Following: NO. R-72

DATE July 15, 19--

DATE NEEDED A.S.A.P.

QUANTITY	STOCK NO.	DESCRIPTION
30		Dolphin clear goggles
30		Olympian clear goggles
12		Assorted earplugs
6		Size 1-4 Swim Wings

REQUISITIONED BY Don B. APPROVED Warren C.

Figure 10.2 *Example of a purchase requisition*

WARRENDON SPORTS

2565 Baseline Road, Ottawa, Ontario K2H 7B3

STORE: 2565 Baseline Road
☐Tel. 829-4444
FACTORY: 5 Melrose Ave.
☐Tel. 729-7100

DATE August 4 19 xx

NO. 4151 **PURCHASE ORDER**

To: Speedquip Ltd.

Ship to: Warrendon Sports Ltd., 2565 Baseline Rd., Ottawa, Ontario. K2H 7E3

Please supply the following by date specified.

REQUIRED BY ______ SHIP BY Parcel Post

QUANTITY	DESCRIPTION
30	Dolphin clear goggles
30	Olympian clear goggles
12	Assorted earplugs
6	Size 1-4 Swim Wings

Provincial Sales Tax License No. 41902211 Per W. Creighton

Figure 10.3 *Example of a purchase order*

A purchase order is a form prepared by the buyer and sent to the seller. It describes the items the buyer wishes to purchase.

Purchase Order It is the responsibility of the purchasing department to acquire the best quality items at the best price. When a supplier has been selected, a *purchase order* is prepared and sent to the supplier. When both the buyer and the seller agree on the terms of the purchase, the purchase order becomes a legal contract. Warrendon Sports uses the purchase order shown in Figure 10.3.

*2

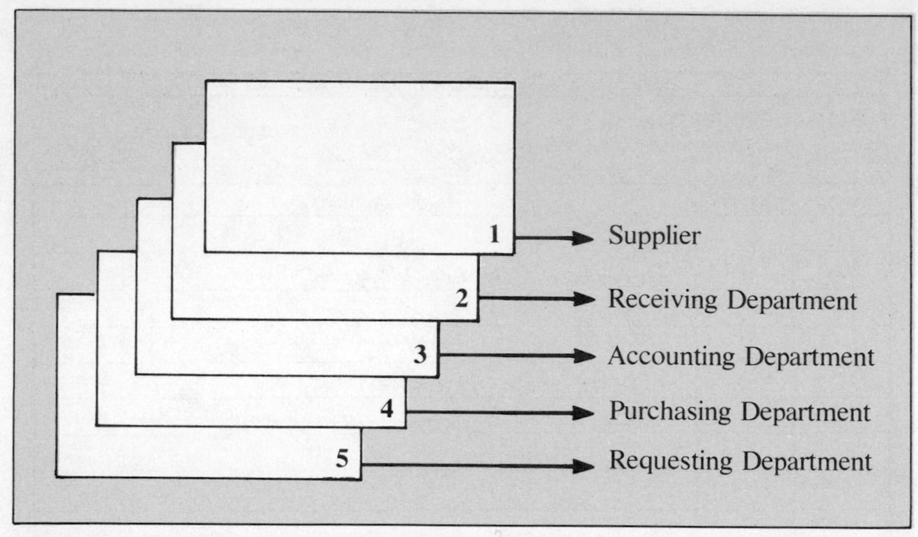

Figure 10.4 *Distribution of purchase order and copies for Warrendon Sports*

Figure 10.4 shows where each copy of the purchase order is sent. The receiving department is sent a copy of the purchase order so that they will know that goods have been ordered and will accept *only* the goods ordered. The accounting department receives a copy of the purchase order so that it will pay only for the goods which have been ordered. The purchasing department retains a copy for their records and the final copy of the purchase order is sent to the requesting department, so that the requesting department is aware that the goods have been ordered and when delivery can be expected.

*3

An invoice is a form sent by the seller to the buyer. It lists the costs of the items shipped, along with details of the shipment.

Purchase Invoice After the goods have been shipped, the seller sends an *invoice* or bill to the buyer. Figure 10.5 is the invoice received by Warrendon Sports. This invoice lists the items shipped to Warrendon that were ordered on August 4 (Figure 10.3).

Among the details presented on the invoice are:

- method of shipment: *Shipped via parcel post*
- date shipped: *September 3*
- responsibility for shipping charges: *FOB Winnipeg* (Warrendon must pay shipping charges from Winnipeg to Ottawa.)
- payment terms: *3% 10 days, net 30 days* (Warrendon may deduct 3% from the total of $139.40 if payment is made within 10 days of the invoice date. If payment is not made in 10 days, the full amount of $139.40 is due 30 days from the invoice date. Notice that there is also a 2% per month charge on accounts not paid on time.
- invoice number: *No. 307*
- date of invoice: *September 3*
- total owed: *$139.40*

The information in the columns headed quantity ordered, quantity shipped, stock number/description, unit price, and amount must be carefully checked and are subject to further detailed controls in Warrendon's purchasing system.

Speed quip ltd

992 St. Mary's Rd., Winnipeg, Manitoba R2M 3S3
Phone: 204 - 256-3489
Telex: 07-55188

INVOICE

SOLD TO
Warrendon Sports Ltd.
2565 Base Line Road
OTTAWA, Ontario K2H 7E3

SHIPPED TO
Same

NO.

DATE Sept. 3/--

YOUR ORDER NO.

Our Order No.	Salesperson	Terms: 3% – 10 DAYS NET 30 DAYS	F.O.B. WINNIPEG	Date Shipped	Shipped Via
4151	Brown				Parcel Post

QUANTITY ORDERED	QUANTITY SHIPPED	STOCK NUMBER/DESCRIPTION	UNIT PRICE		UNIT	AMOUNT	
30	30	Dolphin clear goggles	1	80	1	54	00
30	30	Olympian clear goggles	2	10	1	63	80
12	12	Assorted Earplugs	0	90	1	10	80
6	6	Size 1 -- 4 Swim Wings	1	80	1	10	80
						139	40
		Discount if paid within 10 days = 4.18					
		2% added to overdue accounts					

White – Customer's Copy / *Pink* – Office Copy / *Canary* – Commission Copy / *Green* – Salesperson's Copy / *Blue* – Shipping Copy

Figure 10.5 *Example of a purchase invoice*

Paying for Purchases

To this point, the system for ordering goods from a supplier has been shown. The steps to be followed in receiving the goods and the procedures for paying for them will now be discussed.

*4

Receiving Report Merchandise received from a supplier must be checked to ensure that:

- goods received were actually ordered
- goods are in satisfactory condition
- correct quantity and quality were shipped

The person receiving and checking the goods completes a *receiving report* and sends a copy to the purchasing department (Figure 10.6). Remember that a copy of the purchase order was initially sent to the receiving department when the goods were ordered. This purchase order copy is used to determine if the goods received were in fact ordered.

A receiving report is a form that lists and describes all goods received.

Some firms do not use a receiving report. Instead, the receiver will check off each item on the purchase order when it is received. The receiver then initials the purchase order copy and sends it to the purchasing department.

WARRENDON SPORTS
2565 Baseline Road, Ottawa, Ontario K2H 7B3

RECEIVING REPORT

NO. R-312

FROM: SPEEDQUIP LTD.

DATE SEPT. 10, 19--

P.O. NO. 4151

VIA		PREPAID		COLLECT	

STOCK NO.	QUANTITY	DESCRIPTION	UNIT PRICE	
	30	Dolphin clear goggles		
	30	Olympian clear goggles		
	12	Assorted earplugs		
	6	Size 1 - 4 Swim Wings		

CHECKED BY R. Lee ENTERED IN STORES LEDGER BY

Figure 10.6 *Example of a receiving report*

***5**

The matching process is the comparing of the purchase order, purchase invoice, and receiving report.

Matching Process Before an invoice is approved or recorded, it is checked and compared to the purchase order and the receiving report. This comparison is necessary to ensure that *what was ordered was received,* and *what was charged for, was ordered and received.* Usually, the matching process is the responsibility of the purchasing department. If the three documents match, the invoice is approved and sent to the accounting department.

***6**

An extension is the quantity multiplied by the unit price.

The Approved Invoice The accounting department receives the invoice and supporting documents from the purchasing department and checks their mathematical accuracy. Each *extension* is checked and the amounts are added to verify the total of the invoice.

The account to be debited is indicated on the invoice. An accounting clerk then journalizes and posts the transaction. For example, the Journal entry for the Speedquip invoice is:

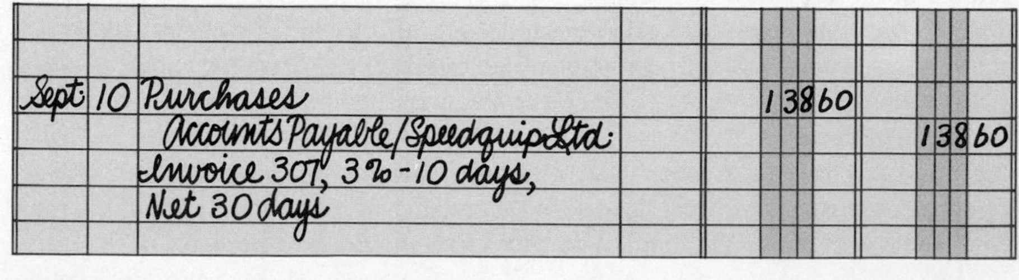

Sept.	10	Purchases		138 60	
		Accounts Payable/Speedquip Ltd.			138 60
		Invoice 307, 3%-10 days,			
		Net 30 days			

Payment on the Due Date After journalizing, the approved invoice is placed in a date file according to the date on which payment is to be made. On that day, the invoice is taken from the file and a cheque is prepared and sent to the supplier. The payment is then journalized and posted. The journal entry to record the payment of the Speedquip invoice is:

*7

Oct.	3	Accounts Payable/Speedquip Ltd.		138 60	
		Cash			138 60
		Invoice 307			

Figure 10.7 illustrates the steps followed when paying an invoice.

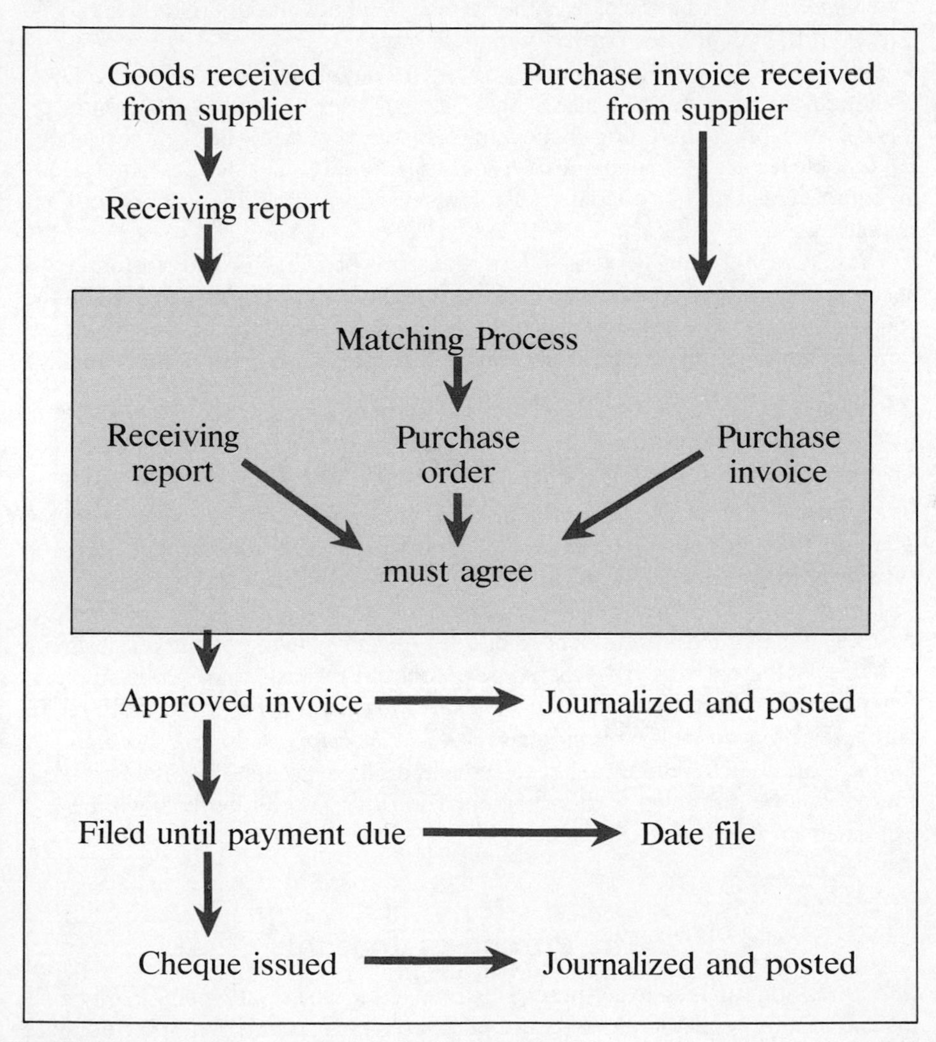

Figure 10.7 *Typical steps followed when paying an invoice*

*8

Terms of sale is the agreement for payment between the buyer and the seller.

Terms of Sale The invoice sent by the supplier to the buyer contains the agreed-upon terms for payment of the items purchased. If payment is to be made immediately, the terms are *cash* or *cash on receipt of invoice*. If the buyer is allowed a period of time for payment, the terms are said to be *on account*, or the purchase is called a credit purchase.

Some firms offer the same terms to all customers. Other firms offer a variety of terms to customers. Here is a list of some commonly used terms of sale:

- *C.O.D.* Payment must be made when the goods are delivered (cash on delivery).
- *Receipt of Invoice* Payment is to be made when the invoice is received.
- *Net 30* The full amount of the invoice is due 30 days from the invoice date.
- *EOM* Payment is due at the end of the month.
- *10th following* Payment is due on the tenth day of the following month.
- *2/10, n/30* The buyer may deduct 2% of the invoice amount if payment is made within 10 days from the date of the invoice. The full amount (net) is due in 30 days if the buyer does not pay within 10 days.
- *1/10, n/30 EOM* A 1% discount may be taken if payment is made within 10 days. The full amount must be paid within 30 days after the end of the month.

It is common practice for firms to negotiate the terms of sale with their customers. Favourable terms, for example 60 days, may be offered to a valued customer. Less favourable terms may be offered to customers who buy small amounts of goods or services.

The nature of the business also affects the terms of sale offered to customers. A business that must maintain a large inventory of goods must pay its suppliers for the goods it buys. Such a business may offer discounts to its customers to encourage early payment so that the business may in turn pay its suppliers more quickly.

Unit 26

*9

Special Journal Systems

In Chapter 8, you learned that a large firm with many customer and creditor accounts uses more than one ledger. Accounts receivable and accounts payable subsidiary ledgers are usually set up in such cases with individual accounting clerks responsible for each of these ledgers. Using the same *division of labour* principle, a business with numerous transactions of one type may use more than one journal.

A special journal system uses separate journals for each type of similar transactions that recur frequently.

A special journal is used for each type of repetitive transaction. For example, a *Sales Journal* is used to record credit sales. A *Purchases Journal* is used to record purchases on account (credit purchases). *Cash Receipts* and *Cash Payments Journals* are used to record cash received and cash payments. Only the Purchases Journal will be discussed in this chapter. The other special journals will be examined in subsequent chapters.

The Purchases Journal

A Purchases Journal is a special journal used to record all purchases on account.

A business that makes many purchases on account uses a *Purchases Journal* instead of a General Journal to record purchases on account. When invoices are received, they are approved and then recorded in the Purchases Journal.

Journalizing Purchases on Account As you know, an invoice received for items purchased on account is called a purchase invoice. After the purchase invoice has been approved, it is journalized. On September 5, these approved invoices were received by the accounting department of Warrendon Sports:

- Invoice 307 dated Sept. 3 from Speedquip Ltd., $138.60 for merchandise, terms 3/10, net 30
- Invoice W 184 dated Sept. 4 from Evans & Kert, $50 for office supplies, terms net 30
- Invoice 3871 dated Sept. 2 from Tops Service Centre, $70 for repairs to the company automobile, terms EOM
- Invoice B-519 dated Sept. 1 from Ontario Hydro, $195 for the August hydro bill, terms EOM
- Invoice 193 dated Sept. 1 from Cooper Bros., $500 for merchandise, terms n/30.

Figure 10.8 shows these transactions recorded in a General Journal.

GENERAL JOURNAL — PAGE 17

DATE		PARTICULARS	PR	DEBIT	CREDIT
19-- Sept.	5	Purchases		138 60	
		Accounts Payable/Speedquip Ltd.			138 60
		Invoice 307, merchandise			
		3% 10, Net 30			
	5	Supplies		50 —	
		Accounts Payable/Evans & Kert			50 —
		Inv. W 184, net 30			
	5	Car Expense		70 —	
		Accounts Payable/Tops			
		Service Centre			70 —
		Inv. 3871, Terms EOM			
	5	Utilities Expense		195 —	
		Accounts Payable/Ontario Hydro			195 —
		Inv. B-519, Terms EOM			
	5	Purchases		500 —	
		Accounts Payable/Cooper Bros.			500 —
		Inv. 193 n/30, merchandise			

Figure 10.8 *Transactions recorded in a General Journal*

PURCHASES JOURNAL PAGE 16

DATE		REF. NO.	CREDITOR	PR	PURCHASES DEBIT	ACCOUNTS PAYABLE CREDIT	UTILITIES EXPENSE DEBIT	OTHER ACCOUNTS	PR	DEBIT
Sept.[19--]	5	307	Speedquip Ltd.		138 60	138 60				
	5	184	Evans & Kert			50 —		Supplies		50 —
	5	B-18	Tops Service Centre			70 —		Car Expense		70 —
	5	519	Ontario Hydro			195 —	195 —			
	5	193	Cooper Bros.		500 —	500 —				

Figure 10.9 *Transactions from Figure 10.8 recorded in a Purchases Journal* ▲

▼ **Figure 10.10** *Cross-balancing the Purchases Journal*

PURCHASES JOURNAL PAGE 16

DATE		REF. NO.	CREDITOR	PR	PURCHASES DEBIT	ACCOUNTS PAYABLE CREDIT	UTILITIES EXPENSE DEBIT	OTHER ACCOUNTS	PR	DEBIT
Sept.[19--]	5	307	Speedquip Ltd.		138 60	138 60				
	5	184	Evans & Kert			50 —		Supplies		50 —
	5	B-18	Tops Service Centre			70 —		Car Expense		70 —
	5	519	Ontario Hydro			195 —	195 —			
	5	193	Cooper Bros.		500 —	500 —				
	6	419	Hall Fuel			200 —	200 —			
	9	801	Coles Ltd.			10 —		Miscellaneous Expense		10 —
	10	331	Speedquip Ltd.		200 —	200 —				
	11	207	Cooper Bros.		40 —	40 —				
	12	H-719	C.N. Express			115 —		Trans. on Purchases		115 —
	16	3461	City Waters Ltd.			360 —	360 —			
	18	219	Cooper Bros.		900 —	900 —				
	20	296	Evans & Kert			97 —		Supplies		97 —
	23	231	Cooper Bros.		120 —	120 —				
	27	B-71	Tops Service Centre			45 —		Car Expenses		45 —
	30	379	Speedquip Ltd.		400 —	400 —				
		4	Debits = 3440.60	1 →	2 298 60	3 440 60	755 —	← 5 →		387 —
			Credits = 3440.60		↑	↑ 3	↑	2		↑

Figure 10.9 shows the same invoices recorded in a Purchases Journal. Compare the recording of the five invoices in the General Journal with the recording procedures followed in the Purchases Journal. *How many lines does each transaction require in the General Journal and in the Purchases Journal? In the recording of these invoices, which journal requires less writing? Why do you think there are special columns headed Purchases debit and Utilities Expense debit? When is the Other Accounts column used?*

Note that only purchases on account appear in the Purchases Journal. Cash purchases would be recorded in the Cash Payments Journal.

Special Column Headings In the Purchases Journal in Figure 10.9, columns are headed Purchases debit, Accounts Payable credit, Utilities Expense debit, and Other Accounts debit. The Accounts Payable credit column is required for every transaction in the Purchases Journal. Merchandise is purchased frequently and that is why there is a special column for Purchases debit in the journal. A special column is headed Utilities Expense debit because for this particular company Utilities Expense is involved in many transactions. Another company might use this column for Supplies or Delivery Expense or any other account used in repetitive transactions.

Special columns are provided for accounts which are used frequently.

The Other Accounts debit section is used to record the debit to accounts other than Purchases or Utilities. Notice that the account title must be shown as well as the name of the creditor when the Other Accounts section is used.

Cross-Balancing the Purchases Journal

*10

Since the Purchases Journal in Figure 10.9 has four money columns it is quite possible to record part of an entry in the wrong column. To locate errors of this type before they are transferred to the ledger in the posting process, each page of the Purchases Journal is *cross-balanced*. Cross-balancing a journal determines if the debits equal the credits on a particular journal page. If the debit column totals equal the credit column totals, that particular page of the Purchases Journal is in balance. These steps should be followed when cross-balancing a Purchases Journal:

Cross-balancing a journal page determines if the debits equal the credits on that page.

1. Add all columns.
2. Add the debit column totals.
3. Add the credit column totals if more than one.
4. If the totals obtained in steps 2 and 3 are the same, show the totals in the Creditor column.
5. Rule a double line across all money columns.

Figure 10.10 illustrates the cross-balancing process for page 16 of the Purchases Journal. The Purchases Journal is cross-balanced at the end of each page and at the end of each month. Note that additional transactions have been posted to the journal in addition to the five transactions already covered. This is done to give the Purchases Journal a more realistic appearance.

Locating Errors If the journal does not balance:

*11

- Start on the first line and check to see if there are equal debit and credit amounts on each line.
- Recheck all addition.
- Follow the *locating error* steps in Chapter 5, pages 99-101.

PURCHASES JOURNAL PAGE 16

DATE		REF. NO.	CREDITOR	PR	PURCHASES DEBIT	ACCOUNTS PAYABLE CREDIT	UTILITIES EXPENSE DEBIT	OTHER ACCOUNTS		
									PR	DEBIT
Sept. 19--	5	307	Speedquip Ltd.	✓	138 60	138 60				
	5	184	Evans & Kert	✓		50 —		Supplies	117	50 —
	5	B-18	Tops Service Centre	✓		70 —		Car Expense	613	70 —
	5	519	Ontario Hydro	✓		195 —	195 —			
	5	193	Cooper Bros.	✓	500 —	500 —				
	6	419	Hall Fuel	✓		200 —	200 —			
	9	801	Coles Ltd.	✓		10 —		Miscellaneous Expense	614	10 —
	10	331	Speedquip Ltd. 1	✓	200 —	200 —				
	11	207	Cooper Bros.	✓	40 —	40 —				
	12	H-719	C.N. Express	✓		115 —		Trans. on Purchases	503	115 —
	16	3461	City Waters Ltd.	✓		360 —	360 —			
	18	219	Cooper Bros.	✓	900 —	900 —				
	20	296	Evans & Kert	✓		97 —		Supplies	117	97 —
	23	231	Cooper Bros.	✓	120 —	120 —				
	27	B-71	Tops Service Centre	✓		45 —		Car Expenses	613	45 —
	30	379	Speedquip Ltd.	✓	400 —	400 —				
			Debits = 3440.60		2298 60	3440 60	755 —		3	387 —
			Credits = 3440.60		(500)	(200)	(615)			
						2				

Figure 10.11 *Posting the Purchases Journal to the General Ledger. How many postings are eliminated by posting column totals to the General Ledger rather than posting every individual transaction?*

Forwarding Totals When a page of a journal is filled it should be cross-balanced and the totals carried forward to the next page. The word *Forwarded* is written in the creditor column on the same line as the totals. On the next journal page, the date, including the year and the month, is written on the first line. The word *Forwarded* is written on the first line in the creditor column and the totals are written in the money columns. Totals are carried forward in this manner until the end of the month. At that time, the journal is cross-balanced and the totals are posted to the General Ledger. *12

Posting the Purchases Journal to the General Ledger

The main advantage of using the Purchases Journal is that it reduces the recording workload since only one line is needed for most transactions. In contrast, three lines of writing are required when transactions are recorded directly in the General Journal. *13

Further efficiencies are achieved in the posting process. When the General Journal in Figure 10.8 is posted, a debit and a credit must be transferred to the General Ledger for every transaction. Individual postings would also be made to the accounts in the Accounts Payable subsidiary Ledger. By using a Purchases Journal, only monthly column totals are posted to the General Ledger from the Purchases Journal. However, individual transactions are posted *daily* to the Accounts Payable subsidiary Ledger. This is necessary in order to keep the creditor account balances continually up to date.

Steps Followed in Posting the Purchases Journal Figure 10.11 illustrates the steps followed in posting the Purchases Journal at the end of the month of September. *14

1. Post each credit in the Accounts Payable column *daily* to the Accounts Payable Ledger. Place a √ in the posting reference (PR) column.
2. Post the totals of each column to the appropriate General Ledger accounts at the end of the month. The account numbers are shown in brackets under each total in Figure 10.11. The Other Accounts column total is not posted.
3. Post the individual transactions in the Other Accounts section to the General Ledger accounts at the end of the month. Show the ledger account number in the PR column.

Posting References Three separate posting references appear in the Purchases Journal as shown in Figure 10.11:

1. When daily postings are made to the subsidiary ledger, a √ is placed in the posting reference (PR) column. The √ indicates that a posting has been made to the subsidiary ledger.
2. When column totals are posted, the General Ledger account numbers are shown below the totals.
3. When the Other Accounts section is posted, the account numbers are shown in the posting reference column beside the transaction. The total is not posted.

Posting references are also made in the ledger accounts as a cross reference back to the Purchases Journal. In the example shown in Figure 10.12, *PJ 16* is written in the posting reference column of the Purchases account in the General Ledger.

DATE		PARTICULARS	PR	DEBIT	CREDIT	DR CR	BALANCE
Sept.[19]--	30		PJ16	2 298 60		DR	2 298 60

ACCOUNT Purchases NO. 500

Figure 10.12 *The Purchases debit column total posted from the Purchases Journal in Figure 10.11 to the Purchases account in the General Ledger*

Advantages of Using the Purchases Journal In summary, there are three advantages to using a Purchases Journal instead of recording transactions directly in a General Journal.

- Most entries require only one line.
- Posting is reduced.
- Explanations are eliminated.

Credit Invoices

*15 When goods are returned to a supplier, a credit invoice is prepared by the supplier and sent to the buyer. The credit invoice indicates to the buyer that Purchases should be decreased and that the Accounts Payable should also be decreased.

Recording Credit Invoices in a Purchases Journal The Purchases Journal in this chapter does not have a *Purchases credit* column. However, a credit invoice may be shown in red or may be circled in the Purchases Debit column. The circled item in Figure 10.13 indicates that the $38.60 should be treated as a credit. When the column is totalled, the circled item is subtracted from the other items.

Sept.[19]--	5	307	Speedquip Ltd.			138 60	138 60	
	8	R-17	Speedquip Ltd.			(38 60)	(38 60)	
			Debits = 100			100 –	100 –	
			Credits = 100					

Figure 10.13 *An example of how a credit invoice would be shown in a Purchases Journal that does not have a Purchases credit column. The circled amounts are subtracted when the columns are totalled.*

Other Methods of Recording Credit Invoices There are several other acceptable methods of recording credit invoices. These include:

- recording credit invoices in the General Journal
- using a special journal, the Purchases Returns and Allowances Journal, to record the credit invoice
- using a Purchases credit column in the Purchases Journal
- using a Purchases Returns and Allowances credit column in the Purchases Journal

Facts to Remember

A *purchase requisition* is a form sent to the purchasing department requesting that goods or services be ordered.

A *purchase order* is a form prepared by the buyer and sent to the seller. It describes the items the buyer wishes to purchase.

An *invoice* is a form sent by the seller to the buyer. It lists the costs of the items shipped along with details of the shipment.

A *receiving report* is a form that lists and describes all goods received.

The *matching process* is the comparing of the purchase order, purchase invoice, and receiving report.

An *extension* is the quantity multiplied by the unit price.

Terms of sale is the agreement for payment between the buyer and the seller.

A *special journal system* uses separate journals for each type of similar transaction that recurs frequently.

A *Purchases Journal* is a special journal used to record all purchases on account.

Cross-balancing a journal page determines if the debits equal the credits on that page.

Checking Your Reading

Questions

1. Answer the following about the purchase requisition shown in Figure 10.2.
   a) Who requested the merchandise?
   b) Who is the supervisor?
   c) Why is it necessary to have the supervisor sign the purchase requisition?
2. What factors does the purchasing department consider before issuing the purchase order?
3. Answer the following about the purchase order in Figure 10.3.
   a) What company was chosen to supply the goods?
   b) Explain why each of the following departments receives a copy of the purchase order:
      i) receiving department
      ii) accounting department
      iii) purchasing department
      iv) requesting department
4. Answer the following about the purchase invoice in Figure 10.5.
   a) Who is the seller?
   b) Who is the buyer?
   c) What is the last day on which the invoice must be paid to obtain the 3% discount?
   d) What is the amount of the discount if the invoice is paid within 10 days?

e) What is the last day on which the invoice must be paid so that no charge for an overdue account will be made?

f) What is the amount of the charge if the payment is overdue by seven days?

g) What will be Warrendon's General Journal entry to record this invoice?

5. Answer the following about the receiving report in Figure 10.6.

a) How does the receiving clerk know that the goods Warrendon Sports has received are those that were ordered?

b) Why does the purchasing department need a copy of the receiving report?

6. Explain the term *matching* and indicate what three documents are matched.

7. What department is responsible for matching the documents?

8. What supporting documents are attached to the purchase invoice?

9. Give the journal entry necessary to record the cheque issued to pay the Speedquip invoice shown in Figure 10.5 if the item is paid on October 3.

Applying Your Knowledge

Exercises Part A

1. a) On what date is the net amount to be paid for each of the following invoices? Discounts are *not* to be taken.

Invoice Date	Terms
March 5	EOM
March 6	n/30
March 8	n/60
March 14	15 EOM
March 17	2/10, n/30
March 19	C.O.D.
March 20	Receipt of Invoice
March 25	1/10 n/30

b) Determine the amount of the discount, the last day for obtaining the discount, and the amount to be paid for each of the following. All invoices are paid on the last day of the discount period.

Amount of Invoice	Terms	Invoice date
$100	2/10,n/30	March 1
$500	1/15,n/30	March 2
$300	3/10,n/60	March 5
$250	2/10,n/30	March 12
$175	1/10,n/60	March 25

2. Record the following in a two-column General Journal:

Jan. 3 Purchased merchandise for $500 from Speedquip Ltd., invoice dated December 30, terms n/30.
4 Purchased office supplies for $63 from Evans & Kert, invoice dated January 2, terms n/30.
4 Purchased merchandise for $700 from Cooper Bros., invoice dated January 2, terms n/30.
5 Purchased office equipment for $500 from Willsons Ltd., invoice 6-110 dated January 2, terms n/30.

3. a) Record the transactions from exercise 2 in a Purchases Journal.
b) Total, cross-balance, and rule the Purchases Journal.

4. a) Enter the following approved invoices in a Purchases Journal for B & M Furniture. Assign page 214 to the Purchases Journal and use the following partial chart of accounts to determine the accounts affected.

B & M Furniture
Partial Chart of Accounts

115	Prepaid Insurance	505	Transportation on Purchases
121	Office Equipment	609	Delivery Expense
201	Accounts Payable	639	Miscellaneous Expense
501	Purchases		

Jan. 3 Carter and Wilson, insurance agents, $3 450 for the insurance premium due on the building and contents.
4 Thornhill's Service Centre, $263 for delivery truck repairs.
4 Teak Manufacturers, $9 756 for dining room furniture.
5 McCall's Stationers, $189 for a new filing cabinet for the office.
7 Thornhill's Service Centre, $580 for a new engine for one of the delivery trucks.
7 Rick's Towing Service, $30 for towing a delivery truck to Thornhill's Service Centre.
9 Ray's Snow Removal, $75 for plowing the parking lot after a storm.
10 Teak Manufacturers, $7 527 for living room furniture.
11 Enders Ltd., $3 651 for a shipment of 10 refrigerators.
11 Hiway Trucking, $750 for furniture shipments.

b) Total and cross-balance the Purchases Journal.

Exercises Part B

5. a) Enter the following approved invoices in a Purchases Journal for the Cycle Shop. Assign page 133 to the journal. Use the partial chart of accounts to determine the accounts affected.

July 1 15 bicycles from CCM Ltd. for $984.50.
3 A purchase of tires and tubes from Dunlop Tires for $157.
4 Repairs to the main entrance by Coastal Glass for $125.

July 4 Transportation of the bicycles received on July 1, $56 from Hi-Way Transport.
5 Gas and oil used in the truck during June, $63 from Craig's Service Station.
8 Advertising space, $120 from the *Daily News*.

Cycle Shop
Partial Chart of Accounts

115	Supplies	505	Transportation on Purchases
125	Office Equipment	620	Delivery Expense
201	Accounts Payable	622	Advertising Expense
302	K. Paul, Drawing	630	Repairs and Maintenance Expense
501	Purchases		

b) Total and cross-balance the Purchases Journal.

c) Assign page 134 to the next journal page and bring the totals forward from page 133, then continue by recording the following approved invoices:

July 9 Repairs to the owner's (K. Paul) cottage, $586 from Denver Contractors.
9 Bicycle accessories from CCM Ltd. for $257.
10 A new typewriter from Jason's Ltd. for $530.
10 10 bicycles from Findley Manufacturers for $879.
11 Paper bags, wrapping paper, and other store supplies from Carter Supplies for $67.

6. a) Set up the following accounts and balances in the partial General Ledger for Discount Stores:

104	Office supplies	$1 340	
201	Accounts Payable Control		$4 520
300	K. Duncan, Capital		4 270
501	Purchases	6 750	
502	Transportation on Purchases	240	
503	Truck Expense	460	
		$8 790	$8 790

b) Set up the following accounts and balances in the Accounts Payable Ledger for Discount Stores:

Canadian Tire	$ 375
Graham Wholesalers	3 470
Whitman Stationers	535
Williams Trucking	140
	$4 520

c) Enter the following approved purchase invoices on page 73 of a Purchases Journal for Discount Stores and cross-balance the journal.

May 4 Merchandise from Graham Wholesalers for $576.
5 Office supplies from Whitman Stationers for $135.
6 Gas and oil used in the truck from Canadian Tire for $35.
7 Transportation of merchandise from Williams Trucking for $47.
8 Merchandise from Graham Wholesalers for $2 348.

d) Post the Purchases Journal to the General Ledger.
e) Post the individual accounts in the Accounts Payable column to the Accounts Payable Ledger.
f) Prepare a trial balance for the General Ledger.
g) Prepare a schedule for the Accounts Payable Ledger.

Exercises Part C

7. Following is a partial chart of accounts for Electronics Unlimited of Vancouver:

100 Cash
121 Office Equipment
201 Accounts Payable
501 Purchases
502 Transportation on Purchases
503 Delivery Expense
510 Building Repairs Expense

a) On page 37 of the Purchases Journal, record the following approved invoices for Electronics Unlimited.
b) Total and cross-balance the Purchases Journal.

BANNEX LTD.
1493 Bridge Road, Toronto, Ontario M6A 1Z5 Phone 594-6655

Sold to Electronics Unlimited
795 Beaver Drive
Vancouver, B.C.
V7N 3H6

INVOICE 17493
DATE Feb. 3, 19--
TERMS net 30 days

Quantity	Description	Price per Unit	Total
5	Spools of #10 Copper Wire	23.50	117.50

Sales Tax Exempt

Received Mar. 2

Received by	BK
Price O.K.	✓
Account	501
Payment O.K.	CD

White & Turner
Heating Contractors
for all your heating supplies

497 Albion Rd., Vancouver, B.C.
V7A 3E4

Telephone 793-8340
or 793-8050

Sold to Electronics Unlimited
795 Beaver Drive
Vancouver, B.C.
V7N 3HG

Invoice No. 86B743

Date Feb. 4, 19--

Terms 2/10, n/30

Received Mar. 4

Stock No.	Description	Quantity	Price	Amount
N-21-2	2 cm x 3 m pipes	7	4.50	31.50
R-63-47	Boxes #3 washers	2	0.75	1.50
Cash ☐ Charge ☐			Prov. Sales Tax	2.31
			Total	35.31

Received by BK
Price O.K. ✓
Account 510
Payment O.K. CD

EVC Limited

Electronics Unlimited
795 Beaver Drive
Vancouver, B.C., Canada
V7N 3H6

Invoice No. E-437073
Terms Net 30 days F.O.B.
Your Order No. 7434
Ship Via WCT
Date Shipped Feb. 28, 19--
Date of Inv. March 1

Received March 5

Quantity	Description	Unit Price	Amount
20	EVC 40 Speakers	109.00	2 180.00
10	EVC 50 Speakers	129.00	1 290.00
10	SP-743-H Receivers	133.00	1 330.00
5	SP-843-H Receivers	152.00	760.00
		Total	5 560.00

Sales Tax Exempt

Received by BK
Price O.K. ✓
Account 501
Payment O.K. CD

WEST COAST TRANSPORT 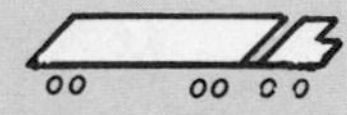

Vancouver - Seattle - Los Angeles

73 Commissioner Rd.	1890 Industrial Rd.	734 Green Street
Vancouver, B.C.	Seattle, Washington	Los Angeles, California
Canada V7R 3T6	U.S.A. 92000	U.S.A. 96300
Phone 937-4370	Phone 347-8650	Phone 474-8503

Shipper:
EVC Limited
1793 Pennfield Drive
Los Angeles, CA 96430 U.S.A.

Consignee:
Electronics Unlimited
795 Beaver Drive
Vancouver, B.C. V7N 3H6

Prepaid Collect X Terms: Net Date: March 4, 19-- Inv. No. W.B. 74343

No. of Containers	Mass	Rate	Amount
45 Boxes	300 kg	$0.40/kg	120.00
		Pay this Amount →	120.00

Received March 8

Received by BK
Price O.K. ✓
Account 502
Payment O.K. CD

Sales Tax Exempt

Local Deliveries

Same Day Delivery

475 Dynes Road
Vancouver, B.C. V7E 3R1
Phone 837-4390

Invoice No. 657
Terms Net
Date March 7, 19--

Charge
Electronics Unlimited
795 Beaver Drive
Vancouver, B.C.
V7N 3H6

Deliver to
Mr. K. Stafford
473 Elm Street
Vancouver, B.C.
V6L 2L4

Description	Amount
4 boxes	10.00

Received March 9

Received by BK
Price O.K. ✓
Account 503
Payment O.K. CD

Jonsson
Office Specialties Ltd.
63 Main Street, Vancouver, B.C. V6A 2S2 Phone 343-7512
For All Your Office Needs

Sold to
Electronics Unlimited
795 Beaver Drive
Vancouver, B.C.
V7N 3H6

Our Invoice No. 73B4973
Your Order No. 7440
Terms 2/10, n/30
Date Shipped March 7, 19--
Date of Invoice March 7, 19--

Quantity	Description	Unit Price	Amount
1	Typewriter	467.50	467.50
		Sales tax	30.73
		Pay this Amount	498.23

Received March 9

Received by	BK
Price O.K.	✓
Account	121
Payment O.K.	CD

EVC Limited
1793 Pennfield Drive, Los Angeles, CA 96430

To: Electronics Unlimited
795 Beaver Drive
Vancouver, B.C. V7N 3H6

Credit No. 1396
March 7, 19--

We credit your account as specified below

Re: Inv. #E-437073, dated January 6, 19--

1 SP-743-H Receiver $133
1 SP-843-H Receiver $152
TOTAL CREDIT DUE $285

Received Mar. 9

CREDIT MEMORANDUM

Accounting in Action

Cash Discounts Tina is an accounting clerk responsible for receiving payments from customers. She is new at her job and anxious to avoid errors.

Case 1

A cheque for $882 was received from a customer. The cheque, dated March 14, was in payment of an invoice for $900, dated March 2. The terms were 2/10, n/30 and it was obvious that the customer had deducted the 2% discount of $18. Since the cheque was issued 12 days after the invoice date and payment was not made within the 10 days stated on the invoice, Tina gave the customer credit for only $882. This left a balance in the account of $18.

a) Did Tina do the correct thing? Give reasons for your answer.
b) What would you have done?

Competitive Discounts You are the accountant for a well-established company with sales of $200 000 a month. Your firm deals with many old and reliable customers who have bought from you for many years.

Case 2

A new competitior has opened a business and has offered one of your best customers a 2% discount for payments made within 15 days of invoice dates. Your firm has never offered such cash discounts.

a) How much would it cost your firm to offer a competitive discount?
b) What factors should be considered before deciding whether cash discounts should be offered to customers?

Financing Purchases General Manufacturing Ltd. produces a household cleaning compound that is sold as a private brand by a very large supermarket chain. Sales to the supermarket chain average $300 000 each month. Payment is received on the thirtieth of every month from the supermarket. No discounts are involved.

Case 3

General Manufacturing Ltd. buys $100 000 worth of raw materials a month. It has received an offer of a 3% discount if payments are made to the materials supplier within 15 days of the invoice date. Invoices are usually dated the first or second day of the month. Present terms of payment are Net 60. It is felt that there would not be enough cash on hand each month to pay the invoices within 15 days of the invoice date in order to take advantage of the 3% discount. Bank loans are readily available at 12% interest a year.

a) What alternatives are available to General Manufacturing Ltd.?
b) What would you do? Support your answer.

The Metropolitan Life Purchasing System Metropolitan Life has been providing personal and group life, health, and disability insurance to Canadians for more than 100 years. Its head office, Figure 10.14, is located in Ottawa and it has over 70 offices across the country. Metropolitan Life employs 3 500 people and provides insurance coverage for over 3 500 000 Canadians. In 1976, the total revenue from insurance premiums, investments, and miscellaneous sources was $346 000 000.

Case 4

A visit to the Ottawa headquarters of Metropolitan Life will show how the

Figure 10.14 *Metropolitan Life head office, Ottawa*

PURCHASING DIVISION
MATERIAL AND EQUIPMENT REQUISITION Date June 18, 19..

QUANTITY	MATERIAL, SIZE, COLOUR, MODEL, ETC.	Account No.	Code
1	Sunar Reception Desk #29-LP 3rd drawer to be lockable black vinyl top Manufactured by Sunar Industries Ltd.		

FOR PURCHASING DIV. USE ONLY

ORDER NUMBER	DATE PLACED
E1503	June 25, 19..
F.O.B. Destination	F.O.B.

Delivery Instructions Verdun District Approved [signature]

Requested by J. Brown Division Field Administration

Figure 10.15 *Metropolitan Life purchase requisition*

accounting paper work is processed for a typical purchase. The divisions and sections within the company that are invovled in a purchase are:

- Purchasing Division
- Supply Division
- Accounting Division – Authenticating Section
  – Accounts Payable Section
  – Financial Records Section
- Auditing Division
- Receipts and Disbursements Division
- Electronic Data Processing Division (EDP Division)

How a Desk is Purchased The description that follows shows the steps involved when J. Brown of the Field Administration Division requests that a new desk be purchased.

Purchase Requisition The purchasing system starts with a purchase requisition that is completed by the Field Administration Division. The requisition is sent to the Purchasing Division where the signature of the person who authorized the requisition, J. Brown, is checked against a file of signature cards. The purchase requisition is illustrated in Figure 10.15.

Purchasing Division A buyer in the Purchasing Division then attempts to find a supplier who will sell the item at an acceptable price. In the case of a large, expensive purchase, bids are requested. When the buyer decides on a supplier, a purchase order with five copies is prepared (Figure 10.16). The first copy is sent to the supplier. A copy of the order is sent to the Accounts Payable Section, and another copy to the Supply Division. Two copies are retained in the Purchasing Division.

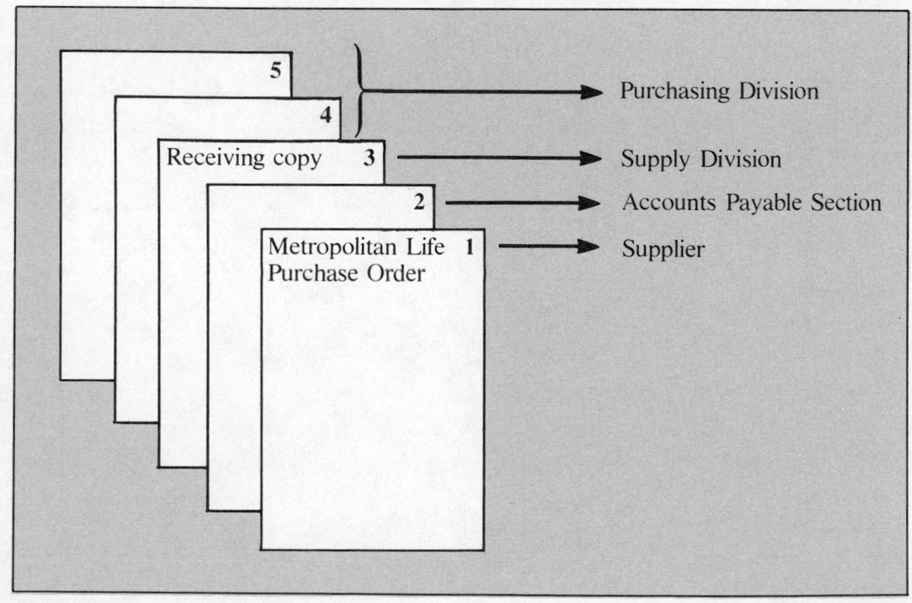

Figure 10.16 *This chart illustrates what happens to the five copies of the purchase order*

The Supply Division When the supplier ships the desk, it is received by the Supply Division which verifies the quantity and quality of all goods received. Remember, they have a copy of the purchase order (called the receiving copy) and therefore know what they should be receiving. After this verification is complete, the Supply Division prepares a receiving report which is a daily summary of orders received. Copies of this summary are sent to the Purchasing Division and also to the Accounts Payable Section along with the receiving copy of the purchase order. The Purchasing Division now knows that the order is completed and the Accounts Payable Section knows that the desk has been received.

The Accounting Division – Accounts Payable Section After the vendor has shipped the desk, an invoice (Figure 10.17) will be mailed to Metropolitan Life.

When the invoice is received by the Accounts Payable Section, it is compared to the purchase order held by Accounts Payable, to the receiving report, and to the receiving copy of the purchase order. This matching process ensures that the correct order has been received, and that the amount billed on the invoice is the same as the amount for the goods received. If the four documents match, the invoice is approved and a cheque request is issued. Figure 10.18 summarizes the steps in this matching process.

The Authenticating Section – Processing the Payment The signature on the cheque request is compared to a file of signature cards in the Authenticating Section and a number is assigned to make the cheque request into a voucher.

A copy of the cheque request voucher is kept on file along with the invoice and receiving report in the Accounts Payable Section. The other copy of the voucher is sent to the Receipts and Disbursements Division.

SIMPSON'S
CONTRACT DIVISION

DATE 07-24-xx 275 SLATER ST., OTTAWA K1P 5H9 INVOICE **NO. 45120**

TO Metropolitan Life
180 Wellington Street
Ottawa, Ontario K1P 5A3

YOUR ORDER NUMBER	E 1503
CHARGE ACCT. NUMBER	W19000
REPRESENTATIVE	A. Madigan

TERMS CHARGE ☐ PAYABLE 30 DAYS FROM DATE OF INVOICE ☐ INSTALMENT

QUANTITY	DESCRIPTION	UNIT PRICE	TOTAL	
1	Re: Montreal Branch		$ 785	00
	Sunar Reception desk		62	80
	+ 8% P.S.T. (Quebec)		$ 847	80

PLEASE FORWARD ALL PAYMENTS TO
SIMPSON'S CONTRACT DIVISION
401 BAY STREET SUITE 700
TORONTO, ONTARIO M2S 1G1

CUSTOMER INVOICE

Figure 10.17 *Invoice received by Metropolitan Life from Simpsons*

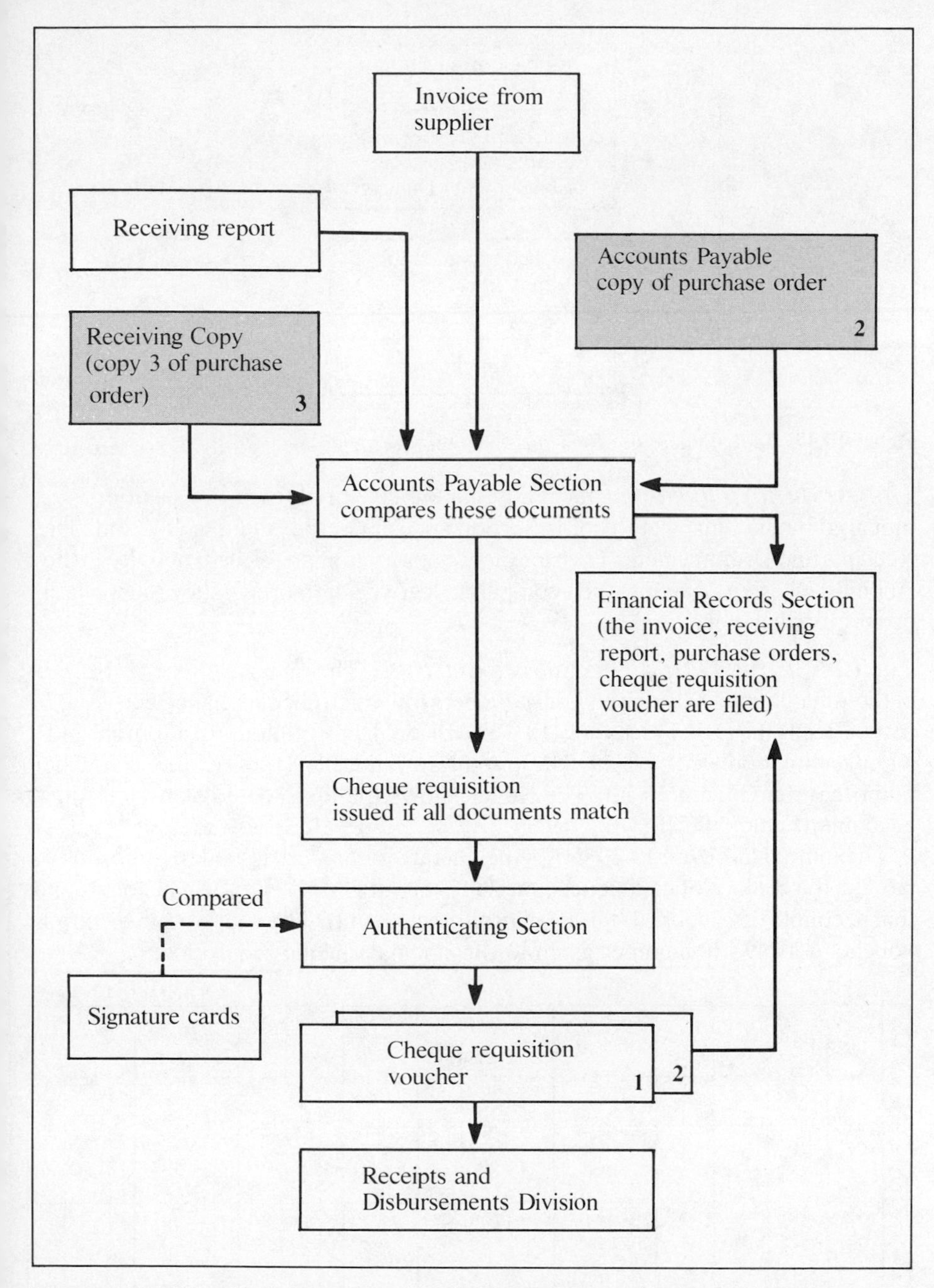

Figure 10.18 *Matching process used by the Accounts Payable Section*

The Receipts and Disbursements Division The Receipts and Disbursements Division prepares a cheque and a stub for each numbered voucher received from the Accounting Division. The amounts on the cheque and the voucher are checked and the cheque is mailed to the supplier. The voucher is then returned to the Accounting Division, Financial Records Section for filing.

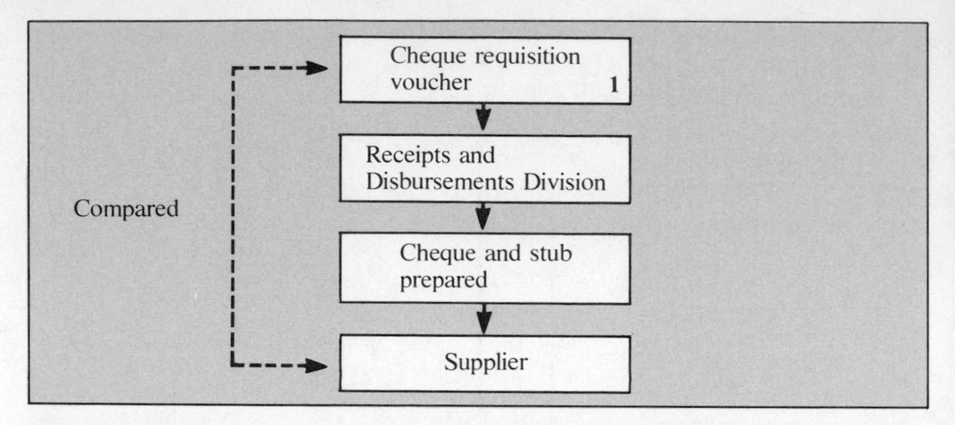

Figure 10.19 *Functions of the Receipts and Disbursements Section*

The Auditing Division Each day a summary of all cash transactions is prepared by the Financial Records Section and sent to the Auditing Division. The Receipts and Disbursements Division also sends a summary of all its activity to the Auditing Division. Auditing then compares the two summaries – they must match or an error has been made.

The Electronic Data Processing Division The Financial Records Section of the Accounting Division sends all vouchers for which cheques have been issued to the Electronic Data Processing (EDP) Division. Daily printouts of a Journal and a Ledger are produced by EDP. The journal is a listing of all transactions in voucher number order (Figure 10.20). The ledger shows the up-to-date balances in the accounts (Figure 10.21).

The journal in Figure 10.20 shows the cheque for $847.80 issued to Simpsons to pay for the desk. Notice that account 760 is credited (this is a Cash account) and that account 705 is debited (this is a Furniture account). The source of this entry is voucher 820249, the number given to the original cheque requisition.

Accounting Division August 1, 19--

DATE			TYPE OF ENTRY	VOUCHER NUMBER	ACCOUNT			CURRENCY CODE	DEBIT	CREDIT
MO.	DAY	YR.			DEPT.	ACCT.	SUB			
07	30	--	1	820248	30	705	01	2	527 73	
07	30	--	1	820248	30	313	51	2		527 73
07	30	--	1	820249	30	705	01	2	847 80	
07	30	--	1	820249	30	760	21	2		847 80
07	30	--	1	820250	30	705	01	2	49 20	
07	30	--	1	820250	30	319	19	2		
07	30	--	1	820250	30	816	01	2		51 66

Figure 10.20 *A computer-prepared journal in voucher number order from the Electronic Data Processing (EDP) Division*

The ledger in Figure 10.21 shows that the balance of the Furniture account when the day started was $2 840.36. To this total was added the desk costing $847.80 to give a balance of $3 688.16 in the Furniture account. Each day's ledger printout provides that day's transactions and a month-to-date total for each account.

Accounting Division   LISTING OF ENTRIES BY ACCOUNT FOR   SEPT. 11, 19--

DATE			TYPE OF ENTRY	VOUCHER NUMBER	ACCOUNT			CURRENCY CODE	DEBIT	CREDIT	BALANCE
MO.	DAY	YR.			DEPT.	ACCT.	SUB				
09	10	--	1	FORWARD	30	705	01	2	2 840 36		2 840 36
09	11	--	1	820249	30	705	01	2	847 80		3 688 16

Figure 10.21 *Computer-prepared ledger showing the updated balance in the Furniture account that is debited for the purchase of the desk*

Metropolitan Life's Computer A Honeywell H8200 computer is used by Metropolitan Life. Input is converted directly to magnetic tape (rather than to punch cards) by a Consolidated Computer Key Edit System. The magnetic tape is then processed by the computer (Figure 10.22).

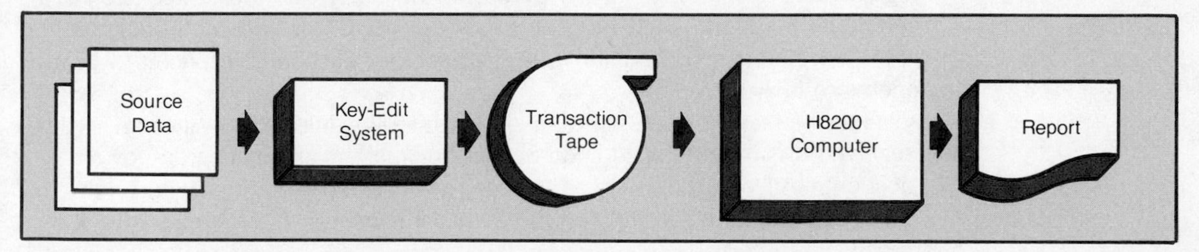

Figure 10.22 *Metropolitan Life uses a Honeywell H8200 computer*

One of the services the computer provides is a *cheques issued* master file. This is a record of each cheque issued and its current status. Each day, cheques that are issued are added to the file. The stubs are used as input. In addition, the status of any cheque cashed is changed from outstanding to cashed. The cancelled cheques returned by the bank are used as input. Reports of each day's activity are produced and sent to the Auditing Division where they are matched against various control totals. For instance, the computer print-out of cheques issued is matched to the previously mentioned summary of cash transactions from the Financial Records Section.

Metropolitan's computer system is used for many other applications. One of its main uses is to maintain master files on all of Metropolitan's policyholders. In addition to maintaining up-to-date information such as address, amount of insurance, premium amount, and the date premiums were paid, this file is used to provide information reports to management and to policyholders. For example, a billing program is used to print billing notices to inform policyholders that their premiums are due.

a) How many different divisions are involved when Metropolitan Life makes a purchase?

b) i) What form did J. Brown complete when he wanted a new desk purchased?
   ii) To which division was the form sent?
c) What form was completed by the Metropolitan Life buyer and sent to the supplier?
d) Why was a copy of the purchase order sent to the Supply Division and to the Accounts Payable Section?
e) How did the Accounts Payable Section know the desk had been received?
f) What is the purpose of the Authenticating Section?
g) Metropolitan Life has a very elaborate purchasing system which involves a number of different people and documents. Why does the company use such an elaborate system?

Career Profile

An Accounts Payable Clerk Fong Hum is an accounts payable clerk with D.S. Fraser & Co. Ltd. This company is a wholesaler of heating and refrigeration equipment. Fong works in the head office of D.S. Fraser and her job involves the recording of purchases and payments in the accounts payable accounts. Fong has worked with D.S. Fraser for two years, since graduating from high school. While in high school, accounting was her favourite subject so she took three accounting courses. Two of these were theory courses. The third was a practical course called applied accounting. In this course, she learned to use accounting machines and the one-write board.

Fong's job at D.S. Fraser Ltd. includes the following duties. When an invoice is received it is date-stamped and checked for mathematical accuracy by an accounting clerk in the cost department. The purchase order, receiving report, and purchase invoice are compared to see that prices, goods ordered, and goods received are correct.

Fong then receives the invoice from the cost department. She records the invoices using a posting machine. Fong uses the batch-posting process. This means that she gathers together all invoices from creditors in alphabetical order. When a number of invoices have been received from a particular creditor, that creditor's account is placed in the posting machine. This allows Fong to post several transactions for a creditor, which is much more efficient than posting them one at a time.

The comptroller of the company is responsible for initiating payment of invoices. A list of accounts to be paid is prepared by the comptroller and sent to Fong. The invoices to be paid are checked against the Accounts Payable accounts. The cheque is then prepared on the posting machine at the same time as the Account Payable is decreased by the machine. The invoice is then marked *paid* and is filed alphabetically in a *paid file*.

The Accounts Payable Ledger is also Fong's responsibility. Most creditors send a monthly statement to her company. This statement shows the balance owing, the charges during the month, and the payments received. Fong checks these statements to see if they agree with her Accounts Payable Ledger accounts. If they do not agree, she tries to determine the cause of the problem. Occasionally it is necessary for her to write to the creditors when she finds they have made errors.

CHAPTER 11

Accounting for Sales

Unit 27

In the last chapter, you learned the procedures for *purchasing* goods and services. In this chapter, the procedures for recording the *sales* of goods and services are discussed.

Renfrew Printing

*1

Renfrew Printing offers a printing service to customers. The company is located in Renfrew, Ontario. In order to earn a profit, it must obtain printing jobs, complete the jobs efficiently, and charge customers an amount which covers the costs of completing the jobs and which includes net income or profit.

In October, Renfrew Printing was asked to quote a price for the printing of 5 000 No. 10 envelopes for MacKillican and Associates, a customer located in Renfrew. Bill McAdam, the manager of Renfrew Printing, quoted the customer a price of $22.00 per 1 000 envelopes. He obtained this figure by considering the materials, labour, and other expenses that would be incurred in completing the job.

After the job was completed, the invoice shown in Figure 11.1 was sent to the customer.

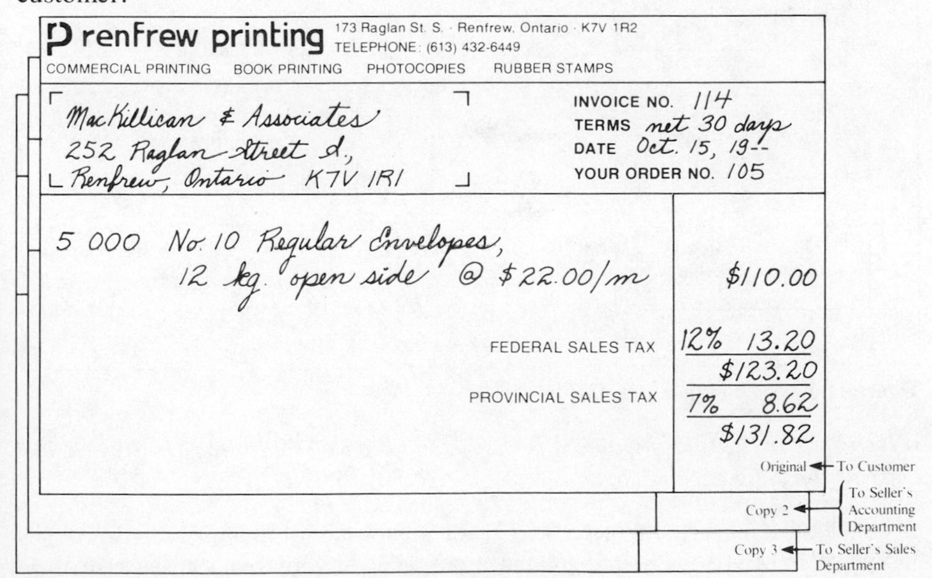
renfrew printing 173 Raglan St. S. · Renfrew, Ontario · K7V 1R2
TELEPHONE: (613) 432-6449
COMMERCIAL PRINTING BOOK PRINTING PHOTOCOPIES RUBBER STAMPS

MacKillican & Associates
252 Raglan Street S.,
Renfrew, Ontario K7V 1R1

INVOICE NO. 114
TERMS net 30 days
DATE Oct. 15, 19--
YOUR ORDER NO. 105

5 000 No. 10 Regular Envelopes, 12 kg. open side @ $22.00/m	$110.00
FEDERAL SALES TAX	12% 13.20
	$123.20
PROVINCIAL SALES TAX	7% 8.62
	$131.82

Figure 11.1 *Distribution of sales invoice copies*

Can you answer the following questions concerning this invoice?

- *Who is the seller?*
- *Who is the buyer?*
- *What is the total to be paid by the customer and when must it be paid?*
- *What is the quantity of the order?*
- *What does $22.00/M mean?*
- *How is the $110.00 calculated?*
- *How are the federal sales tax and the provincial sales tax calculated?*

Credit Sales Since Renfrew Printing gave terms of *net 30 days,* MacKillican and Associates must pay the invoice within 30 days of October 15, the date of the invoice. Payment is due from MacKillican on or before November 14 (October 15 + 30 days). Because the customer is to pay at a later date, the sale is called a *credit sale.*

A credit sale is paid for at a later date.

For each credit sale, a source document called a *sales invoice* is prepared. This document, commonly called a *bill,* is the seller's record of the transaction. Several copies of the sales invoice are prepared (Figure 11.1). The original, or first copy, is sent to the customer to notify him or her of the amount owed and to serve as the customer's record of the sale. A second copy is sent to the seller's accounting department. From this copy, a journal entry is made. A third copy may be prepared and used by the sales department as their record of the sale.

A sales invoice is the source document for a credit sale.

Recording Sales Invoices

*2

Figure 11.2 illustrates the steps in recording a sales invoice.

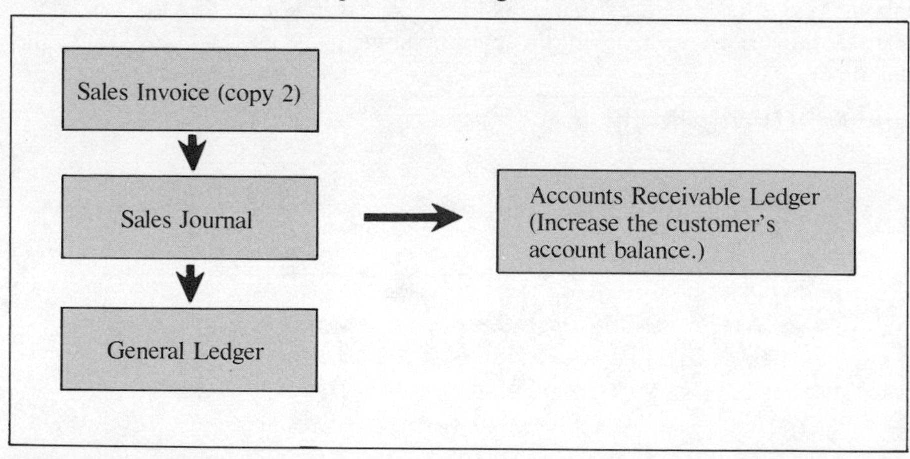

Figure 11.2 *Recording a sales invoice*

Which copy of the sales invoice is referred to in Figure 11.2? Where is the original copy of the sales invoice sent?

On October 15 sales invoice No. 121 for $500 was sent to a customer, Visual Graphics. When the accounting department receives copy 2 of the sales invoice, the credit sale is recorded in the journal as follows:

Oct.	15	Accounts Receivable/Visual Graphics		500 —	
		Sales			500 —
		Sold on account, Invoice No. 121			

After the entry is journalized, it is posted to both the Accounts Receivable Ledger and the General Ledger.

Cash Sale When a customer pays for goods or services as soon as they are sold, the transaction is called a *cash sale*. A source document is prepared for each cash sale. The type of document completed is determined by the type of product being sold. For example, for many low-priced items, a cash sale is recorded on a cash register and the customer receives the cash register receipt as proof of payment.

*3
A cash sale is paid for immediately.

For more expensive items, such as shoes or clothing, a *cash sales slip* is completed. The cash sales slip contains a description of the goods sold. A cash sale is recorded in the Cash Receipts Journal.

A cash sales slip is a source document for a cash sale.

Sales Tax

Both the federal and provincial governments impose sales taxes. A brief description of the two types of sales tax follows.

*4

Federal Sales Tax The federal government collects a 12% sales tax on goods manufactured and imported into Canada. A company which manufactures a product, for example bicycles, must add tax to the wholesale price of each bicycle. This tax is then forwarded to the federal government.

Federal sales tax is charged on the price of goods manufactured or imported into Canada.

Manufacturer's selling price	$60.00
12% federal sales tax	7.20
	$67.20

A number of items are exempt or free from the federal sales tax. These include food, drugs, certain production machinery, farm and fishing equipment, and building materials. As well, materials which become part of other manufactured goods are exempt since the completed product will be taxed when it is sold by the final manufacturer. In this chapter, most problems and examples will deal with companies which do not manufacture or import goods. Therefore, the federal sales tax will not be involved.

Provincial Retail Sales Tax All provinces, except Alberta, impose a sales tax on retail sales. The tax is charged on the price of goods sold to consumers. In most provinces, the tax is charged only on tangible commodities, although a few services (such as telephone service) are taxed. Such items as food, drugs, children's clothes, school supplies, and farm equipment are exempt from sales tax.

*5
Provincial retail sales tax is charged on the price of some goods sold to the final user.

Ontario	7%	Prince Edward Island	8%
British Columbia	5%	Nova Scotia	7%
Saskatchewan	5%	Newfoundland	7%
Manitoba	5%	New Brunswick	8%
Quebec	8%		

The retailer collects the tax when goods are sold to consumers. The retailer then sends the tax to the provincial government. This is usually done each month for the previous month's collections. Figure 11.3 is the form completed in Ontario by retailers when sales tax is remitted (sent) to the government.

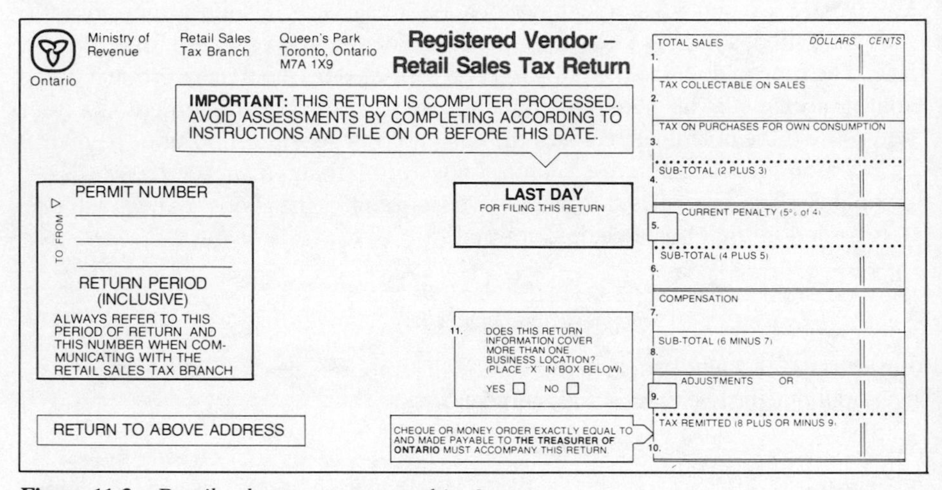

Ontario
Ministry of Revenue
Retail Sales Tax Branch
Queen's Park Toronto, Ontario M7A 1X9

Registered Vendor – Retail Sales Tax Return

IMPORTANT: THIS RETURN IS COMPUTER PROCESSED. AVOID ASSESSMENTS BY COMPLETING ACCORDING TO INSTRUCTIONS AND FILE ON OR BEFORE THIS DATE.

TO FROM ▷ PERMIT NUMBER

RETURN PERIOD (INCLUSIVE)

ALWAYS REFER TO THIS PERIOD OF RETURN AND THIS NUMBER WHEN COMMUNICATING WITH THE RETAIL SALES TAX BRANCH

LAST DAY FOR FILING THIS RETURN

11. DOES THIS RETURN INFORMATION COVER MORE THAN ONE BUSINESS LOCATION? (PLACE X IN BOX BELOW) YES ☐ NO ☐

RETURN TO ABOVE ADDRESS

CHEQUE OR MONEY ORDER EXACTLY EQUAL TO AND MADE PAYABLE TO **THE TREASURER OF ONTARIO** MUST ACCOMPANY THIS RETURN

	DOLLARS	CENTS
1. TOTAL SALES		
2. TAX COLLECTABLE ON SALES		
3. TAX ON PURCHASES FOR OWN CONSUMPTION		
4. SUB-TOTAL (2 PLUS 3)		
5. CURRENT PENALTY (5% of 4)		
6. SUB-TOTAL (4 PLUS 5)		
7. COMPENSATION		
8. SUB-TOTAL (6 MINUS 7)		
9. ADJUSTMENTS OR		
10. TAX REMITTED (8 PLUS OR MINUS 9)		

Figure 11.3 *Retail sales tax return used in Ontario*

*6

The Sales Tax Payable Account On January 10, Office Furniture Ltd. delivers a $450 desk to Sound Corporation and mails the invoice.

Since Sound Corporation will use the desk in their office, and since it is not exempt from provincial sales tax, 7% of the sales price, or $31.50 must be collected from the buyer. Office Furniture will record the invoice by the following journal entry:

Jan.	10	Accounts Receivable/Sound Corp.		481.50	
		Sales			450.—
		Provincial Sales Tax Payable			31.50
		Invoice No. 121			

*7

The amount of sales tax collected by Office Furniture during the month is recorded in the liability account called Provincial Sales Tax Payable. This account is a liability. It increases when taxable goods are sold. It decreases when the seller of taxable goods sends the sales tax to the provincial government.

Provincial Sales Tax Payable		
	Jan. 3	73.43
	4	35.62
	6	55.62
	9	41.74
	10	31.50
	31	43.65
		1 243.62

Provincial Sales Tax Payable	
Debit	Credit
Decrease	Increase
Debit the account when sales tax is remitted to the government.	Credit the account when taxable goods are sold.

At the end of the month, the amount of tax collected is calculated. In January, Office Furniture collected $1 243.62 in provincial sales tax and must remit this amount to the provincial treasurer. When the cheque is issued, the following journal entry is made:

The Sales Tax Payable account is a liability account.

				Debit	Credit
Feb.	15	Provincial Sales Tax Payable		1 243 62	
		Cash			1 243 62
		Cheque No. 299 to Provincial			
		Treasurer for January sales			
		tax collections			

Recording Sales Tax Commission Several provinces pay a commission to companies in return for the collection of sales tax. For example, in New Brunswick, a company receives 2% commission on the first $250 of tax it collects and 1% on amounts over $250. British Columbia pays a commission of 3% on the first $2 500 of tax collected and 1% of the tax collected over $2 500. In Ontario, the retailer is paid a commission of 3% of all tax collected. A maximum commission of $500 may be earned in any one year.

***8**

The commission earned by a company is usually recorded in an account entitled Miscellaneous Revenue or Sales Tax Commission.

***9**

On June 15, Western Supply Ltd. of Vancouver, British Columbia, has a balance of $300 in its Sales Tax Payable account. This balance represents retail tax collected from customers in May. When Western Supply remits the tax to the provincial government, it keeps a 3% commission or $9 ($0.03 \times 300 = 9$). The entry, in General Journal form, to record the payment to the government and the commission earned is:

				Debit	Credit
June	15	Sales Tax Payable		300 —	
		Cash			291 —
		Sales Tax Commission			9 —
		To remit May sales tax and			
		to record commission earned			

The Sales Journal

*10

A Sales Journal is used to record credit sales.

In Chapter 10 you learned that a Purchases Journal is used to record purchases of goods and services on account (credit purchases). The use of special columns saves time and effort in recording and posting purchases. For the same reasons, a *Sales Journal* is used to record sales on account (credit sales) by companies which make many such sales. Figure 11.4 is a Sales Journal for Fraser Enterprises of Vancouver, B.C., in which a number of credit sales have been recorded.

In the Sales Journal, each transaction requires only one line. Notice that in some of the transactions, the customer is charged sales tax and in others, there is no sales tax. This is because some of the sales involve non-taxable items.

*11

Balancing the Sales Journal If transactions have been recorded correctly, the total of the debit columns should equal the total of the credit columns. At the bottom of each page and at the end of the month, this procedure is followed:

1. Add the columns. Write the totals in pencil.
2. If the debit total equals the credit totals, write the totals in ink.
3. Rule double lines across the money column and the date column.

SALES JOURNAL — PAGE

DATE		INV. NO.	CUSTOMER	PR	ACCOUNTS RECEIVABLE DEBIT	SALES CREDIT	PROVINCIAL SALES TAX PAYABLE CREDIT
19— July	5	71	K. Roessler	✓	105 —	100 —	5 —
	7	72	C. Bard	✓	315 —	300 —	15 —
	8	73	M. Wong	✓	75 —	75 —	
	12	74	G. Saikeley	✓	450 —	450 —	
	13	75	K. Rice	✓	735 —	700 —	35 —
	15	76	C. Bard	✓	630 —	600 —	30 —
					2 310 —	2 225 —	85 — (1)
			Debits = $2310		2 310 —	2 225 —	85 — (2)
			Credits = $2310	(3)	(102)	(410)	(222)

Posted daily to the customer accounts in the Accounts Receivable Ledger

Totals are posted to the General Ledger.

Figure 11.4 *A Sales Journal showing correct balancing and posting procedures*

Figure 11.4 is an example of a Sales Journal which has been balanced. If the month has not ended, the totals are carried forward to the next page. At the end of the month, the totals are posted to the General Ledger.

Posting the Sales Journal The following steps describe the posting of the Sales Journal. These steps are illustrated in Figure 11.4.

*12

1. Each day, post the amounts in the Accounts Receivable column to the customer accounts in the Accounts Receivable Ledger. A check mark is placed in the posting reference column of the journal to indicate the completion of the posting. A check mark is used instead of a number since customer accounts are listed alphabetically in the Accounts Receivable Ledger and are not numbered.

Daily postings are made from the Sales Journal to the customer accounts in the Accounts Receivable Ledger.

*13

2. At the end of the month after the Sales Journal is balanced, the columns are posted to the Accounts Receivable, Sales, and Provincial Sales Tax accounts in the General Ledger. Account numbers are shown below the totals.

Ledger Proofs After the Sales Journal has been posted to the individual customer accounts in the Accounts Receivable Ledger and to the General Ledger, it is necessary to prove the accuracy of these ledgers. The accuracy of the Accounts Receivable Ledger is proven by preparing a *schedule of accounts receivable* (Figure 11.5). The total of this schedule should equal the Accounts Receivable Control account in the General Ledger. The mathematical accuracy of the General Ledger is proven by the preparation of a trial balance. The debit total should equal the credit total.

*14

Fraser Enterprises
Schedule of Accounts Receivable
July 15, 19__

K. Roessler	105 —
C. Bard	945 —
M. Wong	75 —
G. Saikeley	450 —
K. Rice	735 —
	2 310 —

Figure 11.5 *Schedule of accounts receivable prepared from individual customer accounts in the Accounts Receivable Ledger. In this simplified example, the total of the schedule of accounts receivable will equal the total of the Accounts Receivable Control account in the General Ledger if the accounts are accurate.*

Sales Tax on Sales Returns and Allowances Since a customer is charged sales tax when goods are purchased, the sales tax should be refunded when goods are returned by the customer. On July 7, $300 worth of merchandise was sold to C. Bard by Fraser Enterprises. After recording the transaction, the accounts in Fraser's ledgers show the following:

*15

Accounts Receivable

C. Bard	
315	

Sales	
	300

Sales Tax Payable	
	15

On July 21, C. Bard returned $50 worth of the merchandise because it was defective. Fraser Enterprises issued a credit invoice for $52.50 to the customer (Figure 11.6). This invoice notifies the customer, C. Bard, that her account balance is reduced by $50 plus the $2.50 sales tax on the returned merchandise.

FRASER ENTERPRISES — CREDIT INVOICE
175 Woodburn Ave., Vancouver, B.C. V75 2W5

Sold to C. Bard
Harmen Ave.
Vancouver, B.C.
V6E 1E5

Ship to Same

No. C-12
Date July 21, 19--

Quantity	Description	Unit Price	Amount
	We have credited your account for returned defective goods.		50 00
	Provincial Sales Tax @ 5%		2 50
	Total Credit to Your Account		52 50

Figure 11.6 *Credit invoice*

The seller, Fraser Enterprises, now owes $2.50 *less* to the provincial government. The effect of the return on the account balances is:

Accounts Receivable/C. Bard		Sales Returns and Allowances		Sales Tax Payable	
315	52.50	50		2.50	15

Figure 11.7 shows these two transactions recorded in General Journal form:

GENERAL JOURNAL — PAGE 33

DATE		PARTICULARS	PR	DEBIT	CREDIT
19-- July	7	Accounts Receivable/C. Bard		315 —	
		Sales			300 —
		Sales Tax Payable			15 —
		Invoice 72, net 30			
	21	Sales Returns & Allowances		50 —	
		Sales Tax Payable		2 50	
		Accounts Receivable/C. Bard			52 50
		C-12, Goods returned			

Figure 11.7 *Transactions recorded in General Journal*

Recording Sales Returns in the Sales Journal In the preceding example, goods returned were recorded in an account called the Sales Returns and Allowances account. The transaction for the goods returned was recorded in the General Journal. *16

For businesses that feel it is not necessary to use a Sales Returns and Allowances account, returns are recorded as decreases in the Sales account on the debit side. Such transactions may be recorded in the Sales Journal using the circling method. Figure 11.8 illustrates a sales return recorded in the Sales Journal using this method.

Circled items in the Accounts Receivable debit column represent decreases in the customer's account. They should therefore be posted as *credits*. When a column containing a circled item is totalled, the circled amount is subtracted from the uncircled amounts. In Figure 11.8 for example, the Sales Credit column total of $2 175 is found by adding the six uncircled items and subtracting $50, the circled amount.

SALES JOURNAL PAGE 17

DATE	INV. NO.	CUSTOMER	PR	ACCOUNTS RECEIVABLE DEBIT	SALES CREDIT	PROVINCIAL SALES TAX PAYABLE CREDIT
19-- July 5	71	K. Roessler		105 —	100 —	5 —
7	72	C. Bard		315 —	300 —	15 —
8	73	M. Wong		75 —	75 —	
12	74	G. Saikelley		450 —	450 —	
13	75	K. Rice		735 —	700 —	35 —
15	76	C. Bard		630 —	600 —	30 —
21	C12	C. Bard		(52 50)	(50 —)	(2 50)
				2 257 50	2 175 —	82 50
				2 257 50	2 175 —	82 50

Figure 11.8 *Circled items representing sales returns are subtracted from uncircled items*

Direct Posting

In Chapter 8, it was shown that information could be posted directly from source documents to customer and creditor accounts. In this chapter, a method of posting from the Sales Journal to the Accounts Receivable Ledger has been described. The latter system is used by small firms with comparatively few customers. *17

When direct posting is used, copies of the invoice are provided to the accounts receivable clerk for direct posting and to the general accountant for journalizing. Some companies send two copies of the invoice to the customer. The second copy is returned by the customer to the seller when the invoice is paid. Thus, the seller knows exactly which invoice a customer is paying.

Statement of Account

*18

Suppose a company has a customer by the name of J. Clarke, and another named J. Clark. A sale of $100 to J. Clarke was incorrectly posted to J. Clark's account. In the seller's Accounts Receivable Ledger, J. Clarke's account balance would be $100 too low and J. Clark's account balance would be $100 too high. *How would this error be discovered?*

A statement of account is a form sent to customers showing charges, amounts credited, and the balance of an account for a period of time, usually one month.

To locate errors of this type, many companies send a *statement of account* to their customers (Figure 11.9). At regular periods, usually every month, a copy of the debits and credits in customer accounts is mailed to every customer. In effect, a copy of the account is sent to the customer. The statement of account serves two purposes:

- It enables a customer to compare his or her records with those of the seller and thus to locate errors.
- It reminds a customer of the balance owing.

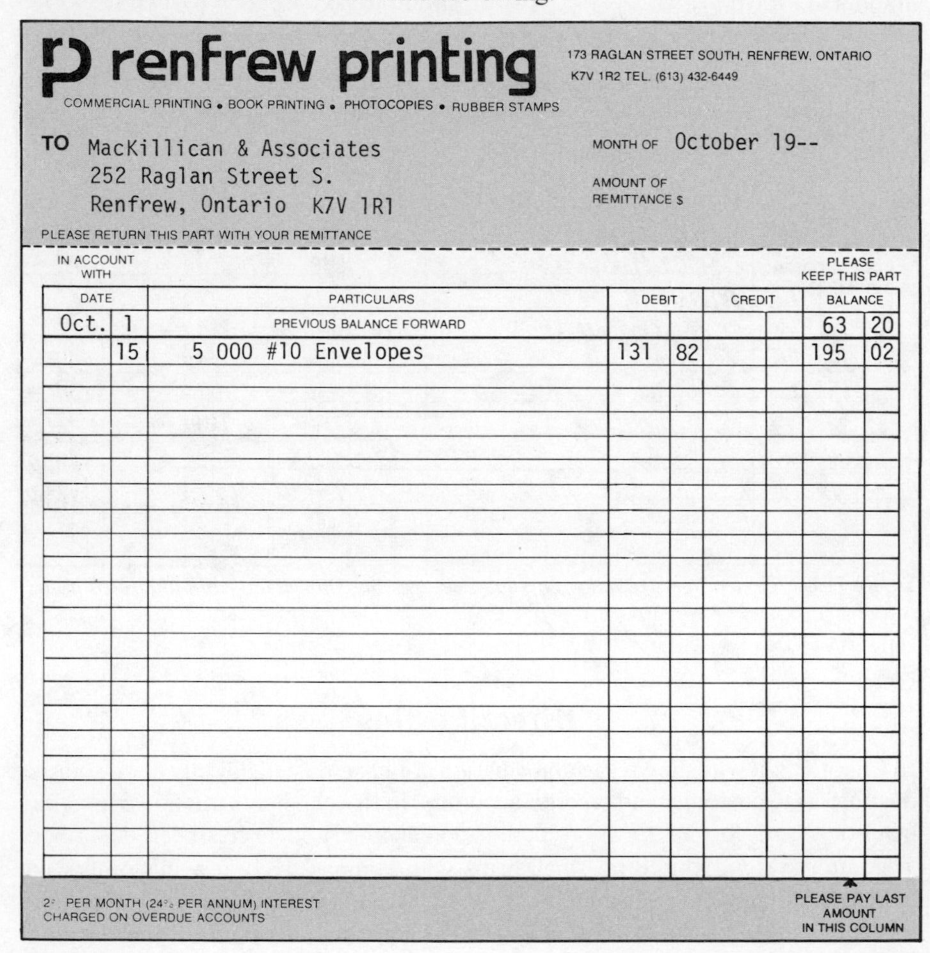

renfrew printing

173 RAGLAN STREET SOUTH, RENFREW, ONTARIO
K7V 1R2 TEL. (613) 432-6449

COMMERCIAL PRINTING • BOOK PRINTING • PHOTOCOPIES • RUBBER STAMPS

TO MacKillican & Associates
252 Raglan Street S.
Renfrew, Ontario K7V 1R1

MONTH OF October 19--

AMOUNT OF REMITTANCE $

PLEASE RETURN THIS PART WITH YOUR REMITTANCE

IN ACCOUNT WITH

PLEASE KEEP THIS PART

DATE		PARTICULARS	DEBIT		CREDIT		BALANCE	
Oct.	1	PREVIOUS BALANCE FORWARD					63	20
	15	5 000 #10 Envelopes	131	82			195	02

2% PER MONTH (24% PER ANNUM) INTEREST CHARGED ON OVERDUE ACCOUNTS

PLEASE PAY LAST AMOUNT IN THIS COLUMN

Figure 11.9 *Statement of account sent each month by Renfrew Printing to its customers. It shows the balance forwarded from the previous month, and the transactions for the current month.*

Preparing the Statement of Account The statement of account may be prepared by hand or using equipment such as an electronic accounting machine, a computer, or a one-write board.

Many smaller firms use an accounting machine to post transactions to customer accounts. The statement of account and the actual customer account are prepared at the same time, using chemically treated paper. The statement and customer account are both inserted into the machine. When a debit or a credit is recorded on the statement, it is reproduced on the account.

Cycle Billing A company which has only a few customers usually sends a statement of account to each customer at the end of the month.

*19

A company with a large number of customers may find it impossible to prepare all the statements at the end of the month. A more efficient method of handling the preparation of the statements is to distribute the work evenly over the month. Statements are prepared and mailed to groups of customers at different times of the month. Figure 11.10 illustrates how the work is scheduled:

Cycle Billing Schedule

Initial of Customer's Last Name:	Includes Transactions Up To:	Day of the Month on which Statement is Prepared:
A - E	5th	6th
F - L	13th	14th
M - R	20th	21st
S - Z	29th	30th

Figure 11.10 *Cycle billing*

In *cycle billing,* the records of transactions (source documents such as invoices and cash receipt lists) for someone like J. Clarke would be accumulated from the date of the last statement. These transactions would be entered in the customer's account and the statement of account would be prepared on the sixth day of each month. The statement of account for Resticon Ltd. would be prepared on the 21st day of each month.

Cycle billing is a method of spreading the work of preparing and mailing statements to customers over the month.

Facts to Remember

A *credit sale* is paid for at a later date.

A *sales invoice* is the source document for a credit sale.

A *cash sale* is paid for immediately.

A *cash sales slip* is a source document for a cash sale.

Federal sales tax is charged on the price of some goods manufactured or imported into Canada.

Provincial retail sales tax is charged on the price of some goods sold to the final user. All provinces except Alberta impose a retail sales tax.

The *Sales Tax Payable account* is a liability account.

A *Sales Journal* is used to record credit sales.

Daily postings are made from the Sales Journal to the customer accounts in the Accounts Receivable Ledger.

A *statement of account* is a form sent to customers showing charges, amounts credited, and the balance of an account for a period of time, usually one month.

Cycle billing is a method of spreading the work of preparing and mailing statements to customers over the month.

Checking Your Reading

Questions

1. What is a credit sale?
2. What source document is prepared for a credit sale?
3. What source document is prepared for a cash sale?
4. In which special journal is a credit sale recorded?
5. What does it mean if a product is exempt from sales tax?
6. What is the amount of your province's retail sales tax? Has it changed since this text was published?
7. A sale of merchandise costing $200 is made with terms of net 30 and sales tax of $14, totalling $214. What accounts are debited and credited in recording this transaction?
8. A cash sale of merchandise for $70 is made. Provincial sales tax is $4.90, totalling $74.90. What accounts are debited and credited in recording this transaction?
9. What type of account (asset, liability, income or expense) is the Sales Tax Payable account?

10. A company collected $510 in retail sales tax during March. What is the journal entry required to record the cheque issued to the provincial treasurer in order to remit the sales tax? (Assume there is no commission paid by the government.)

11. From which column of the Sales Journal are individual entries posted daily?

12. To which ledger are the totals of a Sales Journal posted?

13. A customer returns $60 worth of merchandise. The sales tax is $4.20.
    a) Record this sales return in General Journal form for a seller who uses a Sales Returns and Allowances account.
    b) Record the same transaction in General Journal form for a seller who does *not* use a Sales Returns and Allowances account.

14. There is a $100 entry circled in a Sales Journal's Accounts Receivable column. Should the $100 be posted as a debit or as a credit to the customer's account?

15. To which ledger are copies of a Sales Invoice posted when a company uses direct posting?

16. a) What is a statement of account?
    b) What two purposes are served by the statement of account?

17. a) What is cycle billing? What purpose does it serve?
    b) Using Figure 11.10, on what day of the month is a statement prepared for customers named: Baker, Zircon, Podrebarac?

Applying Your Knowledge

Exercises Part A

1. Answer these questions about the following invoice:
    a) Who is the seller?
    b) Who is the customer?
    c) What is the date of the invoice?
    d) What are the terms of sale?
    e) What is the last day for payment?
    f) What does *$0.60 per M* mean?
    g) Why is sales tax not added to the invoice?

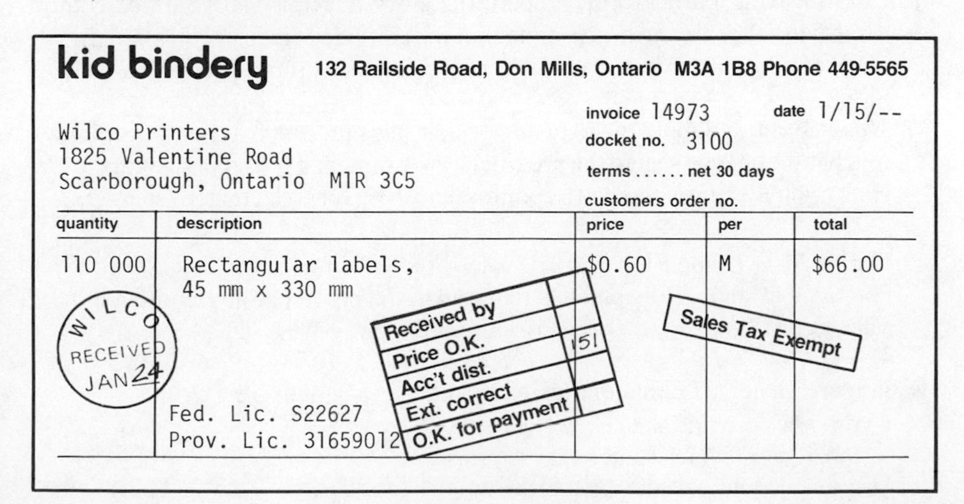

kid bindery 132 Railside Road, Don Mills, Ontario M3A 1B8 Phone 449-5565

invoice 14973 date 1/15/--
docket no. 3100
terms ...... net 30 days
customers order no.

Wilco Printers
1825 Valentine Road
Scarborough, Ontario M1R 3C5

quantity	description	price	per	total
110 000	Rectangular labels, 45 mm x 330 mm	$0.60	M	$66.00

Fed. Lic. S22627
Prov. Lic. 31659012

WILCO RECEIVED JAN 24

Received by
Price O.K. 51
Acc't dist.
Ext. correct
O.K. for payment

Sales Tax Exempt

2. Assuming you are the seller, record the entry for the invoice in exercise 1 in General Journal form.

3. Complete the following chart in your notebook:

	Amount of Sale	Sales Tax (7%)	Total
a)	$ 100.00	—	—
b)	7.95	—	—
c)	650.00	—	—
d)	4 500.00	—	—

4. Kim bought a new car priced at $6 000. The retail sales tax is 7%.
   a) What is the amount of the retail sales tax?
   b) How much does Kim owe the car dealer?
   c) How much does the car dealer owe the government on this sale?

5. Prepare General Journal entries for the following retail sales.
   a) Sold goods for $100 to R. Shadbolt, terms net 30, provincial sales tax $7. Total $107.
   b) Sold goods for $300, sales tax $21, terms 2/10, N/30.
   c) Received $107 cash from R. Shadbolt.

6. Following is a sales tax account:

Provincial Sales Tax Payable

	April 5	70
	12	60
	19	90
	30	120

   a) How much should be remitted to the government for the month of April?
   b) In General Journal form, prepare the entry to remit the April tax to the provincial government. Assume that the company is located in a province which does *not* pay a commission to companies for collecting the tax.

7. Union Electric Supply made taxable retail sales of $3 700 during May. How much is the cheque sent to the provincial government if the retail sales tax is 7% and Union Electric is allowed a commission of 3% for collecting the sales tax?

8. During June, Union Electric made sales of $5 000 of which $900 was paid for non-taxable items. How much is remitted to the provincial government if the sales tax is 7% and the company's commission is 3%?

9. Prepare General Journal entries to record the payment of:
   - the May provincial sales tax, exercise 7
   - the June provincial sales tax, exercise 8

   Use an account called Sales Tax Commission.

10. You are employed by Tanyss' Wholesale Ltd. which sells merchandise to retailers. There is no sales tax on the sales because the retailer is not the end user of the merchandise, but resells it to the public.

a) Record the following invoices in a Sales Journal.

June	3	Sales Invoice 171 to Bayridge Ltd., terms net 15, amount $193.50
	7	Sales Invoice 172 to Dacon Corp., terms 1/10n/30, amount $633.98
	15	Sales Invoice 173 to Frontenac Enterprises, 1/10 n/30, amount $247
	22	Sales invoice 174 to Bayridge Ltd., terms net 15, amount $130
	30	Sales Invoice 175 to Fillion Co., terms n/15, amount $67.50

b) Total, balance, and rule the journal.

11. You have been hired as a junior accounting clerk. One of your duties is to post transactions from the Sales Journal to the customer accounts in the Accounts Receivable Ledger.

a) Open the following accounts in the Accounts Receivable Ledger. Record the debit balances shown:

Fraser Enterprises Schedule of Accounts Receivable January 31, 19__	
C. Bard	1 000 —
D. Meyer	700 —
K. Roesler	800 —
W. Turko	1 000 —
	3 500 —

b) Following is page 12 of a Sales Journal. Post amounts in the Accounts Receivable debit column to the customer accounts:

Sales Journal

Date		Inv.	Name				
19-- Feb.	2	91	C. Bard		52 50	50 —	2 50
	3	92	W. Turko		320 —	320 —	
	3	93	D. Meyer		735 —	700 —	35 —
	4	94	C. Bard		250 —	250 —	
	5	95	K. Roesler		630 —	600 —	30 —
	5	96	W. Turko		315 —	300 —	15 —
	6	97	D. Meyer		75 —	75 —	
					2 377 50	2 295 —	82 50
					2 377 50	2 295 —	82 50

c) Prepare a schedule of accounts receivable. The total should be $5 877.50.

12. Builders Supply Ltd. sells a wide line of building supplies and materials. The company is located in a province which has a 5% retail sales tax. Following are the July invoices:

July 3 Sales Invoice 781 to J. McLean, terms n/30, amount $70, sales tax $3.50, total $73.50.
6 Sales Invoice 782 to R. Vijuk, terms n/30 amount $250, sales tax $12.50, total $262.50.
10 Sales Invoice 783 to M. Swords, terms n/30, amount $93, sales tax $4.65, total $97.65.
15 Sales Invoice 784 to J. McLean, terms n/30, amount $20, sales tax $1, total $21.
17 Sales Invoice 785 to A. Whittaker, terms n/30, amount $146, sales tax $7.30, total $153.30.
19 Sales Invoice 786 to R. Vijuk, terms n/30, amount $317, sales tax $15.85, total $332.85.
24 Sales Invoice 787 to T. Ray, terms n/30, amount $47, sales tax $2.35, total $49.35.
25 Sales Invoice 788 to M. Swords, terms n/30, amount $165, sales tax $8.25, total $173.25.
27 Sales Invoice 789 to J. McLean, terms n/30, amount $450, sales tax $22.50, total $472.50.
29 Sales Invoice 790 to A. Whittaker, terms n/30, amount $67, sales tax $3.35, total $70.35.
30 Sales Invoice 791 to T. Ray, terms n/30, amount $110, sales tax $5.50, total $115.50.

a) Record the invoices in a Sales Journal. Use page 23. Post *daily* from the Sales Journal (Accounts Receivable column) to the Accounts Receivable Ledger. The accounts required are: J. McLean, T. Ray, M. Swords, R. Vijuk, A. Whittaker.
b) Total, balance, and rule the Sales Journal. Post the totals to the General Ledger. Accounts required are: Accounts Receivable No. 102, Sales Tax Payable No. 122, Sales No. 410.
c) Prepare a schedule of accounts receivable. The total should be $1 821.75.

Exercises Part B

13. You are an accounting clerk for Doretas, a high fashion boutique. Sales invoices are recorded in a Sales Journal and credit invoices in a General Journal. Terms of sale for all sales on account are net 30. Sales tax of 7% is charged on all sales.
a) Record the sales invoices listed below on page 37 of the Sales Journal and the credit invoices on page 22 of the General Journal. Post each transaction *daily* to the customer accounts. You require the following accounts in the Accounts Receivable Ledger: M. Conway, L. Matheson, C. L. Ramsey, E. Revell.

Nov. 2 Sales Invoice 201 to customer L. Matheson, amount $70, sales tax $4.90, total $74.90.

Nov. 3 Credit Invoice C-41 to customer L. Matheson, merchandise returned $30, sales tax $2.10, total credit $32.10.

For the following transactions, calculate the 7% tax and add to the amount shown:

Nov. 5 Sales Invoice 202 to customer M. Conway, amount $100.
9 Sales Invoice 203 to customer C. L. Ramsay, amount $49.50.
12 Sales Invoice 204 to customer E. Revell, amount $200.
13 Credit Invoice C-42 to customer E. Revell, allowance of $50.
15 Sales Invoice 205 to customer L. Matheson, amount $19.95.
16 Sales Invoice 206 to customer M. Conway, amount $28.75.
20 Sales Invoice 207 to customer E. Revell, amount $79.
22 Sales Invoice 208 to customer C. L. Ramsay, amount $89.
23 Sales Invoice 209 to customer M. Conway, amount $99.
24 Credit Invoice C-43 to customer M. Conway, goods returned $99.
29 Sales Invoice 210 to customer C. L. Ramsay, amount $140.

b) Total, balance, and rule the Sales Journal.
c) Prepare a schedule of accounts receivable.
d) Open General Ledger accounts: Accounts Receivable No. 102, Sales Tax Payable No. 222, Sales No. 410, Sales Returns and Allowances No. 411.
e) Post the transactions in the General Journal. Post the totals of the Sales Journal to the General Ledger.
f) Prepare a General Ledger trial balance.

14. Fernwood Industries Ltd. does not use a Sales Returns account. Returns and allowances are recorded in the Sales Journal using the circling method. *All* sales are made 2/10, n/30 and are subject to a 7% sales tax.

a) Record the following on page 19 of the Sales Journal. Add 7% sales tax to all amounts in this exercise:

Sept. 4 Sales Invoice 816, R. Dunlop, $400.
5 Sales Invoice 817, R. T. Greer, $250.
7 Credit Memo No. 67, R. T. Greer, $30.
11 Sales Invoice 818, M. Stewart, $775.
15 Sales Invoice 819, R. Ingall, $79.
18 Sales Invoice 820, R. Dunlop, $250.
19 Sales Invoice 821, M. Stewart, $95.
21 Sales Invoice 822, R. Ingall, $150.
23 Credit Memo No. 68, R. Ingall, $75.
25 Sales Invoice 823, R. T. Greer, $350.

b) Total, balance, and rule the Sales Journal.

Exercises Part C

15. You are the accounts receivable clerk for Western Supply of Victoria, B.C. Your job is to post sales invoices and credit invoices directly to the customer accounts. Terms of sale are 1/10, n/30. The sales tax is 7%.

a) Open accounts for these customers in the Accounts Receivable Ledger with the April 1 balances shown.

T. Davis	$295
A. Holt	$750
J. McKay	$ 45
M. Wallace	$150

b) Post the following directly into the customer accounts. Add the sales tax to the amount of each sale or sales return:

April 1 Sales Invoices:
No. 416, A. Holt, $100
No. 417, M. Wallace, $29

3 Sales Invoices:
No. 418, T. Davis, $160
No. 419, J. McKay, $77

5 Credit Invoice:
No. C.I. 36, T. Davis, $295

8 Sales Invoices:
No. 420, M. Wallace, $179
No. 421, A. Holt, $45

12 Sales Invoices:
No. 422, J. McKay, $67
No. 423, T. Davis, $130

15 Sales Invoices:
No. 424, M. Wallace, $460
No. 425, A. Holt, $175
No. 426, T. Davis, $94

19 Credit Invoice:
No. C.I. 37, J. McKay, $45.

23 Sales Invoices:
No. 427, J. McKay, $33
No. 428, M. Wallace, $49.50

26 Credit Invoice:
No. C.I. 38, M. Wallace, $8.95

30 Sales Invoice:
No. 429, T. Davis, $47

c) Prepare a schedule of accounts receivable.
d) Record the April source documents in a Sales Journal on page 77. Use the circling method for any sales returns and allowances.
e) Balance and rule the journal.
f) Open a General Ledger with:

Cash	101	2 000 —	
Accounts Receivable	102	1 240 —	
Inventory	107	13 000 —	
Sales Tax Payable	222		
A. Bruce, Capital	301		16 240 —
Sales	410		

g) Post to the General Ledger.
h) Prepare a trial balance.

Accounting in Action

Provincial Sales Tax Contact the department of your provincial government responsible for the provincial retail sales tax and obtain answers to the following questions. You may be able to get the answers from a regional sales tax office. **Case 1**

a) Which items are exempt from provincial retail sales tax?
b) What is the minimum amount of sale below which sales tax is not charged?
c) What commission, if any, is paid to retailers who collect tax for the government?
d) When must remittances be sent to the government?
e) Obtain a sales tax chart.
f) How is a retail sales tax licence obtained?
g) How is the revenue from retail sales tax used by the government?
h) Explain the retail sales tax law concerning a product (for example, a $2 000 fur coat) bought in a neighbouring province and brought home to your province.

Posting to Customer Accounts Lisa and John work in the accounting department of Ciardella Developments Ltd. Among Lisa's duties is the recording of sales invoices in the Sales Journal. Among John's duties is the posting of the Sales Journal entries to the customer accounts. It seems that whenever Lisa is journalizing invoices in the Sales Journal, John needs the Sales Journal to post the customer accounts. Either Lisa or John then wastes time waiting for the journal. **Case 2**

Can you suggest a solution to this problem?

Sales Returns and Allowances Wilson Distributing handles three main product lines. They are recorded in three separate sales accounts: **Case 3**

- Sales – China, No. 41
- Sales – Silverware, No. 42
- Sales – Miscellaneous, No. 43

For a variety of reasons, there are many sales returns and sales allowances. At the present time, all returns and allowances are recorded in the Sales Journal using the circling method. It has been suggested that it might be worthwhile to use a Sales Returns and Allowances account or possibly three such accounts.

a) What are the advantages and disadvantages of using one Sales Returns and Allowances account?
b) What are the advantages and disadvantages of using three Sales Returns and Allowances accounts?
c) Under the present system, what information concerning returns and allowances would appear on the income statement?

Sales Tax Company A uses a Sales Tax Payable credit column in its journal to record the tax on taxable sales. Once a month, the total of the column is posted to the Sales Tax Payable account in the General Ledger. Each month, the balance of this account is paid to the provincial government. **Case 4**

Company B does not record sales tax in the journal. Once a month it determines the balance of the Sales account in the ledger. This total is multiplied by the rate of the provincial sales tax. The amount calculated is then remitted to the provincial government.

Which company has the better system for the handling of sales tax? Give reasons for your answer.

Case 5 Accounting Systems: The One-Write Board

What is a System? A system is an organized way of doing something. It involves determining what is to be done and then organizing how it is to be done in the most efficient way.

Processing Accounting Data This case study examines the *how* of accounting systems; that is, how accounting data is processed. Three common methods are used in accounting:

- manual
- mechanical
- computer

Manual The term manual accounting is used to describe accounting performed by hand without the use of sophisticated equipment. Journals, ledgers, statements, trial balances, etc., are handwritten.

One-Write Principle When a person requires a copy of a letter, a carbon is used at the time the original is prepared. When a company requires a copy of a sales slip or an invoice the same principle is employed. Carbon paper or specially treated carbonless paper is used when the original is written and a copy (or copies) is produced at the same time.

One-Write Boards In processing accounting data, forms of different sizes and shapes are used. A Sales Journal page is usually larger than a customer statement; a pay cheque is smaller than the Payroll Journal. The differences in size and shape of the forms make it difficult to use carbon sheets and carbonless paper. This problem is overcome by a device called a one-write board.

The one-write board is basically a hard surface on which the accounting forms and carbons are held in place by pegs along the side so that they do not move out of line when written on. One-write boards are also called pegboards and accounting boards.

Accounts Receivable – One-Write System When a sale is made to a customer most companies do the following:

- record the sale in a Sales Journal
- increase the balances in the customer ledger account
- prepare a monthly statement which is mailed to the customer

In completing these three steps for any one sale the following information is recorded separately, three times:

- the date of the transaction
- description of the sale
- amount charged and terms
- new balance
- reference number (invoice number)

With the use of a one-write board this information is written once, not three times.

The Sales Journal is mounted on the pegs of the board, a carbon is placed on top of the journal, the customer ledger account is placed on top of the carbon, and the statement (carbonless paper) is placed on top of the account. The forms are held in place by the pegs.

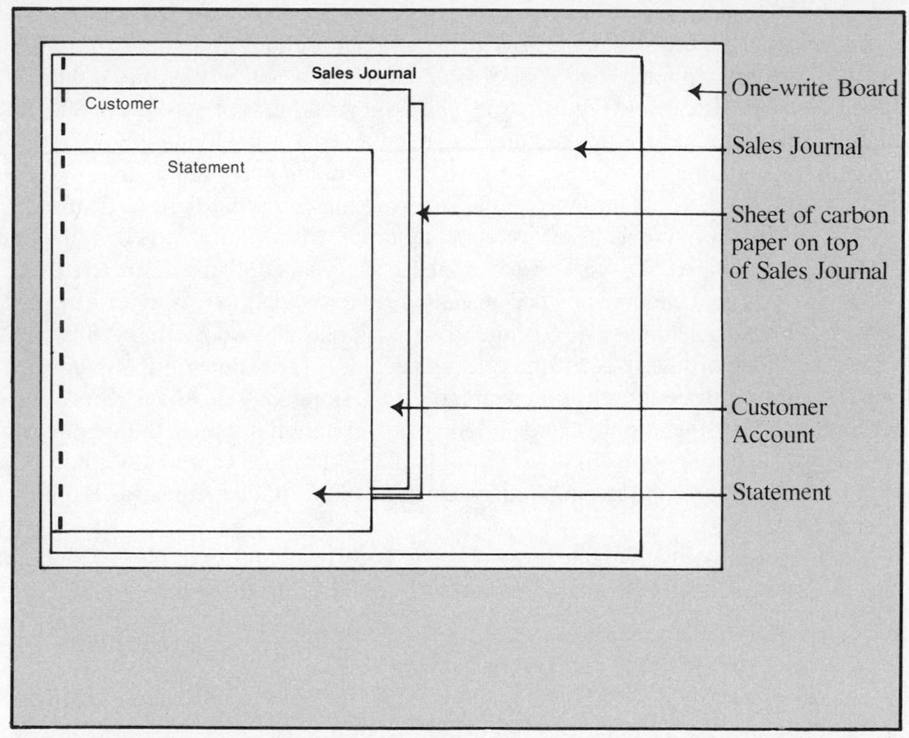

Figure 11.11 *A one-write board with forms used to record a credit sale to a customer*

When the details of the sale are recorded on the statement, they are being recorded simultaneously on the customer account and journal. Thus two-thirds of the writing is eliminated.

In conclusion, the one-write system is an efficient time and work saver when used carefully by a person who writes quickly and accurately. It is commonly used for accounts receivable, payroll, and accounts payable but can be used for any accounting application which utilizes several forms and common data.

a) What is a system?
b) List three common methods used to record accounting data.
c) Explain the one-write principle.
d) What purpose is served by the one-write board?
e) Describe how the forms are placed on a one-write board when recording credit sales.
f) Give three advantages and three disadvantages of the one-write system.

Career Profile

A Computer Accountant *Would you like to combine travel and a business career?* There is nothing to stop you, says Elaine Levy. All it takes is an adventurous spirit.

Elaine graduated from Hants North Royal High School in Kennecook, Nova Scotia. Since completing high school Elaine has lived and worked in Halifax, Calgary, Yellowknife, and Ottawa. She has taken vacation trips across Canada, the U.S.A., Mexico, and Europe. Elaine has been able to enjoy living in a variety of Canadian communities because she possesses banking-accounting skills. These have enabled her to obtain employment in banking firms throughout Canada.

Elaine's first job was as a service representative with Maritime Telephone and Telegraph in Halifax. She worked at this job for two years until the desire to travel led her to a clerical banking position in Calgary. Her next stop was in Yellowknife where she was a secretary at a branch of the Bank of Nova Scotia. After eight months in the Northwest Territories, Elaine decided it was time for a holiday and embarked on a three-month tour highlighted by stops in Vancouver, San Francisco, Reno, and Mexico, and ending up in our nation's capital, Ottawa. Again Elaine was able to obtain employment in banking. For one year she worked as a teller and as a current accounts ledger clerk at the Canadian Imperial Bank of Commerce.

For the past two years Elaine has worked as head teller and computer accountant at the Ottawa/Carleton Education Credit Union. Her duties include:

- supervision of three tellers
- receiving and processing loan applications
- recording deposits, withdrawals, and loan payments of credit union members
- handling members' inquiries about their accounts
- preparing accounting input for a computer service used by the credit union

One of Elaine's main tasks is to work with Computing Devices of Canada, a computer service company. All 5 000 member accounts are stored and processed by CDC's computer using the following system:

- Each transaction is recorded on a source document (deposit slip, cheque, etc.)
- Source documents are recorded in a daily journal. Elaine records the member's code (the account number), the date, and the details of the transaction (deposit, withdrawal, loan payment, etc.)
- The coded journal is sent to CDC.
- A computer print-out is received from CDC. This is an alphabetical listing of all members showing their names, account numbers, previous balances, transactions, and current balances. Elaine checks these for accuracy.
- Every three months the computer prints a customer statement which is mailed out to the credit union members.

The skills required for this job include an ability to deal with the public and to train and supervise employees; neat and accurate recording skills; the ability to handle accounting detail and to work with numbers; and a basic understanding of accounting and computer systems.

CHAPTER 12

Cash Receipts and Cash Payments

Cash Receipts

Unit 29

*1

In the last chapter, the Sales Journal and the procedures for recording credit sales were introduced. For each credit sale, a sales invoice was prepared and sent to the customer. A copy of the invoice was recorded in the Sales Journal and the transaction was posted to the Accounts Receivable Ledger and to the General Ledger.

In Figure 11.1 on page 257, Renfrew Printing made a credit sale of $131.82 (including sales taxes) to MacKillican & Associates. The terms of the sale were net 30 days. This meant that MacKillican & Associates should pay Renfrew Printing $131.82 by November 14, 30 days from the invoice date.

Recording Cash Receipts The cheque received from MacKillican & Associates is shown in Figure 12.1. Notice that this cheque is different from the personal cheques used by most individuals. It is called a *voucher cheque* and contains two parts:

- the cheque
- an attached statement which describes the purpose of the payment.

A voucher cheque is a two-part form with a cheque and an attached statement explaining the purpose for the payment.

CANADIAN IMPERIAL BANK OF COMMERCE
Renfrew, Ont.
Nov.14 19--

PAY TO THE ORDER OF Renfrew Printing $ 131.82

One hundred and thirty-one 82/100 DOLLARS

CURRENT ACCOUNT CHEQUE NUMBER 75039

L. MacKillican

MacKillican & Associates
Chartered Accountants
252 Raglan Street South
Renfrew, Ontario K7V 1R1

⑆00000⑈000⑆

(DETACH AND RETAIN THIS STATEMENT)

THE ATTACHED CHEQUE IS IN PAYMENT OF ITEMS LISTED BELOW

DATE	ITEM	AMOUNT	DISCOUNT	NET AMOUNT
Oct. 15	Order 105	131.82		131.82

Figure 12.1 *Voucher cheque received from MacKillican & Associates*

*2

To record this cheque, the following entry is made:

				Debit	Credit
Nov.	14	Cash		131 82	
		Accounts Receivable/			
		MacKillican & Associates			131 82
		Received cheque No. 75039			
		from MacKillican & Associates			

The debit to Cash will increase the balance in the Cash account. The credit to Accounts Receivable/MacKillican & Associates will decrease the balance in this account.

Cash Discounts

*3

Cash discounts are offered to encourage early payment of customer account balances.

You have learned that sellers offer *discounts* to customers to encourage early payment of account balances. When sales are being made, the buyer and seller agree on payment terms. When the final details of a sale have been completed both parties should understand clearly when and how payment is to be made. The payment terms should appear on the purchase invoice, the sales invoice, and the monthly statement. Any penalty for late payment should also be clearly outlined on the sale documents.

Some companies offer the same terms of sale to all their customers. As an example, the terms offered by Renfrew Printing were *n/30*. This means *net payable in 30 days* or, more precisely, full payment of the account balance is due 30 days from the invoice date.

Companies may offer more favourable terms such as *n/60* which means *net payable in 60 days*. Even better cash discounts are offered to valued customers or to attract new customers. For example, *2/10, n/30* offers the customer a 2% cash discount if payment is made within 10 days from the invoice date. If the discount is not taken, the full amount is due in 30 days. The discount also has the advantage of encouraging customers to be prompt in paying their accounts.

Discounts Offered to Customers On June 2, Renfrew Printing made a non-taxable sale of $620 to W.P. Mulvihill. To encourage early payment, terms of 3/10, n/30 were given to Mulvihill. On June 2, Renfrew Printing's accounts appear as follows:

Accounts Receivable/ W. P. Mulvihill	
June 2 620	

Sales	
	June 2 620

Mulvihill decided that it was worth paying within 10 days because it meant a saving of $18.60 ($0.03 \times 620 = 18.60$). On June 12, exactly 10 days from June 2, payment was made to Renfrew Printing. A cheque for $601.40 was received and recorded by Renfrew as follows:

*4

Cash		Accounts Receivable/ W. P. Mulvihill		Sales Discounts	
June 12 601.40		June 2 620	June 12 620	June 12 18.60	

In General Journal form these entries would appear as follows:

19__ June	2	Accounts Receivable/W.P. Mulvihill		620 —	
		Sales			620 —
		Invoice 107, terms 3/10, N/30			
	12	Cash		601 40	
		Sales Discounts		18 60	
		Accounts Receivable/W.P. Mulvihill			620 —
		Cash received for invoice 107			

After posting these two entries there is a *zero* balance in the Mulvihill Accounts Receivable account. Although only $601.40 was received, the customer receives a full credit of $620, equal to the amount of the invoice.

Sales discounts reduce the total revenue which will be received from sales. Since a reduction in revenue decreases Capital, discounts given to customers are recorded as debits in the Sales Discounts account. Sales Discounts is considered to be a *negative* or *contra* revenue account.

*5

The Sales Discounts account is a negative revenue account.

On the income statement, the total of sales discounts is subtracted from sales in the revenue section as shown in Figure 12.2.

Renfrew Printing Partial Income Statement For the Month of June, 19__			
Revenue			
Sales		3000 00	
Less: Sales Returns	1000 00		
Sales Discounts	300 00	1300 00	
Net Sales			28700 00

Figure 12.2 *The total of sales discounts is subtracted from sales.*

*6

Discounts Received from Creditors On June 4, Renfrew Printing received a purchase invoice for $500 worth of paper from Buntin Reid Co. Ltd. Terms of sale on the invoice were 2/15, n/30. The invoice was checked for accuracy and since the paper was received in good condition the invoice was passed for payment. The invoice was recorded as follows:

Purchases	
June 4 500	

Accounts Payable/ Buntin Reid Co.	
	June 4 500

The invoice was placed in the date file in a folder dated June 19. On June 19, a cheque for $490 was prepared and sent to Buntin Reid. From the cheque copy, the following entry was made:

Cash	
	June 19 490

Accounts Payable/ Buntin Reid Co.	
June 19 500	*June 4* 500

Purchases Discounts	
	June 19 10

In General Journal form these entries would appear as follows:

Date		Particulars	PR	Debit	Credit
June 19--	4	Purchases		500 —	
		Accounts Payable/Buntin Reid			500 —
		Invoice 4918, terms 2/15, net 30			
	19	Accounts Payable/Buntin Reid		500 —	
		Cash			490 —
		Purchases Discount			10 —
		Invoice 4918, less 2% discount			

*7

The Purchases Discounts account is a negative cost account.

Purchase discounts reduce the total cost of goods purchased. In effect, a reduction in cost increases Capital. Discounts received from creditors are recorded as credits in the Purchases Discounts account. Purchases Discounts is considered to be a *negative* or *contra* cost or expense account. It appears in the cost section of the income statement but it reduces the cost of purchases. This is illustrated in the schedule of cost of goods sold in Figure 12.3. Purchase discounts may also be considered to be a miscellaneous revenue account.

Renfrew Printing
Schedule of Cost of Goods Sold
For the Year 19__

Merchandise Inventory Jan. 1			20 000.00
Purchases		37 000.00	
Less: Purchases Returns	2 000.00		
Purchases Discounts	700.00	2 700.00	
Net Purchases		34 300.00	
Add Transportation on Purchases		3 000.00	37 300.00
Total Cost of Merchandise for Sale			57 300.00
Less: Inventory December 31			16 000.00
Cost of Goods Sold			41 300.00

Figure 12.3 *The total of purchases discounts is subtracted from purchases.*

*8

Sales Tax and Cash Discounts A sale of $500 worth of merchandise is made on account to J. Woodsworth. The sales tax at 7% is $35 so the total amount of the sale is $535. The terms of sale are 2/10, n/30.

Suppose that Woodsworth pays for the merchandise within 10 days in order to take advantage of the 2% cash discount. A question arises concerning the amount of the discount. *Should it be 2% of the merchandise only ($500) or should it be 2% of the total owing ($535)?* There are arguments for both alternatives. In actual practice, it is generally accepted that the customer is allowed to take a discount of 2% of $535, which is $10.70 ($0.02 \times 535 = 10.70$).

Cash Receipts Journal

Unit 30

*9

All money received is recorded in the *Cash Receipts Journal*. The items considered to be *money* include cheques, money orders, bills, and coins. Earlier you learned that special columnar journals are used to record repetitive transactions. A Purchases Journal is used to record credit purchases and a Sales Journal is used to record credit sales. A Cash Receipts Journal used by firms with many cash receipts transactions is shown in Figure 12.4.

A Cash Receipts Journal is a special journal used to record all money received.

Columns in the Cash Receipts Journal Figure 12.4 is a five-column journal with a Cash debit column, credit columns for Accounts Receivable, Sales, Provincial Sales Tax Payable, and an Other Accounts Credit column which is used to record credits to any account for which a column is not provided.

An advantage of the Cash Receipts Journal is the reduction of the amount of writing because account titles are shown in the column headings. Most transactions require only one line. However, an occasional compound transaction such as the one for W. Mulvihill in Figure 12.4 requires two lines. When the Other Accounts column is used, the name of the account must be shown in the Customer or Account column. Similarly, the account name must be shown when an entry is made in the Accounts Receivable column. Additional columns may be added to the

CASH RECEIPTS JOURNAL							PAGE	8
DATE	REF. NO.	CUSTOMER OR ACCOUNT	PR	CASH DEBIT	ACCOUNTS RECEIVABLE CREDIT	SALES CREDIT	PROVINCIAL SALES TAX PAYABLE CREDIT	OTHER ACCOUNTS CREDIT
19— Feb. 6		Cash Sale		26 75		25 —	1 75	
6		B. McAdam, capital	300	2000 —				2000 —
6		Interest Earned	420	75 —				75 —
6		W. Mulvihill	✓	196 —	200 —			
		Sales Discount	410					(4 —)
6		T. Davis	✓	200 —	200 —			
7		Cash Sale		128 40		120 —	8 40	
				2626 15	400 —	145 —	10 15	2071 —
				2626 15	400 —	145 —	10 15	2071 —
		Debit Total = $2626.15		(100)	(102)	(400)	(221)	(✓)
		Credit Total = $2626.15						

Accounts Receivable column entries posted to Accounts Receivable Ledger. The √ in the PR column indicates that the entry has been posted to the customer account.

Column totals posted to the General Ledger

Other Accounts column entries posted individually to the General Ledger. The number in the PR column indicates that the entry has been posted and gives the account number.

Figure 12.4 *Five-column Cash Receipts Journal*

journal if a particular account is used frequently. For example, some businesses use a column for Sales Discounts debit.

As well as money received from customers paying the balances in their accounts, cash is received from the following types of transactions:

- cash sales to customers
- owner investments
- cash refunds for purchases returns
- interest earned on bank accounts and other investments
- miscellaneous sources

Source Documents Recorded in the Cash Receipts Journal

*10

Cash Sales Slip A $25 taxable cash sale is made to a customer by Renfrew Printing. The customer pays for the item as soon as it is sold and receives a cash sales slip which describes the transaction and serves as proof of payment. Figure 12.4 illustrates the Cash Receipts Journal entry made to record it.

In T-account form the transaction is recorded as follows:

Cash	
26.75	

Sales Tax Payable	
	1.75

Sales	
	25

*11

Cheque Received – New Investment Bill McAdam, the owner of Renfrew Printing, uses a personal cheque to invest an additional $2 000 in his business. Figure 12.4 shows the entry made to record it in the Cash Receipts Journal. In T-account form the transaction is recorded as follows:

Cash	
26.75	
2 000	

B. McAdam, Capital	
	2 000

*12

Bank Credit Memo A *bank credit memo* is received from the Bank of Nova Scotia. This memo indicates that $75 interest has been earned and added by the bank to the depositor's savings account. Figure 12.4 illustrates the corresponding entry in the Cash Receipts Journal.

A bank credit memo indicates an increase in a customer's bank account.

Like Sales, *Bank Interest Earned* is a revenue account. It increases Capital and therefore is recorded on the credit side.

Bank Interest Earned is a revenue account.

Cash	
26.75	
2 000	
75	

Bank Interest Earned	
	75

A more detailed explanation of the term *bank credit memo* and the relationship of a depositor with the bank is given in Chapter 14.

*13

Cheque Received – Cash Sale with Discount A cheque for $196 is received from W. P. Mulvihill. The voucher section of the cheque indicates that the cheque is in payment of invoice No. 171. The total of the invoice was $200 and the terms of the sale were 2/10, n/30. Since the customer made payment within 10 days, a $4 cash discount ($0.02 \times 200 = 4$) was deducted from the invoice total ($200 - 4 = 196$). Sales Discounts decreases capital and is debited for the amount of cash discount allowed to customers. Figure 12.4 illustrates the resulting entry in the Cash Receipts Journal.

In T-account form, the transaction is recorded as follows:

Cash	
26.75	
2 000	
75	
196	

Accounts Receivable/ W. P. Mulvihill	
	200

Sales Discount	
4	

Cheque Received – Cash Received without a Discount A cheque for $200 is received from a customer, T. Davis. This is recorded in the Cash Debit column and the Accounts Receivable Credit column of the Cash Receipts Journal in Figure 12.4.

Cash Sales Slip The last source document recorded in the Cash Receipts Journal in Figure 12.4 is a cash sales slip for February 7. Merchandise worth $120 is sold to a customer. Tax of $8.40 is added to the selling price and the customer pays a total of $128.40.

Balancing and Posting the Cash Receipts Journal

*14

The Cash Receipts Journal is totalled and balanced at the bottom of each journal page and at the end of the month as shown in Figure 12.5. Refer back to Chapter 10, pages 237-239 for a review of balancing and posting procedures for special journals.

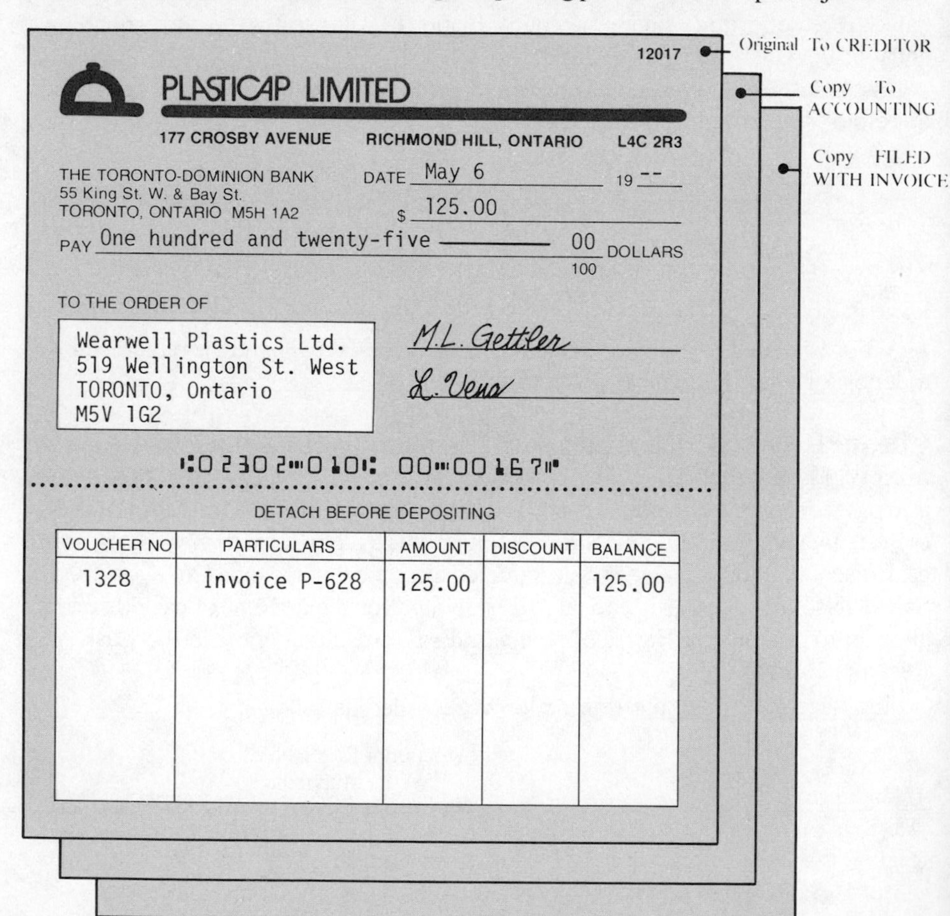
12017

PLASTICAP LIMITED

177 CROSBY AVENUE RICHMOND HILL, ONTARIO L4C 2R3

THE TORONTO-DOMINION BANK
55 King St. W. & Bay St.
TORONTO, ONTARIO M5H 1A2

DATE May 6 19 --

$ 125.00

PAY One hundred and twenty-five 00/100 DOLLARS

TO THE ORDER OF

Wearwell Plastics Ltd.
519 Wellington St. West
TORONTO, Ontario
M5V 1G2

M.L. Gettler
L. Vena

DETACH BEFORE DEPOSITING

VOUCHER NO	PARTICULARS	AMOUNT	DISCOUNT	BALANCE
1328	Invoice P-628	125.00		125.00

Figure 12.5 *Voucher cheque showing distribution of copies*

Figure 12.4 also illustrates the posting of the Cash Receipts Journal. Amounts in the Accounts Receivable and Other Accounts columns are posted individually on a daily basis. All journal totals (except Other Accounts) are posted monthly to the General Ledger. Notice that there is a circled item in Figure 12.4. The $4 in the Other Accounts Credit column would be posted as a *debit* to Sales Discounts because it is circled. When the Other Accounts column was totalled the circled $4 item was subtracted from the uncircled items.

*15

Cash Payments

Unit 31

So far in this chapter the recording of cash received in a special Cash Receipts Journal has been demonstrated. Now the method of recording cash payments will be examined, including how payments are made by cheque, and how a special journal called a Cash Payments Journal is used.

*16

Making Cash Payments A basic accounting principle is that all payments, except very small ones, should be made by cheque. Each cheque request should be authorized and accompanied by documents, such as receiving reports and approved invoices, to support the request.

All payments should be made by cheque.

In many companies a cheque request form is completed before a cheque is issued. This form is called a *cheque requisition*. The cheque requisition is accompanied by all the documents related to the transaction because the person with the responsibility to authorize the issuing of a cheque may wish to trace the entire history of the transaction.

Complete descriptions of how companies carefully process the issuance of cheques are found in the MacVal case study in Chapter 8 and the Metropolitan Life Insurance case study in Chapter 10. A cheque requisition form used by the MacVal Company is shown in Figure 8.17, page 200. This requisition contains all the details required to complete the cheque as well as an authorization for the payment.

Many firms use the voucher form of cheque as shown in Figure 12.5. The cheque is written up with three copies. Copy 2 is used by the accounting department as the source document for the journal entry made to record the transaction. Notice that the cheque requires two signatures.

*17

The Cash Payments Journal

Because of the large number of payments made, many companies record their cheques in a *Cash Payments Journal*. Special columns are provided for accounts which are usually involved in these transactions. In the Cash Payments Journal in Figure 12.6, special columns are headed Cash credit, Accounts Payable debit, Purchases debit, and Purchases Discount credit. The Other Accounts debit column is provided for those accounts which do not fit into the special columns.

*18

A Cash Payments Journal is used to record all payments.

The transactions which follow are recorded in Figure 12.6.

May 1 Purchased merchandise for $500 cash.
Issued cheque No. 101 to Tanyss Trading.

3 Paid Speedquip Ltd. for invoice B-231 dated April 2.
Issued cheque No. 102 for $149.

8 Issued cheque No. 103 to Len's Service Centre for $75 to pay for repairs to the company automobile.

12 Issued cheque No. 104 for $200 to Willsons Ltd. as partial payment of account.

15 Issued cheque No. 105 for $500 to the *Star* for advertising.

17 Issued cheque No. 106 to Angelo's Masonry for $220 to pay for a patio at the home of the owner, B. McAdam.

22 Issued cheque No. 107 to Evans & Kert for the cash purchase of supplies, $49.

23 Issued cheque No. 108 for $127 to the provincial treasurer for last month's sales tax collections.

25 Issued cheque No. 109 to Willsons Ltd. for the cash purchase of merchandise, $270.

28 Issued cheque No. 110 to Tanyss Trading for $343 in payment of invoice 673 (amount of invoice $350, discount taken $7).

31 Issued cheque No. 111 for monthly salaries of $3 400.

CASH PAYMENTS JOURNAL PAGE 14

DATE	CH. NO.	CUSTOMER OR ACCOUNT	PR	CASH CREDIT	ACCOUNTS PAYABLE DEBIT	PURCHASES DEBIT	PURCHASES DISCOUNT CREDIT	OTHER ACCOUNTS DEBIT
19-- May 1	101	Tanyss Trading		500 —		500 —		
3	102	Speedquip Ltd.		149 —	149 —			
8	103	Car Repairs		75 —				75 —
12	104	Willson's Ltd.		200 —	200 —			
15	105	Advertising Expense		500 —				500 —
17	106	B. McAdam, Drawing		220 —				220 —
22	107	Supplies		49 —				49 —
23	108	Sales Tax Payable		127 —				127 —
25	109	Willson's Ltd.		270 —		270 —		
28	110	Tanyss Trading		343 —	350 —		7 —	
31	111	Salaries Payable		3400 —				3400 —
		Debits = $5 840		5833 —	699 —	770 —	7 —	4371 —
		Credits = $5 840		5833 —	699 —	770 —	7 —	4371 —

Figure 12.6 *Transactions recorded in a Cash Payments Journal*

*19

Sales Tax on Cash Refunds On May 1, Jane purchased a pair of tennis shoes for $25 and a racquet for $65. She paid a total of $96.30 cash for her purchases which included sales tax of $6.30 ($90 \times 0.07 = 6.30$). The seller, College Sports, recorded the sale as follows:

May	1	Cash		96 30	
		Sales			90 —
		Sales Tax Payable			6 30
		To record a cash sale			

Jane was unhappy with the quality of the racquet and returned it on May 3. She received a cash refund of $65 plus $4.55 sales tax ($65 \times 0.07 = 4.55$), total $69.55. The refund has this effect on the books of College Sports:

Cash		Sales Returns and Allowances		Sales Tax Payable	
May 1 96.30	*May 3* 69.55	*May 3* 65		*May 3* 4.55	*May 1* 6.30

Since College Sports refunded the $4.55 tax to Jane, they no longer owed this amount to the government. Therefore they decreased their liability to the government by debiting Sales Tax Payable. The refund was a payment made by cheque and therefore is recorded in the Cash Payments Journal in Figure 12.7.

CASH PAYMENTS JOURNAL — PAGE 61

DATE		CH. NO.	CUSTOMER OR ACCOUNT	PR	CASH CREDIT	ACCOUNTS PAYABLE DEBIT	PURCHASES DEBIT	PURCHASES DISCOUNT CREDIT	OTHER ACCOUNTS DEBIT
May 19-	3	601	Sales Returns		69 55				65 —
			Sales Tax Payable						4 55

Figure 12.7 *Cash Payments Journal showing how to record a sales return and the effect on sales tax*

Balancing and Posting the Cash Payments Journal

*20

Procedures similar to those used with the other special journals are followed when balancing and posting the Cash Payments Journal.

1. Each page is totalled and balanced. Page totals are carried forward if the month has not ended.
2. At the end of each month the journal is balanced, ruled, and posted.
3. The column totals are posted to the General Ledger.
4. The Other Accounts column total is not posted.
5. Accounts Payable and Other Accounts column entries are posted individually.

Summary of Special Journals

*21

Since many business transactions are similar in nature, journals may be specially designed to handle the recording of transactions which occur frequently. The following special journals are used by many firms:

- *Purchases Journal* – for recording purchases on account
- *Sales Journal* – for recording sales of merchandise on account
- *Cash Receipts Journal* – for recording all receipts of cash
- *Cash Payments Journal* – for recording all payments of cash

Figure 12.8 summarizes the recording of transactions in the special journal system.

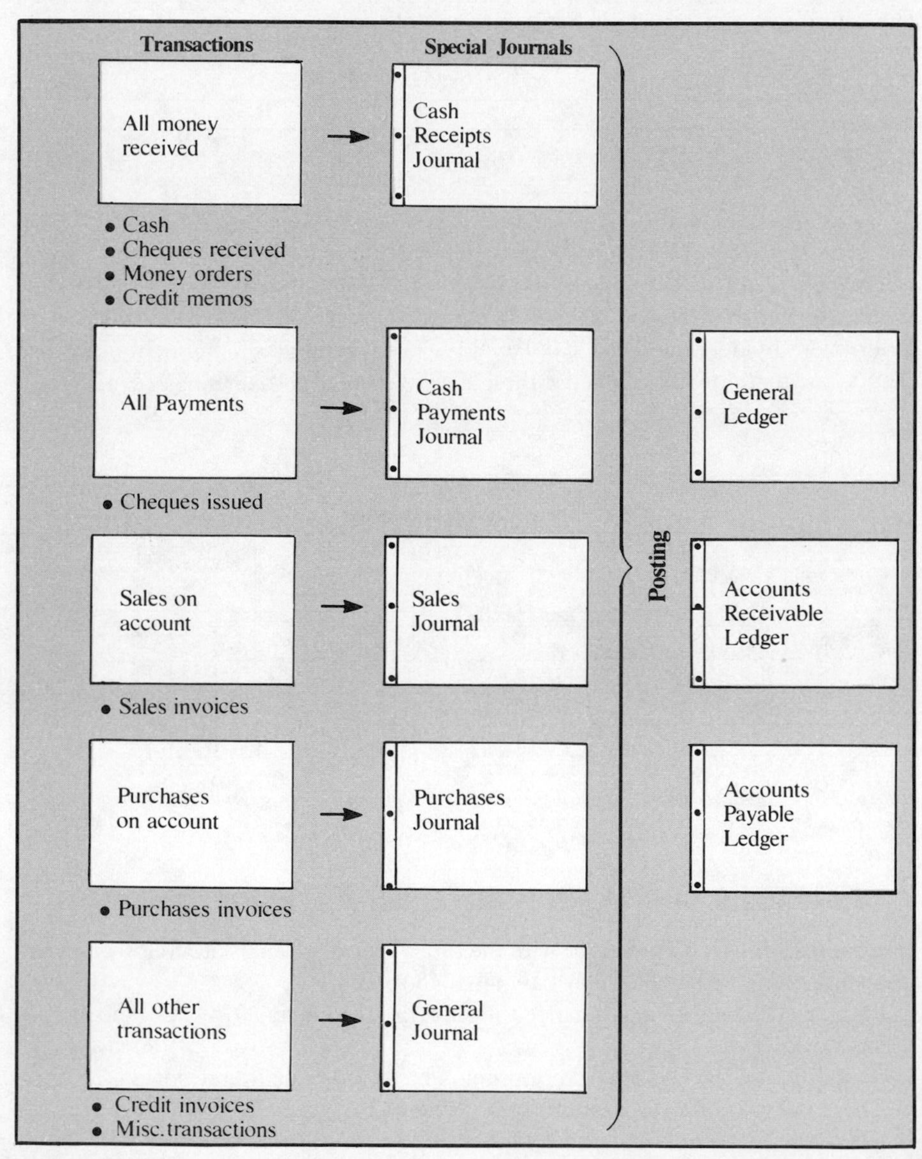

Figure 12.8 *Summary of the special journal system*

Advantages of Special Journals There are two main advantages of special journals:

- *Labour saving* – there is less writing required to record a transaction because the account titles are included in the column headings. Time and effort are saved in posting because column totals are posted rather than all the individual amounts.
- *Division of labour* – different persons can be assigned the job of recording transactions in each special journal.

Facts to Remember

A *voucher cheque* is a two-part form with a cheque and an attached statement explaining the purpose of the payment.

Cash discounts are offered to encourage early payment of customer account balances.

The *Sales Discounts account* is a negative revenue account.

Sales discounts decrease Capital and are recorded as *debits*.

The *Purchasing Discounts account* is a negative cost account.

Purchase discounts increase Capital and are recorded as *credits*.

A *Cash Receipts Journal* is a special journal used to record all money received.

A *bank credit memo* indicates an increase in a customer's bank account.

A *Cash Payments Journal* is used to record all payments.

Reviewing Your Reading

Questions

1. What is a voucher cheque?
2. What is the purpose of the voucher which is attached to the voucher cheque?
3. On November 10, your company received an invoice with terms 2/10, n/30 for $550 plus $38.50 provincial sales tax.
   a) By what date must the invoice be paid to take advantage of the discount?
   b) Will the discount be taken on the $550 or on $588.50?
   c) Calculate the amount of the cheque that must be issued to pay the invoice.
4. Not all stores use a cash sales slip as a source document for a cash sale. What are other source documents that can indicate that a cash sale has taken place?
5. The cheque for $2 000 from Bill McAdam was recorded as a payment to the business in Figure 12.4. Why is it recorded as a cash receipt and not a cash payment?
6. A bank credit memo for $75 showing that cash has been deposited in the company's bank account is recorded in Figure 12.4.

a) What is the reason for the deposit?
b) For what other reasons could a bank credit memo be issued?

7. Figure 12.4 records a cheque received from W. P. Mulvihill in payment of invoice 171.
a) Why is the payment only $196, while the invoice is $200?
b) How is Capital affected by the granting of a discount?

8. a) Why is the $4 in the Other Accounts Credit column in Figure 12.4 circled?
b) Should the $4 be posted as a debit or a credit?
c) Why is the total of that column not posted?

9. a) Why would a purchase order, a receiving slip, and a purchase invoice be attached to the cheque requisition?
b) Why do MacVal and Metropolitan Life use cheque requisitions while the smaller company, Renfrew Printing, does not?

10. a) The voucher cheque in Figure 12.5 is made out in triplicate. What is the purpose of each of the copies?
b) Why does the cheque have two signatures?
c) Prepare the General Journal entry to record the payment made by this cheque.

Applying Your Knowledge

Exercises Part A

1. a) Journalize the following source documents for Renfrew Printing:

Aug. 11 Sales invoice issued to MacKillican & Associates for $236.57 (sales tax exempt), terms net 30 days.
Sept. 10 Voucher cheque received from MacKillican & Associates for $236.57 in payment of the August 11 invoice.

b) Head up T-accounts for the following: Accounts Receivable/MacKillican & Associates; Cash; Sales. Post the journal entries from part a) to the T-accounts.

2. a) Set up the following T-accounts:

101 Cash
102 Accounts Receivable/C. Beaulne
103 Accounts Receivable/P. Garner
104 Accounts Receivable/L. Trenholme
401 Sales
403 Sales Discounts

b) Journalize and post the following source documents related to sales made on January 10. Use page 73 for the General Journal.

Jan. 10 Sales invoices issued (all sales are tax exempt):
No. 703 to C. Beaulne, $507, terms 2/10, n/30
No. 704 to L. Trenholme, $109, terms 2/10, n/30
No. 705 to P. Garner, $375, terms 2/10, n/30

Jan. 16 Cheque received from L. Trenholme for $106.82 for invoice No. 704 with a sales discount of $2.18

20 Cheque received from P. Garner for $367.50 for invoice No. 705.

25 Cheque received from C. Beaulne for $507 for invoice No. 703.

3. a) Set up the following T-accounts for Parker's Men's Wear:

101 Cash
102 Accounts Receivable/C. Baker
103 Accounts Receivable/A. Jonsson
104 Accounts Receivable/T. Mathews
401 Sales
402 Sales Returns and Allowances
403 Sales Discounts

b) Journalize and post the following source documents in a **General Journal**. Use page 94 for the General Journal.

Feb. 10 Sales invoices issued (all sales are tax exempt):
No. 1035 to A. Jonsson, $2 506, terms 2/10, n/30
No. 1036 to C. Baker, $709, terms 2/10, n/30
No. 1037 to T. Mathews, $1 750, terms 2/10, n/30

14 Credit invoice issued to A. Jonsson, $506 for goods returned. Goods were sold to Jonsson on February 10. It was agreed to change the discount period to date from February 14.

17 Cheque received from C. Baker, $694.82 for invoice No. 1036.

20 Cheque received from T. Mathews, $1 715 for invoice No. 1037.

24 Cheque received from A. Jonsson, $1 960 for invoice No. 1035 less credit invoice $506, and less discount.

4. Calculate the net sales for Doreen's Dress Shoppe if some of the General Ledger accounts show the following balances:

401 Sales $107 503 credit
402 Sales Returns and Allowances $3 597 debit
403 Sales Discounts $845 debit

5. Calculate the net sales for Parker's Men's Wear (exercise 3).

6. a) Set up the following T-accounts:

101 Cash
202 Accounts Payable/CN Express
203 Accounts Payable/Greater Wholesalers
204 Accounts Payable/Winnipeg Manufacturers
501 Purchases
502 Purchases Returns and Allowances
503 Purchases Discounts
504 Transportation on Purchases

b) Journalize and post the following documents related to purchase invoices received on August 10. Use page 107 for the General Journal.

Aug. 10 Purchase invoices received from:
Greater Wholesalers for $3 507, dated August 8, terms 3/10, n/30
CN Express for $105, dated August 9, payable on receipt of invoice
Winnipeg Manufacturers for $7 017, dated August 7, terms 2/10, n/30
11 Copy of cheque No. 331 issued to CN Express for $105.
16 Credit invoice dated August 14, from Greater Wholesalers, for $215 worth of goods received in damaged condition. Discount period to begin August 16.
17 Copy of cheque No. 332 for $6 876.66, issued to Winnipeg Manufacturers to pay invoice dated August 7.
24 Copy of cheque No. 333 for $3 193.24 to Greater Wholesalers for invoice dated August 8, less credit invoice.

Exercises Part B

7. a) Set up the following T-accounts for Dupuis Clothiers:

101 Cash
202 Accounts Payable/Cytrex Manufacturing
203 Accounts Payable/Karl's Service Centre
204 Accounts Payable/Tarneaud Ltd.
501 Purchases
502 Purchases Returns and Allowances
503 Purchases Discounts
606 Car Repairs Expense

b) Journalize and post the following documents related to purchase invoices received on October 9. Use page 291 for the General Journal:

Oct. 9 Purchase invoices received from:
Cytrex Manufacturing for $7 115, dated October 7, terms 1/20, n/30
Tarneaud Ltd., for $5 074, dated October 8, terms 2/10, n/30
Karl's Service Centre for $160, dated October 8, payable on receipt of invoice.
10 Copy of cheque No. 1070 for $160, to Karl's Service Centre for invoice dated October 8.
14 Credit invoice received from Tarneaud Ltd. dated October 12, for $270 worth of goods returned because they were not as ordered. Discount period to begin October 14.
17 Copy of cheque No. 1071 for $7 043.85, to Cytrex Manufacturing for invoice dated October 7.
22 Copy of cheque No. 1072 for $4 707.92, to Tarneaud Ltd. for invoice dated October 8, less credit note.

8. Calculate the net purchases for Bleeper Stereo Ltd. if some of the General Ledger accounts show the following balances:
501 Purchases $93 560 debit
502 Purchases Returns and Allowances $2 145 credit
503 Purchases Discounts $867 credit

9. Calculate the net purchases for Dupuis Clothiers in exercise 7.

10. Record the following source documents in a General Journal:

Aug. 23 Cash Sales Slip for $25.00 plus $1.75 sales tax.
23 Cheque received from the owner, B. McAdam, for $2 000 as an additional investment in the business.
23 Bank credit memo from the Bank of Montreal showing that $75 in interest has been added to the bank account.
23 Cheque received from M. Mulvihill for $196 to pay invoice No. 405 of $200 less $4 discount allowed.
23 Cheque received from T. Davis for $200 to pay invoice No. 399, no discount.
24 Cash sales slip for $120 plus $8.40 sales tax, total $128.40.

11. a) Record the following source documents on page 307 of a Cash Receipts Journal:

June 1 Cash register tape shows sales of $945 plus sales tax of $58.
2 Cheque received from C. Ballard for $524 to pay invoice No. 803, $524.
Cheque received from L. Noble for $317.52 to pay invoice No. 799, $324 less $6.48 discount.
3 Bank credit memo, $25 for interest deposited into the bank account.
4 Cheque received from K. Engel, the owner, for $2 500 as an additional investment in the business.
7 Bank credit memo, $9 000 for a bank loan that was deposited in the company bank account.
8 Cheque received from C. Drago for $548.80 to pay invoice No. 805, $560 less $11.20 discount.
9 Cash sales slips No.'s 940 to 955 for $2 155 plus $115.76 sales tax.
10 Cash register tape for sales of $890 plus $52.30 sales tax.
11 Money order received from C. Tierney for $875.14 to pay invoice No. 810, $893 less $17.86 discount.

b) Total and balance the Cash Receipts Journal.

12. a) Record the following source documents on page 193 of a Cash Receipts Journal:

Sept. 1 Cheque received for $3 000 from the owner, C. Black, as a further investment in the business.

Sept. 2 Cash sales invoices No.'s 340 to 355 for $975 plus $68.25 sales tax.
3 Cheques received:
$336 from A. Derouin on account
$428.26 from V. Williams to pay invoice No. 6061 for $437 less $8.74 discount
4 Bank credit memo for $346 the bank collected for us from B. Jennings on account.
5 Cheque received from A. Derouin for $749.70 to pay invoice No. 6059 for $765 less $15.30 discount.
5 Cash sales invoices No.'s 356 to 382 for $2 750 plus $192.50 sales tax.

b) Total and balance the Cash Receipts Journal.
c) Set up a General Ledger and an Accounts Receivable Ledger with the following accounts and balances, then post the Cash Receipts Journal.

Account	No.	Debit	Credit
Cash	101	1 000 —	
Accounts Receivable/Control	102	3 869 —	
Sales Tax Payable	205		350 —
C. Black, Capital	301		15 000 —
Sales	401		—
Sales Discount	402	—	

Schedule of Accounts Receivable
September 1, 19__

A. Derouin	2 576 —
B. Jennings	346 —
V. Williams	947 —
	3 869 —

13. Record the following source documents on page 705 of a Cash Receipts Journal.

Nov. 1 Bank credit note of $3 000 for a bank loan that was approved and deposited in the bank account.
3 Cheques received:
$344.86 from K. Bandy to pay invoice No. 756 for $352 less $7.14 discount
$463.44 from L. Kessba to pay invoice No. 754 for $473 less $9.56 discount

Nov. 4 Cash register tape showing $976 in sales plus $58 in sales tax.
5 Bank credit memo, $43 for interest earned from the bank.
5 Money order received from C. Taylor for $565 to pay invoice No. 601, no discount.

b) Total and balance the Cash Receipts Journal.
c) Set up a General Ledger and an Accounts Receivable Ledger with the following accounts and balances, then post the Cash Receipts Journal:

Account	No.	Debit	Credit
Cash	101	7050 —	
Accounts Receivable	103	2453 —	
Sales Tax Payable	205		256 —
Bank Loan	206		—
Sales	401		—
Sales Discount	402	—	
Interest Income	403	—	

Schedule of Accounts Receivable
September 1, 19__

Customer	Amount
K. Bandy	730 —
L. Kessler	473 —
C. Taylor	1250 —
	2453 —

Exercises Part C

14. Record the following source documents in a General Journal:

May 1 Cheque No. 101 for $500 issued to Tanyss Trading for merchandise purchased.
3 Cheque No. 102 for $149 issued to Speedquip Ltd. for invoice B-231, no discount.
8 Cheque No. 103 for $75 issued to Len's Service Station for car repairs.
12 Cheque No. 104 for $200 issued to Willsons Ltd. for a payment on account.
15 Cheque No. 105 for $500 issued to the *Star* for advertising.
17 Cheque No. 106 for $220 issued to Angelo's Masonry for a patio for the owner, B. McAdam.
22 Cheque No. 107 for $49 to Evans & Kert for the cash purchase of supplies.

May 23 Cheque No. 108 for $127 to the provincial treasurer for sales tax collected in April.

25 Cheque No. 109 for $270 issued to Willsons Ltd. for the cash purchase of merchandise.

28 Cheque No. 110 for $343 issued to Tanyss Trading for payment of invoice No. 673, $350 less $7 discount.

31 Cheque No. 111 for $3 400 to get cash to pay the employees' salaries for the month.

15. a) Record the following documents on page 319 of a Cash Payments Journal:

May 1 Cheque No. 1890, $230 to K. Bellamy for a week's salary.

3 Cheque No. 1891, $350 to P. Meikle, the owner, for personal use.

5 Bank debit memo, $3.50 for service charges.

6 Cheque No. 1892, $833 to General Distributors for $850 less $17 discount.

Cheque No. 1893, $73.60 to Bill's Service Centre on account.

7 Bank debit memo, $300 for monthly payment on the bank loan.

9 Cheque No. 1894, $4 410 to Electronic Wholesalers, for $4 500 invoice less $90 discount.

b) Total and balance the Cash Payments Journal.

c) Set up a General Ledger and an Accounts Payable Ledger with the following accounts and balances, then post the Cash Payments Journal.

Account	No.	Debit	Credit
Cash	101	8 493 —	
Bank Loan	201		15 000 —
Accounts Payable	202		9 458 —
P. Meikle, Drawing	302	—	
Purchases Discount	503		—
Salaries Expense	600	—	
Bank Charges Expense	615	—	

Schedule of Accounts Payable
May 1, 19__

Bill's Service Centre	145 —
Electronic Wholesalers	7 056 —
General Distributors	2 257 —
	9 458 —

16. a) Record the following documents on page 109 of the Cash Payments Journal:

Dec. 3 Cheque No. 705, $2 600 to Clark Realtors for the December rent.
Cheque No. 706, $14 355 to Colonial Manufacturers for $14 500 invoice less $145 discount.
4 Bank debit memo, $4.75 for bank service charges.
6 Cheque No. 707, $172.92 to C. Bartoli, a customer, for a $156 coffee table plus $16.92 tax, returned for a cash refund.
Cheque No. 708, $2 656 to Dupuis Cabinets, on account.
7 Cheque No. 709, $7 409.68 to General Electric for $7 561 less $151.32 discount.
8 Cheque No. 710, $500 to L. Colby for personal use.

b) Total and balance the Cash Payments Journal.

c) Set up a General Ledger and Accounts Payable Ledger with the following accounts and balances, then post the Cash Payments Journal.

Cash	101	56 793 56	
Accounts Payable	202		35 696 67
L. Colby, Drawing	302	13 490 44	
Sales Returns and Allowances	403	2 376 49	
Purchases Discounts	503		5 976 56
Rent Expense	600	28 600 —	
Bank Charges Expense	613	1 673 55	

Schedule of Accounts Payable
December 1, 19__

Colonial Manufacturers	14 500 —
Dupuis Cabinets	9 400 23
General Electric	11 796 44
	35 696 67

Accounting in Action

Case 1

Discounts Henry Oldtimer has been an accounting clerk for Wellandvale Ltd. for 30 years. His main task is to process, record, and pay purchase invoices. In the last few years Wellandvale's business has greatly increased.

Henry keeps invoices in two large files, one for *unpaids* and one for *paids*. About once a week, or whenever he gets around to it, Henry checks the unpaid file and issues cheques for invoices which have become due.

The controller of the company has noticed that a number of cash discounts have been lost because payments were not made within the discount period. When confronted, Henry said he was overworked and should not be blamed.

a) What changes would you recommend in the handling of purchase invoices?
b) How would you get Henry to accept your suggestions?

Case 2

Recording Cash Payments J. Ballast is the owner of Canadian Enterprises Ltd., a large company in the entertainment business. The revenue of the business is about $6 000 000 a year. In the past several years Ballast has spent the following:

- $10 000 for a swimming pool built at his home
- $8 000 on renovations to his cottage
- $2 000 on landscaping around his home
- $4 000 plumbing and air conditioning installed in his home

Although each of these expenditures was of a personal nature, Ballast requested that invoices for the charges be sent to his company, Canadian Enterprises. All of the expenditures were recorded in the books of the company in various expense accounts. Payments were made from company funds. Examples of the accounting procedures used follow.

June	1	Building Repairs Expense		10 000 —	
		Cash			10 000 —
		Cheque No. 1190 to Modern			
		Contractors			
June	30	Maintenance Expense		2 000 —	
		Cash			2 000 —
		Cheque 1264 to Valley Landscaping			

a) From an accounting theory point of view what is wrong with recording the transactions as expenses of the business?
b) What is the effect on the company's net income and income tax?

Case 3

Cash Discounts Mavis Porter manages Studio Sound, a stereo components specialty shop. She is in the process of negotiating a $5 000 order from one of her main suppliers. The supplier has offered a 3% discount if payment is made within 15 days. Studio Sound does not have cash on hand to take advantage of the discount. However, the bank will lend money to Studio Sound for 30 days at an annual rate of interest of 12%. Mavis is sure that within 30 days there will be enough cash on hand to repay the bank.

Should Mavis take the 3% discount using money borrowed from the bank? How much will be gained or lost if the loan is taken?

Case 4

Terms of Sale You are the credit manager for a large manufacturer of sporting goods. One of your main jobs is to decide if a new customer is to be allowed to buy on credit. Depending on the customer, your firm allows *one* of the following terms of payment:

- C.O.D. (cash on delivery)
- 30 days
- 90 days

Astro Sports, a new customer, has ordered $10 000 worth of merchandise from you. Which term of payment would you grant to Astro Sports? Their balance sheet follows. Give reasons for your answer.

Astro Sports
Balance Sheet
October 31, 19__

Assets		Liabilities	
Cash	3 000 00	Accounts Payable	95 000 00
Accounts Receivable	14 000 00	Bank Loan	35 000 00
Inventory	90 000 00	Mortgage Payable	100 000 00
Equipment	30 000 00	Total Liabilities	230 000 00
Building	195 000 00		
		Owner's Equity	
		M. Cassidy, Capital	102 000 00
		Total Liabilities	
Total Assets	332 000 00	and Owner's Equity	332 000 00

Case 5

Designing Journals H. Bloos Ltd. is a speciality gift shop. It has three main types of merchandise: jewellery, china, and silverware. Some of the sales are taxable and some are not, and most sales are made on a cash basis. When a sale is made, a prenumbered sales slip is completed. The original, marked *paid*, is given to the customer. A copy is used by the acountant to record the sale.

Design a Cash Receipts Journal for H. Bloos Ltd. You may use as many columns as you wish.

Career Profile

Accounting Department Manager for a Public Accounting Firm Winspear Higgins Stevenson & Company is a national accounting firm with offices in many Canadian cities. The firm offers accounting services such as:

- the auditing of financial records prepared by customers' own accountants
- preparation of financial statements
- complete accounting services for small businesses
- tax and general business consultations
- organizing of accounting systems and procedures

John Kisel is the accounting department manager in the Welland, Ontario office of Winspear Higgins Stevenson & Company. This profile will examine John's job function and his educational background.

John grew up in Welland and obtained his Honours Secondary Graduation Diploma from Welland High and Vocational School. His first full-time job was as a *student-in-accounts* with the public accounting firm of Peters, Brown & Co. in Fort Erie, Ontario. A student-in-accounts is an employee of an accounting firm who is enrolled in a professional accounting program. John worked in the daytime and spent approximately 10 hours a week studying towards a C.A. (Chartered Accountant) degree. John has successfully completed four and a half years of the five-year C.A. program offered by the Institute of Chartered Accountants of Ontario.

After working in Fort Erie for five years, John obtained employment with Winspear Higgins Stevenson & Company in his home town. For over 10 years now John has worked for the same firm. His present position is Accounting Department Manager and he is responsible for these duties:

- hiring of accounting department staff
- advising staff who have various accounting and tax problems
- checking income tax returns and financial statements of clients
- advising clients on tax and general business matters
- valuation of businesses for possible purchase by clients
- establishing accounting systems for clients
- client billing, time budgeting, and job scheduling

John enjoys his job, with its pleasant working atmosphere, and benefits from professional relationships with members of the firm and in the Welland business community. He especially likes the involvement with people that goes with his hiring, training, and supervisory duties.

The Special Journal System

Project 2

Allan Jonsson, owner of Jonsson's Furniture, has exclusive rights of distribution for the products of Teak Manufacturers and of General Appliances Ltd. The store has been operating successfully for a number of years and the accounting records for Jonsson's Furniture include the following journals:

- Sales Journal
- Purchases Journal
- Cash Receipts Journal
- Cash Payments Journal
- A General Journal which is used for returns and allowances and for correcting entries.

On January 10 the balances in the accounts of the company are:

Jonsson's Furniture
Trial Balance
January 10, 19__

ACCOUNT TITLE	ACC. NO.	DEBIT	CREDIT
Cash	101	27 678.50	
Accounts Receivable	102	10 617.08	
Merchandise Inventory	103	255 673.84	
Office Equipment	110	4 763.35	
Trucks	120	24 897.88	
Fixtures	121	11 342.89	
Land and Building	130	305 768.—	
Accounts Payable	200		14 550.06
Sales Tax Payable	201		5 369.90
Bank Loan	210		15 765.31
Mortgage on Building	211		105 675.35
A. Jonsson, Capital	300		501 819.08
A. Jonsson, Drawing	301	1 700.—	
Sales	400		13 658.73
Sales Returns and Allowances	401	146.51	
Purchases	500	9 105.82	
Purchases Returns and Allowances	501		97.33
Transportation on Purchases	502	278.85	
Salaries Expense	600	2 376.51	
Truck Repairs Expense	601	138.64	
Heating Expense	602	173.56	
Utilities Expense	603	78.53	
Bank Charges Expense	604	45.20	
Advertising Expense	605	2 150.60	
		656 935.76	656 935.76

Jonsson's Furniture
Schedule of Accounts Receivable
January 10, 19__

A. Bartoli	4 687 35
D. Crankshaw	390 47
L. Larivière	491 60
M. St. Amour	3 673 38
S. Walli	1 374 28
	10 617 08

Jonsson's Furniture
Schedule of Accounts Payable
January 10, 19__

Campbell Heating	493 70
CKNH T.V.	767 00
General Appliances Ltd.	5 358 61
Hi-Way Transport	478 90
Teak Manufacturers	6 798 50
Welland Motors Ltd.	653 35
	14 550 06

Part A

1. Open the five journals.
2. Open the ledgers with the balances on January 10, 19__.
3. Record the following transactions in the appropriate journals.

Jan. 13 Cash sales invoice No. 7339. (Prepare one batch entry.)

JF Jonsson's Furniture
359 Portage Ave.,
Ottawa, Ontario
K2A 7N9

INVOICE

Order No.

Date Jan. 13. 19--

Sold to P. Mitchell Ship to Same

Invoice No. 7339

Terms Cash

Cash ✓ Charge

Quantity	Description	Unit Price	Amount
1	Washing Machine		$469 98
1	Dryer		319 98
		Sub-total	789 96
		Sales Tax	55 30
		Pay this Amount	$845 26

Jan. 13 Other cash sales invoices:
No. 7340, $299.96 + $21 sales tax = $320.96
No. 7342. $83.98 + $5.88 sales tax = $89.86
No. 7343, $119.98 + $8.40 sales tax = $128.38
No. 7344, $1 355.74 + $94.90 sales tax = $1 450.64

13 Charge sales invoice No. 7341, $649.90 + $45.49 sales tax = $695.39 from L. Larivierre.

13 Cash receipt No. 671, $300 from A. Bartoli.

13 Cheque No. 345 issued to Elgin Cabinets, $476.58 for merchandise

14 Cheque No. 346 issued.

$ 359.00
BAL. 27 678.50
DEP. 3 135.10
TOTAL 30 813.60
CHEQUE 359.00
BAL. 30 454.60
PAY TO Hi-Way Transport
on account
SUM OF $359.00
Jan. 14/77 346

THE BANK OF NOVA SCOTIA
Preston & Norman Branch
Ottawa, Ont.
346 January 14, 19--
DATE
PAY TO THE ORDER OF Hi-Way Transport $ 359.00
SUM OF Three hundred and fifty-nine ——— DOLLARS
ACCOUNT NO. 43519
A. Jonsson
Jonsson's Furniture
⑆70276⑈002⑆

Jan. 14 Other cheque issued:
No. 347 to Bell Telephone, $35.67

14 Cash sales:
No. 7345, $530 + $37.10 sales tax = $567.10
No. 7346, $164.98 + $11.55 sales tax = $176.53
No. 7348, $549.98 + $38.50 sales tax = $588.48
No. 7349, $239.98 + $16.80 sales tax = $256.78

14 Sales invoices (on account):
No. 7347, to M. St. Amour, $574.98 + $40.25 sales tax = $615.23
No. 7350, to D. Crankshaw, $356.90 + $24.98 sales tax = $381.88

14 Purchase invoices:
From Welland Motors Ltd. for truck repairs, $235.63
From Campbell Heating, for fuel, $565.64

14 Correcting entry:
An error was made in recording an amount of $57.53 to the Fixtures account when it should have been recorded in the Office Equipment account. Record a correcting entry.

15 Credit invoice No. 3470 received from Teak Manufacturing, $35 overcharge on invoice No. 110985.

Jan. 15 Cash sales:
No. 7352, $609.50 + $42.67 sales tax = $652.17
No. 7353, $79.96 + $5.60 sales tax = $85.56
No. 7354, $499.98 + $35 sales tax = $534.98
No. 7355, $419.98 + $29.40 sales tax = $449.38
No. 7356, $799.98 + $56 sales tax = $855.98

15 Sales invoice No. 7351 to S. Walli, $359.98 + $25.20 sales tax = $385.18

15 Cash receipts:
No. 9147 from M. St. Amour, $350 on account
No. 9148 from D. Crankshaw, $120 on account

15 Purchase invoices
From General Appliances Ltd., for merchandise, $2 567.56
From Hi-Way Transport, for transportation on merchandise, $467.50

15 Cheques issued:
No. 348 to the provincial treasurer, $4 265.14 for sales tax collected in December
No. 349 to Teak Manufacturers, $1 567.50 on account
No. 350 to CKNH T.V., $450 on account

16 Credit invoice No. 175 issued

JF Jonsson's Furniture
359 Portage Ave.,
Ottawa, Ontario
K2A 7N9

CREDIT INVOICE

Sold to L. Lariviere
4935 rue Champlain
Ottawa, Ontario
K1C 3P1

Order No.
Date Jan. 16, 19--
Credit Invoice No. CR 175

Quantity	Description	Unit Price		Amount	
4	Chairs	20	00	80	00
	Sales tax			5	60
	Total Credit			85	60
	Overcharge on invoice No. 7341				

Jan. 16 Cash sales:
No. 7357, $209.50 + $14.67 sales tax = $224.17
No. 7359, $549.98 + $38.50 sales tax = $588.48
No. 7361, $355 + $24.85 sales tax = $379.85
No. 7362, $322 + $22.54 sales tax = $344.54
No. 7363, $79.98 + $5.60 sales tax = $85.58

Jan. 16 Sales invoices (on account):
No. 7358, to A. Bartoli, $289.98 + $20.30 sales tax = $310.28
No. 7360, to M. St. Amour, $539.98 + $37.80 sales tax = $577.78

16 Cash receipts:
No. 9149, from L. Larivierre, $250 on account
No. 9150, from S. Walli, $95 on account

16 Purchase invoices:
From CKNH T.V., $1 200 for advertising
From Teak Manufacturers, $1 563.69 for merchandise

16 Cheques issued:
No. 351 to Welland Motors Ltd., $450 on account
No. 352 to Bank of Nova Scotia, $2 000 payment on the bank loan
No. 353 to Commercial Realtors, $1 500 payment on the mortgage

17 Bank debit memo for $54 received for bank charges.

17 Cash sales:
No. 7364 $298.98 + $20.93 sales tax = $319.91
No. 7365 $74.95 + $5.25 sales tax = $80.20
No. 7367 $599.98 + $42 sales tax = $641.98
No. 7368 $239.98 + $16.80 sales tax = $256.78
No. 7369 $209.98 + $14.70 sales tax = $224.68

17 Sales invoice No. 7366 to D. Crankshaw, $408.96 + $28.63 sales tax = $437.59 on account

17 Purchase invoices:
From Hi-Way Transport, $367.50 for transportation of merchandise
From Welland Motors Ltd., $198 for truck repairs

17 Cheques issued:
No. 354 to A. Jonsson, the owner, $1 450 for personal use
No. 355 to General Appliances Ltd., $3 600 on account
No. 356 to Campbell Heating, $493.70 on account

Part B

1. Post to the subsidiary ledgers.
2. Total and balance the journals.
3. Post the journals to the General Ledger.

Part C

1. Prepare schedules for the subsidiary ledgers.
2. Prepare a trial balance of the General Ledger.

Part D

1. Prepare schedule of cost of goods sold and an income statement for the two weeks ended Janaury 17, 19__. The January 17 merchandise inventory is $257 931.12.
2. Prepare a balance sheet for January 17, 19__, with an ending inventory of $257 931.12.

CHAPTER 13

The Synoptic Journal

Unit 32 Recording Repetitive Transactions

*1

Special journals are used by fairly large companies which have a number of repetitive transactions. Several persons are usually involved in the journalizing phase of the accounting cycle. In a smaller company where all the transactions are

SYNOPTIC JOURNAL

DATE		ACCOUNT AND EXPLANATION	REF. NO.	CASH		PR	GENERAL	
				DEBIT	CREDIT		DEBIT	CREDIT
19— May	1	A. Walker	75					
	2	Cash Sales Slips	20-24	535 —				
	4	National Wholesale	B-117					
	4	Rent Expense	171		600 —		600 —	
	5	Telephone Expense	172		95 —		95 —	
	6	B. Baldwin		200 —				
	8	Butler Mfg.	173		700 —			
	10	G. LePensée, Drawing	174		300 —		300 —	
	11	A. Walker		209 72				
		Sales Discount					4 28	
	12	National Wholesale	175		196 —			
		Purchases Discount						4 —
	15	G. LePensée, Drawing					100 —	
		Purchases						100 —
		1 →		944 72	1 891 —		1 099 28	104 —
6 →		Forwarded		944 72	1 891 —		1 099 28	104 —
4 →		Debits = $3 558	5 ↗					
		Credits = $3 558						

(Callouts 2 and 3 point to the Cash Debit column totals.)

Figure 13.1 *A typical Synoptic Journal*

recorded by one person, a *Synoptic Journal* may be used. A Synoptic Journal has special columns for repetitive transactions and offers some of the advantages of special journals: less time, effort, and space are required for the recording of each transaction.

A Synoptic Journal is a columnar journal that combines several journals.

The Synoptic Journal combines two or more of the special journals into one journal and is sometimes called a *combination journal*. The Synoptic Journal illustrated in Figure 13.1 combines five journals into one. It is used to record various types of transactions which in the five-journal system are recorded in the Cash Receipts, Cash Payments, Sales, Purchases, and General Journals.

Combination Journal is another name for a Synoptic Journal.

Recording Transactions in a Synoptic Journal

*2

The recording of transactions in a Synoptic Journal is very similar to recording transactions in the special journals. The transactions which follow are recorded in the Synoptic Journal in Figure 13.1.

- *May 1 Sales invoice No. 75, for merchandise sold to A. Walker for $200 plus sales tax of 7%, terms 2/10, n/30.*

The name of the customer is written in the Account and Explanation column. This is necessary because the amount will be posted to the customer's account in the

PAGE 61

ACCOUNTS RECEIVABLE		SALES CREDIT	PROVINCIAL SALES TAX PAYABLE CREDIT	PURCHASES DEBIT	ACCOUNTS PAYABLE	
DEBIT	CREDIT				DEBIT	CREDIT
214 —		200 —	14 —			
		500 —	35 —			
				400 —		400 —
	200 —					
				700 —		
	214 —					
					200 —	
214 —	414 —	700 —	49 —	1100 —	200 —	400 —
214 —	414 —	700 —	49 —	1100 —	200 —	400 —

Accounts Receivable subsidiary Ledger. The invoice number is recorded in the No. column. The debit ($214) is written in the Accounts Receivable column. The credit for the selling price of the merchandise ($200) is recorded in the Sales column. The 7% tax ($0.07 \times 200 = 14$) is recorded in the Provincial Sales Tax Payable column.

- *May 2 Cash sales slips No. 20 to 24 for $500. Five sales of merchandise were made for cash.*

In this transaction, five cash sales slips (No. 20 to 24) are combined. The sales slip numbers are shown in the No. column. The names of the cash customers are not recorded since these cash transactions will not be posted to the customer accounts.

- *May 4 Purchase invoice B-117, for merchandise purchased from National Wholesale for $400, terms on account.*

The name of the creditor is recorded in the Account and Explanation column because the credit of $400 will later be posted to the National Wholesale account in the Accounts Payable subsidiary Ledger. The invoice number is shown in the No. column.

- *May 4 Cheque copy No. 171 for $600 was issued to Royal Real Estate to pay rent.*

Because rent is paid only once a month, a special column has not been provided. The $600 is shown in the General Debit column and Rent Expense is written in the Account and Explanation column. Later the $600 debit will be posted to Rent Expense in the General Ledger.

*3

- *May 5 Cheque copy No. 172 for $95 was issued to pay the telephone bill.*

The debit of $95 is recorded in the General Debit column and the account debited is identified by writing Telephone Expense in the Account and Explanation column.

- *May 6 Cash receipt for $200 from B. Baldwin on account.* The $200 amount is recorded in the Debit column and in the Accounts Receivable Credit column. To indicate that the credit is also to be posted to the customer's account, the customer's name, B. Baldwin, is written in the Account and Explanation column.
- *May 8 Cheque copy No. 173 for $700 was issued to Butler Manufacturing to pay for a cash purchase of merchandise.*

Since both the debit (Purchases) and the credit (Cash) are recorded in special columns, it is not necessary to write an account name in the Account and Explanation column. However, this space may be used as an explanation of the transaction. The cheque number is shown in the No. column.

- *May 10 Cheque copy No. 174 for $300 was issued to the owner, G. LePensée, for personal use.*

The cheque is recorded in the General Debit column and in the Cash Credit column. The Account and Explantion column is used to identify the account that is debited in the General Debit column.

- *May 11 Cash receipt for $209.72 from A. Walker in payment of invoice No. 75 ($214). A $4.28 cash discount was taken by the customer since payment was made within 10 days.*

Two lines are required to record this transaction. A debit of $209.72 is recorded in the Cash Debit column. The debit of $4.28 in the General Debit column is identified by writing the name of the account, Sales Discount, in the Account and Explanation column. The credit of $214 is identified by writing A. Walker, the customer account to be credited, in the Account and Explanation column.

- *May 12 Cheque copy No. 175 for $196 was issued as a payment of an account to a creditor, National Wholesale. A $4 purchase discount was taken.*

This payment is recorded on two lines by crediting Cash and Purchases Discount (in the General Credit column) and debiting Accounts Payable. National Wholesale is written in the Account and Explanation column because the creditor's account must be debited $200 in the Accounts Payable subsidiary Ledger when the journal is posted.

- *May 15 The owner, G. LePensée, took home merchandise worth $100 for personal use.*

Two lines are used to record this transaction since neither the debit (LePensée, Drawing) nor the credit (Purchases), can be recorded in the special columns. The Purchases Debit column is not used in this example because this transaction causes a decrease (a credit) in the Purchases account. However, the circling method may be used to record the decrease in purchases. If it is used, the $100 is written in the Purchases column and is circled. The circle identifies the $100 as a credit to purchases *despite* the column heading which is Purchases Debit, and the amount is subtracted when the column is totaled.

In some provinces, the company is responsible for charging sales tax if the goods withdrawn by the owner are taxable. If this is the case, debit the Drawing account to include the sales tax. A credit would be recorded in the Sales Tax Payable account for the amount of the tax as shown in the following journal entry:

May	15	G. LePensée, Drawing		107 —	
		Purchases			100 —
		Sales Tax Payable			7 —
		Merchandise for personal use			

Account and Explanation Column Note that when a transaction causes a change in a customer or a creditor account, the name of the customer or creditor is shown in the Account and Explanation column. This is required so that the entry may be posted to the subsidiary ledger account.

*4

General Section When a transaction includes a debit or a credit for which there is not a special column in the Synoptic Journal, the General column is used. The account title is written in the Account and Explanation column so that the entry may be posted to that account in the General Ledger.

Source Document Reference Numbers A number column is located next to the account and explanation column. This column is used to record, for referencing purposes, the number of the source document from which the transaction was recorded. For a sale on account, the number of the sales invoice is recorded in the number column. For other transactions, the cheque number, purchase invoice number, or credit invoice number is shown.

Balancing the Synoptic Journal

*5
The Synoptic Journal should be balanced at the bottom of each page and at the end of the month.

If transactions have been recorded properly, the debits should equal the credits on every page of the Synoptic Journal. At the bottom of each page and at the end of each month, the totals of each column are shown. The total of all the debit column totals must equal the total of all the credit column totals. If a machine has been used to prove the totals, the tape may be attached to the journal.

Steps in Balancing the Synoptic Journal The steps followed in balancing the Synoptic Journal shown in Figure 13.1 are:

1. Rule a single line across the money columns.
2. Add the columns and record the totals in pencil.
3. Add the debit column totals and the credit column totals. Use a machine or pencil and paper.
4. If the debit totals equal the credit totals, write the column totals in ink. Write the debit and credit totals in the Account and Explanation column or attach machine tapes.

SYNOPTIC JOURNAL

DATE		ACCOUNT AND EXPLANATION	REF. NO.	CASH DEBIT	CASH CREDIT	PR	GENERAL DEBIT	GENERAL CREDIT
May 19--	15	Forwarded		944 72	1891 —		1099 28	104 —

Figure 13.2 *Column totals Forwarded to a new page in the Synoptic Journal*

SYNOPTIC JOURNAL

DATE		ACCOUNT AND EXPLANATION	REF. NO.	CASH DEBIT	CASH CREDIT	PR	GENERAL DEBIT	GENERAL CREDIT
May 19--	1	A. Walker	75			✓		
	2	Cash Sales Slips	20-24	535 —				
	15	G. LePensee, Drawing				302	100 —	
		Purchases				411		100 —
				944 72	1891 —		1099 28	104
		Forwarded		944 72	1891 —		1099 28	104
		Debits = $3558		(100)	(100)			
		Credits = $3558						

Post all column totals (except General column) monthly to the General Ledger.

Post individual column amounts monthly to the General Ledger.

Figure 13.3 *Posting the Synoptic Journal*

5. Rule a double line across all money totals.
6. If a new page of the Journal is being opened, use the following procedure: Write *Forwarded* in the Account and Explanation column on the same line as the totals (Figure 13.1). On the next page, write the year, month, and day in the date column. Write *Forwarded* again (Figure 13.2) in the Account and Explanation column and record each total in the appropriate column. *6

Locating Errors in the Synoptic Journal Because each page of the Synoptic Journal is balanced before proceeding to the next page, the balancing procedure will immediately identify an error in which the debits do not equal the credits. It is a mathematical check of the equality of the debits and credits. If the journal page does not balance, these procedures are followed: *7

1. Calculate the difference between the debit totals and the credit totals. Divide the difference by two. Look for this amount in the wrong column of your balancing list of debit and credit totals.
2. Check the addition. If a machine has been used, audit the tape to locate errors in entering data on the machine.

PAGE 62

ACCOUNTS RECEIVABLE		SALES CREDIT	PROVINCIAL SALES TAX PAYABLE CREDIT	PURCHASES DEBIT	ACCOUNTS PAYABLE	
DEBIT	CREDIT				DEBIT	CREDIT
214 —	414 —	700 —	49 —	1100 —	200 —	400 —

PAGE 61

ACCOUNTS RECEIVABLE		SALES CREDIT	PROVINCIAL SALES TAX PAYABLE CREDIT	PURCHASES DEBIT	ACCOUNTS PAYABLE	
DEBIT	CREDIT				DEBIT	CREDIT
214 —		200 —	14 —			
		500 —	35 —			

214 —	414 —	700 —	49 —	1100 —	200 —	400 —
214 —	414 —	700 —	49 —	1100 —	200 —	400 —
(102)	(102)	(401)	(202)	(411)	(201)	(201)

Post individual column amounts daily to the Accounts Receivable Ledger.

Post individual column amounts daily to the Accounts Payable Ledger.

3. If the addition is correct, check each entry on the journal page. There should be equal debit and credit amounts for every transaction.
4. Follow the steps suggested on page 99 of Chapter 5.

Unit 33

Posting the Synoptic Journal

*8

Many businesses wish to maintain up-to-date balances in the customer and creditor accounts. For this reason, information is posted directly to the Accounts Receivable and Accounts Payable subsidiary Ledgers from the source documents. The source documents are then journalized in the Synoptic Journal.

Another way to maintain up-to-date balances in the subsidiary ledgers is to journalize the source documents in the Synoptic Journal and post each day to the Accounts Receivable and Accounts Payable subsidiary Ledgers. The rest of the posting is done at the end of the month after the Synoptic Journal has been balanced.

*9

Steps in Posting the Synoptic Journal There are three basic steps in posting a Synoptic Journal as shown in Figure 13.3:

1. Each day, post the amounts in the Accounts Receivable and Accounts Payable columns *individually* to the customer and creditor accounts in the subsidiary ledgers. The names of the customers and creditors are given in the Account and Explanation column of the Synoptic Journal. Because customer and creditor accounts are filed alphabetically and not numbered, a check mark is written in the posting reference columns of the journal as the postings to the subsidiary ledgers are completed.

*10

2. At the end of the month, post the amounts in the General column *individually* to the General Ledger. The names of the accounts are given in the Account and Explanation column. As the postings from this General column are completed, the account number is shown in the posting reference column of the Synoptic Journal.

*11

3. At the end of the month, post all column totals, except the General column, to the General Ledger. When each column total has been posted, the number of the account is written in brackets under each total.

Posting References in the Ledgers When a business uses one journal only, the page number from which the posting is made is shown in the Posting Reference column of the ledger accounts. When there is more than one journal, a letter and page number are used. For example, *S61* indicates that a posting was made from page 61 of the Synoptic Journal.

Advantages of the Synoptic Journal

*12

There are three main advantages to the Synoptic Journal.

- The use of special columns saves time and space in recording transactions.
- Posting is reduced compared to the posting of a two-column journal.
- All transactions are found in one book, in chronological order.

Disadvantages of the Synoptic Journal

There are also three disadvantages to using the Synoptic Journal.

- The multi-column journal may be cumbersome and inconvenient to use.
- The risk of error is increased by the large number of columns.
- The use of the Synoptic Journal is restricted to a business with relatively few transactions which can be recorded by one person.

Journalless Accounting

Journalless accounting is *not* a system without journals. Journalless accounting is a system in which one or more of the special journals is eliminated and replaced by a group of source documents. For example, a collection of sales invoices replaces the Sales Journal.

*13

In journalless accounting a special journal is replaced by a group of source documents.

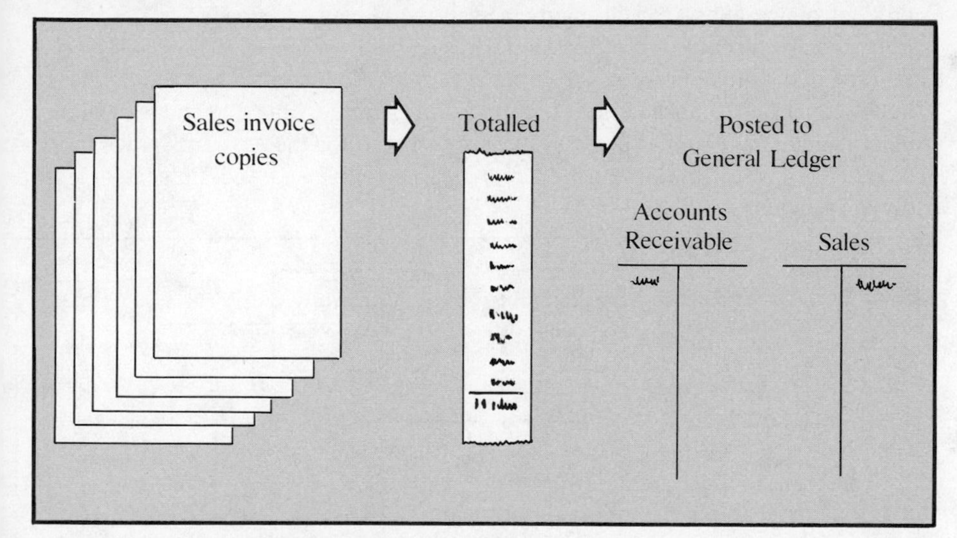

Figure 13.4 *A batch of sales invoices is totalled and posted directly to the General Ledger.*

Figure 13.4 illustrates how a batch of sales invoice copies is totalled and posted directly to the General Ledger. The journalizing step is eliminated. In effect, the batch of invoice copies becomes the Sales Journal.

Ledgerless Accounting

Ledgerless accounting refers to an accounting system in which subsidiary ledgers are replaced by files for each customer and for each creditor. A General Ledger is still used, but subsidiary ledgers are eliminated. Figure 13.5 illustrates a ledgerless accounting system.

*14

In ledgerless accounting subsidairy ledgers are replaced by files for each customer and for each creditor.

In a ledgerless system, at least three copies of the sales invoice are required. The original copy of the invoice is sent to the customer. Copy 2 of the invoice is the source document used to journalize the transaction. The journal entry is:

Jan.	7	Accounts Receivable Control		100 —	
		Sales			100 —
		Invoice 171			

Copy 3 is placed in the customer file folder. The set of files, which includes a file for each customer, replaces the Accounts Receivable subsidiary ledger. When a customer pays for an invoice, the receipt of cash is recorded in the General Journal. The invoice being paid is pulled from the customer's file folder and marked or stamped *PAID*. The invoice is then removed and placed in a paid file.

*15

Proof of Accounts Receivable and Accounts Payable In ledgerless accounting, the subsidiary ledgers are replaced by file folders for each customer and for each creditor. Invoices are still journalized and posted to the general ledger and control accounts are still maintained in the General Ledger.

Periodically a proof of the Accounts Receivable is prepared. This consists of a listing of all the unpaid invoices from the customer file folders. The total of this list should equal the balance of the Accounts Receivable Control account in the General Ledger. A similar proof system is prepared for the accounts payable. A summary of a ledgerless system for Accounts Receivable and Accounts Payable is shown in Figure 13.5.

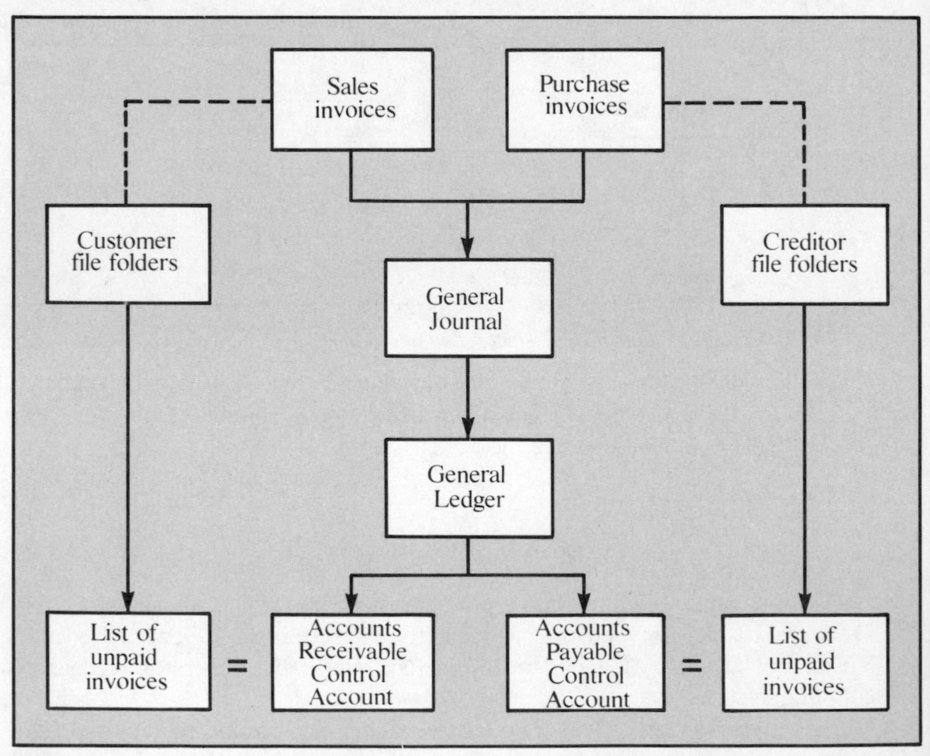

Figure 13.5 *Summary of the ledgerless system for Accounts Receivable and Accounts Payable*

Credit Card Companies Credit card companies have made it possible for small retailers to bring the ledgerless system a step further. Any business that has an arrangement with *Master Charge* or *Visa* can sell on credit to customers and receive the cash within a short period of time from the credit card company. Instead of carrying hundreds of different accounts receivable, businesses need only have one or two accounts. There is naturally a charge attached to this service, but this cost is usually offset by an increase in sales and a decrease in the cost of keeping track of, and collecting, accounts. ***16**

The buyer must present such a personalized credit card when making a credit purchase. Along with a sales invoice, the seller will prepare a sales draft as shown in Figure 13.6.

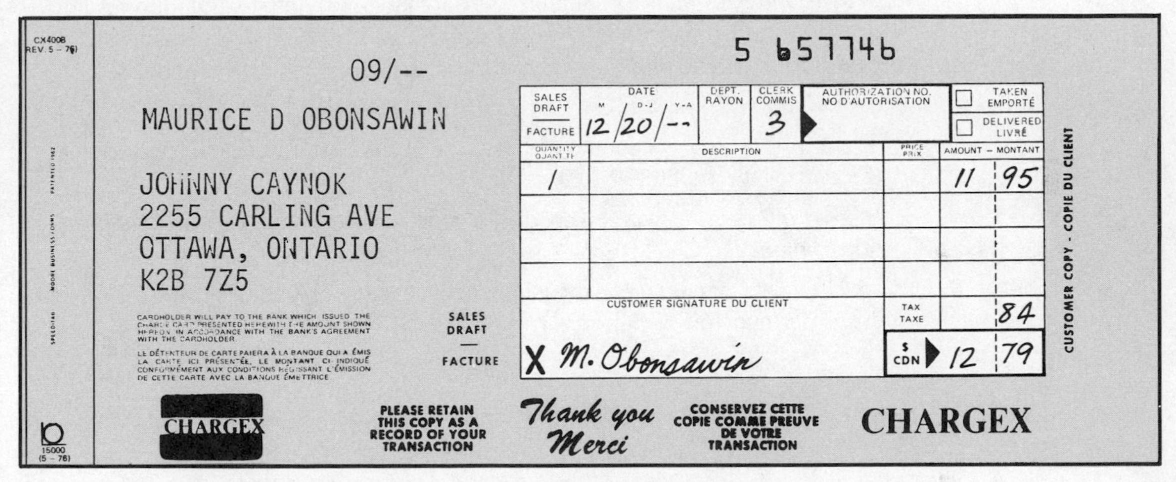
CX4008
REV. 5 – 76

5 657746

09/--

MAURICE D OBONSAWIN

JOHNNY CAYNOK
2255 CARLING AVE
OTTAWA, ONTARIO
K2B 7Z5

SALES DRAFT / FACTURE	DATE 12/20/--	DEPT. RAYON	CLERK COMMIS 3	AUTHORIZATION NO. NO D'AUTORISATION	TAKEN EMPORTÉ / DELIVERED LIVRÉ

QUANTITY QUANT.	DESCRIPTION	PRICE PRIX	AMOUNT – MONTANT
1			11 95
CUSTOMER SIGNATURE DU CLIENT		TAX TAXE	84
X M. Obonsawin		$ CDN	12 79

CARDHOLDER WILL PAY TO THE BANK WHICH ISSUED THE CHARGE CARD PRESENTED HEREWITH THE AMOUNT SHOWN HEREON IN ACCORDANCE WITH THE BANK'S AGREEMENT WITH THE CARDHOLDER

LE DÉTENTEUR DE CARTE PAIERA À LA BANQUE QUI A ÉMIS LA CARTE ICI PRÉSENTÉE, LE MONTANT CI-INDIQUÉ CONFORMÉMENT AUX CONDITIONS RÉGISSANT L'ÉMISSION DE CETTE CARTE AVEC LA BANQUE ÉMETTRICE

SALES DRAFT — FACTURE

CHARGEX

PLEASE RETAIN THIS COPY AS A RECORD OF YOUR TRANSACTION

Thank you Merci

CONSERVEZ CETTE COPIE COMME PREUVE DE VOTRE TRANSACTION

CHARGEX

CUSTOMER COPY - COPIE DU CLIENT

15000 (5 – 76)

Figure 13.6 *A sales draft prepared for a Visa (Chargex) credit purchase*

When the seller has accumulated a certain number of such sales drafts from various customers, they are presented to the credit card company which will immediately pay for the total value of the sales that were made, less a certain commission. The commission varies from 2% to 5% depending on the amount of business brought to the credit card company.

Transactions involving Visa and Donna's Beauty Salon would be handled as follows. At the end of each day, Donna makes a list of all the sales in which customers used a Visa credit card. Assuming that all the Visa sales drafts on May 4 totalled $153.34, the journal entry to record these sales would be:

May	4	Visa Receivable		153 34	
		Sales			153 34
		Sales drafts 5-875505 to			
		5-875511			

On May 6, Donna took these sales drafts to Visa and a deposit was made to her bank account for the amount owing to her, less a 5% commission. The entry in her General Journal would be:

May	6	Cash		145 67	
		Commission Expense		7 67	
		Visa Receivable			153 34
		Bank deposit from Visa			

Facts to Remember

A *Synoptic Journal* is a columnar journal that combines several journals into one book of original entry. Small businesses, in which one person records transactions, generally use a Synoptic Journal.

Combination Journal is another name for a Synoptic Journal.

The *Synoptic Journal* should be balanced at the bottom of each page and at the end of the month.

In *journalless accounting,* a special journal is replaced by a group of source documents.

In *ledgerless accounting,* subsidiary ledgers are replaced by files for each customer and for each creditor.

Checking Your Reading

Questions

1. a) What type of business generally uses a Synoptic Journal?
b) What is another name for the Synoptic Journal?

2. Why does the entry on May 11 in Figure 13.1 take two lines to record?

3. a) When is a debit or a credit amount recorded in the General section of the Synoptic Journal?
b) Where is the name of the account that is debited or credited recorded?

4. When is an account given its own column in the Synoptic Journal?

5. a) What is meant by auditing an adding machine tape?
b) List the steps you should follow to locate errors in a Synoptic Journal.

6. a) When is the Synoptic Journal balanced?
b) When is the Synoptic Journal posted?

7. List the three basic steps followed in posting the Synoptic Journal.

8. What Synoptic Journal column totals are not posted?

9. It is necessary to post the amounts in some of the Synoptic Journal columns individually. To which columns does this apply?

10. When posting from the Synoptic Journal's Accounts Receivable and Accounts Payable columns, what is shown in the posting reference column of the journal?
11. When column totals have been posted, where are the posting references shown in the journal?
12. When are two lines required to record a transaction in the Synoptic Journal?
13. Give three advantages and three disadvantages of the Synoptic Journal.
14. In journalless accounting, to which ledger are batch totals of invoices posted?
15. In ledgerless accounting, which ledgers are eliminated?
16. In ledgerless accounting, what should the balance of the Accounts Receivable Control account equal?

Applying Your Knowledge

Exercises Part A

1. Record the following source documents in a General Journal.

May 1 Sales invoice No. 75, issued to A. Walker for $200 plus 7% sales tax (200 + 14 = 214).
2 Cash sales slips No. 20 to No. 24, total $500 plus 7% sales tax (500 + 35 = 535).
4 Purchase invoice B-117 of $400, from National Wholesale for merchandise.
4 Cheque copy No. 171 for $600, issued to Royal Real Estate for the rent.

2. a) Journalize the June transactions for Costello Enterprises in a Synoptic Journal. Label the journal page 13.

June 1 Issued cheque No. 76 for $800 to pay the June rent.
1 Cash sales slips totalled $395, all non-taxable.
5 Sales invoices, terms 2/10, n/30:
No. 171, M. Swords, $75, sales tax $5.25, total $80.25.
No. 172, W. Kranz, $180, sales tax $12.60, total $192.60.
No. 173, J. Moore, $130, sales tax $9.10, total $139.10.
5 Purchased merchandise for $750 from Tanyss Trading, Invoice B-316, terms net 30.
8 Bought office supplies for $55 with cheque No. 77.
10 Cash purchase of merchandise for $200, cheque No. 78.
13 Paid $370 to the *Star* for advertising, cheque No. 79.

b) Total, rule, and balance the Synoptic Journal.

3. a) Continue to journalize transactions for Costello Enterprises in the Synoptic Journal, page 14. Forward the totals from page 13.

June 15 Received cheques from customers:
M. Swords, $78.64 for invoice No. 171. Amount of invoice $80.25; discount taken $1.61.
J. Moore, $136.32 for invoice No. 173. Amount of invoice $139.10; discount taken $2.78.

17 Purchased merchandise for $250 from National Wholesale, terms 1/10, n/30.

19 Cash sales slips totalled $500, sales tax $35, total cash received $535.

22 Issued cheque No. 80 to Tanyss Trading for $250 on account.

22 The owner, P. Costello, invested an additional $4 000 in the business.

23 Sales invoices, terms 2/10, n/30:
No. 174, M. Swords $200, sales tax $14, total $214.
No. 175, L. Usher $730, sales tax $51.10, total $781.10.

25 Issued cheque No. 81 for $2 700 to pay the month's wages.

26 Received credit invoice N-17 for goods returned to National Wholesale, $75.

26 Issued cheque No. 82 to National Wholesale for invoice of June 17, less credit invoice of June 26. Amount of cheque $173.25; amount of discount taken $1.75.

29 Cheque received for $192.60 from W. Kranz.

30 Issued cheque No. 83 for $95 to pay Utilities Expense for the month.

b) Total, rule, and balance the journal.

4. Following is the chart of accounts and trial balance for the Jean Shop:

Jean Shop
Trial Balance
May 1, 19__

ACCOUNT TITLE	ACC. NO.	DEBIT	CREDIT
Cash	101	1 500 —	
Accounts Receivable	102	1 756 —	
Store Supplies	104	6 551 —	
Accounts Payable	201		4 407 —
Sales Tax Payable	202		
L. Flynn, Capital	301		5 400 —
Sales	401		
Purchases	411		
Transportation on Purchases	412		
Advertising Expense	501		
Salaries Expense	502		
		9 807	9 807

a) Record the following documents on page 47 of the Synoptic Journal, then total and prove the journal.

May 1 Sales invoices issued:
No. 703 to K. Prentice of $450 plus $31.50 sales tax.
No. 704 to Clayton High for $376, no sales tax.
No. 705 to C. Mathers for $133 plus $9.31 sales tax.

2 Purchase invoices received:
Northern Wholesalers, $2 576 for merchandise.
CCKK T.V., $378 for T.V. advertising.
Robinson Trucking, $56 for transportation of merchandise from Northern Wholesalers.

3 List of cash receipts from:
Clayton High, $538.
C. Mathers, $346.
L. Flynn, the owner, $2 000 extra investment.

4 Copies of cheques issued:
No. 931 for $350 for employees' weekly salaries.
No. 932 for $1 270 to Northern Wholesalers, on account.
No. 933 for $37 to Robinson Trucking, on account.

b) Set up an Accounts Receivable Ledger and an Accounts Payable Ledger with the following balances:

Jean Shop Schedule of Accounts Receivable May 1, 19__	
Clayton High	675 —
C. Mathers	346 —
K. Prentice	735 —
	1 756 —

Jean Shop Schedule of Accounts Payable May 1, 19__	
CCKK T.V.	532 —
Northern Wholesalers	3 573 —
Robinson Trucking	302 —
	4 407 —

c) Post the Synoptic Journal to the subsidiary ledgers.

d) Post the individual accounts from the general column of the Synoptic Journal to the General Ledger.

e) Post the totals of each column, except for the general column, to the General Ledger.

f) Prepare proofs for the three ledgers.

5. a) Use the following chart of accounts and trial balance to record transactions on page 26 of the Synoptic Journal of Crawford Enterprises, a wholesaler.

Crawford Enterprises
Trial Balance
March 1, 19__

ACCOUNT TITLE	ACC. NO.	DEBIT	CREDIT
Cash	100	2 000 —	
Accounts Receivable	102	710 —	
Office Supplies	103	800 —	
Equipment	104	6 000 —	
Accounts Payable	201		954 —
Bank Loan	202		
P. Crawford, Capital	301		8 556 —
P. Crawford, Drawing	302		
Sales	401		
Sales Returns	402		
Sales Discounts	403		
Purchases	411		
Purchases Returns	412		
Purchases Discounts	413		
Transportation on Purchases	414		
Advertising Expense	501		
Utilities Expense	502		
		9 510 —	9 510 —

b) Total and balance the Synoptic Journal at the end of each page and at March 28.

March 2 Sales Invoices, terms 2/10, n/30; all sales are non-taxable:
Invoice 76-25 to W. Squire, $355.
Invoice 76-26 to R. Mask, $37.

5 Cash Sales Slips for the week, No. 69 to 85, total $2 970.

9 Purchase Invoices:
Wilson Supply, invoice K 297, for $987, terms 1/10, n/30.
Grant Ltd., invoice 491, for $500, terms 3/15, n/30.

10 Cash Receipts:
R. Mask, $125 for invoice 76-20.
W. Squire, $155 for invoice 76-24.

10 Credit Invoice issued:
No. CI-16 for $130 to T. Campbell for goods returned (goods were sold to Campbell on Feb. 15).

March 12 Cheques issued:
No. 122 to Corbett's for $160 in payment of invoice 225.
No. 123 to Grant Equipment for $722.70 in payment of invoice No. 420, less the purchase discount of $7.30, total $730.
No. 124 to the *Citizen* for advertising, $450.

12 Cash Receipts:
W. Squire $347.90 for invoice 76-25, discount taken $7.10.

15 Sales Invoices:
T. Campbell, invoice 76-27 for $476.
R. Mask, invoice 76-28 for $670.
G. Thompson, invoice 76-29 for $1 490.

15 Credit Invoice Received:
Grant Ltd., for $85 worth of defective merchandise on invoice No. 491, dated March 9.

20 Cheque Issued:
No. 125 for $175 to Roadway Transport Ltd. for transportation on purchases of merchandise.

25 Purchase Invoices:
Wilson Supply, $75 for office supplies.
Noonan Ltd., $250 for merchandise.

26 Bank Credit Memo:
Bank loan for $2 500 has been deposited by the bank in Crawford Enterprises account.

27 Cheques Issued:
No. 126 for $2 000 to pay for a vacation trip for the P. Crawford family.
No. 127 to City Hydro, $160 for the company's hydro bill.

28 Sales Invoice:
No. 76-30 to W. Squire for $790.

c) Head up a General Ledger, Accounts Receivable Ledger, and Accounts Payable Ledger and record the March 1 balances. The following accounts are in the subsidiary ledgers as of March 1:

Crawford Enterprises
Schedule of Accounts Receivable
March 1, 19__

T. Campbell		430 —
R. Mask		125 —
W. Squire		155 —
G. Thompson		
		710 —

Crawford Enterprises Schedule of Accounts Payable March 1, 19__	
Corbett's Service Station	160 —
Grant Ltd.	730 —
Noonan Ltd.	40 —
Wilson Supply	24 —
	954 —

d) Post the Synoptic Journal to the three ledgers.
e) Prepare three trial balances.

6. You are an accounting clerk for Holmes Consulting Services. Your accounting system does not include a Sales Journal. Sales invoices are not journalized. Batches of sales invoices are totalled and posted directly to the General Ledger each week.

a) Head up a General Ledger with the following October 1 balances:

Holmes Consulting Service
Trial Balance
October 1, 19__

ACCOUNT TITLE	ACC. NO.	DEBIT	CREDIT
Cash	100	1 000 —	
Accounts Receivable Control	110	2 185 —	
Equipment	120	10 500 —	
Accounts Payable Control	201		755 —
A. Holmes, Capital	301		11 745 —
Sales	401		1 185 —
		13 685 —	13 685 —

On October 1, the sales invoices that customers had not yet paid are:

No. 10, M. Wong, $645.
No. 13, Quinn Inc., $367.
No. 22, Morgan Co., $861.
No. 27, Quinn Inc., $312.

b) Post the totals for the October 8, October 18, and October 29 invoices directly to the General Ledger for the following transactions:

Oct. 8 No. 31, Morgan Co., $160.
No. 32, Quinn Inc., $325.
No. 33, M. Wong, $270.
No. 34, Morgan Co., $150.
No. 35, Battista Ltd., $200.

Oct. 18 No. 36, M. Wong, $100.
No. 37, Battista Ltd., $600.
No. 38, Quinn Inc., $230.
No. 39, Morgan Co., $75.

Oct. 29 No. 40, Battista Ltd., $265.
No. 41, M. Wong, $190.
No. 42, Quinn Inc., $1400.
No. 43, Morgan Co., $60.

c) Prepare a General Ledger trial balance.

7. Holmes Consulting Services uses a ledgerless system of Accounts Receivable. They have no customer accounts but maintain a file folder for each customer. Invoices are placed in each customer's file until they are paid. At any time, the total of all the unpaid invoices should equal the Accounts Receivable Control account in the General Ledger. Assume you have a file folder for each of the following customers:

- Battista Ltd.
- Quinn Inc.
- Morgan Co.
- M. Wong

a) If you file all the sales invoices from exercise 6 in the proper customer file, what is the total owing by each customer?

b) List and total all unpaid invoices. What is the total owed to your company? Explain why this total equals the balance in the Accounts Receivable Control account from exercise 6.

Exercises Part B

8. a) Use the following chart of accounts and April 2 trial balance to record transactions on page 35 of the Synoptic Journal of Sporting Wholesalers.

ACCOUNT TITLE	ACC. NO.	DEBIT	CREDIT
Cash	100	21 576 53	
Accounts Receivable	110	2 147 07	
Building	120	235 000 —	
Accounts Payable	201		2 306 75
Sales Tax Payable	202		2 476 53
Bank Loan	203		4 560 —
R. Dundee, Capital	301		211 213 73
R. Dundee, Drawing	302	4 563 47	
Sales	401		74 751 87
Sales Returns	402	2 156 39	
Purchases	501	24 573 90	
Purchases Returns	502		1 397 88
Purchases Discounts	503		176 35
Salaries Expense	601	4 753 91	
Advertising Expense	602	1 376 53	
Bank Charges Expense	603	735 31	
		296 883 11	296 883 11

April 2 Sales Invoices, terms n/20:
No. C-5730 to Carver Basketball League for $276 plus $19.32 sales tax.
No. C-5731 to Action Sporting Goods for $476, sales tax exempt.

4 Cash Sales Slips for the week:
No. 795 to No. 863, $759.63 plus $35.17 sales tax.

7 Purchase Invoices:
Invoice 9767M from Cadieux Textiles, $896.00 for merchandise, terms 2/10, n/30.
Invoice 35-7402 from Croydon Manufacturing, $1 796.43 for merchandise, terms 1/15, n/30.
Invoice 8739 from *Daily Star,* $163.00 for advertising, terms n/15.

9 Cheques Issued:
No. 670, $797.53 to Croydon Manufacturing for invoice 35-5309.
No. 671, $563.45 to Cadieux Textiles for invoice 6391M.
No. 672, $2 476.53 to the Provincial Treasurer for sales tax collected in March.

10 Credit Invoice issued:
No. CR 893 to the Carver Basketball League, $33.00 plus $2.31 sales tax for defective crests on invoice C-5730 dated April 2.

10 Cash Receipts:
Vernon Athletics, $376.50 for invoice C-5103
Action Sporting Goods, $593.03 for invoice C-5117.

11 Cash Sales Slips for the week:
No. 864 to No. 983, $893.55 plus $42.45 sales tax.

13 Cheques issued:
No. 673, $46.50 to CKCH Radio for advertising.
No. 674, $375.00 to L. Savage for his salary.
No. 675, 250.00 to R. Dundee, the owner, for personal use.

15 Sales Invoices, terms n/20:
No. C-5732 to Vernon Athletics for $573.54 plus $40.15 sales tax.
No. C-5733 to Action Sporting Goods for $638.53, sales tax exempt.

16 Cheque issued:
No. 676 for $878.08 to Cadieux Textiles to pay invoice 9767M, $896.00 less $17.92 discount.

17 Credit Invoice received:
Invoice 35-7402 from Croydon Manufacturing, $192.12 for damaged goods, dated April 7.

18 Cash Sales Slips for the week:
No. 984 to No. 1117, total $695.03 plus $37.65 sales tax.

20 Cash Receipts:
Carver Basketball League, $497.50 for invoice C-5105.
Action Sporting Goods, $875.03 for invoice C-5213.

April 22 Cheques Issued:
No. 677 for $1 778.47 to Croydon Manufacturing to pay invoice 35-7402 for $1 796.43, less $17.96 discount.
No. 678 for $250.00 to the Bank of Commerce as payment on the bank loan.

24 Sales Invoices, terms n/20:
No. C-5734 to Action Sporting Goods, $397.55, sales tax exempt.
No. C-5735 to Vernon Athletics, $137.35 plus $9.61 sales tax.

25 Cash Sales Slips for the week:
No. 1118 to No. 1304, $934.15 plus $47.39 sales tax.

28 Bank Debit Memo:
Bank of Commerce; $27.53 was taken out of the bank account for bank charges.

30 Cheques Issued:
No. 679 for $389.00 to R. Dundee for personal use.
No. 680 for $375.00 to L. Savage for his salary.

b) Total, balance, and rule the Synoptic Journal.

9. a) From the following trial balance, open the Accounts Receivable Ledger accounts and post those transactions from exercise 8 that affect these accounts:

Sporting Wholesalers
Schedule of Accounts Receivable
April 2, 19__

Action Sporting Goods	1 273 07
Carver Basketball League	497 50
Vernon Athletics	376 50
	2 147 07

b) From the following trial balance, open the Accounts Payable Ledger accounts and post those transactions from exercise 8 that affect these accounts:

Sporting Wholesalers
Schedule of Accounts Payable
April 2, 19__

Cadieux Textiles	1 373 59
Croydon Manufacturing	797 53
Daily Star	135 63
	2 306 75

c) From the chart of accounts given in exercise 8, open General Ledger accounts and post the Synoptic Journal.
d) Prepare the three trial balances.

Exercises Part C

10. Following is the chart of accounts and trial balance for The Tiny Tot, a store specializing in young children's clothing.

The Tiny Tot Trial Balance June 7, 19__			
ACCOUNT TITLE	**ACC. NO.**	**DEBIT**	**CREDIT**
Cash	101	6 573 65	
Visa Receivable	102	4 396 77	
Accounts Payable	201		2 795 63
A. Becker, Capital	301		1 700 91
Sales	401		30 975 11
Sales Returns	402	753 91	
Purchases	411	19 371 75	
Salaries Expense	501	2 798 67	
Advertising Expense	502	848 23	
Utilities Expense	503	274 82	
Visa Commission Expense	504	453 85	
		35 471 65	35 471 65

Notice that there is no Accounts Receivable account. The Tiny Tot does not extend credit to its customers, but does accept payment by Visa, a major credit card company. This provides certain advantages such as the elimination of checking up on customers' credit ratings and also eliminates the need for an Accounts Receivable Ledger. Visa takes over that responsibility.

a) Set up a Synoptic Journal with appropriate headings.
b) Record the following documents that were issued or received in the first week of June.

June 7 Cash Sales Slips No. 1347 to No. 1682, $3 533.46 plus $247.34 sales tax.

7 Sales Draft No. 5-379552 to 5-379701 issued and mailed to Visa for $2 654.33 plus $185.80 sales tax. (Note that the sales drafts should be handled in the same way as a sales invoice and represent sales on account.)

7 Cheques issued:
No. 351, $175.00 to C. Cathcart for the week's salary.
No. 352, $126.00 to CKFM Radio for invoice 933-A dated May 10.
No. 353, $635.00 to National Manufacturers for invoice 33-6697 dated May 12.
No. 354, $47.95 to City Hydro for electricity used.

June 7 Cheque received from Visa for $3 576.53 less $107.30 commission. The $3 469.23 cheque is in payment of sales drafts No. 5-379130 to 5-379393 that were sent in two weeks ago.

7 Purchase invoices received:
Gaynor Textiles, invoice L 39047 for $576.34 in merchandise, terms 1/10, n/30.
National Manufacturers, invoice 35-7654 for $837.63 in merchandise, terms n/30.
CKFM Radio, invoice 1797-B $79.00 for spot advertising, terms n/30.

7 Credit Sales draft number 5-387592 for $35.49 plus $2.48 sales tax. Goods had to be returned to a customer because they were unsatisfactory; a credit note was sent to Visa to reduce the account.

c) Total, balance, and rule the Synoptic Journal.
d) Open General Ledger accounts, including the opening balances, for the accounts listed in the chart of accounts.
e) Post the Synoptic Journal.
f) Prepare a trial balance.

Accounting in Action

Case 1

Designing a Sales System Superior Manufacturing produces specialized equipment. About 90% of its sales are made to four customers. The remaining 10% of sales are made to companies who make one or two purchases a year. An average of 10 invoices is issued each week. As the new accountant, you have been given the task of designing a system for recording sales and handling accounts receivable.

a) Consider each of the following systems for the recording of sales invoices:
  - Synoptic Journal and Accounts Receivable Ledger
  - a ledgerless system with file folders for each customer (sales to be recorded in a Sales Journal)
  - a ledgerless system with file folders for each customer and a journalless system of recording sales in which batch totals of sales invoices are directly posted to the General Ledger

b) Give advantages and disadvantages of each of the preceding alternatives. Select one method as your choice.

Case 2

Recording Sales Invoices Clifford's Wholesale Auto Parts is an old and well-established business. It has over 100 customers who buy on credit. It purchases merchandise on credit from about 15 different creditors. The bookkeeper for Clifford's Wholesale uses a system which consists of a two-column General Journal and a General Ledger. File folders are used instead of subsidiary ledgers.

The company auditor has pointed out that many customers do not follow the net 30 days payment terms. It is not unusual to have thousands of dollars many days overdue. As a result, there always seems to be a cash crisis, with little money on hand to meet necessary payments. It has been very easy to arrange an open line of credit with a bank of up to $10 000 at 12% interest. There is normally $5 000 owing to the bank.

Clifford's Wholesale is operating profitably and the bookkeeper is not sure that changes are needed in the system. Suggest a different way of handling sales invoices and customer accounts. Give the advantages and disadvantages of the old system and of your recommended methods.

Case 3

Survey of Accounting Systems Make a list of 10 wholesalers, 10 retailers, and 10 manufacturers located in your area. Prepare a questionnaire which will determine the following:

a) the number of sales invoice copies prepared by each company,
b) the journal system used,
c) the ledger system used,
d) whether the systems are: i) manual ii) mechanical iii) electronic.

Case 4

Accounting Systems Your business has experienced rapid growth in the last few years. The number of customers has increased from 200 to over 800. The number of creditors has increased from 10 to 70. A manual accounting system using special journals and subsidiary ledgers is used. Monthly financial statements are prepared and except for electronic calculators and adding machines, no special accounting machines are used.

Because of the growth of the business and the need to hire additional accounting clerks, it seems necessary to investigate the use of specialized equipment and accounting procedures. The possibilities include:

- The purchase and use of a one-write accounting board system for accounts receivable, accounts payable, and payroll.
- The purchase and use of electronic accounting machines for accounts receivable, accounts payable, and payroll.
- The purchase of a small computer.
- The use of an accounting service company to perform the accounts receivable, accounts payable, payroll, and financial statement functions.

Prepare a list of questions you would require to be answered by companies capable of providing the four services listed.

Case 5

The Social Costs of Business Decisions Metalco is a very large producer of several types of metals. It mines, refines, and ships metal products to customers located in many different countries. The following chart presents a summary of operating results for the last five years and projected results for the next two years.

	Operating Results (in millions of dollars)					Projected Results (Loss)	
	19_1	19_2	19_3	19_4	19_5	19_6	19_7
Sales	500	490	480	470	460	400	390
Costs and Expenses	380	390	390	400	400	410	410
Net Income	120	100	90	70	60	(10)	(20)

This chart illustrates a decrease of $40 000 000 in sales from 19_1 to 19_5. Costs and expenses have increased slightly. Net income has decreased dramatically from $120 000 000 to $60 000 000.

Management of Metalco is aware of the causes of the unfavourable trends. World prices and the demand for its products have decreased. In the next two years sales and net income are projected to decrease even more substantially. This forecast is based on increased competition from foreign producers located in countries with very low labour costs compared to Canada.

Metalco is faced with a very difficult problem. The major company expense is wages. The company does not need the services of about 3 000 of its workers because production is decreasing. In the last five years these unneeded people have been kept on staff because the company felt a loyalty towards its workers. If they had been laid off their families would have suffered severe economic hardships. However, had they been laid off the company net income would have averaged about $80 000 000 a year.

Metalco must decide what to do in the next two years. If it does not lay off unneeded workers the company will suffer certain losses. If unneeded workers are laid off the company will be able to decrease total expenses by about $50 000 000.

a) What will be the estimated net income for 19_6 and 19_7 if unneeded workers are let go?
b) What are the *social costs* to the community if workers are let go?
c) What are the the *economic costs* to the community if the workers are let go?
d) What obligation does Metalco have to the shareholders who have invested their savings in Metalco shares?
e) What do you feel is the correct decision to make in the interest of each of these:
   i) the community
   ii) the shareholders
   iii) the company's future
f) Do you feel the government has the right to step in and to order the company to retain all 3 000 employees?
g) If you were a member of Metalco's management team, what decision would you make? Why?

Case 6

Making a Business Decision T. Hood worked for many years as a machinist for a large automobile manufacturer. Hood lived very frugally and saved money to satisfy a dream – to own his own business. Three years ago Hood mortgaged his home, borrowed money, and invested in his own business. Hood now employs six persons and the business has earned a modest net income for two years.

This year there has been a general slump in the economy. Hood's business has suffered with sales decreasing 30%. Hood's accountant has predicted a loss of $36 000 if three full-time workers are not laid off. Hood feels that his employees are almost part of his family. They have been loyal and are partly responsible for the business success of the past two years. If Hood does not lay off the workers he will not be able to make his mortgage payments and will likely lose his home and perhaps his business as well.

a) If you were Hood, what would you do?
b) Do you see any similarities and differences between this case and the one involving Metalco?

Career Profile

Peter Carter is general manager of Congdon Van and Storage, (Edmonton) Ltd., a subsidiary of North American Van Lines. He is totally responsible for the operation of the company – including sales, employee relations, services, and accounting. His main task is to see that the company operates profitably. This career profile follows Peter's development from his first job as an accounting clerk to his present position of general manager of a company with 30 employees, doing about $1 000 000 worth of business each year.

Peter enjoyed the accounting courses he took at high school, and shortly after graduating he started working as a junior accounting clerk at North American Van Lines in Ottawa. He realized that to get ahead he would have to work hard to further his education. He enrolled in the C.G.A. program. After two years, during which Peter put in many hours of study and extra effort on the job, he was appointed comptroller of the Ottawa office. He was responsible for setting up an efficient system of financial controls and for making recommendations which would make the operation more profitable.

After a short time as comptroller in Ottawa, Peter was transferred to a similar position in North American Van Lines' Toronto office. After two years in Toronto, Peter was promoted to the position of comptroller, Western Region. This meant that he was responsible for the accounting functions of the Edmonton, Calgary, and Vancouver offices of North American Van Lines. His new position involved a lot of travel and creative work in establishing effective accounting systems in each office.

The position of general manager of the Edmonton office was offered to Peter after he had served one year as Western Region comptroller. Peter is now twenty-seven years old. He enjoys his work as manager and feels that his years of strenuous effort and study have been rewarded.

Peter and his wife Michelle like living in western Canada. They enjoy skiing, photography and music. Peter is involved in community work in Edmonton with the Kinsmen Club, of which he is treasurer. He has completed two years of the C.G.A. program and hopes to complete the five-year program sometime in the future.

CHAPTER 14

Cash Control

Control of Cash

Unit 34

*1

Leslie H. works for Finest Flowers Ltd. One of Leslie's duties is to handle cash sales. When a customer buys merchandise for cash, a cash sales slip is completed in duplicate. One copy is given to the customer and the second is placed in a cash box with the money received from the sale. Leslie is often left alone in the store and has learned that a sale can be made, a cash sales slip given to the customer, the duplicate copy destroyed, and the money placed in Leslie's pocket instead of in the company's cash box.

This little story is an example of why all companies, both large and small, require accounting systems which provide control over dishonesty and error.

Because of the ease with which cash may be lost or stolen, and errors made in counting cash, systems are needed which give effective control over all cash received and all payments made. No two businesses operate in exactly the same way. Some have many cash sales every day while others have only a few. It is the accountant's task to design a system that suits the particular needs of a company. The system should effectively control cash, but it should not be overly complicated or expensive to operate.

In the case of Finest Flowers, the solution can be as simple as prenumbering all the sales slips and having Leslie's supervisor check them periodically to ensure that none are missing.

In this chapter, the basic accounting procedures used to control a company's cash will be examined. It should be understood that the term *cash* as used in this chapter includes cheques, money orders, bills, and coins.

Cash includes cheques, money orders, bills, and coins.

Principles of Cash Control

*2

A business owned and operated by one person or by a small family has little need for control procedures. However, as a company grows and employs an increasing number of people, it is often necessary to pass to others tasks which include financial responsibilities. This makes it necessary to control theft, fraud, and errors made by people within the company. As well, control procedures can result in more efficient use of employee time. There are a number of established accounting principles which have been designed to provide internal control over cash. Seven such cash control principles will be discussed in this chapter.

Principle One: Deposit all Cash and Pay by Cheque

*3

Deposit all cash received in the bank. Pay all bills by cheque.

As cash is received, either through the mail or across the counter in a store or office, a source document should be prepared to record the receipt of the money. The money should then be deposited in the bank as soon as it is practical to do so.

The cash received is never used to pay bills. It is deposited intact. All payments are made by cheques drawn on the company bank account. In this way, there is a record of payment both in the company's set of books and in the bank's records. If discrepancies occur, the two sets of records can be compared. If it is necessary to make payments with cash, a petty cash fund should be used.

Principle Two: Petty Cash

*4

It is often necessary to make a payment by cash because the amount involved is small or because a cheque is not acceptable. For example:

- $1.50 parcel post C.O.D. charge
- 50¢ shortage of postage on incoming mail
- $5 taxi charge for a rush order of supplies
- $2 payment for office supplies

The petty cash fund is an amount of cash used to make small payments.

To meet these situations, a small amount of cash is kept on hand. Called the *petty cash fund,* it is given to one person, called the *petty cashier*. This person usually has no connection with the accounting system of the company.

Setting Up the Petty Cash Fund To establish the petty cash fund, a cheque is issued and given to the petty cashier. The cheque is cashed and the money is usually kept in a petty cash box.

The petty cash voucher is a signed authorization for small payments.

Making Payments The petty cashier is the only person who handles petty cash. Payments made must be authorized by a properly supporting *petty cash voucher* (Figure 14.1).

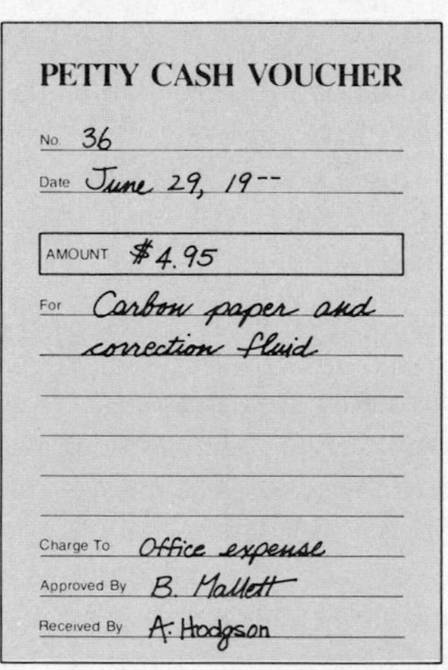
PETTY CASH VOUCHER

No. 36

Date June 29, 19--

AMOUNT $4.95

For Carbon paper and correction fluid

Charge To Office expense

Approved By B. Mallett

Received By A. Hodgson

Figure 14.1 *Petty cash voucher*

Petty cash vouchers are kept in the petty cash box with the remaining cash. The vouchers prove that legitimate, authorized payments were made because they have been signed by the party receiving the cash payment.

Proving the Petty Cash Suppose a petty cashier starts with $100 cash in the petty cash fund. At any time, the petty cash can be *proven* by adding the total of the cash in the box to the total of the vouchers in the box. Cash plus vouchers should always equal $100. *5

Replenishing the Petty Cash Fund When the petty cash fund runs low, the petty cashier presents the vouchers to the accountant. The vouchers prove that authorized payments were made. The accountant will then issue a cheque equal to the total of the vouchers. The petty cashier cashes the cheque and places the money in the petty cash box. The petty cash fund will now be back to its original amount. The fund is replenished when it runs low and at the end of the fiscal period before financial statements are prepared. *6

Replenishing the petty cash fund means bringing its total back to the original amount.

Journal Entries for Petty Cash When a petty cash fund is established, this entry is made: *7

Jan.	2	Petty Cash		100 —	
		Cash			100 —
		Cheque 171 to set up a			
		petty cash fund			

The Petty Cash account is found in the General Ledger. It is an asset and appears in the current asset section of the balance sheet.

The Petty Cash account is a current asset.

On January 23, the petty cashier noted that there was only $12 cash left in the petty cash fund. Along with this cash were 17 vouchers for payments made. Since the original amount of the fund was $100 and there was only $12 left, the payment vouchers should total $88. *8

The petty cashier added the 17 vouchers. They totalled $88. This meant that there were no errors in handling the petty cash. The vouchers were then presented to the accountant. A replenishing cheque for $88 was issued by the accountant. This journal entry was made: *9

Jan.	23	K. Martin, Drawing		20 —	
		Office Expense		29 —	
		Delivery Expense		17 —	
		Miscellaneous Expense		22 —	
		Cash			88 —
		Cheque 207 to replenish			
		petty cash, vouchers 1 to 17			

A journal entry similar to the one above is made each time the petty cash fund is replenished. The accounts to be debited are determined by referring to the vouchers submitted by the petty cashier.

The petty cashier is usually given a set of guidelines like the following:

- amount of fund, $100
- an approved voucher is required for every payment
- replenish when the cash level reaches $10
- maximum for any one payment, $15
- approved vouchers must be presented to the accountant when requesting a replenishing cheque

Unit 35

Principle Three: Separation of Duties

*10

The tasks of recording cash received and actually handling the cash should be carried out by different people.

The principle of *separation of duties* is used by Fraser Enterprises, a large wholesaler of heating and refrigeration equipment, to control and record cash receipts. Each day, a list of all cash received is prepared. This list shows the name of the customer, the amount received, and the invoice which is being paid. Two copies of the list are prepared. They are sent to the accounting department where the money received is recorded.

The actual cash is taken to the bank each day. Cheques received are endorsed using a restrictive endorsement stamp as shown in Figure 14.2. This endorsement ensures that the cheque is deposited in the company account. It cannot be cashed by anyone. A duplicate deposit slip is prepared and one copy is kept by the bank. The second copy, signed by the bank teller, is kept by the company.

DEPOSIT TO THE CREDIT OF
CEDARHILL GOLF AND COUNTRY CLUB

The Bank of Nova Scotia
Carlingwood & Woodroffe Branch
794-13 Ottawa, Ontario 794-13

Figure 14.2 *A restrictive endorsement stamp on the back of a cheque*

*11

The List of Cash Received Two copies of the list of cash received are sent to the accounting department. One copy goes to the accounts receivable posting clerk and the other copy goes to the junior accountant responsible for journalizing.

The Accounts Receivable Clerk From the list of cash received, the accounts receivable clerk posts to the customer accounts. Each account is lowered with a credit, as was seen in Chapter 8. Once every week, the accounts receivable clerk prepares a schedule of accounts receivable. This is a list showing the amounts owing by each customer and the total owed by all the customers as a group.

Once a month a statement is sent to each customer. The statement shows the balance, charges, and credits for cash received and it acts as a reminder of the amount owing. The statement also is used to check on the accuracy of both Fraser Enterprises' and the customer's records. The customer is sure to complain if the balance owing shown on the statement is too high. Figure 14.3 illustrates the handling of copy one of the list of cash received.

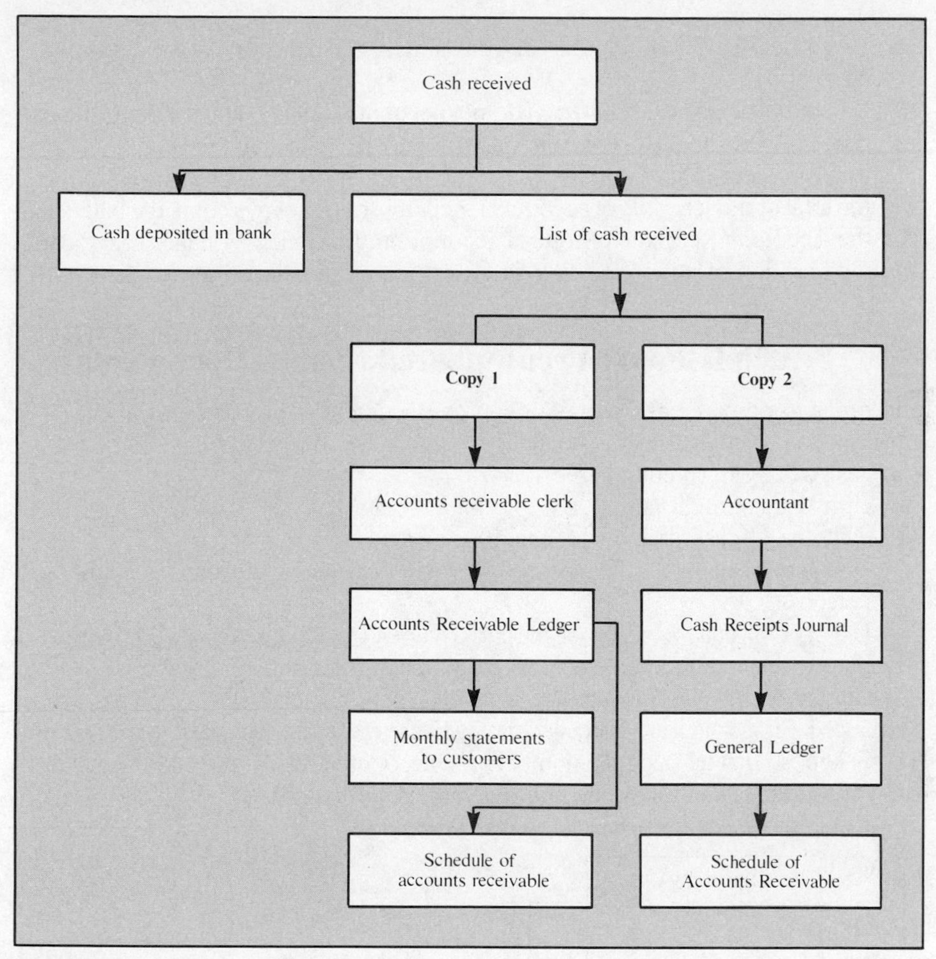

Figure 14.3 *The duties of depositing and recording cash received are carried out by three separate people.*

The Accountant The second copy of the list of cash receipts is sent to the accountant who is responsible for recording cash received in the Cash Receipts Journal. The total recorded in the Cash Receipts Journal each day must equal the total of the daily bank deposit. The Cash Receipts Journal is posted to the General Ledger. A trail balance is prepared to prove the accuracy of the General Ledger. One of the accounts on the General Ledger trial balance is the *Accounts Receivable Control account*. The balance in this account must equal the total of the schedule of accounts receivable prepared by the accounts receivable clerk. Figure 14.3 illustrates the tasks performed by the accountant in recording the second copy of the list of cash received.

*12

Control Features In the system just described, three persons are involved in the cash receipts procedures. One person prepares the deposit and takes the money to the bank. The duty of recording the receiving of cash is handled by two other people. The duties are separated. This separation of duties has several built-in control features:

- the entries in the Cash Journal each day should equal the total of the day's bank deposit
- the credits posted each day to customer accounts should equal the day's deposit
- the customer should discover amounts not posted to the customer account when the statement is sent out
- the total of the schedule of accounts receivable must always equal the balance of the Accounts Receivable Control account on the General Ledger trial balance

The separation of duties principle is observed by most large companies.

Principle Four: Prenumbered Source Documents

*13

In order to prepare cash proofs, a source document is prepared for every transaction. The documents include:

- cash sales slip (prenumbered)
- cash register audit tape
- daily list of cash receipts received by mail
- customer receipts and copies issued when customers pay their accounts in person

The type of daily cash proof prepared varies from company to company. Brighton Cleaners records every sale on a cash sales slip. Each slip is prenumbered. All slips must be accounted for at the end of the day when the cash is balanced. Slips which are cancelled or which are rewritten, are marked *VOID* and a copy kept so that all sales slip numbers are accounted for. At the end of each day, the slips are totalled on an adding machine (Figure 14.4).

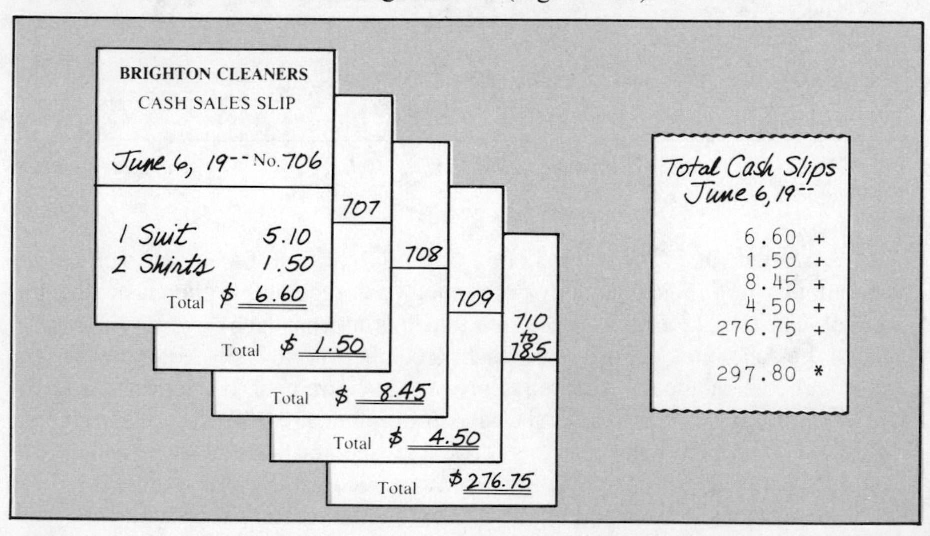

Figure 14.4 *Prenumbered sales slips are totalled on an adding machine.*

The cash is counted and a $50 *float* (change fund) is removed from the cash and kept for the next day's business. The cash is deposited in the bank. A copy of the deposit slip is used to compare the total cash with the total of the sales slips (Figure 14.5).

*14

A float is a small change fund that is put into the cash register at the start of the day.

THE BANK OF NOVA SCOTIA
CREDIT CURRENT ACCOUNTS

NO. 00-91835 June 6, 19--
DATE
NAME Brighton Cleaners
DEPOSITED BY E. Plata

16 X 1	16	–
10 X 2	20	–
11 X 5	55	–
14 X 10	140	–
3 X 20	60	–
X 50		
X 100		
COIN	1	50
BONDS/COUPONS		
SUB-TOTAL	292	50
CHEQUES	5	–
TOTAL	297	50
LESS EXCHANGE		
TELLER $	297	50

Figure 14.5 *Bank deposit slip*

If all documents are prenumbered, all of them must be accounted for. It is therefore impossible for the sales clerk to destroy a cash sales slip and pocket the money, since it would mean that one of the numbered slips would be destroyed. If a sales slip is spoiled or cancelled, it must be marked *VOID* and kept with the rest of the day's source documents. The principle of prenumbering documents is applied to many forms. For example, cheques, sales invoices, and petty cash vouchers are all prenumbered. This ensures that every document is accounted for.

Cancelled invoices are marked *void* and are kept on file.

Principle Five: Daily Cash Proof

Each day, the cash received should be balanced against the source documents used to record the cash transactions.

*15

Journal Entries In the case of Brighton Cleaners, a daily cash proof form is completed by the owner of the business, E. Plata (Figure 14.6).

DAILY CASH PROOF

DATE June 7 19 --	
TOTAL CASH	$347.50
LESS FLOAT	50.00
TOTAL DEPOSITED	297.50
SALES SLIPS NO.'s 706 to 785	297.80
CASH SHORT	0.30
or	
CASH OVER	
AUTHORIZED E. Plata	

Figure 14.6 *Daily cash proof*

The daily cash proof is the source document for a journal entry to record the day's sales. For June 6, the journal entry is:

Cash *shortages* are recorded as *debits* in the Cash Short and Over account.

June	6	Cash		297 50	
		Cash Short and Over		30	
		Sales			297 80
		To record sales slips 706 to 785			

The daily cash proof for the next day, June 7, is shown in Figure 14.7.

DAILY CASH PROOF

DATE June 7 19 --	
TOTAL CASH	$366.73
LESS FLOAT	50.00
TOTAL DEPOSITED	316.73
SALES SLIPS NO.'s 786 to 861	315.73
CASH SHORT	
or	
CASH OVER	1.00
AUTHORIZED E. Plata	

Figure 14.7 *Daily cash proof showing a cash overage*

Notice that the total cash deposited is $1 more than it should be according to the cash sales slips. In this entry, the overage is recorded as a credit to *Cash Short and Over*. The journal entry for June 7 is:

June	7	Cash		316 73	
		Sales			315 73
		Cash Short and Over			1 –
		To record sales slips 786			
		to 861			

Cash *overages* are recorded as *credits* in the Cash Short and Over account.

Cash Short and Over Account In the daily cash proof in Figure 14.6, the cash was short by 30¢. This shortage represents a loss to the company and is charged as a debit (a decrease in owner's equity) to the account Cash Short and Over. If the cash is *over* (Figure 14.7), the amount is recorded in the same Cash Short and Over account. However, an overage is recorded as a credit (an increase in owner's equity).

*16

The Cash Short and Over account is used to record shortages and overages of cash.

Income Statement When an income statement is prepared, the Cash Short and Over account may appear in *either* the revenue or the expense section. It appears in the revenue section if the account has a *credit* balance, or the overages have been greater than the shortages. It appears in the expense section if the account has a *debit* balance, or the shortages have been greater than the overages.

Some companies prefer to use a separate section at the bottom of the income statement for miscellaneous items such as cash short and over. This section, called Other Income and Expenses, includes such items as bank interest earned, cash short and over, and gain or loss on sale of assets. The use of this section clearly indicates how much of the net income comes from the regular operations of the business and how much comes from miscellaneous sources.

Cash Short and Over Policy A company which handles a lot of cash transactions and prepares a daily cash proof is faced with a problem. *What should be done about shortages and overages?* There are several possibilities, including these:

*17

- absorb all shortages and overages
- deduct shortages from the cashier's pay

Many companies prefer to keep all shortage information from the cashier. The daily cash proof is prepared by someone from the accounting office. Shortages and overages are absorbed by the company and are not mentioned to the cashier, unless they are frequent and fairly large. If this occurs, the situation is discussed with the cashier. Retraining may be necessary. If errors still continue on a large scale, the cashier may be transferred or fired.

Principle Six: Periodic Audits

*18

An audit is a periodic check on the accuracy of an accounting system.

Periodically, a check or an *audit* is made to determine that all cash is properly accounted for. Any system, no matter how complicated or fool-proof, can break down. Those involved in the system can devise ways to break the system. People can get together and contrive to defraud a company. The periodic, often unannounced audit is designed to thwart such attempts.

An auditor, employed either by the company or by an outside accounting firm, is given the task of checking the company records. Transactions are traced from their source documents to their posting in the ledgers. Invoices and deposit slips are checked for accuracy. Principle Four stated that prenumbered documents should be used to record cash. However, if a check is not made to ensure that all documents and cash are accounted for, the system breaks down.

Principle Seven: Bank Reconciliation Statement

*19

Principle Seven will involve making sure that a company's record of its money agrees with the bank's record of the company's money. This requires an understanding of the relationship between a bank and its depositors.

The Banking Connection *What is the relationship between a company or person who deposits money and the bank? Do banks follow the same accounting rules and the theory of debits and credits that everyone else does?* The following example is a good illustration of the banking connection.

Renfrew Printing makes cash sales of $1 500 and deposits the $1 500 in a savings account at the Bank of Nova Scotia. In the books of Renfew Printing, the following occurs:

Renfrew Printing's Books

Cash		Sales	
1 500			1 500

Renfrew Printing has more money: their Cash account increases (debit) and their Sales account increases (credit). When the Bank of Nova Scotia receives the deposit, their books change as follows:

Bank of Nova Scotia's Books

Cash		Renfrew Printing	
1 500			1 500

The Bank of Nova Scotia has more money: their asset Cash increases (debit). The bank *owes* this $1 500 to Renfrew Printing. At any time the depositor can demand the money owing and withdraw cash from the account. The bank records the debt by placing a credit of $1 500 in the liability account, Renfrew Printing.

The Bank's Source Documents Some of the bank's source documents are the same as those of other companies. For example, banks receive purchase invoices and write cheques. The source document which is evidence that a depositor has withdrawn money from the bank is the *withdrawal slip*. The *deposit slip* is the source document proving that money was deposited by a depositor. Two other source documents commonly used by banks are the *bank credit memo* and the bank *debit memo*. Transactions involving these two documents follow.

*20

Bank Debit Memo The Bank of Nova Scotia made a service charge of $2.50 for cashing cheques on Renfrew Printing's account. They deduct the $2.50 by debiting Renfrew's account. Remember, a liability decreases on the debit side.

A depositor's account is a liability of the bank. Service charges decrease the liability of the bank.

Bank of Nova Scotia's Books

Renfrew Printing	
2.50 Decrease	1 500 Increase

No. 221

THE BANK OF NOVA SCOTIA

001840 — Account Number

June 10, 19-- — Date

DEBIT Service charge for month $2.50

Authorized by C.S. Checked by H.G. Entry made by M.S.

This slip must be initialled by an authorized signing officer.

PRINTED IN CANADA

Figure 14.8 *A bank debit memo is the source document prepared when the bank decreases a customer's account.*

When the depositor, Renfrew Printing, receives the debit memo, the following changes are made:

A bank *debit* memo is a source document indicating a *decrease* in a depositor's account.

Renfrew Printing's Books

Cash	
1 500	2.50

Bank Charges	
2.50	

Since this transaction is a payment, it is recorded in the Cash Payments Journal of Renfrew Printing.

Bank Credit Memo If Renfrew Printing has a savings account, it will earn interest, which is periodically calculated by the bank. Suppose interest amounting to $67.39 has been earned by Renfrew Printing. This means that the bank owes Renfrew more money and the bank will increase the amount in their liability account, Renfrew Printing.

*21

Bank of Nova Scotia's Books	Renfrew Printing	
	2.50	1 500
		67.39

A bank *credit* memo is a source document indicating an *increase* in a depositor's account.

A bank credit memo (Figure 14.9) is completed and serves to instruct the bank's clerk to increase the Renfrew account. A copy of the memo is sent to Renfrew to inform them that their bank account has been increased.

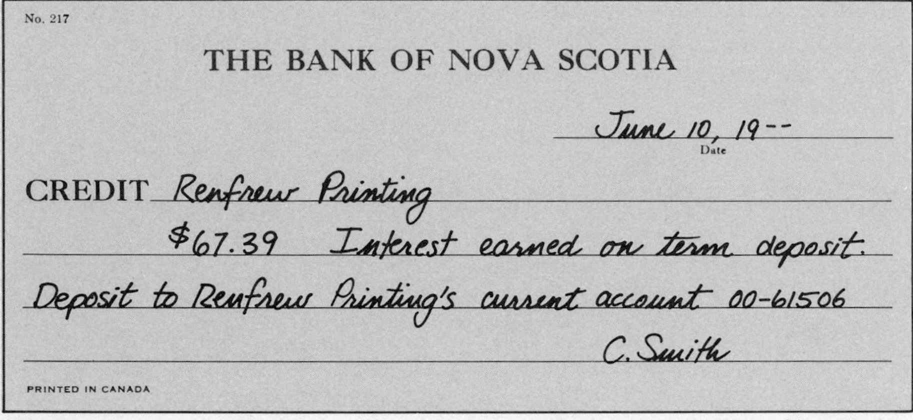
No. 217

THE BANK OF NOVA SCOTIA

June 10, 19--
Date

CREDIT Renfrew Printing
$67.39 Interest earned on term deposit.
Deposit to Renfrew Printing's current account 00-61506
C. Smith

PRINTED IN CANADA

Figure 14.9 *A bank credit memo is the source document prepared when the bank increases a customer's account.*

When the depositor, Renfrew Printing, receives the credit memo, they will change their accounts as follows:

Renfrew Printing's Books	Cash		Interest Earned	
	1 500	2.50		67.79
	67.79			

This transaction represents cash received and is recorded in the Cash Receipts Journal. *After the debit and credit transactions, what is the balance in the bank's liability account, Renfrew Printing? What is the balance in Renfrew Printing's Cash account?*

A company's Cash account should, theoretically, always have the same balance as the bank's record of the company's bank account. However, in actual practice this is rarely the situation. Look at Principle Seven: Bank Reconciliation Statement to see what is done to determine if the bank's records agree with the depositor's records.

A Personal Bank Reconciliation Statement

We All Make Mistakes!

*22

Pat and Bob Hunter are a young couple striving to make ends meet. Because they are making payments on their new home and on furniture, they have little money left over for savings. Several months ago, they received telephone calls from the company holding their house mortgage and their insurance company.

Both said that the cheques given to them by Pat and Bob had *bounced* – that is, the cheques had been returned by the bank with the explanation that there was *not-sufficient funds* in the Hunter account to cash the cheques.

The Hunters were quite upset because, according to their records, there was enough money in their bank account to cover the cheques. They called the bank and suggested that the bank had made an error. They were right. Somehow, the deposit for their last pay cheques had ended up in someone else's account. The Hunters felt good about discovering this error because they kept a good record of their bank account balance. Principle Seven illustrates how the Hunters check the accuracy of the bank's records.

An NSF cheque is one for which there is not sufficient money in the depositor's account to pay the cheque.

Do banks make errors? Of course they do! People who work in banks are human and can make mistakes just like anyone else. *Can you remember instances of banks making errors in your own or your family's bank account?*

Personal Chequing Account The Hunters have a joint personal chequing account at the Bank of Nova Scotia. They use this account to make payments for their personal expenses such as mortgage payments, utilities, and charge accounts. Every month, the bank sends them a bank statement and returns their cancelled cheques. At the end of July, the Hunters received the bank statement as shown in Figure 14.10 from the bank. According to the bank statement the Hunters' balance is $287.76. Enclosed with the bank statement were four *cancelled cheques,* numbered 73, 74, 75, and 76 (Figure 14.11).

***23**

Cancelled cheques are cheques which have been cashed by the bank.

THE BANK OF NOVA SCOTIA – LA BANQUE DE NOUVELLE-ÉCOSSE

Pat and Bob Hunter
675 Willow Place, Apt. 702
OTTAWA, Ontario
K1R 6W3

ACCOUNT NUMBER
NUMERO DE COMPTE
00-21830

STATEMENT OF / RELEVE DE COMPTE DE   FROM / DU July 1   TO / AU July 31   PAGE 1

DEBITS - DEBITS		CREDITS - CREDITS	DATE M	D/J	BALANCE SOLDE
			FORWARD REPORT		
			07	01	486.79
		900.00	07	02	1 386.79
12.84			07	05	1 373.95
386.29			07	09	987.66
499.00			07	15	488.66
200.00			07	17	288.66
0.90	SC		07	29	287.76

SCOTIA CARD EXP DATE	SCOTIA CARD LIMIT	NO ENCLOSURES	MORE ITEMS ON PAGE	NO DEBITS	TOTAL AMOUNT DEBITS	NO CREDITS	TOTAL AMOUNT CREDITS
		4		5	1 099.03	1	900.00
DATE D'EXPIRATION DE LA CARTE DE CHÈQUES GARANTIS	LIMITE DE LA CARTE DE CHÈQUES GARANTIS	NOMBRE D'EFFETS CI-JOINTS	AUTRES ECRITURES PAGE	NOMBRE DE DEBITS	MONTANT TOTAL DES DEBITS	NOMBRE DE CREDITS	MONTANT TOTAL DES CREDITS

PLEASE EXAMINE THIS STATEMENT PROMPTLY AND REPORT ANY ERRORS OR OMISSIONS TO THE BANK WITHIN 30 DAYS
VERIFIEZ SANS DELAI LE PRESENT RELEVE DE COMPTE ET SIGNALLER A LA BANQUE, DANS LES 30 JOURS, TOUTE ERREUR OU OMISSION

Figure 14.10 *Bank statement received by the Hunters*

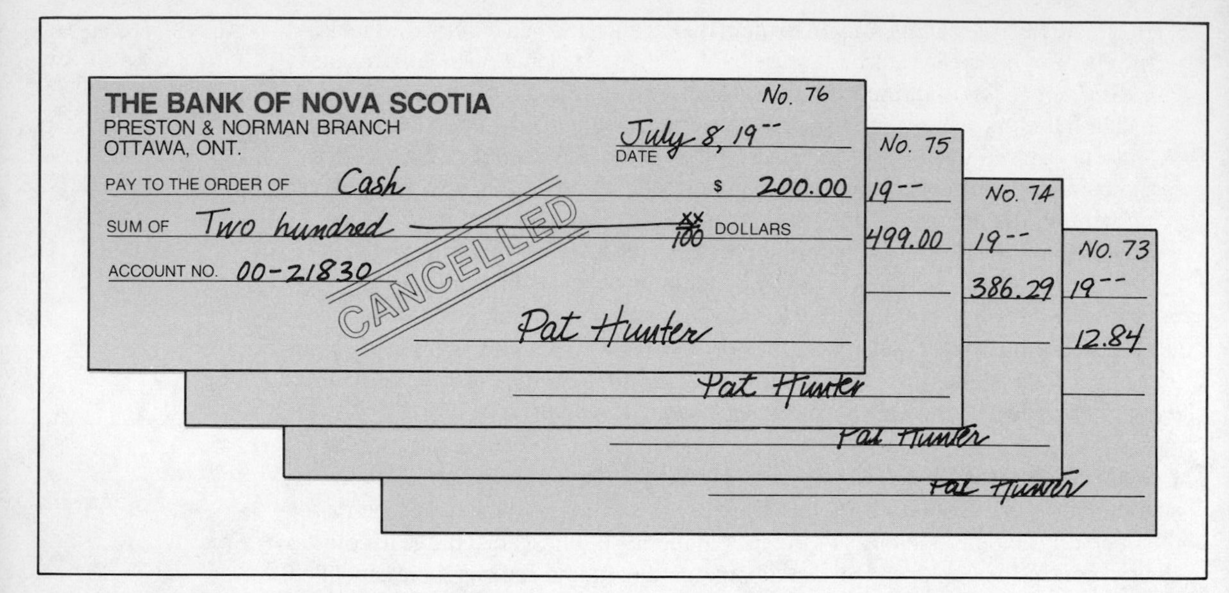
THE BANK OF NOVA SCOTIA
PRESTON & NORMAN BRANCH
OTTAWA, ONT.
No. 76
DATE July 8, 19--
PAY TO THE ORDER OF Cash $ 200.00
SUM OF Two hundred xx/100 DOLLARS
ACCOUNT NO. 00-21830
CANCELLED
Pat Hunter

No. 75
19--
499.00
Pat Hunter

No. 74
19--
386.29
Pat Hunter

No. 73
19--
12.84
Pat Hunter

Figure 14.11 *Cancelled cheques enclosed with bank statement*

***24** The cheque book provided to the Hunters by the bank includes cheque record pages as shown in Figure 14.12. These provide the Hunters with a record of cheques written, desposits made, and the balance. According to their cheque record, the Hunters have a balance of $533.48. *Which is correct – the bank statement balance of $287.76, or the Hunters' balance of $533.48, or neither?*

CHEQUE NO.	DATE	CHEQUE ISSUED TO	AMOUNT OF CHEQUE			DEP. DATE	AMOUNT OF DEPOSIT		BALANCE	
	July 1	Balance							486	79
	2	Deposit				July 2	900 ✓		1386	79
72	3	Mastercharge	48	60					1338	19
73	3	Bell Canada	12	84	✓				1325	35
74	3	Mortgage Payment	386	29	✓				939	06
75	12	CIAG Insurance	499	–	✓				440	06
76	17	Withdrawal	200	–	✓				240	06
77	23	The Bay	62	08					177	98
78	29	Exxon Ltd.	44	50					133	48
	30	Deposit				July 30	400	–	533	48

Figure 14.12 *A page from the Hunters' cheque book showing their record of banking transactions*

To determine the correct balance, the Hunters did the following:

Outstanding cheques are cheques issued but not yet cashed.

1. In their cheque record (Figure 14.12) they ticked off (√) each of the cancelled cheques returned by the bank. The three unticked items in the same column are *outstanding*, that is, they are cheques which have been issued but have not yet been cashed by the bank. Cheques 72, 77, and 78 are outstanding.

2. They matched and ticked off the deposits on the bank statement with deposits in their cheque book record. The last deposit of $400 was not shown in the bank statement. This is probably because the statement was being prepared and mailed before the Hunters made the deposit.
3. They looked for items that appeared on the bank statement but not on their records. The Hunters then prepared a *reconciliation statement* (Figure 14.13) which brought into agreement their records with the bank's records. This statement indicates that their correct balance is $532.58.

A reconciliation statement is a statement which brings into agreement the bank's records with the depositor's records.

Pat and Bob Hunter
Bank Reconciliation Statement
July 31, 19__

Bank Statement Balance			$ 287.76
add unrecorded deposit of July 30			400.00
			687.76
Less Outstanding Cheques:			
	No. 72	$ 48.60	
	No. 77	62.08	
	No. 78	44.50	155.18
Correct Bank Balance			$532.58
Cheque Record Balance			$533.48
Less service charge			0.90
Correct Cheque Book Balance			$532.58

Figure 14.13 *Bank reconciliation statement prepared by the Hunters*

4. After preparing the reconciliation statement, the Hunters recorded the service charge on their cheque record. They did this by recording the 90¢ SC (service charge) in the cheque column. Their new balance in the cheque record is now $532.58.

People like the Hunters wisely prepare monthly bank reconciliation statements. This ensures that their records and the bank's records agree. Reconciliation statements will bring to light errors made by the bank or by the depositor. Companies follow similar procedures. An example of how companies prepare reconciliation statements follows.

A Business Bank Reconciliation Statement Fraser Enterprises has a current account with the Bank of Nova Scotia. Each month, the bank sends a statement to Fraser Enterprises and encloses cancelled cheques that were paid out of Fraser's account. The company accountant compares the bank statement balance with the balance in Fraser's books. A reconciliaiton statement is then prepared to bring the two into agreement. Figure 14.14 is the bank statement received by Fraser Enterprises. It shows a balance of $2 039.12 on June 30. Figure

*25

14.15 is the company's cash records. The Cash account shows a balance of $3 251.02 on June 30.

THE BANK OF NOVA SCOTIA – LA BANQUE DE NOUVELLE-ÉCOSSE

Fraser Enterprises
680 Norman Street
OTTAWA, Ontario
R1S 3K6

ACCOUNT NUMBER
NUMERO DE COMPTE
00-3192

STATEMENT OF
RELEVE DE COMPTE DE

FROM / DU June 1 TO / AU June 30 PAGE 1

DEBITS – DÉBITS			CREDITS – CRÉDITS	DATE M	D/J	BALANCE – SOLDE
				FORWARD REPORT		
				06	01	780.22
			395.00	06	02	1 175.22
75.00			1 200.00	06	05	2 300.22
149.50				06	10	2 150.72
50.00	RI		250.00	06	12	2 350.72
675.00		1 500.00	1 800.00	06	19	1 975.72
29.60				06	28	1 946.12
2.00	SC		95.00 CM	06	30	2 039.12

SCOTIA CARD EXP. DATE	SCOTIA CARD LIMIT	NO ENCLOSURES	MORE ITEMS ON PAGE	NO DEBITS	TOTAL AMOUNT DEBITS	NO CREDITS	TOTAL AMOUNT CREDITS
		6		7	2 481.10	5	3 740.00
DATE D'EXPIRATION DE LA CARTE DE CHÈQUES GARANTIS	LIMITE DE LA CARTE DE CHÈQUES GARANTIS	NOMBRE D'EFFETS CI-JOINTS	AUTRES ÉCRITURES PAGE	NOMBRE DE DÉBITS	MONTANT TOTAL DES DÉBITS	NOMBRE DE CRÉDITS	MONTANT TOTAL DES CRÉDITS

PLEASE EXAMINE THIS STATEMENT PROMPTLY AND REPORT ANY ERRORS OR OMISSIONS TO THE BANK WITHIN 30 DAYS
VERIFIEZ SANS DELAI LE PRESENT RELEVE DE COMPTE ET SIGNALLER A LA BANQUE, DANS LES 30 JOURS, TOUTE ERREUR OU OMISSION

Figure 14.14 *Bank statement received by Fraser Enterprises*

CASH RECEIPTS JOURNAL PAGE 21

DATE		REF. NO.	CUSTOMER OR ACCOUNT	PR	CASH DEBIT	ACCOUNTS RECEIVABLE CREDIT	SALES CREDIT	PROVINCIAL SALES TAX PAYABLE CREDIT	OTHER ACCOUNTS CREDIT
19-- May	31		Deposit		395 —				
			May total		1 175 22				
June	5				1 200 —				
	12				250 —				
	19				1 800 —				
	30				2 200 —				
					5 450 —				
					(101)				

Deposits made in June

CASH PAYMENTS JOURNAL								PAGE
DATE	CH. NO.	CUSTOMER OR ACCOUNT	PR	CASH CREDIT	ACCOUNTS PAYABLE DEBIT	PURCHASES DEBIT	PURCHASES DISCOUNT CREDIT	OTHER ACCOUNTS DEBIT
19-- June 1	171			75 —				
4	172			149 50				
11	173			50 —				
16	174			675 —				
17	175			1 500 —				
26	176			29 60				
27	177			68 10				
28	178			827 —				
				3 374 20				
				(101)				

Cheques written in June

ACCOUNT Cash					NO.	
DATE	PARTICULARS	PR	DEBIT	CREDIT	DR CR	BALANCE
May 31	Balance	✓			DR	1 175 22
June 30	Cash Receipts	CR21	5 450 —		DR	6 625 22
30	Cash Payments	CP32		3 374 20	DR	3 251 02

Cash account in the General Ledger

Figure 14.15 *Fraser Enterprises' cash records*

Which of the two balances is correct – the bank's or Fraser's? Or is neither correct? The following procedures are followed in preparing the bank reconciliation statement. This statement will bring into agreement the bank's balance with the company's balance.

Preparing the Reconciliation Statement

1. Prepare a list of outstanding cheques. This is done by ticking off all the cancelled cheques returned by the bank in the *Cash Payments Journal*. Unticked cheques are outstanding; they have not been cashed by the bank. The cancelled cheques are also ticked off on the bank statement debit column. The outstanding cheques are subtracted from the bank statement balance on the reconciliation statement.

***26**

Subtract outstanding cheques.

2. Compare the deposits shown in the Cash Debit column of the Cash Receipts Journal with those shown in the credit or deposit column of the bank statement. Tick off the deposits on both records. Deposits not recorded on the bank statement are added to the bank statement balance.

Add outstanding deposits.

3. Locate all unticked items on the bank statement. Add unticked items in the creditor deposit column to the company's record of the cash balance. In this case, *CM* or credit memo indicates $95 in interest must be added. Subtract the

Add credit memos. Subtract debit memos.

unticked items in the debit or withdrawal of the bank statement from the company's record of the cash balance. Two items must be subtracted in this example: *SC* (service charge) of $2 and *RI* (non-sufficient funds) of $50. RI stands for returned item and in this case is a non-sufficient funds cheque.

4. Adjust both the bank's and the company's balance for any obvious errors. For example, cheque amounts could have been recorded incorrectly or arithmetic errors may have been made.

Figure 14.16 is the bank reconciliation statement prepared after completing the preceding four steps. It shows that the correct Cash account balance is $3 294.02.

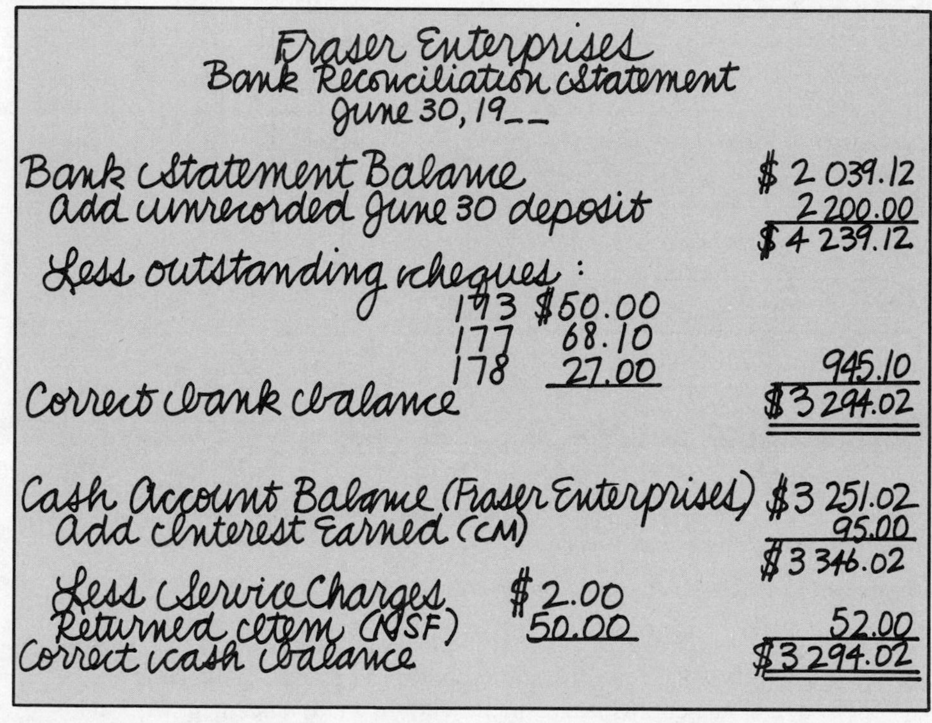

Fraser Enterprises
Bank Reconciliation Statement
June 30, 19__

Bank Statement Balance		$2 039.12
Add unrecorded June 30 deposit		2 200.00
		$4 239.12
Less outstanding cheques:		
193	$50.00	
177	68.10	
178	27.00	945.10
Correct bank balance		$3 294.02
Cash Account Balance (Fraser Enterprises)		$3 251.02
Add Interest Earned (CM)		95.00
		$3 346.02
Less Service Charges	$2.00	
Returned Item (NSF)	50.00	52.00
Correct cash balance		$3 294.02

Figure 14.16 *Bank reconciliation statement prepared by Fraser Enterprises*

*27

Journal Entries after Bank Reconciliation After the reconciliation statement has been prepared, the company's Cash account balance must be brought up to date. Remember, Figure 14.16 shows that, according to the company's Cash account, the cash balance is $3 251.02. However, the correct balance is $3 294.02, as shown on the reconciliation statement. The company's Cash account is brought up to date by preparing journal entries for any unrecorded items brought to light by the reconciliation statement. A journal entry decreasing cash is made for items such as service charges, NSF cheques, and interest charged. A journal entry increasing cash is made for items such as interest earned and added by the bank.

Service Charges The bank has deducted this amount, therefore the company should record an expense and decrease its cash.

				Debit	Credit
July	1	Bank Service Charges		2 —	
		Cash			2 —
		To record bank service			
		charges			

NSF Cheques An NSF cheque is usually a customer's cheque which has been deposited by the company and subsequently *bounces* when the bank tries to cash it. Since the bank cannot collect from the writer of the cheque, it will deduct the amount of the cheque from the depositing company's account. The company charges the amount back to its customer's account as an account receivable and tries to collect the amount.

				Debit	Credit
July	1	Accounts Receivable/G. Symons		50 —	
		Cash			50 —
		NSF cheque charged back to			
		G. Symons			

Interest Earned The bank adds interest earned to the depositor's account. A journal entry is made to record the revenue earned and to increase cash.

				Debit	Credit
July	1	Cash		95 —	
		Interest Earned			95 —
		To record interest earned on			
		the company's saving account			

Interest Charged Interest charged by the bank has been deducted by the bank. An entry is made to record the interest expense and to decrease cash. This transaction was not shown in the Fraser Enterprises example.

				Debit	Credit
July	1	Interest Expense		120 —	
		Cash			120 —
		To record interest charged			
		on a bank loan and deducted			
		by the bank			

Seven Cash Control Principles

In summary, this chapter has examined seven principles of cash control:

1. Cash received should be deposited intact. Payments are made by cheque.
2. Small payments are made through a petty cash fund.
3. The tasks of recording cash received and actually handling the cash should be separated.
4. Prenumbered source documents are prepared for all cash received.
5. Daily cash proofs are prepared.
6. Periodic audits are made.
7. A monthly bank reconciliation statement should be prepared.

Facts to Remember

Cash includes cheques, money orders, bills, and coins.

The *petty cash fund* is an amount of cash used to make small payments.

The *petty cash voucher* is a signed authorization for small payments.

The *Petty Cash* account is a current asset.

A *float* is a small change fund that is put into the cash register at the start of the day.

The *Cash Short and Over* account is used to record shortages and overages of cash.

An *audit* is a periodic check of the accuracy of an accounting system.

A *depositor's account* is a liability of the bank.

A *bank debit memo* is a source document indicating a decrease in a depositor's account balance.

A *bank credit memo* is a source document indicating an increase in a depositor's account balance.

A *NSF cheque* is one for which there is not sufficient money in the depositor's account to pay the cheque.

Cancelled cheques are cheques which have been cashed by the bank.

Outstanding cheques are cheques issued but not yet cashed.

A *reconciliation statement* is a statement which brings into agreement the bank's records with the depositor's records.

Checking Your Reading

Questions

1. Why is control of cash necessary?

2. What two factors must be considered when a system of cash control is designed?

3. What items are included when cash control is discussed?
4. What type of business must consider cash control systems?
5. What is the first principle of cash control?
6. Give an advantage of making all payments by cheque.
7. If all the day's receipts are deposited intact, what two sets of records will show the total of the day's receipts?
8. What is the purpose of a petty cash fund?
9. What is a petty cash voucher?
10. How does the petty cash voucher prove that a legitimate payment was made?
11. For any one company, how often is the petty cash replenished?
12. The first principle of cash control states that all payments must be made by cheque. Explain how the petty cash fund is designed so that this principle is followed.
13. What accounts are debited and credited when a petty cash fund is established?
14. What type of account is petty cash?
15. When the petty cash fund is replenished, what accounts are debited?
16. What is a restrictive endorsement, and what is its main advantage?
17. Who receives the two copies of the deposit slip?
18. When all the day's cash receipts are deposited, both the company's records and the bank's record show the cash the company has received on that day. How is this an advantage for the company?
19. Who receives each of the two copies of the cash received list?
20. What does the accounts receivable clerk do with a copy of the cash received list?
21. To what is the balance in the Accounts Receivable Control account compared?
22. What is the purpose of prenumbering source documents?
23. What should be done with cancelled or voided cash sales slips in a prenumbered system?
24. What is a float?
25. In which General Ledger account are both shortages and overages recorded?
26. The cash received total for one day is $765.80. The sales slips total $766. Is the cash short or over and by how much?

27. The day's cash total is $583.39. The sales slips total $582.13. Is the cash short or over and by how much?

28. Is a cash shortage recorded as a debit or a credit in the Cash Short and Over account? How is an overage recorded?

29. The Cash Short and Over account has a debit balance of $19 at the end of a fiscal period. Is this considered a revenue or an expense? Does it increase or decrease net income?

30. Explain the role of the auditor.

31. Jan O'Dacre has a savings account with the Toronto Dominion bank. On which section of their ledger will the bank locate O'Dacre's account – the asset, liability, owner's equity, revenue, or expense section?

32. Will a debit memo increase or decrease the balance of a depositor's account?

33. Will a credit memo increase or decrease the balance of a depositor's account?

34. In which journal is a bank credit memo recorded? A bank debit memo?

35. What is the journal entry to record:
 a) bank service charges of $2.50?
 b) interest earned of $190?
 c) loan interest charged by the bank of $120?
 d) a partial repayment of $500 on a bank loan?

36. What is an NSF cheque?

37. What is a bank statement?

38. What is a cancelled cheque?

39. What is an outstanding cheque?

40. Some cheques that have been issued will not appear on the bank statement. Explain how such a situation can happen.

41. Some deposits that have been recorded in the depositor's records may not appear on the bank statement. Explain how such a situation can happen.

42. Give examples of certain items that appear on a bank statement but not on the depositor's records.

43. A bank reconciliation statement brings into agreement two sets of records. What are they?

44. Who prepares the bank reconciliation statement, the bank or the depositor?

45. When a company prepares a bank reconciliation statement, to what is the balance on the bank statement compared?

46. List seven principles of cash control.

Applying Your Knowledge

Exercises Part A

1. A petty cash fund was established with $100. At present the petty cash box contains:

- 6 vouchers for payments totalling $37.50
- 2 twenty-dollar bills
- 1 ten-dollar bill
- 2 five-dollar bills
- 1 one-dollar bill

Have any errors been made in the handling of the petty cash?

2. A petty cash box contains 16 payment vouchers which total $46.25. The fund was started with $50. How much cash should be in the cash box?

3. Mechanical Services Ltd. has decided to establish a petty cash fund. The Office supervisor is given $100 and is responsible for the petty cash. The accountant issued cheque No. 171 for $100 on June 1 and gave it to the supervisor to establish the fund. Record the $100 cheque in a General Journal.

4. On June 19, a summary of vouchers in a petty cash box shows:

Office Expenses	$41.50
G. LePensée, Drawing	25.00
Donations Expense	15.00
Miscellaneous Expense	14.50
Total	$96.00

In General Journal form, record the $96 cheque issued by the accountant to replenish the petty cash fund.

5. On July 7, the following summary of 15 petty cash vouchers was prepared:

Office Expense	$31.50
Entertainment Expense	30.20
Owners, Drawing	10.00
Advertising Expense	23.00
Total	$94.70

This summary was presented to the accountant who issued a cheque, No. 216, to replenish the petty cash. Record cheque No. 216 in a General Journal.

6. On September 7, Print-o-matic Ltd. decided to begin using a petty cash fund. A cheque for $25 was issued and cashed. The $25 cash was given to the receptionist who was to act as petty cashier. The receptionist/petty cashier was told to obtain authorized vouchers for all payments. No payments could exceed $10. The petty cash was to be replenished when the balance in the cash box reached $10. When this happened, a summary of vouchers was to be prepared and given to the accountant.

a) Record the $25 cheque to establish the fund on September 7.
b) On September 13, this summary was prepared:

Office Expense	$10
Miscellaneous Expense	5
Advertising Expense	5
Total	$20

Record the cheque to replenish the petty cash.

c) On September 19, this summary was prepared:

Delivery Expense	$ 5.75
Miscellaneous Expense	12.25
Office Expense	6.33
Total	$24.33

Prepare the entry to replenish the petty cash.

d) It was decided to increase the amount of the petty cash fund from $25 to $75. A cheque for $50 was issued. Record this cheque.

7. At the end of the day, the manager of a business totalled the cash on hand and prepared a deposit slip. The total of the deposit was $277.35. The cash sales slips issued during the day were totalled. They came to $275.50. Prepare the daily cash proof. Is the cash short or over?

8. a) The cash on hand for Brighton Cleaners follows. Remove the $50 change fund and then prepare a deposit slip:

Currency	**Coin**
3 × $20	40 × 25¢
12 × $10	29 × 10¢
20 × $5	41 × 5¢
18 × $2	26 × 1¢
39 × $1	

b) Prepare the daily cash proof. A calculator tape total of the cash sales slips follows:

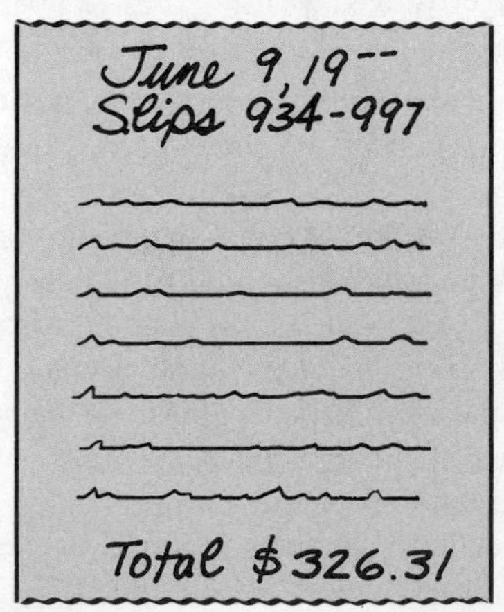

9. Prepare journal entries to record the authorized daily proofs prepared for exercises 7 and 8.

10. Record the following transactions in a General Journal for Mechanical Services Ltd.:

Nov. 7 Cash sales slips total $895. Cash was deposited.

7 Sales Invoice 87-B to A. Michaels, terms 3/15, n/30, amount $200, non-taxable.

8 Bank credit memo: $89 interest had been earned by the company.

9 Bank debit memo: $8.75 for the annual charge for a safety deposit box.

15 Cash Receipt: a cheque for $194 received from A. Michaels. Discount deducted, $6, for invoice 87-B. Amount of invoice, $200. Deposited the cheque.

30 Bank debit memo: $4.50 service charges on current account.

11. Record the following transactions in a General Journal for Mechanical Services Ltd.:

Dec. 1 Bank credit memo: A $1 000 loan has been granted and deposited in the company account, term two months, interest at 12% payable monthly.

Dec. 31 Bank debit memo: $10 interest on the loan has been deducted from the company account.

Jan. 31 Bank debit memo: $1 010 has been deducted from the company account ($1 000 repayment of the bank loan, $10 interest on the loan).

12. At the end of August, Pat and Bob Hunter have a balance of $1 240 in their cheque record. The statement received from their bank shows a balance of $1 583.75.

The bank statement contains a deduction of $1.60 for service charges. A comparison of the cheques issued in the Hunters' cheque record and the cheques cashed on the statement indicates that cheque No. 72 for $48.60, cheque No. 86 for $250, and cheque No. 89 for $46.75 are outstanding.

Prepare a bank reconciliation statement dated August 31.

13. At the end of September, the Hunters have a balance of $865.84 in their cheque record. The bank statement shows a balance of $1 588.40. The bank statement contains a service charge deduction of $2.54 and a deposit made on September 15 for $400. This deposit is not recorded in the Hunters' cheque record. Cheque No. 92 for $48.60, cheque No. 94 for $89, and cheque No. 95 for $187.50 are outstanding.

Prepare the September reconciliation statement.

Exercises Part B

14. a) Prepare the April reconciliation statement for K. Martin Painting Contractors using the following information:

Company Records
- Cash account balance $1 970.11
- These cheques are recorded in the cash payments journal but *not* on the bank statement:
  No. 161 $ 49.50   No. 170 $150   No. 176 $ 75
- A deposit for $400 was recorded in the cash receipts journal on April 30 but did not appear on the bank statement

Bank Statement
- Bank statement balance is $1 839.86
- Bank service charges of $4.75 are shown on the bank statement

b) In a General Journal, prepare any entries required to bring the company records up to date.

15. Prepare the May reconciliation statement for K. Martin Contractors using the following information:
- Cash account balance $2 060.51
- Bank statement balance $1 684.51
- These cheques were recorded in the Cash Payments Journal but did not appear on the bank statement:
  No. 176 $ 75   No. 193 $297.30   No. 199 $924.60
- A deposit for $1 910 dated May 31 was recorded in the Cash Receipts Journal but did not appear on the bank statement
- Service charges of $5.75 are shown on the bank statement
- A cheque for $37.50 has been cashed (correctly) by the bank but was incorrectly recorded in the company's Cash Payments Journal as $375.50
- An NSF cheque for $95.15 appeared on the bank statement as a returned item. It was deducted by the bank. It had been received from J. Barkley and was recorded in the company's Cash Receipts Journal.

16. Record the following selected transactions in a General Journal for The Sundowner:

May 1 Establish a petty cash fund by issuing cheque No. 178 for $100.

5 Cash sales slips for the week total $2 400. Sales tax on taxable sales is $84. Total cash $2 484.

5 The cash proof indicated a shortage of $1.50.

8 Issued cheque No. 179 for $795 for a cash purchase of merchandise from Carswell Ltd.

10 Sales Invoices: (all non-taxable, terms 2/10, n/30)
No. 818: $500 to Warrendon Ltd.
No. 819: $79.80 to Tisi and Zotta
No. 820: $465 to J. Mocson & Sons
No. 821: $720 to L. Gojmerac

May 12 Cash sales slips for the week total $1 700.
Sales tax is $53. Total $1 753.

12 Bank credit memo for $160, interest received on a term deposit.

15 Replenished the petty cash. Issued cheque No. 180. Summary of petty cash vouchers:

Office Expense	$39
Advertising Expense	$33
Postage Expense	$25

Exercises Part C

17. Continue recording transactions in a General Journal for The Sundowner.

May 15 Received a cheque for $78.20 from Tisi and Zotta in payment of invoice No. 819 less $1.60 discount.

16 The cash proof indicated that cash was over by $2.15.

19 Received a bank debit memo for $78.20 plus $2 service charge. Tisi & Zotta's cheque was returned NSF.

20 Purchased merchandise on account from Finlays Inc., $915, terms 30 days.

20 Received a cheque for $455.70 from J. Mocsan & Sons in payment of invoice No. 820. Discount taken, $9.30.

29 The monthly bank reconciliation was prepared. The bank statement included a debit of $2.50 for bank service charges.

18. M. Monroe Ltd. has a current account with the Bank of Nova Scotia. The October bank statement that follows was sent to M. Monroe Ltd. by the bank.

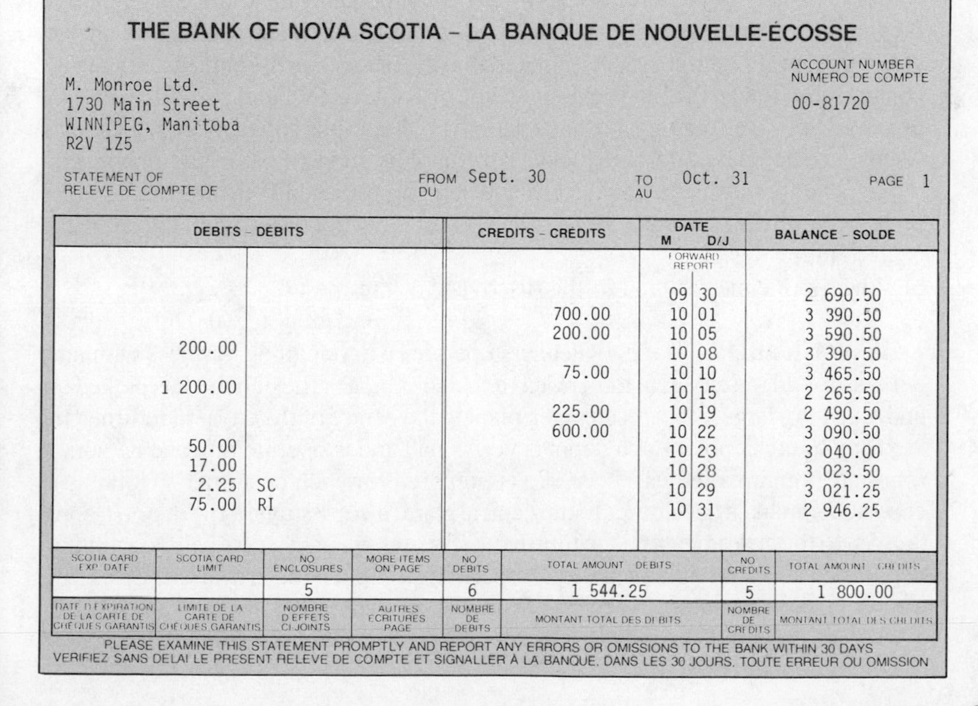

THE BANK OF NOVA SCOTIA – LA BANQUE DE NOUVELLE-ÉCOSSE

M. Monroe Ltd.
1730 Main Street
WINNIPEG, Manitoba
R2V 1Z5

ACCOUNT NUMBER
NUMERO DE COMPTE
00-81720

STATEMENT OF
RELEVE DE COMPTE DE

FROM / DU Sept. 30 TO / AU Oct. 31 PAGE 1

DEBITS – DEBITS		CREDITS – CREDITS	DATE M	DATE D/J	BALANCE – SOLDE
			FORWARD REPORT		
			09	30	2 690.50
		700.00	10	01	3 390.50
		200.00	10	05	3 590.50
200.00			10	08	3 390.50
		75.00	10	10	3 465.50
1 200.00			10	15	2 265.50
		225.00	10	19	2 490.50
		600.00	10	22	3 090.50
50.00			10	23	3 040.00
17.00			10	28	3 023.50
2.25	SC		10	29	3 021.25
75.00	RI		10	31	2 946.25

SCOTIA CARD EXP. DATE	SCOTIA CARD LIMIT	NO. ENCLOSURES	MORE ITEMS ON PAGE	NO. DEBITS	TOTAL AMOUNT DEBITS	NO. CREDITS	TOTAL AMOUNT CREDITS
		5		6	1 544.25	5	1 800.00
DATE D EXPIRATION DE LA CARTE DE CHÈQUES GARANTIS	LIMITE DE LA CARTE DE CHÈQUES GARANTIS	NOMBRE D EFFETS CI-JOINTS	AUTRES ÉCRITURES PAGE	NOMBRE DE DÉBITS	MONTANT TOTAL DES DÉBITS	NOMBRE DE CRÉDITS	MONTANT TOTAL DES CRÉDITS

PLEASE EXAMINE THIS STATEMENT PROMPTLY AND REPORT ANY ERRORS OR OMISSIONS TO THE BANK WITHIN 30 DAYS
VERIFIEZ SANS DELAI LE PRESENT RELEVE DE COMPTE ET SIGNALLER À LA BANQUE, DANS LES 30 JOURS, TOUTE ERREUR OU OMISSION

The bank also sent four cancelled cheques, Nos. 301, 303, 304, and 305 and an NSF cheque for $75 which had been deposited by Monroe Ltd. The NSF cheque was signed by A. Bloom, a customer of M. Monroe Ltd. Outstanding cheques are #302, $100; #306, $250; #307, $170. A deposit of $450 has not been recorded by the bank.

The following records were kept by M. Monroe Ltd.: Cash Receipts Journal, Pg. 14, Cash Payments Journal, Pg. 17, Cash account No. 101, $2 953.50 (see Study Guide 2, pages 13-15).

a) Prepare a bank reconciliation statement dated October 31, 19__.
b) Prepare the necessary journal entries.

Accounting in Action

Case 1

Dr. Clark Faye B. worked as a receptionist-secretary for Dr P. Clark, a dentist, for five years. Her duties included billing patients, receiving cash from customers and issuing receipts, depositing money, and handling the patients' accounts. One day Faye reduced a patient's account to zero by mistake. A month later the patient paid $50 which was actually still owing. Faye *pocketed* the $50. Nothing happened.

Yielding to temptation, Faye began to embezzle money from Dr Clark on a regular basis. When money was received from patients she would lower the patients' accounts and prepare a bank deposit but keep some of the cash for herself. The deposit was always lower than the cash received. For example, one week she received $1 900 from customers, kept $200 and deposited $1 700. She lowered the customers' accounts by $1 900. Over a period of 30 weeks she stole $3 500. She is now awaiting trial on criminal charges! *How was she caught?*

While Faye was in Bermuda on a two-week holiday, Dr Clark's accountants prepared the annual income statement and balance sheet. The accountant arrived at a normal profit for the year but noticed that the balance in the bank account was considerably lower than in previous years. A bank reconciliation statement was prepared but it was out by thousands of dollars. A comparison of the receipt copies issued to customers and the weekly deposit slips showed what had happened.

Faye had a surprise waiting for her when she returned from Bermuda.

a) Which principles of accounting cash control were not followed in the dentist's accounting system?
b) Which principle resulted in the discovery of the theft?

Case 2

Lafleur Cleaners Lafleur Cleaners operates a drycleaning business with nine depots around the city. Customers leave their clothing at the depots. It is picked up and taken to a large, efficient cleaning plant in the centre of the city and returned the next day to the depots. Each depot is very small and is operated by one person. A four-part prenumbered cash sale slip is prepared for each customer's clothing. A copy accompanies the clothes to the central plant, a copy stays at the depot, a copy is given to the customer, and the fourth copy is sent to the head office's accounting department. It is possible for a person operating a depot to destroy a cash sales slip and to pocket the money received from a customer.

Prepare a control procedure which will prevent an employee from taking company money.

Petty Cash You are the assistant to the office manager of a very large company. She asks you to develop a system and procedures for a petty cash fund. At present there is no such fund. Prepare a report with a recommended system. **Case 3**

Cash Short and Over Assume that you are the owner of Brighton Cleaners. There is one person handling all transactions in your cleaning outlet. This person meets about 75 customers a day, organizes pick-ups and deliveries, prepares sales slips, and handles the cash. At the end of each day, you, the owner, count and deposit all the cash and prepare a daily cash proof. The cash never seems to balance. In the past week the results were: **Case 4**

June 13 short 75¢
14 over 5¢
15 short 15¢
16 over $1
17 short 25¢

You realize that your one clerk is responsible for these shortages and overages but also that the clerk is very busy. There is no time for a coffee break and only 40 minutes for lunch.

a) Would you make the clerk pay for cash shortages? Why or why not?
b) What changes do you think should be considered in the operation of this business?

Cash Shortages You are the senior accountant for Ogilvy's, a department store. Sales for the year are $2 000 000. There are 27 cashiers in the store. Each cashier prepares a daily cash proof. The cash short and over account is shown with the year's balance and a summary of the entries for all 27 cashiers. **Case 5**

Cash Short and Over

125 debits Total debits $176	91 credits Total credits $49
Balance $127	

a) What action, if any, would you recommend?
b) What additional information would you like to have?

Public Relations Mr and Mrs Doe have two accounts in a bank where they have been dealing for 12 years. One is a joint chequing account and the other a true savings account in Mrs Doe's name. Mr Doe's monthly pay cheque is deposited directly to the chequing account by his employer and he receives a pay statement showing the amount and date of deposit. Each month Mrs Doe visits the bank to withdraw money for household expenses. **Case 6**

As the time for the monthly visit drew near, the Does were looking over their bank books and realized that a substantial amount had built up in their chequing account. They received no interest on this account. They decided that during Mrs Doe's regular visit to the bank, she would transfer some of the money to her savings account.

Since it was her habit to visit the bank early in the day, she always took Mr Doe's pay statement with her in case the bank had not had time to enter the deposit yet. When her turn at the teller's wicket came, Mrs Doe found herself facing a new teller to whom she gave her withdrawal slip and request for the transfer to her savings account. The teller disappeared for a moment, then returned and announced in a loud voice, "You don't have enough money in your account." This really did not surprise Mrs Doe since she realized that the pay for the month would not have been entered in their account yet. She explained this to the teller and showed her the pay statement which had that day's date. The teller glanced at the statement and said indignantly, "Well, just because you got this today doesn't mean the money is here today. It could take a couple of days." Mrs Doe was surprised and embarrassed and asked the teller to check it again. The teller refused.

Mrs Doe left, very angry. She telephoned the bank manager later in the day and described what had happened.

a) If you were the manager what would you say to the irate customer? What would you say to your teller?
b) What changes would you recommend in your bank's recording procedures?

Case 7

Bank Transfer John Southcott has been transferred by his company from Toronto to British Columbia. He has $1 200 in a bank account in Toronto. Rather than withdraw the $1 200 and take it with him, John asks the bank to transfer the money to a B.C. branch of the bank. When John arrives in B.C., he receives a statement from his new bank showing a balance in his account of $12 000.

a) Does the extra $10 800 in his account belong to John?
b) How could such an error occur?

Career Profile

A Bank Accountant Chuck Smith is married and has two sons, Michael and Ian. His wife Louise is a legal secretary. The Smith family lives in Pembroke, Ontario, where Chuck is the accountant with a branch of the Bank of Nova Scotia. After graduating from Sir Wilfrid Laurier High School in Ottawa, Chuck enrolled in the Business Administration program at Algonquin College. While he was in high school Chuck had taken three accounting courses and he continued his interest by taking accounting courses at Algonquin.

The Bank of Nova Scotia hired Chuck as a management trainee when he graduated from Algonquin College. For one year he was trained at most of the clerical jobs in the bank. He was then promoted to the position of branch assistant accountant where he became responsible for the tellers and for the Ledger Department. After two more years, Chuck was promoted again to the position of accountant at the Preston and Norman branch of the Bank of Nova Scotia in Ottawa.

While in Ottawa, Chuck enrolled in the Institute of Canadian Bankers' program (ICB) at Carleton University. The bank encouraged Chuck by paying for his tuition and books, as well as providing a bonus for successfully completing sections of the program. Chuck left Ottawa when he was promoted to a larger branch in Pembroke, Ontario. In his present position Chuck is responsible for 33 people in the branch and has three main job functions:

- to organize and supervise the routine work and the accounting records and procedures;
- to motivate, train, and supervise the employees;
- to ensure a high standard of service to customers.

In the next five years Chuck's goals are to obtain the experience necessary for an assistant manager's job and then a bank manager's job. The bank provides continuous development programs, such as seminars and courses, to its staff in order to develop and to improve their banking experience.

Chuck enjoys his present position because he is in continuous contact with the public and the employees for whom he is responsible. Surprisingly, although Chuck is an accountant, he does very little actual accounting. Instead, he is mostly involved in training and supervising those who perform the bank's actual accounting work.

Chuck works hard at furthering his career but he also has many outside interests such as skating, bowling, and stamp collecting. He and Louise enjoy curling and Chuck contributes to community life in Pembroke as a member of the Kinsmen Club and the Chamber of Commerce.

Banking

Project 3

You are employed as the accountant for Sandy's Personnel Agency. Your firm locates job applicants for clients who have positions to be filled. In this project you will write cheques and prepare deposit slips for the month of June. You will require eight blank cheques, with stubs, and three current account deposit slips.

Part A

1. Complete the cheque stub first before writing the cheque.
2. Decrease the cheque stub balance each time a cheque is written. Increase the balance each time a deposit is made.
3. Sign your name to all cheques.
4. Assume that another employee is responsible for journalizing and posting the transactions.

Cheques and Deposits

June 1 Record the bank balance of $4 350 on the first cheque stub (cheque No. 21).

1 Write cheque No. 21 for $132.50 to Willson's Ltd. to pay for a cash purchase of office supplies.

5 Write cheque No. 22 to Bell Canada for May telephone service, $127.58.

5 Prepare a deposit slip to include:
Coins: $5.50
Bills: 2 × $20
6 × $5
Cheques: $164.50 from Atlas Ltd.
$135.72 from Murphy Gamble Ltd.

8 Issue a $272.50 cheque to Advertising Specialties Ltd. for desk pad sets to be used as gifts to clients.

10 Issue a $765 cheque to Sherman's Real Estate for June rent.

11 Pay Welland Hydro $153.75 for electricity.

12 Deposit:
Coins: $5.75
Bills: 9 × $20
15 × $10
3 × $5
14 × $2
7 × $1
Cheque: $172.50 from Warrendon's Ltd.

18 Pay Echo Systems Ltd. $25.50 for repairs to office equipment.

26 Pay Welland Evening Tribune $349.50 for advertising.

27 Pay R. Parent Insurance Ltd. $82 for insurance of office equipment.

29 Deposit:
Coins: $5
Bills: 5 × $20
6 × $10
4 × $2
12 × $1

Cheques: $187 from Welmet Co.
$220 from Union Carbide

Part B

The following documents are received from the bank at the end of June: the bank statement, a bank debit memo, and a group of cancelled cheques. Notice that the ending balance on the bank statement does not agree with the balance on the last cheque stub prepared in Part A.

THE BANK OF NOVA SCOTIA – LA BANQUE DE NOUVELLE-ÉCOSSE

Sandy's Personnel Agency
10 Broadway Avenue
WELLAND, Ontario
L3C 5L3

ACCOUNT NUMBER
NUMERO DE COMPTE
0021840

STATEMENT OF / RELEVE DE COMPTE DE — FROM / DU June 1 — TO / AU June 30 — PAGE 1

DEBITS - DÉBITS		CREDITS - CRÉDITS	DATE M	DATE D/J	BALANCE - SOLDE
			FORWARD REPORT		
			06	01	4 350.00
127.58			06	08	4 222.42
		375.75	06	08	4 598.17
272.50			06	12	4 325.67
132.50			06	14	4 193.17
		558.25	06	15	4 751.42
765.00					3 986.42
25.50			06	21	3 960.92
150.00	DM		06	22	3 810.92
82.00			06	28	3 728.92
2.00	SC		06	29	3 726.92

SCOTIA CARD EXP DATE	SCOTIA CARD LIMIT	NO ENCLOSURES	MORE ITEMS ON PAGE	NO DEBITS	TOTAL AMOUNT - DEBITS	NO CREDITS	TOTAL AMOUNT - CREDITS
		7		8	1 557.08	2	934.00
DATE D EXPIRATION DE LA CARTE DE CHEQUES GARANTIS	LIMITE DE LA CARTE DE CHEQUES GARANTIS	NOMBRE D EFFETS CI-JOINTS	AUTRES ECRITURES PAGE	NOMBRE DE DEBITS	MONTANT TOTAL DES DEBITS	NOMBRE DE CREDITS	MONTANT TOTAL DES CREDITS

PLEASE EXAMINE THIS STATEMENT PROMPTLY AND REPORT ANY ERRORS OR OMISSIONS TO THE BANK WITHIN 30 DAYS
VERIFIEZ SANS DELAI LE PRESENT RELEVE DE COMPTE ET SIGNALLER À LA BANQUE, DANS LES 30 JOURS, TOUTE ERREUR OU OMISSION

EXPLANATION OF SYMBOLS – ABRÉVIATIONS

SC	SERVICE CHARGE / FRAIS D ADMINISTRATION	OC	OVERDRAFT CHARGE / FRAIS DE DECOUVERT	AC	SCOTIA CARD ADVANCE CHARGE / FRAIS D AVANCE - CARTE DE CHEQUES GARANTIS
NS	NSF CHEQUE CHARGE / FRAIS DE CHEQUES SANS PROVISION	DM	DEBIT MEMO / NOTE DE DEBIT	CM	CREDIT MEMO / NOTE DE CREDIT
RC	NSF CHEQUE / CHEQUE SANS PROVISION	RD	CHARGE BACK / EFFET RETOURNE	IN	INTEREST / INTERÊT
MD	MORTGAGE PAYMENT / VERSEMENT SUR HYPOTHEQUE	LD	LOAN PAYMENT / VERSEMENT SUR EMPRUNT	LC	LOAN / PRÊT
		EC	ERROR CORRECTION / CORRECTION		

THE BANK OF NOVA SCOTIA

0021840 — Account Number
June 22, 19-- — Date

DEBIT

Interest charges $150.00

Authorized by B.V. Checked by L.D. Entry made by L.S.

This slip must be initialled by an authorized signing officer.

PRINTED IN CANADA

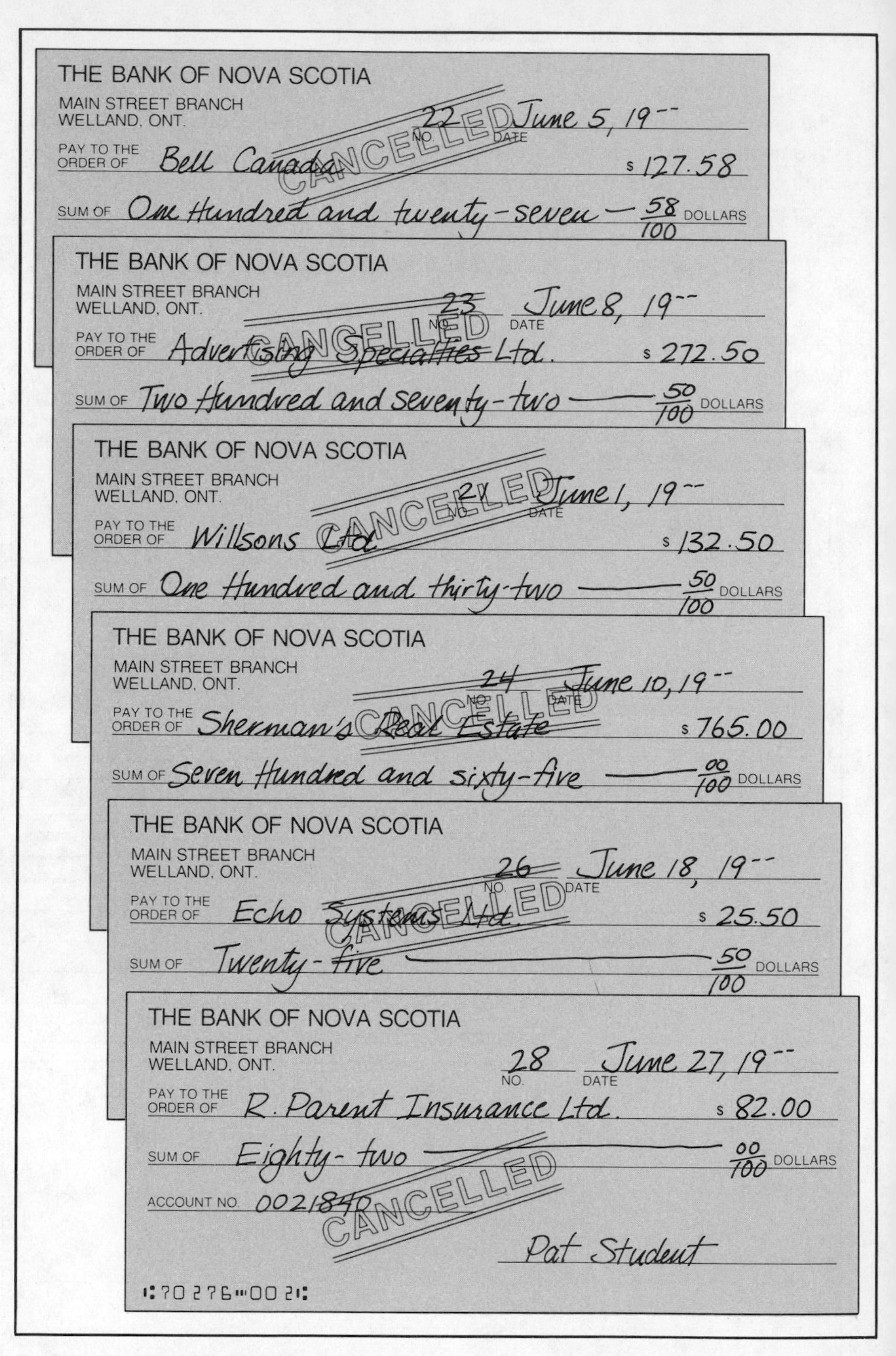

THE BANK OF NOVA SCOTIA
MAIN STREET BRANCH
WELLAND, ONT.
NO. 22 DATE June 5, 19--
PAY TO THE ORDER OF Bell Canada $ 127.58
SUM OF One Hundred and twenty-seven — 58/100 DOLLARS
CANCELLED

THE BANK OF NOVA SCOTIA
MAIN STREET BRANCH
WELLAND, ONT.
NO. 23 DATE June 8, 19--
PAY TO THE ORDER OF Advertising Specialties Ltd. $ 272.50
SUM OF Two Hundred and seventy-two — 50/100 DOLLARS
CANCELLED

THE BANK OF NOVA SCOTIA
MAIN STREET BRANCH
WELLAND, ONT.
NO. 21 DATE June 1, 19--
PAY TO THE ORDER OF Willsons Ltd. $ 132.50
SUM OF One Hundred and thirty-two — 50/100 DOLLARS
CANCELLED

THE BANK OF NOVA SCOTIA
MAIN STREET BRANCH
WELLAND, ONT.
NO. 24 DATE June 10, 19--
PAY TO THE ORDER OF Sherman's Real Estate $ 765.00
SUM OF Seven Hundred and sixty-five — 00/100 DOLLARS
CANCELLED

THE BANK OF NOVA SCOTIA
MAIN STREET BRANCH
WELLAND, ONT.
NO. 26 DATE June 18, 19--
PAY TO THE ORDER OF Echo Systems Ltd. $ 25.50
SUM OF Twenty-five — 50/100 DOLLARS
CANCELLED

THE BANK OF NOVA SCOTIA
MAIN STREET BRANCH
WELLAND, ONT.
NO. 28 DATE June 27, 19--
PAY TO THE ORDER OF R. Parent Insurance Ltd. $ 82.00
SUM OF Eighty-two — 00/100 DOLLARS
ACCOUNT NO. 0021840
CANCELLED
Pat Student
⑆70276⑈0021⑆

1. Why do the two balances not agree?
2. What is the correct balance?

CHAPTER 15

Payroll

Paying Employees

Unit 37

***1**

For the past two years, Dennis Obonsawin has been working for the International Nickel Company of Canada, Limited (INCO), in Copper Cliff, Ontario. INCO is one of the world's major mining companies. In the Sudbury area, INCO mines various metals, the most important being nickel and copper. Dennis is part of a crew of men who have the responsibility of loading the refined metal into various containers that may be shipped anywhere in the world.

Figure 15.1 shows the *T-4 slip* that Dennis has received from INCO reporting his total earnings and deductions for the past calendar year. A T-4 slip or Statement of Remuneration Paid is given to each employee in order that he or she can complete an individual income tax return. The T-4 slips must be given to employees by February 28 for the previous year's earnings and deductions.

T-4 slips must be given to employees by February 28 and provide the previous year's earnings and payroll deductions which affect employees' income taxes.

A rather large portion of Dennis' earnings goes to the government. Both Dennis and the federal government (specifically, a department called Revenue Canada – Taxation) are concerned about the details of his earnings.

Dennis can check the figures reported by keeping track of the hours he has worked during each week to see if his total pay per week is correct. The total of these weekly pay figures must add up to the amount reported in box (c) of the T-4 slip. In Dennis' case, this total is $14 450.90. Revenue Canada – Taxation is

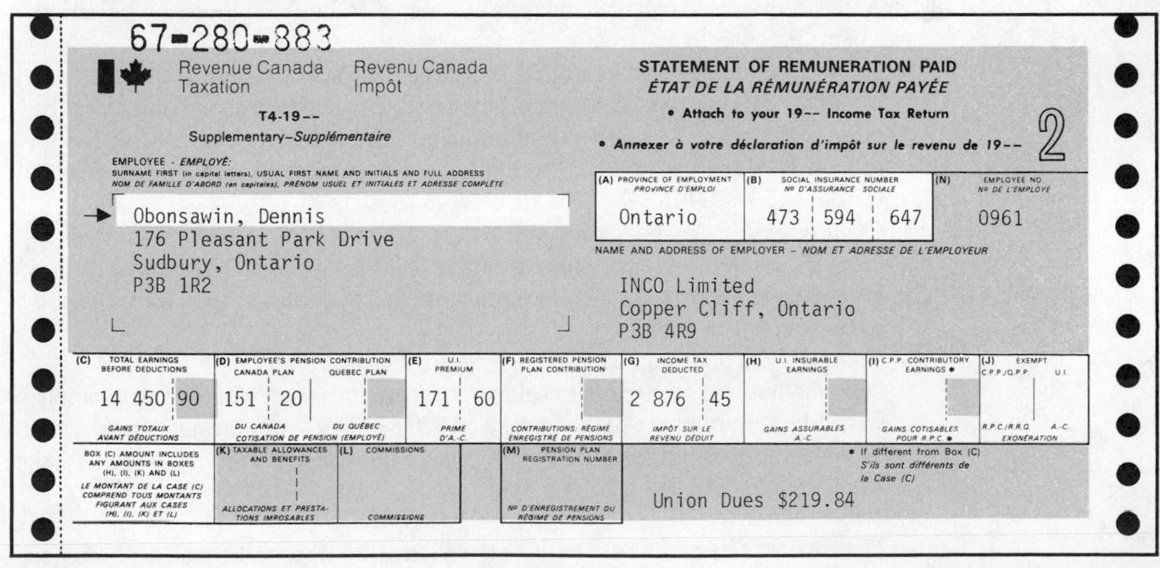

67-280-883

Revenue Canada Taxation — Revenu Canada Impôt

STATEMENT OF REMUNERATION PAID
ÉTAT DE LA RÉMUNÉRATION PAYÉE

T4-19--
Supplementary–*Supplémentaire*

• Attach to your 19-- Income Tax Return
• *Annexer à votre déclaration d'impôt sur le revenu de 19--*

2

EMPLOYEE - *EMPLOYÉ:*
SURNAME FIRST (in capital letters), USUAL FIRST NAME AND INITIALS AND FULL ADDRESS
NOM DE FAMILLE D'ABORD (en capitales), PRÉNOM USUEL ET INITIALES ET ADRESSE COMPLÈTE

Obonsawin, Dennis
176 Pleasant Park Drive
Sudbury, Ontario
P3B 1R2

(A) PROVINCE OF EMPLOYMENT / *PROVINCE D'EMPLOI*	(B) SOCIAL INSURANCE NUMBER / *Nº D'ASSURANCE SOCIALE*	(N) EMPLOYEE NO / *Nº DE L'EMPLOYÉ*
Ontario	473 594 647	0961

NAME AND ADDRESS OF EMPLOYER – *NOM ET ADRESSE DE L'EMPLOYEUR*

INCO Limited
Copper Cliff, Ontario
P3B 4R9

(C) TOTAL EARNINGS BEFORE DEDUCTIONS / *GAINS TOTAUX AVANT DÉDUCTIONS*	(D) EMPLOYEE'S PENSION CONTRIBUTION CANADA PLAN / *DU CANADA*	QUEBEC PLAN / *DU QUÉBEC*	(E) U.I. PREMIUM / *PRIME D'A.-C.*	(F) REGISTERED PENSION PLAN CONTRIBUTION / *CONTRIBUTIONS: RÉGIME ENREGISTRÉ DE PENSIONS*	(G) INCOME TAX DEDUCTED / *IMPÔT SUR LE REVENU DÉDUIT*	(H) U.I. INSURABLE EARNINGS / *GAINS ASSURABLES A.-C.*	(I) C.P.P. CONTRIBUTORY EARNINGS * / *GAINS COTISABLES POUR R.P.C. **	(J) EXEMPT C.P.P./Q.P.P. U.I. / *R.P.C./R.R.Q. A.-C. EXONÉRATION*
14 450 90	151 20		171 60		2 876 45			

BOX (C) AMOUNT INCLUDES ANY AMOUNTS IN BOXES (H), (I), (K) AND (L) / *LE MONTANT DE LA CASE (C) COMPREND TOUS MONTANTS FIGURANT AUX CASES (H), (I), (K) ET (L)*	(K) TAXABLE ALLOWANCES AND BENEFITS / *ALLOCATIONS ET PRESTATIONS IMPOSABLES*	(L) COMMISSIONS / *COMMISSIONS*	(M) PENSION PLAN REGISTRATION NUMBER / *Nº D'ENREGISTREMENT DU RÉGIME DE PENSIONS*

* If different from Box (C)
S'ils sont différents de la Case (C)

Union Dues $219.84

Figure 15.1 *T-4 slip received by Dennis Obonsawin from INCO*

concerned that the correct amount of income tax has been deducted from all employees and forwarded to the department. As a result, the department may audit or check INCO's or any other employer's records from time to time.

Several laws require employers to keep detailed records of their payroll and to file reports with the government. These laws include:

- Canada Pension Plan Act
- Income Tax Act
- Unemployment Insurance Act
- provincial acts governing minimum wages and employment standards

Various government departments such as provincial labour departments administer these laws and investigate employee complaints of unfair treatment. The provincial laws outline payroll records which must be kept and give provincial labour department auditors the right to inspect company records.

The accounting procedures required to pay employees and to fulfill government requirements will now be studied.

*2

Pay Periods At INCO, Dennis is paid once a week and his pay is based on the number of hours he worked. However, this is only one method of paying employees and many employers, including INCO, will also use other methods. Employers work out payrolls at different time periods such as:

- *Weekly:* once a week, or 52 times a year
- *Bi-weekly:* every two weeks, or 26 times a year
- *Semi-monthly:* twice a month, or 24 times a year
- *Monthly:* once a month, or 12 times a year
- *Daily:* at the end of each day (This method is sometimes used by companies who need workers for special jobs such as on construction jobs, that may last only for a day or two.)

*3

Payment Methods Depending on the work being done, employers may use a variety of methods to calculate the gross earnings of their employees. The various payment methods include:

- *Salary:* The employee's earnings are calculated according to a set weekly, monthly or yearly rate. A common practice is to calculate the rate on a monthly basis. If this rate is $1 600 per month, and is to be paid on a semi-monthly basis, at the end of each pay period the employee will receive gross earnings of $800 ($1\,600 \div 2 = 800$).
- *Commission:* Sales personnel are often paid on a commission basis; their earnings are determined by the amount of sales they make. The gross earnings for a salesperson who gets a 5% commission and had sales of $6 570 are $328.50 ($0.05 \times 6\,570 = 328.50$).

*4

- *Combination of Salary and Commission:* It is more common to see a combination of a set minimum salary plus a commission on sales. An example would be a minimum weekly salary of $200 plus 3% of all sales made above $7 000. The gross earnings in a week, where the salesperson's sales are $9 000, would be $200 plus 3% of $2 000, which works out to $260 ($200 + 0.03 \times 2\,000 = 260$).

*5

- *Piece Rate:* To provide an incentive to workers, some jobs are paid according to the number of units the worker produces. If an employee is paid $1.25 per unit and completes 203 units, the employee's gross earnings will be $253.75 (203 × 1.25 = 253.75).

- *Hourly Rate:* Most labourers are paid according to the number of hours they work in the time period. An employee working at the rate of $6.10/h, and who works 40 h in the week, would earn $244 (610 × 40 = 244).

*6

Overtime Provincial laws require that extra pay be given after a certain number of hours have been worked in a week. For example, if 44 h was the maximum number of hours at regular pay, an employee who works more than 44 h would receive extra pay for the time worked over the 44 h. Suppose a person earns $6.00/h plus time and one half for overtime ($9.00/h for each hour worked over the maximum of 44 h). If the employee works a total of 48 h in the pay period, $300 would be earned for this period. The amount of pay would be calculated as follows:

$$\begin{aligned} 6.00 \times 44 &= 264.00 \\ 9.00 \times 4 &= \underline{36.00} \\ & 300.00 \end{aligned}$$

Overtime regulations are set by the provincial governments and by agreements between the employer and the employees.

Determining Hours Worked

Of the five basic pay methods noted, the amount of *gross earnings* in a certain pay period is easiest to calculate if the employee is paid by the salary method. By this method, the employee usually receives a set amount per pay period.

Gross earnings are the total earnings of an employee before deductions.

The calculation of gross earnings for other methods, however, is more involved. If the employee is paid on an hourly rate, a record must be kept of the hours that have been worked. This is usually done by having the worker record hours worked on a time card each day (Figure 15.2).

No. 101 Pay Period Ending Jan. 7, 19--

E.P. Rooney

	Hours	Rate	Earnings
Regular	40	$4.70	$188.00
Overtime	4	$7.05	28.20
		Gross Earnings	$216.20

Day	Morning		Afternoon		Extra		Hours	
	IN	OUT	IN	OUT	IN	OUT	Regular	Overtime
M	07:54	12:00	13:00	17:01			8	–
T	07:55	12:05	12:57	17:00			8	–
W	07:53	12:07	12:56	17:05			8	–
T	07:55	12:07	12:54	17:07	18:00	22.01	8	4
F	07:51	12:06	12:55	17:08			8	–
S								
S								
						Total	40	4

Figure 15.2 *Time card for E.P. Rooney with a record of hours worked*

Regular Earnings + Overtime Earnings = Gross Earnings

For example, E. P. Rooney's employer pays time and one half for hours worked in excess of 8 h in any one day. Rooney is paid \$4.70 for the first 8 h and \$7.05 ($4.70 \times 1.5 = 7.05$) for overtime. On Thursday, Rooney worked an extra 4 h, so the regular earnings for the week are \$188.00 ($4.70 \times 40 = 188.00$) and the overtime earnings are \$28.20 ($7.05 \times 4 = 28.20$). The total gross earnings work out to \$216.20 ($188.00 + 28.20 = 216.20$).

Lates In an agreement worked out between Wilco Printers and its employees, it has been agreed to pay employees time and one half for overtime. It has also been agreed that employees will lose 15 min pay (0.25 h) for every 15 min, or part thereof, that they are late.

Payroll Deductions

THE INTERNATIONAL NICKEL COMPANY OF CANADA LIMITED
Ontario Division

Statement of Wages and Deductions

Period Ended Mo.	Dy.	Yr.	Total Hours Worked	Allowance Hours	Gross Earnings	Total Deductions	Net Earnings	Plant	Employee No.	Name
01	11	--	48.0	8.00	317.20	69.70	247.50	Matte Proc.	0961	D. H. OBONSAWIN

Income Tax	Unemp. Insur.	Canada Pension	Other Deductions – Code List on Reverse									
			Code	Amount	Code	Amount	Code	Amount	Code	Amount	Code	Amount
48.80	3.60	5.38	280	11.92								

Regular Earnings									Incentive Earnings	Misc. Earnings	
Hours	Rate	Amount	Allowance	Hours	Rate	Amount	Allowance	premium		Code	Amount
40.0	6.10	244.00		8.0	9.15	73.20					

Figure 15.3 *Statement of wages and deductions*

*7

Deductions are amounts subtracted from an employee's gross earnings.

Returning to the example of Dennis Obonsawin and his job at INCO, it can be seen that Dennis received a *statement of wages and deductions* (Figure 15.3) showing he had gross earnings of \$317.20 for the week ending January 11. However, the amount of take-home pay he received from INCO was only \$247.50 because there were *deductions* from his pay totalling \$69.70.

Gross Earnings – Deductions = Net Earnings

Net earnings is the balance remaining after deductions have been subtracted from gross earnings.

Legislation provides that every employee must receive an explanation of how his or her *net earnings* are determined. INCO, therefore, gives each employee a statement of wages and deductions as illustrated in Figure 15.3. Dennis' deductions add up to \$69.70 and are made up of \$48.80 for income tax, \$3.60 for unemployment insurance, \$5.38 for the Canada Pension Plan, and \$11.92 for union dues.

*8

Compulsory Deductions Employers are required to make three payroll deductions from all their employees. The three payroll deductions required by law in all provinces are:

- federal income tax
- unemployment insurance contributions
- Canada Pension Plan contributions

In some provinces health insurance is a compulsory deduction. In Ontario, employers with 15 or more employees must also deduct the Ontario Health Insurance Plan premium from their workers' earnings.

Employers may also have collective agreements with unions that require union dues to be deducted as compulsory deductions.

Voluntary Deductions There are a large number of items which a person may elect to pay through payroll deductions. Some of these are:

- group life insurance premiums
- company pension plans or registered retirement plans
- credit union deposits
- extended health insurance
- disability insurance premiums
- charitable donations
- savings bond purchases

A company pension plan may be registered with Revenue Canada – Taxation. Contributions by an employee to a registered retirement plan are tax deductible and lower the income on which income tax is paid. Usually the employer contributes to the registered retirement plan as well as the employee. The company's contribution is an expense and is recorded in an account called Registered Retirement Plan Expense.

Canada Pension Plan Every employee who is over 18 and under 70 years of age and working in Canada (with minor exceptions), must contribute to the Canada Pension Plan (C.P.P.). Upon retirement, anyone who has contributed will receive a pension at the age of 65. (In the event of death, his or her dependents will receive a pension). The employer is supplied with a booklet of tables listing the contribution required from each employee.

*9

Since Dennis Obonsawin's gross earnings were $317.20 as shown in Figure 15.3, he must contribute $5.38 per week to the Canada Pension Plan. This deduction will be made every week until a maximum for the year as determined by Revenue Canada – Taxation, has been reached. Each employee contributes 1.8% of his or her gross earnings subject to contributions to the Canada Pension Plan. Every employer is required to make a matching contribution for each employee.

It should be noted that the maximum contribution changes every year. The amount of change is determined by the *consumer price index*. This index is a measure of the current cost of living compared to the buying power of the dollar in a previous year (or what is called a base year). Benefits received at retirement age are also adjusted in accordance with changes in the consumer price index.

The consumer price index is a measure of the changes in the cost of living.

Unemployment Insurance If, for some reason, an employee loses a job, he or she can collect unemployment insurance benefits if a minimum number of weekly contributions have been recorded and if other criteria are satisfied (for example, the person should be actively trying to get a new job). The same booklet used to

*10

calculate Canada Pension Plan deductions is used to calculate unemployment insurance premiums. Dennis' unemployment insurance premium deduction of $3.60 based on gross earnings of $317.20.

With minor exceptions, all full-time employees are required to make unemployment insurance contributions. The employer must contribute 1.4 times the employee deduction for each employee. For example, since Dennis' unemployment insurance premium is $3.60, INCO must contribute an additional $5.04 (3.60 × 1.4 = 5.04) on his behalf.

*11

A TD-1 form shows an employee's claim for personal exemptions and must be filled in yearly by all employees.

Income Tax Since the amount of income tax an employee pays varies according to gross earnings, the number of dependants, and the amount of tax deductible items, it is necessary for each employee to fill out a Tax Deduction Return *(TD-1)* form. The TD-1 form indicates the total claim for personal exemptions for each employee. This is the amount of yearly earnings which is tax-free. Every employee is required by law to fill out this form when hired and once a year thereafter, or whenever there is a change affecting personal exemptions.

By filling out the TD-1 form, INCO can determine that Dennis has a *Net Claim Code* of 8. The Income Tax Deductions tables, as shown in Figure 15.4, may now be used to calculate the amount of Dennis' income tax deduction. Dennis' tax deductions will be based on his taxable earnings only. Taxable earnings are gross earnings less the amount contributed to the Canada Pension Plan and the unemployment insurance premiums. His tax deduction will be based on $308.22 (317.20 − 5.38 − 3.60 = 308.22).

Gross Earnings − C.P.P. Contributions − U.I. Premiums = Taxable Earnings

TABLE 325

WEEKLY TAX DEDUCTIONS
Basis—52 Pay Periods per Year

DÉD
B

20

WEEKLY PAY Use appropriate bracket — PAIE PAR SEMAINE Utilisez le palier approprié	IF THE EMPLOYEE'S "NET CLAIM CODE" ON FORM TD1 IS — SI LE «CODE DE RÉCLAMATION								ST DE	See note on page 18. Voir remarque p. 18.
	1	2	3	4	5	6	7	8	13	
	DEDUCT FROM EACH PAY — DÉDUISEZ SUR C									Column A Colonne A
$ 289.00 - 293.99	59.50	57.75	55.15	53.10	51.00	48.30	46.05	44.15	.05	1.90
294.00 - 298.99	61.05	59.30	56.75	54.75	52.65	49.95	47.55	45.70	.60	1.90
299.00 - 303.99	62.60	60.85	58.30	56.40	54.30	51.60	49.25	47.20	.10	1.90
304.00 - 308.99	64.15	62.40	59.85	57.95	55.95	53.25	50.90	48.80	.60	1.90
309.00 - 313.99	65.70	63.95	61.40	59.50	57.50	54.95	52.55	50.45	.10	1.90
314.00 - 318.99	67.25	65.50	62.95	61.05	59.05	56.55	54.20	52.10	.65	1.90
319.00 - 323.99	68.90	67.10	64.50	62.60	60.60	58.10	55.85	53.80	.15	1.90
324.00 - 328.99	70.60	68.75	66.10	64.15	62.15	59.65	57.40	55.45	.65	1.90
329.00 - 333.99	72.25	70.45	67.75	65.70	63.75	61.20	58.95	57.00	.15	1.95
334.00 - 338.99	73.95	72.15	69.45	67.40	65.30	62.75	60.50	58.55	.70	2.05
339.00 - 343.95	75.65	73.85	71.15	69.05	66.95	64.30	62.05	60.10	.35	2.05
344.00 - 348.99	77.35	75.50	72.85	70.75	68.60	65.85	63.60	61.65	00	2.05
349.00 - 353.99	79.00	77.20	74.50	72.45	70.30	67.55	65.15	63.20	.65	2.05
354.00 - 358.99	80.70	78.90	76.20	74.15	72.00	69.25	66.80	64.75	.30	2.05
359.00 - 363.99	82.40	80.60	77.90	75.80	73.70	70.90	68.50	66.35	.95	2.05

Figure 15.4 *Tables used to calculate the amount of Dennis Obonsawin's income tax*

The table in Figure 15.4 shows that for taxable earnings from $304.00 to $308.99, and with a Net Claim Code of 8, the income tax deducted will be $48.80.

When an employee contributes to a private pension (registered retirement plan), these contributions are also subtracted along with C.P.P. and unemployment insurance contributions in arriving at taxable earnings. To find the taxable earnings of employees who have a registered retirement plan, the calculation is:

Gross Earnings	–	C.P.P. Contributions	–	U.I. Premiums	–	Registered Retirement Plan Contributions	=	Taxable Earnings

Union Dues Because of a collective bargaining agreement between the company and the union, all hourly rated employees at INCO must pay union dues. On Dennis' statement of wages and deductions (Figure 15.3), code 280 refers to the union dues INCO has deducted.

*12

Health Insurance All provinces provide health insurance plans. The benefits provided by provincial health insurance plans generally include:

- doctor's fees for required services
- hospital expenses

The cost to the public for this insurance varies from province to province. In Ontario, the cost is $19 a month for single persons and $38 for a family. The family rate applies to a married couple and their dependents, regardless of number. A married couple without children pays $38 a month, the same as a married couple with four dependent children.

Health insurance is generally free to persons with no income and to persons over 65 years of age. It is subsidized for persons with low income.

Many companies pay part or all of the health insurance premium as a fringe benefit for their employees. The portion of the monthly premium paid by the company is an expense of operating the business and is recorded in an account called Health Insurance Expense or in an account called Payroll Expenses.

Provincial Health Plans Because of the terms of the collective bargaining agreement, INCO pays 100% of the provincial health plan premiums. As a result, there is no health plan deduction shown on Dennis' statement of wages and deductions. In many companies, however, there would be a deduction for a provincial or private plan, the amount of which varies from province to province.

Group Life Insurance Many companies provide a group life insurance plan for their employees. Because of the large number of people joining such plans, the insurance companies provide a good premium rate which is usually based on the amount of insurance each employee takes. For example, an employee who decides to purchase $35 000 worth of insurance for a premium of 19¢ per $1 000 per week, would have a deduction from wages of $6.65 per week. INCO does provide for such insurance but pays 100% of the premiums for employees. Consequently, the deduction does not show up on Dennis' statement of wages and deductions. The company's payment to this plan is an expense of operating the business. The expense is called Group Insurance Expense.

*13

Credit Union Many companies sponsor a credit union for their employees. A credit union is a *non-profit banking organization* operated by its members. It receives deposits from members and gives interest on the deposits. Funds contributed by employees are loaned to other members who pay interest on money borrowed. The expenses of a credit union are low because it is operated by its own members, facilities are often provided by the employer, and bad debts on loans are rare since loans are only made to members.

Credit unions provide many banking services including:

- chequing accounts
- savings accounts
- mortgages
- loans
- registered retirement savings plans

Extended Health Insurance Plans Many employees feel a need for health insurance in addition to the provincial government plan. Extended Health Insurance Plans provide benefits such as:

- semi-private or private hospital accommodation
- cost of prescription drugs
- home nursing care
- cost of special medical services and supplies

Some companies pay all or part of the cost of this insurance for their employees.

Social Insurance Number

In order to receive unemployment insurance or Canada Pension Plan benefits, a person must have contributed to these plans. To accurately record contributions, every contributor must have a social insurance number. *Can you imagine how many John Millers or Marcel Leblancs there are in Canada?* By assigning numbers to each person, the possibilities of error due to similarities in names is eliminated.

Unit 38

Recording the Payroll

*14

The previous unit outlined how INCO determined the gross earnings, payroll deductions, and net earnings for one of its employees. In order to provide Dennis Obonsawin with his T-4 slip as shown in Figure 15.1, a number of records and calculations were completed. In this unit, the details of a payroll accounting system used by a small company, Wilco Printers, will be examined.

John Carver's pay cheque for the week ending February 6 is shown in Figure 15.5. Attached to the cheque is the statement of wages and deductions which his employer, Wilco Printers, is required to provide to its employees. John Carver separates the statement from the cheque before cashing the cheque. The statement is kept as his record of his earnings and deductions.

EMP. NO.	REGULAR HR.	REGULAR RATE	REGULAR PAY	OVERTIME HR.	OVERTIME RATE	OVERTIME PAY	TOTAL EARNINGS	Deductions C.P.P.	Deductions U.I.C	Deductions REG. PFNS.	Deductions F.I.T.	Deductions HTH INS.	Deductions MISC. CD.	Deductions MISC. AMT.	TOTAL DEDUCTIONS	NET EARNINGS	TOTAL C.P.P. TO DATE	C.K. NO.	PAY PERIOD ENDING
103	40	6 80	272 –	3	10 20	30 60	302 60	5 11	3 60	9 98	41 15	11 –	3	7 –	77 84	224 76	25 85	502	6/2/1-

Statement of Wages and Deductions

MISCELLANEOUS DEDUCTIONS

1 PENSION ______

2 BONDS ______

3 UNION 7·00

4 ______

5 ______

WILCO PRINTERS
1825 VALENTINE ROAD
SCARBOROUGH, ONTARIO

PAYROLL ACCOUNT

CHEQUE NO. 502

DATE Feb·6, 19 –

PAY TO THE ORDER OF J. Corver $ 224·76

Two hundred and twenty-four —— 76/100 DOLLARS

ROYAL BANK OF CANADA

B. Wilson
WILCO PRINTERS

Cheque

Figure 15.5 *Pay cheque with statement of wages and deductions received by John Carver from Wilco Printers*

Payroll Journal

In determining the net earnings for an employee, a number of calculations are made. The gross earnings are determined and a number of deductions are subtracted to arrive at the net earnings. These steps are performed on a sheet of columnar paper called a *Payroll Journal*.

*15

Figure 15.6 is the Payroll Journal used by Wilco Printers as the basic record of its payroll. The Payroll Journal records the payroll details for all employees for one pay period.

A Payroll Journal is a form used to record gross earnings, deductions, and net earnings for all of a firm's workers.

Steps in Preparing a Payroll Journal

1. Record the gross earnings. For hourly rated workers, the gross earnings are obtained from the time cards.
2. Calculate and record the deductions.
3. Determine the net earnings by subtracting the deductions from the gross earnings.
4. Balance the Payroll Journal.

Balancing the Payroll Journal In order to reduce the chance of mathematical errors, the Payroll Journal is balanced by doing the following proofs:

*16

1. Regular Earnings column total + Overtime Earnings column total = Gross Earnings column total.
2. The total of all the Deduction columns = Total Deductions column total.
3. Gross Earnings column total – Total Deductions column total = Net Earnings column total.

PAY PERIOD ENDING: February 6							PAYROLL JOURNA
EMPL. NO.	NAME OF EMPLOYEE	NET CLAIM CODE	EARNINGS		GROSS EARNINGS		
			REGULAR	OVERTIME		C.P.P.
101	L. Penny	9	288 —		288 —	4.84
102	B. Simpson	1	272 —	40.80	312.80	5.29
103	J. Carver	8	272 —	30.60	302.60	5.11
104	A. Baker	10	297.50		297.50	5.02
105	T. Regimbal	8	288 —	54 —	342 —	5.83
106	C. Duquette	1	272 —	61.20	333.20	5.65
			1689.50	186.60	1876.10	31.74

Figure 15.6 *Payroll Journal used by Wilco Printers*

Employee's Earnings Record

*17

An employee's earnings record is a form containing all the payroll information for an employee for one year.

Every employer is required to supply a record of the year's earnings and deductions, called a T-4 Statement of Renumeration Paid to each employee. Before February 28 of every year, the T-4 slip must be given to the employee and a copy sent to Revenue Canada – Taxation. The T-4 slip shows the totals of the previous year's earnings and deductions. In order to prepare T-4 slips, employers must keep a record of the year's payroll information for each employee. This record is called the employee's earnings record.

Journal Entries

*18

After the Payroll Journal has been proven, the information is processed in one of two ways.

- Post the Payroll Journal directly to the General Ledger.
- Make a General Journal entry which is then posted to the General Ledger.

Wilco Printers uses the second method. The gross earnings of all Wilco's employees in the pay period ending February 6 was $1 876.10 (see Figure 15. 6). However, the company will only pay employees $1 373.49. The balance of $502.61 in deductions will be sent by the company to the different parties for whom the deductions have been made. These amounts will be paid at a later date and must therefore be recorded as liabilities for the moment. The company must record an expense of $1 876.10 for the total of the gross earnings, and also the following liabilities: Wages Payable $1 373.49, C.P.P. Payable $31.74, U.I. Payable $21.60, Registered Pension Payable $61.97, Income Tax Payable $290.30, Health

ON-TAXABLES		TAXABLE EARNINGS	OTHER DEDUCTIONS					TOTAL DEDUCTIONS	NET EARNINGS
U.I.	REG. PEN.		F.I.T.	HEALTH	GROUP INS.	CODE	OTHER		
3.60	9.50	270.06	35 —	11 —		3	7 —	70.94	217.06
3.60	10.38	293.53	59.50	5.50		3	7 —	91.27	221.53
3.60	9.98	283.91	41.15	11 —		3	7 —	77.84	224.76
3.60	9.82	279.06	35.15	11 —		3	7 —	71.59	225.91
3.60	11.29	321.28	53.80	11 —		3	7 —	92.52	249.48
3.60	11	312.95	65.70	5.50		3	7 —	98.45	234.75
21.60	61.97		290.30	55 —			42 —	502.61	137349

Insurance Payable $55.00, and Union Dues Payable $42.00.

The General Journal entry to record Wilco Printers' payroll for the pay period ending February 6 will be:

GENERAL JOURNAL				PAGE
DATE	PARTICULARS	PR	DEBIT	CREDIT
19-- Feb. 6	Wages Expense		1 876 10	
	Wages Payable			1 373 49
	C.P.P. Payable			31 74
	U.I. Payable			21 60
	Registered Pension Payable			61 97
	Income Tax Payable			290 30
	Health Insurance Payable			55 —
	Union Dues Payable			42 —
	To record the payroll for the week ended February 6			

Figure 15.7 shows the General Ledger accounts affected when the preceding General Journal entry is posted.

Wages Expense	
Feb. 1 1 876.10	

C.P.P. Payable	
	Feb. 6 31.74

U.I. Payable	
	Feb. 16 21.60

Income Tax Payable	
	Feb. 6 290.30

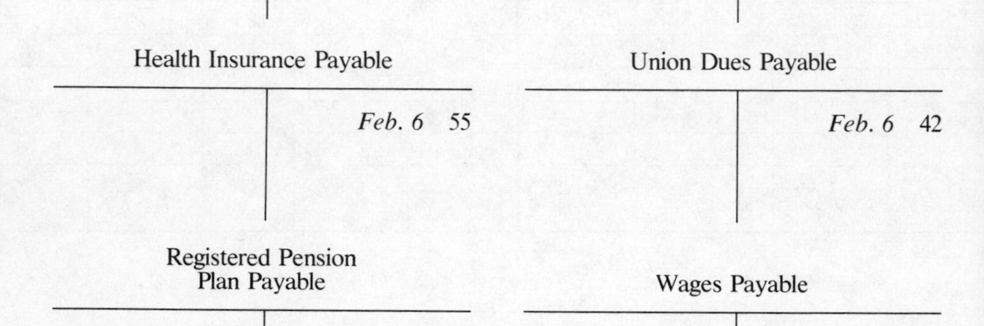

Health Insurance Payable	
	Feb. 6 55

Union Dues Payable	
	Feb. 6 42

Registered Pension Plan Payable	
	Feb. 6 61.97

Wages Payable	
	Feb. 6 1 373.49

Figure 15.7 *General Ledger accounts needed to record Wilco Printers' payroll*

*19

When the employees are paid, the following General Journal entry is recorded:

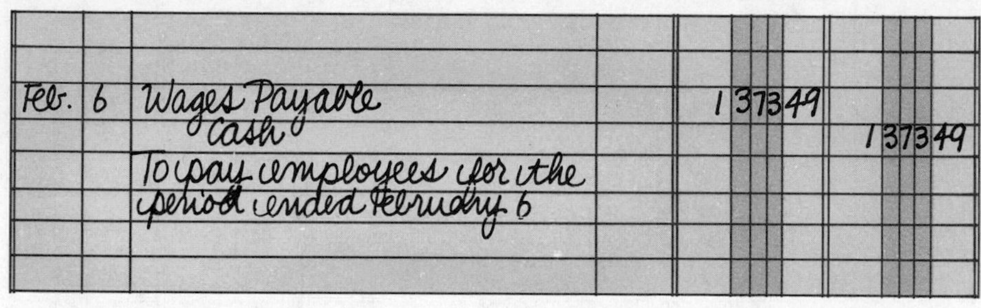

Date		Account	PR	Debit	Credit
Feb.	6	Wages Payable		1 373 49	
		Cash			1 373 49
		To pay employees for the			
		period ended February 6			

Wages Payable	
Feb. 6 1 373.49	Feb. 6 1 373.49

Cash	
	Feb. 6 1 373.49

Figure 15.8 *General Ledger accounts affected by the entry to record wages paid to employees*

Figure 15.8 shows the effect on the General Ledger when the preceding General Journal entry is posted.

Employer's Share of C.P.P. and U.I. Legislation requires that employers match employee contributions to the Canada Pension Plan. Figure 15.6 shows that Wilco Printers deducted a total of $31.74 from their employees for the pay period ending February 6. This amount must be paid to the government along with an equal contribution from Wilco Printers. To record the employer's matching contribution of $31.74, the following entry must also be journalized: *20

				Debit	Credit
Feb.	6	C.P.P. Expense		31 74	
		C.P.P. Payable			31 74
		To record the company's			
		share of the C.P.P. contribution			

Employers must also contribute to employees' unemployment insurance. However, the employer must contribute 1.4 times the employee's amount (or, in this case, $30.24 (21.60 × 1.4 = 30.24). The following entry must be journalized to record Wilco's contribution to unemployment insurance:

				Debit	Credit
Feb.	6	U.I. Expense		30 24	
		U.I. Payable			30 24
		To record the company's			
		share of U.I. premium			

When these two entries are posted, the General Ledger accounts for C.P.P. Payable and U.I. Payable will appear as in Figure 15.9.

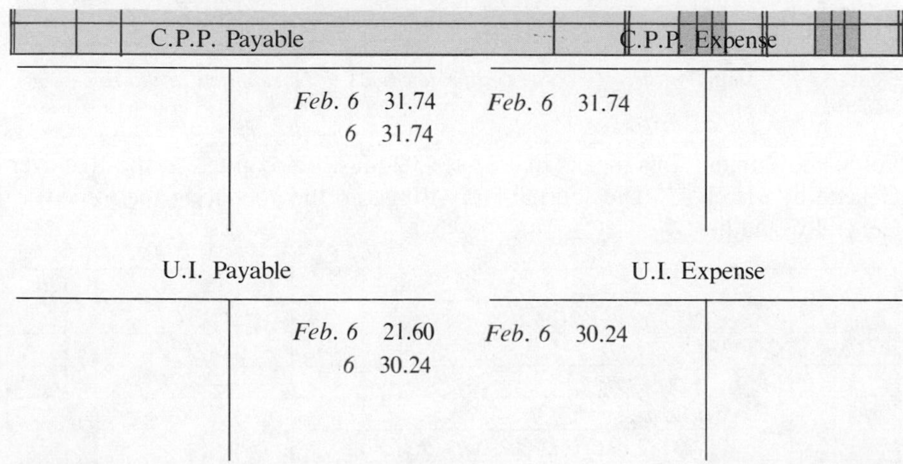

Figure 15.9 *General Ledger accounts affected by entry to record the employer's share of C.P.P. Payable and U.I. Payable*

***21** **Remittances to the Federal Government** During the month of February, which involved four pay periods, the totals of the amounts deducted for the employees of Wilco Printers is shown in Figure 15.10. All amounts held back from employees during the month for C.P.P., U.I., and income tax must be remitted to the Receiver General for Canada by the fifteenth day of the following month.

C.P.P. Payable

Debit	Credit	
	Feb. 6	31.74
	6	31.74
	13	33.81
	13	33.81
	20	31.62
	20	31.62
	27	33.19
	27	33.19
		260.72

U.I. Payable

Debit	Credit	
	Feb. 6	21.60
	6	30.24
	13	19.80
	13	27.72
	20	18.92
	20	26.49
	27	19.80
	27	27.72
		192.29

Income Tax Payable

Debit	Credit	
	Feb. 6	290.30
	13	297.80
	20	242.11
	27	272.80
		1 103.01

Health Insurance Payable

Debit	Credit	
	Feb. 6	55
	13	55
	20	55
	27	55
		220

Registered Pension Plan Payable

Debit	Credit	
	Feb. 6	61.97
	13	62.40
	20	58.73
	27	60.30
		243.40

Union Dues Payable

Debit	Credit	
	Feb. 6	42
	13	42
	20	42
	27	42
		168

Figure 15.10 *Totals of three General Ledger accounts to be remitted to the Receiver General*

For Wilco Printers, this means that $1 556.02 must be remitted to the Receiver General by March 15. The Journal entry to record the cheque to the Receiver General would be:

Date		Particulars		Debit	Credit
Mar.	15	Income Tax Payable		1 103 01	
		C.P.P. Payable		260 72	
		U.I. Payable		192 29	
		Cash			1 556 02
		To record cheque No. 430			
		to the Receiver General			

This entry is normally recorded in the Cash Payments Journal. The accounts are shown, after posting, in Figure 15.11.

Cash

Debit date	Debit amount	Credit date	Credit amount
		March 15	1 556.02

C.P.P. Payable

Debit date	Debit amount	Credit date	Credit amount
		Feb. 6	31.74
		6	31.74
		13	33.81
		13	33.81
		20	31.62
		20	31.62
		27	33.19
March 15	260.72	*27*	33.19
		Balance	260.72

U.I. Payable

Debit date	Debit amount	Credit date	Credit amount
		Feb. 6	21.60
		6	30.24
		13	19.80
		13	27.72
		20	18.92
		20	26.49
		27	19.80
		27	27.72
March 15	192.29	Balance	192.29

Income Tax Payable

Debit date	Debit amount	Credit date	Credit amount
		Feb. 6	290.30
		13	297.80
		20	242.11
		27	272.80
March 15	1 103.01	Balance	1 103.01

Figure 15.11 *General Ledger accounts after posting*

Other Remittances Separate cheques will also have to be made out for the health insurance and the union dues deductions and recorded in the Cash Payments Journal. Figure 15.12 is a summary of the payroll procedures covered in this chapter. *22

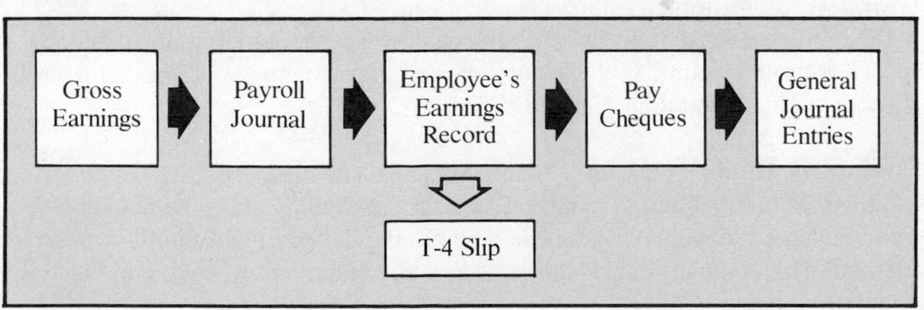

Figure 15.12 *Summary of Wilco Printers' payroll procedures*

Paying the Employees

There are three common methods of paying employees: *23

- by cash
- by cheque
- by bank deposit (or bank transfer)

Paying by Cash Although this method is *not* preferred by most employers, it is sometimes necessary to pay by cash, because of agreements with unions or the preference of workers.

In order to pay by cash, a change sheet is completed to determine the number of coins and bills of each denomination required to pay the workers. Next, a currency requisition is completed. This form is a summary of the coins and bills required. It is taken to the bank along with a cheque for the total. The bank cashes the cheque and provides the necessary number of coins and bills as outlined on the currency requisition. Finally, the pay for each worker is counted and placed in individual pay envelopes. Usually a pay statement is printed on the envelope. This provides the worker with a summary of gross earnings, deductions, and net earnings.

Paying by cash is risky and time-consuming; it also increases the chance of error because of the extra work involved.

Paying by Cheque Many companies prefer to pay their employees by cheque. To simplify the end-of-the-month bank reconciliations, a separate payroll bank account is opened at the bank. Each month a cheque is written on the regular account. The amount of this cheque is exactly the total required to pay all the employees. This cheque is deposited in the special payroll bank account. The General Journal entry to record this transaction is:

Feb.	28	Salaries Payable		1 963 51	
		Cash			1 963 51
		To transfer funds to the			
		special payroll account			

Next, pay cheques are issued to each employee. These cheques have the pay statements attached and are usually identified as payroll cheques by the words *Payroll Account,* printed on the cheque face.

When workers cash their cheques, the bank will cash them from the company's special payroll account. If all workers cashed their cheques, the special payroll account balance would be reduced to zero.

Paying by Bank Transfer Some companies (such as INCO) provide a summary of their payroll to a bank. Each worker then receives the pay directly from the bank by means of a deposit equal to the net pay placed in the worker's account. The company must still provide a pay statement to each employee as required by law.

Canadian banks offer a complete payroll service to companies. For a fee, they will process the entire payroll, pay the workers, and provide required records to the company.

Workmen's Compensation

*24

All provinces provide an insurance plan for the protection of workers who suffer personal injuries or occupational diseases related to their jobs. Compensation is paid to injured workers from an accident fund administered by a provincial Workmen's Compensation Board. Employers supply the money for the fund. The amount paid into the fund by an employer varies according to the type of business. In return for providing money to the fund the employer is relieved of liability for injuries suffered by workers. The amount of compensation received by an injured worker is based on the average salary earned while working.

The employer's payment to the fund is an expense of operating the business. When premiums are paid this entry is made:

June	30	Workmen's Compensation Expense		150 —	
		Cash			150 —
		To pay semi-annual premium			

Ledger Accounts

Payroll accounting involves a number of expense accounts. For example, Wages Expense is the account used for earnings of hourly rated workers. Salaries Expense is used for the earnings of salaried employees.

Several expense accounts are used to record employer's contributions required by various laws. These include C.P.P. Expense, U.I. Expense, and Workmen's Compensation Expense. Rather than use these three individual accounts, some companies prefer to use one account called *Payroll Expense* to record required contributions. This account may also be used to record payments on behalf of workers required by the negotiated collective agreement. These payments might include health insurance, life insurance, and dental insurance. A sample entry using the Payroll Expense account follows.

June	30	Payroll Expense		274 —	
		C.P.P. Payable			74 —
		U.I. Payable			60 —
		Workman's Compensation Payable			20 —
		Group Insurance Payable			30 —
		Health Insurance Payable			90 —
		To record employer's			
		Payroll Expenses			

The One-Write System

*25

Payroll accounting procedures involve considerable repetitive work. The same payroll data for each employee is recorded three times:
- in the Payroll Journal
- on the pay cheque or pay statement
- on the employee's earnings record

One device used to cut down the payroll recording work is the one-write board. The one-write board makes it possible to record on three sets of forms at one time. It consists of a board with a series of pegs along the side. Each accounting form is held in place by the pegs. The forms are separated by carbon paper. When data is entered on the pay cheque it is automatically made on the Payroll Journal and earnings record card as well.

Facts to Remember

T-4 slips must be given to employees by February 28 and provide the previous year's earnings and payroll deductions which affect employees' income taxes.

Gross earnings are the total earnings of an employee before deductions.

Deductions (income tax, Canada Pension Plan, unemployment insurance, and others) are amounts subtracted from an employee's gross earnings.

Net earnings is the balance remaining after deductions have been subtracted from gross earnings.

Compulsory payroll deductions include income tax, Canada Pension Plan, and unemployment insurance.

The *statement of wages and deductions* is provided to all employees and shows how net earnings are determined.

The *consumer price index* is a measure of the changes in the cost of living.

A *TD-1 form* shows an employee's claim for personal exemptions and must be filled in yearly by all employees.

A *Payroll Journal* is the form used to record gross earnings, deductions, and net earnings for all of a firm's workers.

An *employee's earnings record* is a record of all the payroll information for an employee for one year.

Cash, cheque, and *bank transfer* are three common methods of paying workers.

Reviewing Your Reading

Questions

1. a) What is a T-4?
   b) Why does an employee need a copy?
   c) Why does the federal government (Revenue Canada – Taxation) receive a copy?
2. What is an audit?
3. List the different government departments which may from time to time audit a company's payroll records.
4. Explain why an employee who is paid twice a month has 24 pay periods a year while one who is paid every two weeks has 26 pay periods.
5. How were the gross earnings of $317.20 in Figure 15.3 calculated?
6. What are Dennis Obonsawin's deductions in Figure 15.3? What are his net earnings?
7. Why must every employee receive a statement of earnings and deductions which explains how pay is determined?
8. What are the compulsory deductions in your province?
9. a) What are the seven voluntary deductions listed in the text?
   b) Name three of the many other voluntary deductions possible.
10. a) Who must contribute to the Canada Pension Plan?
    b) What percentage of gross earnings must be contributed by employees?
    c) What is the maximum contribution for the year?
    d) If all the employees of a company contributed $327.10 in the week, what must the company also contribute?
11. a) Who must pay unemployment insurance premiums?
    b) What is an employee's maximum premium for one year?
    c) If all the employees of a company paid premiums of $297.46, what is the amount of the premium to be paid by the company?
12. a) What is a TD-1?
    b) Why does Dennis Obonsawin have a net claim code of 8?
13. a) Dennis Obonsawin does not contribute to a registered retirement plan. How are his taxable earnings calculated?
    b) Dennis' social insurance number is 473-594-647. What purpose is served by this number?
14. a) What are the two parts of J. Carver's cheque in Figure 15.5?
    b) What is the purpose of the pay statement?
15. What is the purpose of the employee's earnings record?
16. Name three common methods of paying employees.
17. What is the purpose of a change sheet and the currency requisition?

18. Why do companies prefer to pay by cheque rather than by cash?

19. Explain the bank transfer method of paying employees.

20. a) What insurance compensates workers injured on the job?
    b) Who pays the premiums for this insurance?

21. What single expense account may be used instead of C.P.P. Expense, U.I. Expense, and Workmen's Compensation Expense?

22. Name the three payroll forms which are prepared simultaneously when a one-write board is used.

Applying Your Knowledge

Exercises Part A

1. Calculate gross earnings for Ken Thorpe, a salesman who receives a 3% commission on all sales, if his sales for the week were $10 535.00.

2. What are Nancy Koosman's gross earnings if she receives a 2.5% commission and had sales of $13 570 during the week?

3. a) Andy Mather is paid a basic salary of $110 per week plus 1.5% commission on his sales. Calculate his gross earnings from the following list of sales for the month and total the month's earnings.
   Week 1 $11 680
   Week 2 $13 493
   Week 3 $18 514
   Week 4 $ 9 617
   b) What would Andy's earnings have been for each week and for the month in part a) if he had remained on a straight commission basis of 2.5% of sales?
   c) Which method would you prefer – salary and commission or commission only? Why?

4. Dave Zwicker works for a firm producing hand-held calculators. He is paid according to the number of calculators he assembles. Calculate Dave's gross earnings for each day of the week, if he is paid 55 cents for each assembly.

Day	No. of Calculators
Monday	70
Tuesday	74
Wednesday	81
Thursday	87
Friday	75

5. Lois Belincki is paid at the rate of $4.50/h and time and one half for overtime. Any work over eight h in one day is considered overtime. Calculate her week's gross earnings if she worked the following hours:

Monday	8 h
Tuesday	7.5 h
Wednesday	10 h
Thursday	7.75 h
Friday	8 h

6. During the month of August, Veronica Davies had the following gross earnings:

Week 1	$196.75
Week 2	$207.53
Week 3	$175.34
Week 4	$193.54

Using an up-to-date Canada Pension Plan Contributions and Unemployment Insurance Premium booklet, calculate the C.P.P. and U.I. premium for the month of August.

7. a) Charles Mazer contributes $12 per week to the company pension plan as well as the regular deductions for C.P.P. and U.I. premiums. Calculate his taxable earnings in July if his gross earnings for the four weeks were:

Week 1	$298.75
Week 2	$325.64
Week 3	$319.26
Week 4	$307.49

b) Charles Mazer is married and has one three-year-old child. His wife does not work, so his net claim code for income tax purposes is 8. Using the chart in Figure 15.4 or an up-to-date income tax deduction booklet, calculate his income tax deductions for the four weeks in July that are given in part a).

c) As well as the deductions that you calculated in parts a) and b), Charles also has the following weekly deductions: health insurance of $11.00; union dues, $7.50; group life insurance for $30 000 at a premium of 15¢ per $1 000. In the fourth week he chose to buy a Canada Savings Bond at $25 per week. Calculate his total deductions and his net earnings for the four weeks.

8. Grace Trumball contributes $11.25 per week to her company's pension plan. She also has the following weekly deductions: health insurance, $5.50; group life insurance for $25 000 at a cost of 17¢ per $1 000; union dues of $5.55. Since she is single, her net claim code for tax purposes is 1. Her gross earnings in July were as follows:

Week 1	$347.50
Week 2	$299.56
Week 3	$358.61
Week 4	$302.66

a) Calculate the C.P.P. contributions, the U.I. premium, and the taxable earnings using an up-to-date contribution booklet.

b) Calculate the income tax deductions using the table in Figure 15.4.

c) Calculate the net earnings.

Exercises Part B

9. Wilco Printers has six employees on their hourly payroll. Relevant information on the employees follows:

No.	Name	Net Claim Code	Hours Reg.	Hours O.T.	Rates Reg.	Rates O.T.	Deductions Pension	Deductions Health	Deductions Union
103	John Coleman	9	40	3	$7.80	$11.70	$9.50	$11.00	$7.00
104	Bill Strahan	1	35	–	8.70	12.75	9.50	5.50	7.00
105	Linda Sherman	10	40	4	6.80	10.20	9.50	11.00	7.00
106	Lesley Durvan	1	40	–	8.10	12.15	9.50	5.50	7.00
107	Stan Houser	9	40	6	6.80	10.20	9.50	11.00	7.00
108	Tracey St. James	1	40	3	6.80	10.20	9.50	5.50	7.00

a) Calculate the gross earnings for each employee.
b) Calculate the C.P.P. contributions and the U.I. premiums, and the taxable earnings of each worker.
c) Calculate the income tax deductions of each worker.
d) Calculate the net earnings of each worker.

10. a) Record the payroll for exercise 9 in a Payroll Journal.
b) Total and prove the Payroll Journal.

11. The Payroll Journal for the pay period ending on May 7 showed the following totals: gross earnings $5 783.20; C.P.P. contributions $104.09; U.I. premiums, $62.70; federal income tax, $983.14; health insurance, $132.00; union dues, $142.50; net earnings $4 358.77. Prepare journal entries to record:
a) the Payroll Journal;
b) the paying of the employees;
c) the owner's share of the C.P.P. contributions and U.I. premiums.

12. The Payroll Journal for the pay period ending on May 14 showed the following totals: gross earnings, $46 793.55; C.P.P. contributions, $842.28; U.I. premiums, $495.00; registered pension plan, $1 544.19; income tax, $7 954.90; health insurance, $1 122.00; union dues $1 325.25; group insurance, $797.53; net earnings, $32 712.40. Prepare journal entries to record:
a) the Payroll Journal;
b) the paying of the employees;
c) the owner's share of the C.P.P. contributions and U.I. premiums.

13. The payroll information for McDivott Manufacturers for the week ending May 7 is shown at the top of the next page.
Every employee also has $30 000 worth of group life insurance for which 12¢ per $1 000 is contributed, and union dues of $6.55 weekly.

Emp. No.	Name	Social Insurance Number	Net Claim Code	Hours Reg.	Hours O.T.	Rate Reg.	Rate O.T.	Health Insurance Deduction
101	P. Dagenais	731-502-671	11	40	2	$7.10	$10.65	$11.00
102	L. Grace	371-307-407	8	40	–	7.90	11.85	11.00
103	C. Nichols	933-008-973	1	39.5	–	7.80	11.70	5.50
104	T. Stewart	407-909-981	9	40	4	7.20	10.80	11.00
105	F. Brammel	347-978-392	9	38	–	8.05	12.75	11.00
106	C. Turner	507-673-097	1	40	1.5	8.20	12.30	5.50

a) Record the payroll in a Payroll Journal using the tables for C.P.P. contributions, U.I. premiums, and income tax deductions provided in the current tables available from Revenue Canada – Taxation.
b) Total and prove the Payroll Journal.
c) Prepare a General Journal entry to record the payroll.
d) Prepare General Journal entries to record the company's share of C.P.P. contributions and U.I. premiums.
e) Prepare a General Journal entry to record the paying of the employees.

14. The payroll information for Western Distributors for the week ending June 15 follows:

Emp. No.	Name	Social Insurance Number	Net Claim Code	Hours Reg	Hours O.T.	Rate Reg	Rate O.T.	Health	Co. Pension
201	T. Moore	705-079-032	1	40	2	$7.20	$10.80	$ 5.50	$1.80
202	A. Adams	673-902-307	9	38.75	–	7.80	11.70	11.00	1.95
203	A. Covington	347-991-137	10	40	3	6.90	10.35	11.00	1.73
204	C. Trant	507-870-345	1	40	–	8.05	12.75	5.50	1.76
205	P. Singer	511-422-617	1	37	–	8.10	12.15	5.50	1.78
206	S. Betterworth	115-716-242	11	40	8	7.40	11.10	11.00	1.85

Every employee also has $35 000 worth of group life insurance for which 15¢ per $1 000 is contributed, and union dues of $4.05 weekly.

a) Record the payroll in a Payroll Journal, using an up-to-date contributions booklet for C.P.P., U.I., and income tax.
b) Total and prove the Payroll Journal.
c) Prepare a General Journal entry to record the payroll.
d) Prepare General Journal entries to record the company's share of C.P.P. contributions and U.I. premiums.
e) Prepare a General Journal entry to record the paying of the employees.

15. McDivott Manufacturers pays its salaried employees once a month. The Payroll Journal at the end of May for these employees follows:

PAY PERIOD ENDING: May 31, 19__ PAYROLL JOURNA

EMPL. NO.	NAME OF EMPLOYEE	NET CLAIM CODE	EARNINGS REGULAR	EARNINGS OVERTIME	GROSS EARNINGS	C.P.P.
65	P. O'Connell	9	1574 —		1574 —	26.82
66	C. Dooner	1	862 —		862 —	14.02
67	L. Greenspoon	1	1433 —		1433 —	24.30
68	F. Ritcher	10	1729 —		1729 —	29.61
69	C. Lapchinski	9	1325 —		1325 —	22.32
70	A. Karklins	1	1325 —		1325 —	22.32
			8248 —		8248 —	139.39

Prepare journal entries to record:

a) the payroll at the end of May;
b) the employer's share of the C.P.P. contributions and the U.I. premiums;
c) the cheques to pay the employees;
d) the remittance to the Receiver General on June 15;
e) the remittance to Metropolitan Life for the group insurance and pension;
f) the remittance to the provincial treasurer for the health insurance.

Exercises Part C

16. The time cards for the week ended February 6 and other payroll information for Claymore Industries' employees follow:

NO. 101 Pay Period Ending Feb. 6, 19--
NAME J.L. Carter
Regular Hours ______ Regular Rate $6.80
Overtime Hours ______ Overtime Rate $10.20
Total Earnings ______

	MORN IN	NOON OUT	NOON IN	NIGHT OUT	EXTRA IN	EXTRA OUT	HOURS
M	07:58	12:01	13:00	17:00			
T	08:00	12:01	13:00	17:00			
W	07:56	12:04	13:00	17:01	18:00	21:00	
T	07:59	12:03	12:55	17:01			
F	07:58	12:02	12:56	17:02			
S							
S							

NO. 102 Pay Period Ending Feb. 6, 19--
NAME P.S. Stelmack
Regular Hours ______ Regular Rate $7.10
Overtime Hours ______ Overtime Rate $10.65
Total Earnings ______

	MORN IN	NOON OUT	NOON IN	NIGHT OUT	EXTRA IN	EXTRA OUT	HOURS
M	07:59	12:01	12:59	17:01			
T	07:58	12:02	12:58	17:00	18:00	21:00	
W	08:02	12:01	13:02	17:02			
T	08:03	12:03	13:05	17:03			
F	07:59	12:01	13:00	17:05			
S							
S							

PAGE 307

ON-TAXABLES		TAXABLE EARNINGS	OTHER DEDUCTIONS					TOTAL DEDUCTIONS	NET EARNINGS
U.I.	REG. PEN.		F.I.T.	HEALTH	GROUP INS.	CODE	OTHER		
15.60	55.09	1476.49	243.55	44—	23.61			408.67	1165.33
12.93	30.17	804.88	117.90	22—	12.93			209.95	652.05
15.60	50.16	1342.94	284.70	22—	21.50			418.26	1014.74
15.60	60.52	1623.27	280.90	44—	25.94			456.57	1272.43
15.60	46.38	1240.70	173.80	44—	19.88			321.98	1003.02
15.60	46.38	1240.70	253.65	22—	19.88			379.83	945.17
90.93	288.70		1354.50	198—	123.74			2195.26	6052.74

Emp. No.	Name	Social Insurance Number	Net Claim Code	Health Deduction	Company Pension Plan	Group Insurance
101	J. L. Carter	707-307-977	1	$ 5.50	$1.70	$25 000
102	P. S. Stelmack	354-975-406	9	11.00	1.78	35 000
103	A. A. Humphreys	397-103-507	10	11.00	1.80	45 000
104	B. M. Logan	576-300-397	1	5.50	1.78	20 000

NO. 103 Pay Period Ending Feb. 6, 19--
NAME A. A. Humphreys
Regular Hours ________ Regular Rate $7.20
Overtime Hours ________ Overtime Rate $10.80
Total Earnings ________

	MORN IN	NOON OUT	NOON IN	NIGHT OUT	EXTRA IN	EXTRA OUT	HOURS
M			12:50	17:01			
T	07:59	12:00	12:51	17:02			
W	07:58	12:01	12:57	17:00	17:59	21:02	
T	07:57	12:04	12:55	17:05			
F	07:56	12:05	12:50	17:04			
S							
S							

NO. 104 Pay Period Ending Feb. 6, 19--
NAME B. M. Logan
Regular Hours ________ Regular Rate $7.10
Overtime Hours ________ Overtime Rate $10.65
Total Earnings ________

	MORN IN	NOON OUT	NOON IN	NIGHT OUT	EXTRA IN	EXTRA OUT	HOURS
M			12:52	17:02			
T	08:00	12:00	13:04	17:02			
W	07:55	12:02	13:00	17:01			
T	07:58	12:01	12:59	17:00	18:00	21:01	
F	07:58	12:02	12:59	17:01			
S							
S							

Every employee pays weekly group insurance premiums of 20¢ per $1 000.

a) Record the Payroll Journal.
b) Total and prove the Payroll Journal.
c) Prepare the General Journal entries to record:
   i) the Payroll Journal;
   ii) the employer's share of C.P.P. contributions and U.I. premiums;
   iii) the transfer of funds to the employees' bank accounts.
d) Post the journal entries to the general ledger (you may use T-accounts). The accounts required are:

101	Cash	215	Company Pension Payable
210	Wages Payable	216	Group Insurance Payable
211	C.P.P. Payable	610	Wages Expense
212	U.I. Payable	611	C.P.P. Expense
213	Income Tax Payable	612	U.I. Expense
214	Health Insurance Payable		

17. The gross earnings for the week ended February 13 for the four employees in exercise 16 follow:

101	J . L. Carter	$289.55
102	P. S. Stelmack	$313.60
103	A. A. Humphreys	$325.35
104	B. M. Logan	$309.47

All other information is the same as in exercise 16.

a) Record the Payroll Journal.
b) Total and prove the Payroll Journal.
c) Prepare the General Journal entries to record:
   i) the Payroll Journal;
   ii) the employer's share of C.P.P. contributions and U.I. premiums;
   iii) the transfer of funds to the employees' bank accounts.
d) Post the General Journal entries to the same T-accounts used in exercise 16.

18. Follow the same instructions as in exercise 16 for the week ended February 20. The gross earnings for the four employees are:

101	J. L. Carter	$299.76
102	P. S. Stelmack	$305.60
103	A. A. Humphreys	$337.55
104	B. M. Logan	$315.73

19. a) Follow the same instructions as in exercise 16 for the week ended February 27. The gross earnings for the four employees are:

101	J. L. Carter	$290.76
102	P. S. Stelmack	$323.75
103	A. A. Humphreys	$340.96
104	B. M. Logan	$319.80

b) On March 15, prepare the General Journal entries to record:
   i) the remittances to the Receiver General for Canada for the income tax, C.P.P. contributions and U.I. premiums for the month of February;
   ii) all other remittances that apply.

Accounting in Action

Ethics in Business Wellington's is a large department store which employs many students part time. Minimum wage laws specify the number of hours of work per week above which a student must be paid the general worker's rate. There is about a 10% difference between the general rate and the student rate. Wellington's offers several fringe benefits to its full-time employees. These include a free life insurance policy, 50% of the cost of a medical plan, and 20 days' annual sick leave. Part-time employees do not receive fringe benefits. **Case 1**

The owner of the store encourages the use of many part-time students because the minimum rate for students is lower and because they do not receive fringe benefits.

The personnel manager occasionally but deliberately contravenes the minimum wage law by not paying overtime as required. The owner is not aware of this.

The manager of the sporting goods department has hired his son-in-law as a salesman and often offers him overtime work. No one else in the department works overtime.

a) Who do you think is the most ethical person in the store? Who is the least ethical?
   Rank the following in an *ethical* scale, from 1 to 4 with 4 being the least ethical:
   i) the owner;
   ii) the personnel manager;
   iii) the sporting goods manager;
   iv) the son-in-law.
b) What do you understand by the word *ethical?*
c) Suppose you worked for Wellington's and felt that you were not being treated fairly according to several of your province's employment standards laws:
   i) What would you do? List your alternatives.
   ii) What are the possible consequences of each alternative?

Unemployment Insurance Visit a library or visit or call your region's federal Manpower Department office and obtain answers to the following: **Case 2**

a) Who pays into the unemployment insurance fund?
b) In general, who receives benefits from the fund?
c) How long must a person make contributions in order to qualify for benefits?
d) How long may benefits be received?

Evaluating Two Job Offers Marion has worked for a large insurance company for seven years. During this period of time, Marion has received a number of promotions and raises in pay. Although highly regarded by her employers, Marion has only limited opportunities for advancement with the present company. **Case 3**

After applying to a number of firms, Marion has received two offers of jobs at the management level. Both companies are progressive and growing and appear to be able to supply the type of future Marion is seeking.

Company A offers the following:
Salary: $25 000
Fringe benefits:
- free life insurance
- free long-term disability insurance
- free extended health-care insurance
- a company pension which is partly paid by the company (the employee pays approximately $500 a year)

Company B offers the following:
Salary: $26 000
A bonus of $3 000 if employee work goals are successfully met.
A number of benefits which are paid by *the workers:*
- life insurance $400 a year
- disability insurance $100 a year
- extended health insurance $200 a year
- provincial medical insurance $264 a year
- company pension $1 700

Which of the two positions would you accept if you were Marion? Why?

Case 4

Employment Standards Contact the provincial government department which administers your province's minimum wage and employment standards act.

a) Prepare a report which covers at least the following:
   - the minimum wage for general workers, construction workers and students
   - the number of hours worked above which a student must be paid the general minimum wage
   - vacation pay and overtime regulations
   - statutory holidays

b) Invite a person from your province's labour department to speak to your class on the minimum wage act and how it is administered.

c) Obtain a copy of the law in your province which governs minimum wages and employment standards. Present a summary of this law to your class.

Case 5

Valuing Honesty Canada's unemployment insurance plan provides insurance against job loss. It is designed to provide benefits to persons unemployed through no fault of their own. Money in the fund comes from three sources: employees, employers, and the federal government. Employees contribute 1.5% of their gross earnings. Thus, a worker earning $200 contributes $3 in unemployment insurance. The first $48 earned each week is exempt from contributions. On earnings over $48 and up to $240 a week, 1.5% is the required contribution. The contribution does not increase after weekly earnings of $240. Employers are required to contribute 1.4 times the employee premium. Thus for a worker earning $200 the employer must contribute $4.50 ($1.4 \times 3 = 4.50$). For many years the unemployment insurance fund has operated at a deficit. The federal government must make up the deficit from general tax revenues. There are several reasons for the deficit including:

- improved benefits paid to the unemployed
- rising unemployment
- claimants cheating the fund

Read each of the following mini-cases.

A Joe is an employee working for a small firm owned by Don. They have an agreement that Don does not deduct unemployment insurance from Joe's earnings. This saves Joe about $180 a year and Don about $285. *Besides being party to an illegal act, what risk is Joe taking?*

B Janet has worked for several years and never been unemployed. She decides to take a six-month trip. After deliberately getting herself laid off from her job, Janet completes the required forms and begins receiving unemployment insurance benefits. She has her friend Romi complete forms for her indicating that Janet is actively looking for employment. Janet is far away enjoying her extended vacation. Romi forges Janet's name on government cheques and deposits them in Janet's bank account.

C Jon and Marie are both working and earning good salaries. Each year one of them deliberately becomes unemployed and receives benefits for several months then goes back to work. Although both could be employed full time they feel they deserve the unemployment insurance benefits because they have contributed premiums for so many years. An employer realizes the game they are playing, but does not report them because the employer does not wish to become involved in a court case.

D Toni has worked for 30 years at a number of low-level jobs and has never had to claim benefits because of unemployment. Toni is about a year away from retirement and knows that a retirement benefit of several weeks pay is provided by unemployment insurance regulations. Toni does not feel that this is fair because of the 30 years of contributions without benefits. Therefore, Toni has worked out a plan to be laid off for about a year and will claim full benefits without trying to find employment.

Discuss each of the mini-cases with several of your classmates and prepare answers to these questions.

a) Rank each of these people according to honesty: Joe, Don, Janet, Romi, Jon, Marie, the employer in C, and Toni. Give each a number from 1 to 8 with 1 being the most dishonest.
b) Do you think each of the eight persons is guilty of wrongdoing? If not, which person has done nothing wrong?
c) In each mini-case, suggest procedures the government could use to prevent wrongdoing by the persons involved.
d) In each mini-case, suggest a fair penalty for those you feel have committed an illegal action.

Career Profile

A Payroll Clerk Accounting offers many career opportunities at various levels of responsibility. The following career profile is an example of a person who is beginning a business career immediately after completing high school.

Virginia Larkin is 20 years old. When she obtained her secondary school graduation diploma she decided to look for a job. Since she had liked accounting courses in high school she applied for jobs in that field.

Virginia was hired as an accounting clerk by the International Grenfell Association. This is a non-profit organization which operates hospitals and nursing stations in Labrador and northern Newfoundland. Virginia has now been with this association for two years and is responsible for completing the payroll for 350 employees of the association.

Her payroll duties include calculating earnings, determining the payroll deductions such as income tax, Canada pension, unemployment insurance, and medical insurance, and preparing pay cheques and bank transfers. She is also responsible for preparing reports and sending payroll deductions to the federal and provincial governments.

Virginia enjoys the people she works with and plans to make a career in accounting.

CHAPTER 16

The Voucher System

Internal Control

Unit 39

*1

Internal control refers to the need to eliminate errors, waste, and fraud by company employees.

Throughout Part Two of this text systems of *internal control* have been emphasized. Internal control refers to the need to eliminate errors, waste, and fraud on the part of the employees of a company. In Chapter 8, procedures were described which ensured that information in the Accounts Receivable and Accounts Payable Ledgers was correct and agreed with information in the General Ledger. In Chapter 14 methods of controlling cash receipts and payments, particularly petty cash payments, were introduced. Two examples of control procedures used by modern businesses were outlined in the *MacVal* case study, Chapter 8, and the *Metropolitan Life Insurance* case study, Chapter 10.

All these control procedures are based on a widely used accounting system called the *voucher system*. Many companies use the principles of the voucher system to control payments. In this chapter, the internal control procedures of the voucher system will be examined in detail, to show how the errors, waste, and fraud described in the following six examples are controlled by the procedures of the voucher system.

- A company orders 60 items, is sent 70, and is billed for 70. The bill is paid.
- A company orders 60 items at $12 and is billed for 60 items at $12.50. The bill is paid.
- A company receives and pays a bill for 60 items at $12. The bill is paid. The items were never ordered.
- A dishonest accounting clerk issues cheques to a fictitious company and cashes the cheques himself.
- An accounts payable clerk authorizes invoices which contain incorrect prices. She receives a *kick-back* from the supplier.
- An inventory clerk completes requisitions for unnecessary goods. She also receives a kick-back from the supplier.

All of these examples show a lack of control over purchases and payments. *How could this happen? How can it be avoided?* Large companies design systems to control payments so they can be sure that:

- the goods were actually received
- what was received was in fact ordered
- prices charged and terms of payment are correct

The Voucher System

The voucher system is a method used to control payments.

The *voucher system* is a method of controlling all payments. It contains procedures to ensure that:
- prices and calculations on purchase invoices are correct
- all payments are authorized by a responsible person
- items which are paid for have been ordered and received
- payments are charged to the correct accounts
- payments are made on time

A voucher is a form which provides all the important information about a transaction.

The Voucher A *voucher* is a special form that provides detailed information about a specific transaction. The information usually provided on a voucher includes:
- name and address of the supplier
- account to be debited
- account to be credited
- departmental approval
- details of the invoice
- details of payment
- records of the supporting documents

A Voucher Register is a book of original entry in which all approved invoices are recorded.

The Voucher Register In the standard special journal system, a Purchases Journal is used to record all purchases on account. In the voucher system, the *Voucher Register* is used to record *all* purchases including cash and credit purchases.

The Voucher Register can be considered to be a special columnar journal designed for the voucher system. It has special columns so that repetitive transactions may be efficiently recorded. The register usually contains columns for Vouchers Payable (credit), Purchases (debit), and Other Accounts (debit and credit). Additional columns may be provided for any accounts which occur frequently in the company's transactions.

Using the Voucher System

*2

The following description of the voucher system used by Print-O-Matic is an example of how one company controls its purchases using this system. Print-O-Matic received the invoice shown in Figure 16.1 on January 27. The invoice was stamped and initialled to indicate that the price had been checked, the items had been received, the extensions had been checked, and the account to be charged was shown.

*3

Voucher No. 71 shown in Figure 16.2 was prepared from the invoice. The voucher shows that the cheque was issued by the treasurer's office, but the recording of the transaction was done by the accounting department. There were three different departments involved in the completion of the voucher: Accounting, Purchasing, and Treasurer's Office. As well, a number of different people within the departments had specific tasks to perform before payment was made.

SIGNAL

SIGNAL CHEMICALS LIMITED 12 CARLAW AVENUE TORONTO, ONTARIO M4M 2R7 451-8181

WI-60372
PLEASE QUOTE THIS NUMBER WHEN REFERING TO OR PAYING THIS INVOICE.

SOLD TO PRINT-O-MATIC
77 Beverly St.
VICTORIA, British Columbia
V8S 3Z8

SHIPPED TO Same

RECEIVED JAN. 27

Received by	WB
Price O.K.	SZ
Acc't dist.	AB
Ext. correct	DV
O.K. for payment	dB

SHIP VIA	PPD.	COLL.	CUSTOMER'S ORDER NO.	TERMS	SALESPERSON	DATE
Delivery	x		1246	XB-23	O. Smith	01 25 --

NO.	SIZE	TYPE	DESCRIPTION		UNIT	AMOUNT
55	4 L Drums		One-step Hand Cleaner	55	4.00	220.00
			Drum deposit			25.00
			Note: Sales Tax not applicable to drum			
			FEDERAL SALES TAX LICENSE 8329103 AMT.			
			PROVINCIAL SALES TAX LICENSE AMT.			11.00
			SHIPPING CHARGES			
			PLEASE PAY THIS AMOUNT			256.00

DEPOSIT MUST BE PAID FOR WITH THE MERCHANDISE. IT WILL BE REFUNDED IF CONTAINERS ARE RETURNED IN GOOD CONDITION WITHIN 60 DAYS FREIGHT PREPAID.

Figure 16.1 *An invoice that has been received and checked by Print-O-Matic*

No. 71 **PAYMENT VOUCHER**

Purchased from Signal Chemicals
Address 12 Carlaw Ave. Toronto, Ontario M4M 2R7

ACCOUNT DEBITED	AMOUNT
Purchases	
Trans. on Purchases	
Delivery Expense	
Salaries Payable	
Utilities Expense	
Other: Cleaning Supplies	$256
Vouchers Payable Credit	$256

APPROVALS	NAME	DATE
Extensions	Domenica Vena	
Quantities agree with receiving report	Steve Zinic	
Prices agree with P.O.	Steve Zinic	
Payment terms agree with P.O.	A. Bunker	
Accounting Distribution	Alice Belker	
Recorded in Voucher Reg.	R. Dylan	
Recorded in Cheque Reg.	Abe Linklet	

INVOICE DETAILS

Invoice No. WI 60372
Terms Net 30
Due Date or Disc. Date Feb 24
Description Cleaner
Quantity 55 4L cans
Price $4.00 / can
Federal Tax Exempt
Prov. Tax $11
Total $256

PAYMENT DETAILS

Amount of Cheque $256
Cash Discount
Net Amount $256
Paid by Cheque No. 871
Date of Cheque Feb 21
Approved for Payment. (Treasurer's Dept.)

DOCUMENTATION ENCLOSED: Purchase Order ✓ Receiving Report ✓ Purchase Invoice ✓ Cheque Copy ✓

Figure 16.2 *Voucher No. 71 prepared for the invoice in Figure 16.1*

Form of the Voucher The voucher illustrated in Figure 16.2 is actually a file folder with printing on the front. All the documentation concerning a transaction is placed in the voucher file folder. This allows the persons responsible for authorizing the payment of the voucher to check the records of the transaction. For example, Steve Zimic of the Purchasing Department would not sign the voucher unless he saw that the price on the purchase order agreed with the price on the purchase invoice and that the quantities on the purchase invoice, purchase order, and receiving report were the same.

Some of the documents which may be included inside the voucher folder are:

- purchase order copy
- purchase invoice
- receiving report
- cheque copy
- credit invoice
- correspondence concerning the order

A simpler version of the voucher is a sheet of paper with the voucher information printed on it. Supporting documents are clipped or attached to the voucher form. This has obvious disadvantages because documents may become separated from the voucher.

*4

Processing the Voucher After a voucher has been prepared for an invoice, the voucher is recorded in a Voucher Register (Figure 16.3) or a type of journal which replaces the Purchases Journal. The voucher is then filed in a date file under the date on which it will be paid. This date is the *discount date*, if a cash discount is to be taken, or the *due date*. The due date is the date on which the full amount of the invoice must be paid. For example, the terms of the invoice from Signal Chemicals (Figure 16.1) are *Net 30*. Therefore, the invoice must be paid within 30 days from the date on the invoice. Voucher No. 71 would be filed under February 24 in the date file. The supporting documents are filed with the voucher. Figure 16.4 summarizes the processing of the voucher to the point where it is placed in the date file.

*5

Purchase Invoices Payable on Receipt Every payment in a voucher system must be supported by a voucher. If an invoice is received and must be paid immediately, a voucher must be prepared and a cheque issued for payment. The voucher is recorded as paid and filed with the paid vouchers. This ensures that all payments are supported by a voucher.

A voucher is required for all payments.

*6

Payment of the Voucher On February 24, the voucher is pulled from the date file and is presented to the company official who is responsible for authorizing payments. (This may be the company treasurer or another person who is responsible for the bank account and issuing cheques.) Voucher No. 71 has been approved for payment by J. Burrows of the Treasurer's office.

A cheque is prepared payable to Signal Chemicals in the amount of $256. The cheque is then recorded in the *Cheque Register* (Figure 16.5). This is a book of original entry which replaces the Cash Payments Journal.

A Cheque Register is a book of original entry in which all cheques issued are recorded.

DATE		VO. NO.	CREDITOR	PAYMENT DATE	PAYMENT CH. NO.	VOUCHERS PAYABLE CREDIT	PURCHASES DEBIT	TRANS. ON PURCHASES DEBIT	OTHER ACCOUNTS ACCOUNT TITLE	PR	DEBIT	CREDIT
Jan.	4	63	Wilson's Ltd.	14/1	868	56 —			Office Supplies		56 —	
	6	64	Pringle & Son	15/1	869	500 —	500 —					
	8	65	Roadway Transport			76 —		76 —				
	10	66	Chalmers Ltd.			895 —	895 —					
	15	67	Receiver General	15/1	870	120 —			Sales Tax Payable		120 —	
	17	68	C.P.R.			156 —		156 —				
	21	69	Wilson's Ltd.			120 —			Office Furniture		120 —	
	23	70	P. Doyle Co.			2000 —	2000 —					
	27	71	Signal Chemicals	Feb. 24	940	256 —			Cleaning Supplies		256 —	
	28	72	Petty Cash	28/1	871	44 —	16 —	12 —	Misc. Expense		12 —	
									Office Supplies		4 —	
	31	73	Salaries Payable	31/1	872	1992 —			Salaries Payable		1992 —	
			Totals			6215 —	3411 —	244 —			2560 —	

Figure 16.3 *Voucher Register showing the entry for voucher 71*

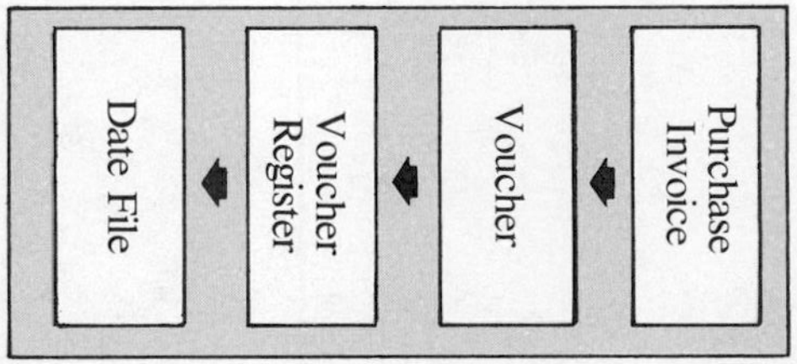

Purchase Invoice → Voucher → Voucher Register → Date File

Figure 16.4
Processing a voucher

CHEQUE REGISTER PAGE

DATE		PAYEE	VO. NO.	VOUCHERS PAYABLE DEBIT	PURCHASES DISCOUNT CREDIT	CASH CREDIT	CH. NO.
19– Jan.	14	Wilson's Ltd.	63	56 —		56 —	868
	15	Pringle & Son	64	500 —	10	490 —	869
	15	Receiver General	67	120 —		120 —	870
	28	Petty Cashier	72	44 —		44 —	871
Feb.	24	Signal Chemicals	71	256 —		256 —	940

Figure 16.5 *Cheque Register showing the entry made on February 24 to pay voucher 71 with cheque No. 940*

The cheque number and date are then recorded in the payment column of the Voucher Register. Any entry in the Voucher Register which does not have a cheque number and date recorded is an unpaid voucher. In Figure 16.3, there are six paid and five unpaid vouchers. Figure 16.6 summarizes all the steps involved in processing the voucher:

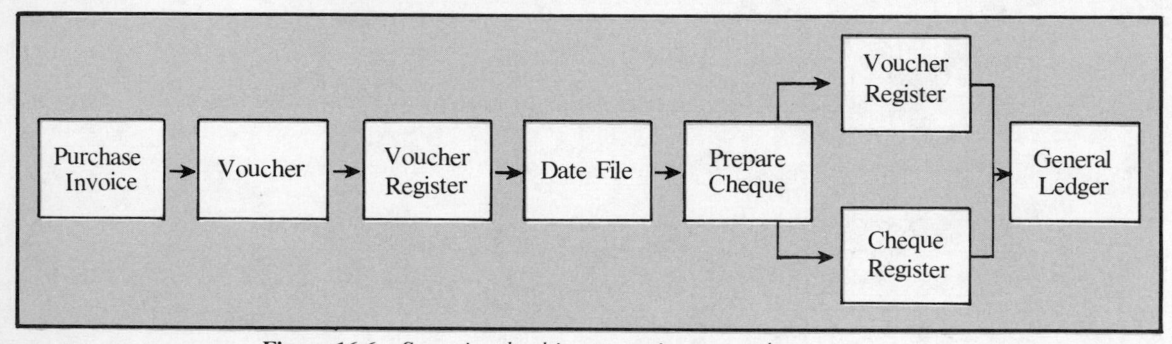

Figure 16.6 *Steps involved in processing a voucher*

*7

In the voucher system, there is no Accounts Payable Ledger.

Lack of an Accounts Payable Ledger Look carefully at the steps involved in the voucher system as summarized in Figure 16.6. *Did you notice that these steps do not include posting to the Accounts Payable Ledger?* One feature of the voucher system is the lack of an Accounts Payable Ledger. There is no individual Account Payable account for each creditor in the voucher system. This can be seen as an advantage because some of the time and effort involved in posting is eliminated.

The lack of individual Account Payable accounts can also be a major disadvantage of the system. Suppose someone wanted to know how much is owing to a certain creditor. To obtain the total owing, it would be necessary to go to the unpaid voucher file and locate all the unpaid vouchers for that particular creditor. This information could also be obtained by totalling the unpaid vouchers in the Voucher Register. However, both of these methods of obtaining information about a creditor are not as convenient as having an up-to-date record in an Accounts Payable Ledger.

Some companies feel it is important to have a historical record of all transactions with their creditors. They keep a separate card for each creditor to record the details of every transaction. A second method of providing information about creditors is to use an alphabetical file. For each creditor, a folder is used to keep a copy of all invoices involving that creditor.

Filing Paid Vouchers A paid voucher will have a cheque number and date recorded on it. The paid voucher and supporting documents are filed in a Paid Vouchers file. Some companies use a paid file for each creditor. Other companies file the paid vouchers numerically according to the voucher number.

Balancing and Posting the Voucher Register

***8**

The Voucher Register is totalled, balanced, and posted at the end of each month.

Like any other columnar journal, each page of the Voucher Register is totalled and cross-balanced to prove the equality of the debits and credits. The totals of each page are carried forward to the next page. At the end of the month the Voucher Register is totalled, balanced, and posted. Posting is done to the General Ledger only. Remember, there is no Accounts Payable Ledger in this system. In the voucher system, the Accounts Payable account is replaced by an account called *Vouchers Payable*. This is a control account in the General Ledger. The two steps followed in posting the Voucher Register are:

The Vouchers Payable account is a control account in the General Ledger.

1. Each entry in the Other Accounts section is posted individually to the General Ledger. The General Ledger account numbers are recorded in the Posting Reference column next to the debit column in the Other Accounts column.
2. The *totals* of the three special columns (Vouchers Payable credit, Purchases debit, and Transportation on Purchases debit) are posted to the General Ledger. The General Ledger account numbers are recorded below the totals in the Voucher Register.

Balancing and Posting the Cheque Register

***9**

The Cheque Register is totalled, balanced, and posted at the end of each month.

The cheque register is totalled and cross-balanced at the end of each page. The totals in the Cheque Register are posted at the end of each month. Since individual transactions are not posted, the posting procedures are very simple:

1. Post the totals of the three columns to the General Ledger.
2. Record the account numbers (posting references) below the register totals.

***10**

The balance in the Vouchers Payable account in the General Ledger must equal the total of the list of unpaid vouchers.

List of Unpaid Vouchers Since there are no individual creditor accounts in the voucher system, there is no need for an Accounts Payable summary (trial balance). Instead, a list is prepared of the unpaid vouchers. The total of the list as shown in Figure 16.7 must equal the Vouchers Payable Control account in the General Ledger. The unpaid vouchers may be obtained from the unpaid voucher file or from the Voucher Register.

Print-O-Matic		
List of Unpaid Vouchers		
January 31, 19--		
Voucher Number	Creditor	Amount
65	Roadway Transport	$ 76.00
66	Chalmers Ltd.	895.00
68	C. P. R.	156.00
69	Wilsons Ltd.	120.00
70	P. Doyle Co.	2 000.00
		$3 247.00

Figure 16.7 *The total of unpaid vouchers must equal the Vouchers Payable Control account in the General Ledger. Look at Figure 16.3 to see how this list of unpaid vouchers was prepared.*

Special Recording Procedures

*11

The voucher system requires special methods for recording purchases returns and allowances, partial payments of invoices, and banking transactions.

Purchases Returns and Allowances On May 9, $300 worth of merchandise was purchased from Signal Chemicals. Voucher No. 193 was completed and recorded in the Voucher Register. The following T-accounts show the debits and credits for this transaction:

Vouchers Payable		Purchases	
	May 9 300	*May 9* 300	

Some of the merchandise was unsatisfactory and had to be returned to Signal Chemicals. On May 16, a credit invoice for $53 was received. The following procedure is used to handle the credit invoice:

1. A new voucher (No. 227) is prepared in the amount of $247 (300 - 53 = 247) since only $247 is now owed.
2. The original voucher (No. 193) for $300 is cancelled. It is marked *Cancelled – replaced by voucher No. 227* and placed in the paid file.
3. The new voucher (No. 227) for $247 is recorded in the Voucher Register by crediting Vouchers Payable $247 and Purchases Returns $53, and debiting Vouchers Payable $300 in the Other Accounts section (Figure 16.8).

VOUCHER REGISTER PAGE

DATE		VO. NO.	CREDITOR	PAYMENT DATE	PAYMENT CH. NO.	VOUCHERS PAYABLE CREDIT	PURCHASES DEBIT	TRANS. ON PURCHASES DEBIT	OTHER ACCOUNTS ACCOUNT TITLE	PR	DEBIT	CREDIT
May 19--	9	193	Signal Chemicals	See Vo.	227	300 —	300 —					
May	16	227	Signal Chemicals			247 —			Vouchers Payable		300 —	
									Purchases Returns			53 —

Figure 16.8 *Recording Purchases Returns and Allowances in the Voucher Register*

4. *See Vo. 227* is written in the Voucher Register in the payment column (beside the old voucher No. 193). In T-account form, these procedures can be summarized as follows:

Vouchers Payable	
May 16 300	*May 9* 300
	16 247

Purchases	
May 9 300	

Purchases Returns	
	May 16 53

Notice that there is no change in the Purchases account. The original $300 in Vouchers Payable has been cancelled and replaced by the new amount owing ($247) and a Purchases Return of $53 has been recorded.

*12

Partial Payments of Invoices If an invoice is to be paid in two separate payments at different times, two vouchers should be prepared, one for each payment. The vouchers are recorded in the Voucher Register and filed according to their payment dates in the unpaid file. Occasionally it is decided to make separate payments *after* the transaction has been recorded on a single voucher. The original voucher should be cancelled and a new voucher prepared for each of the instalment payments.

For example, a purchase of $9 000 was made on May 12 (Figure 16.9). Voucher No. 203 was prepared and recorded in the Voucher Register. The payment date for voucher No. 203 is May 31.

On May 29, an agreement is made with the creditor to make three separate payments of $3 000 on June 10, June 20, and June 30 instead of one payment of $9 000 on May 31. The following steps were taken:

1. On May 29 three new vouchers, No. 251, No. 252, and No. 253, each for $3 000 are prepared.
2. The original voucher (No. 203) is cancelled. It is marked *Cancelled - replaced by Vouchers No. 251, No. 252, and No. 253* and is placed in the paid file.
3. The new vouchers are recorded in the Voucher Register by debiting Vouchers Payable $9 000 in the Other Accounts column and crediting each of the new vouchers in the Vouchers Payable column.
4. A notation *See vouchers 251, 252, 253* is placed in the Voucher Register on the line for Voucher No. 203, the old voucher.

*13

Banking Transactions Occasionally banks add or deduct amounts from depositors' accounts. Some of the reasons for these transactions are: payments for interest earned, interest expense deductions, loan repayments, and service charges. Usually the bank notifies the depositor of these changes by sending debit and credit memos. Service charges on current accounts are noted on the monthly bank statement so a debit memo is not sent to the depositor.

In the voucher system, a voucher must be prepared for each debit memo or deduction by the bank. The voucher is recorded as usual in the Voucher Register (Figure 16.10). A cheque is not issued of course, because the deduction has already been made by the bank. However, the deduction is recorded in the cheque register (Figure 16.11).

VOUCHER REGISTER — PAGE

DATE		VO. NO.	CREDITOR	PAYMENT DATE	PAYMENT CH. NO.	VOUCHERS PAYABLE CREDIT	PURCHASES DEBIT	TRANS. ON PURCHASES DEBIT	OTHER ACCOUNTS ACCOUNT TITLE	PR	DEBIT	CREDIT
May 19–	12	203	Excello Corp.	See Vo. 251, 252, 253		9000 —	9000 —					
	29	251	Excello Corp.			3000 —			Vouchers Payable		9000 —	
		252	Excello Corp.			3000 —						
		253	Excello Corp.			3000 —						

Figure 16.9 *Recording a partial payment of an invoice in the Voucher Register*

VOUCHER REGISTER — PAGE 71

DATE		VO. NO.	CREDITOR	PAYMENT DATE	PAYMENT CH. NO.	VOUCHERS PAYABLE CREDIT	PURCHASES DEBIT	TRANS. ON PURCHASES DEBIT	OTHER ACCOUNTS ACCOUNT TITLE	PR	DEBIT	CREDIT
Sept.	7	91	Scotia Bank	Sept. 5	D.M.	15 —			Bank Charges		15 —	
	30	127	Scotia Bank	Sept. 29	D.M.	2 75			Bank Charges		2 75	

Figure 16.10 *A bank debit memo and a current account service charge recorded in the Voucher Register*

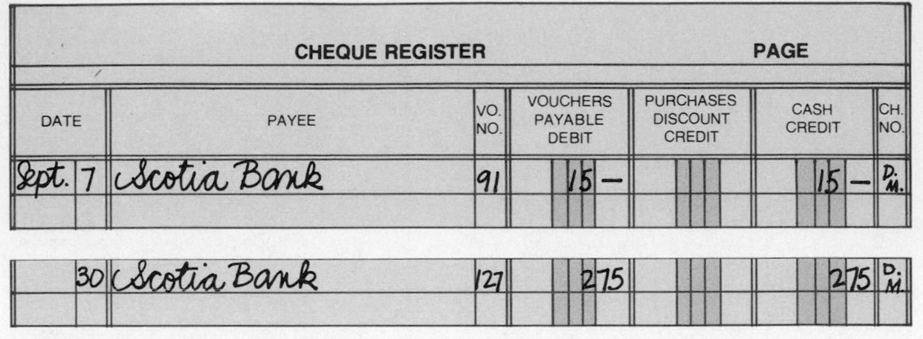

CHEQUE REGISTER PAGE

DATE		PAYEE	VO. NO.	VOUCHERS PAYABLE DEBIT	PURCHASES DISCOUNT CREDIT	CASH CREDIT	CH. NO.
Sept.	7	Scotia Bank	91	15 —		15 —	D.M.
	30	Scotia Bank	127	2 75		2 75	D.M.

Figure 16.11 *In the Voucher System, a bank debit memo and a current account service charge are recorded in the Cheque Register even though no cheque is issued*

Advantages and Disadvantages of the Voucher System

It is important to realize that no accounting system is perfect. If a particular system does suit a business at a particular point in time, the probability remains that there will be a need to alter the system at some stage, as the business grows, or laws affecting it change. Following is a short summary of the advantages and disadvantages of the voucher system.

Advantages of the Voucher System

- Every payment is carefully checked before a cheque is issued.
- The paid voucher contains all the information about a transaction. Related documents are stored in the voucher if it is a file folder type of voucher; or are stapled to the voucher if it is a single sheet.
- Payments are organized so that all cash discounts are received.
- The elimination of the Accounts Payable Ledger reduces the paperwork.
- Opportunities for fraud or dishonesty are minimized.

Disadvantages of the Voucher System

- There is no complete record of transactions with each creditor since there is no Accounts Payable Ledger.
- A voucher is required for *every* payment, thus adding some paperwork.
- Procedures for recording partial payments and purchases returns and allowances are a bit complicated.

Facts to Remember

The *voucher system* is a method used to control payments.

In the *voucher system*, all purchases for cash or on credit require the preparation of a voucher. Every voucher is recorded in the Voucher Register.

A *voucher* is a form which provides all the important information about a transaction.

A *Voucher Register* is a book of original entry in which all approved invoices are recorded.

A *Cheque Register* is a book of original entry in which all cheques issued are recorded.

In the *voucher system,* there is no Accounts Payable Ledger.

The *Voucher Register* is totalled, balanced, and posted at the end of each month.

The *Vouchers Payable* account is a control account in the General Ledger.

The *Cheque Register* is totalled, balanced, and posted at the end of each month.

The balance in the *Vouchers Payable account* in the General Ledger must equal the total of the list of unpaid vouchers.

Reviewing Your Reading

Questions

1. Why do large companies require a system of internal control over payments and purchases?
2. What is a Voucher Register?
3. How are unpaid vouchers filed?
4. What is a Cheque Register?
5. How does the Voucher Register show that a voucher has been paid?
6. Figure 16.3 shows a Voucher Register. What vouchers are shown as having been paid?
7. List advantages and disadvantages of the voucher system.
8. Following is a list of vouchers numbered from 150 to 154. All have been prepared from purchase invoices dated May 10. Calculate the date on which payment should be made and indicate with numbers from 1 to 5 the order in which they will be filed in the unpaid file.

Voucher Number	Terms	Date of Payment	Order of Filing
150	2/10, n/30	________	
151	net 30	________	
152	1/15, n/60	________	
153	e.o.m.	________	
154	net 15	________	

9. Explain why the Vouchers Payable account is a control account.

Applying Your Knowledge

Exercises Part A

1. a) Would you approve this invoice for payment? Why or why not?

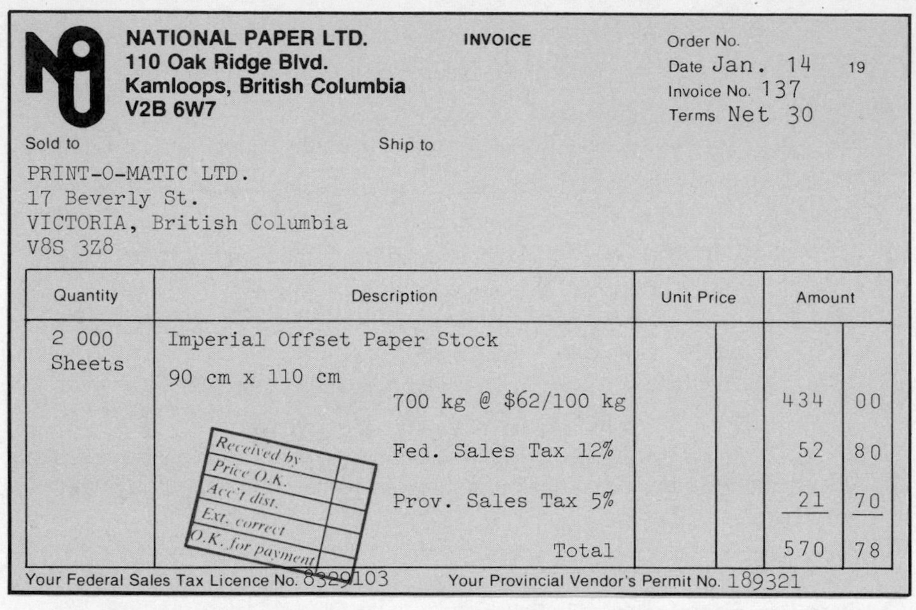

NATIONAL PAPER LTD.
110 Oak Ridge Blvd.
Kamloops, British Columbia
V2B 6W7

INVOICE

Order No.
Date Jan. 14 19
Invoice No. 137
Terms Net 30

Sold to
PRINT-O-MATIC LTD.
17 Beverly St.
VICTORIA, British Columbia
V8S 3Z8

Ship to

Quantity	Description	Unit Price	Amount
2 000 Sheets	Imperial Offset Paper Stock 90 cm x 110 cm		
	700 kg @ $62/100 kg		434 00
	Fed. Sales Tax 12%		52 80
	Prov. Sales Tax 5%		21 70
	Total		570 78

Received by
Price O.K.
Acc't dist.
Ext. correct
O.K. for payment

Your Federal Sales Tax Licence No. 8329103 Your Provincial Vendor's Permit No. 189321

b) What do the federal and provincial sales tax licence numbers indicate?

c) Make the necessary corrections and then prepare a voucher (No. 672) for the invoice.

2. a) Prepare a voucher (No. 673) for Print-O-Matic Ltd. Use the invoice from Wilson Munroe Company and the following information:

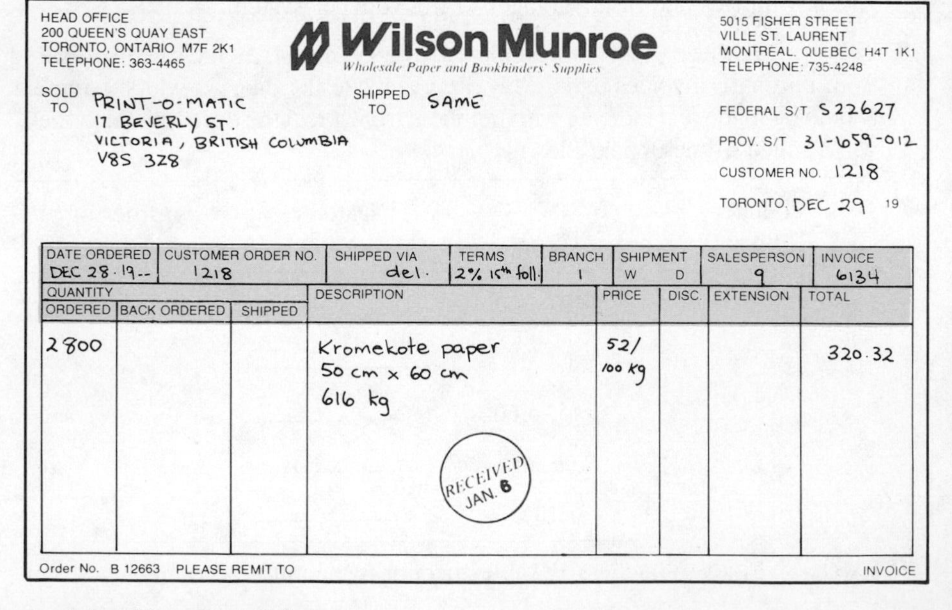

HEAD OFFICE
200 QUEEN'S QUAY EAST
TORONTO, ONTARIO M7F 2K1
TELEPHONE: 363-4465

Wilson Munroe
Wholesale Paper and Bookbinders' Supplies

5015 FISHER STREET
VILLE ST. LAURENT
MONTREAL, QUEBEC H4T 1K1
TELEPHONE: 735-4248

SOLD TO PRINT-O-MATIC
17 BEVERLY ST.
VICTORIA, BRITISH COLUMBIA
V8S 3Z8

SHIPPED TO SAME

FEDERAL S/T S22627
PROV. S/T 31-659-012
CUSTOMER NO. 1218
TORONTO DEC 29 19

DATE ORDERED	CUSTOMER ORDER NO.	SHIPPED VIA	TERMS	BRANCH	SHIPMENT W D	SALESPERSON	INVOICE
DEC 28 19--	1218	del.	2% 15th foll.	1		9	6134

QUANTITY ORDERED	BACK ORDERED	SHIPPED	DESCRIPTION	PRICE	DISC.	EXTENSION	TOTAL
2800			Kromekote paper 50 cm x 60 cm 616 kg	52/100 kg			320.32

RECEIVED JAN. 6

Order No. B 12663 PLEASE REMIT TO INVOICE

- Accounting distribution was authorized by J. Carter
- Cheque number is 372
- Date of cheque is January 15
- Payment approval: W. Shouldice
- Extensions: F. Craig
- Prices: D. Del Rio
- Quantities: J. Backus
- Payment Terms: D. Del Rio
- Voucher Register: J. Carter
- Cheque Register: W. Shouldice

b) How many departments are involved in the processing of this voucher? How many different people?

3. a) A voucher has been prepared for each of the following transactions. Enter the vouchers in a Voucher Register

Sept. 2 Purchased $900 worth of merchandise from Connors Ltd. Invoice dated Aug. 28. Terms 2 /10, n/30. Voucher No. 1.

4 Received an invoice from C.P.R. for freight on incoming goods, $79. Voucher No. 2, terms 10 days.

5 Established a petty cash fund, $100. Voucher No. 3.

9 Purchased $1 500 worth of merchandise from Acres Wholesale. Terms n/30. Voucher No. 4.

11 Purchased $700 worth of office equipment from Evans & Kert Ltd. Terms n/30. Voucher No. 5.

12 Paid freight charges to Direct Transport Ltd. on merchandise purchased, $120. Voucher No. 6.

17 Made a $25 donation to United Appeal (Miscellaneous Expense). Voucher No. 7

19 Received an invoice for office supplies of $119 from Evans & Kert. Terms *on account*. Voucher No. 8.

30 Issued a voucher for salaries, $2 200 (Salaries Payable). Voucher No. 9.

b) Total, balance, and rule the Voucher Register.

4. a) Enter the following cheques in a Cheque Register. This Cheque Register accompanies the Voucher Register in exercise 3. Enter the date and cheque number in the Voucher Register when cheques are issued.

Sept. 5 Issued cheque No. 1 to the petty cashier, $100 for voucher No. 3

6 Issued cheque No. 2 to Connors Ltd., $882 for voucher No. 1.

12 Issued cheque No. 3 to Direct Transport for voucher No. 6

14 Issued cheque No. 4 to C.P.R. for voucher No. 2.

17 Issued cheque No. 5 to the United Appeal for voucher No. 7.

21 Issued cheque No. 6 to Evans & Kert for voucher No. 8

30 Issued cheque No. 7 to Payroll for voucher No. 9.

b) Total, balance, and rule the Cheque Register.

5. a) Prepare a General Ledger with these accounts:

ACCOUNT TITLE	ACC. NO.	DEBIT	CREDIT
Cash	100	5 000 —	
Petty Cash	101		
Office Supplies	131		
Office Equipment	141		
Automotive Equipment	142	30 000 —	
Vouchers Payable	200		
Bank Loan	220		3 000 —
Salaries Payable	222		2 200 —
J. Branscombe, Capital	300		29 800 —
Purchases	500		
Purchases Discounts	501		
Transportation on Purchases	502		
Miscellaneous Expense	601		

b) Post the Voucher Register from exercise 3 to the General Ledger.
c) Post the Cheque Register from exercise 4 to the General Ledger.
d) From the Voucher Register, prepare a list of unpaid vouchers.
e) Prepare a General Ledger trial balance.

Exercises Part B

6. a) Enter the transactions in a Voucher Register and a Cheque Register.

May 1 Issued voucher No. 101 to Regal Trust for rent, $700. Issued cheque No. 90.

3 Bought merchandise from Greer Ltd. for $1 200. Invoice dated May 1. Terms 1/10 n/30. Voucher No. 102.

5 Received an invoice from Gary's Service Station for gas and oil for company vehicles, $120. Issued a cheque.

8 Bought merchandise from R. Wilson & Sons for $750. Invoice dated May 3. Terms 3/10, n/30.

10 Received freight bill from C.N.R. for transportation on purchases, $131.50. Issued cheque.

12 Paid voucher 102.

15 Received invoice for new office desk for $375. Terms cash. Issued cheque to Office Analysts Ltd.

15 Issued cheque to Receiver General of Canada, $450 for last month's payroll deductions; Income Tax, $260; C.P.P. $92, U.I. $98.

May 16 Received a $100 credit invoice for goods returned to R. Wilson & Sons, on invoice dated May 3.

19 Received freight bill from Wallace Transport for incoming purchases, $76.75.

19 Issued voucher No. 110 to replenish the petty cash fund, $46. (Summary of payments: Office Supplies $14; Miscellaneous Expense $23; Transportation on Purchases, $9). Issued cheque.

22 Issued a cheque to the provincial treasurer, $765 for sales tax collected last month.

24 Bought merchandise from Pringle & Son for $1 800. Invoice dated May 19. Terms net 30.

26 Received an invoice from Frangione Cartage, $96 for deliveries to customers.

30 Issued voucher to pay salaries, $2 800. Issued cheque.

b) Total, balance, and rule the registers.
c) Head up a T-account for Vouchers Payable. Post both registers to this T-account.
d) Prepare a list of unpaid vouchers.

7. a) Record the following in Voucher and Cheque registers:

Dec. 1 Prepare voucher No. 133 to S. Symons, $500 for rent. Issued cheque No. 121.

3 Received invoice of goods from M. Chalmers, $1 375. Invoice dated Dec. 1. Terms 2/10 n/30.

5 Purchased goods from Bachman Overly Ltd. for $1 545. Invoice dated Dec. 2, terms n/30.

8 Received credit invoice from M. Chalmers for $39 for goods returned.

9 Prepared a voucher for $100 to establish a petty cash fund. Issued a cheque.

12 Negotiated an agreement with Bachman Overly Ltd. concerning their invoice dated Dec. 2. Terms n/30. $500 will be paid to Bachman Overly Ltd. on Dec. 15 and the balance on January 31.

13 Issued cheque to M. Chalmers Ltd. for voucher No. 136.

15 Issued cheque for $500 to Bachman Overly.

19 Received an invoice for merchandise from Brooks Ltd. for $700. Payment will be made in two instalments: $500 on Dec. 31 and $200 on Feb. 28.

23 Received a $156 freight bill for incoming merchandise from Intercity Transport.

29 Issued cheque and voucher to replenish petty cash, $94. (Summary of payments: Delivery Expense $14; Office Supplies Expense $36; Advertising Expense $29; Miscellaneous Expense $15.)

b) Total and rule the registers.
c) Head up a T-account for Vouchers Payable. Post both registers to this T-account.
d) Prepare a list of unpaid vouchers.

8. a) Record these transactions in Voucher and Cheque Registers:

July 1 Purchase invoices for merchandise:
W. McDonald Ltd., $500, terms n/30.
P. Doyle Co., $1 200, terms $200 cash, balance in 60 days.
Issued vouchers No. 1, No. 2, and No. 3 and cheque No. 1

7 Credit invoice for incorrect merchandise, $125 from W. McDonald Ltd.

10 Bank debit memo:
$175 bank charges for payroll services.

12 Purchase invoices: G. Wiens Designs Ltd., $800 for office furniture, terms cash, issued cheque.
T. Murphy Inc. for merchandise, $9 000, terms $1 000 cash, $4 000 in 30 days, $4 000 in 60 days, issued cheque.

15 Bank debit memo:
$25 bank charges for preparing a credit rating on a prospective customer.

16 Purchase invoices for merchandise:
J. Amireault Co., $490, terms n/30.
J. Andrews & Sons, $795, terms 2/10 n/30.

20 Credit invoice for defective goods, $95 from J. Amireault Co.

26 Issued a cheque to pay for voucher No. 12.

30 Issued a voucher for $4.50 bank charges. This amount has been deducted by the bank. Record the payment in the cheque register.

b) Total, balance, and rule the registers.
c) Open a T-account for Vouchers Payable. Post the registers to the T-account.

Exercises Part C

9. a) B. Neeb and Associates employ a voucher system. Record the following transactions in Voucher and Cheque Registers. The next voucher is No. 66.

Feb. 1 Purchase invoices for merchandise:
Snetsinger Ltd., $1 710, terms n/30.
Babcock Corp., $1 400, terms 2/10, n/30.
Prepared vouchers No. 66 and No. 67.

7 Purchase invoice for electronic calculators from K. Towsley Ltd., $875 plus $45 shipping charges (Miscellaneous Expense).

11 Paid Babcock Corp. $980 on their Feb. 1 invoice. Discount taken $20. Balance of $400 is being disputed because of quality of goods Issued cheque No. 51.

Feb. 15 Received an allowance of $175 from K. Towsley Ltd. because calculators do not perform one of the stipulated functions. Credit invoice received today.

16 Purchased display equipment from L. Jones Equipment for $4 500. Cash payment of $1 500 made with balance due in 30 and 60 days in two equal instalments.

16 Issued cheque to Receiver General for January payroll deductions (Income Tax, $760; C.P.P., $76; U.I., $92).

20 Issued a cheque and voucher for $670 to the provincial treasurer for January collections.

21 Received a credit invoice of $300 from Babcock Corp. as an allowance for poor quality goods on invoice dated Feb. 1.

23 Issued cheque $100 in full payment of balance owing to Babcock Corp.

23 Purchased merchandise for $760 from S. Gyme Ltd., terms 3/10, n/30.

25 Received an invoice for $160 for transportation on purchases from C.N.R., terms n/30.

28 Received a bank statement showing service charges of $1.75 and a debit memo of $160 (interest on loan).

28 Issued cheque to S. Gyme Ltd. in payment of Feb. 23 invoice.

28 Issued cheque and voucher for monthly salaries, $4 900.

b) Total, balance, and rule the registers.
c) Open a T-account General Ledger containing these accounts: Cash $16 598; Office Equipment; Display Equipment; Vouchers Payable; Income Tax Payable $760 (credit); C.P.P. Payable $76 (credit); U.I. Payable $92 (credit); Sales Tax Payable $670 (credit); Salaries Payable $4 900 (credit); B. Neeb, Capital $10 100; Purchases; Purchases Discounts; Purchases Returns and Allowances; Transportation on Purchases; Bank Charges Expense; Miscellaneous Expense.
d) Post the registers to the T-account ledger and prepare a trial balance.
e) Prepare a list of unpaid vouchers.

10. The post-closing trial balance of the R. Harkness Corp. follows:

R. Harkness Corp.
Post-Closing Trial Balance
December 31, 19__

ACCOUNT TITLE	ACC. NO.	DEBIT	CREDIT
Cash	100	9 600 —	
Petty Cash	101	100 —	
Inventory	110	22 000 —	
Office Supplies	120	600 —	
Equipment	131	16 000 —	
Vouchers Payable	200		
Sales Tax Payable	201		700 —
Income Tax Payable	202		990 —
C.P.P. Payable	203		180 —
U.I. Payable	204		230 —
Salaries Payable	205		—
Bank Loan	220		6 000 —
R. Harkness, Capital	300		40 200 —
R. Harkness, Drawing	301		
Sales	400		
Purchases	500		
Transportation on Purchases	501		
Purchases Returns and Allowances	502		
Purchases Discounts	503		
Salaries Expense	600		
Selling Expense	601		
Office Expense	602		
Bank Charges Expense	603		
		48 300 —	48 300 —

Harkness Corp. uses these books of original entry: Voucher Register, Cheque Register, Payroll Journal, and General Journal.

a) Selected transactions for January follow. Record them in the appropriate book of original entry.

Jan. 3 Purchase invoices for merchandise:
Westco Ltd., $900, terms 2/10, n/30, (voucher No. 1).
Hamilton Supply, $1 200, terms 2/10, n/30.
Norco Ltd., $1 450, terms $500 immediately, balance on Jan. 25.

5 Received invoice for freight charges on incoming goods for $225 from Overnight Express.

7 Cash Sales to date $4 000. Sales tax on taxable sales, $170. Total $4 170.

7 Credit invoice received from Westco Ltd., $200 for defective goods refused on delivery of January 3.

Jan. 12 Issued cheque No. 2 for office supplies from Office Associates Ltd., $175.

13 Issued cheque to Hamilton Supply for voucher No. 2.

15 Cash Sales $6 700. Sales tax $295. Total $6 995.

15 Issued cheque and voucher to the Receiver General for December deductions for C.P.P., U.I., and Income Tax. Total $1 400.

15 Issued voucher and cheque to the Provincial Treasurer for $700 to remit the sales tax collected in December.

18 Issued voucher and cheque to Francis Fuels for $270 Office Expenses (heat).

19 Received a bank debit memo, $10.50 for loan interest. Issued voucher.

21 Received purchase invoice No. 780 for merchandise from Norco Ltd. $350. Terms n/30.

22 Received an invoice for radio advertisements from CFRB, $780. Terms n/20 (Selling Expense).

22 Cash Sales $7 403. Sales tax $357. Total $7 760.

25 Issued cheque for voucher No. 4

28 Replenished petty cash. (Summary of payments: Selling Expense $45; Office Expense $31; R. Harkness, Drawing $22.) Issued cheque and voucher for $98.

28 Paid Westco Ltd. for voucher No. 6

29 Purchase invoice No. 370 for merchandise from C. Kraft, $675, terms n/60.

30 Received the bank statement which indicated service charges of $4.50 had been deducted from the company bank account.

30 Issued cheque and voucher for salaries payable, $2 485.

30 Issued cheque and voucher to R. Harkness for the owner's salary, $2 000.

30 Cash Sales, $8 309; Sales tax $435. Total $8 744.

b) Total, balance, and rule the books of original entry.

c) The Payroll Journal has the following totals:

Salaries Expense	$3 500	(DR.)
C.P.P. Payable	150	(CR.)
U.I. Payable	165	(CR.)
Salaries Payable	2 485	(CR.)
Income Tax Payable	700	(CR.)

Post these totals to the General Ledger.

d) Record the employer's share of the C.P.P. and U.I. in the General Journal.

e) Post all journals to the General Ledger.

f) Prepare a trial balance and a list of unpaid vouchers.

g) Prepare an income statement and a balance sheet. The ending inventory is $20 500.

Accounting in Action

Case 1

Designing Accounting Forms Assume that you work for a fairly small company which is owned by one person, D. Ryan. At a recent business meeting Ryan heard about the voucher system and is impressed by the control procedures built into the system. Ryan suggests that you develop procedures similar to the voucher system.

Your task is to create a voucher form similar to the one in Figure 16.2. However, your firm is fairly small and involves only a few employees in Accounting and Purchasing transactions. One person in the Accounting Department (not yourself) records all purchases and payments. One person handles the purchasing function in the Purchasing Department. You are responsible for all payments and your signature as well as Ryan's is required on all cheques.

Design a voucher form which is at least one third the size of the one in Figure 16.2. Remember that you work for a smaller firm. You may make any assumptions you wish about your firm's accounting system.

Case 2

Variations of the Voucher System Your company uses a voucher system similar to the one described in this chapter. A friend of yours is an accountant with Metropolitan Life Insurance. Your friend claims that Metropolitan uses a form of the voucher system.

a) Read the Metropolitan Life Insurance case study in Chapter 10.
b) Compare Metropolitan's system to the voucher system described in this chapter.
   i) How is it similar?
   ii) In what ways is it different?

Case 3

The Voucher System and Fraud It is claimed that the voucher system makes it almost impossible for one person in the accounting department of a business to be successful in defrauding a business by authorizing phony invoices for payment. Is this so? Give reasons for your answer.

Case 4

The Voucher System and the Computer J. Enns, a data processing specialist, claims that the voucher system is outdated. Enns says that the computer can handle purchases and payments automatically and that the voucher system is unnecessary. Present arguments against Enn's claims.

Case 5

Financial Control The Brandon Mfg. Co. is a very large firm with sales of about $100 000 000 a year. It uses a form of the voucher system for internal control of purchases and payments.

Purchase invoices are approved by the purchasing department after they have been matched with the receiving report and purchase order. The accounting department checks the mathematical accuracy of the invoice, prepares a voucher, and requests a cheque on the due date of the invoice. Cheques are issued by the treasurer of the company, who receives the voucher and all supporting documents.

Jack is a senior member of the Purchasing Department and Jean is the senior accountant. They approve and record the invoices and vouchers. Jack and Jean have concocted a "get rich" scheme. They have agreed to approve phony invoices for inflated amounts for two of their major suppliers. In return, they will get kick-backs.

Their scheme will probably not work. Describe why they will be caught.

Case 6

Accounting System Analysis Gelder Construction makes numerous purchases from only a few creditors. Each creditor offers a cash discount. One voucher folder is prepared each month for each creditor and all the invoices from a particular creditor are placed in the one voucher folder.

Once a month the total of all invoices in the folder is recorded in the Voucher Register. One large cheque is then issued. This cheque covers all the month's invoices in the voucher folder.

What are the advantages and disadvantages of this system?

Career Profile

Keeping the Books Muriel Pue has worked for Griff Building Supplies of Coquitlam, British Columbia for the last 15 years. During this period, sales of the business have climbed from $35 000 a year to a figure 10 times that amount. Muriel is responsible for all the accounting functions of the company. Her job responsibilities can basically be divided into five segments:

- *Accounts Receivable* Delivery slips are matched with purchase invoices to insure accuracy before the goods are priced and put on display in the store or lumber yard.
- *Accounts Payable* Invoices received by mail from suppliers are matched with the delivery slips and purchase orders and recorded using a one-write system. Cheques and payment records are also recorded on the one-write board.
- *Payroll* The 14 employees are paid twice a month with the necessary payroll deductions being calculated at the end of each month.
- *Cash Sales* Cash sales are recorded daily.
- *Planning* Short and long range cash requirements are computed by comparing accounts receivable to accounts payable, taking into account customer paying habits which range from 30 to 120 days.

What kind of experience is required for this type of job? In high school, Muriel specialized in commercial subjects with a stress on consumer mathematics. On graduation, Muriel began work in retail sales for a large department store, quickly rising to the position of buyer. Marriage and a family took her out of the business world for a number of years, but when Muriel's brother started Griff Building Supplies she was asked to keep the books for the new company. "I was a bit rusty at first, but with the help of a six-month night-school course in accounting I was soon able to handle the job without any problems. The business has been a great success and I like to think that I have done my share."

In Muriel's opinion, the current accounting system is able to efficiently handle the volume of business being generated. She can see the day, however, when the growth of Griff Building Supplies will require conversion to an automated accounting machine and eventually a computer system. When that time comes it will be back to night school to learn about the latest techniques!

CHAPTER 17

Completing the Accounting Cycle

Unit 40

Purpose of Accounting

*1

The basic accounting cycle was introduced in the first seven chapters of this text. Chapters 8 to 16 described special accounting systems and control procedures. In Chapters 17 and 18, the accounting procedures performed at the end of the accounting cycle will be introduced. These procedures include *adjustments, financial statements,* and *closing the books*.

*2

One of the main purposes of accounting is to provide information for decision-making. The information is presented in the form of financial statements. If decisions are to be made based on data on the financial statements, it is essential that the statements be as accurate as possible.

It is not enough that the debits equal the credits and that the statements are mathematically correct. All revenue and expenses must be recorded. All asset, liability, and equity account balances must be correct. The purpose of *adjusting the books* is to ensure that the accounts and the financial statements are accurate.

Adjustments are necessary so that the financial statements are correct.

Investors often base decisions about whether they should buy or sell a company's shares on the results shown on the financial statements. Banks and other lending agencies decide whether or not to grant loans to a company because of the figures on the financial statements. Governments accept or reject tax returns because of financial statements. Managers make many decisions about running their companies as a result of what appears on the financial statements.

Therefore, it is important that the financial statements be accurate. The balance sheet must show the true value of all the assets, liabilities, and equity accounts at the end of the fiscal period. The income statement must show the true value of all the revenue and expenses for the fiscal period it covers.

Adjusting the Books

*3

Suppose that employees work overtime or earn bonuses which have not been recorded by the end of the fiscal period. *What will be wrong with the financial statements*? Both the income statement and the balance sheet will be incorrect. The expenses will be too low because the Salaries Expense does not include the overtime. The liabilities will be incorrect because the debt owing to the workers, Salaries Payable, will not be shown on the balance sheet.

It is necessary to *adjust* the books to ensure that all accounts have the correct balances. In this chapter, some of the accounts of a business called Management Consultant Services will be examined and the adjustments to the accounts, which are required before the financial statements are prepared, will be described. J. Turner is the owner of Management Consultant Services. This business provides management advice to other companies and is located in a rented office. The rental lease requires that rent of $700 a month be paid in advance for three months.

On April 1, a cheque for $2 100 was issued in payment of the April, May, and June rents. Because the rent was being paid in advance for three months, Rent Expense was *not* debited. Instead, an account called Prepaid Rent was debited.

Prepaid Expenses

*4

Payments made in advance for items such as rent, insurance, and supplies are called *prepaid expenses*. Often, the payments are made in advance for more than one fiscal period. Prepaid expenses are items of value. They are assets. They generally appear in the current asset section of the balance sheet.

*5

Prepaid expenses are expense payments made in advance.

Prepaid expenses are current assets.

At the end of April, Management Consultant Services prepares financial statements covering one month. *Should Prepaid Rent be shown as a current asset with a value of $2 100?* The answer is no. After one month, one third of the asset, Prepaid Rent, has been used. The business has used up one third, or $700, of the value of the prepaid rent. The value of the prepaid rent must be reduced by $700 if the asset, Prepaid Rent, is to be correct. It is now worth $1 400, not $2 100.

Furthermore, since $700 of the rent has been used, an expense of $700 must be recorded. The following entry, called an *adjusting entry*, is made:

April	30	Rent Expense		700 —	
		Prepaid Rent			700 —
		To record one month's Rent Expense			

This adjusting entry has two effects:

- It records the Rent Expense for April
- It decreases the asset, Prepaid Rent, by $700

The entry in T-account form is:

Prepaid Rent		Rent Expense	
April 1 2 100	*April 30* 700	*April 30* 700	
Balance 1 400			

*6

When the financial statements for the month ended April 30 are prepared, Rent Expense of $700 will be shown on the income statement. Prepaid Rent of $1 400 will appear on the balance sheet. If this adjusting entry is not made, the expenses would be too low and as a result, the net income would be too high. Also, the assets would be too high.

*7

Supplies The Supplies account is another prepaid asset. During the month of April, supplies worth $900 were purchased by Management Consultant Services. These supplies will last for several fiscal periods.

Each working day in April, small amounts of the supplies were used up. The Supplies account was not decreased because it would be time-consuming and inconvenient to record a decrease in the Supplies account every time supplies were used. Thus, the Supplies account was deliberately allowed to become incorrect. However, at the end of April when financial statements were prepared, the Supplies account was adjusted. This is how it is done.

First, a count of all supplies *left* on April 30 is made. The value of the unused supplies is $600. Then, the amount of supplies *used* is determined by this calculation:

Supplies *purchased*	$900
Less: Supplies *left*	600
Supplies *used*	$300

Supplies Expense is the value of supplies used.

The value of supplies used is the Supplies Expense. The asset Supplies should be decreased by the amount used. The following adjusting entry is made:

April	30	Supplies Expense		300 —	
		Supplies			300 —
		To adjust the Supplies account			
		and to record the Supplies			
		Expense for the month			

The effect of this adjusting entry is shown in these T-accounts:

Supplies

Debit		Credit	
April 2	900	*April 30*	300
Balance	600		

Supplies Expense

Debit		Credit
April 30	300	

When the April 30 financial statements are prepared, the asset Supplies, with a value of $600, appears on the balance sheet. The Supplies Expense of $300 appears on the income statement.

*8

Prepaid Insurance On April 1, a comprehensive insurance policy covering fire, theft, and accidental damage to all office furniture and equipment is purchased. The cost of the insurance for one year is $240.

At the end of April, one month's insurance has been used and must be recorded as an expense. The cost of one month's insurance is 1/12 of $240, or $20. This adjusting entry is made:

April	30	Insurance Expense		20 —	
		Prepaid Insurance			20 —
		To record one month's			
		Insurance Expense and to			
		decrease the asset Prepaid			
		Insurance			

The effect of this adjusting entry is shown in these T-accounts:

Prepaid Insurance

Debit	Credit
April 1 240	*April 30* 20
Balance 220	

Insurance Expense

Debit	Credit
April 30 20	

On the April financial statements, Prepaid Insurance of $220 appears on the asset section of the balance sheet. Insurance Expense of $20 appears on the income statement.

Depreciation

Management Consultant Services purchased office equipment for $12 000. This purchase is recorded by decreasing Cash and increasing the fixed asset account Equipment.

*9

The equipment will be used to help operate the business. Typewriters, calculators, duplicating machines, and dictaphones are only some of the equipment used by companies. Such equipment is necessary for the operation of most businesses.

Early in this text you learned a simple definition of an expense: money spent on things used to operate a business over the years. Since the equipment is *used up* in operating the business, it does in some way contribute to the expenses of the business. For example, Management Consultant Services may estimate that the equipment purchased will probably last for five years. After that time, it will be worthless. The $12 000 spent on the equipment will have been used up.

An expense is money spent on things used to operate a business.

However, the equipment does not suddenly become worthless – it loses value each year. The cost of the equipment should be assigned or allocated as an expense to each year's operation. Each year, part of the equipment cost should become an expense.

*10

Depreciation is the allocation of the cost of an asset to the fiscal periods in which it is used.

Depreciation is an expense and appears on the income statement.

Depreciation Expense The assignment of costs, or division of the initial cost over the life of the asset, is called *depreciation*. By dividing the initial cost ($12 000) over the life (five years) of the equipment, the depreciation figure would be $2 400 each year. This assumes that the equipment is worthless after five years and has no *scrap value* or *trade-in value*.

The allocation of the cost of assets is recorded in an expense account called Depreciation Expense. The depreciation or *using up of fixed assets* is an expense of operating a business.

The entry to record the depreciation of the equipment is:

Dec.	31	Depreciation Expense: Equipment		2 400 —	
		Accumulated Depreciation:			
		Equipment			2 400 —
		To record depreciation for			
		the year			

After this entry has been posted, there are three accounts relating to the equipment and its depreciation:

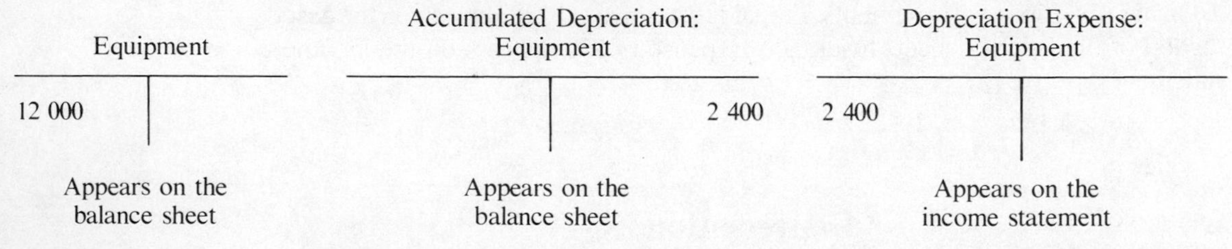

*11

Accumulated Depreciation appears on the balance sheet.

The Depreciation Expense account will appear on the income statement in the expense section. Both Equipment and Accumulated Depreciation: Equipment appear on the balance sheet. They are in the fixed assets section. Accumulated Depreciation is a deduction from Equipment as shown in the partial balance sheet in Figure 17.1.

Management Consultant Services Partial Balance Sheet December 31, 19__		
Fixed Assets		
Equipment	12 000 00	
Less: Accumulated Depreciation	2 400 00	9 600 00

Figure 17.1 *Accumulated Depreciation appears in the fixed assets section of the balance sheet.*

Accumulated Depreciation Account You might ask why it is necessary to use an Accumulated Depreciation account. *Why not simply credit Equipment to show the decrease in its value*? The use of the Accumulated Depreciation account as well as the asset account, Equipment, provides two types of information. One is the *original cost* of the equipment. This is found in the asset account, Equipment. The other is the *total amount of depreciation* recorded over the years. The Accumulated Depreciation account is sometimes called a *valuation account* because it is used to arrive at the value of an asset.

There is a separate Depreciation Expense account and a separate Accumulated Depreciation account for each group of fixed assets such as Buildings, Equipment, Delivery Trucks, and Machinery. Once an asset has been depreciated 100%, no further depreciation is allowed. Suppose an asset cost $10 000 and, over the years, 20% was deducted each year. When the Accumulated Depreciation account reaches $10 000, no further depreciation is available.

Depreciation is not Valuation In Figure 17.1, a current figure of $9 600 is shown for the equipment. This does *not* mean that the equipment is worth $9 600. It does *not* mean the equipment can be sold for $9 600. The figures simply mean:

*12

- that the equipment *cost* $12 000
- that depreciation of $2 400 has been recorded
- that $9 600 remains to be depreciated

The term *book value* is used to describe the $9 600 undepreciated cost.

Book Value When an asset is purchased it is recorded at its cost price. Each year, depreciation builds up in the Accumulated Depreciation account. The book value of the asset is the cost minus the accumulated depreciation. This value is the value according to the books of the company. It is not the *actual* value, which is the amount received if the asset is sold.

Book value is the cost of an asset minus the accumulated depreciation.

Methods of Calculating Depreciation

There are several methods for calculating depreciation. The two methods that will be discussed in this chapter are:

*13

- straight-line method
- declining-balance method, fixed percentage

Straight-line Method A widely used method of calculating depreciation is the *straight-line method*. As shown in Figure 17.1, the equipment depreciated $2 400 a year. After five years, a total of $12 000 depreciation will have been recorded (5 x 2 400 = 12 000). Each year the same amount of depreciation, or $2 400, is recorded. The table in Figure 17.2 summarizes the calculation of depreciation by the straight-line method.

The straight-line method of depreciation allocates the same amount of depreciation to each fiscal period.

Depreciation Schedule – Equipment
Straight-Line Method

Year	Calculation	Depreciation Expense	Accumulated Depreciation
1	20% × 12 000	$ 2 400	$ 2 400
2	20% × 12 000	2 400	4 800
3	20% × 12 000	2 400	7 200
4	20% × 12 000	2 400	9 600
5	20% × 12 000	2 400	12 000
		$12 000	

Figure 17.2 *Depreciation by the straight-line method*

*14

The declining balance method of depreciation allocates a greater amount of depreciation to the first years of an asset's life.

Declining-balance Method, Fixed Percentage The straight-line method of depreciation allocates an equal amount of depreciation to each fiscal period. It can be argued that this is not accurate because depreciation is greatest in the first few years of an asset's life. For example, an automobile's depreciation is greatest in its first year.

A greater amount of depreciation is allocated to the first years when the *declining-balance method* is used. Suppose that equipment, worth $12 000, is depreciated using the declining-balance method. Each year, a fixed percentage, for example 20%, of the *declining balance* is charged. Here is how it works.

The table in Figure 17.3 shows the calculation of depreciation using the declining-balance method.

Depreciation Schedule – Equipment
Declining-Balance Method

Year	Undepreciated Cost	Amount of Depreciation 20%	Declining Balance, End of Year
1	12 000	2 400	9 600
2	9 600	1 920	7 680
3	7 680	1 536	6 144
4	6 144	1 228.80	4 915.20
5	4 915.20	983.04	3 932.16

Figure 17.3 *Depreciation by the declining-balance method*

Notice that each year as the asset grows older, the depreciation is smaller. The cost of the fixed asset is never completely written off as long as the asset is being used. However, each year's depreciation is progressively smaller.

*15

Journal Entries for the Declining-balance Method The adjusting entry used for the declining-balance method of depreciation is the same as for the straight-line method. Only the amount differs.

Year 1	Depreciation Expense: Equipment		2400 —	
	Accumulated Depreciation:			
	Equipment			2400 —
	To record the first year's			
	depreciation			
Year 2	Depreciation Expense: Equipment		1920 —	
	Accumulated Depreciation:			
	Equipment			1920 —
	To record the second year's			
	depreciation using the			
	declining-balance method			

Depreciation and Income Taxes Two methods of calculating depreciation have been described. However, for income tax purposes in Canada, the declining-balance method must be used. This method is called *capital cost allowance* under the Income Tax Act.

*16

For income tax purposes, depreciation is called capital cost allowance.

The maximum percentage of depreciation (capital cost allowance), as well as the method used, is controlled by the government. Assets are grouped into classes and a maximum percentage of depreciation allowed for income tax purposes is set for each class. A few of the classes are shown in Figure 17.4.

Class	Capital Cost Allowance Description of Asset	Maximum Percentage
3	Buildings of brick, stone, cement	5%
6	Buildings of frame, log, stucco, galvanized or corrugated iron	10%
8	Machinery and equipment	20%
10	Trucks, tractors, automobiles, trailers, buses, wagons	30%

Figure 17.4 *Depreciation for income tax purposes*

Figure 17.4 describes only a few assets and their maximum percentage rates of capital cost allowance. The income tax regulations provide a listing of all types of assets and the classes to which they belong. The rates vary from 5% a year for Class 1 to 100% for Classes 12, 23, and 25. Class 1 includes items such as bridges and airplane runways. Class 12 includes tools and dental instruments costing less than $100.

It is important to note that land is not depreciable. For income tax purposes, a business may not claim depreciation expense (capital cost allowance) on land. It is

Land is not depreciable.

also important to remember that, except for a few isolated items such as fishing and farming assets, the straight-line method may not be used for income tax purposes. The declining-balance method, called capital cost allowance in the Income Tax Act, must be used for any depreciation expense used as an income tax expense.

The capital cost allowance regulations under the Income Tax Act set out the *maximum* amount of depreciation expense which may be deducted for income tax purposes. However, a company may decide to use no depreciation in a particular year. *Can you think of a situation in which a business might decide to use no depreciation expense?*

A business does not have to use depreciation expense.

Suppose a business is having a poor year. The accountant knows that a loss will be suffered even without including depreciation as an expense. The accountant may decide to save the year's depreciation expense and use it in future years. If the company suffers a loss during the year, no income tax will be payable for that year. In future years, when the business operates profitably, the depreciation expense will be available to decrease the net income and thus to reduce income taxes.

A company may use any amount of depreciation *up to the allowable amount* for each class of asset (Figure 17.4). The amount of depreciation used in a particular year is often determined by the estimated profits or losses and the estimated income tax.

Two Sets of Books!!! Business people are often sarcastically accused of having two sets of books – one for themselves and one for the government. In certain circumstances, it is legal to have separate records of the same business results. The following are examples.

An accountant feels that the straight-line method of calculating depreciation is the best method. It allots the same amount of depreciation to each fiscal period. The straight-line method, therefore, is used on the company's books. For income tax purposes, the accountant must use the capital cost allowance (declining-balance) method. This means that the net income which is reported to the government is different from the net income on the company books. The difference is caused by the use of the two methods of calculating depreciation.

Another example involves the amount of depreciation expense recorded each year. Suppose a company foresees a loss at the end of the year. It might record depreciation on its books. But in order to save income tax on future net income, it might choose *not* to show any depreciation on its income tax return. This will save depreciation for future years.

So you see, it is possible to have two sets of books – legally.

Unit 41

*17

Adjustments on the Work Sheet and Financial Statements

So far in this chapter you have learned:
- that adjustments are necessary if financial statements are to be correct
- how to adjust prepaid expenses such as Supplies, Rent, and Insurance
- how to adjust fixed assets by recording Depreciation Expense

In this part of the chapter, you will learn how the adjustments are prepared on the work sheet and how the financial statements are prepared.

Adjustments are first prepared on the work sheet.

The Eight-Column Work Sheet

The trial balance for Management Consultant Services is shown in Figure 17.5 on an eight-column work sheet. In Chapter 6, you learned how a six-column work sheet is used to help organize the financial statements. The trial balance is written on a work sheet. The accounts on the trial balance are then transferred to either the income statement section or the balance sheet section of the work sheet. The revenue and expense items are transferred to the income statement section. The difference in the totals of the income statement section is the net income or the net loss for the accounting period. The difference in the totals of the balance sheet section is also the net income or the net loss. This difference should of course be the same as that obtained in the income statement section.

The eight-column work sheet serves the same purpose. It is prepared in the same way as a six-column work sheet, but an *adjustments* section is added. It is also used by the accountant to *rough out* or plan the necessary adjustments so that the financial statements will be correct. There are four sections on an eight-column work sheet as shown in Figure 17.5:

- the trial balance
- a section to plan the adjustments
- an income statement section
- a balance sheet section

In the next few pages, the work sheet will be completed for Management Consultant Services. The period of time covered by this work sheet will be one full year. The first step in preparing the work sheet is to gather the information required to complete the adjustments. This information includes: *18

- A count made of all supplies on hand shows $400 worth left on December 31
- On January 1, a three-year insurance policy was purchased. One year of the policy is now expired
- The balance in the Prepaid Rent account represents a payment on October 1 for the October, November, and December rents
- The equipment depreciates 20% a year. The declining-balance method is used.

Using this information the adjustments are prepared on the work sheet.

Preparing Adjustments

In this example four accounts need to be adjusted. They are: *19

- Supplies
- Prepaid Insurance
- Prepaid Rent
- Office Equipment

Supplies The asset account Supplies has a $1 000 balance. However, the inventory taken at the end of the fiscal period indicates only $400 worth of supplies are left. This means that $600 worth of supplies have been *used* and should be recorded as an *expense*.

It is necessary to record the Supplies Expense of $600 and to decrease the asset Supplies by $600. This is done by debiting Supplies Expense and crediting Supplies. Figure 17.6 shows how this adjustment is prepared on the work sheet.

Management Consultant Services
Work Sheet
For the Year Ended December 31, 19__

	ACCOUNT TITLE	ACC. NO.	TRIAL BALANCE		ADJUSTMENTS		INCOME STATEMENT		BALANCE SHEET		
			DEBIT	CREDIT	DEBIT	CREDIT	DEBIT	CREDIT	DEBIT	CREDIT	
1	Cash	100	13 000 —								1
2	Accounts Receivable	102	7 000 —								2
3	Supplies	131	1 000 —								3
4	Prepaid Insurance	132	900 —								4
5	Prepaid Rent	133	2 100 —								5
6	Office Equipment	141	12 000 —								6
7	Accumulated Depreciation: Equip.	142		2 400 —							7
8	Accounts Payable	200		1 000 —							8
9	Bank Loan	221		3 000 —							9
10	J. Turner, Capital	300		10 400 —							10
11	J. Turner, Drawing	301	15 000 —								11
12	Fees Earned	400		132 000 —							12
13	Salaries Expense	500	89 500 —								13
14	Utilities Expense	501	1 300 —								14
15	Rent Expense	502	6 300 —								15
16	Miscellaneous Expense	503	700 —								16
17			148 800 —	148 800 —							17
18											18
19											19
20											20
21			1		2		3		4		21
22											22
23			Trial Balance		Adjustments		Income Statement		Balance Sheet		23
24											24
25											25

Figure 17.5 *The eight-column work sheet*

In preparing the adjustment, it is necessary to add the account Supplies Expense to the bottom of the trial balance because the account Supplies Expense does not appear on the trial balance. The new account, Supplies Expense, is debited $600 in the adjustments debit column. The asset Supplies is reduced by entering a credit of $600 in the adjustments credit column in the same line as Supplies. The effect of this adjustment, in T-account form, is:

Supplies				Supplies Expense			
	1 000	*Dec. 31*	600	*Dec. 31*	600		
Balance	400						

This adjustment decreases the asset Supplies by $600 to the correct balance of $400. It also records the amount of supplies used ($600) in the Supplies Expense account.

Prepaid Insurance In January, a $900, three-year insurance policy was purchased. At the end of the current year, two years of insurance remain. One third of the policy has expired or been used up and it is necessary to reduce the Prepaid Insurance by $300 ($\frac{1}{3} \times 900 = 300$) and record an expense of $300. This is done by adding the account Insurance Expense to the work sheet. A debit of $300 is written beside Insurance Expense in the adjustments debit column. The asset Prepaid Insurance is reduced by entering a credit of $300 in the adjustments column opposite Prepaid Insurance. The work sheet in Figure 17.6 illustrates how Prepaid Insurance is adjusted.

The effect of this adjustment is to lower the asset Prepaid Insurance to $600 and to record the Insurance Expense for one year of $300.

Prepaid Rent On October 1, the rent of $2 100 was prepaid for October, November, and December. On December 31, the rent for those three months is no longer prepaid. It has been *used up* and an expense must be recorded. ***20**

Since there is already a Rent Expense account on the trial balance, all that is required to adjust Prepaid Rent is to decrease the asset by a credit of $2 100. The rent expense for the three months is recorded by debiting Rent Expense $2 100. Because the rent is no longer prepaid, the effect of the credit to Prepaid Rent is to reduce this asset to zero. Figure 17.6 illustrates the rent adjustment.

Depreciation Fixed assets such as equipment depreciate each year. Equipment may be depreciated at a rate of up to 20% a year. For income tax purposes, the declining-balance method must be used. The year's depreciation on equipment using a 20% rate on the declining balance is $1 920.

To record the depreciation, a debit is entered in the Depreciation Expense account and a credit is entered in the Accumulated Depreciation account. It is necessary to add Depreciation Expense: Equipment to the work sheet. This account is debited $1 920 in the adjustments column. The Accumulated

Management Consultant Services
Work Sheet
For the Year Ended December 31, 19__

	ACCOUNT TITLE	ACC. NO.	TRIAL BALANCE		ADJUSTMENTS		INCOME STATEMENT		BALANCE SHEET		
			DEBIT	CREDIT	DEBIT	CREDIT	DEBIT	CREDIT	DEBIT	CREDIT	
1	Cash	100	13 000 —						13 000 —		1
2	Accounts Receivable	102	7 000 —						7 000 —		2
3	Supplies	131	1 000 —			(a) 600 —			400 —		3
4	Prepaid Insurance	132	900 —			(b) 300 —			600 —		4
5	Prepaid Rent	133	2 100 —			(c) 2 100 —					5
6	Office Equipment	141	12 000 —						12 000 —		6
7	Accumulated Depreciation: Equip.	142		2 400 —		(d) 1 920 —				4 320 —	7
8	Accounts Payable	200		1 000 —						1 000 —	8
9	Bank Loan	221		3 000 —						3 000 —	9
10	J. Turner, Capital	300		10 400 —						10 400 —	10
11	J. Turner, Drawing	301	15 000 —						15 000 —		11
12	Fees Earned	400		132 000 —				132 000 —			12
13	Salaries Expense	500	89 500 —				89 500 —				13
14	Utilities Expense	501	1 300 —				1 300 —				14
15	Rent Expense	502	6 300 —		(c) 2 100 —		8 400 —				15
16	Miscellaneous Expense	503	700 —				700 —				16
17			148 800 —	148 800 —							17
18	Supplies Expense	504			(a) 600 —		600 —				18
19	Insurance Expense	505			(b) 300 —		300 —				19
20	Depreciation Expense: Equipment	506			(d) 1 920 —		1 920 —				20
21					4 920 —	4 920 ·	102 720 —	132 000 —	48 000 —	18 720 —	21
22	Net Income						29 280 —			29 280 —	22
23							132 000 —	132 000 —	48 000 —	48 000 —	23
24											24
25											25

Figure 17.6 *Completing the work sheet*

Depreciation account is credited $1 920 in the adjustments column. Figure 17.6 illustrates this adjustment.

Four adjustments have been made on the work sheet and were placed in the adjustments section; each adjustment was labelled. For example, the supplies adjustment has an a) beside the debit and an a) beside the credit. The other adjustments were labelled b), c), and d) respectively. These labels ensure that there is a debit for every credit and provide a reference for checking the adjustments.

The mathematical accuracy of the adjustments section of the work sheet is proven by adding the two columns. The debit column total should equal the credit column total. If this is the case, the columns are double-ruled.

Completing the Work Sheet

*21

After the adjustments have been completed and the adjustments columns totalled, the items on the trial balance are transferred to either the income statement or balance sheet sections of the work sheet. The income and expenses are transferred to the income statement section. The assets, liabilities, and equity accounts are transferred to the balance sheet section.

For example, Figure 17.6 shows that Cash, $13 000, is transferred to the balance sheet debit column (line 1). Accounts Receivable, $7 000, is also transferred to the balance sheet debit column (line 2). However, there is a complication on line 3 of the work sheet. The asset Supplies has a *debit* of $1 000 and a *credit* of $600 in the adjustments column. The difference between a debit of $1 000 and a credit of $600 is $400. Because Supplies is an asset account, the $400 balance is transferred to the balance sheet debit column.

*22

Prepaid Insurance is handled in the same way as Supplies. The difference between the $900 debit and the $300 credit is $600. This amount ($600) is transferred to the balance sheet debit column (line 4). On line 5, the difference in the Prepaid Rent account is zero (2 100 debit - 2 100 credit = 0). Therefore there is no balance shown in the balance sheet section for Prepaid Rent. There is no change in the Office Equipment account. Thus $12 000 is transferred to the balance sheet debit column (line 6). On line 7, there are two credits for Accumulated Depreciation. These are added and the balance, $4 320, is transferred to the balance sheet credit column. Accounts Payable, Bank Loan, and J. Turner, Capital are all transferred to the balance sheet credit column and J. Turner, Drawing is transferred to the balance sheet debit column.

Fees Earned, on line 12, is the revenue of Management Consultant Services and is transferred to the income statement credit column.

Salaries Expense, Utilities Expense, and Miscellaneous Expense did not require adjustment and are transferred to the income statement debit column. Rent Expense on line 15 has two debits. These are added and the total of $8 400 appears in the income statement debit column. At the bottom of the work sheet are found the remaining expenses, including Supplies Expense, Insurance Expense, and Depreciation Expense, which required adjustments. These expenses are transferred to the income statement debit column.

*23

Determining the Net Income or Net Loss After all the amounts have been transferred to either the balance sheet or income statement columns, it is quite simple to determine the net income or net loss. First, add the income statement debit and credit columns and then find the difference between them. This difference is the net income or the net loss. There is net income if the credit column total is bigger than the debit column total. Conversely, there is net loss if the debit column has a bigger total than the credit column. Looking at Figure 17.6, it can be seen that the credit column total of the income statement section is bigger and thus shows a net income ($29 280).

Next, add the balance sheet debit and credit columns and determine the difference between them. The difference is the net income or net loss. There is net income if the debit column total is bigger than the credit column total, and net loss if the credit column total is the larger of the two. Notice that the debit column total in Figure 17.6 is bigger and the difference is the *same* as the difference in the income statement columns – both differences are $29 280. This should come as no surprise as both differences are measuring the same thing – net income.

*24

Balancing the Work Sheet After the net income (or net loss) has been determined, the amount (in this example $29 280) is added to the smaller column total of both the income statement and the balance sheet section of the work sheet. The net income figure is added to both the debit column of the income statement section and to the credit side of the balance sheet section. A net loss would be added to the credit side of the income statement section and to the debit side of the balance sheet section. The columns are then double-ruled as shown in Figure 17.6.

*25

Steps in Preparing the Work Sheet To summarize, these are the steps followed when preparing an eight-column work sheet.

1. Write the heading on the work sheet.
2. Write the trial balance on the work sheet.
3. Gather the data needed to prepare the adjustments.
4. Prepare the adjustments and total, balance, and rule the adjustment columns.
5. Transfer all items to either the income statement or balance sheet columns.
6. Total the income statement and balance sheet columns and determine the net income or net loss.
7. Balance and rule the work sheet.

Preparing the Financial Statements

*26

When the work sheet has been completed, the formal financial statements are prepared. All the information necessary for the preparation of the income statement is found on the work sheet in the income statement columns. Similarly, all the necessary data for the balance sheet is found on the work sheet in the balance sheet columns.

Financial statements are prepared from information on the work sheet.

Figures 17.7 and 17.8 illustrate the financial statements prepared from the completed work sheet. Note the following about these two statements:

Management Consultant Services Income Statement For the Year Ended December 31, 19__		
Revenue		
Fees Earned		132 000 00
Expenses		
Salaries	89 500 00	
Utilities	1 300 00	
Rent	8 400 00	
Miscellaneous	700 00	
Supplies	600 00	
Insurance	300 00	
Depreciation: Equipment	1 920 00	102 720 00
Net Income		29 280 00

Figure 17.7 *Income statement prepared from the work sheet*

Management Consultant Services Balance Sheet December 31, 19__			
Assets			
Current Assets			
Cash		13 000 00	
Accounts Receivable		7 000 00	
Supplies		400 00	
Prepaid Insurance		600 00	21 000 00
Fixed Assets			
Equipment		12 000 00	
Less: Accumulated Depreciation		4 320 00	7 680 00
Total Assets			28 680 00
Liabilities and Owner's Equity			
Current Liabilities			
Accounts Payable		1 000 00	
Bank Loan		3 000 00	4 000 00
Owner's Equity			
Capital, Jan. 1		10 400 00	
Add: Net Income for year	29 280 00		
Less: Drawing	15 000 00		
Increase in Capital		14 280 00	
Capital, Dec. 31			24 680 00
Total Liabilities and Owner's Equity			28 680 00

Figure 17.8 *Balance sheet prepared from the work sheet*

- The new expenses resulting from the adjustments are included on the income statement. These are Supplies Expense, Insurance Expense, and Depreciation Expense
- The Accumulated Depreciation is shown as a subtraction from Equipment in the fixed asset section of the balance sheet

Unit 42

Adjusting and Closing Entries

*27

The books of a company consist of the various journals and ledgers. The work sheet is not part of a company's permanent records. The work sheet is used by the accountant as an aid in organizing data used to prepare the financial statements.

In the example used in this chapter, the assets Supplies, Prepaid Insurance, Prepaid Rent, and Equipment were adjusted. Changes were made in some expenses and three expenses were added: Insurance Expense, Supplies Expense, and Depreciation Expense. All these adjustments were made on the work sheet. The accounts themselves in the Ledger have not as yet been changed. The Ledger accounts are incorrect and must be changed to reflect the adjustments made on the work sheet. The purpose of *adjusting entries* is to record the adjustments in the Ledger accounts.

The Ledger accounts must be updated to be in agreement with the adjusting entries on the work sheet.

Adjusting Entries

*28

The recording of adjusting entries is quite simple because the adjustments have already been made on the work sheet. It is only necessary to record the adjustments in journal form and to post them to the Ledger.

When the adjustments were made on the work sheet, they were coded a), b), c), and d). The debit and credit for the supplies adjustment were coded a). By referring to the work sheet and finding the a) adjustment (Figure 17.6), this entry is journalized:

Dec.	31	Supplies Expense		600 —	
		Supplies			600 —
		To record supplies used			

Similar entries are recorded in the General Journal for each of the adjustments. These are shown in Figure 17.9.

*29

Posting the Adjusting Entries

After the adjusting entries have been journalized, they are posted to the General Ledger. Some of the General Ledger accounts of Management Consultant Services are shown in Figure 17.10. These T-accounts contain the end-of-the-fiscal-period balances found on the trial balance *before* adjustments have been made.

Adjusting entries are necessary to record the adjustments in the ledger accounts.

DATE		PARTICULARS	PR	DEBIT	CREDIT
Dec. 19--	31	Supplies Expense		600 —	
		Supplies			600 —
		To record supplies used			
	31	Insurance Expense		300 —	
		Prepaid Insurance			300 —
		To record the Insurance expense for the year			
	31	Rent Expense		2100 —	
		Prepaid Rent			2100 —
		To record Rent Expense for three months			
	31	Depreciation Expense: Equipment		1920 —	
		Accumulated Depreciation: Equipment			1920 —
		To record one year's depreciation, declining balance method			

Figure 17.9 *General Journal entries to record the adjustments*

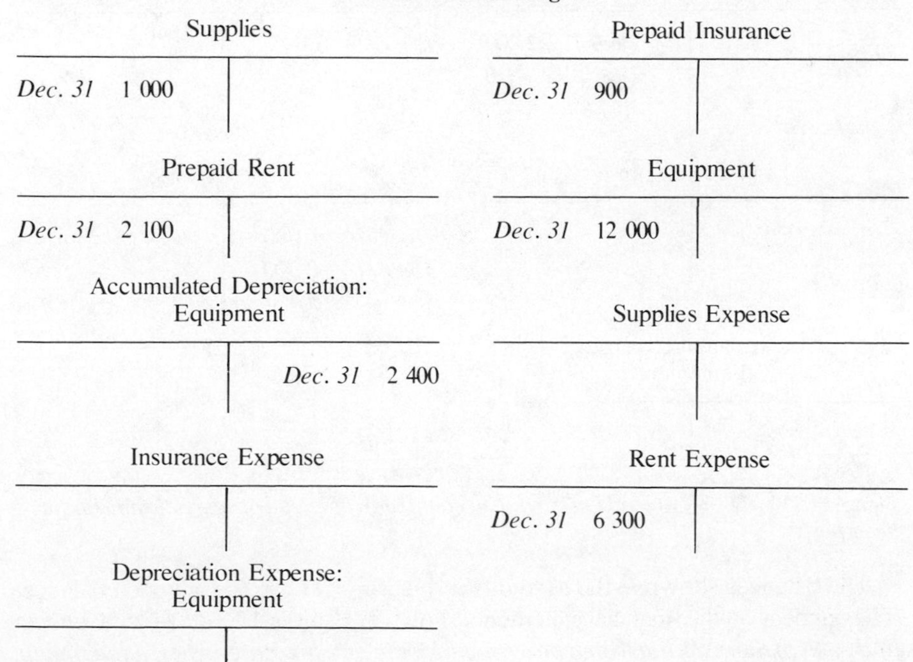

Figure 17.10 *Partial General Ledger in T-account form before end of year adjustments have been posted*

In the accounts shown in Figure 17.11, several expense accounts have no balance. If the adjustments are not journalized and posted, Supplies Expense, Insurance Expense, and Depreciation Expense: Office Equipment would all have *nil* balances at the end of the fiscal period. That would be wrong, since supplies were used, insurance did expire, and depreciation is an expense. As well, the balance of $6 300 in the Rent Expense account is incorrect since it does not include the $2 100 rent for the last three months.

Figure 17.11 is the partial General Ledger showing the accounts after the adjusting entries have been posted. *Can you trace the entries from the General Journal in Figure 17.9 to this ledger?*

Partial General Ledger

Supplies

Dec. 31	1 000	*Dec. 31*	600
Balance	400		

Prepaid Insurance

Dec. 31	900	*Dec. 31*	300
Balance	600		

Prepaid Rent

Dec. 31	2 100	*Dec. 31*	2 100
Balance	0		

Equipment

Dec. 31	12 000		

Accumulated Depreciation: Equipment

		Dec. 31	2 400
		Dec. 31	1 920
		Balance	4 320

Supplies Expense

Dec. 31	600		

Insurance Expense

Dec. 31	300		

Rent Expense

Dec. 31	6 300		
Dec. 31	2 100		
Balance	8 400		

Depreciation Expense: Equipment

Dec. 31	1 920		

Figure 17.11 *Partial General Ledger in T-account form after end of year adjustments have been posted*

The balances shown in the accounts in Figure 17.11 are the adjusted balances. They appear on the financial statements shown in Figures 17.7 and 17.8. *Can you find each of them? What would be wrong with the income statement if adjustments had not been made? What would be wrong with the balance sheet if adjustments had not been made?*

Closing the Books

In Chapter 7 you learned that revenue and expense accounts are closed at the end of the fiscal period. This means that each revenue account and each expense account is reduced to a zero balance. Closing the books serves two purposes:

- to prepare the revenue and expense accounts for the next accounting period
- to update the Owner's Equity account

*30

Closing entries are necessary to prepare the revenue and expense accounts for the next fiscal period and to update the equity accounts.

Revenue and Expense Accounts The revenue accounts are used to record the sales of goods and services. The expense accounts are used to record the costs of operating the business. The net income or net loss for a fiscal period is the difference between the revenue and expenses.

The revenue and expense accounts provide the information to determine the net income or net loss for a given fiscal period. The information for each fiscal period must be kept separate. This is done by reducing the revenue and expense account balances to zero before the new fiscal period starts. Their balances are transferred to an account called the Income Summary account.

Revenue, expense, and drawing accounts are closed at the end of a fiscal period.

Updating the Equity Accounts Before closing entries are prepared, the owner's Capital account in the Ledger does not include the net income or net loss. On the balance sheet (Figure 17.8) the net income or net loss is added or subtracted from the owner's Capital balance of the previous fiscal period.

The closing entries do the same thing. They add or subtract the net income or net loss from the owner's Capital. This results in the Capital account being brought into agreement with the balance sheet. The Owner's Equity account is now updated.

The owner's Drawing account affects the owner's Capital account. It must also be closed. The closing of the Drawing account is part of updating the Capital account. Also, the Drawing account should have a zero balance to start the next fiscal period.

Closing the Books from the Work Sheet The completed work sheet for Management Consultant Services is found in Figure 17.6. The revenue and expense accounts are found in the income statement columns.

Closing Revenue Accounts On the work sheet (Figure 17.6), the revenue account Fees Earned has a credit balance of $132 000. To reduce it to zero, the Fees Earned account is debited $132 000. This closing entry is journalized:

Dec.	31	Fees Earned		132 000 —	
		Income Summary			132 000 —
		To close the Revenue account			

Closing Expense Accounts There are seven expenses in the debit column of the income statement section of the work sheet. Each is credited to reduce it to zero This entry is journalized:

*31

Date		Particulars	PR	Debit	Credit
Dec.	31	Income Summary		102 720 —	
		Salaries Expense			89 500 —
		Utilities Expense			1 300 —
		Rent Expense			8 400 —
		Miscellaneous Expense			700 —
		Supplies Expense			600 —
		Insurance Expense			300 —
		Depreciation Expense			1 920 —
		To close the expense accounts			

*32

Updating the Equity Accounts There are two entries required to update the Owner's Equity account. The first is to transfer the net income or net loss to the Capital account from the Income Summary. The net income of $29 280 earned during the year increases the owner's Capital account. In very simple terms, *the net income belongs to the owner*. For this reason, the net income is credited to the owner's Capital account. This increases the owner's Capital. If there was a net loss, Capital is decreased. This entry is journalized:

Date		Particulars	PR	Debit	Credit
Dec.	31	Income Summary		29 280 —	
		J. Turner, Capital			29 280 —
		To transfer net income to			
		the owner's Capital account			

*33

A second entry involving Owner's Equity is needed to close the Drawing account into the Capital account. This entry is journalized:

Date		Particulars	PR	Debit	Credit
Dec.	31	J. Turner, Capital		15 000 —	
		J. Turner, Drawing			15 000 —
		To close the Drawing account			
		into the Capital account			

The closing entries just described are all recorded in the General Journal. The source of information is the income statement columns of the work sheet except for the Drawing account which is found in the balance sheet columns of the work sheet.

*34

After the closing entries have been journalized, they are posted to the General Ledger. Selected ledger accounts from the General Ledger are shown in Figure 17.12. This ledger contains the adjusting entries and the closing entries which have been posted from the General Journal. All the revenue and expense accounts have a zero balance. They are double-ruled and are now ready to receive data for the new fiscal period. Notice that the Drawing account and the Income Summary account are also closed. The asset, liability, and owner's Capital accounts are not closed. Their balances continue into the next fiscal period.

Asset, liability, and owner's capital accounts are not closed at the end of a fiscal period.

ACCOUNT Cash NO. 100

DATE		PARTICULARS	PR	DEBIT	CREDIT	DR CR	BALANCE
Dec. 19--	31		✓			DR	13 000 —

ACCOUNT Supplies NO. 131

DATE		PARTICULARS	PR	DEBIT	CREDIT	DR CR	BALANCE
Dec. 19--	31		✓			DR	1 000 —
	31	Adjusting Entry	J34		600 —	DR	400 —

ACCOUNT Prepaid Insurance NO. 132

DATE		PARTICULARS	PR	DEBIT	CREDIT	DR CR	BALANCE
Dec. 19--	31		✓			DR	900 —
	31	Adjusting Entry	J34		300 —	DR	600 —

ACCOUNT Office Equipment NO. 141

DATE		PARTICULARS	PR	DEBIT	CREDIT	DR CR	BALANCE
Dec. 19--	31		✓			DR	12 000 —

ACCOUNT Acc. Depreciation: Office Equipment NO. 142

DATE		PARTICULARS	PR	DEBIT	CREDIT	DR CR	BALANCE
Dec. 19--	31		✓			CR	2 400 —
	31	Adjusting Entry			1 920 —	CR	4 320 —

ACCOUNT Accounts Payable NO. 200

DATE		PARTICULARS	PR	DEBIT	CREDIT	DR CR	BALANCE
Dec. 19--	31		✓			CR	1 000 —

ACCOUNT J. Turner, Capital NO. 300

DATE		PARTICULARS	PR	DEBIT	CREDIT	DR CR	BALANCE
Dec. 19--	31					CR	10 400 –
	31	Net Income for Year	J35		29 280 –	CR	39 680 –
	31	Drawings	J35	15 000 –		CR	24 680 –

ACCOUNT J. Turner, Drawing NO. 301

DATE		PARTICULARS	PR	DEBIT	CREDIT	DR CR	BALANCE
Dec. 19--	31		✓			DR	15 000 –
	31	Closing entry	J35		15 000 –		–0–

ACCOUNT Revenue and Expense Summary NO. 302

DATE		PARTICULARS	PR	DEBIT	CREDIT	DR CR	BALANCE
Dec. 19--	31	To close Fees Earned	J35		132 000 –	CR	132 000 –
	31	To close Expenses	J35	102 720 –		CR	29 280 –
	31	To close Revenue and Expense Summary	J35	29 280 –		–	–0–

ACCOUNT Supplies Expense NO. 504

DATE		PARTICULARS	PR	DEBIT	CREDIT	DR CR	BALANCE
Dec. 19--	31		✓			DR	600 –
	31	Closing Entry	J35		600 –	–	–0–

ACCOUNT Insurance Expense NO. 505

DATE		PARTICULARS	PR	DEBIT	CREDIT	DR CR	BALANCE
Dec. 19--	31		✓			DR	300 –
	31	Closing entry	J35		300 –	–	–0–

ACCOUNT Depreciation Expense: Equipment						NO. 506
DATE	PARTICULARS	PR	DEBIT	CREDIT	DR CR	BALANCE
Dec. 19-- 31		✓			DR	1 920 —
31	Closing entry	J35		1 920 —	—	-0-

Figure 17.12 *General Ledger for Management Consultant Services after adjusting and closing entries have been posted*

Post-closing Trial Balance After the adjusting and closing entries have been posted to the General Ledger, a post-closing trial balance is prepared (Figure 17.13). The purpose of this trial balance is to prove the mathematical accuracy of the General Ledger. If the debit total equals the credit total, the Ledger is assumed to be *in balance*. It is ready for the next fiscal period. The post-closing trial balance is quite a bit shorter than other General Ledger trial balances. This is because it contains only asset, liability, and capital accounts with balances. The revenue, expense and drawing accounts have been reduced to zero and do not appear on this final trial balance.

*35
The post-closing trial balance is prepared after the closing entries have been posted to the General Ledger.

The post-closing trial balance contains only asset, liability and capital accounts.

Management Consultant Services Post-Closing Trial Balance December 31, 19--			
ACCOUNT TITLE	ACC. NO.	DEBIT	CREDIT
Cash	100	13 000 —	
Accounts Receivable	102	7 000 —	
Supplies	131	400 —	
Prepaid Insurance	132	600 —	
Office Equipment	141	12 000 —	
Accumulated Depreciation: Equipment	142		4 320 —
Accounts Payable	200		1 000 —
Bank Loan	221		3 000 —
J. Turner, Capital	300		24 680 —
		33 000 —	33 000 —

Figure 17.13 *The post closing trial balance which is prepared after the closing of the books*

Accounting Cycle

In this chapter, several steps have been added to the accounting cycle. Figure 17.14 summarizes the complete accounting cycle and illustrates the different stages of the cycle during the fiscal period.

*36

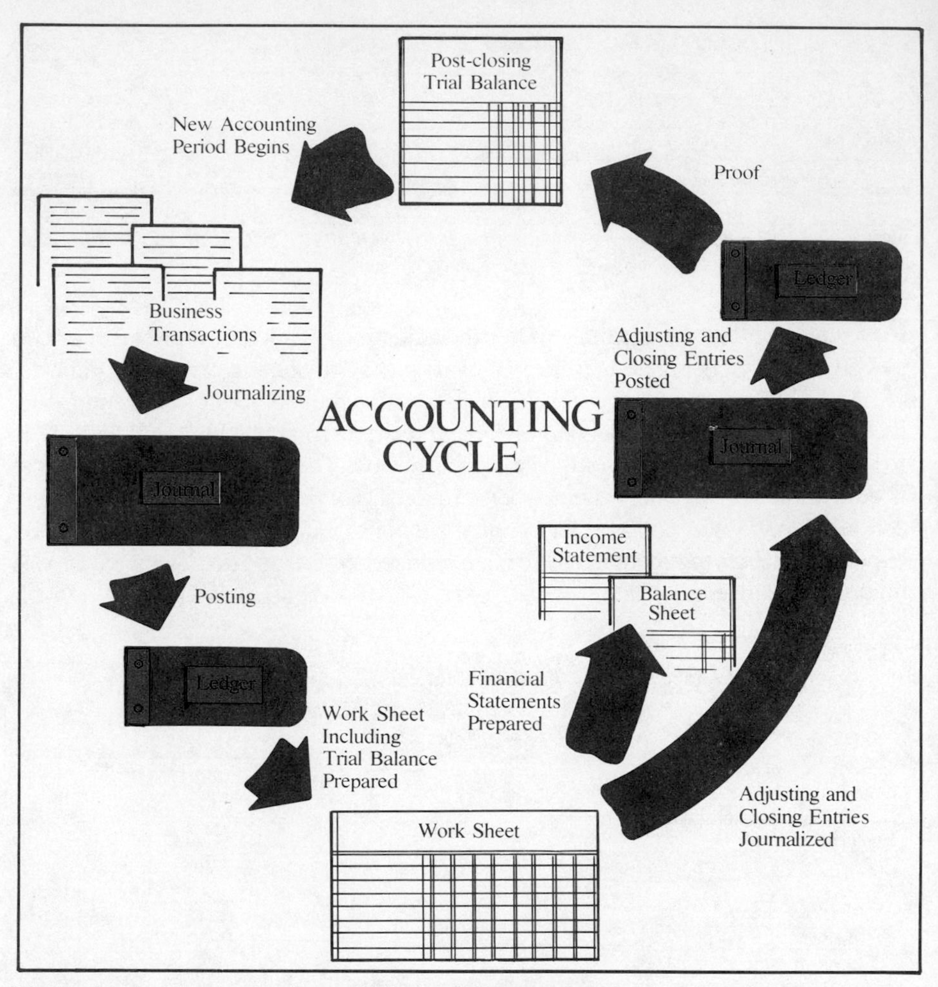

Figure 17.14 *The accounting cycle is a continuous process.*

Facts to Remember

Adjustments are necessary so that the financial statements are accurate.

Prepaid expenses are expense payments made in advance.

Prepaid expenses are current assets.

Depreciation is the allocation of the cost of an asset to the fiscal periods in which it is used.

Depreciation is an expense and appears on the income statement.

Accumulated Depreciation is a valuation account and appears in the fixed assets section of the balance sheet.

The straight-line method of depreciation allocates the same amount of depreciation to each fiscal period.

The declining balance method of depreciation allocates a greater amount of depreciation to the first years of an asset's life.

Capital-cost allowance is the income tax terminology for depreciation. The capital-cost allowance method is similar to the declining balance method of depreciation.

The maximum amount of depreciation chargeable in any one tax year is set out in the Income Tax Act.

Land is not depreciable.

Adjustments are first prepared on the work sheet.

Financial statements are prepared from information on the work sheet.

Adjusting entries are necessary to record the adjustments in the Ledger accounts.

Closing entries are necessary to prepare the revenue and expense accounts for the next fiscal period and to update the equity accounts.

Revenue, expense, and drawing accounts are closed at the end of a fiscal period.

Asset, liability, and *owner's capital* accounts are not closed at the end of a fiscal period.

The *post-closing trial balance* is prepared after closing entries have been posted to the General Ledger.

Checking Your Reading

Questions

1. a) What is meant by the term *adjusting the books*?
b) Why are adjustments necessary?
c) List three parties that would be interested in studying accurate financial statements.

2. a) What type of accounts are Prepaid Expenses?
b) On which financial statement do they appear?

3. a) Why is the account Supplies allowed to become incorrect?
b) Why is it not credited each time supplies are used?
c) On which financial statement does the account Supplies appear? Which statement shows Supplies Expense?

4. What type of account is Prepaid Insurance? What type is Insurance Expense?

5. Define depreciation.

6. Which assets depreciate?

7. On which financial statement does Depreciation Expense and Accumulated Depreciation appear?

8. "Depreciation is not valuation." What does this mean?
9. Two methods of calculating depreciation are the straight-line method and the declining-balance method. Explain each of them.
10. What is capital cost allowance?
11. For income tax purposes, which method of depreciation must be used?
12. How is the net income or net loss determined on the work sheet?
13. When there is a net loss, which column of the income statement section of the work sheet is greater? Which column of the balance sheet section is greater?
14. When there is a net income, to which columns on the work sheet is the amount of the net income added?
15. List the seven steps in preparing a work sheet.
16. Why are adjusting entries recorded after the work sheet has been completed?
17. What two purposes are served by closing the books?
18. What type of accounts are closed?
19. Is a revenue account debited or credited in order to close it?
20. In order to close an expense, is a debit or a credit necessary in the expense account?
21. Into which account are revenue and expenses closed?
22. Into which account are the Income Summary account and the Drawing account closed? Why?
23. Which accounts appear on the post-closing trial balance?

Applying Your Knowledge

Exercises Part A

1. Set up T-accounts for Cash, Prepaid Rent and Rent Expense.
   a) In the T-accounts, record the following entry:
   May 1, cheque No. 467 for $2 400 was issued to Triangle Realtors as advance payment for four months' rent.
   b) On May 31, record an adjustment to record one month's rent expense.
   c) Indicate what type of accounts Prepaid Rent and Rent Expense are, and indicate the financial statement on which each appears.

2. The asset account Supplies is shown below. At the end of the fiscal period, an inventory shows supplies worth $100 on hand.

Supplies	
700	

Supplies Expense	

a) What was the value of supplies used during the fiscal period?
b) What is the Supplies Expense for the fiscal period?
c) What should the balance in the asset account Supplies be at the end of the fiscal period?
d) Prepare the adjusting entry to record the supplies used.
e) What is the amount of the Supplies Expense which will appear on the income statement?
f) What is the value of the asset Supplies which will appear on the balance sheet?

3. On August 31, the trial balance showed a balance of $1 575.67 in the Supplies account. An actual count of supplies, however, showed that there was $347.72 worth on hand. Give the General Journal entry required to adjust the Supplies account.

4. On September 30, the trial balance for Grayson Enterprises showed the following balances:
Office Supplies, $796.53; Cleaning Supplies, $1 375.84.
a) Set up T-accounts with the following balances:
Office Supplies, $796.53; Cleaning Supplies, $1 375.84; Office Supplies Expense, Nil; Cleaning Supplies Expense, Nil.
b) An actual count of supplies showed values of $179.25 for office supplies and $467.31 for cleaning supplies. Prepare General Journal entries to record the necessary adjustments.
c) Post the adjustments to the T-accounts

5. Prepare adjusting entries for each of the following:
a) Balance in the Supplies account, $700. Supplies on hand, February 28, $500.
b) Balance in the Supplies account, $1 300. Supplies on hand, March 31, $940.
c) Balance in the Supplies account, $300. Supplies on hand, April 30, $180.

6. Prepare adjusting entries for the month of February for the following:
a) Balance in Prepaid Rent account, $3 000. Monthly rent is $1 000.
b) Balance in Prepaid Rent account, $1 800. Monthly rent is $900.
c) A 12-month insurance policy costing $360 was purchased on February 1.
d) A 3-year insurance policy costing $756 was purchased on February 1.

7. On January 1, a three-year insurance policy was purchased for $750 cash. Prepare the December 31 adjusting entry to record one year's insurance expense.

8. Three accounts related to the fixed asset account Automobile (which was bought one year ago) follow:

Automobile		Accumulated Depreciation: Automobile		Depreciation Expense: Automobile	
8 000					

a) On December 31, prepare the General Journal adjusting entry to depreciate the automobile for one year at the rate of 30%.
b) Post the entry to T-accounts.
c) Give the accounts and balances which appear in the balance sheet and the income statement.

9. It has been estimated that equipment bought for $24 000 will have a useful life of six years, at which time it will be thrown away.
a) Using the straight-line method of depreciation, what will be the amount of depreciation each year?
b) Complete the following chart for a period of six years:

Year	Value at beginning of year	Depreciation for the year	Accumulated depreciation	Value at end of year
1	$24 000	$4 000	$4 000	$20 000
2	20 000	4 000	8 000	16 000
3				
4				
5				
6				

10. After one year's depreciation, several T-accounts related to fixed assets were as follows:

Equipment	
20 000	

Accumulated Depreciation: Equipment	
	4 000

Depreciation Expense: Equipment	

Automobiles	
15 000	

Accumulated Depreciation: Automobiles	
	4 500

Depreciation Expense: Automobiles	

Prepare the necessary adjusting entries to record a year's depreciation if the straight line method of depreciation is used. The rates of depreciation are 20% for equipment and 30% for automobiles.

11. a) Complete the following chart for the depreciation of equipment purchased for $55 000, which depreciates at the rate of 20% a year on the declining balance.
b) Show the journal entries required to record the depreciation expenses in the first four years.

Year	Value at beginning of year	Depreciation for the year	Accumulated depreciation	Value at end of year
1	$55 000	$	$	$
2				
3				
4				

12. Priddle Plumbing prepares monthly financial statements. Fixed assets owned by the company include equipment valued at $14 000 and a truck worth $10 000. Accumulated depreciation on the equipment is $7 170. Accumulated depreciation on the truck is $6 500. Prepare adjusting entries to record one month's depreciation, using the declining-balance method. The rate of depreciation for one year for the equipment is 20%, and for the truck, 30%.

Exercises Part B

13. The trial balance for Music Man Disco follows. Prepare the work sheet for the year ended December 31 using the additional information given.

Music Man Disco
Trial Balance
December 31, 19__

ACCOUNT TITLE	ACC. NO.	DEBIT	CREDIT
Cash	100	2 000 —	
Accounts Receivable	102	4 000 —	
Supplies	131	700 —	
Equipment	141	15 000 —	
Accumulated Depreciation: Equipment	142		5 400 —
Accounts Payable	200		1 000 —
M. Bathurst, Capital	300		13 600 —
M. Bathurst, Drawing	301	8 000 —	
Sales	400		60 000 —
Salaries Expense	500	42 000 —	
Rent Expense	501	4 000 —	
Telephone Expense	502	400 —	
Miscellaneous Expense	503	900 —	
Office Expense	504	3 000 —	
		80 000 —	80 000 —

Additional Information:

- Supplies on hand on December 31 are valued at $200
- The declining-balance method of depreciation is used, and the equipment depreciates at the rate of 20%

14. Prepare a work sheet for Treliving Consultants using the trial balance and additional information given. The fiscal period is one year.

Treliving Consultants Trial Balance December 31, 19__			
ACCOUNT TITLE	ACC. NO.	DEBIT	CREDIT
Cash	100	4500 —	
Accounts Receivable	102	17000 —	
Supplies	131	2000 —	
Prepaid Insurance	132	2400 —	
Office Equipment	141	11 000 —	
Accumulated Depreciation: Office Equip.	142		3760 —
Automobile	143	12000 —	
Accumulated Depreciation: Automobile	144		5760 —
Accounts Payable	200		1500 —
J. Treliving, Capital	300		27980 —
J. Treliving, Drawing	301	18 000 —	
Fees Income	400		120 000 —
Salaries Expense	500	80000 —	
Rent Expense	501	7200 —	
Car Expense	502	800 —	
Utilities Expense	503	1100 —	
Office Expense	504	3000 —	
		159 000 —	159 000 —

Additional Information:

- Supplies on hand on December 31 are valued at $700
- The three-year insurance policy was purchased on January 1 for $2 400
- The declining-balance method of depreciation is used (Figure 17.4)

15. a) Prepare financial statements for exercise 13.
    b) Prepare financial statements for exercise 14.

16. Using the completed work sheet for C. Hall, Electrical Contractor, carry out the following procedures.
    a) Prepare the financial statements.
    b) Journalize the adjusting entries.
    c) Post the adjusting entries.
    d) Journalize and post the closing entry for Service Income.
    e) Journalize and post the closing entry for Expenses.
    f) Journalize and post the closing entry for the Income Summary account.
    g) Journalize and post the closing entry for the Drawing account.
    h) Prepare a post-closing trial balance.

C. Hall Electrical Contractor
Work Sheet
For the Month Ended October 31, 19__

	ACCOUNT TITLE	ACC. NO.	TRIAL BALANCE		ADJUSTMENTS		INCOME STATEMENT		BALANCE SHEET		
			DEBIT	CREDIT	DEBIT	CREDIT	DEBIT	CREDIT	DEBIT	CREDIT	
1	Cash	100	5500 —						5500 —		1
2	Accounts Receivable	102	2300 —						2300 —		2
3	Supplies	131	7200 —			(a) 500 —			6700 —		3
4	Prepaid Rent	132	1800 —			(b) 600 —			1200 —		4
5	Equipment	143	21000 —						21000 —		5
6	Accumulated Depr. - Equipment	144		7560 —		(c) 224 —				7784 —	6
7	Accounts Payable	200		3500 —						3500 —	7
8	C. Hall, Capital	300		24640 —						24640 —	8
9	C. Hall, Drawing	301	900 —						900 —		9
10	Service Income	400		5700 —				5700 —			10
11	Salaries	500	2200 —				2200 —				11
12	Equipment Repairs	501	200 —				200 —				12
13	Miscellaneous Expense	502	300 —				300 —				13
14			41400 —	41400 —							14
15	Supplies Expense	510			(a) 500 —		500 —				15
16	Rent Expense	511			(b) 600 —		600 —				16
17	Depreciation - Equipment	512			(c) 224 —		224 —				17
18					1324 —	1324 —	4024 —	5700 —	37600 —	35924 —	18
19	Net Profit						1676 —			1676 —	19
20							5700 —	5700 —	37600 —	37600 —	20
21											21
22											22

17. a) Prepare adjusting and closing entries for the work sheet in exercise 13.
b) Post the adjusting and closing entries to the General Ledger.
c) Prepare a post-closing trial balance.

Exercises Part C

18. a) Prepare adjusting and closing entries for exercise 14.
b) Open T-accounts for the Drawing, Capital, and Income Summary accounts. Post to these accounts.

19. For each of the following transactions for the Dry Doc Diaper Service, prepare a Journal entry to record the transaction and also the adjusting entry dated May 31, when the one-month fiscal period ends.

May 1 Purchased a 12-month insurance policy for $600 cash.
1 Paid the rent for May, June, and July, a total of $3 000.
1 Purchased a delivery van costing $8 000. Made a down-payment of $3 000; balance to be paid in two years.
3 Purchased supplies by cheque, $1 500. An inventory taken on May 31 showed unused supplies worth $800.

20. The trial balance of the Stoney Creek Travel Service follows:

Stoney Creek Travel Service
Trial Balance
December 31, 19__

ACCOUNT TITLE	ACC. NO.	DEBIT	CREDIT
Cash	100	9 000 —	
Accounts Receivable	102	22 000 —	
Supplies	131	2 000 —	
Office Equipment	141	15 000 —	
Accumulated Depreciation: Office Equip.	142		5 000 —
Automobile	143	9 000 —	
Accumulated Depreiation: Automobile	144		4 800 —
Accounts Payable	200		2 000 —
Bank Loan	220		3 000 —
F. Katch, Capital	300		21 500 —
F. Katch, Drawing	301	13 000 —	
Sales	400		105 000 —
Advertising Expense	500	2 500 —	
Salaries Expense	501	57 000 —	
Rent Expense	502	7 800 —	
Office Expense	503	4 000 —	
		141 300 —	141 300 —

Additional Information:
- Supplies on hand at end of the year are worth $600
- Use the declining-balance method of depreciation (Figure 17.4)

a) Complete a work sheet for the year.
b) Prepare adjusting and closing entries.
c) Open accounts for each item on the trial balance. Post the adjusting and closing entries.
d) Prepare a post-closing trial balance.
e) Record these transactions in a Synoptic Journal. In this exercise, merchandise sold is exempt from sales tax.

Jan. 5 Cash Sales for the week, $1 200.
Charge Sales, $800.
5 Cheque Copies:
No. 101, rent, $650, Royal Realty.
No. 102, advertising, $400, *Stoney Creek Sentinel.*
12 Cash Sales, $925.
Charge Sales, $1 095.
15 Purchase invoices:
Supplies, $720, Grand & Toy.
Gas and oil for automobile, $35, Exxon Ltd.
15 Record the semi-monthly payroll:
Salaries Expense, $6 000
Income Tax Payable, $1 280.
C.P.P. Payable, $108.
U.I. Payable, $84.
Salaries Payable, $4 528.
15 Recorded company's share of C.P.P. ($108) and U.I. ($117.60).
15 Issued payroll cheque (No. 103) to the bank for $4 528, for deposit to employees' accounts.
29 Reduced the Bank Loan by $500.
29 Issued cheques for office expenses:
No. 104, $45, Bell Canada
No. 105, $115, City Hydro.
No. 106, $25, water bill.
No. 107, $190, fuel.
30 Cash Sales, $2 000.
Charge Sales, $1 600.
30 Issued cheques:
No. 108, Grand & Toy, on account, $720.
No. 109, Exxon Ltd., on account, $35.
30 Record the payroll:
Salaries Expense, $6 000.
Income Tax Payable, $1,280.
C.P.P. Payable, $108.
U.I. Payable, $84.
Salaries Payable, $4 528.
30 Record company's share of C.P.P. and U.I.
30 Issued payroll cheque (No. 100), $4 528.

f) Total, rule, and post the Synoptic Journal to the General Ledger.
g) Complete the work sheet for January, using this information:
- supplies on hand, $590.
- record one month's depreciation on the fixed assets.

h) Prepare financial statements for January.

Accounting in Action

Case 1

Comparative Financial Positions Company A has current assets totalling $15 000. One of the current assets is Cash, $2 000. It has recently paid its rent for three months in advance. Prepaid Rent, $1 500, is one of the current assets. Company B has current assets totalling $15 000. It has Cash of $2 500. Rent of $500 is paid monthly. This month's payment has been made. Both companies have current liabilities of $12 000.

Considering only the facts given, which company is in the better financial position, Company A or B? Give reasons.

Case 2

Overstating Net Income At the end of the year, the accountant for Martin Painting Contractors prepared financial statements but neglected to prepare the adjustment for the Supplies account. The balance in the Supplies account at the end of the year is $1 500. An actual count shows that the value of supplies on hand at the end of the year is $700.

The net income for the year as calculated by the accountant is $22 000 and the total assets are $110 000. However, these figures are incorrect because Supplies was not adjusted.

a) By how much is the net income overstated?
b) By how much are the assets overstated?
c) What are the correct figures for the net income and the total assets?

Case 3

Looking Beyond the Figures The Revenue and Expense accounts of Johnson Enterprises are shown below:

Revenue	
	Year 1 100 000

Expenses	
Year 1 75 000	

Financial statements were prepared at the end of the fiscal period. The net income was $25 000. The accountant quit after preparing the statements and a new accountant began work in the new year. At the end of the second year the accounts appear as summarized below:

Revenue		Expenses	
	Year 1 100 000	*Year 1* 75 000	
	Year 2 130 000	*Year 2* 90 000	
	Total 230 000	*Total* 165 000	

Financial statements prepared at the end of the second year indicated a net income of $65 000. The owner thought this was too good to be true. The owner was right!

a) Why is the $65 000 net income figure incorrect?
b) What is the correct net income for the second year?

What is a business worth? Jeremy Crunch owns the Great Sounds Disco. He wishes to sell his business and approaches you with this offer: he will sell you his business, including all its assets and liabilities, for $15 000. Jeremy states that the business has earned a net income every year for the last eight years. He provides this balance sheet information: **Case 4**

Assets			
Cash		2000 —	
Accounts Receivable		500 —	
Supplies		1 000 —	
Equipment		20 000 —	
Accumulated Depreciation : Equipment			14 750 —
Delivery Van		9 000 —	
Accumulated Depreciation : Del. Van			7 562 —
Liabilities			
Bank Loan			2000 —

Jeremy states that the business is well worth $15 000 since the van and equipment cost a total of $29 000.

a) What is the Owner's Equity in this business?
b) What is the book value of the van and equipment?
c) Approximately how many years have the equipment and van been owned by the business?
d) What do you think is a fair selling price based only on the figures provided?
e) What other factors might affect the setting of a fair price for this business?

Recording Depreciation J. Allin is the owner of a furniture restoration and refinishing business. The business has a delivery van worth $9 000 and equipment worth $14 000. Depreciation has not been recorded on these fixed assets. **Case 5**

a) What effect has the omission of depreciation on the operating results of the business?
b) How is income tax affected?
c) Why might depreciation have been deliberately not recorded?

Career Profile

The Asset of Good Secretarial Skills Frances Burke was born in Nova Scotia and, after graduating from high school, went on to commercial college where she studied typing, shorthand, and accounting. On completion of her college courses, she wrote the Civil Service secretarial examinations for the Department of External Affairs, passing with flying colours. After a waiting period of about six months, Frances was offered a position at the Canadian Embassy in Washington, where she stayed for five enjoyable years. Her typing ability stood her in good stead here, as diplomatic despatches are typed on very heavy, embossed paper, and erasures do not exist – if an error is made, the whole despatch is retyped. She did well in her work, and was offered the position of Junior Passport Officer, a post that would have carried diplomatic status. However, marriage was in the offing, and Frances declined the job offer to return to Canada, settling in Vancouver with her husband.

After nearly four years of happy married life, and a baby boy, her husband was killed in an automobile accident, and Frances was forced to return to the job market. A good friend advised her: "Get out of the secretarial field and into the managerial. Get some public relations and advertising agency experience; then apply for a managerial job." She did just that, working for a public relations office for two years, then for a large advertising agency for two years, and finally applied for, and got, the position of Assistant Public Relations Director for a large book publishing firm.

In the early part of her career, Frances used her secretarial skills to the best advantage. As she obtained more responsible positions, her training in accounting became invaluable to her various jobs. Such tasks as budgeting, salary negotiations, and promotional expense transactions became part of her day-to-day tasks. During the years, contacts she made in the publishing industry took her to many far ranging locations including California for five years, Fort Lee, New Jersey for a year, and back to California for another four years. By the time her son had grown, finished college, and married, Frances was nearing retirement age and she decided to return to Canada.

After reviewing her financial situation, she discovered she would have to have more than just retirement income if she wished to have a few luxuries besides her bread-and-butter. She applied for, and obtained, a position as manuscript typist for a textbook publishing firm. At the age of 66 when most of her peers have retired on a limited income, Frances is securely entrenched in a job that is not physically taxing, is extremely interesting, and shows every evidence of being as permanent as she wants it to be.

CHAPTER 18

Completing the Accounting Cycle

A Merchandising Company

Unit 43

*1

In the last chapter, you were introduced to the accounting procedures performed at the end of the fiscal period. These included adjustments, financial statements, adjusting and closing entries, and the post-closing trial balance. A service business, Management Consultant Services, was used to explain the closing procedures.

In this chapter, the procedures for completing the accounting cycle for a merchandising company called Fraser Enterprises will be described. Fraser Enterprises is a distributor of mechanical and heating equipment such as furnaces, humidifiers, air conditioners, and dehumidifiers. Fraser Enterprises purchases these products from manufacturers and sells them to customers who are heating contractors, electrical contractors, and builders.

Adjusting the Books

*2

A merchandising firm must prepare adjustments for the same reason a service company must – so that the financial statements will be accurate. Adjustments to prepaid expense accounts and fixed assets are similar to those prepared for a service business. However, additional adjustments are necessary for merchandising companies. These include adjusting the Merchandise Inventory account, setting up an Allowance for Bad Debts, and recording amounts owing.

Credit Sales Almost all companies and all consumers buy *on credit* at some time. They buy when they need or desire goods or services and they pay when they have the cash to settle their debts. Our economy relies heavily on credit: there are more credit sales made than cash sales. In many product areas, a business cannot survive if it does not offer its customers the privilege of *buying now and paying later*.

Selling on credit is a necessity for most companies.

Sometimes Customers Do Not Pay An accounting problem arises when customers do not pay their debts. Suppose that for the year 19__1, Fraser Enterprises made sales worth $320 000. The net income for the year is $69 600. If in the next year, 19__2, customers defaulted on 19__1 sales worth $2 000, the net income of $69 600 would be incorrect. It includes sales of $2 000 for which money will never be received. A more accurate net income figure is $67 600.

*3

Figure 18.1 shows part of the balance sheet for 19__1. The Accounts Receivable figure of $53 000 includes the $2 000 in credit sales, which will never be paid by customers.

Fraser Enterprises Partial Balance Sheet December 31, 19__	
Current Assets	
Cash	12 000 00
Accounts Receivable	53 000 00

Figure 18.1 *Partial balance sheet for Fraser Enterprises*

At the time the balance sheet was prepared at the end of 19__1, the business hoped to collect all $53 000 of the Accounts Receivable. However, during 19__2, $2 000 worth of the Accounts Receivable proved to be uncollectable. The $53 000 Accounts Receivable in Figure 18.1 is therefore not accurate. A figure of $51 000 more correctly describes the value of the Accounts Receivable.

*4

Bad debts are amounts owed by customers which are uncollectable

The Accountant's Problem Because of past experience, the accountant knows that despite anything a business does, there will be *bad debts.* Some customers will not, or cannot, pay their debts. However, the accountant does not know which customers will not pay, nor does the accountant know the exact amount that will not be paid. Past experience only indicates that there *will* be a loss due to bad debts.

Bad Debts Expense is the loss due to uncollectable accounts.

If there will be a loss due to bad debts, the books of a company must be adjusted to reflect the *expected* bad debts so that the financial statements will be more accurate. In Figure 18.2, an expense of $2 000, called Bad Debts Expense, has been included in the expense section of the income statement. This results in an adjusted net income for the year of $67 600.

Fraser Enterprises Income Statement For the Year Ended December 31, 19__		
Revenue:		
Sales		320 000 00
Cost of Goods Sold:		
Cost of Goods Sold		114 000 00
Gross Profit		206 000 00
Operating Expenses:		
Bad Debts Expense	2 000 00	
Other Expenses	136 400 00	
Total Expenses		138 400 00
Net Income		67 600 00

Figure 18.2 *Income statement with Bad Debts Expense included*

In the partial balance sheet shown in Figure 18.3, Accounts Receivable is shown with a net value of $51 000. Compare the Accounts Receivable amounts in Figures 18.1 and 18.3. *Which is more accurate? Why?*

Fraser Enterprises Partial Balance Sheet December 31, 19__		
Current assets		
Cash		12 000 00
Accounts Receivable	53 000 00	
Less: Allowance for Bad Debts	2 000 00	51 000 00

Figure 18.3 *Partial balance sheet with Allowance for Bad Debts included*

Adjustment for Bad Debts

A business which grants credit to its customers can use its past history to *estimate* its bad debts. Suppose Fraser Enterprises estimates that $2 000 worth of its Accounts Receivable on December 31, 19__1, will eventually become bad debts. This adjusting entry is made:

Date		Particulars	PR	Debit	Credit
19_1					
Dec.	31	Bad Debts Expense		2 000 —	
		Allowance for Bad Debts			2 000 —
		To record the estimated bad			
		debts for the year 19-1			

The effect of this entry is shown in T-account form as follows:

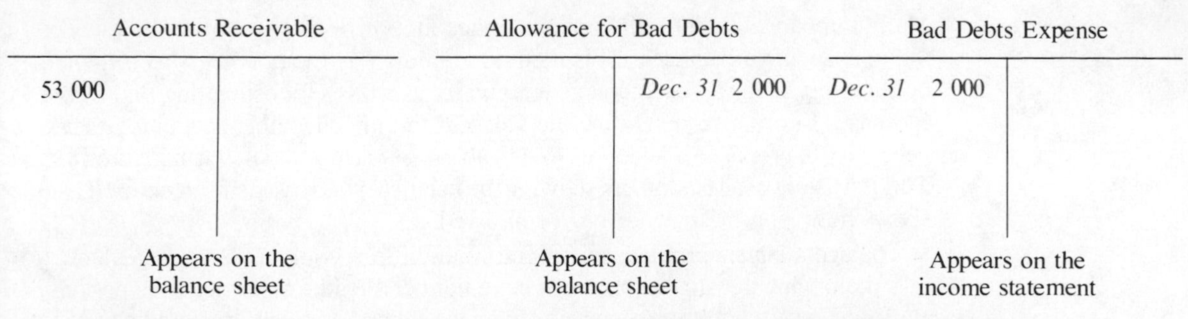

Bad Debts Expense Bad Debts Expense appears as an expense account on the income statement as shown on Figure 18.2. At the end of the fiscal period, Bad Debts Expense is closed into the Revenue and Expense Summary account. During the fiscal period, there is no balance in the Bad Debts Expense account. It is opened with the adjustment made at the end of the fiscal period. It is then reduced to a zero balance when the closing entries are prepared.

*5

The Bad Debts account is an expense account.

*6

Allowance for Bad Debts is a valuation account in the asset section of the balance sheet.

Allowance for Bad Debts The balance sheet in Figure 18.3 contains the Accounts Receivable Control account with a balance of $53 000. Fraser Enterprises estimates that $2 000 of the Accounts Receivable balance will become bad debts. *Why is the asset Accounts Receivable not credited $2 000 when the adjustment is made?*

This is not done because it is not known which customer balances will become uncollectable. Therefore, it is not possible to credit any customer in the Accounts Receivable Ledger. Furthermore, it is not possible to credit the Accounts Receivable Control account in the General Ledger because the control account must always be equal to the total of the individual customer balances in the Accounts Receivable Ledger. This is why the account *Allowance for Bad Debts* is credited with the estimated uncollectable amount.

The Allowance for Bad Debts account appears in the asset section of the balance sheet but is considered to be a *contra* account or a *valuation* account. It is used to determine a realistic valuation for the Accounts Receivable. Another valuation or contra account is the Accumulated Depreciation account (see page 425). A contra account or a valuation account is really a *negative* account. It is used to produce the correct balance sheet value for an asset.

*7

Estimating Bad Debts Expense Before the financial statements are prepared at the end of the fiscal period, an adjustment for bad debts must be made. The amount of the adjustment can only be an estimate based on past experience.

A company may use any one of several methods for estimating Bad Debts Expense. Whichever method is used it should be consistently followed. It is not considered good accounting practice to alternate between methods. Following are descriptions of two methods of estimating Bad Debts Expense – the *balance sheet method* and the *income statement method*.

Balance Sheet Method

The balance sheet method uses a percentage of Accounts Receivable as a basis for estimating Bad Debts Expense.

Many companies examine their customer accounts in order to estimate the value of the uncollectable balances. This method is known as the *balance sheet method* because it uses the asset Accounts Receivable as a basis for estimating Bad Debts Expense. In order to determine the value of the uncollectable accounts, it is necessary to prepare an Accounts Receivable *age analysis* as shown in Figure 18.4. This is a listing of all customers showing the balance owed by each customer. It also shows how long the balance has been owed.

The age analysis provides useful information to a company's management. It tells them which customer balances have not been paid for various time periods. With this information, a manager can decide when to stop giving credit to a customer or when to start *collection proceedings* against a customer.

At the end of a fiscal period, the age analysis is used to determine the amount required for the Bad Debt Expense adjustment. Here is how it is done. For each age group, the accountant estimates a percentage loss. For example, past experience might indicate that 50% of all debts over 90 days past due will be uncollectable. Figure 18.4 shows that $1 900 is over 90 days old. Therefore,

Accounts Receivable Age Analysis
December 31, 19__

Customer	Balance of Accounts Receivable	Current Accounts Receivable	1 d to 30 d Overdue	31 d to 60 d Overdue	61 d to 90 d Overdue	91 d Overdue
Axon	$ 400	$ 400				
Bell	200	50	$ 50	$ 100		
Clark	2 600	2 600				
Dervin	800				$ 800	
Elichuk	600	600				
All Others	48 400	40 000	4 800	900	800	$1 900
Total	$53 000	$43 650	$4 850	$1 000	$1 600	$1 900

Figure 18.4 *Age analysis prepared for Accounts Receivable*

$950 (0.50 × 1 900 = 950) will probably be uncollectable. In a similar way, estimates are made for each of the age groups. Figure 18.5 shows the percent considered uncollectable for each group and the total amount of estimated bad debts.

Estimated Bad Debts
For the Year 19__

Age of Accounts	Amount	Percent Estimated to be Uncollectable	Bad Debts Estimate
Current	$43 650	1%	$ 436
1 d to 30 d	4 850	4%	194
31 d to 60 d	1 000	10%	100
61 d to 90 d	1 600	20%	320
Over 90 d	1 900	50%	950
	$53 000		$2 000

Figure 18.5 *Estimated amount of Accounts Receivable that will become bad debts*

The total of $2 000 shown in Figure 18.5 is the amount required in the Allowance for Bad Debts account. This adjusting entry is made:

				Debit	Credit
Dec.	31	Bad Debts Expense		2 000 —	
		Allowance for Bad Debts			2 000 —
		To record estimated bad debts			

*8

When using the balance sheet method of estimating Bad Debts Expense any existing balance in the Allowance for Bad Debts account must be considered.

Previous Balance in the Allowance Account When using the balance sheet method of estimating bad debts, any existing balance in the contra account (Allowance for Bad Debts) *must* be considered. For example, suppose the age analysis indicates an estimate for bad debts of $2 000, but there is already a credit balance of $50 in the Allowance for Bad Debts account. A credit of only $1 950 is required. This would be the adjusting entry:

Dec.	31	Bad Debts Expense	1 950 —	
		Allowance for Bad Debts		1 950 —
		To increase the allowance		
		account to $2000		
		Previous credit balance 50		
		Adjustment 1950		
		Total 2000		

The result of the adjusting entry in T-account form would appear as follows:

Bad Debt Expense			Allowance for Bad Debts	
Dec. 31	1 950		*Balance*	50
			Dec. 31	1 950
			New Balance	2 000

Appears on the income statement

Appears on the balance sheet

Where does the $50 beginning balance in the Allowance for Bad Debts account originate? The answer is that the balance comes from the estimate of the previous fiscal period. Remember the adjustment for bad debts is an *estimate* only. It is usually impossible to estimate the exact amount of the bad debts. There will generally be a debit or a credit balance in the allowance account. When using the balance sheet method of adjusting bad debts, the previous balance must be considered.

It is possible to have a debit balance in the Allowance for Bad Debts account. Suppose the age analysis indicates an estimate of $2 000 for bad debts. There is an existing debit balance of $100 in the Allowance for Bad Debts account. An adjustment of $2 100 is necessary. This is the entry:

Dec.	31	Bad Debts Expense	2 100 —	
		Allowance for Bad Debts		2 100 —
		To increase the allowance		
		account to $2000		
		Previous debit balance 100		
		Adjustment, credit 2100		
		New Balance, credit 2000		

When using the balance sheet method of estimating bad debts, these points must be remembered.

- An accounts receivable age analysis is prepared.
- From the age analysis, the estimated bad debts total is determined.
- The adjustment must take into consideration any existing balance in the Allowance for Bad Debts account.

Income Statement Method

*9

The balance sheet approach is based on the question *"How much of the Accounts Receivable will be uncollectable?"* The second approach, called the income statement method, is based on the question *"How much of this year's sales will become bad debts?"*

The income statement method uses a percentage of net sales as the basis for estimating Bad Debts Expense.

This is how the income statement method works. The accountant examines the bad debt losses in the past years. If, for instance, the losses have consistently been about 1% of net sales, then the same percentage is used for the current year's adjustment. If sales are $210 000 and sales returns are $10 000, the net sales are $200 000. 1% of $200 000 is $2 000. This adjustment is made.

Dec.	31	Bad Debts Expense		2000 —	
		Allowance for bad debts			2000 —
		To record bad debts of 1%			
		of net sales			

Previous Balance in the Allowance Account When the income statement method is used, the previous balance in the Allowance for Bad Debts account is ignored. This method stresses the relationship of the income statement accounts, bad debts, and sales of the current period. It does not take into consideration the asset, Accounts Receivable.

When using the income statement method of estimating Bad Debts Expense the previous balance in the Allowance for Bad Debts account is ignored.

Writing Off Uncollectable Accounts

*10

Three accounts are involved in the adjustment for bad debts. They are Accounts Receivable, Allowance for Bad Debts, and Bad Debts Expense. The first two accounts appear in the asset section on the balance sheet. The third, Bad Debts Expense, is an expense on the income statement. It is closed at the end of the fiscal period. At the beginning of the new fiscal period, these three accounts will appear in T-account form as follows:

Accounts Receivable			
Dec. 31	53 000		

Appears on balance sheet

Allowance for Bad Debts			
		Balance	50
		Dec. 31	1 950
		New Balance	2 000

Appears on balance sheet as a *contra* asset account

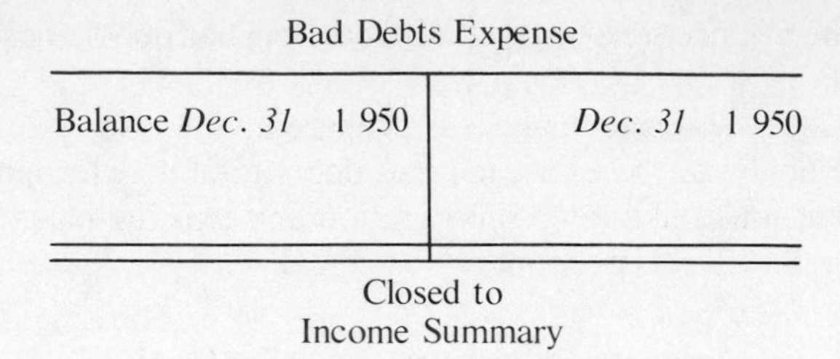

Notice that when the new period begins, there is a zero balance in the Bad Debts Expense account. There is a credit balance of $2 000 in the Allowance for Bad Debts account to take care of the expected uncollectable accounts.

What does a company do when it determines that it will never be able to collect a debt owed by a customer? Examine the following system used by Fraser Enterprises. Suppose that after several months a customer of Fraser Enterprises, J. Wilson, declares bankruptcy. By March 12, it is clearly determined that the $750 owed by J. Wilson will never be collected. The following entry is made:

Mar.	12	Allowance for Bad Debts		750 —	
		Accounts Receivable, J. Wilson			750 —
		To write off J. Wilson's			
		account as uncollectable			

Notice that in this entry, Bad Debts Expense is not used. The loss is written off against the Allowance for Bad Debts account which was set up in expectation of, or to allow for, such losses. Remember that a total of $2 000 was recorded in the Bad Debts Expense account when the adjustment was made. To record the $750 loss in the Bad Debts Expense account would be wrong because this would mean the expense would be recorded twice: once in the adjustment and once in the write-off.

After writing off J. Wilson's account, the T-accounts would appear as follows:

Accounts Receivable	
Dec. 31 53 000	

Allowance for Bad Debts	
March 12 750	*Dec. 31* 2 000

Bad Debts Expense	
Dec. 31 1 950	*Dec. 31* 1 950

No change to this account

Accounts Receivable/ J. Wilson	
Balance 750	*March 12* 750

This account is now closed

During the year, write-off entries are made whenever it is certain that a debt is uncollectable. At the end of the year, there will probably be a balance in the

Allowance for Bad Debts account. It is almost impossible to be exactly correct in estimating a year's uncollectable accounts. When the next fiscal period ends, the balance in the Allowance for Bad Debts account must be considered if the balance sheet method of adjusting for bad debts is used. The income statement method ignores any such balance.

Bad Debts for a Service Business A service business may also have bad debts. The procedures for adjusting and closing entries and the methods of determining the amount of Bad Debts Expense are the same for a service business as those procedures described in this chapter for a merchandising company.

Unrecorded Expenses

An adjusting entry is required for any expense which is owed, but has not been recorded. An example is interest owed on loans but not recorded. Suppose $10 000 was borrowed by Fraser Enterprises from a bank on October 1 and is to be repaid in six months. Interest at 9% is charged by the bank. The following entry is made when the money is borrowed: ***11**

Oct.	1	Cash		10 000 —	
		Bank Loan			10 000 —
		Borrowed $10 000 for six			
		months at 9% interest			

On December 31, at the end of the fiscal period, the bank is owed three months' interest. This amount owing is an expense and should be on the income statement. The interest figure for three months is $225. This amount must be shown in an account called Interest Expense. The adjustment necessary is:

Dec.	31	Interest Expense		225 —	
		Interest Payable			225 —
		To record October, November,			
		and December interest			
		(10 000 x 0.09 x 3/12 = 225)			

After this entry has been posted, the Bank Loan, Interest Expense, and Interest Payable accounts appear as follows:

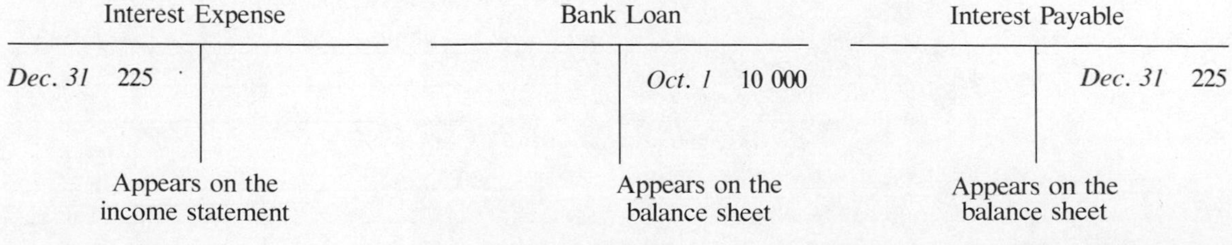

What would be wrong with the financial statements if this adjustment were not made? First of all, the expenses would be too low and this would cause the net income to be $225 too high. Because net income would be overstated, the final owner's equity total would also be too high.

*12

A second example of unrecorded expenses is salaries earned but not yet paid. Fraser Enterprises pays a commission to its sales staff of 10% of their monthly sales. The commission is paid the following month for the previous month's sales. In December, the sales staff made sales of $12 000. The commission of $1 200 ($0.10 \times 12\,000 = 1\,200$) is paid at the end of January. However, since it was earned in December, the amount of commission should be part of the financial statements prepared in December. This adjustment is necessary:

Dec.	31	Salaries Expense		1 200 —	
		Salaries Payable			1 200 —
		To record December commissions			
		owing sales staff			

When this entry is posted, the accounts appear as follows:

Salaries Expense

Dec. 31	110 000	
31	1 200	
Balance	111 200	

Salaries Payable

	Dec. 31	1 200

If this entry were not made, by how much would the expenses be understated? By how much would the net income be overstated? By how much would the liabilities be understated?

*13

Accrued Expenses The two adjustments for interest and salaries were made because expenses had accumulated or built up, but had not been recorded. The term *accrued expenses* is sometimes used to describe such expenses.

*14

Accrued Revenue It is also possible to accumulate revenue but not record the revenue by the end of the fiscal period. The term *accrued revenue* is used to describe such a transaction. For example, a sale may have been agreed upon with a customer, but the documents may not have been completed or recorded. The following entry is made:

Dec.	31	Accounts Receivable		1 000 —	
		Sales			1 000 —
		To record sales made but			
		not recorded			

Adjustments and the Work Sheet

*15

In the first part of this chapter, you learned how to prepare adjusting entries for bad debts, interest owing, and salaries owing. These adjustments were described in General Journal form. In this part of the chapter, the work sheet will be used to plan adjustments for a merchandising company.

The accountant for Fraser Enterprises has prepared the trial balance for the fiscal period ended December 31. It is shown on the work sheet in Figure 18.6. The following information is used to prepare the adjustments on the work sheet.

- The age analysis indicates that a balance of $2 000 is required in the Allowance for Bad Debts account.
- There is $2 000 worth of supplies left at the end of the year.
- Depreciation is recorded using the declining balance method. The equipment depreciates 20% and the building 5%.
- $225 Interest Expense is owed on the bank loan.
- $1 200 Salaries Expense is owed to the employees.

Adjustment for Bad Debts Fraser Enterprises uses the balance sheet method for estimating bad debts. The age analysis indicates that $2 000 is required in the Allowance for Bad Debts account. Since there is already a credit balance, an adjustment of $1 950 is made. Bad Debts Expense is added to the work sheet and is debited $1 950. A credit of $1 950 is written on line three opposite Allowance for Bad Debts. An *(a)* is written beside the debit and credit amounts in the adjustment columns.

*16

Adjustment for Supplies An inventory of supplies shows a $2 000 total for supplies on hand at the end of the year. The Supplies account on the work sheet had a $4 500 balance. An adjustment of $2 500 is required. Supplies Expense is added to the work sheet and is debited $2 500, the amount of the supplies used. Supplies (line five) is credited $2 500. This adjustment is coded *(b)*.

*17

Adjustment for Depreciation The declining balance method of depreciating fixed assets is used by Fraser Enterprises. The declining balance of the Equipment account is $12 800 (23 000 – 10 200 accumulated depreciation = 12 800). The rate of depreciation is 20% per year. Therefore, Depreciation Expense of $2 560 (0.20 × 12 800 = 2 560) is added to the work sheet. Accumulated Depreciation, Equipment, is credited $2 560 (line seven). The adjustment is coded *(c)*. The building depreciates at the rate of 5% per year on the declining balance which is now $111 800. Depreciation Expense for the building is $5 590 (111 800 × 0.05 = 5 590). This adjustment is coded *(d)*.

*18

Adjustment for Accrued Interest Three months' interest is owed on the bank loan and amounts to $225 (10 000 × 0.09 × 3/12 = 225). Both Interest Expense and Interest Payable are added to the work sheet. The $225 adjustment is coded *(e)*.

*19

Adjustment for Accrued Salaries The salaries adjustment is made to record the $1 200 owed to the employees. Salaries is debited $1 200. Salaries Payable is added to the work sheet and is credited $1 200.

Fraser Enterprises
Work Sheet
For the Year Ended December 31, 19__

	ACCOUNT TITLE	ACC. NO.	TRIAL BALANCE		ADJUSTMENTS		INCOME STATEMENT		BALANCE SHEET		
			DEBIT	CREDIT	DEBIT	CREDIT	DEBIT	CREDIT	DEBIT	CREDIT	
1	Cash	100	12 000 —						12 000 —		1
2	Accounts Receivable	102	53 000 —						53 000 —		2
3	Allowance for Bad Debts	103		50 —		(a) 1 950 —				2 000 —	3
4	Merchandise Inventory Jan. 1	120	90 000 —				90 000 —	86 000 —	86 000 —		4
5	Supplies	131	4 500 —			(b) 2 500 —			2 000 —		5
6	Equipment	140	23 000 —						23 000 —		6
7	Accumulated Depreciation: Equipment	141		10 200 —		(c) 2 560 —				12 760 —	7
8	Building	142	160 000 —						160 000 —		8
9	Accumulated Depreciation: Building	143		48 200 —		(d) 5 590 —				53 790 —	9
10	Accounts Payable	200		23 450 —						23 450 —	10
11	Bank Loan	221		10 000 —						10 000 —	11
12	Mortgage Payable	231		88 000 —						88 000 —	12
13	D. S. Fraser, Capital	300		97 000 —						97 000 —	13
14	D. S. Fraser, Drawing	301	8 000 —						8 000 —		14
15	Sales	400		320 000 —				320 000 —			15
16	Purchases	500	110 000 —				110 000 —				16
17	Advertising Expense	520	5 000 —				5 000 —				17
18	General Expense	521	4 000 —				4 000 —				18
19	Salaries Expense	522	120 000 —		(f) 1 200 —		121 200 —				19
20	Utilities Expense	523	7 400 —				7 400 —				20
21			596 900 —	596 900 —							21
22	Bad Debts Expense	524			(a) 1 950 —		1 950 —				22
23	Supplies Expense	525			(b) 2 500 —		2 500 —				23
24	Depreciation Expense: Equipment	526			(c) 2 560 —		2 560 —				24
25	Depreciation Expense: Building	527			(d) 5 590 —		5 590 —				25
	Interest Expense	528			(e) 225 —		225 —				
	Interest Payable	201				(e) 225 —				225 —	
	Salaries Payable	202				(f) 1 200 —				1 200 —	
					14 025 —	14 025 —	350 425 —	406 000 —	344 000 —	288 425 —	
	Net Income						55 575 —			55 575 —	
							406 000 —	406 000 —	344 000 —	344 000 —	

Adjustments for Merchandise Inventory

The work sheet in Figure 18.6 contains the account Merchandise Inventory with a January balance of $90 000. This means that at the beginning of the fiscal period, there were goods on hand which cost $90 000. During the year, merchandise was sold and the sales transactions were recorded in the Sales account. Merchandise was purchased when it was required and recorded in the Purchases account.

*20 The Merchandise Inventory account shows the cost of goods on hand at a specific date.

At the end of the year, the Merchandise Inventory account must be adjusted since it contains the cost of the merchandise on hand at the beginning of the year, January 1. This figure is incorrect. It has changed because of sales and purchases of merchandise during the year. The Merchandise Inventory must be adjusted so that it contains the value of the inventory on hand at the end of the year (December 31).

Taking Inventory During the fiscal period, entries are not made in the Merchandise Inventory account. At the end of the fiscal period, a physical count, called *taking an inventory,* is made of merchandise on hand. This results in a new dollar amount for the Merchandise Inventory account of $86 000, which is the actual value of the merchandise on hand. The new amount is used in making the adjustment to the account. This entry is made to record the new inventory figure:

During the fiscal period entries are not made in the Merchandise Inventory account.

Dec.	31	Merchandise Inventory		86 000 —	
		Income Summary			86 000 —
		To record the ending			
		inventory			

This entry is necessary because the inventory on hand at the end of the year is an asset and must be recorded. The following T-account shows that the Merchandise Inventory account now has two debits. The beginning-of-the-year figure of $90 000 and the new end-of-the-year figure of $86 000 are shown:

	Merchandise Inventory		
Beginning inventory ⟶	*Jan. 1*	90 000	
Ending inventory ⟶	*Dec. 31*	86 000	

*21

A second entry is made to remove the beginning inventory figure. This is necessary because the beginning merchandise value has been replaced by the end-of-the-year merchandise inventory figure of $86 000. This entry is made to transfer out the beginning inventory to the Income Summary account:

Dec.	31	Income Summary		90 000 —	
		Merchandise Inventory			90 000 —
		To close the beginning			
		inventory into the			
		summary account			

◄ **Figure 18.6** *Completed work sheet for Fraser Enterprises*

The merchandise inventory account now appears as follows:

Merchandise Inventory

Jan. 1	90 000	*Dec. 31*	90 000
Dec. 31	86 000		

The balance of the inventory account is now $86 000, the value of the ending inventory. When the financial statements are prepared, Merchandise Inventory, $86 000 will appear in the current asset section of the balance sheet.

The Income Summary T-account follows. Note that it has a debit and a credit in it as a result of the inventory adjustments.

Income Summary

90 000	86 000

The beginning inventory of $90 000 is on the left, or expenses and cost side, of the summary account. The new inventory figure of $86 000 is on the revenue side. Figure 18.6 shows how the debit of $90 000 and credit of $86 000 are recorded on the work sheet.

Two entries involving inventory have been described. One entry reduces the inventory account to zero by transferring the *beginning* inventory to the Income Summary account. The second entry records the *ending* inventory in the Merchandise Inventory account. Since both of these entries involve the Income Summary account they are prepared as part of the closing entries.

*22

Recording the Inventory Adjustment on the Work Sheet The two entries that have just been described show how the Merchandise Inventory Account is adjusted at the end of the fiscal period. These steps are followed on the work sheet in Figure 18.6:

1. Transfer the beginning inventory ($90 000) to the debit column of the income statement section. This decreases the net income.
2. Record the new inventory ($86 000) in the credit column of the income statement section. This increases the net income.
3. Record the new inventory ($86 000) in the debit column of the balance sheet section. This records the ending inventory as an asset.

Completing the Work Sheet

*23

After the inventory adjustment has been made, the individual amounts on the trial balance are transferred to either the income statement section or the balance sheet section of the work sheet. The columns are totalled and the net income is determined. Then, the work sheet columns are balanced and double ruled.

Figure 18.6 shows the completed work sheet for Fraser Enterprises. The major difference between this work sheet and that of a service company is the addition of the Purchases and Merchandise Inventory accounts. The Purchases account is transferred to the income statement section. The new inventory value is shown in the debit column on the balance sheet and in the credit column of the income statement section. The old, or beginning, inventory value is shown on the debit side of the income statement section.

Financial Statements

Unit 45

When the work sheet has been completed, financial statements are prepared. These include the schedule of cost of goods sold, the income statement, and the balance sheet.

*24

Schedule of Cost of Goods Sold The first statement prepared is the schedule of cost of goods sold. The cost information used to prepare this schedule is found in the income statement section of the work sheet. The cost information used by Fraser Enterprises includes the beginning and ending inventories and the purchases. Fraser Enterprises' schedule of cost of goods sold is shown in Figure 18.7.

Fraser Enterprises Schedule of Cost of Goods Sold For the Year Ended December 31, 19__		
Merchandise Inventory Jan. 1	90 000 —	
Purchases	110 000 —	
Total Cost of Merchandise for Sale	200 000 —	
Merchandise Inventory Dec. 31	86 000 —	
Cost of Goods Sold		114 000 —

Figure 18.7 *Schedule of cost of goods sold for Fraser Enterprises*

Other cost accounts which appear in the schedule of cost of goods sold of some merchandising companies are:

- Transportation on Purchases
- Purchases Returns
- Purchases Discounts
- Duty on Purchases

Income Statement Now that the cost of goods sold figure has been determined from the schedule of cost of goods sold, the income statement can be prepared. Figure 18.7 indicates that the goods sold during the year cost $114 000. This figure is now used on the income statement (Figure 18.8) to determine the gross profit. The items in the revenue and the expenses sections of the income statement are obtained from the work sheet.

*25

Fraser Enterprises Income Statement For the Year Ended December 31, 19__		
Revenue:		
Sales		320 000.00
Cost of Goods Sold (per schedule)		114 000.00
Gross Profit		206 000.00
Operating Expenses:		
Advertising	5 000.00	
General	4 000.00	
Salaries	121 200.00	
Utilities	7 400.00	
Bad Debts	1 950.00	
Supplies	2 500.00	
Depreciation: Equipment	2 560.00	
Depreciation: Building	5 590.00	
Interest	225.00	
Total Expenses		150 425.00
Net Income		55 575.00

Figure 18.8 *Income statement for Fraser Enterprises prepared after cost of goods sold has been determined*

*26

Balance Sheet The data required for the balance sheet is found on the balance sheet section of the work sheet. The classified balance sheet of Fraser Enterprises is shown in Figure 18.9. Notice how Capital is updated in the equity section. The difference between the net income and the Drawing account is added to the Capital shown on the work sheet.

Adjusting and Closing Entries

*27

In the last chapter, you learned that adjusting entries are required so that the adjustments made on the work sheet become part of the permanent records. By coding the adjustments with letters such as *(a)*, *(b)*, *(c)*, and so on, the preparation of the adjusting entries is made quite simple. The adjusting entries made for Fraser Enterprises are shown in the General Journal in Figure 18.10. See if you can trace these entries back to the work sheet (Figure 18.6).

Closing entries are required to prepare the ledger for the next fiscal period and to update the owner's Capital account. The revenue, expense, and cost accounts are closed into the Income Summary account. The Income Summary and Drawing accounts are closed into the Capital account. Four basic closing entries are prepared. They are:

1. Close the credits from the income section of the work sheet.
2. Close the debits from the income section of the work sheet.
3. Close the Income Summary account into the Capital account.
4. Close the Drawing account into the Capital account.

Fraser Enterprises Balance Sheet December 31, 19__			
Assets			
Current Assets			
Cash		12 000 00	
Accounts Receivable	53 000 00		
Less Allowance for Bad Debts	2 000 00	51 000 00	
Merchandise Inventory		86 000 00	
Supplies		2 000 00	151 000 00
Fixed Assets			
Equipment	23 000 00		
Less Accumulated Depreciation	12 760 00	10 240 00	
Building	160 000 00		
Less Accumulated Depreciation	53 790 00	106 210 00	116 450 00
Total Assets			267 450 00
Liabilities and Owner's Equity			
Current Liabilities			
Accounts Payable		23 450 00	
Bank Loan		10 000 00	
Interest Payable		225 00	
Salaries Payable		1 200 00	34 875 00
Long Term Liabilities			
Mortgage Payable			88 000 00
Owner's Equity			
D. S. Fraser, Capital Jan. 1		97 000 00	
Add Net Income for year	55 575 00		
Less Drawings	8 000 00		
Increase in Capital		47 575 00	
D. S. Fraser, Capital December 31			144 575 00
Total Liabilities & Owner's Equity			267 450 00

Figure 18.9 *Balance sheet for Fraser Enterprises*

Included in these entries are two entries involving the adjustment for the Merchandise Inventory account. One entry closes the beginning entry amount and the other records the ending inventory amount in the Merchandise Inventory account.

The General Journal in Figure 18.11 contains the closing entries prepared from the work sheet (Figure 18.6). *Can you trace each entry back to the work sheet? What effect does the credit of $90 000 have on the Merchandise Inventory account? What effect does the debit of $86 000 have on the Merchandise Inventory account?*

GENERAL JOURNAL				PAGE 33
DATE	PARTICULARS	PR	DEBIT	CREDIT
19-- Dec. 31	Bad Debts Expense		1950 —	
	Allowance for Bad Debts			1950 —
	To record estimated bad debts according to Age Analysis Summary			
31	Supplies Expense		2500 —	
	Supplies			2500 —
	To record supplies used			
31	Depreciation Expense: Equipment		2560 —	
	Accumulated Depreciation: Equipment			2560 —
	To record depreciation at 20% using declining balance method			
31	Depreciation Expense: Building		5590 —	
	Accumulated Depreciation: Building			5590 —
	To record depreciation at 5% using declining balance method			
31	Interest Expense		225 —	
	Interest Payable			225 —
	To record 3 months interest owed on bank loan (0.09 × 10 000 × 3/12 = 225)			
31	Salaries Expense		1200 —	
	Salaries Payable			1200 —
	To record salaries owed to employees			

Figure 18.10 *Adjusting entries in General Journal*

GENERAL JOURNAL				PAGE 34	
DATE		PARTICULARS	PR	DEBIT	CREDIT
19-- Dec.	31	Merchandise Inventory		86 000 —	
		Sales		320 000 —	
		Income Summary			406 000 —
		To record the new inventory and to close the Sales account			
	31	Income Summary		350 425 —	
		Merchandise Inventory			90 000 —
		Purchases			110 000 —
		Advertising Expense			5 000 —
		General Expense			4 000 —
		Salaries Expense			121 200 —
		Utilities Expense			7 400 —
		Bad Debts Expense			1 950 —
		Supplies Expense			2 500 —
		Depreciation Expense: Equipment			2 560 —
		Depreciation Expense: Building			5 590 —
		Interest Expense			225 —
		To close the inventory account, the cost accounts, and the expense accounts			
	31	Income Summary		55 575 —	
		D. S. Fraser, Capital			55 575 —
		To transfer the year's net income to the capital account			
	31	D. S. Fraser, Capital		8 000 —	
		D. S. Fraser, Drawings			8 000 —
		To close the drawings account			

Figure 18.11 *Closing entries in General Journal*

ACCOUNT Inventory NO. 120

DATE		PARTICULARS	PR	DEBIT	CREDIT	DR CR	BALANCE
Jan. 19--	1	Beginning Balance	✓	90 000 —		DR	90 000 —
Dec.	31	To close	J34		90 000 —	—	-0-
	31	To record new inventory	J34	86 000 —		DR	86 000 —

ACCOUNT D. S. Fraser, Capital NO. 300

DATE		PARTICULARS	PR	DEBIT	CREDIT	DR CR	BALANCE
Jan. 19--	1	Balance	✓			CR	97 000 —
Dec.	31	Net Income	J34		55 575 —	CR	152 575 —
	31	Drawings	J34	8 000 —		CR	144 575 —

ACCOUNT D. S. Fraser, Drawing NO. 301

DATE		PARTICULARS	PR	DEBIT	CREDIT	DR CR	BALANCE
Dec. 19--	31	Balance	✓			DR	8 000 —
	31	To close	J34	8 000 —		—	-0-

ACCOUNT Income Summary NO. 302

DATE		PARTICULARS	PR	DEBIT	CREDIT	DR CR	BALANCE
Dec. --	31	Inventory and Sales	J34			CR	406 000 —
	31	Inventory, Costs and Expenses	J34	350 425 —		CR	55 575 —
	31	To transfer net income to capital	J34	55 575 —		—	-0-

ACCOUNT Sales NO. 400

DATE		PARTICULARS	PR	DEBIT	CREDIT	DR CR	BALANCE
Dec. 19--	31	Balance	✓			CR	320 000 —
	31	To close	J34	320 000 —		—	-0-

Figure 18.12 *General Ledger accounts after posting of the adjusting and closing entries. Not all the accounts are shown.*

Posting to the Ledger

*28

The adjusting and closing entries in the General Journal are posted to the General Ledger. After this is done, the revenue and expense accounts will have *zero* balances. They will be ready to receive the revenue and expense transactions for the new fiscal period. The Merchandise Inventory account will contain the new inventory figure. The Capital account will be updated. It will contain the new balance which takes into consideration the operating results for the fiscal period.

In Figure 18.12 several of the General Ledger accounts are shown after the adjusting and closing entries have been posted.

Notice that the Sales account is prepared for the next fiscal period. It has a *zero* balance and has been ruled closed. The Inventory account has been closed and re-opened. It contains the new inventory of $86 000. The Capital account has a balance of $144 575, the same as the new capital on the balance sheet in Figure 18.9.

Post-Closing Trial Balance

*29

A final proof is required to ensure that the General Ledger is in balance to start the new fiscal period. Figure 18.13 shows the trial balance prepared after the closing entries have been posted. It contains only asset, liability, and equity accounts. All the revenue, expense and cost accounts have been closed and do not have to be shown on the last trial balance.

Eraser Enterprises
Post Closing Tiridl Balance
December 31, 19__

ACCOUNT TITLE	ACC. NO.	DEBIT	CREDIT
Cash	100	12 000 —	
Accounts Receivable	102	53 000 —	
Allowance for Bad Debts	103		2 000 —
Merchandise Inventory	120	86 000 —	
Supplies	131	2 000 —	
Equipment	140	23 000 —	
Accumulated Depreciation: Equip.	141		12 760 —
Building	142	160 000 —	
Accumulated Depreciation: Building	143		53 790 —
Accounts Payable	200		23 450 —
Bank Loan	221		10 000 —
Interest Payable	201		225 —
Salaries Payable	202		1 200 —
Mortgage Payable	231		88 000 —
D. S. Fraser, Capital	300		144 575 —
		336 000 —	336 000 —

Figure 18.13 *Post-closing trial balance proves the accuracy of the recording process in preparation for the new fiscal period*

Classified Financial Statements

*30

The grouping of accounts using a standardized format is an aid to those who examine and interpret financial statements. Owners, managers, creditors, and government officials examine the financial statements of a variety of companies. Their task is made easier by the use of standard or classified financial statements.

Current assets are listed according to order of liquidity.

Classified Balance Sheet Assets are divided into two sections on the balance sheet – current and fixed as was shown in Figure 18.9. The current assets are listed in order of *liquidity:* that is, in the order in which they will be converted into cash.

In the fixed asset section, the assets which have the longest life are generally listed first.

Order of liquidity is the order in which current assets will be converted into cash.

Current Assets	**Fixed Assets**
Accounts Receivable	Land
Merchandise Inventory	Building
Prepaid Expenses	Equipment

Classified Income Statement There are three main sections in the classified income statement. They are revenue, cost of goods sold, and operating expenses. Two separate categories may be found in the expenses sections of merchandising companies. They are administrative expenses and selling expenses.

Administrative expense is money spent in the general day-to-day operations of a business.

Administrative Expenses Money spent in the general operation of a business is usually classed as an administrative expense. This would include expenses involved in the operation of the business offices and departments other than sales. Office salaries, office supplies, and building maintenance are a few examples.

Selling expense is money spent for the direct purpose of selling goods.

Selling Expenses Money spent for the direct purpose of selling goods is classed as a selling expense. Some examples include sales salaries, advertising, deliveries, and selling supplies.

*31

Allocating Responsibility for Expenses Classifying expenses as administrative or selling expenses provides a detailed breakdown of where the money is being spent. It also allows the top management of a company to allocate responsibility for the spending of money. For example, if the sales manager were to be held responsible for all selling expenses, it would be the responsibility of the sales manager to justify the spending of money for all the selling expenses. The responsibility for administrative expenses may be allocated to someone in the same manner. A person such as an office manager may be held responsible for controlling the administrative expenses.

Some expenses may be allocated as both selling and administrative expenses. For example, Insurance Expense may be incurred on behalf of the office and the sales department. Depreciation Expense may have to be divided between the administrative and the sales sections. It is the accountant's task to determine a fair basis for allocating the expense. For example, if the office occupies 30% of the building, then 30% of the Building Expense would be charged as an administrative expense. If the remaining 70% is occupied by the sales sections, then 70% of the Building Expense would be charged as a selling expense.

Reversing Entries

Earlier in this chapter you learned how to adjust accrued expenses. The example used was $225 interest which was owed on a bank loan. The loan was for six months. At the end of the fiscal period, three months' interest or $225 was owed but had not been recorded because it was not due to be paid until the end of the six months' March 31. *32

The following T-accounts illustrate the adjusting and closing entry dated December 31 and the payment of the six months' interest on March 31.

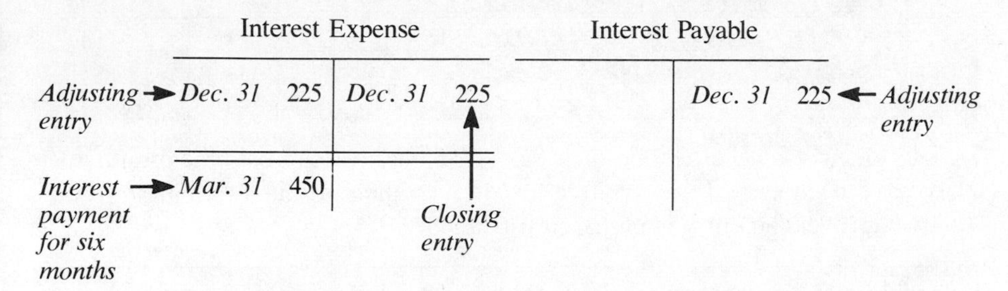

On March 31, payment was made to the bank for six months' interest ($450). This covered the period of the loan, October 1 to March 31. When this entry was made, Interest Expense was debited and Cash was credited. *How much interest has been recorded in the Interest Expense account? Can you see the dilemma?*

Because of the adjusting entry, the interest for October 1 to December 31 was recorded twice, once when the adjustment was made and again when the interest for the period October 1 to March 31 was actually paid to the bank. This double recording of interest is avoided by the use of a reversing entry. On January 3, the first working day after the end of the fiscal period, this entry is made:

19–– Jan.	3	Interest Payable		225 —	
		Interest Expense			225 —
		To reverse the adjusting			
		entry of December 31			

The effect of this entry is shown in the following T-accounts:

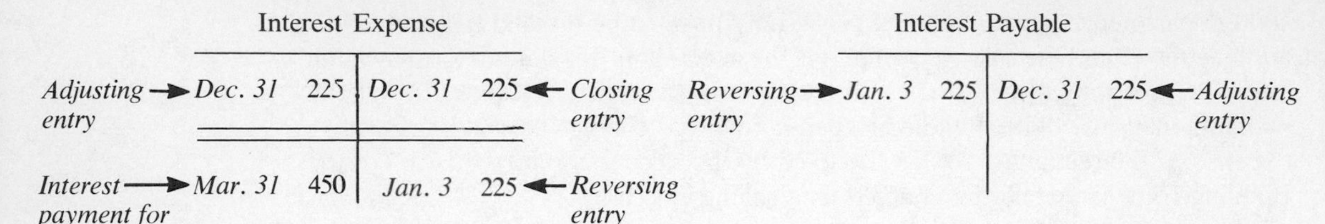

Notice that the reversing entry of January 3 has the effect of allocating half of the actual interest paid to the new fiscal period and half to the previous fiscal period. This is correct and results in accurate financial statements for both fiscal periods.

Reversing entries are necessary to make adjustments to accrued expense and accrued revenue accounts.

Other Reversing Entries Reversing entries are required for all accrued expense and revenue adjustments. Earlier in this chapter an adjusting entry for salaries owed ($1 200) was explained. The adjusting entry was:

Dec.	31	Salaries Expense		1 200 —	
		Salaries Payable			1 200 —
		To record December commissions			
		owed but not yet paid			
		to sales staff			

This entry was necessary because sales commissions are paid the month after they have been earned. To avoid a double recording of this information, the following reversing entry is prepared on January 3:

Jan.	3	Salaries Payable		1 200 —	
		Salaries Expense			1 200 —
		To reverse December 31			
		adjusting entry for			
		accrued commissions			

On January 31, the commissions are paid and this entry is made:

Jan.	31	Salaries Expense		1 200 —	
		Cash			1 200 —
		To pay December commissions			

Can you see the purpose served by the reversing entry? It is required to avoid the double recording of the $1 200. Similar reversing entries are required for all accrued expense and accrued revenue adjustments. The reversing entries for these accrued adjustments are prepared on the first working day of the new fiscal period.

Could reversing entries be avoided by simply debiting the payable account when actual payment is made in the new fiscal period? This avoids the double recording of data in the expense account. The reason this is not done is that it requires great accuracy and a good memory on the part of the accountant. With a number of accrueds and payments spread out over months it would be easy to forget to handle the transactions correctly. To avoid errors and reliance on one person's memory, it is standard accounting practice to use the reversing entry procedure.

Interpreting Accounting Data

Unit 46

*33

Throughout this book, it has been stressed that accounting provides information for decision-making. A good accounting system provides the management of a company with a great deal of data which enables the management to make informed decisions. For example, sales figures can be provided which show total sales for each month. The sales for each month can then be compared with the same month in the previous year. Similar comparisons can be made for expenses, assets, and liabilities. Such comparisons indicate trends both favourable and unfavourable. Management is able to take action when unfavourable trends begin to develop and is able to take advantage of favourable trends. Examples of information provided to management for decision-making purposes have been provided in case studies throughout this book.

Accounting Analysis

The figures on any one set of financial statements are not especially revealing by themselves. They gain significance when compared to other statements. They also become important when they are expressed in a manner that indicates developing trends. Following is a description of several techniques used by accountants to interpret accounting data.

Comparative Financial Statements Changes in financial position are indicated when comparative figures for a series of years are provided. This is often done by using *condensed comparative* statements such as the one in Figure 18.14.

Comparative figures for a series of years show changes in financial position.

Cosentino Enterprises
Comparative Income Statements
For the years 19–9, 19–0, 19–1, 19–2
(in thousands of dollars)

	19–9	19–0	19–1	19–2
Net Sales	$101	$125	$132	$141
Cost of Goods Sold	50	72	78	85
Gross Profit	51	53	54	56
Operating Expenses	35	40	43	47
Net Income	16	13	11	9

Figure 18.14 *Comparative income statements by dollar amounts*

An analysis of the figures shows that sales are increasing, and that gross profit is increasing slightly. However, net income is decreasing. The cause of the downward trend is the increase in expenses and the large increase in the cost of goods sold. Figure 18.15 compares these changes in percentage terms rather than in dollars.

Percentage Change from a Base Year It is helpful to compare the changes in terms of percentages and to relate these changes to a *base year*. In Figure 18.15, figures for the years 19__0, 19__1, 19__2, are compared to a base year, 19__9. The results for 19__9 are considered to be 100%. Results for the three following years are stated as a percentage of the base year figures.

Cosentino Enterprises
Percentage Changes
Base Year 19–9

	19–9	19–0	19–1	19–2
Net Sales	100%	124%	131%	139%
Cost of Goods Sold	100%	144%	156%	170%
Gross Profit	100%	104%	106%	110%
Operating Expenses	100%	114%	123%	134%
Net Income	100%	81%	69%	56%

Figure 18.15 *Comparative income statements by percentages*

Ratios

*34

A ratio is a mathematical relationship of one item to another.

A frequently used technique in accounting analysis is the presentation of financial statement items as ratios. A ratio is a mathematical relationship of one item to another. The use of ratios can be used to place attention on the *inter-relationship* of financial data. Some of the commonly used ratios are:

- current ratio
- debt ratio
- equity ratio
- quick ratio

Each of these ratios is examined by working the various types out for the condensed balance sheet in Figure 18.16.

The current ratio is the relationship between current assets and current liabilities.

Current Ratio One method of measuring a company's ability to pay its current debts is to calculate the *current ratio*. The current ratio is determined by dividing the total current assets by the total current liabilities.

The current ratio for Levesque Sales is 2.8:1. This was obtained by dividing the current assets ($170 000) by the current liabilities, ($60 000) and expressing the result as a ratio. *But what significance has a current ratio of 2.8:1?* Basically it means that the company has 2.8 dollars' worth of current assets for each dollar of current liabilities. This indicates that the company should be able to generate enough cash from its current assets to pay its current debts when they become due.

Levesque Sales
Condensed Balance Sheet
December 31, 19_

Assets		
Current Assets		
Cash	10 000 00	
Accounts Receivable	90 000 00	
Merchandise Inventory	60 000 00	
Prepaid Expenses	10 000 00	
Total Current Assets		170 000 00
Fixed Assets		300 000 00
Total Assets		470 000 00
Liabilities and Owner's Equity		
Current Liabilities		60 000 00
Long-term Liabilities		200 000 00
Owner's Capital		210 000 00
Total Liabilities and Owner's Equity		470 000 00

Figure 18.16 *Balance sheet for Levesque Sales*

A general rule is that a current ratio of 2:1 is satisfactory and suggests that a company can pay its debts. A ratio of 1:1 or less is unfavourable in the eyes of creditors. A very high ratio, for example, 6:1, is not necessarily good. It may indicate poor management. Perhaps too much money is tied up in inventory or by customers not paying their debts on time.

The current ratio is of special interest to creditors and to potential lenders such as banks. A favourable current ratio is a positive factor in obtaining credit or loans. It means that the borrower is in a good position to repay debts and is a good credit risk.

Quick Ratio The *quick ratio* compares the current assets which are very easily converted to cash with the current liabilities. These assets are cash, accounts receivable, and marketable securities. Items such as government bonds and shares in other companies are marketable securities if they can be readily converted to cash.

***35**
The quick ratio is the relationship between current assets that can quickly be converted to cash and current liabilities.

The quick assets are Cash ($10 000) and Accounts Receivable ($90 000) which total $100 000. The current liabilities are $60 000. The quick ratio is obtained by this calculation:

$$\textbf{Quick Ratio} = \frac{100\ 000}{60\ 000} = 1.7:1$$

A quick ratio of 1:1 is considered satisfactory.

The quick ratio and the current ratio when considered together provide a good indication of a company's ability to pay its debts. They are used by creditors as factors in deciding if credit or loans should be granted to a company. The term *acid* ratio is sometimes used instead of quick ratio.

*36

The equity ratio is the relationship between owner's equity and total assets.

Equity Ratio The assets of a company have two financial sources. The money to purchase assets comes from the liabilities or from the owners. The *equity ratio* and the *debt ratio* are methods of comparing the amount of funds to purchase assets supplied by the creditors to the amount supplied by the owners.

In Figure 18.16, the total assets are $470 000. The owner's Capital is $210 000. The equity ratio expressed as a percentage is 45%. That is, 45% of the assets are financed by owner's equity. This is obtained by the calculation:

$$\frac{\textbf{Owner's Equity}}{\textbf{Total Assets}} \times 100 = \frac{210\ 000}{470\ 000} \times 100 = 45\%$$

The debt ratio is the relationship between total debts and total assets.

Debt Ratio In the Levesque Sales balance sheet, the total debts are $260 000 and the total assets are $470 000. The *debt ratio* is determined by this calculation:

$$\frac{\textbf{Total Debts}}{\textbf{Total Assets}} \times 100 = \frac{260\ 000}{470\ 000} \times 100 = 55\%$$

The two ratios, equity and debt, when considered together, indicate that 55% of the assets are financed through debt and 45% by the owners. Generally the owners of a business favour a *low* equity ratio and a higher debt ratio. This is especially true if earnings are satisfactory and interest on the debt is relatively low. However, if the company must pay high interest on its debt the situation is unfavourable because the company must pay out interest and there could be a problem earning enough income to pay the interest.

From a creditor's point of view, the higher the equity ratio, the better. A high equity ratio, for example 70%, indicates that the owners themselves are financing the assets to a great extent. The company should be in a fairly good position to repay its debts because its debt ratio is low. Also, the company should be able to afford to pay its interest on borrowed funds.

Developing Trends Those persons involved in analysing and interpreting accounting data generally do not examine one set of financial statements in isolation. It is common practice to examine several years' data. Some analysts prepare comparative figures for ten years. This points out developing trends and is a help in forecasting what will happen in the future.

Facts to Remember

Bad debts are amounts owed by customers which are uncollectable.

Bad Debts Expense is the loss due to uncollectable accounts.

Bad Debts Expense appears on the income statement.

Allowance for Bad Debts is a valuation account in the asset section of the balance sheet.

The *balance sheet method* uses a percent of Accounts Receivable as a basis for estimating Bad Debts Expense.

When using the *balance sheet method* of estimating Bad Debts Expense, any existing balance in the Allowance for Bad Debts account *must* be considered.

The *income statement method* uses a percentage of net sales as the basis for estimating Bad Debts Expense.

When using the *income statement method* of estimating Bad Debts Expense, the previous balance in the Allowance for Bad Debts account is *ignored.*

Bad Debts Expense is closed at the end of the fiscal period.

Uncollectable accounts are written off against the Allowance for Bad Debts account.

Accrued expense is an expense which has been incurred but not yet recorded in the books.

Accrued revenue is revenue earned during the fiscal period but not yet recorded in the books.

The *Merchandise Inventory* account shows the cost of goods on hand at a specific date.

Current assets are listed according to order of liquidity.

Order of liquidity is the order in which current assets will be converted into cash.

Fixed assets are listed with those having the longest life coming first.

Reversing entries are necessary to make adjustments to accrued expense and accrued revenue accounts.

Comparative figures for a series of years show changes in financial position.

A *ratio* is a mathematical relationship of one item to another.

The *current ratio* is the relationship between current assets and current liabilities.

The *quick ratio* is the relationship between current assets that can be quickly converted to cash and current liabilities.

The *equity ratio* is the relationship between owner's equity and total assets.

The *debt* ratio is the relationship between total debts and total assets.

Checking Your Reading

Questions

1. Explain the difference between a trading company and a merchandising company.
2. Explain why many companies purchase on credit instead of paying cash immediately for their purchases.
3. On which financial statements do the following two accounts appear:
   a) Bad Debts Expense, b) Allowance for Bad Debts?

4. a) What is the General Journal entry to record Estimated Bad Debts?
   b) Name the financial statement on which each account in the entry from a) would appear.
   c) Which of the two accounts in a) are closed at the end of the fiscal period?
5. Explain the term *contra account*.
6. a) Name the two methods of estimating bad debts.
   b) Which method takes into consideration the previous balance in the Allowance for Bad Debts account?
7. What is the General Journal entry to write off an uncollectable account?
8. When is an account written off as uncollectable?
9. What is the adjusting entry to record interest owed but not recorded?
10. What is the adjusting entry to record salaries owed to employees?
11. Define accrued expenses and give two examples.
12. Define accrued income and give two examples.
13. What is the General Journal entry required to set up the new inventory taken at the end of the fiscal period?
14. What is the General Journal entry required to close the beginning inventory?
15. What is the purpose of classifying financial statements?
16. What are the five separate sections on a classified balance sheet?
17. What are the two classes into which operating expenses may be divided?
18. Explain why reversing entries are necessary.
19. Which adjusting entries require reversing entries?
20. Explain the term *comparative financial statements*.
21. Explain the terms:
    a) current ratio b) quick ratio c) debt ratio d) equity ratio
22. How are each of these ratios calculated:
    a) current ratio b) quick ratio c) debt ratio d) equity ratio
23. How do persons who interpret accounting data identify developing trends?

Applying Your Knowledge

Exercises Part A

1. At the end of the fiscal period, Boutique Anne Marie has a balance of $13 000 in the Accounts Receivable account. It is estimated that the bad debts will be $135.
   a) Prepare the adjusting entry to record the estimated bad debts of $135.
   b) Post to T-accounts.

Accounts Receivable		Allowance for Bad Debts		Bad Debts Expense	
13 000					

c) How much will appear on the income statement for Bad Debts Expense?
d) Show how Accounts Receivable and Allowance for Bad Debts appear on the balance sheet.
e) Which of the three accounts affected by this transaction requires a closing entry? Prepare the closing entry.

2. The accounts receivable age analysis for the Gaylor Trading Company on December 31, 19__1, shows the following totals:

		Days Overdue			
Balance	Current	1 d to 30 d	31 d to 60 d	61 d to 90 d	over 90 d
95 800	78 600	7 700	2 600	3 200	3 700

a) Calculate the allowance for bad debts if it is estimated that the following percentages are uncollectable: Current, 3%; 1 d to 30 d, 10%; 31 d to 60 d, 15%; 61 d to 90 d, 25%; over 90 d, 45%.
b) Calculate the estimated value of the Accounts Receivable.

3. a) Head up the T-accounts that follow:

Accounts Receivable		Allowance for Bad Debts		Bad Debts Expense	
Jan. 31 46 000			*Jan. 31* 145		

b) An age analysis shows that $465 of the Accounts Receivable is estimated to be uncollectable. Journalize and post the necessary adjusting entry.

4. a) Head up the T-accounts that follow:

Accounts Receivable		Allowance for Bad Debts		Bad Debts Expense	
Feb. 28 75 000		*Feb. 28* 265			

b) An age analysis shows that $753 of the Accounts Receivable is estimated to be uncollectable. Journalize and post the necessary adjusting entry.
c) Journalize and post the closing entry.

5. For each of the following cases, give the adjusting entry for bad debts:
a) Estimated bad debts, $13 500; balance in the Allowance for Bad Debts account, $175 credit.
b) Estimated bad debts, $47 600; balance in the Allowance for Bad Debts account, $890 debit.

6. The three companies in the following description all use the income statement method of estimating bad debts. For each, prepare the adjusting entry.
   a) *Company A:* Sales were $90 000. Bad debts are estimated to be 1% of sales.
   b) *Company B:* Sales were $200 000. Bad debts are estimated to be 0.5% of sales.
   c) *Company C*: Sales were $150 000. Bad debts are estimated to be 0.5% of sales.

7. a) Head up the T-accounts that follow:

Accounts Receivable		Allowance for Bad Debts		Bad Debts Expense	
20 000			290		

   b) Record these transactions in a General Journal and post the entries to the T-accounts.

Jan. 17 Write off T. Tallman's account of $85 as uncollectable. Tallman is bankrupt.
25 Write off M. Swords' account of $190 as uncollectable. Swords has left town and cannot be located.
30 An age analysis shows that $300 of Accounts Receivable is estimated to be uncollectable. Prepare the necessary adjusting entry. Use the balance sheet method, remembering that the balance in the Allowance for Bad Debts account must be considered.
30 Close the Bad Debts Expense account.

8. Journalize these transactions in a General Journal:

May 1 No entry required. The balance in the Allowance for Bad Debts is $150 credit.
9 Write off Joyce Turner's account of $115 as uncollectable.
23 Write off E. McKurcher's account of $40 as uncollectable.
30 The age analysis indicates that $180 is required in the Allowance for Bad Debts account. The balance sheet method is being used. Prepare the adjusting entry.
30 Close the Bad Debts Expense account.

9. a) Head up the T-accounts that follow:

Bank Loan		Interest Payable		Interest Expense	
	6 000				

   b) At the end of the fiscal period, $300 interest has accrued. Prepare the adjusting entry to record the $300 interest.
   c) Post the adjusting entry to the T-accounts. Prepare the necessary closing entry and post.

10. For each of the following cases, give the adjusting entry for interest owing:
   a) $2 400 interest for 12 months to be paid on June 30. Date of adjustment: February 28.
   b) $1 873 interest for nine months to be paid on September 30. Date of adjustment: June 30.
   c) $3 768 interest for six months to be paid on March 31. Date of adjustment: January 31.

11. For each of the following cases, give the adjusting entry for interest owing:
   a) One-year loan for $8 000 at annual interest of 9% to be repaid on March 31. Date of adjustment: August 31.
   b) Six-month loan for $12 000 at annual interest of 8%, to be repaid on October 31. Date of adjustment: June 30.
   c) Four-month loan for $6 500 at annual interest of 9%, to be repaid on July 31. Date of adjustment: April 30.

12. a) Head up the T-accounts that follow:

Salaries Expense	
Dec. 31 29 000	

Salaries Payable	

   b) At the end of the fiscal period, $290 is owed to the employees. Prepare the adjusting entry to record the salaries owing.
   c) Post the adjusting entry to the T-accounts.
   d) Prepare the necessary closing entry and post to the T-account.

13. For each of the following cases, give the adjusting entry for salaries owing:
   a) Sales staff receive a 5% commission on their monthly sales. In May, they sold $26 000 worth of goods for which they are to be paid on June 30. The date of the adjustment is May 31.
   b) The total earnings of all hourly employees is $3 500 per day, excluding Saturdays and Sundays. They are paid every Friday. What will the adjusting entry be if the financial statements are prepared at the end of the working day on Wednesday?

Exercises Part B

14. From the year-end trial balance and the additional information that follows, prepare a work sheet.

   Additional Information:
   - Merchandise Inventory, December 31, valued at $58 000.
   - Supplies on hand, December 31, valued at $2 200.
   - Increase the Allowance for Bad Debts to $600 using the balance sheet method.
   - Fixtures depreciate 20% using the declining balance method.
   - Interest owing but unrecorded, $750.
   - Salaries owed to employees total $500.

Jeans Unlimited
Trial Balance
December 31, 19__

ACCOUNT TITLE	ACC. NO.	DEBIT	CREDIT
Cash	100	14 000 —	
Accounts Receivable	102	30 000 —	
Allowance for Bad Debts	103		50 —
Merchandise Inventory, Jan. 1	120	60 000 —	
Supplies	131	5 000 —	
Store Fixtures	141	15 000 —	
Accumulated Depreciation:			
Store Fixtures	142		7 300 —
Accounts Payable	200		9 000 —
Bank Loan	221		8 000 —
L. Steeves, Capital	300		54 475 —
L. Steeves, Drawing	301	19 000 —	
Sales	400		260 000 —
Purchases	500	80 000 —	
Advertising Expense	510	8 000 —	
Office Expense	511	4 000 —	
Store Expense	512	9 000 —	
Rent Expense	513	14 000 —	
Salaries Expense	514	80 000 —	
Interest Expense	515	825 —	
		338 825 —	338 825 —

15. a) Prepare a work sheet for Ross Stores using the trial balance at the top of page 491.

Additional Information:

- Merchandise Inventory, December 31 valued at $2 400.
- Supplies on hand valued at $450.
- Insurance expired, $1 200.
- Building depreciates 5%, equipment 20%.
- Record bad debts of 1% of net sales.

b) Prepare a schedule of cost of goods sold.
c) Prepare an income statement.
d) Prepare a balance sheet.
e) Journalize the adjusting and closing entries.
f) Post the adjusting and closing entries.
g) Prepare a post-closing trial balance.

Ross Stores
Trial Balance
December 31, 19--

ACCOUNT TITLE	ACC. NO.	DEBIT	CREDIT
Cash	100	3 000 —	
Accounts Receivable	102	8 000 —	
Inventory, Jan. 1	120	21 000 —	
Supplies	121	1 700 —	
Prepaid Insurance	122	2 000 —	
Land	140	40 000 —	
Building	141	120 000 —	
Equipment	143	40 000 —	
Accounts Payable	200		13 700 —
Mortgage Payable	210		50 000 —
M. Ross, Capital	300		140 000 —
M. Ross, Drawing	301	6 000 —	
Sales	400		195 000 —
Sales Returns	401	1 000 —	
Sales Discounts	402	300 —	
Purchases	500	95 000 —	
Transportation on Purchases	501	7 000 —	
Purchases Returns	502		3 300 —
Purchases Discounts	503		3 000 —
Salaries Expense: Selling	510	30 000 —	
Salaries Expense: Administrative	511	20 000 —	
Delivery Expense	512	7 000 —	
General Expense	513	2 000 —	
Property Tax Expense	514	1 000 —	
		405 000 —	405 000 —

16. Prepare schedules of cost of goods sold for each of the following companies. The fiscal period is the month of May, 19--.

Company A: Beginning inventory, $14 000
Purchases, $60 000
Transportation on Purchases, $1 200
Purchases Returns, $3 000
Ending inventory, $12 000

Company B: Beginning inventory, $50 000
Purchases, $80 000
Transportation on Purchases, $4 900
Duty, $6 000
Purchases Returns, $6 000
Purchases Discounts, $1 800
Ending Inventory, $52 000

17. a) Following is a list of expenses. Divide the list into two sections, administrative and selling. Insurance is to be allocated 60% to selling and 40% to administrative. Utilities, Telephone and Depreciation–Building are also divided 60% selling and 40% administrative.
b) What is the total of the selling expenses and the total of the administrative expenses?
c) What is the net income if the gross profit is $32 000?
d) What is the net sales figure if the cost of goods sold is $20 000?

Advertising	$2 000
Utilities	1 200
Salaries – Office	5 000
Delivery	6 000
Office Supplies (used)	400
Insurance	300
Depreciation – Building	2 000
Depreciation – Truck	1 000
Store Supplies (used)	800
Telephone	200

18. a) Prepare a classified income statement for exercise 14. Jeans Unlimited classifies Bad Debts as a selling expense and allocates Supplies Expense, Rent Expense, Depreciation Expense and Salaries Expense 70% to selling expenses and 30% to administrative expenses.
b) Prepare financial statements for Ross Stores in exercise 15. When classifying the income statement, distribute Supplies Expense, Insurance Expense, and Depreciation Expense 75% to selling expense and 25% to administrative expense. Bad Debts Expense is an administrative expense.

Exercises Part C

19. The adjustments presented below were prepared on December 31. In a General Journal prepare the reversing entries which would be made on January 3.

Date		Particulars		Debit	Credit
19-- Dec.	31	Interest Expense		350 –	
		Interest Payable			350 –
		To record interest owed but			
		not yet paid			
Dec.	31	Salaries Expense		195 –	
		Salaries Payable			195 –
		To record salaries owed to			
		workers but not yet paid			

20. A company pays its workers every two weeks. The next pay day is January 4. Employees are owed (but have not been paid) $1 800 for work in December.
a) Prepare the adjusting entry to record salaries owing.
b) Prepare the reversing entry.

21. At the end of the fiscal period, a company has earned, but not yet received, interest of $1 200 on a long-term deposit. Prepare the adjusting and reversing entries. The accounts involved are Interest Receivable and Interest Income Accrued.

22. Comparative income statements for five years follow.
a) What trends are developing?
b) Suggest action management might take.

Ramsay Enterprises
Comparative Income Statements
For Years 1, 2, 3, 4, 5
(in thousands of dollars)

	Year 1	Year 2	Year 3	Year 4	Year 5
Revenue	$120	$140	$130	$125	$122
Expenses	67	72	77	82	87
Net Income	$ 53	$ 68	$ 53	$ 43	$ 35

23. Present the Ramsay Enterprises data in exercise 22 in terms of percentages. Use Year 1 as the base year (100%).

24. a) From the condensed income statement of Susan Toth Sales Co. prepare percentages to compare the dollar figures for years 2, 3, 4 and 5 to the base year, year 1.

Susan Toth Sales Co.
Condensed Income Statement
For years 19–1, 19–2, 19–3, 19–4, 19–5
(in thousands of dollars)

	19–1	19–2	19–3	19–4	19–5
Net Sales	225	243	292	330	375
Cost of Goods	175	180	181	201	220
Gross Profit	50	63	111	129	155
Operating Expenses	75	77	87	99	118
Net Income or (Net Loss)	(25)	(14)	24	30	37

b) Prepare a line graph showing sales and net income for years 1 to 5.
c) Describe the trends which are developing.

25. a) The total current assets are $250 000 and total liabilities are $190 000. What is the current ratio?
b) Calculate the quick ratio using the appropriate data from the following: Cash $6 000; Accounts Receivable $90 000; Government Bonds $20 000; Building $200 000; Current Liabilities $100 000.

c) Calculate the equity ratio and the debt ratio from the following: Total Assets $490 000; Total Liabilities $300 000; Owners's Equity $190 000.

26. a) Calculate the current ratio, quick ratio, debt ratio, and equity ratio for the P. Scobie Co.

b) Prepare a general comment on the financial position of the company.

P. Scobie Company Balance Sheet December 31, 19__		
Assets		
Current Assets		
Cash	85 000 00	
Accounts Receivable	350 000 00	
Merchandise Inventory	400 000 00	
Prepaid Expenses	80 000 00	
Total Current Assets		915 000 00
Fixed Assets		1 300 000 00
Total Assets		2 215 000 00
Liabilities and Owner's Equity		
Current Liabilities		400 000 00
Long-term Liabilities		900 000 00
Owner's Equity		915 000 00
Total Liabilities and Owner's Equity		2 215 000 00

Accounting in Action

Case 1

Taking Inventory At the end of the fiscal period, employees for Trans Canada Distributors made a count of all merchandise on hand. However, a complete section of the warehouse was missed when the inventory was taken. The cost of the merchandise which was missed and not included in the ending inventory figure was $7 500. What effect has this error on the income statement and on the balance sheet?

Case 2

Interpreting Accounting Data 1 The following table presents the net sales and the *actual* bad debts for five years. For each of these years calculate the percentage of bad debts in relation to sales. Then project (or estimate) the percentage of sales which will become bad debts for 19__6.

Year	Net Sales	Actual Bad Debts	Percentage
19–1	$250 000	$2 000	%_____
19–2	$400 000	$6 000	_____
19–3	$425 000	$4 000	_____
19–4	$470 000	$9 000	_____
19–5	$450 000	$8 000	_____

Bad Debts A company does not adjust its Accounts Receivable by estimating bad debts at the end of the fiscal period. It uses a method called *direct write-off*. With this method, Accounts Receivable are written off when they are determined to be uncollectable. For example, on January 31 a debt of $1 500 was determined to be uncollectable because the customer, P. Kully, had declared bankruptcy. The sale of $1 500 had been made in the previous fiscal period. **Case 3**

This entry was made on January 31, 19__2:

Date		Particulars		Debit	Credit
19–2 Jan.	31	Bad Debts Expense		1 500 —	
		Accounts Receivable/			
		P. Kully			1 500 —
		To write off, customer has			
		declared bankruptcy.			

a) How does the fact that an adjustment for estimated bad debts was not made in 19__1 affect the financial statements for that year?

b) How does the write-off entry affect the financial statements of 19__2?

Age Analysis Part of an age analysis for Canada Imports follows: **Case 4**

Partial Age Analysis
December 31, 19__

Customer	Total	Current	1 d to 30 d past due	31 d to 60 d past due	61 d to 90 d past due	over 90 d past due
A. Abrams	400	400				
K. Allen	700		100	300		300
J. Allin	120				120	
M. Ambler	220	120		100		
Others	42 000	19 000	11 000	2 000	5 100	4 900
Total	43 440	19 520	11 100	2 400	5 220	5 200
Percent	100					

The accounting department of Canada Imports is very small. The employees in accounting prepare the age analysis and send it to the sales department which is also responsible for granting credit and collecting overdue accounts. Canada Imports is often required to borrow from its bank in order to pay its creditors.

a) Calculate the percentage of total for each column of the age analysis.
b) Prepare recommendations for the management of Canada Imports regarding their credit and collections procedures.

Case 5

Interpreting Accounting Data 2 You are a loan manager and have received an application for a loan from J. Traskle Ltd. From the financial statements provided by J. Traskle the data following has been calculated. Considering the data provided, would you grant the loan? Give reasons for your answer.

	19–3	19–4	19–5	19–6	19–7
Current Ratio	3:1	2.7:1	2:1	2:1	2:1
Quick Ratio	1:1	0.9:1	0.7:1	1:1	1:1
Debt Ratio	45%	55%	50%	49%	48%
Equity Ratio	55%	45%	50%	51%	52%

Career Profile

An Accounting Teacher Not all accountants work for a living – some teach!!

Pat O'Neill spent a number of years working as an accountant with the federal government before he started a career in teaching. Pat was born in Amherst, Nova Scotia and attended St. Charles High School before graduating from St. Francis Xavier University with a Bachelor of Commerce degree.

Pat's first job was with Revenue Canada – Taxation in Halifax. A government training program prepared Pat for a career in taxation. Pat was transferred to the Toronto regional tax office where he stayed for six years.

While he worked in Toronto Pat enrolled in the C.G.A. (Certified General Accountant) program. Night lectures offered at Ryerson kept Pat very busy on his studies. Because he was given a number of credits for the subjects he had studied while at St. Francis Xavier University, Pat was able to complete the C.G.A. requirements in three years.

Pat continued to work with the federal government during this period with his next move being to the Taxation Data Centre in Ottawa.

Pat's interest in people and the human side of business led him to apply for a teaching position at Algonquin College. In his ten years at Algonquin, Pat has taught a variety of courses including Cost Accounting, Financial Accounting, and Intermediate Accounting. At the present time Pat is head of the Department of Accounting at the college. He is responsible for supervising 12 professional accounting teachers and, although Pat spends a great deal of time on matters of administration, his primary love is teaching. Pat has been the president of the Ottawa chapter of the C.G.A. Association. He has also lectured C.G.A. courses at Carleton University.

CHAPTER 19

Inventory Control

Van Leeuwen Boomkamp

Unit 47
*1

Bob and Louise Bennett are shopping for new livingroom furniture. While visiting the Van Leeuwen Boomkamp store they see just the style of leather chair they are looking for. However, the chairs on display are tan and the Bennetts require dark brown. They approach a salesperson and ask if two chairs in brown leather are available. Within minutes they are loading their new brown leather chairs into their stationwagon.

How did the salesperson know that the items wanted by the customer were on hand in the warehouse? Here is what the salesperson did. First the inventory stock cards in the store office were consulted. A card for the brown leather chairs wanted by the Bennetts (Figure 19.1) was located. This card indicated that there were four chairs and two matching footstools in the warehouse. Because the salesperson had this information the sale was quickly completed. The customer did not have to wait while someone went to the warehouse or while a telephone call was made to see if the chairs were available. The inventory system used by Van Leeuwen Boomkamp is called a *perpetual inventory system.* It provides a continuous record of all merchandise on hand.

Description Chair, leather, brown, rosewood | Stock No. X 128 | Minimum 2
Location Row 3 | Unit Price $156 | Maximum 10

Date		Reference Number	Quantity Ordered	Rec'd	Unit Cost	Sold	Balance
Feb	10	Req. 94	10	10			10
	19	Inv. 1420				2	8
	25	1504				1	7
Mar	15	1647				3	4
	30	2926				2	2
	30	Req. 109	8				2
Apr.	19			8			10

Figure 19.1 *A perpetual inventory stock card showing the two chairs sold to the Bennets as well as eight more chairs ordered and received by Van Leeuwen Boomkamp*

Perpetual Inventory Systems

*2

A perpetual inventory system is a continuous record of all merchandise on hand.

There is a stock card for every item sold.

The perpetual inventory system used by Van Leeuwen Boomkamp is a relatively simple but effective method of controlling inventory. For every item of merchandise sold by the company there is a *stock card* like the one in Figure 19.1. Each stock card shows the balance on hand for that particular item. The stock card also shows:

- the location of the merchandise
- its stock number
- date and price of goods received
- date and quantity of goods sold

When sales are made, the stock card balances are lowered. The balances are raised when merchandise is purchased. The inventory clerk receives copies of all sales invoices and receiving reports. The clerk uses these source documents to raise and lower the stock cards.

Sales Invoice Copies A sales invoice is prepared for every sale. The original copy is given to the customer and one copy is used by the inventory clerk. The inventory clerk records the sale of two chairs by reducing the number of chairs on the stock card.

*3

A receiving report lists all merchandise received.

Receiving Reports When goods purchased by Van Leeuwen Boomkamp are received in the warehouse a *receiving report* is completed as shown in Figure 19.2.

Van Leeuwen Boomkamp Ltd.

RECEIVING REPORT

FROM RUSSELL FURNITURE MFG.
MONCTON, NEW BRUNSWICK

NO. R-306
DATE APRIL 19
P.O. NO. 4-001

VIA		PREPAID		COLLECT	
STOCK NO.	QUANTITY	DESCRIPTION		UNIT PRICE	
X128	8	ROSEWOOD LEATHER CHAIRS, BROWN			

CHECKED BY R. Lee ENTERED IN INVOICE LEDGER BY T.W.

Figure 19.2 *Receiving report prepared by the warehouse when stock arrives*

A copy of the report is sent to the purchasing department where it will be compared to the purchase order and to the purchase invoice received from the supplier. If the details on these three forms agree, the invoice will be approved for payment.

Another copy of the receiving report is sent to the inventory clerk. The report indicates that merchandise has been received and that the balance on the stock cards should be raised. Figure 19.1 shows the stock card for the leather chairs. Notice that entries have been made in the *Received* and *Sold* columns. The source document for the Sold column entry is the sales invoice copy. The source document for the Received column entry is the receiving report.

Each stock card contains a minimum figure of stock to be on hand. When the balance of an item reaches the minimum, additional stock must be purchased. The minimum for brown leather chairs is 2. When this is reached a *purchase requisition* is completed.

A purchase requisition is a form requesting the purchase of an item.

Purchase Requisition The inventory clerk is responsible for requesting the purchase of merchandise. This is done by completing a purchase requisition. Whenever a stock card balance reaches its minimum point the inventory clerk completes a purchase requisition and sends it to the purchasing department. A notation is made on the stock card in the *Qty. Ordered* column so that duplicate requisitions are avoided.

*4

Inventory Clerk The duties of the inventory clerk at Van Leeuwen Boomkamp are:

- to record sales of merchandise in the Sold column of the stock cards
- to record purchases of merchandise in the Received column of stock cards
- to issue purchase requisitions when balances on stock cards reach the minimum point

Physical Inventory If an error is made in the recording on the stock cards or if goods are damaged or stolen, the figures on the stock cards will be incorrect. To check the accuracy of the perpetual inventory records, all goods on hand are counted. This *physical inventory* serves as a check on the accuracy of the system. A complete physical inventory is taken at least once a year – although many firms take inventory more frequently. Some spot-check each department at random several times a year.

*5

A physical inventory is a count of all merchandise on hand.

Stock Cards The perpetual inventory system is a continuous record of all merchandise on hand. The record of the merchandise is kept in the form of stock cards in the manual perpetual inventory system. There is one stock card for every different item of merchandise sold by the company; this could mean hundreds and even thousands of stock cards. The stock cards as a group make up a subsidiary ledger called the *Inventory Ledger*. In the Inventory Ledger there is one account (or stock card) for every item of merchandise sold.

In the General Ledger there is a control account for the merchandise called *Merchandise Inventory*. The balance of the Merchandise Inventory account should equal the total of all the stock cards in the Inventory Ledger.

The Inventory Ledger is a subsidiary ledger containing stock cards.

The Merchandise Inventory account is a control account in the General Ledger.

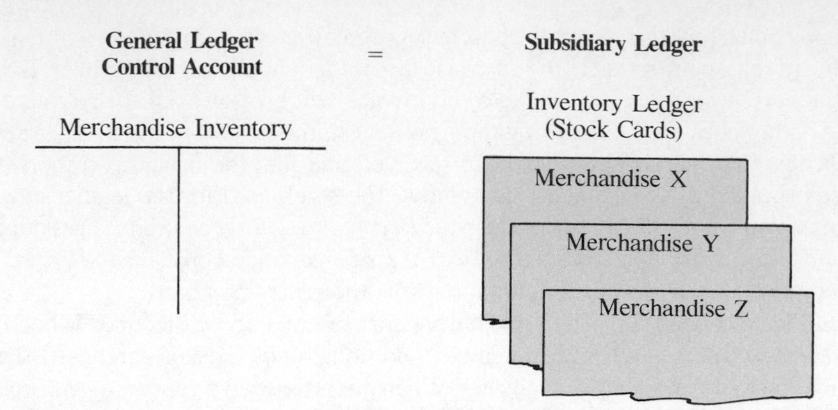

Figure 19.3 *The total of the stock cards in the Inventory Ledger should equal the balance of the Merchandise Inventory account in the General Ledger.*

*6

Who Uses a Perpetual Inventory System?

Many small firms do not require a continuous written record of their stock. The manager or owner knows what is on hand and reorders stock when needed. Past experience indicates when the heavy selling times are and the owner acts accordingly.

Larger businesses and those which sell or manufacture high-value products, such as automobiles or boats, generally use a perpetual inventory system. Such a system helps to ensure that sales are not lost nor production halted by a lack of merchandise or parts; it enables management to keep adequate stock on hand.

*7

Merchandise Inventory Account

All merchandise costs are recorded in the Merchandise Inventory account.

In the perpetual inventory system, numerous entries are made in the Merchandise Inventory account. It is used to record all costs involving merchandise purchased. It is increased (debited) for the value of goods purchased, for transportation charges on merchandise purchased, and for the cost of sales returns made by customers.

The Merchandise Inventory account is decreased (credited) for the cost price of all goods sold. It is also credited for the cost of goods returned to the supplier and for allowances and cash discounts received from suppliers. All transactions involving merchandise must be recorded in the Merchandise Inventory account.

Merchandise Inventory (an asset)

Increase	**Decrease**
Used to record merchandise purchased at cost, transportation charges on purchases and sales returned by customers at cost	Used to record goods returned to suppliers at cost, allowances and discounts received from suppliers, and sales made at cost

Cost of Goods Sold (a cost account)

Increase	**Decrease**
Used to record sales made at cost.	Used to record goods returned by customers (sales returns) at cost.

Figure 19.4 *Merchandise Inventory and Cost of Goods Sold accounts of the perpetual inventory system*

Cost of Goods Sold Account The Cost of Goods Sold account is an important account in the perpetual inventory system. At the end of the fiscal period, the balance in this account is used on the income statement. The balance is subtracted from sales to determine the gross profit.

Cost of Goods Sold is an account used in the perpetual inventory system.

Journal Entries – Perpetual Inventory System To illustrate the use of the two new accounts, six transactions will now be recorded using perpetual inventory procedures.

*8

Purchase Invoice No. B-710 for merchandise purchased from Buntin Reid, $500, terms 2/10, n/30. This transaction results in an increase of merchandise on hand. The increase is shown in the Merchandise Inventory account. This entry is made:

The value of merchandise purchased is recorded in the Merchandise Inventory account.

June	6	Merchandise Inventory		500 —	
		Accounts Payable/Buntin Reid			500 —
		Bought merchandise, terms			
		2/10, n/30			

Credit Invoice No. C-21, $75 credit for defective goods returned to Buntin Reid. This transaction results in a decrease in merchandise. The decrease is recorded by crediting Merchandise Inventory.

*9

The value of goods returned to suppliers is recorded in the Merchandise Inventory account.

June	10	Accounts Payable/Buntin Reid		75 —	
		Merchandise Inventory			75 —
		Defective goods returned to			
		supplier			

Purchase Invoice No. 635 from Roadway Transport, $125 for freight charges on incoming merchandise. The freight charges increase the cost of the merchandise. The increase is shown by debiting Merchandise Inventory.

*10

Transportation charges are recorded in the Merchandise Inventory account.

June	15	Merchandise Inventory		125 —	
		Accounts Payable/			
		Roadway Transport			125 —
		Freight charges on incoming			
		goods			

*11
Purchase discounts are recorded in the Merchandise Inventory account.

Cheque Copy Cheque No. 37 to Buntin Reid for invoice B-710 less $75 credit invoice and 2% discount. The $75 credit invoice was recorded in the June 10 entry. The 2% cash discount results in a decrease in the cost of the merchandise. This decrease is shown by crediting Merchandise Inventory.

				Debit	Credit
June	16	Accounts Payable/Buntin Reid		425 —	
		Cash			416 50
		Merchandise Inventory			8 50
		Cheque No. 3 for Invoice			
		B-710, less goods returns			
		and 2% discount			

*12
Sales are recorded as a decrease in Merchandise Inventory using the cost price of the goods sold.

Cash Sales Slip No. 437, goods sold for $1 000 cash to B. Wiseman. All sales transactions require two entries in the perpetual inventory system.

				Debit	Credit
June	17	Cash		1 000 —	
		Sales			1 000 —
		Cash sale to B. Wiseman,			
		Cash Sales Slip 437			
June	17	Cost of goods sold		600 —	
		Merchandise Inventory			600 —
		Cash sales slip no. 437			

Because merchandise has been sold, the account Merchandise Inventory must be decreased to show the decrease in goods on hand. This decrease is recorded by using the cost price of $600. The cost price is obtained from the original purchase invoice. When a sale is made some companies note the cost price on their copy of the sales invoice. When the sales invoice is journalized (for example, the $1 000 entry in the last transaction), the cost price ($500) is obtained from the copy of the invoice and is used for the second entry. It is not always a simple matter to obtain the cost price of the sales. This is a disadvantage of the perpetual inventory system.

All sales are recorded in the Cost of Goods Sold account using the cost price.

All sales must be recorded using the cost price in the Cost of Goods Sold account. At the end of the fiscal period, this account will contain the total cost of goods sold.

*13
Goods returned by customers increase the Merchandise Inventory account and decrease the Cost of Goods Sold account.

Cheque Copy Cheque No. 38 for $100 to B. Wiseman as refund on goods returned because they were the wrong colour. Two entries are required for this transaction. The first entry records the return and the decrease in Cash. The second entry is required because the goods are placed back in stock. The business has more merchandise. The increase in merchandise is recorded by debiting Merchandise Inventory.

June	6	Sales Returns and Allowances		100 —		
		Cash				100 —
		Cheque No. 38, goods returned,				
		wrong colour				
June	6	Merchandise Inventory		60 —		
		Cost of Goods Sold				60 —
		Goods returned to stock				
		at cost price, $60				

Notice that in the second entry, the cost price is used. The second entry is really a reversal of the original entry recording the sale at cost price.

Calculating the Cost of Goods Sold It is quite simple to calculate the cost of goods sold for a merchandising company when the perpetual inventory system is used. The account, Cost of Goods Sold, contains the costs of all the sales made during the fiscal period. Remember that every time a sale is made, two entries are recorded, one entry to record the sale at the selling price and a second entry to record the cost of the item sold. The cost is debited to the Cost of Goods Sold account. The balance of this account is used on the income statement; it is subtracted from sales to determine the gross profit.

*14

The Cost of Goods Sold account contains the cost of all sales made during the fiscal period.

Cost of Goods Sold		Merchandise Inventory	
Income Statement		**Balance Sheet**	

Gross profit is the difference between Sales and the Cost of Goods Sold.

*15

In the perpetual inventory system, the Merchandise Inventory account is a continuous record of all merchandise owned. It is an asset and appears in the current asset section of the balance sheet.

Financial Statements The income statement and the balance sheet are the same in format as those you have already studied with one exception: the Cost of Goods Sold account balance is used on the income statement.

Adjusting and Closing Entries In the perpetual system, the only cost account to be closed is the Cost of Goods Sold account. The Merchandise Inventory account is always up-to-date and does not require entries. When closing the books for the perpetual inventory system, follow these steps:

1. Revenue accounts are closed into the Income Summary account.
2. The Cost of Goods Sold account is closed into the Income Summary account.
3. The Expenses are closed into the Income Summary account.
4. The Income Summary account is closed into the Capital account (or, in the case of a corporation, into Earned Surplus).

Figure 19.5 illustrates the closing entries for the perpetual inventory system.

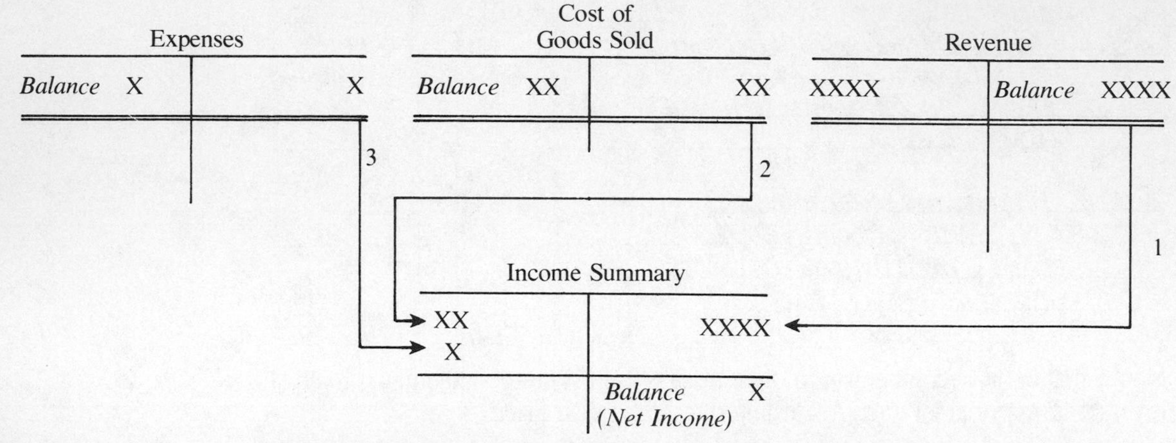

Figure 19.5 *Closing the books for the perpetual inventory system*

Facts to Remember

A *perpetual inventory system* is a continuous record of all merchandise on hand.

A *receiving report* lists all merchandise received.

A *purchase requisition* is a form requesting the purchase of an item.

A *physical inventory* is a count of all merchandise on hand.

The *Inventory Ledger* is a subsidiary ledger containing stock cards.

The *Merchandise Inventory account* is a control account in the General Ledger.

All *merchandise costs* are recorded in the Merchandise Inventory account.

A *schedule of cost of goods sold* is prepared in the periodic inventory system.

Cost of Goods Sold is an account used in the perpetual inventory system.

The *Cost of Goods Sold* account contains the cost of all sales made during the fiscal period.

Gross profit is the difference between sales and the Cost of Goods Sold.

Checking Your Reading

Questions

1. Refer to Figure 19.1 and answer the following:
   a) How many chairs were on hand on March 15?
   b) How many were on hand on February 19?
   c) Explain what happened on February 10 and on February 25.
2. Explain the following: perpetual inventory, physical inventory, receiving report, purchase requisition.
3. How many stock cards are found in a perpetual inventory system?

4. a) What source document indicates that a stock card balance should be increased?
   b) What source document indicates that a stock card balance should be decreased?
5. What are the advantages of a perpetual inventory system?
6. What kind of business uses a perpetual inventory system?
7. In the perpetual inventory system, when is the Merchandise Inventory account debited? When is it credited?
8. What is the name of the subsidiary ledger which is composed of stock cards?
9. How may the accuracy of the balances in the Inventory Ledger be proven?

Applying Your Knowledge

Exercises Part A

1. Prepare a stock card for: a television set, cost $105, minimum 10, order quantity 15. Record the following on the stock card:

May 1 Balance 25, unit cost $105
Sales Invoices:
May 2 Quantity sold, 3
4 Quantity sold, 5
5 Quantity sold, 1
8 Quantity sold, 4
May 15 Receiving report
Received 15 sets, unit cost $105
Sales Invoices:
May 16 Quantity sold, 2
18 Quantity sold, 5
19 Quantity sold, 1

2. In this exercise you will perform some of the tasks of an inventory control clerk.
   a) Head up stock cards for the five items on the following list.
   b) Update the stock cards by increasing the balance when purchases are made and by decreasing the balance when sales are made.

Stereo Styles Inventory List — May 1, 19__

Code	Description	Quantity on Hand	Unit Cost	Value
R-51	S-120, 5 RMS	37	$ 75	$2 775
R-52	K-2400, 15 RMS	22	100	2 200
R-53	S-5800, 55 RMS	8	300	2 400
R-54	Viking, 8 RMS	43	95	4 085
R-55	SX 450, 15 RMS	59	130	7 670

May 2 Sales Invoice:
No. 7165 to Wackid Stereo, quantity 10, item R-55; quantity 5, item R-51

9 Receiving Report:
No. M-61, received 10, R-53 receivers, unit cost $300; and 25, R-52 receivers, unit cost $100

12 Sales Invoices:
No. 7167 to Studio Sound, quantity 10, item R-51
No. 7168 to Wackid Stereo, quantity 8, item R-52; quantity 2, item R-53; quantity 5, item R-54

15 Sales Invoice:
No. 7169 to Pegasis, quantity 5, item R-51; quantity 10, item R-52; quantity 10, item R-55

20 Receiving Report:
No. M-62, received 25, R-51 receivers, unit cost $75

20 Sales Invoice:
No. 7170 to Audio Town, quantity 5, item R-53; quantity 15, item R-55; quantity 10, item R-54; quantity 6, item R-52

c) Prepare an inventory list dated May 30 which shows the unit cost, description, balance, and value of the five stock items.

Exercises Part B

3. Feature Systems Ltd. specializes in selling stereo system components. Their marketing program is geared toward weekly specials which are heavily advertised in local newspapers. Terms of sale offered to customers are cash, Visa, or three equal payments, 30 days apart.

a) Head up stock cards for the five products shown on the April 1 inventory list.

Feature Systems Ltd. Inventory List — April 1, 19__

Stock No.	Description	Unit Cost	Balance	Minimum	Order Quantity
S-9	Speakers, Sherwin 22	$175	28	20	20
R-81	Receiver, STR 7035 24 RMS	$195	35	25	50
T-4	Turntable, LP 211	$ 69	33	25	30
A-4	Amplifier, A.T. 2650	$135	25	10	15
C-22	Cartridge, Shore m-81	$ 24	50	30	35

b) Record the transactions for April on the stock cards. Raise the stock card balances when goods are received and decrease the balances when goods are sold.

c) Open an Accounts Receivable Ledger with these accounts:

Visa balance	$3 800
P. Craig	Nil
M. Fleming	Nil
R. Klabouch	Nil
K. Larkin	Nil
A. Morena	Nil

d) Post to the accounts in part c) directly from the source documents given in the April transactions listed below. Prepare the April 30 schedule of accounts receivable.
e) Record the transactions in a General Journal.
f) Open T-accounts for Accounts Receivable, (balance $3 800), Cost of Goods Sold, and Merchandise Inventory (balance $18 577).
g) Post the transactions involving the three T-accounts in part f).
Your April 30 balances should be:

• Accounts Receivable	$ 9 840.76
• Cost of Goods Sold	$13 119.00
• Merchandise Inventory	$20 643.00

April Transactions

April 2 Cash Sales:
$3 450, sales tax $241.50, total $3 691.50

Charge Sales:
P. Craig $499, sales tax $34.93, total $533.93. Down payment received $177.98.
K. Larkin $899, sales tax $62.93, total $961.93. Down payment received $320.64.
A Morena $138, sales tax $9.66, total $147.66. Down payment received $49.22

Visa Sales:
$1 965, sales tax $137.55, total $2 102.55.

Inventory Analysis:
The following items were sold on April 2:
- 7 cartridges No. C-22
- 2 amplifiers No. A-4
- 7 turntables No. T-4
- 5 receivers No. R-81
- 10 speakers No. S-9

Purchase Requisition:
Issued for speakers (S-9). Record in the *On Order* column of the stock card.

April 9 Cash Sales:
$1 875, sales tax $131.25, total $2 006.25.

Charge Sales:
R. Klabouch, $699, sales tax $48.93, total $747.93. Down payment received $249.31.
M. Fleming, $799, sales tax $55.93, total $854.93. Down payment received $284.98.

Visa Sales:
$3 100, sales tax $217, total $3 317

Inventory Analysis:
The following items were sold since April 2:
- 17 cartridges No. C-22
- 4 amplifiers No. A-4
- 15 turntables No. T-4
- 4 receivers No. R-81

Purchase Requisitions:
Issued for cartridges (No. C-22) and turntables (No. T-4). Record these in the *On Order* column of the stock cards.

16 Cash Sales:
$1 900, sales tax $133, total $2 033

Visa Sales:
$1 095, sales tax $76.65, total $1 171.65

Credit Invoice Issued:
To K. Larkin for a turntable (No. T-4) returned, $138, sales tax $9.66, total credit $147.66. (The turntable was placed back in inventory.)

Inventory Analysis:
The following items were sold since April 9:
- 5 amplifiers No. A-4
- 5 turntables No. T-4
- 6 receivers No. R-81
- 4 speakers No. S-9

Purchase Requisition:
Issued for receivers (No. R-81)

21 Receiving Report and Purchase Invoice:
30 turntables (T-4) were received. Unit cost price $69, terms n/30

23 Cash Sales:
$1 195, sales tax $83.65, total $1 278.65

Charge Sales:
K. Larkin $156, sales tax $10.92, total $166.92. Down payment $55.64

April 23 Receiving Report and Purchase Invoice:
50 receivers R-81 were received. Unit cost price $195.
Terms 2/10 n/30.
20 speakers were received. Unit cost $175. Terms 2/10 n/30

Inventory Analysis:
The following items were sold since April 16:
- 12 cartridges No. C-22
- 2 amplifiers No. A-4
- 1 turntable No. T-4

30 Cash Sales:
$1 275, sales tax $89.25, total $1 364.25

Visa Sales:
$1 700, sales tax $119, total $1 819

Charge Sales:
A. Morena, $436, sales tax $30.50, total $466.50. Down payment $155.50

30 Credit Invoice Received:
$975 for 5 receivers (R-81) returned to the supplier

Receiving Report and Purchase Invoice:
35 cartridges were received, unit cost $24. terms n/30

Inventory Analysis:
The following items were sold since April 23:

- 14 cartridges No. C-22
- 4 turntables No. T-4
- 10 receivers No. R-81
- 4 speakers No. S-9
- 5 receivers No. R-81 were returned to the supplier (see credit invoice received)

30 Cheques Received:
P. Craig $177.98
M. Fleming $284.98
R. Klabouch $249.31
K. Larkin $246.82
A. Morena $49.22
Visa $3 686, commission deducted $114, total $3 800

4. a) R. Conroy invested $50 000 in an equipment sales company. The results for each of the first five years of operation were:

Year 1: $3 000 net loss
Year 2: $4 000 net income
Year 3: $9 000 net income
Year 4: $6 000 net income
Year 5: $7 000 net income

What is the percentage return on investment for each year?

b) After the five years what is the average annual return on investment?

c) Conroy could have invested $50 000 in secured mortgages at 9% interest annually. Which investment would provide Conroy with the best annual return over five years?

Accounting in Action

Case 1

Inventory Losses Ajax Co. is a manufacturer of household appliances. From its manufacturing plant in central Canada, it ships appliances to 26 district branch sales offices across Canada. Each branch consists of a sales manager, a small office staff, and a sales team. As sales are made, a copy of each sales slip is sent to the head office. All cash received is deposited to a company account. All payments are made from head office. Each branch keeps a large stock of appliances on hand in its warehouse. The sales staff sell door-to-door; when a sale is made, the merchandise is immediately shipped from the branch warehouse. The sales staff is paid on a commission basis. The branch manager receives a base salary plus a bonus based on total yearly sales.

Rich Quick, the manager of the Edmonton branch, has just been fired and arrested for theft of company appliances. He has been selling appliances, collecting the cash, but not reporting the sales or depositing the cash to the company account. How was he caught?

Case 2

Analysing Accounting Data Leslie T. is the manager of a large retail outlet. Each month Leslie receives marketing and financial information from Statistics Canada about companies in the same retail business. Leslie has prepared a comparison of several account balances which matches Leslie's company's results with averages for other companies. This comparison follows:

Type of Account	Leslie's Company (in 000's)	Industry Average (in 000's)
Cash	$ 7	$ 15
Accounts Receivable	250	175
Merchandise Inventory	300	200
Accounts Payable	90	45
Bank Loan	40	10
Sales	800	800
Cost of Goods Sold	400	400
Gross Profit	400	400
Interest Charges	5	1
Warehouse Expense	60	35
Bad Debts Expense	5	2
Net Income	58	90

Based only on the data presented, prepare recommendations for improving the financial position of Leslie's company.

Case 3

Inventory Control George Palmas operates three discount appliance stores in a large metropolitan area. His operation has been very profitable. There are three rules which have guided George's decision-making:

- Keep costs and expenses to a minimum.
- Offer as few services as possible.
- Offer low prices.

George has a niece, Jodie, studying for her PhD in business administration. This summer, while working for her uncle, Jodie noticed that many sales were lost because the stores ran out of merchandise. Customers asked for advertised items but had to be told that the items were sold out.

Jodie mentioned the lost sales to her uncle, who stated that he would rather lose a few sales than get stuck with a lot of unsold merchandise. Jodie offered to study the problem. After several weeks of research, Jodie presented these facts to her uncle:

- Approximately $9 000 worth of sales are lost every month because of poor inventory control.
- Present buying decisions are based on hunches and experience.
- A manual inventory system could be installed in each store for $15 000 a year per store.
- A mini computer could be purchased and used for several different functions. The cost allocated to the inventory function would be about $68 000 a year.
- A computer service would provide a weekly inventory listing of all items sold for a cost of $12 000 a year. A daily inventory listing could be provided at a cost of $40 000. This would provide a list of all items showing:
  balance on hand, previous day's sales, and sales to date for the year.
- There would also be $5 000 a year in additional clerical costs to the company.
  a) What would you recommend that George do?
  b) What other factors might affect the final decision?

Career Profile

Audit Technician Tina Ilkiw is 19 years old and has been out of school for two years. While in high school, Tina won several academic awards. She was on the honor roll every year and represented her school in provincial typing and accounting contests. Tina was not only an honours student but participated in numerous extra curricular activities. She was on the students council every year and in her graduating year was head girl. She was also selected the outstanding accounting student in the City of Ottawa by the Administrative Management Society.

After graduating Tina worked as a payroll clerk. Her duties included coding time sheets for the computer, checking payroll deductions, cross-balancing time sheets, and maintaining time sheet files. While on this job Tina enrolled in the C.G.A. program which involved taking night courses at Carleton University. Tina did not find the payroll clerk's job very challenging and after six months left to work with a public accounting firm, Thorne Riddell & Company. Tina's job title is audit technician. She is part of an accounting team which visits clients and audits their books. Auditing is the process of checking the accuracy of an accounting system and includes checking accounting records to ensure that the accounting functions are being correctly carried out. Tests are performed to see if cash and company funds are being correctly handled. For example, in an accounts payable test, cheques are selected at random. For each cheque the purchase requisition, purchase order, and receiving report are all analysed to see if the transaction is correct. A typical audit involves a visit of about three weeks to the client's office.

Tina feels she is fortunate to have a position with Thorne Riddell because many of her fellow workers are graduate accountants who help and advise her with her C.G.A. courses. The practical work experience she is receiving helps her to better understand the theoretical courses she is taking. Tina's long term goals include completing her C.G.A. degree and perhaps obtaining a university degree in business administration. Because of her interest in helping and working with people Tina could eventually become a teacher or enter the field of business management.

The Accounting Cycle

Project 4

Project 4 takes you through the accounting cycle for a merchandising company.

On May 1 T. Clements started a business called Metro Sales Co. J. Kisel recommended a Synoptic Journal, a General Ledger, an Accounts Payable Ledger, and an Accounts Receivable Ledger. The accounts are :

100 Cash
101 Petty Cash
102 Accounts Receivable
103 Merchandise Inventory
104 Office Supplies
105 Prepaid Insurance
120 Equipment
121 Acc. Dep.: Equipment
200 Accounts Payable
201 Sales Tax Payable
202 Salaries Payable
203 C.P.P. Payable
204 U.I. Payable
205 Health Insurance Payable
206 Employee's Income Tax Pay
300 T. Clements, Capital
301 T. Clements, Drawing
302 Income Summary
400 Sales
401 Sales Returns and Allowances
402 Sales Discounts
500 Purchases
501 Purchases Returns and Allowances
502 Transportation on Purchases
503 Purchases Discounts
600 Advertising Expense
601 Delivery Expense
602 Accounting Fees Expense
603 C.P.P. Expense
604 U.I. Expense
605 Miscellaneous Expense
606 Rent Expense
607 Salaries Expense
608 Telephone Expense
609 Utilities Expense

May 1 T. Clements invested $20 000 and started Metro Sales Company.

2 Cheque Copies:
No. 1 to J. Kisel C.A., $150 for organizing an accounting system.
No. 2 to Dot Personnel, $100 for hiring services.
No. 3 to Maxwell Realty Ltd., $2 000 for May rent.
No. 4 to Lambton Mfg. Ltd., for a cash purchase of merchandise, $3 500.
No. 5 to *Daily Express,* $450 for advertising.

3 Purchase Invoices:
Burford Supply, $1 700 for merchandise, terms net 60 days.
Willson's Ltd., $250 for letterhead, business forms, and miscellaneous office supplies, terms net 30 days.
Halton Interiors, $9 000 for office equipment and furnishings, terms 3 equal payments, May 15, May 30, and June 30.
Stevensville Mfg. Ltd., $2 000 for merchandise, terms 2/10, n/30.

4 Cash sales, $1 250 plus tax, total $1 337.50, sales invoices No. 1 to No. 4.

5 Sales Invoices:
No. 5, $200 to J. Barnes, 7% sales tax $14, total $214. Terms 2/10, n/30 for all sales on account.
No. 6, $300 plus 7% sales tax, to Mr. Charters.
No. 7, $1 200 plus sales tax, to A. Falcone.
No. 8, $140 plus sales tax to L. Parrish.

8 Purchase Invoices:
Bell Canada, $90 for installation services.
C.P.R., $120 for transportation on merchandise purchases.
Jenkins Enterprises, $2 900 for merchandise, terms 3/10, n/60.

9 Credit Invoices Received:
Burford Supply, $120 for defective merchandise.

Halton Interiors, $250 allowance off the price of scratched furnishings.

May 10 Cash Sales, $2 400 plus sales tax. Invoices No. 9 to No. 12.

11 Credit Invoice Issued to M. Charters, $107 for $100 worth of merchandise returned and $7 sales tax.

12 Sales Invoices:
No. 13 to L. Becker, $1 200 plus sales tax.
No. 14 to T. Gabriel, $500 plus sales tax.
No. 15 to M. Charters, $220 plus sales tax.

12 Cheque Copies:
No. 6 to Bell Canada, $90 on account.
No. 7 to C.P.R., $120 on account.
No. 8 to Halton Interiors, $3 000 on acccount.
No. 9 to Stevensville Mfg., $1 960 for invoice of May 3 less 2% discount.

14 Record the biweekly payroll in the journal:
Salaries Expense $2 265, C.P.P. Payable $39.90, U.I. Payable $19.20, Income Tax Payable $385, Health Insurance Payable $64, Salaries Payable $1 756.90.

14 Record the company's liability for C.P.P. and U.I. The employer pays 1.4 times the employees' unemployment insurance premium.

15 Purchase Invoices:
Stevensville Mfg., $275 for merchandise, terms 2/10, n/30

15 Cheque Copies:
No. 10, $1 200 for a twelve-month comprehensive business insurance policy to Metropolitan Life.
No. 11, $1 756.90 to pay the biweekly payroll.
No. 12, $100 to establish a petty cash fund.

15 Cash Received from Customers:
J. Barnes, $209.72 for May 5 invoice less 2% cash discount.
L. Parrish, $146.80 for May 5 invoice less 2% cash discount.

16 Sales Invoices:
No. 16 to L. Becker, $400 plus sales tax.
No. 17 to T. Gabriel, $650 plus sales tax.
No. 18 to M. Braganolo, $940 plus sales tax.
No. 19 to N. Lumsden, $895 plus sales tax.

18 Cheque Copies:
No. 13 for $126 to pay for an invoice received today from Mac's Delivery Service, terms, cash.
No. 14 for $500 to T. Clements for personal use.
No. 15 for $2 813 to Jenkins Enterprises for May 8 invoice, less 3% cash discount

19 Cash Sales, $3 170 plus sales tax. Invoices 20 to 26.

22 Purchase Invoices:
C.P.R., $79 for transportation on purchases of merchandise.
Willson's Ltd., $46 for office supplies.

May 24 Credit Invoice Issued:
To N. Lumsden, $45 plus sales tax for defective merchandise.

25 Cheque Copy:
No. 16 for $93 to replenish petty cash.
Summary of petty cash vouchers:
Office Supplies, $40; Miscellaneous Expense, $33; T. Clements, Drawing, $20.

25 Sales Invoices:
No. 27 to J. Barnes, $798 plus sales tax.
No. 28 to T. Gabriel, $240 plus sales tax.

29 Record the biweekly payroll in the journal:
Salaries Expense $2 379, C.P.P. Payable $42.82, U.I. Payable $23.80, Income Tax Payable $415, Health Insurance Payable $64, Salaries Payable $1 833.38.

30 Record the company's liability for C.P.P. and U.I.

30 Cheque Copies:
No. 17 for $3 000 to Halton Interiors on account.
No. 18 for $1 200 to T. Clements for personal use.
No. 19 for $1 833.38 for biweekly payroll.
Purchase Invoices:
Bell Canada $39.
City Light and Power, $85 for hydro bill.
Daily Express, $870 for newspaper advertising.

1. Record the transactions in the subsidiary ledgers by following these steps:
a) Post sales invoices, cash received, and credit invoices issued directly into the customer accounts. Open accounts as required.
b) Post purchase invoices, cheques issued, and credit invoices received directly into the accounts payable ledger. Open accounts as required.
c) On May 31 prepare schedules for each of the subsidiary ledgers.

2. a) Record the May transactions in the Synoptic Journal.
b) Total, cross-balance, and rule the Synoptic Journal.
c) Post the Synoptic Journal to the General Ledger.
d) Prepare a General Ledger trial balance on work sheet paper.

3. Complete the work sheet and prepare financial statements using this information:
a) Equipment depreciates 30% per year.
b) One month of the 12-month insurance policy has expired.
c) At the end of the month there is $90 worth of supplies on hand.
d) The ending inventory is $1 150.

4. a) Journalize the adjusting and closing entries in a General Journal and post.
b) Prepare a post-closing trial balance.

CHAPTER 20

Partnership Accounting

Types of Business Ownership

Unit 48

In the first part of this book most of the accounting theory involved businesses owned by one person. For example, Chapter 5 described the journal and ledger system used by K. Martin, the owner of Martin Painting Contractors. A business owned by one person is known as a *sole proprietorship*. Two other types of ownership are the *partnership* and the *corporation*.

*1

A sole proprietorship is a business owned by one person.

Sole Proprietorship

The owner of a sole proprietorship is legally responsible for all its debts and legal obligations. Many small businesses are sole proprietorships. These include small stores, restaurants, and many service businesses such as barbershops, T.V. repair firms, and hairstylists.

*2

In a sole proprietorship, the proprietor has unlimited personal liability for the debts and legal obligations of the business.

Advantages of Proprietorships

- pride of ownership
- ease of formation and dissolution
- freedom of action
- privacy
- simplified decision-making
- owner receives all the net income
- personal satisfaction
- possible tax savings

Disadvantages of Proprietorships

- unlimited personal liability
- limited capital
- heavy personal responsibilities
- lack of continuity
- limited talent

Taxation and the Proprietorship A proprietorship does not pay income tax on its net income. The owner must add the net income of the business to his or her own income and then pay personal income tax on the total. There can be a tax advantage with this form of ownership when the combined net income is quite low. However, when net income becomes fairly high there may be a tax advantage in switching to a corporate form of ownership. This is explained in detail in Chapter 21.

*3

Partnerships

*4

A partnership is a business owned by two or more persons.

In a partnership, the partners have unlimited personal liability for the debts and legal obligations of the business.

Two or more persons may find it worthwhile to combine their talents and money to form a *partnership*. Doctors, lawyers, dentists, and small retail and service businesses are frequently owned by partners. Some of the characteristics of the partnership are similar to those of the proprietorship. The net income or net loss belongs to the owners and they have unlimited personal liability for the debts of the business. The net income becomes the personal income of the individual partners for income tax purposes.

Advantages of Partnerships Some of the disadvantages of the proprietorship are overcome by the partnership form of ownership. In a partnership two or more persons are available to share the work and the responsibilities. Between them they may possess many of the skills and talents required to operate a business successfully. The partners each contribute personal savings and borrowing capacities to the business. The partners may complement each other and be able to combine to operate an efficient business.

Disadvantages of Partnerships Both partners are responsible for the debts of the business. Unlimited personal liability is a disadvantage of a partnership just as it is for a proprietorship. When two people work closely together day in and day out and are responsible for the success of a business, there is a good possibility of personality conflict. Partners must be able to work with each other. If they cannot get along, it could be difficult to get out of the partnership unless they mutually agree to dissolve it. If one partner dies, the partnership may have to be dissolved in order to settle the estate of the deceased partner.

The sharing of net income could be another disadvantage. In a proprietorship all net income belongs to the one owner. In a partnership the partners must share the net income of the business. Disagreements may occur when a partner is not satisfied with his or her share. Sometimes a partner may feel that the other partners are not contributing enough effort to the business.

Corporations

*5

A corporation is a business owned by three or more persons and has a legal existence of its own.

In a corporation, the owners' liability is limited to their investment in the corporation.

Unlike a sole proprietorship or a partnership, a corporation has a legal existence of its own and may have many owners. However, the owners are not personally responsible for the debts and obligations of the corporation. In the partnership and proprietorship, the owners have unlimited personal liability for the business and risk the loss of their own personal assets. The owners of a corporation do not risk their personal assets but only their direct investment in the corporation. For this reason the term *limited company* is sometimes used to describe the corporate form of ownership.

Advantages of the Corporate Form of Ownership Limited liability of the owners of a corporation is an important advantage of the corporate form of ownership. However, there are several others. A corporation has access to more capital. It may sell shares if it requires more financing. Corporations probably will be able to borrow more funds than partners or proprietors.

A corporation does not cease to exist if a shareholder dies or wishes to get out of the business. The shareholder may sell the shares owned and the business will continue to operate.

Disadvantages of the Corporate Form of Ownership A corporation is more complicated to form than partnerships or proprietorships. This is due to the legal requirements imposed by governments. A lawyer is generally required and start-up costs can be high. Shareholders elect a board of directors and hire managers to operate their business. This can complicate the decision-making process especially when persons with many shares wish to be involved in the business operations. Employees of a corporation may not be as dedicated, loyal or industrious as the owners of a proprietorship or a partnership. As a result it may cost a corporation more to operate.

Accounting Procedures for Partnerships

Unit 49

Two or more persons may agree orally or in writing to establish a partnership. Each of the provinces has a Partnership Act which establishes rules and regulations for partnerships. It is a general practice to prepare a written contract of partnership. This contract outlines the rights and responsibilities of each of the parties concerned.

***6** The partnership agreement outlines the rights and responsibilities of the partners.

Formation of a Partnership There are several ways in which a partnership may be formed. Five basic examples and the journal entries involved follow.

***7**

Example 1 Ron Kendall and Betty McArthur agree to contribute $10 000 each to form a partnership. A Capital account is required for each partner. The entry to open the books of Kendall and McArthur Services is:

				Debit	Credit
		Cash		20 000 —	
		R. Kendall, Capital			10 000 —
		B. McArthur, Capital			10 000 —
		To record the investments of R. Kendall and B. McArthur			

Example 2 J. Hill and D. Love have been operating businesses of their own. Their balance sheets are shown in Figure 20.1.

***8**

J. Hill			
Balance Sheet			
January 1, 19__			
Assets		Liabilities and Equity	
Cash	2 000 00	Accounts Payable	2 000 00
Accounts Receivable	3 000 00	J. Hill, Capital	20 000 00
Inventory	12 000 00		
Equipment	5 000 00		
	22 000 00		22 000 00

D. Love			
Balance Sheet			
January 1, 19__			
Assets		Liabilities and Equity	
Cash	2 000 00	Accounts Payable	4 000 00
Accounts Receivable	4 000 00	Bank Loan	20 000 00
Inventory	9 000 00	Mortgage Payable	46 000 00
Building	95 000 00	D. Love, Capital	40 000 00
	110 000 00		110 000 00

Figure 20.1 *Balance sheets for J. Hill and D. Love*

They decide to merge their companies and to form a partnership. A separate journal entry is made for each of the partner's contributions to the new business.

Jan.	1	Cash		2 000 —	
		Accounts Receivable		3 000 —	
		Inventory		12 000 —	
		Equipment		5 000 —	
		Accounts Payable			2 000 —
		J. Hill, Capital			20 000 —
		To record J. Hill's assets,			
		liabilities, and Capital			

Date		Account		Debit	Credit
Jan.	1	Cash		2 000 —	
		Accounts Receivable		4 000 —	
		Inventory		9 000 —	
		Building		95 000 —	
		Accounts Payable			4 000 —
		Bank Loan			20 000 —
		Mortgage Payable			46 000 —
		D. Love, Capital			40 000 —
		To record D. Love's assets,			
		liabilities, and capital			

Example 3 F. Pearen, the sole owner of Pearen Security Services, decides that in order to expand his business he will take in a partner. B. Nicols invests $30 000 and becomes a partner in Pearen, Nicols Security Services. The entry to record Nicols as a partner in the firm is:

***9**

Date		Account		Debit	Credit
		Cash		30 000 —	
		B. Nicols, Capital			30 000 —
		To record Nicols' investment			

The same ledger used by the Pearen Security Services will continue to be used by the new partnership. The $30 000 contributed by Nicols was deposited into the bank account of the business. The Cash account increased and a new Capital account was opened.

Example 4 Bill Dolman, the sole proprietor of Dolman TV Services, has agreed to sell part of his business. Bill's Capital account has a balance of $90 000. Ab Salman has offered $45 000 to become an equal partner in the firm. Dolman accepts the offer. Dolman will personally receive the $45 000. In return he will give up half of his capital in the business. The Cash account of the business does not change since the transaction is between Dolman and Salman and not Salman and the business. The only change in the books of the business is a decrease in Dolman's capital and the addition of a second Capital account, A. Salman, Capital. The entry to record the new account is:

***10**

A proprietor sells an interest in a business to a partner. Cash is paid to the owner personally.

Date		Account		Debit	Credit
		B. Dolman, Capital		45 000 —	
		A. Salman, Capital			45 000 —
		Admission of a partner			
		to the business			

It should be noted that this is a private exchange of money outside of the business. The assets and the total capital remain the same, but there are now two Capital accounts.

*11

Example 5 W. Henry and W. Gordon operate competing businesses. Henry's firm is thriving, profitable, and uses modern equipment. Gordon's business is not as successful. Simplified versions of the accounts of the two businesses follow:

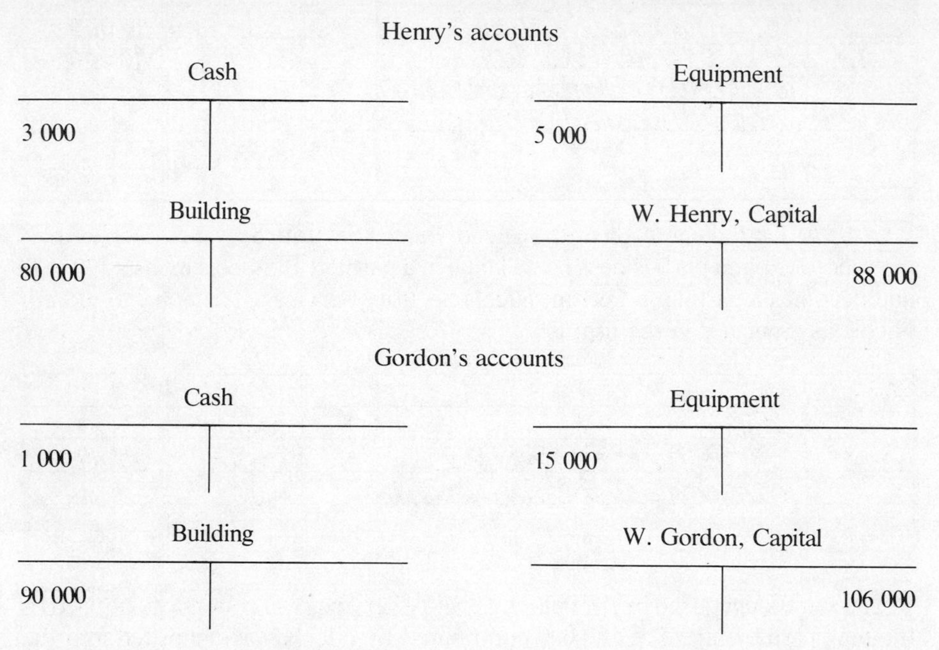

Two proprietorships merge to form a partnership. Assets are revalued and Goodwill is established on the books.

Goodwill is an intangible asset which recognizes above average earnings expected in the future.

The two men agree to merge their business assets with the following provisions:

- Gordon's assets are to be devalued by $31 000 (Equipment to be decreased by $10 000 and Building by $21 000).
- Henry is to receive credit for the established clientele and promising future of his business by the setting up of a *Goodwill account* of $12 000 and an increase in his capital of $12 000. Goodwill is an asset account. It is a recognition of the good reputation and promising future of the business.

Before the books of the new partnership are opened, it is necessary to record the Goodwill and to revalue Gordon's account. This entry is made on Henry's books:

		Goodwill		12 000 —	
		W. Henry, Capital			12 000 —
		To record Goodwill and			
		to increase the owner's			
		capital according to			
		partnership agreement			

The entry to decrease the assets of the Gordon business is:

				Debit	Credit
		W. Gordon, Capital		31 000 —	
		Equipment			10 000 —
		Building			21 000 —
		To devalue equipment and building according to partnership agreement			

After the two entries above have been posted, the two businesses close their books and a new set of books is opened for the partnership, Henry & Gordon Associates. The following two entries are made to open the partnership's books:

				Debit	Credit
		Cash		3 000 —	
		Equipment		5 000 —	
		Building		80 000 —	
		Goodwill		12 000 —	
		W. Henry, Capital			100 000 —
		To record the assets and capital of W. Henry			

				Debit	Credit
		Cash		1 000 —	
		Equipment		5 000 —	
		Building		69 000 —	
		W. Gordon, Capital			75 000 —
		To record the assets and capital of W. Gordon			

After posting this entry, the accounts of the partnership appear as follows:

Cash

Debit	Credit
3 000	
1 000	
Balance 4 000	

Equipment

Debit	Credit
5 000	
5 000	
Balance 10 000	

Building

Debit	Credit
80 000	
69 000	
Balance 149 000	

Goodwill

Debit	Credit
12 000	

W. Gordon, Capital

Debit	Credit
	75 000

W. Henry, Capital

Debit	Credit
	100 000

Partnerships and Income Taxes

*12

As a business, a partnership does not pay income taxes on its net income. Each partner is taxed on his or her share of the partnership's net income, in addition to any income received from other sources.

The partners in a business pay personal income tax on their share of the partnership's net income.

Suppose the partnership of R. Kendall and B. McArthur (Example 1, page 517) earned a net income of $28 000 and the partnership agreement stipulated that the partners were to share the net income equally. The business, Kendall and McArthur Services, is not taxed. The net income is treated as personal income of the owners. Kendall must include his share of the partnership's net income ($14 000) on his personal income tax return. McArthur must include her share ($14 000) on her personal income tax return.

Unit 50

Ledger Accounts of a Partnership

*13

The accounts in the Ledger of a partnership are the same as those of a proprietorship except that there is one Drawing account and one Capital account for *each* partner.

Drawing Accounts The Drawing account of each partner is used in the same way in a partnership as the Drawing account in a sole proprietorship. The relevant Drawing account is debited whenever assets are withdrawn by a partner from the business. Typical transactions involving Drawing accounts are:

There is a Drawing account and a Capital account for each partner in the ledger of a partnership.

- payment of salaries to partners
- withdrawal of cash or other business assets by a partner
- payments of a personal nature for a partner using partnership funds

It should be emphasized that salaries paid to partners during the year *must* be recorded in the Drawing accounts. They cannot be treated as a company expense and debited to Salaries Expense. One of the difficulties encountered by accountants is to decide if a transaction involves a legitimate business expense or should be treated as a personal withdrawal and recorded in the owner's Drawing account. Personal expenses charged to the business have the effect of lowering the net income of the business and in the long run, the income taxes paid by the owners. By charging expenses to the business, owners can obtain free fringe benefits illegally.

Salaries paid to partners must be recorded in the Drawing account.

Closing the Partnership Books

*14

In a proprietorship, revenue and expense accounts are closed into an Income Summary account. The balance of the summary account would be the net income or the net loss. This balance is then transferred to the owner's Capital account. The owner's Drawing account is then closed into the Capital account.

The books of a partnership are closed in a similar way but with one difference. The balance of the Income Summary account is closed into each of the partner's Capital accounts according to the partnership agreement for dividing net income and net loss. Figure 20.2 illustrates the closing of the books when there is a net income of $30 000 to be divided equally between the two partners. In General Journal form this entry is:

Dec.	31	Income Summary		30 000 —	
		Partner A, Capital			15 000 —
		Partner B, Capital			15 000 —
		To divide the net income equally as per partnership agreement			

After the net income has been transferred to the partners' Capital accounts, the partners' Drawing accounts are closed into the Capital accounts. The partners' Drawing accounts contain the salaries paid to the owners during the year as well as any other personal withdrawals. The debit balance of the Drawing accounts represents a decrease in equity and this decrease is reflected by closing the Drawing account into the Capital account with this entry:

Dec.	31	Partner A, Capital		8 000 —	
		Partner B, Capital		8 000 —	
		Partner A, Drawing			8 000 —
		Partner B, Drawing			8 000 —
		To close the Drawing accounts			

The steps in closing the books of a partnership include:
1. Close revenue accounts into the Income Summary account.
2. Close expense accounts into the Income Summary account.
3. Close the Income Summary account into the partners' Capital accounts (based on the terms of the partnership agreement).
4. Close the partners' Drawing accounts into the partners' Capital accounts.

These steps are illustrated in Figure 20.2.

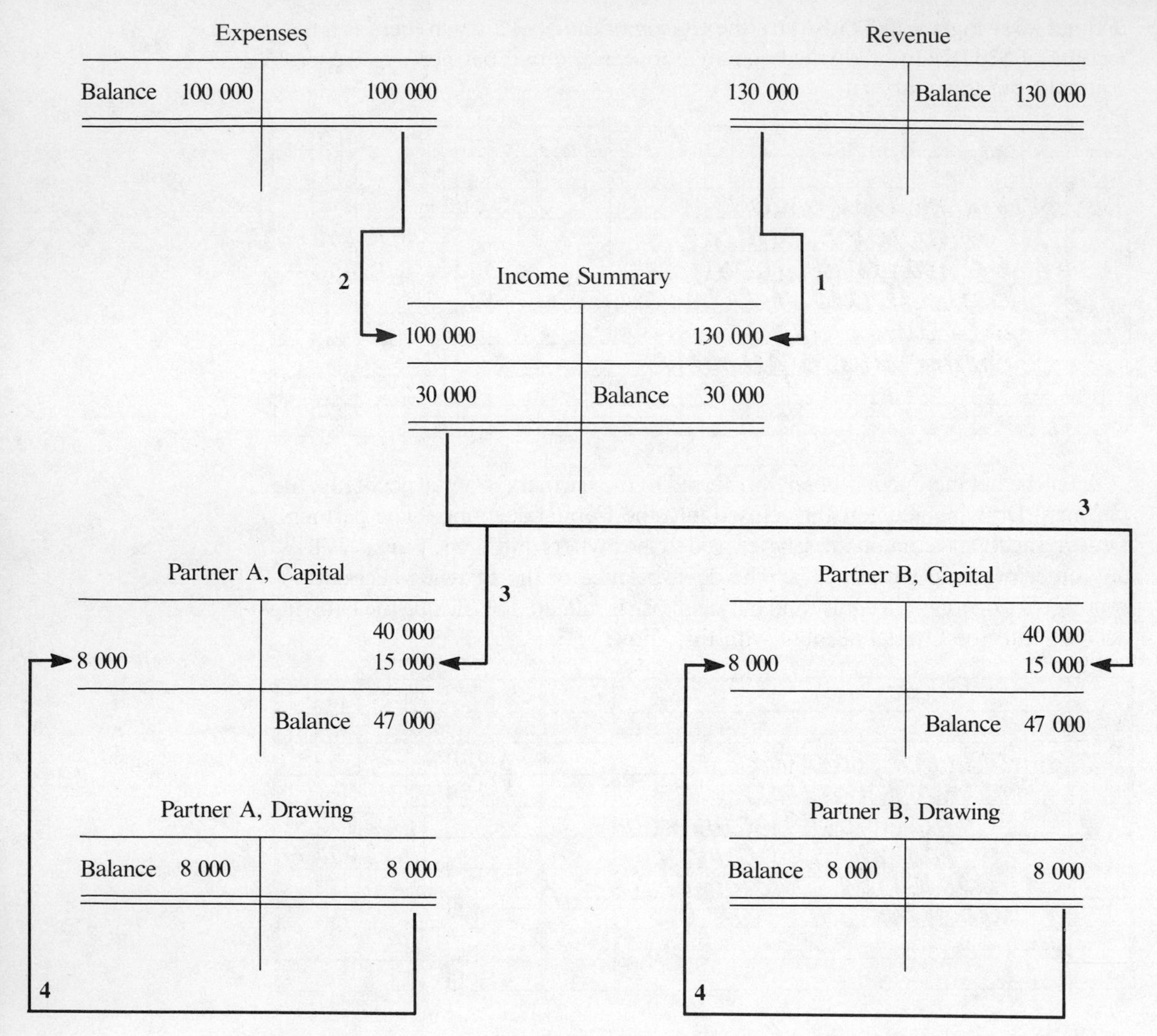

Figure 20.2 *The partnership agreement in this example states that the net income is to be divided equally between partners A and B.*

Dividing Net Income

***15**

The partnership contract states how net income or net losses are to be shared.

Partners may make any agreement they wish for the division of the partnership's net income or net loss. One of the most important clauses of the partnership contract is the one stating how these will be shared. Four factors considered by partners in coming to agreement on the sharing of net income and net loss are:

- payment for amount of work performed
- return on capital
- amount of capital invested
- skills, talent, reputation

Payment for Amount of Work Performed Suppose one partner is very actively engaged in running a business while another contributes money but does not work in the business. It seems fair that the working partner should be paid for the work performed. In some partnerships both partners work in the business but one has a more responsible position or puts in more hours of work than the other. In preparing the partnership agreement, the partners may consider the amount of work performed in deciding how to share net income or net loss.

Return on Capital If a partner invested money in government bonds, term deposits or mortgages, interest would be earned on that money. Likewise, if a partner invests in a partnership, it seems reasonable to pay interest on the money invested. This is especially so when one partner invests more funds in the partnership than the others. If interest is paid on all funds contributed to a partnership proportionately to all partners, the partner who invested more money would appropriately receive more interest.

Amount of Capital Invested If partners contribute an equal amount of money, work, time, and skills to a partnership, it seems fair to distribute net income equally to the partners. However, if one of the partners contributes more money, that partner could expect to receive a greater share. Suppose one partner contributes $10 000 and another partner contributes $20 000. The second partner could demand a greater share of net income because of the larger investment.

Skills, Talent, Reputation Sometimes partners use factors such as skills, talents, and reputation of the owners in deciding on how to share net income or net losses. It can be argued that if a net income is earned it is because of the personal contributions of the partners. The differing levels of skills, talent and reputation of partners may be reflected in how the partners agree to share net income or net loss.

Methods of Dividing Net Income or Net Loss

*16

Among the many methods used to divide net income and net loss are:

- fixed ratio
- capital ratio
- salaries and remaining net income (or net loss) to partners on a fixed ratio
- interest on capital, salaries, and remaining net income (or net loss) to partners on a fixed ratio.

Fixed Ratio On forming their partnership, Kendall and McArthur (Example 1, page 517) agreed to divide net income and net loss equally. Thus 50% of net income will belong to Kendall and 50% to McArthur. They felt that a 50:50 ratio was fair since both contributed the same amount of capital, both would work full time in the business, and both had special skills to offer to the new business. At the end of a year, net income is $28 000. According to the partnership agreement this amount is divided 50:50. When the books are closed, the division is made by the following entry:

	Income Summary	28 000 —	
	R. Kendall, Capital		14 000 —
	B. McArthur, Capital		14 000 —
	To divide the net income equally between the partners, per partnership agreement		

Figure 20.3 shows how the division of net income is included on the bottom of the income statement.

Kendall and McArthur Services Income Statement December 31, 19__		
Revenue		
Sales		138 000 00
Expenses		
Selling Expenses	90 000 00	
Administrative Expenses	20 000 00	110 000 00
Net Income		28 000 00
Distribution of net income		
R. Kendall (50%)	14 000 00	
B. McArthur (50%)	14 000 00	28 000 00

Figure 20.3 *Distribution of net income as shown on the income statement*

*17

Capital Ratio The capital ratio method is used when the success of the business depends to some extent on the contribution of capital. In some businesses, such as auto dealerships, substantial investments in equipment, buildings, and merchandise are required. The capital ratio method recognizes the importance of capital to the business and divides the net income or net loss accordingly.

J. Hill and D. Love (Example 2, page 517) have invested $20 000 and $40 000 respectively in their partnership. They agree to share net income and net loss in the ratio of their beginning capital. The ratio is determined as follows:

	Beginning Capital	Percentage of Total
J. Hill	$20 000	33.3%
D. Love	40 000	66.7%
Total	$60 000	100%

Hill receives 33.3% of any net income and Love 66.7%. They share net losses in the same way, that is in the ratio of 33.3:66.7. Suppose there is net income of $10 000. The division of the net income would be calculated as follows:

		Share of Net Income
J. Hill	0.333 × 10 000 =	$ 3 330
D. Love	0.667 × 10 000 =	6 670
	Total	$10 000

The entry to record the division of net income is: *18

Date		Account		Debit	Credit
Dec.	31	Income Summary		10 000 —	
		J. Hill, Capital			3 330 —
		D. Love, Capital			6 670
		To divide net income in the ratio of 33.3:66.7, per partnership agreement			

The division of the net income would be shown on the bottom of the income statement as was the case in Figure 20.3.

Salaries and Remaining Profits in a Fixed Ratio In their partnership agreement (Example 3, page 519), F. Pearen and B. Nicols agreed to the following: *19

- A salary of $12 000 to Pearen and $10 000 to Nicols per year
- Any remaining net income after salaries to be shared 50:50

At the end of the year, there is a net income of $25 000. A special report called a *statement of distribution of net income* is prepared as shown in Figure 20.4.

Pearen & Nicols Security Services
Statement of Distribution of Net Income

	F. Pearen	B. Nicols	Total
Net Income to be divided			$25 000
Salaries	$12 000	$10 000	$22 000
Remaining net income shared equally (50:50)	1 500	1 500	3 000
Totals	$13 500	$11 500	$25 000

Figure 20.4 *Statement of distribution of net income for two partners, Pearen and Nicols*

The statement of distribution of net income outlines clearly to the partners how the net income is shared between them. There are two entries required in the ledger.

Dec.	31	Income Summary		22 000 —	
		F. Pearen, Capital			12 000 —
		B. Nicols, Capital			10 000 —
		To credit partners with their salaries, per partnership agreement			
Dec.	31	Income Summary		3 000 —	
		F. Pearen, Capital			1 500 —
		B. Nicols, Capital			1 500 —
		To divide remainder of net income on a 50:50 ratio, per partnership agreement			

*20

Interest, Salaries, and Fixed Ratio In forming their partnership, W. Gordon and W. Henry (Example 5, page 520) agreed on the following division of net income and net loss:

- each partner to receive a $14 000 salary per year
- 12% interest on the beginning capital to be credited annually to each partner from net income
- any remaining net income or net loss after interest and salaries to be divided equally

In the last fiscal year, the partnership earned net income of $53 000. The statement of distribution of net income was prepared to divide the net income.

Gordon & Henry Company
Statement of Distribution of Net Income
December 31, 19__

Net income to be divided			$53 000
	W. Gordon	W. Henry	Total
Salaries	$14 000	$14 000	$28 000
Interest on beginning capital 12%	9 000	12 000	21 000
Remaining Net Income shared equally	2 000	2 000	4 000
Total	$25 000	$28 000	$53 000

Figure 20.5 *Statement of distribution of net income for Gordon & Henry Company*

There are three entries required to record this division of net income in the General Ledger accounts.

Date		Particulars	PR	Debit	Credit
Dec.	31	Income Summary		28 000 —	
		W. Gordon, Capital			14 000 —
		W. Henry, Capital			14 000 —
		To credit each partner with salaries, per partnership agreement			
Dec.	31	Income Summary		21 000 —	
		W. Gordon, Capital			9 000 —
		W. Henry, Capital			12 000 —
		To credit each partner with 12% interest based on beginning capital, per partnership agreement			
Dec.	31	Income Summary		4 000 —	
		W. Gordon, Capital			2 000 —
		W. Henry, Capital			2 000 —
		To divide remainder ($4 000) of net income equally, per partnership agreement			

Dividing Net Loss and Insufficient Net Income

*21

In each of the situations discussed to this point there was a net income large enough to give each partner what was owing according to the partnership agreement. However, businesses often suffer losses or do not earn enough net income to pay the partners according to the agreement. Two examples of such situations follow.

For example, S. Hill and D. Love agreed to share net income and net loss in the ratio of their beginning capital balances. This ratio was 33.3:66.7. This means that if there is a net loss, Hill absorbs 33.3% of the net loss and Love 66.7%. Suppose the partnership suffers a net loss of $8 000. The division of the net loss would be calculated as follows:

		Share of Net Loss
J. Hill	0.333 × 8 000 =	$2 664
D. Love	0.667 × 8 000 =	5 336
	Total	$8 000

The entry to record this division of the net loss is:

Date		Account / Explanation	PR	Debit	Credit
Dec.	31	J. Hill, Capital		2 664 —	
		D. Love, Capital		5 336 —	
		Income Summary			8 000 —
		To close the Income Summary account and to divide the net loss per partnership agreement			

Partners' Salaries

*22

Journal entries involving partners' salaries occur in two ways. A debit entry is made during the year each time salaries are paid to the partners, and when personal withdrawals are made. Another entry is made at the end of the year when the net income or net loss is divided between the partners. For example, suppose Creaco and Costanza invest $18 000 each and become partners in a masonry business. Their partnership agreement states that they are to receive salaries and to share equally any remaining net income or net loss after salaries. Each receives a salary of $15 000 a year. Once a month, each partner receives a cheque for $1 250 a month. At the end of the year each partner will have received cash payments of $15 000. The following T-accounts show the entries for salaries on the debit side of the Drawing accounts.

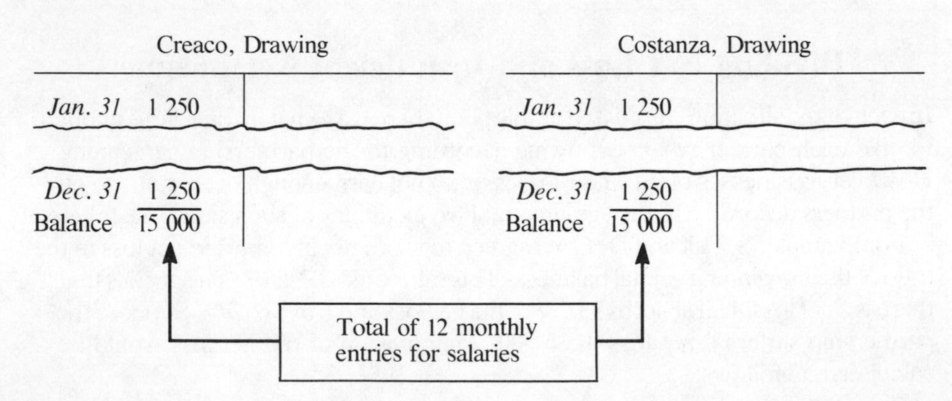

Suppose the partnership has earned a net income of $40 000 for the year. According to the partnership agreement the partners share this $40 000 by:

- receiving salaries of $15 000 each (total $30 000)
- sharing the remainder ($10 000) equally

These entries are made to distribute the net income:

Date		Account	PR	Debit	Credit
19-- Dec.	31	Income Summary		30 000 —	
		Creaco, Capital			15 000 —
		Costanza, Capital			15 000 —
		To credit each partner with $15 000 salary, per the partnership agreement			
Dec.	31	Income Summary		10 000 —	
		Creaco, Capital			5 000 —
		Costanza, Capital			5 000
		To distribute the remaining net income equally, per the partnership agreement			

Finally the Drawing accounts are closed into the Capital accounts with this entry:

Date		Account	PR	Debit	Credit
19-- Dec.	31	Creaco, Capital		15 000 —	
		Costanza, Capital		15 000 —	
		Creaco, Drawing			15 000 —
		Costanza, Drawing			15 000 —
		To close the Drawing accounts			

See if you can understand these principles:

1. The debits in the Drawing accounts represent actual withdrawals of cash made during the year.
2. Each partner's share of the net income, ($20 000 in this example which is made up of $15 000 salary and $5 000 remainder) appears as a credit in each Capital account.
3. Although each partner's share of the net income is $20 000, the partners' Capital accounts only increase by $5 000 each because they withdrew $15 000 during the year as salaries.

Financial Statements

In a partnership, the following four financial statements may be prepared: *23

- income statement
- statement of distribution of net income
- balance sheet
- statement of partners' equity

Income Statement The income statement of a partnership is very similar to that of a proprietorship. However, a section may be added to the bottom to show the division of the net income or net loss (Figure 20.3).

Statement of Distribution of Net Income If the division of the net income or net loss is not shown on the income statement, a *statement of distribution of net income* is prepared (Figure 20.5). This is a more formal report that is prepared when there are salaries, interest, and a remainder of net income or loss to be divided.

The Balance Sheet There are at least two people in every partnership. For every partner there is a Capital account. Each partner's capital appears in the equity section of the balance sheet as shown in Figure 20.6.

Gordon & Henry Company Balance Sheet December 31, 19__			
Assets			
Current Assets			
Cash		9 000 —	
Accounts Receivable		12 000 —	
Inventory		30 000 —	
Total Current Assets			51 000 —
Fixed Assets			
Equipment	10 000 —		
Less Accumulated Depreciation	1 000 —	9 000 —	
Building	149 000 —		
Less Accumulated Depreciation	7 000 —	142 000 —	
Total Fixed Assets			151 000 —
Other Assets			
Goodwill			12 000 —
Total Assets			214 000 —
Liabilities and Partners' Equity			
Current Liabilities			
Accounts Payable			4 000 —
Partner's Equity			
W. Gordon, Capital		91 000 —	
W. Henry, Capital		119 000 —	210 000 —
Total Liabilities and Partners' Equity			214 000 —

Figure 20.6 *Balance sheet for Gordon & Henry Company*

Statement of Partners' Equity Partners are usually interested in seeing the changes in their Capital accounts from year to year. A *statement of partners' equity* is prepared to provide this information (Figure 20.7). The information in this statement could be placed in the equity section of the balance sheet if it did not make the balance sheet unduly long.

*24

Gordon & Henry Company
Statement of Partners' Equity
For the year ended Dec. 31, 19__

	Gordon	Henry	Total
Capital, Jan. 1	$75 000	$100 000	$175 000
Add: Additional Investment	5 000	5 000	10 000
Share of Net Income	25 000	28 000	53 000
Total	$105 000	$133 000	$238 000
Less: Withdrawals	14 000	14 000	28 000
Total Capital, Dec. 31	$ 91 000	$119 000	$210 000

Figure 20.7 *Statement of partners' equity for Gordon & Henry Company*

The statement of partners' equity is a picture of all the activity involving the partners' investments; it shows additions to the business contributed during the year; it shows all withdrawals made; it shows the share of the net income or net loss credited to each partner.

Facts to Remember

A *sole proprietorship* is a business owned by one person.
In a *sole proprietorship*, the proprietor has unlimited personal liability for the debts and legal obligations of the business.
A *partnership* is a business owned by two or more persons.
In a *partnership*, the partners have unlimited personal liability for the debts and legal obligations of the business.
A *corporation* is a business owned by three or more persons and has a legal existence of its own.
The term *limited company* is sometimes used to describe the corporate form of ownership.
In a *corporation*, the owners' liability is limited to their investment in the corporation.
Goodwill is an *intangible asset* which recognizes above-average earnings expected in the future.

Reviewing Your Reading

Questions

1. Explain what is meant by the following:
   a) sole proprietorship b) partnership c) corporation
2. Explain the term *unlimited personal liability*.
3. If a proprietorship does not pay income tax on its net income, how does the net income get taxed?
4. How many persons may form:
   a) a partnership? b) a corporation?
5. Give three advantages and three disadvantages for each of the three forms of business ownership.
6. What do you think are the three main items which should be included in a partnership agreement?
7. Why might some assets be revalued when two persons combine their businesses to form a partnership?
8. Explain the term *goodwill*. Where does the Goodwill account appear on a balance sheet?
9. Explain how income tax is paid on the income of a partnership.
10. Which account is used to record the payment of salaries to partners?
11. What accounts are debited and credited when a partner withdraws merchandise from the business for personal use?
12. In closing partnership books at the end of a fiscal period, into which account (or accounts) are the following closed:
    a) the balance of the Income Summary account?
    b) revenue and expenses?
    c) the drawing account?
13. List the four steps followed in closing the books of a partnership.
14. List four methods of dividing the net income of a partnership.
15. Chow and Wong use the ratio of beginning capital balances as their method of dividing net income. Chow's capital balance is $27 000 and Wong's is $18 000. In what ratio is the net income divided?
16. Name the four financial statements which may be prepared for a partnership.

Applying Your Knowledge

Exercises Part A

1. For each of the following, prepare General Journal entries to record the formation of the partnership.
   a) D. Renshaw, J. Heward, and B. Malloy each contribute $7 000 cash to a new partnership.

b) S. Signer and L. Harris agree to form a new business. Signer contributes $18 000 and Harris $20 000.

c) S. Brucculieri and M. Scornaiencki form a partnership with Brucculieri contributing cash, $5 000 and a building worth $80 000. Scornaiencki invests $20 000 cash and equipment worth $20 000.

2. M. Bondar and C. Church agree to join their two businesses to form a partnership. Bondar's assets and liabilities are: Cash $1 200; Accounts Receivable $2 000; Equipment $7 000; Accounts Payable $1 100. Church's assets and liabilities are: Cash $2 000; Accounts Receivable $3 000; Building $80 000; Mortgage Payable $50 000; Bank Loan $10 000. Prepare General Journal entries to set up the partnership.

3. M. Ross wishes to expand her business and agrees to take K. Golumbia in as an equal partner. M. Ross has a capital balance of $25 000. K. Golumbia contributes $25 000 cash to the business. Prepare the General Journal entry to record Golumbia's investment in the business.

4. C. DeGagne has an investment of $40 000 in a sole proprietorship. In order to share the work of running the company, he sells an equal share of the company to R. Francis. In return, he personally receives $20 000 cash from Francis. The assets of the business do not change. Prepare the General Journal entry to admit Francis as a partner.

5. Moffat and Mottola agree to join their businesses and to form a partnership.

Moffat's Accounts		**Mottola's Accounts**	
Cash	$ 5 000	Cash	$ 2 000
Accounts Receivable	20 000	Accounts Receivable	7 000
Equipment	30 000	Building	40 000
Accounts Payable	7 000	Equipment	19 000
		Mortgage Payable	10 000

Their agreement includes the following:

- Moffat's equipment is to be reduced in value to $20 000 from the balance of $30 000.
- Mottola's building is to be increased in value to $70 000 from $40 000.
- Mottola's equipment is to be reduced in value to $9 000 from $19 000.

a) Prepare General Journal entries to revalue assets for Moffat and for Mottola.

b) Prepare General Journal entries to set up the partnership.

6. a) Prepare General Journal entries to record these transactions for Ron Kendall and Betty McArthur:

May 10 McArthur withdrew cash for personal use, $150.
20 Kendall took home merchandise worth $75.
31 Paid salaries, $1 000 each to partners.

June 15	Paid $75 for golf lessons for Kendall's daughter.
30	Paid partners' salaries $1 000 each.
July 25	Kendall invested an additional $5 000 in the business.

b) After closing the expense and revenue accounts, there is a credit balance of $19 000 in the Income Summary account. This net income is to be divided equally between Kendall and McArthur. Prepare the General Journal entry to close the Income Summary account and to divide the net income between the partners.
c) Kendall's Drawing account has a debit balance of $6 000 and McArthur's a debit balance of $8 000. Prepare the General Journal entry to close the Drawing accounts.
d) The next year, the firm of Kendall & McArthur Services incurs a net loss of $7 000. This is represented by a debit balance in the Income Summary account. Prepare the General Journal entry to close the Income Summary account and to divide the net loss equally.

7. a) Stewart & Smith divide net income and net loss according to the ratio of their beginning capital balances. Stewart has a capital balance of $25 000 and Smith $75 000. What is the ratio used?
b) Using the ratio from part a), how much is received by each partner if the net income is $16 000?
c) If Stewart and Smith incurred a net loss of $6 000, how much of the net loss would be shared by each partner?

8. Hill and Love divide net income from their partnership in the ratio of their capital. The ratio is 33.3:66.7.
a) The net income or net loss for each of three years follows. For each year determine how much of the net income or net loss is allocated to Hill and how much is allocated to Love.

Year I	Net Income	$10 000
Year II	Net Loss	6 000
Year III	Net Income	22 000

b) Prepare General Journal entries to close the Income Summary account and to divide the net income or net loss each year.

9. Pearen and Nicols divide net income and net loss on the following basis:
- Pearen's salary is $12 000 and Nicols' salary is $10 000.
- Any remaining net income or net loss after salaries is shared equally.

a) Prepare a statement of distribution of net income for each of these years:

Year I	Net Income	$23 000
Year II	Net Income	30 000
Year III	Net Income	36 000

b) Prepare General Journal entries to distribute the net income each year.

10. Gordon and Henry share the net income of their partnership in the following manner:
 - Salaries are $14 000 each.
 - Interest on beginning capital is 12%. Gordon's capital if $75 000, Henry's $100 000.
 - Remaining net income or loss after salaries and interest is shared equally.

 a) Prepare a statement of distribution of net income for each of these years:

Year I	Net Income	$59 000
Year II	Net Income	30 000
Year III	Net Loss	5 000

 b) Prepare the General Journal entries to distribute the net income or net loss each year.

Exercises Part B

11. Prepare a statement of partners' equity for Klemba and Swords on December 31, using this information:
 - January 1 capital balances: Klemba $30 000; Swords $40 000.
 - Additional investment: Klemba $5 000.
 - Withdrawals: Klemba $18 000; Swords $21 000.
 - Share of net income: Klemba $18 000; Swords $21 000.

12. Prepare a December 31 statement of partners' equity for Doyle and Durivage:
 - January 1 capital balances: Doyle $20 000; Durivage $15 000.
 - Additional investment: $7 000 each.
 - Withdrawals: Doyle $12 000; Durivage $11 000.
 - Share of net income: Doyle $20 000; Durivage $16 000.

13. S. Gomes, the owner of a proprietorship, has the following assets and liabilities:

Cash	$ 2 000
Supplies	1 000
Equipment	25 000
Accounts Payable	2 000

 He has agreed to sell an equal share of the business to L. Borel for $33 500 after $7 500 worth of goodwill has been recorded.

 a) Record the goodwill in a General Journal entry.
 b) Prepare an entry to record Gomes' contribution to the new partnership.
 c) Record the contribution of $33 500 cash to the new business by L. Borel.

Exercises Part C

14. Kay Martin owns a company with assets of $190 000 and liabilities of $40 000. She agrees to sell an equal share of the business to Ray Robert after her capital account has been increased to $175 000 by the recording of goodwill.

 a) What is the amount of goodwill to be recorded?
 b) How much must Robert invest for an equal share of the business?

15. Stewart and Todkill decide to form a partnership. Stewart invests $25 000 cash and Todkill $20 000 cash. They are each to receive a salary of $9 000 and interest of 12% on their beginning capital. The balance of the net income or net loss is to be divided in the ratio of the Capital accounts at the time of formation.
   a) Prepare General Journal entries to record the formation.
   b) Prepare a statement of distribution of net income if the year's net income is $26 000.

16. Following is the trial balance of F. Addario and W. Box who are partners. They share net income and net loss in the ratio of 2:1. Each receives a salary of $11 000. The ending inventory, December 31, is $51,000. Prepare:
   a) an income statement
   b) a statement of distribution of net income
   c) a statement of partners' equity
   d) a balance sheet
   e) the closing entries

Addario & Box
Trial Balance
December 31, 19__

ACCOUNT TITLE	ACC. NO.	DEBIT	CREDIT
Cash		5 000 —	
Accounts Receivable		22 000 —	
Inventory, January 1		46 000 —	
Equipment		40 000 —	
Accumulated Depreciation: Equipment			8 000 —
Accounts Payable			14 000 —
Addario, Capital			27 000 —
Box, Capital			24 000 —
Addario, Drawing		13 000 —	
Box, Drawing		12 000 —	
Sales			257 000 —
Purchases		90 000 —	
Transportation on Purchases		2 000 —	
Selling Expense		70 000 —	
Administrative Expense		30 000 —	
		330 000 —	330 000 —

Accounting in Action

Case 1

Starting Your Own Business For the past few years Don has been a mechanic for a large garage. He has been especially adept at repairing cars made in Germany. He has been so successful that many customers insist that he be the only mechanic to work on their cars. Having saved a substantial amount of money, he wants to open his own garage in which he would specialize in the repair of German cars. He would be the only mechanic.

a) Discuss the reasons why starting your own business, as Don is doing, is so attractive to many individuals.
b) Explain some of the factors that Don should consider in starting his own business.

Case 2

Taking on a Partner Don was concerned about the reduction in net income that occurred in the fifth year of his business. He felt his garage had grown as much as it could for a sole proprietorship. He had managed to train Jim, another mechanic, to help him, but felt that the business would do better if the helper could put more effort into his work. As a result, Don offered to take in Jim as a partner if he would invest $20 000 cash in the business and help to run the garage.

a) Explain some of the advantages of taking in a partner.
b) Discuss some of the disadvantages of taking in a partner.
c) If Jim decided to order a piece of equipment worth $15 000 without Don's knowledge, would Don have to help pay for it?
d) To what extent would Don be responsible for the actions of Jim?

Case 3

Partnership Problems R. Lee and B. Scinto have been partners for eight years. Their net incomes for the eight years have risen from $1 000 the first year to $90 000 last year. Lee and Scinto share net income and net loss equally. They have always gotten along well together and have been able to make business decisions with little argument. They have no written partnership contract.

When they were establishing their business both partners worked 70 to 80 hours a week. Lee still works long hours, but Scinto has decided to enjoy life now that the company is doing so well. He puts in about half the time of Lee. Scinto feels that Lee does much of the work which could be done by employees. Lee feels he should be receiving more of the net income.

What are the potential difficulties for the partnership? Suggest action to forestall these difficulties.

Case 4

Interpreting Accounting Data Jake Meyers is a young lawyer who operated a law office as a proprietorship for five years. The results for the five years are summarized as follows:

	19–1	19–2	19–3	19–4	19–5
Revenue	$20 000	$30 000	$59 000	$65 000	$66 000
Expenses	25 000	26 000	28 000	33 000	34 000
Net Income (or Net Loss)	(5 000)	4 000	31 000	32 000	32 000
Net Income (or Net Loss) as a Percent of Revenue	(25%)	13.3%	52.5%	49.2%	48.5%
Meyers' Share of Net Income or Net Loss	(100%)	100%	100%	100%	100%

At the beginning of 19_6 Jake joined three other lawyers in a partnership. Jake receives 25% of the net income or net loss. The partnership agreement is renewable every five years. The results for the five years of the partnership follow:

	19–6	19–7	19–8	19–9	19–10
Revenue	$200 000	$300 000	$400 000	$450 000	$500 000
Expenses	180 000	272 000	290 000	293 000	330 000
Net Income	20 000	28 000	110 000	157 000	170 000
Net Income as a Percent of Revenue	10%	9.33%	27.5%	34.9%	34%
Meyers' Share of Net Income	25%	25%	25%	25%	25%

Jake must now decide whether to stay in the partnership or to leave and form his own business again. Compare the financial results for the ten years shown and prepare a recommendation for Jake.

Career Profile

A Bookkeeper The terms *accounting* and *bookkeeping* are sometimes confusing to readers. In general, accounting refers to the total set of accounting functions, from recording, to the preparation of reports, to making financial recommendations based on the reports. Bookkeeping is a more narrow area and is generally concerned with recording functions.

D. Kemp Edwards Ltd. is a building supply company which provides specialized services and products for its customers. It stocks a variety of special hardwoods required by hobbyists and cabinetmakers. D. Kemp Edwards employs skilled workers and is often involved in supplying specialized quality finished products. For example, one of their jobs was to build a solid oak desk worth over $5 000 for the reception area of a large office complex.

Louise Holdham holds a bookkeeping position with D. Kemp Edwards. After graduating from the High School of Commerce in Ottawa, Louise was hired as a receptionist-cashier at D. Kemp Edwards. She then was promoted to a secretarial position in which she learned basic bookkeeping tasks. Louise is now mainly involved in bookkeeping and performs a wide range of work. Here is a summary of what she does:

- *Accounts Receivable:* Louise records sales invoices in customer accounts, sends monthly statements to customers, and, on occasion, helps to balance the Accounts Receivable Ledger with the General Ledger Control account. She uses an Audit 402 posting machine for the customer accounts.
- *Accounts Payable:* Purchase invoices are checked for mathematical accuracy and matched with the purchase order and receiving report.
- *Sales:* Louise prepares journal entries to record each day's sales in the Sales Journal.
- *Cash Receipts:* Louise handles the *cash float,* prepares the daily cash register proof, and records cash sales slips and cash received in a Cash Receipts Journal. She prepares a daily bank deposit.

As well as these duties, Louise performs many miscellaneous accounting jobs as they are required. For example, she helps out with the inventory records.

CHAPTER 21

Accounting for Corporations

Unlimited Liability

Unit 51

*1

The proprietorship and partnership forms of ownership, discussed in previous chapters, have several disadvantages. One of these is illustrated by the following example.

John Bowers operated a very successful business as a sole proprietorship for fifteen years. Through hard work and good management, John's company earned substantial net income for him. Over the years, John invested the money earned by his business by purchasing a cottage, two expensive cars, and several apartment buildings, which he rented out.

However, his business suddenly became unprofitable as new products and competitors caused several large losses in consecutive years. John's business was unable to pay a number of debts on time and as a result, the business was forced into bankruptcy. To pay off his creditors, John was ordered by the court to sell his cottage and the apartment buildings. John had to do so despite the fact that the properties belonged to him, personally, and not to his business.

John was personally liable for all the business debts. He lost his business investment and some of his personal assets.

The proprietor of a business is personally responsible for its debts.

The case of John Bowers illustrates a major disadvantage of partnerships and proprietorships – that of unlimited liability. It also points out one of the advantages of forming a corporation. In the corporate form of ownership, an investor risks the investment in the business, but not personal assets. Limited liability is an important advantage of the corporate form of ownership. Because of this characteristic, the term *limited company* is often used instead of *corporation*. Other advantages of the corporate form of ownership were given in Chapter 20.

What is a Corporation?

*2

A corporation is a business that has a legal existence of its own. It is separate from its owners. It has the right to sue and can be sued by others. In a partnership or proprietorship, the owners are not separate from the business.

*3

A business corporation is a legal entity owned by shareholders.

Forming a Corporation A corporation is formed by applying to a provincial government or to the federal government for a certificate of incorporation. The application, signed by one or more persons, must include the following information:

- name and address of the corporation
- types and number of shares to be authorized for issue
- names of directors
- nature of the business to be conducted

Generally, a corporation that will do business in only one province will apply to that province for incorporation. A business that will operate in more than one province usually applies to the federal government for incorporation.

Corporation Name *Have you ever wondered why so many businesses use Limited or Ltd. in their names?* The reason for this is that the corporation laws require the words *Limited, Limitée, Incorporated* or *Incorporée* to be part of the name. The short forms *Ltd.* or *Ltée.* or *Inc.* may be used. Other requirements for the corporation name are:

- the proposed name must differ from any other Canadian business
- the name must be acceptable to the public
- the name must be clearly displayed on the outside of the business in all its locations and in notices and advertisements

After the application has been accepted by the government, and the incorporation fee paid, the limited company or corporation comes into existence. The persons who applied for incorporation receive a document from the government. It is called a *charter* or *certificate of incorporation* if issued by the federal government, or *letters patent* or *memorandum of association* depending on the province involved.

Once a business is incorporated, a meeting is held to elect directors of the corporation. The directors then hire people to manage the business. Shares are sold or exchanged for assets and the company is in business.

Types of Business Corporation

*4

There are two types of business corporation:

- private corporation
- public corporation

Private Corporation A private business corporation is limited in the number of shareholders it may have and in the way it raises its capital. It may not have more than 50 shareholders and it must obtain its funds privately. It cannot sell shares or bonds to the public. Many small proprietorships and partnerships change their form of ownership to that of a private corporation in order to take advantage of the limited liability feature of the corporation. The owners still control and own the business, and yet have protection for their personal assets.

Public Corporation A public business corporation can have any number of shareholders. It can sell shares and bonds to the public.

Accounting Procedures for Corporations

Share Certificates Ownership of a corporation is represented by shares in the company. A person who invests in a corporation buys a portion or a share of the corporation. A share certificate is a form issued by a corporation showing the number of shares owned. The person purchasing the shares receives the share certificate and is called a *shareholder*. The terms *stock* and *stockholder* are sometimes used in place of *share* and *shareholder*.

*5

A share certificate is a form issued by a corporation indicating the number of shares owned.

Shareholders' Equity Accounts The books and accounts of a corporation are similar to those of proprietorships and partnerships except for differences in the equity section.

Shareholders are owners of shares in a corporation.

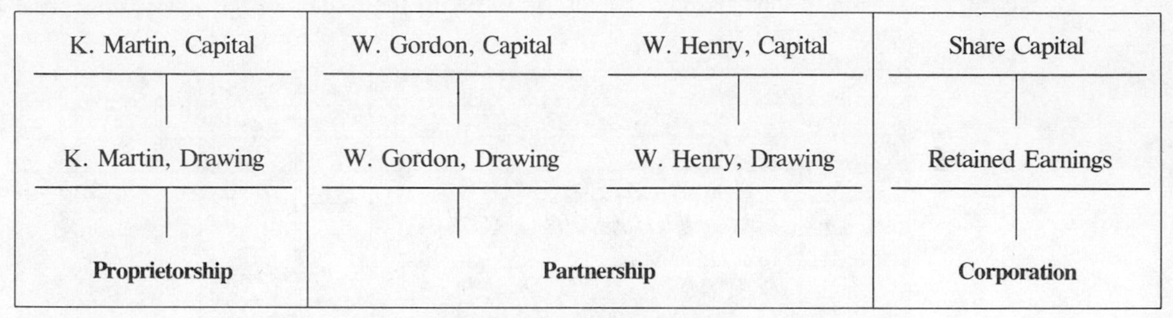

Figure 21.1 *Owner's Equity accounts for the three types of business ownership*

Figure 21.1 illustrates the different types of Owner's Equity accounts. In the corporate form of ownership, there are no Drawing accounts. The shareholders or owners of a corporation may not withdraw assets. They may, however, receive a portion of the corporate net income in the form of *dividends*.

Dividends are the portion of a corporation's net income paid to the shareholders.

Excello Corporation Balance Sheet December 31, 19__		
Assets		
Cash		5 000 00
Other Assets		100 000 00
Total Assets		105 000 00
Liabilities and Shareholders' Equity		
Current Liabilities:		
Accounts Payable		20 000 00
Shareholders' Equity:		
Share Capital	45 000 00	
Retained Earnings	40 000 00	85 000 00
Total Liabilities and Shareholders' Equity		105 000 00

Figure 21.2 *Equity section on the Excello Corporation balance sheet*

The Retained Earnings account is an equity account containing the balance of undistributed net income.

The equity section of a corporate balance sheet is shown in Figure 21.2. Note that in this simplified balance sheet, there are two new accounts in the equity section. The *Share Capital* account is a record of shares sold. The *Retained Earnings* account contains the balance of net income earned by the corporation after dividends have been paid.

*6

Journal Entries W. Gordon and W. Henry operate a business as a partnership. In order to have the benefits of limited liability, they have applied to their provincial government for permission to incorporate their company. They have received permission to incorporate as a private corporation with 10 000 authorized shares at a par value of $50 each.

Four hundred shares are sold in the new corporation to Gordon, Henry, and to several of their friends. The entry to record the issuing of the shares in general journal form is:

Feb.	1	Cash		20 000 —	
		Share Capital			20 000 —
		Sold 400 shares at $50			
		par value:			
		W. Gordon 100 shares			
		W. Henry 100 shares			
		D. Thomas 75 shares			
		M. Thomas 25 shares			
		J. Bak 100 shares			
		400 shares			

Shares for Assets W. Gordon and W. Henry turned over to the corporation the assets of their previous business in return for shares in the corporation. Equipment worth $10 000 and a building valued at $150 000 are exchanged for company shares.

Feb.	2	Equipment		10 000 —	
		Building		150 000 —	
		Share Capital			160 000 —
		Issued 3 200 shares for			
		property at $50 par value:			
		W. Gordon 1 200 shares			
		W. Henry 2 000 shares			
		3 200 shares			

The corporation, Gordon & Henry Ltd., is now formally established. Its balance sheet is shown in Figure 21.3. In the equity section of the balance sheet it is necessary to show both the *authorized* shares and the value of the shares actually issued or sold.

Gordon & Henry Ltd. Balance Sheet February 2, 19__		
Assets		
Current assets:		
Cash		20 000 00
Fixed assets:		
Equipment	10 000 00	
Building	150 000 00	160 000 00
Total assets		18 000 00
Shareholders' Equity		
Share Capital		
Authorized 10 000 shares, $50 par value		
Issued 3 600 shares		180 000 00

Figure 21.3 *Balance sheet for the new corporation – Gordon & Henry Ltd.*

Organization Expenses A number of expenses are incurred in organizing a corporation. These include legal fees, a fee to the government, and miscellaneous items such as share certificates and a company seal. These expenses are charged to an account called *Organization Expense*. Generally, this account is treated in one of two ways: *7

- as an expense charged to the first year's operations
- as an asset that is *written off* as an expense over a number of years. Each year, the balance in the account, Organization Expense, is shown after the fixed assets on the balance sheet

The first of these two methods is used when the amount involved is small. Whichever method is followed, the entry to record organizational costs is:

Organization Expense is an account used to record costs of organizing a business.

	Organization Expense	2 000 —	
	Cash		2 000 —
	Paid organizing costs		

Corporate Net Income The net income of a corporation increases the shareholders' equity. The decision concerning what happens to the net income is made by the board of directors. The board has several alternatives: *8

- distribute all of the net income to the shareholders
- leave all of the net income in the corporation
- a combination of the above – leave part of the net income in the business and distribute part to the shareholders

The shareholders do not participate directly in deciding what is done with corporate net income. However, if they are not satisfied with the decision of the board of directors, they can make their displeasure known at the annual shareholders' meeting. Every business corporation must hold a meeting of shareholders each year. At this meeting, the board of directors is elected by the shareholders. If enough shareholders are displeased with the operation of the corporation, some or all of the directors may be replaced. Elections are based on a majority vote of shareholders with one vote allowed for each share owned.

Dividends

*9

Generally speaking, the owners of a proprietorship or partnership may withdraw money from their business as they wish. The Drawing account is a record of withdrawals.

There is no opportunity for shareholders in a corporation to withdraw cash in the way that proprietors or partners do. Because of the limited liability feature of corporations, the creditors must be protected from the possibility of corporate owners withdrawing the assets and leaving no funds for the payment of corporate debts. In that event, the creditors would lose their investment since shareholders are not personally liable for the corporation's debts.

Dividends are the portion of a corporation's net income paid to the shareholders.

Dividends are paid out of retained earnings.

The portion of a corporation's net income distributed to the shareholder is called a *dividend*. Corporate laws allow dividends to be paid to owners or shareholders only out of accumulated net income. The accumulated net income is recorded in the Retained Earnings account. This account appears in the shareholders' equity section of the balance sheet (Figure 21.2). If there is a balance in this account, dividends may be declared.

*10

Closing the Books of a Corporation The closing phase of the accounting cycle for a corporation is very similar to those of partnerships and proprietorships. The steps in closing the books include:

1. Close Revenue and Expense accounts into the Income Summary account.
2. Close the Income Summary account balance (which is the net income or the net loss) into the Retained Earnings account. These steps are illustrated in Figure 21.4.

There is no change in the Share Capital account. The Retained Earnings account balance represents the accumulated net income (credit balance) or net loss (debit balance) of the corporation. It presents a historical picture of the company's profitability.

If dividends are to be paid, the Retained Earnings account must have a credit balance. Dividends may be paid in a year when the corporation has sustained a loss, as long as the net income from previous years leaves a credit balance in the Retained Earnings account.

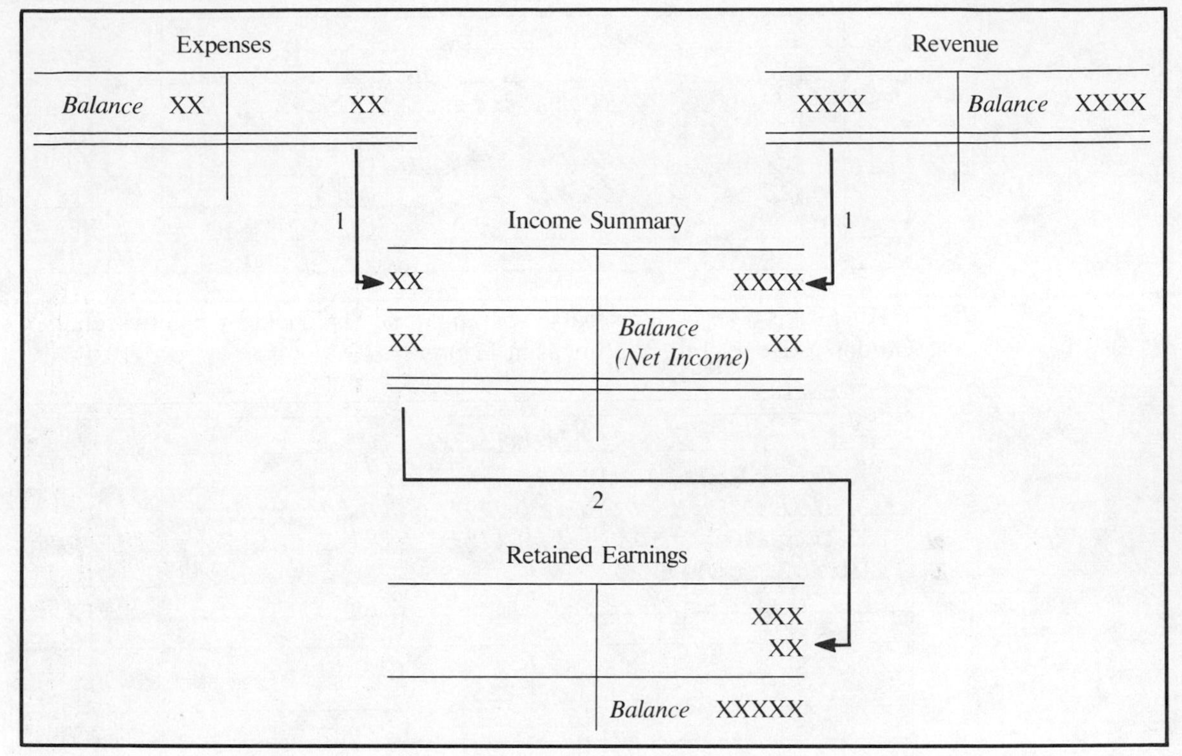

Figure 21.4 *Closing the books*

Distributing Dividends The board of directors has decided to pay a dividend of $2 to each of the outstanding shares of Gordon & Henry Ltd. June 15 was the date that the decision was made. It was also decided that the $2 dividend would be paid to all owners of shares on record as of June 25. The dividend cheques would be issued on July 10. This entry is made on June 15 to establish a liability on the corporate books: *11

June	15	Retained Earnings		7 200 —	
		Dividends Payable			7 200 —
		Declared a $2 dividend on			
		the 3 600 outstanding shares			

This entry results in a decrease in the shareholders' equity because some of the accumulated net income will be taken out of the business. The debit to Retained Earnings reduced the equity. This entry also establishes a current liability called *Dividends Payable*.

On July 10, cheques are issued to the shareholders of record on June 25. The entry to record the payment is:

July	10	Dividends Payable		7 200 —	
		Cash			7 200 —
		Issued dividend cheques			
		to shareholders			

After several years of profitable operation, the Shareholders' equity section of Gordon & Henry Ltd. appears as in Figure 21.5.

Shareholders' Equity	
Share Capital	
Authorized 10 000 shares, $50 par value	
Issued 3 600 shares	180 000 00
Retained Earnings	90 000 00
	270 000 00

Figure 21.5 *Shareholders' Equity portion of the balance sheet*

The balance of $90 000 in retained earnings indicates that a net income has been earned and that not all the net income was distributed in the form of dividends.

*12

Statement of Retained Earnings The shareholders' equity section of the balance sheet shown in Figure 21.5 indicates retained earnings of $90 000 when the balance sheet was prepared at the end of the fiscal period. However, it does not show the beginning balance or changes during the year.

Gordon & Henry Ltd. Statement of Retained Earnings December 31, 19__	
Retained earnings, January 1, 19__	55 200 —
Add: net income for the year	42 000 —
Total	97 200 —
Less: dividends	7 200 —
Retained earnings, December 31, 19__	90 000 —

Figure 21.6 *The statement of retained earnings provides a complete description of changes to retained earnings*

A *statement of retained earnings* as shown in Figure 21.6 provides a complete description of changes in retained earnings. It shows the beginning balance, net income added, dividends paid, and ending balance or retained earnings. A statement of retained earnings is prepared in addition to the income statement and the balance sheet.

Corporate Income Tax

*13

A corporation has a legal existence of its own and is a taxpayer. Corporations pay income tax on their net income to the federal government (46% of taxable income) and to the provinces in which it earns income (10% to 13%, depending on the province). A special income tax rate is available to small Canadian-owned corporations. This deduction, if applicable, results in a small Canadian business paying income tax at a rate of 25% rather than 46%. Special accounting procedures must be followed if the reduced rate is to be obtained.

The income tax paid by a corporation is an expense of operating the business and appears as a deduction on the income statement, as shown in Figure 21.7.

Gordon & Henry Ltd. Income Statement For the Year Ended December 31, 19__		
Revenue:		
Sales		120 000 00
Expenses:		
Selling	39 000 00	
Administrative	24 000 00	
Depreciation	2 500 00	65 500 00
Operating Income		54 500 00
Other Income:		
Investments		1 500 00
Net income before income taxes		56 000 00
Income taxes		14 000 00
Net income after income taxes		42 000 00

Figure 21.7 *Income statement for Gordon & Henry Ltd.*

Gordon & Henry Ltd. had a net income of $56 000 *before* income taxes. From the information on the income statement, there was a net income of $42 000 *after* taxes. This amount is the increase in the shareholders' equity as a result of the year's activity and appears on the statement of retained earnings as shown in Figure 21.6. Figure 21.6 also shows that $7 200 in dividends was distributed to the shareholders during the year.

Double Taxation A shareholder receiving a dividend from a corporation like Gordon & Henry Ltd. must add the dividend to personal income. As a result, the shareholder ends up paying income tax on this dividend. The corporation also paid income tax on the same income from which the shareholder received a dividend. This can be considered to be a case of double taxation: the corporation was taxed and so was the shareholder on the *same net income*.

To alleviate the burden of double taxation, the federal government allows a personal deduction of up to $1 000 from taxable income. This deduction, called *interest and divident deduction*, is available to a taxpayer who earns interest or who receives dividends from a taxable Canadian corporation. The amount that can be deducted is the actual amount of interest or dividends received, up to $1 000 in any one tax year.

Unit 53

Types of Shares

*14

The capital of a corporation takes the form of shares. Shares are sold for cash or exchanged for assets or for services performed for the corporation. Shares may be issued with a *par value* (a stated value) or *without par value* (see page 553). The shares may be *common shares* alone or a mixture of *common shares* and *preferred shares*.

Common shares have one vote per share but no guaranteed dividend.

Common Shares The basic shares issued by a corporation are common shares. Each common share entitles the owner to one vote at shareholders' meetings. There is no guarantee that owners of common shares will receive a dividend since only the board of directors may decide if dividends are to be paid on common shares. The board also decides the amount of any dividend. The person or group owning a majority of common shares controls the voting at shareholders' meetings – and thus the make up of the board of directors and how the business will be managed.

When a corporation offers additional shares for sale, it usually provides common shareholders the first opportunity to purchase the shares, often at less than the current market price. The term *rights* is used to describe the privilege of buying new shares at special prices.

*15

Preferred shares do not have voting rights but have prior claim on assets and net income over common shares.

Preferred Shares Sometimes a corporation, in order to attract investors and cash, offers shares with special features. These shares, called preferred shares, have the following advantages:

- fixed dividend
- preferred position for dividends and assets

For instance, a $2 preferred share is one which is entitled to a $2 dividend if the corporation earns a profit. A 5% preferred share is one which is entitled to a dividend of 5% of the par value of the share. Thus a 5% preferred share, par value $30, would pay a dividend of $1.50 on each preferred share. These dividends must be paid before any dividends are allocated to the common shares. In the event that a corporation dissolves or goes into bankruptcy, the holders of preferred shares have a right to the assets *before* the holders of common shares. Normally, preferred shares do *not* carry voting rights.

Other special features which may be attached to preferred shares are: *16

- cumulative dividends
- convertibility
- participating
- callable

Cumulative preferred share A share for which the dividends build up or accumulate if they are not paid. For example, a $2 cumulative preferred shareholder might not be given the $2 dividend in a year when a loss is suffered by the corporation. However, the next year, a $4 dividend is paid before any portion of the net income is given to common shareholders.

Convertible preferred share A share which the owner may exchange for common shares at a set price. For example, the owner might be given the right to exchange each convertible preferred share for two common shares.

Callable preferred share Gives the corporation the right to repurchase the share at a set price.

Participating preferred share A share which has the right to share in any remaining net income along with the common shares. This means that the preferred shareholder receives the fixed dividend and may also share in any remaining net income after dividends have been paid to the common shareholders.

Journal Entries Separate equity accounts are used for each class of share. The following entries record the issue of both common and preferred shares: *17

Jan.	2	Cash		20 000 —	
		Share Capital-Common			20 000 —
		Issued 1 000 common			
		shares, par value $20			
	3	Cash		30 000 —	
		Share Capital-Preferred			30 000 —
		Issued 1 000, 5% preferred			
		shares, par value $30			

The accounts for the different classes of shares are shown below:

Share Capital – Preferred	
	Jan. 3 30 000

Share Capital – Common	
	Jan. 2 20 000

The shareholders' equity section of the balance sheet is shown in Figure 21.8. For each class of share, the total number of shares authorized and issued is shown. *18

Dividends – Common and Preferred The board of directors of a corporation decides if dividends are to be paid and their amount. Suppose net income is $90 000. The board of directors declares a dividend of 5% of the par value for preferred shares and of $1 for common shares. Since there is a total of 4 000 *19

Shareholders' Equity	
Share Capital	
Authorized	
10 000 5% preferred shares, $30 par value	
70 000 common shares, $20 par value	
Issued	
4 000 preferred shares	120 000 00
30 000 common shares	600 000 00
	720 000 00
Retained earnings	400 000 00
	1120 000 00

Figure 21.8 *Number of shares authorized and issued is shown on the balance sheet.*

preferred shares outstanding at $30 each, the preferred share dividend is $1.50 per share ($30 × 5%) or a total of $6 000 ($1.50 × 4 000 shares). The dividend for the common shares amounts to $30 000 or $1 for each of the 30 000 common shares that have been issued. The entry to record the declaration of dividends is:

Apr.	15	Retained Earnings		36 000 —	
		Dividends Payable-Preferred			6 000 —
		Dividends Payable-Common			30 000 —
		Dividends declared, $1 per common share and $1.50 per 5% preferred share			

When the dividends are paid, this entry is made:

May	1	Dividends Payable-Preferred		6 000 —	
		Dividends Payable-Common		30 000 —	
		Cash			36 000 —
		Issued dividend cheques			

*20

Suppose that in the next fiscal period, the net income went down to $20 000. The board of directors decided to pay the 5% dividend on the preferred shares, but to pay nothing to the common shareholders. They felt that a common share dividend would put a strain on the corporation's finances by removing too much cash. They hoped that by keeping the cash in the corporation the operations and net income would improve in the next fiscal period. An entry for $6 000 was made to record only the preferred dividend.

In the next fiscal period, the net income of the corporation increased dramatically to $200 000. The board of directors was right! The board decided to again declare a 5% dividend on each preferred share, but to raise the dividend on the common shares to $4. This entry was made:

Apr.	17	Retained Earnings		126 000 —	
		Dividends Payable-Preferred			6 000 —
		Dividends Payable-Common			120 000 —
		Dividends declared, $4 per			
		common share and $1.50			
		per 5% preferred share			

The three examples just covered illustrate some of the differences in types of shares and dividend payments. The preferred shares have first claim on net income. Common shares may receive no dividend at all when net income is low. However, common shares may receive high dividends when net income increases significantly. It should be noted that the preferred shareholders could also miss their dividends if the directors decide that sufficient funds are not available.

Par-Value and No-Par-Value Shares Shares which are issued with a value are said to have a *par value*. For example, a company may issue common shares with a $20 par value. This does not mean that each share is worth $20. A share is worth whatever buyers will pay for it.

*21

Some corporations prefer to issue no-par-value shares. These shares are recorded on the corporate books at the price for which they are sold. The par value of a share (if any) is the amount entered in the Share Capital account. It represents legal capital per share. It does not mean market value. By law, dividends may *not* be declared if the payment of the dividend causes the shareholders' equity to fall below the par value of the outstanding shares.

Market Value of Shares W. Gordon and W. Henry own the majority of shares in a private corporation, Gordon & Henry Ltd. The corporation has no need of additional funds and does not plan to issue more shares. Both Gordon and Henry paid $50 a share when the corporation was formed.

*22

J. Probyn is aware of the success of the corporation and feels that Gordon & Henry Ltd. will continue to be successful in the future. She would like to invest in the company, but it is not issuing any new shares. She offers W. Gordon $83 a share for 100 of his shares. Gordon agrees and receives $8 300. He has made a gain of $33 per share, a total of $3 300 on the 100 shares sold, since he originally paid only $50 per share. This example illustrates the *market value* of a share. Market value is the price at which a buyer and seller agree to exchange shares.

Market value is the price at which buyers and sellers agree to exchange shares.

The Stock Market

***23**
The stock market is a place where shares in a corporation are bought and sold after they have been issued.

The stock market is a place where shares in a corporation are bought and sold after they have been issued. It is a place where a shareholder who wishes to sell shares may find a buyer willing to purchase the shares. Large public corporations such as the Ford Motor Company of Canada, Inco, and John Labatt Limited know it is important to make it easy for the public to buy and sell their shares. One reason for this is that these corporations may wish to expand their operations. Expansion requires financing, which can be obtained by issuing more shares.

To facilitate this process, large public corporations list their companies on a *stock exchange* where shares are bought and sold. In order to be listed on a stock exchange, a corporation must follow detailed regulations and must provide the public with much information concerning the operation of the company. In Canada, there are stock exchanges in Vancouver, Toronto, and Montreal. Stockbrokers act as agents for those who wish to buy and sell shares. The brokers arrange the sale in return for a commission on the sale. As well as handling the sale of shares between shareholders and people who wish to buy shares, stockbrokers sell large blocks of new shares for corporations in need of funds.

Facts to Remember

A *business corporation* is a legal entity owned by shareholders.

Shareholders are owners of shares in a corporation.

A *board of directors* is a group of persons, elected by the shareholders, who are responsible for the operation of the corporation.

The *officers* of a corporation are hired employees who manage the day-to-day operations of the corporation.

The *Share Capital* account is a record of shares sold.

The *Retained Earnings* account is an equity account containing the balance of undistributed net income.

Organization Expense is an account used to record the costs incurred in organizing a business.

Dividends are the portion of the corporation's net income paid to the shareholders.

Dividends are paid out of retained earnings.

The *statement of retained earnings* provides a complete description of changes in the retained earnings account.

Common shares have one vote per share but no guaranteed dividend.

Preferred shares do not have voting rights but have prior claim on assets and net income over common shares.

Market value is the price at which buyers and sellers agree to exchange shares.

Checking Your Reading

Questions

1. Explain why unlimited liability is an advantage of the corporate form of ownership.
2. Explain what is meant by the phrase *a corporation has a legal existence of its own*.
3. a) Why do creditors need to know whether the company applying for credit is a corporation?
   b) Why must the name of the corporation be clearly displayed in all its notices and advertisements?
4. The firm of Gordon & Henry Ltd. is a corporation, not a partnership. How does the public know this?
5. What is the board of directors?
6. What is the difference between a private and a public business corporation?
7. What is the name of the form that indicates that a person owns shares in a corporation?
8. Name the two main equity accounts in a corporation's Shareholders' Equity section of the balance sheet.
9. What information does the Retained Earnings account provide?
10. What is the difference between shares authorized and shares issued?
11. What account is debited to record the costs of forming a corporation?
12. What are the three options for distributing the net income of a corporation?
13. Who decides what will be done with the net income of a corporation?
14. What is the name given to the portion of a corporation's net income that is paid to the shareholders?
15. What is the name of the account that is used to record the accumulated net income of a business?
16. Into which account are the Revenue and Expense accounts of a corporation closed?
17. Into which account is the balance of the Income Summary account closed?
18. What does the balance of the Retained Earnings account represent?
19. a) What effect do dividends declared have on the Retained Earnings account?
    b) What effect does net income have on the Retained Earnings account?
    c) What effect does net loss have on the Retained Earnings account?
20. What is a common share?
21. Explain three main features of common shares.
22. What are rights?

23. What is a preferred share?

24. Explain why preferred shares are generally considered to be a safer investment than common shares.

25. Explain the following terms:
a) cumulative preferred shares
b) convertible preferred shares
c) callable preferred shares
d) participating preferred shares

26. What does the par value of a share mean?

27. What is the market value of a share?

28. After a corporation has sold its shares to the public, how can a person purchase shares in that corporation?

Applying Your Knowledge

Exercises Part A

1. A group of business people have received a certificate of incorporation to operate a Canadian corporation called General Distributors Ltd. They were authorized to issue 20 000 shares of $24 par value per share. Record the following in a General Journal using these accounts: Cash; Equipment; Building; Share Capital.

June 1 Sold 1 000 shares for $24 000 cash ($24 per share).
5 Issued 500 shares to G. Devine, a founding shareholder, in return for equipment
(500 × $24 = $12 000).
6 Issued 3 000 shares to A. Galla in return for a building
(3 000 × $24 = $72 000).

2. I. Grant Ltd. has been incorporated with authorized share capital of 70 000 common shares having a $25 par value. Journalize the following transactions using these accounts: Cash; Delivery Equipment; Organization Expense; Share Capital.

April 1 I. Grant, F. Grant, and W. McMichael purchased 2 000 shares each for cash at par value.
2 I. Grant was issued 400 shares in return for a new delivery van.
3 I. Grant and F. Grant each received 3 000 shares in return for a building.
15 A cheque for $100 was issued in payment for printing of share certificates.
15 W. McMichael was issued 80 shares in return for legal services for incorporating the business.

3. O. Muma, a sole proprietor, has received letters patent which allow him to organize his business as a private corporation to be called Brookfield Products

Ltd. The accounts of the proprietorship are exchanged for common shares in the new company. Brookfield Products Ltd. has authorized 100 000 common shares with a $100 par value per share. The accounts of the proprietorship had these balances:

ACCOUNT TITLE	ACC. NO.	DEBIT	CREDIT
Cash		1 000 —	
Supplies		500 —	
Equipment		15 000 —	
Land & Building		200 000 —	
Goodwill		20 000 —	
O. Muma, Capital			236 500 —

a) Record journal entry to take over the accounts of the proprietorship in return for common shares.

b) Record the following transactions:

Sept. 1 Issued shares in return for assets of the proprietorship.
1 Issued 15 shares to D. Adams in return for legal services.
10 Issued shares at par for cash:
D. Adams 50 shares,
R. Bradfield 100 shares,
J. Scobie 100 shares.
15 Paid $10 000 cash for delivery equipment.
20 Paid $5 000 cash for advertising.

4. a) Prepare closing General Journal entries using the balances in the following T-accounts:

Expense Account	
75 000	

Revenue Account	
	100 000

Income Summary	

Retained Earnings	
	135 000

b) Close the Expense account into the Income Summary account.
c) Close the Revenue account.
d) Close the Income Summary account into the Retained Earnings account.
e) Post the journal to the T-accounts.

5. An Income Summary account has a credit balance (net income) of $70 000. Prepare the Journal entries from the following information:

- Close the Income Summary account and transfer net income into the Retained Earnings account.
- Dividends of $30 000 are declared.
- Dividends are paid by cheque.

6. An Income Summary account has a credit balance of $25 000. Prepare the General Journal entries from the following information:

- Close the Income Summary account.
- Dividends of $7 000 are declared.
- Dividends are paid by cheque.

7. Prepare a statement of retained earnings dated December 31, 19__ for Gordon & Henry Ltd. using the following information:

- net income for the year, $70 000
- dividends paid, $30 000
- retained earnings, beginning balance January 1, $90 000

8. Prepare the next year's (from exercise 7) statement of retained earnings dated December 31, 19__ for Gordon & Henry Ltd. using the following information:

- net income for the year, $10 000
- dividends paid, $30 000
- retained earnings, January 1, $130 000

9. Mayfair Enterprises Ltd. pays income tax at the rate of 25%. This year, the corporation's net income before taxes is $70 000.
a) What is the income tax expense for this year?
b) What is the net income after taxes?

Exercises Part B

10. Broadway Mfg. Ltd. was organized on October 1 with the following capital authorized:

- 5 000, 7% cumulative preferred shares, par value $50
- 100 000 common shares, par value $5

Record the following transactions in a General Journal.

Oct. 1 Issued 400 preferred shares for cash.
6 Received cash for 10 000 common shares sold at par.
10 Paid legal fees for incorporation of $2 000 by issuing common shares at par.
15 Received title to land in exchange for 2 000 preferred shares and 10 000 common shares at par.
20 Sold 500 preferred shares and 10 000 common shares at par for cash.

11. Prepare the shareholders' equity section of a balance sheet from the following information:

- 100 000 common shares authorized, no par value
- 50 000 common shares issued with a total value of $300 000
- 10 000 5% preferred shares authorized, no par value
- 1 000 preferred shares issued with a total value of $50 000
- retained earnings, $65 000

12. Prepare the shareholders' equity section of a balance sheet from the following:

- 200 000 common shares authorized, $10 par value
- issued 90 000 shares at par
- 30 000 preferred shares authorized, $20 par value
- issued 10 000 shares at par
- retained earnings, $170 000

13. Prepare a statement of retained earnings and the shareholders' equity section of the balance sheet dated April 30, 19__ for Brookfield Products Ltd.

- authorized share capital, 100 000 common shares
- shares issued, 2 630 common shares valued at $263 000
- retained earnings, beginning balance April 1, $75 000
- net income for the year, $60 000

14. Broadway Mfg. Ltd. has issued 2 900 7% cumulative preferred shares, par value $50.

a) How much is the total annual dividend on the preferred shares?

b) Assume no dividends were paid the first year. How much is the total of dividends owing to preferred shareholders at the end of the second year?

Exercises Part C

15. Chateau Holdings Ltd. was formed with the following capitalization:

- authorized Share Capital:
  20 000 5% preferred shares, par value $30
  100 000 common shares, no par value

a) Record the following transactions in a General Journal:

Jan. 3 Sold 10 000 common shares for $6 each. Received cash, $60 000.
4 Issued for cash, 500 preferred shares at par value.
10 Purchased equipment for $7 000 cash. Issued a cheque.
12 Paid legal fees of incorporation by issuing 100 preferred shares to the company lawyers.
15 Sold 10 000 common shares for $6 cash.
16 Purchased a building valued at $200 000 in return for $100 000 cash, a $40 000 mortgage and 10 000 common shares at $6 per share.

b) Prepare T-accounts and post the General Journal entries.

16. Prepare the year's income statement for Chateau Holdings Ltd. from the adjusted trial balance that follows. Use an income tax rate of 25%.

Chateau Holdings Ltd.
Adjusted Trial Balance
December 31, 19__

ACCOUNT TITLE	ACC. NO.	DEBIT	CREDIT
Cash		15 000 —	
Supplies		5 000 —	
Accounts Receivable		90 000 —	
Building		200 000 —	
Accumulated Depreciation: Building			10 000 —
Equipment		7 000 —	
Accumulated Depreciation: Equipment			1 400 —
Accounts Payable			7 000 —
Mortgage Payable			38 000 —
Share Capital: Common			180 000 —
Preferred			18 000 —
Retained Earnings			—
Sales			317 600 —
Selling Expense		230 000 —	
Administrative Expense		25 000 —	
		572 000 —	572 000 —

17. a) Record these General Journal entries for Chateau Holdings Ltd.:

Nov. 1 Declared a 5% dividend on preferred shares and a 10¢ per share dividend on common shares.

25 Issued dividend cheques.

b) Prepare closing entries for revenue and expenses including Income Tax Expense.

c) Post the closing entries to a T-account for Income Summary.

d) Journalize and post the entry to close the Income Summary account into the Retained Earnings account.

18. Prepare a statement of retained earnings and the shareholders' section of the Chateau Holdings Ltd. balance sheet using information from exercises 15 to 17 and the following:

- dividends paid, $3 900
- net income after taxes, $46 950

19. The trial balance for Ashford Co. Ltd. follows:

a) What is the net income before income taxes?

b) What is the net income after income taxes? Use a 46% tax rate.

c) Prepare a statement of retained earnings using this information:

- dividends paid, $80 000
- beginning balance for retained earnings, $210 000
- net income, $270 000 (after taxes)

Ashford Co. Ltd. Trial Balance May 31, 19__			
ACCOUNT TITLE	ACC. NO.	DEBIT	CREDIT
Cash		20 000 —	
Other Assets		940 000 —	
Liabilities			30 000 —
Share Capital			300 000 —
Retained Earnings			130 000 —
Sales			2 000 000 —
Selling Expense		1 100 000 —	
Administrative Expense		300 000 —	
Other Expenses		100 000 —	
		2 460 000 —	2 460 000 —

d) Open a T-account ledger with these accounts:
Sales; Selling Expense; Administrative Expense; Other Expenses; Income Tax Expense; Income Tax Payable; Retained Earnings; Income Summary.

i) Record the balances on the trial balance in the T-account ledger.

ii) Record these entries in a General Journal:

- the income tax liability
- close the Revenue and Expense accounts
- close the Income Summary account

Accounting in Action

Case 1

Forms of Ownership Maurice Howard is a very wealthy person. He accumulated his wealth as a professional hockey player and through family inheritance. After retiring from hockey, Maurice opened up Astro Sports, a retail sporting goods business. Astro Sports has been moderately successful. However, several very large chain stores offer tough price competition to Astro Sports. Maurice feels that he can meet the competition's prices if he expands his business and opens several branches of Astro Sports. This will allow him to buy merchandise in large quantities at lower cost, and to lower prices to the level of the large chain stores. The financing for his new branch stores would come from his savings, from cashing in some of his personal investments, and from loans. He has a good credit rating and feels that his name alone could get him a substantial loan.

Astro Sports is presently organized as a sole proprietorship. Suggest the best form of ownership for Astro Sports assuming that it expands to a five-store business. Give reasons for your suggestion.

Case 2

Personal Liability Judy Taglioni was injured in an automobile accident. The driver of a vehicle owned by the General Distilling Ltd. was clearly at fault and Judy has several reliable witnesses to prove this. Judy's losses due to the accident total

$40 000. These include loss of salary, personal suffering, and personal expenses. Judy knows that E. P. Naylor is the principal owner of General Distillery Ltd. and Judy has decided to sue E. P. Naylor for $40 000 since it was Naylor's company which caused Judy's financial losses.

Do you think Judy will be successful in her lawsuit against Naylor? Why?

Case 3

Corporate Names Marjorie and Phil Kelly plan to incorporate their appliance repair business. They decide that the name General Electric Repairs Ltd. will attract business. Do you think this name will be accepted by the government? Why?

Case 4

Corporate and Personal Income Tax Steve McKing is the sole owner of McKing Sales Co. Most of his income comes from his business and he is concerned about the amount of personal income tax he is paying. Last year he was in the 45% tax bracket. He asks you if it would be to his advantage to change his proprietorship into a private corporation. He feels it might be to his advantage for tax purposes. These are the facts he gives you:

- As president of the corporation Steve would receive a salary of $40 000 but receive no dividends.
- The corporation's net income before taxes would be $40 000. The tax rate on the $40 000 would be 25%.
- As a proprietorship the business net income would be $80 000. This is $40 000 higher than the corporate net income because Steve's salary of $40 000 is not allowed as a proprietorship expense.
- As a proprietorship, the $80 000 net income becomes the income of the owner. Steve would pay personal income tax at the rate of 47% on his income. After subtracting allowable exemptions and deductions, his taxable income would be $70 000.
- As president of the corporation Steve would have personal taxable income of $32 000. The tax rate on this income would be 37%.

Assume that the business will earn $80 000 next year. Prepare a recommendation concerning the tax advantages or disadvantages of incorporating the business.

Case 5

Corporate Dividends Squire Mfg. Ltd. had a net income of $30 000 in its last fiscal period. I. A. McGreedy owns 1 000 shares of the 100 000 common shares issed by the corporation. The board of directors has decided not to declare a dividend this year. I. A. McGreedy feels she should receive a dividend on her shares and plans to demand one at the annual shareholders meeting. Will McGreedy be successful? Give reasons for your answer.

Case 6

Return on Investment Premier Distilleries Ltd. is a public corporation. Its shares are traded on the Toronto Stock Exchange. An analysis of the last year's results provides the following data about Premier Distilleries:

- 300 000 shares issued and outstanding
- Net Income after taxes, $6 000 000
- Dividends paid, $1 per share
- Current market price, $10 per share

a) What was the rate of dividends paid per share, based on the current market price?
b) What are the earnings per share (that is, the amount of net income earned per share)?
c) If you had money to invest would you purchase shares in Premier Distilleries Ltd. at $10 per share or would you invest them in government bonds at 9% interest? What factors will affect your decision?

Career Profile

Corporate Comptroller R.L. Crain Limited is a leader in the business forms industry. It operates five manufacturing plants, 44 sales offices and eight distribution warehouses across Canada. The plants are located in Moncton, Hull, Ottawa, Toronto, and Medicine Hat. Annual sales approximate $43 000 000 and there are about 1 100 employees working for the company.

A corporation of the size of R.L. Crain Limited must emphasize accounting control systems and procedures in order to operate at a profitable level. Two of the top financial positions in the company are those of Treasurer and Corporate Comptroller. In general, the Treasurer is responsible for the handling of the company's cash and investments and the Comptroller handles the accounting systems and records. In some companies, the title Controller is sometimes used instead of Comptroller.

In this career profile, the job held by Barry Henson, the Comptroller of R.L. Crain Limited, will be examined. Barry grew up and went to school in Birmingham, England. He came to Canada while still in his early twenties. His first job was a navigator for Spartan Air Services. Barry enjoyed flying, but when he married, he decided he wanted a more stable career and more time at home.

Barry obtained a position with Thorne, Riddell & Co., a public accounting firm. He also enrolled in the C.A. (Chartered Accountant) program and after five years of study he completed the C.A. requirements. While with Thorne Riddell, one of Barry's clients was R.L. Crain Limited. Barry was part of the audit team which examined the accounting systems and procedures at R.L. Crain each year. On completion of his C.A. degree, Barry was offered a job with Crain.

Barry has now been with R.L. Crain Limited for 12 years. He has held the positions of Sales Controller, Assistant Comptroller, and his present job of Corporate Comptroller. As Comptroller, Barry supplies and interprets financial information for the division managers, senior management, and the corporate directors. More specifically, Barry is responsible for these areas of accounting:

- cost accounting
- budget control
- pricing
- invoicing
- accounts payable
- payroll
- some aspects of inventory control
- general ledger and preparation of financial reports
- accounting systems, procedures, and internal control

There are 40 accounting personnel involved in these tasks including the Plant Accountants, a Manager of Accounting, a Budget Co-ordinator, a Supervisor of Cost Accounting, and a Payroll Supervisor.

APPENDIX A Chart of Accounts

Following is a chart of accounts for the Canadian Tire Store located in the Town and Country Square, Willowdale, Ontario.

Assets

Current Assets

103 Cash on Hand
104 Cash in Bank – General
105 – Savings
110 Accounts Receivable General
112 Accounts Receivable Budget
114 NSF Cheques
119 Allowance Doubtful Accounts
120 Inventory – CTC
122 – Other
137 – Discount
140 Prepaid – Insurance
– General
154 Gas Coupons
155 Store Coupons

Investments

159 Shares in Dealer Hold
161 Buildings and Land

Fixed Assets

168 Store Equipment
169 Accumulated Depreciation
170 Display Equipment
171 Accumulated Depreciation
172 Office Equipment
173 Accumulated Depreciation
174 Garage Equipment
175 Accumulated Depreciation
176 Leasehold Improvements
177 Accumulated Amortization
178 Auto and Truck
179 Accumulated Depreciation
180 Cafeteria Equipment

Other Assets

199 Organization Expense
201 Deposits

Liabilities

Current Liabilities

203 Bank Advances
210 Accounts Payable – CTC
212 – Plan/Prom
213 – Other
215 Canada Pension Plan
217 Employee Tax Deductions
223 Unemployment Insurance
225 Group OHIP
227 Group Disability
229 Stock Purchase Plan
231 Sales Tax Payable
232 Federal Income Tax Payable
234 Provincial Income Tax Payable
235 Current Tax Provision
236 Accrued Vacation Pay
238 Accrued Wages
239 Accrued General
243 Computer
245 Payroll Clearing
246 Loans to Employees
247 Suspense

Non-Current Liabilities

263 Loan Payable Bank
279 Loan Shareholders

Shareholders Equity

286 Common Shares Issued
288 Retained Earnings
297 Net Earnings to Date

Merchandise Sales

391 Sports
392 Hardware
393 Parts
395 Sale Items
398 Refunds

Cost of Sales

495 Opening Inventory
496 Purchases – CTC
497 – Other
499 Less Ending Inventory

500 Salaries and Benefits

01 Wages – Store manager
02 – Store
03 – Office
04 Group Insurance – OHIP
05 – Disability
06 Stock Purchasing Plan
07 Unemployment Insurance
08 Workmen's Compensation
09 Canada Pension Plan
10 Transfer to Garage Expense

550 Occupancy

01 Rent
02 Building Maintenance
03 Heat
04 Light and Power
05 Amortization and Leasehold
06 Transfer to Garage Expense

600 Store Operation

01 Auto and Truck
02 Cleaning
03 Display
04 Equipment Main
05 Supplies Store Use
06 Security Service
07 Stock Control System
08 Uniforms
09 Parking and Traffic Control

650 Administrative

01 Salaries Management
02 Accounting
03 Association Fees
04 Bad Debts
05 Business Tax
06 Bank Charges
07 Cash Over/Short
08 Capital Tax
09 Insurance
10 Legal
11 Miscellaneous
12 Returned Cheques
13 Stationery
14 Telephone
15 Travelling
16 Transfer to Garage Expense
18 Entertainment

700 Other

01 Advertising
02 Freight Net
03 Coupons Out
04 Purchases Discount
05 Budget Income/Expense

725 Depreciation

01 Equipment – Office
02 – Store
03 Truck
04 Display

750 Financial

01 Bank Interest
02 Other Interest

775 Miscellaneous Income

01 Commission Sales Tax
02 Discounts Earned
03 Bonus CTC
04 Other

800 Garage Income/Expense

01 Labour Income
02 Wages – Manager
03 – Tire Changer
04 – Maintenance
05 – Mechanics
06 Garage Supplies
07 Repairs Equipment
08 Depreciation Equipment
09 Heat and Hydro
10 Rent
11 Miscellaneous
12 Telephone
13 Uniforms
14 Warranty
15 Workmen's Compensation
16 Employee Benefits

850 Cafeteria

01 Income Cafeteria
02 Purchases
03 Wages
04 Supplies
05 Depreciation
06 Miscellaneous
07 Maintenance Equipment

899 Provision for Income Tax
999 Ledger Posting Control

B Professional Accounting Programs

Information concerning admission requirements, programs, etc., of the three main professional accounting associations may be obtained from the following addresses.

Registered Industrial Accountant (R.I.A.)

Canada

The Society of Management Accountants of Canada
154 Main Street E.
P.O. Box 176
Hamilton, Ontario
L8N 3C3

Write to The Society of Management Accountants at the following provincial addresses:

British Columbia
Suite 401 - 750 West Pender Street
Vancouver, British Columbia
V6C 2T7

Yukon
P.O. Box 4823
Whitehorse, Yukon Territory

Alberta
Suite 3120
700 - 2nd Street S.W.
Calgary, Alberta
T2P 2W2

Saskatchewan
2221 - 14th Avenue
Regina, Saskatchewan
S4P 0X9

Manitoba
220 Grant Park Plaza
1120 Grant Avenue
Winnipeg, Manitoba
R3M 2A6

Ontario
154 Main Street E.
P.O. Box 176
Hamilton, Ontario
L8N 3C3

Victoria Towers
Suite 617
25 Adelaide Street East
Toronto, Ontario
M5C 1Y2

9th Floor, 410 Laurier Ave. West
Ottawa, Ontario
K1R 7T3

Newfoundland
Regional Office
P.O. Box 543
Halifax, Nova Scotia
B3J 2R7

Nova Scotia
Regional Office
P.O. Box 543
Halifax, Nova Scotia
B3J 2R7

New Brunswick
Regional Office
P.O. Box 543
Halifax, Nova Scotia
B3J 2R7

Prince Edward Island
Regional Office
P.O. Box 543
Halifax, Nova Scotia
B3J 2R7

Quebec
Suite 1 - The Linton
1509 Sherbrooke St. W.
Montreal, Quebec
H3G 1L7

Chartered Accountant (C.A.)

Canada

Canadian Institute of Chartered Accountants
250 Bloor Street East
Toronto, Ontario
M4W 1G5

Write to the Institute of Chartered Accountants at the following provincial addresses:

Alberta
207 - 10080 Jasper Avenue
Edmonton, Alberta
T5J 1V9

British Columbia
562 Burrard Street
Vancouver, British Columbia
V6C 2K8

Manitoba
607 - 213 Notre Dame Avenue
Winnipeg, Manitoba
R3B 1N3

New Brunswick
Box 6644, 66 Waterloo Street
Saint John, New Brunswick
E2L 4S1

Newfoundland
197 Water Street
St. John's, Newfoundland
A1C 1B4

Nova Scotia
Box 489
Halifax, Nova Scotia
B3J 2R7

Ontario
69 Bloor Street East
Toronto, Ontario
M4W 1B3

Prince Edward Island
Box 301
Charlottetown, Prince Edward Island
C1A 7K7

Saskatchewan
1200 - 1867 Hamilton Street
Regina, Saskatchewan
S4P 2C2

Order of Chartered Accountants of Quebec
680 Sherbrooke Street West,
7th Floor
Montreal, Quebec
H3A 2S3

Certified General Accountant (C.G.A.)

Canada

General Accountants Association
535 Thurlow Street, Suite 800
Vancouver, British Columbia
V6E 3L2

Write to the C.G.A. Association at the following provincial addresses:

Ontario
25 Adelaide Street East,
18th Floor
Toronto, Ontario
M5C 1Y6

Quebec
5165 Queen Mary Road,
Suite 412
Montreal, Quebec
H3W 1X7

British Columbia
1555 West 8th Avenue,
Vancouver, British Columbia
V6J 1T5

Manitoba
419 Graham Avenue,
Suite 202
Winnipeg, Manitoba
R3C 0M3

Newfoundland
Prince Edward Island
Nova Scotia
New Brunswick
Atlantic Region
Administrative Office
Courtenay Centre
Suite 195
P.O. Box 5100
Postal Station "C"
Saint John, New Brunswick
E2L 3W1

Alberta
Saskatchewan
Northwest Territories
Yukon Territory
Prairie Region
Administrative Office
808 First Street, S.W.
Suite 310
Calgary, Alberta
T2P 1N1

Index

Page references in bold type indicate a definition.

7 8 9 #010165 85 84